INSTRUCTIONAL-DESIGN THEORIES
AND MODELS
Volume II

A New Paradigm
of Instructional Theory

INSTRUCTIONAL-DESIGN THEORIES AND MODELS
Volume II

A New Paradigm of Instructional Theory

Edited by

Charles M. Reigeluth
Indiana University

LAWRENCE ERLBAUM ASSOCIATES, PUBLISHERS

1999   Mahwah, New Jersey   London

Lawrence Erlbaum Associates, Inc., Publishers
10 Industrial Avenue
Mahwah, NJ 07430

Library of Congress Cataloging-in-Publication Data

Main entry under title:

Instructional-design theories and models.

Bibliography: p.

Includes index.

ISBN 0-8058-2859-1

Books published by Lawrence Erlbaum Associates are printed on acid-free paper, and their bindings are chosen for strength and durability.

Printed in the United States of America
10   9   8   7   6   5   4   3   2   1

*I dedicate this book to my loving wife, Maitena,
who has understandingly endured the countless days
that this book has stolen from our relationship.*

*I further dedicate this book to our three children,
Jennifer, Mikel, and Kevin, with the hope that
it will in some small way help to improve
learning for them and their children.*

—C.M.R.

Contents

Preface

How to help people learn better. That is what instructional theory is all about. It describes a variety of methods of instruction (different ways of facilitating human learning and development), and when to use—and not use—each of those methods.

Volume I of *Instructional-Design Theories and Models* provided a "snapshot in time" of the status of instructional theory in the early 1980's. But the nature of instructional theory has changed dramatically since then, partly in response to different needs in educational and training environments, partly in response to advances in knowledge about the human brain and learning theory, partly due to a change in educational philosophies and beliefs, and partly in response to advances in information technologies, which have made new methods of instruction both possible and necessary—necessary to take advantage of the new instructional capabilities offered by the technologies. These changes are so dramatic that many argue they constitute a new paradigm of instruction, which requires a new paradigm of instructional theory.

In short, there is a need for a Volume II of *Instructional-Design Theories and Models*, to provide a concise summary of a broad sampling of the new methods of instruction currently under development, but also to help show the interrelationships among these diverse theories and to highlight current issues and trends in instructional design. To attain this broad sampling of methods and theories, and to make this book more useful for practitioners as well as graduate students interested in education and training, this volume contains twice as many chapters, but each half as long, as the ones in Volume I, and the descriptions are generally less technical than in Volume I.

Because this volume contains a lot of theories to understand and compare, I have tried to make this task easier for the reader by preparing a rather unconventional kind of chapter foreword that summarizes the major elements of each instructional-design theory. Hopefully, these forewords will be as useful for reviewing and comparing theories after you have read them, as they will for previewing a theory to decide whether or not it interests you and developing a general schema that will make it easier to understand. Furthermore, the editor's notes, which are also rather unconventional for an edited volume, will hopefully help you in this task of understanding and comparing the theories. Finally, Units 2 and 4 both have introductory chapters that are intended to help you analyze and understand the theories in those units.

Unit 1 describes what instructional-design theory is like, the ways it is changing, and why. It also discusses current issues and trends in instructional-design theory. I strongly recommend reading the two chapters in this unit *before* reading any of the theory chapters. Unit 2 provides concise summaries of a broad sampling of new instructional-design theories (methods and when to use them), currently under development in the cognitive domain; Unit 3 provides the same for one highly integrative theory in the psychomotor domain, and Unit 4 provides the same for five theories in the affective domain. Finally, Unit 5 provides a general discussion of the various theories presented in Units 2 and 4, and a research methodology for further developing this emerging knowledge base about the new paradigm of instruction.

I hope you will enjoy exploring these fascinating new approaches to fostering human learning and development. They have helped me greatly to think "outside the box" about ways to better meet the needs of learners in all kinds of learning contexts.

—C.M.R.

Unit I
FOREWORD

About Instructional-Design Theory

This unit has two chapters that are intended to help the reader analyze and understand:

- The nature of the theories in this book.
- The ways this new paradigm of instructional-design theory differs from the previous paradigm.
- Some issues about instructional-design theories that are of interest to researchers and some of interest to practitioners.

I strongly recommend reading these two chapters prior to reading any of the theory chapters.

In this volume, I use the term "design theory" in place of "prescriptive theory," which was used in Volume I as the alternative to descriptive theory. This change is because the connotations of "prescription" are those of rigidity and inflexibility, which are inaccurate conceptions of most instructional-design theories, especially in the new paradigm. This change also makes the term "instructional-design theory" more obviously a kind of design theory. In addition, many people use the term "instructional theory" with the same meaning as instructional-design theory. Therefore, I have sometimes done the same in this volume for the sake of brevity.

This unit introduces you to many of the issues that are addressed throughout this volume. The following questions represent some of the more important of those issues.

- What are the key characteristics of the **new paradigm** of instruction?
- What is an **instructional theory**, and how does it differ from learning theory and instructional systems development (ISD) processes?
- What role should **values about instruction** play in the design of instruction?

1

- To what extent should instructional theory and curriculum theory be **integrated**?
- To what extent should instruction address all three domains—**cognitive, psychomotor, and affective** (thinking, doing, and feeling)—in an integrated manner?
- To what extent should a **diversity of methods** be offered to practitioners, as opposed to methods from a single theoretical perspective?
- How much **flexibility** should an instructional theory offer to practitioners?
- How much **detail** should an instructional theory offer in its guidance to practitioners?
- To what extent should **culture** or **climate** of the learning environment be a method in an instructional theory?
- What role do methods of **motivating students** play in the new paradigm of instruction?
- What role do student **self-regulation** and **reflection on learning** play in the new paradigm of instruction?
- What should **student assessment** be like for the new paradigm of instruction?
- What is **systemic thinking**, and to what extent is it important to designing and implementing a new paradigm of instruction?
- How does **"either-or" thinking** relate to the new paradigm of instructional theory?
- What additional **kinds of learning** are dealt with by the new paradigm of instructional theory?
- How are the **roles** of teachers and students different in the new paradigm of instruction? And what are the implications of those new roles for pre-service and in-service **professional development** of teachers?

These questions are addressed to some extent in chapters 1 and 2, but for the most part they remain for you to answer as you read through the theories in Units 2–4. The editor's notes throughout the theory chapters should help you to keep those questions in mind and consider some answers that have occurred to me. Furthermore, a few of these questions were addressed in Unit 1 of Volume 1 (Reigeluth, 1983), so you might find it helpful to look at those three chapters, especially chapter 1.

One of the themes in this volume is that cognitive, affective, and behavioral (psychomotor) development are inextricably linked. Nonetheless, ways of fostering development (i.e., instructional methods) are often quite different for the cognitive aspects of development than for the affective aspects. It is important to understand both the differences and the interrelatedness of these domains of human learning and development.

Another theme has to do with interrelatedness on a broader scale. Curriculum theory and instructional theory are interrelated. Instructional theory, learning theory, and the ISD process (development theory) are interrelated. The different domains of learning are interrelated, and within each of these domains, the different subject areas are interrelated, thematically and in other ways. Interrelationships between instruction and such other areas as student motivation and assessment are also powerful. Learning is related to (influenced by) the climate or culture within which it occurs. Furthermore, other aspects (or subsystems) of the educational system can have powerful influences on the success of implementation of the new paradigm of instruction in a school, such as the administrative system, the professional development system, the record-keeping system, the technological support system, the transportation system, and so forth (and the similar influences exist in corporate training settings). Systems thinking (see, e.g., Boulding, 1985; Checkland, 1981; Hutchins, 1995; Senge, 1990) and chaos theory (Gleick, 1987; Prigogine & Stengers, 1984) provide powerful tools for identifying and understanding the interrelationships that are likely to impact practitioners' ability to successfully implement the new paradigm of instructional theory as well as theorists' ability to successfully build comprehensive instructional theory. Some useful applications of systems thinking to education have been published by Banathy (1991, 1996), Fullan (1993), Jenlink (1995), Reigeluth and Garfinkle (1994), and Schlechty (1990). Given the extent to which interrelationships are important to the new paradigm of instruction, you may find it useful to explore the tools provided by systems thinking and chaos theory.

—C.M.R.

REFERENCES

Banathy, B. H. (1991). *Systems design of education.* Englewood Cliffs, NJ: Educational Technology Publications.

Banathy, B. H. (1996). *Designing social systems in a changing world.* New York: Plenum Press.

Boulding, K. E. (1985). *The world as a total system.* Beverly Hills, CA: Sage.

Checkland, P. (1981). *Systems thinking, systems practice.* Chichester, NY: Wiley.

Fullan, M. (1993). *Change forces.* London: The Falmer Press.

Gleick, J. (1987). *Chaos.* New York: Vilroy.

Hutchins, C. L. (1995). *Systems thinking.*

Jenlink, P. M. (1995). *Systemic change: Touchstones for the future school.* Palatine, IL: Skylight Training and Publishing, Inc.

Prigogine, I., & Stengers, I. (1984). *Order out of chaos: Man's new dialogue with nature.* Boulder, CO: New Science Library.

Reigeluth, C. M. (Ed.); (1983). *Instructional-design theories and models: An overview of their current status.* Hillsdale, NJ: Lawrence Erlbaum Associates.

Reigeluth, C. M., & Garfinkle, R. J. (1994). *Systemic change in education.* Englewood Cliffs, NJ: Educational Technology Publications.

Schlechty, P. C. (1990). *Schools for the 21st century: Leadership imperatives for educational reform.* San Francisco, CA: Jossey-Bass.

Senge, P. (1990). *The fifth discipline: The art and practice of the learning organization.* New York: Doubleday.

1 What Is Instructional-Design Theory and How Is It Changing?

Charles M. Reigeluth
Indiana University

The purpose of this chapter is to provide some ideas that will help you analyze and understand the instructional-design theories presented in this book. First, we will explore what an instructional-design theory is. This will include a discussion of the role that values play in instructional-design theories and a discussion of what an instructional-design theory is not. In the second half of the chapter, we will explore the need for a new paradigm of instructional-design theory. In particular, we will look at the need for a paradigm of training and education in which the learner is at the top of the organizational chart rather than the bottom. Then we will look at the implications that such a paradigm has for instructional-design theory, including the extent to which some of the design decisions should perhaps be made by the learners while they are learning.

WHAT IS AN INSTRUCTIONAL-DESIGN THEORY?

An instructional-design theory is a theory that offers explicit guidance on how to better help people learn and develop. The kinds of learning and development may include cognitive, emotional, social, physical, and spiritual. For example, in *Smart Schools*, Perkins describes an instructional-design theory, called "Theory One," which offers the following guidance for what the instruction should include to foster cognitive learning. The instruction should provide:

- *Clear information*. Descriptions and examples of the goals, knowledge needed, and the performances expected.

Sections of this chapter are excerpted or adapted from Reigeluth, C. M. (1996). A new paradigm of ISD? *Educational Technology, 36*(3), 13–20, with permission of the publisher.

- *Thoughtful practice*. Opportunity for learners to engage actively and reflectively whatever is to be learned—adding numbers, solving word problems, writing essays.
- *Informative feedback*. Clear, thorough counsel to learners about their performance, helping them to proceed more effectively.
- *Strong intrinsic or extrinsic motivation*. Activities that are amply rewarded, either because they are very interesting and engaging in themselves or because they feed into other achievements that concern the learner (Perkins, 1992, p. 45).

This is an instructional-design theory. Of course, Perkins elaborates on each of these guidelines in his book, but this overview provides a good example of what an instructional-design theory is like. So what are the major characteristics that all instructional-design theories have in common?

First, unlike more familiar kinds of theories, instructional-design theory is *design-oriented* (focusing on means to attain given goals for learning or development), rather than description oriented (focusing on the results of given events). In the case of Theory One, the goal is to enhance learning "for any performance we want to teach" (p. 45). Being design oriented makes a theory more directly useful to educators, because it provides direct guidance on how to achieve their goals.

Second, instructional-design theory identifies *methods* of instruction (ways to support and facilitate learning) and the *situations* in which those methods should and should not be used. In the case of Theory One, the methods (at this general level of description) are: clear information, thoughtful practice, informative feedback, and strong motivators. Perkins goes on to say, "Good teaching demands different methods for different occasions" (p. 53), and he describes how Theory One can underlie each of Adler's (1982) three different ways of teaching: didactic instruction, coaching, and Socratic teaching.

Third, in all instructional-design theories, the methods of instruction can be broken into *more detailed component methods*, which provide more guidance to educators. In the case of Theory One, Perkins provides considerable information about components for each of the four basic methods. For example, within the didactic framework, Perkins describes some of the components for clear information, based on Leinhardt's (1989) research:

- identification of goals for the students;
- monitoring and signaling processes toward the goals;
- giving abundant examples of the concepts treated;
- demonstration;
- linkage of new concepts to old ones through identification of familiar, expanded, and new elements;
- legitimizing a new concept or procedure by means of principles the students already know, cross-checks among representations, and compelling logic (Perkins, 1992, pp. 53–54).

And fourth, the methods are *probabilistic* rather than deterministic, which means they increase the chances of attaining the goals rather than ensuring attainment of the goals. In the case of Theory One, "Giving abundant examples of the concepts treated" will not ensure that the goals for the students will be attained. But, it will increase the probability that they will be attained.

So, instructional-design theories are design oriented, they describe methods of instruction and the situations in which those methods should be used, the methods can be broken into simpler component methods, and the methods are probabilistic. Each of these characteristics of instructional-design theories is described in more detail next.

Design-Oriented Theories

An important characteristic of instructional-design theories is that they are design oriented (or goal oriented). This makes them very different from what most people usually think of as theories. Theories can be thought of as dealing with cause-and-effect relationships or with flows of events in natural processes, keeping in mind that those effects or events are almost always probabilistic (i.e., the cause increases the chances of the stated effect occurring) rather than deterministic (i.e., the cause always results in the stated effect). Most people think of theories as descriptive in nature, meaning that the theory describes the effects that occur when a given class of causal events occurs, or meaning that it describes the sequence in which certain events occur. For example, information-processing theory is descriptive. Among other things, it says that new information enters short-term memory before it enters long-term memory. It doesn't tell you how to facilitate learning. Descriptive theories can be used for prediction (given a causal event, predict what effect it will have; or, given one event in a process, predict what event will likely occur next) or for explanation (given an effect that has occurred, explain what must have caused it or preceded it).

But design-oriented theories are very different from descriptive theories (see e.g., Cronbach & Suppes, 1969; Simon, 1969; Snelbecker, 1974; Reigeluth, 1983b, which is chapter 1 in Volume 1 of this book). Design theories are prescriptive in nature, in the sense that they offer guidelines as to what method(s) to use to best attain a given goal. (They are not usually prescriptive in the sense of spelling out in great detail exactly what must be done and allowing no variation. Prescription in that sense only applies to deterministic—or positivistic—theories, which are almost nonexistent in the social sciences.) For example, if you want to help long-term retention of some new information to occur (an instructional goal), you should help the learner to relate that information to relevant prior knowledge (an instructional method).

Simon (1969) referred to the distinction between descriptive theories and design theories as "the natural sciences" and "the sciences of the artificial," respectively. Cronbach and Suppes (1969) referred to it as "conclusion-oriented inquiry" and "decision-oriented inquiry." Whatever you choose to call them, they are very different kinds of theories that have very different purposes and require very different kinds of research. Design theories are intended to provide direct guidance to practitioners about what methods to use to attain different goals, whereas descriptive theories attempt to provide a deeper understanding of effects that result from phenomena. Therefore, descriptive theories are also useful to practitioners, because they provide an understanding of why a design theory works and because they can help practitioners to generate their own design theories for those many situations for which no adequate ones exist. The major concern for people developing and testing descriptive theories is validity, whereas for design theories, it is preferability (i.e., does this method attain your goals for your situation better than any other known method?). This is why design theories require different research methodologies from descriptive theories (see chap. 26, this volume, for a description of a methodology for advancing design theories).

Methods and Situations

Instructional-design theory requires at least two components: methods for facilitating human learning and development (which are also called methods of instruction), and indications as to when and when not to use those methods (which I call situations). Although the term "context," has a similar meaning in lay language and is often used in education, not all aspects of the context influence what methods should be used. Therefore, I use the term "situation" to refer to those aspects of the context that do influence selection of methods. An essential feature of instructional-design theories is that the methods they offer are situational rather than universal. In other words, one method may work best in one situation, while another may work best in a different situation.

There are two major aspects of any instructional situation (see Fig. 1.1): the conditions under which the instruction will take place and the desired outcomes of the instruction. *Instructional conditions*, which should not be confused with Gagné's conditions of learning, include:

- the nature of what is to be learned (e.g., understandings are learned differently from the way skills are learned);
- the nature of the learner (e.g., prior knowledge, learning strategies, and motivations);
- the nature of the learning environment (e.g., independently at home, in a group of 26 students at school, in a small team in a business); and
- the nature of the instructional development constraints (e.g., how much time and money you have for planning and developing the instruction).

All of these conditions may influence which methods will work best to attain your desired outcomes. Gagné's internal conditions of learning fall within the sec-

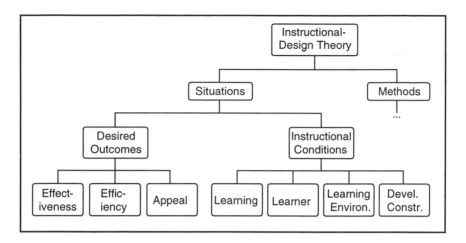

FIG. 1.1.   The components of instructional-design theories.

ond item above (the nature of the learner), so they are instructional conditions; but his external conditions of learning are actually instructional methods, not instructional conditions.

The second major aspect of any instructional situation is the *desired instructional outcomes.*[1] These are different from learning goals. They do not include the specific learnings that are desired. Remember, the first item for conditions (see the previous bulleted list) was "the nature of what is to be learned." Instead, desired instructional outcomes include the levels of effectiveness, efficiency, and appeal you want or need from the instruction.

- Level of effectiveness is a matter of how well the instruction works, as indicated by how well (to what degree of proficiency) the learning goals are attained. The desired instructional outcomes are not concerned with what the learning goals are, but with how well they are achieved. The term "criterion" is often used to refer to the level of effectiveness. An example is correctly solving 8 out of 10 real-world problems that require the use of $a^2+b^2 = c^2$ in a right triangle.
- Level of efficiency is the level of effectiveness of the instruction divided by the time and/or cost of the instruction. An example is how long it takes stu-

---

[1]As Landa (1983) indicated in Volume I, descriptive instructional theory (as opposed to instructional-design theory) is concerned with actual outcomes, rather than with desired outcomes. See also, chapter 1 of Volume I (Reigeluth, 1983b) for a discussion of the difference between desired and actual outcomes.

dents to reach the criterion mentioned above: correctly solving 8 out of 10 real-world problems that require the use of $a^2+b^2 = c^2$ in a right triangle.

* Level of appeal is the extent to which the learners enjoy the instruction. An example is students asking where they could learn more about a topic.

Some trade-offs are often necessary among the three desired outcomes (effectiveness, efficiency, and appeal). The more effective you want the instruction to be, the more time and expense it may require, making it less efficient. And sometimes the more appealing (motivational) you want the instruction to be, the less efficient it will be. In this book, the instructional-design theories (see Units 2 and 3) explicitly state the situations for which their methods are recommended.

Component Methods

So, instructional-design theories are design oriented; they have methods, which are situational; and they specify the situations (instructional conditions and desired outcomes) for which the methods are appropriate or inappropriate. Their methods are also componential, meaning that each can be done in different ways and is therefore made up of different components (or features). For example, problem-based learning (PBL) can be viewed as a method of instruction. But PBL is made up of many smaller methods, such as presenting the problem and the scenario in which it occurs, forming teams, providing support for the teams' efforts, reflecting on the results of the individuals' and teams' efforts, and so forth. These are *parts* of the more general method.

In addition, there are usually many different ways in which a method can be performed. The problem can be presented in different ways, the scenario can have different kinds of characteristics, and so forth. These are *kinds* of their more general method. Sometimes one of those kinds is better than the others (better for a given set of conditions and desired outcomes), but sometimes they are equally efficacious. Often, it depends on the situation.

Finally, more detail can be provided for a method by offering *criteria* that the method should meet. These are neither parts nor kinds of the more general method; rather they indicate specifications that the method should meet. For example, realism might be specified as a criterion for designing the scenario in problem-based learning.

It should be apparent all of these components[2] (whether they are parts, kinds, or criteria) can usually be broken down into more detailed guidelines; in other words, they usually have subcomponents, which in turn can have subsubcomponents, and so

---

[2]I use the term "components" even though that is often viewed as synonymous with "parts," because the three kinds of "break-downs" (parts, kinds, and criteria) comprise, or are contained in, the more general method.

forth, down to what have been called "elementary components" (components that for practical purposes have insignificant variation and therefore are not usefully analyzed into their components; see the Landa and Scandura theories in Volume I: Reigeluth, 1983a). Of course, those components are highly interrelated and usually highly situational in their effects on attaining the desired outcomes. An instructional-design theory is much simpler and easier to understand if it describes methods on a relatively general level. In other words, in a diagram that breaks the methods down into components and then breaks those components into their components, the general methods are those higher up in the diagram. But such a simple theory is also less useful to educators, because there are so many different ways that those methods can be performed, and educators have no guidance about which way (or ways) is (are) likely to work best for their situations. Therefore, an instructional-design theory is easier to apply if it describes methods on a relatively detailed level.

So, instructional-design theories can vary greatly in terms of the level of guidance they provide, ranging from very general theories to highly detailed theories. But just because a theory is detailed does not mean it is not flexible, in the sense of being adaptable to different situations. In the present book, the authors have only enough space to summarize their respective theories, so the level of guidance provided herein may be much lower than what the same authors have given elsewhere. In such cases, the authors provide references to their more thorough works, so readers can find additional guidance for using their methods.

Probabilistic Methods

Another characteristic of methods of instruction is that they are probabilistic. This means that methods do not guarantee the desired instructional and learning outcomes. They only increase the probability that the desired results will occur. This is because there are so many factors (situation, variables) that influence how well a method of instruction works. It is probably impossible to develop an instructional method that will work better than any other method 100% of the time, in the situations for which it is intended. But the goal of an instructional-design theory is to attain the highest possible probability of the desired results (which often include cost-effectiveness) occurring.

It would be nice if instructional-design theories could specify probabilities for each method component, but those probabilities likely differ for different situations and differ depending on what other method components are being used with them (an "interaction effect"). This makes it difficult to specify probabilities for each method in anything less than an electronic performance support system, though the theorist would still have the formidable problem of empirically determining or validating all the probabilities for all the qualitatively different situations. So, unfortunately, probabilities are rarely included in instructional-design theories.

Values

A major implication of design theory's goal (or design) orientation and emphasis on preferability of methods for attaining its goals is that values play an important role for design theories, whereas any talk of values for descriptive theories is usually considered unscientific. Values (or philosophy, if you prefer) are especially important to design theory in two ways. First, they play an important role in deciding what *goals* to pursue. Traditionally, instructional-design process models (see the "Instructional-Design Process" section below) have relied solely on needs-analysis techniques (a data-based approach) to decide what to teach. We need greater recognition of the important role that values play in such decisions, and instructional-design process models need to offer guidance on how to help all people who have a stake in the instruction reach consensus on such values. Second, for any given goal, there is almost always more than one *method* that can be used to attain it. Traditionally, instructional-design process models have relied primarily on research data about which methods work best. But which methods work best depends on what criteria you use to judge the methods. Those criteria reflect your values. In this book, all the instructional-design theories (see Units 2–4) state explicitly what values guide their selection of goals and what values guide their selection of methods.

So, instructional-design theories are design oriented, and they offer methods which are situational, componential, and probabilistic. They identify the situations for which the methods should be used. They also identify the values that underlie the goals they pursue and the methods they offer to attain those goals. So what kinds of things do not constitute instructional-design theories, but are often confused with such theories?

WHAT IS NOT AN INSTRUCTIONAL-DESIGN THEORY?

To understand what instructional-design theory is, it is helpful to contrast it with what it is not. It differs in important ways from *learning theory, instructional-design process*, and *curriculum theory*. But instructional-design theory is also closely related to each of these, and it is important for teachers and instructional designers to know about them. Each of them is discussed in what follows.

Learning Theory

Learning theories are often confused with instructional-design theories. But learning theories are descriptive. They describe how learning occurs. For example, one kind of learning theory, called schema theory, proposes that new knowledge is acquired by accretion into an existing schema, by tuning that schema when minor inconsistencies emerge, and by restructuring that schema when major inconsistencies arise (Rummelhart & Norman, 1978). But how does that understanding help me to teach, say, English grammar? If I'm creative and have a lot of time, I may be able to develop instructional methods that facilitate accretion, tuning, and restructuring of schemata. But it is very difficult, and I may completely miss the mark. If I'm successful in identifying useful methods for particular situations, I've created an instructional-design theory. It may only apply to a very narrow slice of situations, but those methods and situations comprise an instructional-design theory.

In contrast to learning theories, instructional-design theories are more directly and easily applied to educational problems, for they describe specific events outside of the learner that facilitate learning (i.e., methods of instruction), rather than describing what goes on inside a learner's head when learning occurs. The same kind of analysis applies to theories of human development. They are descriptive and apply only indirectly to teaching (fostering learning and development of all sorts).

Nevertheless, that does not mean that theories of learning and human development are not useful to educators. As Winn (1997) put it, "any successful practitioner or researcher needs to be thoroughly versed in at least the immediately underlying discipline to his or her own. A good instructional designer knows [theories of learning and human development]" (p. 37). Indeed, learning and developmental theories are useful for understanding why an instructional-design theory works, and, in areas where no instructional-design theories exist, they can help an educator to invent new methods or select known instructional methods that might work.

So, instructional-design theories and theories of learning and human development are both important, and, like a house and its foundation, they are closely related. In fact, they are often so closely related that several of the theories in Units 2–4 provide some discussion of learning theory as well as instructional-design theory (see, e.g., chap. 7 in which Mayer has a section on the "SOI Model of Learning" as well as on the "Instructional Methods Suggested by the SOI Model"). But these kinds of theories also differ from each other in important ways, and it is difficult to adequately understand how to facilitate learning without understanding the differences between them.

Instructional-Design Process

Another thing that isn't instructional-design theory is the instructional-design process. Instructional-design theory concerns what the instruction should be like (i.e., what methods of instruction should be used) not what process a teacher or instructional designer should use to plan and prepare for the instruction. Other common terms that characterize this distinction are instructional theory, instructional model, and instructional strategies to represent instructional-design theory; and instructional development (ID) model or instructional systems development (ISD) process to represent instructional-design process.

However, instructional-design theories and instructional-design processes are also closely related. Different theories require differences in the process used to apply those theories to particular situations. Therefore, some of the chapters in Units

2–4 of this book contain brief summaries of the new aspects of the design process that are necessary to use their theory; for example, in chapter 23 Kamradt and Kamradt talk about "attitudinal needs analysis."

Curriculum Theory

In Volume I of this book (Reigeluth, 1983a), I discussed the distinction between what to teach and how to teach; and I indicated that decisions about what to teach have been viewed as the province of curriculum theories, whereas decisions about how to teach have been the province of instructional-design theories. However, the interrelationships between these two kinds of decisions are so strong that it often makes sense to combine the two. And, in fact, many curriculum theories have offered guidance for methods of instruction, while many instructional-design theories have offered guidance for what to teach. Therefore, although it is helpful to recognize the difference between deciding what to teach and how to teach it, some of the theories presented in Units 2 and 3 appropriately address both, for example, chapter 4, in which Gardner talks about "Topics Worth Understanding" as well as about ways of fostering understanding.

A fundamental question concerns bases for making decisions about what to teach and how to teach. Regarding what to teach (goals), the ISD process has traditionally looked only at what works, through the process of needs analysis, as I mentioned in the section on "Values" earlier. But many curriculum theories are based on a philosophy (a set of values). In fact, both empirics (data about what is needed) and values (opinions about what is important) are relevant and should be addressed in the ISD process for deciding what to teach, perhaps with different degrees of emphasis for different situations. Similarly, regarding decisions about how to teach (what methods to use), instructional-design theories have traditionally relied exclusively on data obtained through research, summative evaluations, and formative evaluations, typically assuming that the criteria used to judge "what works" are universal (indisputable). But they aren't. Criteria often differ from one situation to another, because people differ in their values about what outcomes are important. Thus, both values and empirics are important for making decisions about how to teach as well as what to teach, so elements of curriculum theory and the ISD process should be combined.

In this chapter, we have already explored what an instructional-design theory is. It is design oriented (or goal oriented), offering guidelines about what methods to use in what situations. Its methods are componential, offering varying levels of guidance for educators. The methods are also probabilistic, not always fostering the desired results. And we have seen that values play an important role in an instructional-design theory in that they underlie both the goals it pursues and the methods it offers to attain those goals. We have also explored what an instructional-design theory isn't. It isn't the same as a learning theory, an ISD process model, or a curriculum theory; but it is closely related to all three, and educators should supplement their knowledge of instructional-design theory with all three. In fact, it is often useful to combine instructional-design theory and curriculum theory.

Given this understanding of what an instructional-design theory is and isn't, we can move on to the question of why it is important.

Why Is Instructional-Design Theory Important?

Pogrow (1996) points out that "The history of educational reform is one of consistent failure of major reforms to survive and become institutionalized.... Cuban [1993] refers to the historical success of attempted curriculum reform as 'pitiful.'" (p. 657). Pogrow goes on to say that "The single biggest tool in promoting reform has been advocacy" (p. 658), which originates primarily from the "REsearch/Academic/Reform (REAR) community," made up of educational reformers and the academicians and researchers who develop ideas and rationales for them. Pogrow states that "The feeling is widespread in the REAR community that its responsibility is to produce general theory and that it is up to practitioners to figure out how to apply that theory" (p. 658).

What Pogrow is calling for is the need for design theory rather than descriptive theory. He goes on to say:

> It is far more difficult to figure out how to implement [descriptive] theory than it is to generate it. I am reasonably intelligent, and it took me 14 years of almost full-time effort to figure out how to consistently work just four thinking skills into a detailed and effective curriculum.... My own experience is that it is indeed possible for the right type of research to develop techniques and determine implementation details that are applicable to most local conditions—if REAR is so disposed. (p. 658)

To really help educators to improve education, it is essential that more people in the REAR community devote their efforts to generating design theories, rather than, as Pogrow puts it, "prefer[ing] to philosophize and preach" (p. 658). The purpose of this book is to summarize and publicize some of the promising work that is being done to generate design theories in the field of instruction. We leave it to others to do the same in other areas of education, including administration and governance/policy. We also leave it to others to generate design theories that deal with systemic change in the entire educational system (see e.g., Banathy, 1991; Reigeluth & Garfinkle, 1994).

Having addressed what instructional-design theory is and why it is important, I turn now to how and why it is changing in such a dramatic way as to require a Volume II, rather than a second edition, of the previous work on this topic (Reigeluth, 1983a).

WHY AND HOW ARE INSTRUCTIONAL-DESIGN
THEORIES CHANGING?

It is helpful to think in terms of two basic kinds of change: piecemeal and systemic. Piecemeal change leaves the structure of a system unchanged. It often involves finding better ways to meet the same needs, such as using an analogy to help your students learn the science concepts you taught in an otherwise similar manner last year. In contrast, systemic change entails modifying the structure of a system, usually in response to new needs. For example, you may find that your students' characteristics (such as their entering knowledge, learning styles, interests, and motivations) are more diverse than they used to be and that they have very different goals (such as college, vocational school, or immediate employment). To respond to these changed needs, you may decide to use customized, team-based, problem-based learning with continuous progress and to use advanced technology more extensively. Piecemeal change usually changes one part of a system in a way that is still compatible with the rest of the system, whereas systemic change entails such a fundamental change that it requires changes throughout the system, because the other parts of the system are not compatible with the change.

So, does instructional-design theory need piecemeal change or systemic change? As we discussed earlier, instructional-design theory is a knowledge base that guides educational practice: how to facilitate learning. In turn, instructional practice is a subsystem that is a part of different kinds of systems, such as public education systems, higher education systems, corporate training systems, health agencies, the armed forces, museums, informal learning systems, and many others. I shall refer to the instructional practice subsystems as simply the "instructional systems."

Systems thinkers know that, when a human-activity system (or societal system) changes in significant ways, its subsystems must change in equally significant ways to survive. This is because each subsystem must meet one or more needs of its supersystem in order for the supersystem to continue to support it (Hutchins, 1996). So, if the supersystems for instructional systems are undergoing systemic changes, then—and only then—do instructional systems, and consequently instructional-design theory, need to undergo systemic change or risk becoming obsolete.

Instruction's Supersystem

So, are instruction's supersystems changing dramatically? In the agrarian age, businesses were organized around the family: the family farm, the family bakery, and so forth. In the industrial age, the family was replaced by the bureaucracy and departments, which became the predominant form of business organization. Now, as we evolve deeper into the information age, corporations are doing away with many of the midlevels of the bureaucracy and are reorganizing on the basis of holistic processes rather than fragmented departments; they are also organizing their staffs into teams that are being given considerable autonomy to manage themselves within the purview of the corporate vision, rather than being directed from above (Drucker, 1989; Hammer & Champy, 1993). This allows the corporations to respond much more quickly and appropriately to their customers' and clients' needs. These changes certainly fit the definition of systemic change.

Increasingly, other organizations in the private, public, and "third" (nonprofit) sectors are undergoing similar transformations (see, e.g., Osborne & Gaebler, 1992). Fig. 1.2 shows some of the "key markers" that characterize the differences between industrial-age organizations and information-age organizations.

Industrial Age	Information Age
Standardization	Customization
Bureaucratic organization	Team-based organization
Centralized control	Autonomy with accountability
Adversarial relationships	Cooperative relationships
Autocratic decision making	Shared decision making
Compliance	Initiative
Conformity	Diversity
One-way communications	Networking
Compartmentalization	Holism
Parts oriented	Process oriented
Planned obsolescence	Total quality
CEO or boss as "king"	Customer as "king"

FIG. 1.2.   Key markers that distinguish industrial-age and information-age organizations.

These fundamental changes in instruction's supersystems have important implications for instruction. Employees need to be able to think about and solve problems, work in teams, communicate, take initiative, and bring diverse perspectives to their work. Also, "people need to learn more, yet they have less time available in which to learn it" (Lee & Zemke, 1995, p. 30), and they need to demonstrate an impact on the organization's strategic objectives (Hequet, 1995). Can our systems of education and training meet those needs by merely changing the content (what we teach) or do we need to make more fundamental changes? To answer this question, we must take a closer look at our current paradigm of training and education.

The Current Paradigm of Education and Training

Fig. 1.2 indicates that our current paradigm in education and training is based on *standardization*, much like the mass production of industrial-age manufacturing, which is now giving way to customized production in the information-age economy. We know that different learners learn at different rates and have different learning needs. Yet our current paradigm of education and training entails teaching a large group of learners the same content in the same amount of time. Why? One reason is that group-based learning represents logistical and economic efficiencies, even though it does not do a good job of meeting learners' needs. As Campbell and Monson (1994) state, "We challenge this key assumption of traditional instruction that asserts that walking all learners through the content in the same way can be effective. This may be a model for efficiency, but certainly not for effectiveness" (p. 9).

When you consider that student assessment has typically been norm based and that teachers sometimes withhold information from students to see who the really bright ones are, it becomes clear that at least part of the reason for standardized instruction has been to sort learners in K–12 schooling, higher education, and corporate training. Standardized instruction allows valid comparisons of students with each other, which was an important need in the industrial age: separating the laborers from the managers. After all, you couldn't afford to—and didn't want to—educate the common laborers too much, or they wouldn't be content to do boring, repetitive tasks, nor to do what they were told to do without questions. So our current paradigm of training and education was never designed for learning; it was designed for sorting (Reigeluth, 1994).

But assembly-line workers acting as automatons are becoming an endangered species in the United States. The migration of manufacturing jobs abroad, the increasing complexity of equipment, and the current corporate restructuring movement's emphasis on quality combine to require ever-increasing numbers of employees who can take initiative, think critically, and solve problems. To meet this need in industry and the need for life-long learners, we must now focus on learning instead of on sorting. But how can we refocus our systems on learning? Educators agree that different people learn at different rates. So, when an educational or training system holds time constant, achievement must vary, as has been the case in our industrial-age educational system ever since it replaced the one-room schoolhouse. The alternative is to allow time to vary—to give each learner the time he or she needs to reach the learning goals. That would be a learning-focused system, which we show signs of moving toward (see, e.g., the special issue of *Educational Technology*, 1994, on goal-based scenarios developed by Northwestern University and Andersen Consulting Education). This means we need a focus on *customization*, not standardization. This is true in all instructional contexts: corporations and other organizations, as well as K–12 schools and institutes of higher education. Merely changing the content of what we teach will not meet this new need of instruction's supersystems.

Figure 1.2 indicates that our current paradigm of training and education is also based on *conformity* and *compliance*. Trainees and students alike are usually expected to sit down, be quiet, and do what they are told to do. Their learning is directed by the trainer or teacher. But employers now want people who will take *initiative* to solve problems and who will bring *diversity*—especially diverse perspectives—to the workplace. Both of these enhance the ability of a team to solve problems and keep ahead of the competition. Communities and families also need people who will take initiative and honor diversity. Changing the content of what we teach is not sufficient to meet these new needs of the supersystems, for the very structure of our systems of training and education discourages initiative and diversity.

I could continue this process of analyzing how each of the key markers of our current paradigm of training and education (Fig. 1.2) are counterproductive for meeting the emerging needs of the information age, but the message should already be clear: the paradigm itself needs to be changed. This is the focus of the emerging field called educational systems design (ESD) (see, e.g., Banathy, 1991; Reigeluth, 1995), which is concerned both with what kinds of changes are required to better meet the needs of supersystems and learners (a product issue) and with how to go about making those changes (a process issue). So the next question is, does that mean instruction has to change?

Implications for Instructional-Design Theory

From the above discussion, we have seen that the current paradigm of education and training needs to change from one focused on sorting to one focused on learning—from the Darwinian notion of "advancement of the fittest" to the more spiritually and humanistically defensible one of "advancement of all"—and on helping everyone to reach their potential. This means that the paradigm of *instruction* has to change from standardization to customization, from a focus on presenting material to a focus on making sure that learners' needs are met, from a focus on putting things into learners' heads to a focus on helping learners understand what their heads are into: a "learning-focused" paradigm. This, in turn, requires a shift from passive to active learning and from teacher-directed to student-directed (or jointly directed) learning. It requires a shift from teacher initiative, control, and responsibility to shared initiative, control, and responsibility. It requires a shift from decontextualized learning to authentic, meaningful tasks. And, most importantly, it requires a shift from holding time constant and allowing achievement to vary, to allowing each learner the time needed to reach the desired attainments.

But to change the paradigm of instruction in this way, the teacher can't teach the same thing to a whole "class" at the same time. This means the teacher has to be more of a "guide on the side" rather than a "sage on the stage." So, if the teacher is a facilitator rather than the agent of most of the learning, what other agents are there? Well-designed resources are one, and instructional-design theory and instructional technology can play particularly large roles in developing these. But others include fellow learners (e.g., students or trainees), local real-world resources (e.g., practitioners), and remote resources (e.g., those available through the Internet). Instructional-design theories are needed to offer guidance for the use of all these kinds of resources for the learning-focused paradigm of instruction. Furthermore, this paradigm requires that our definition of *in*struction include what many cognitive theorists refer to as "*con*struction" (see, e.g., Ferguson, 1992): a process of helping learners to build their own knowledge, as opposed to (or in addition to) a process of merely conveying information to the learner. Instruction must be defined more broadly as anything that is done to facilitate purposeful learning.

Clearly, this new paradigm of instruction requires a new paradigm of instructional-design theory. But does this mean we should discard current instructional-design theories? To answer this question, let's consider some of the major contributions of current theories. If someone wants to learn a skill, then demonstrations of the skill, generalities (or explanations) about how to do it, and practice doing it, with feedback, will definitely make learning easier and more successful. Behaviorists recognized this, and called these elements examples, rules, and practice with feedback. Cognitivists also recognized this, but naturally had to give these elements different names, such as cognitive apprenticeship and scaffolding. And, yes, constructivists also recognize this, and even radical constructivists walk the walk, though they may not talk the talk. An analysis of instruction designed by some radical constructivists reveals a plentiful use of these very instructional strategies. Should we seriously consider discarding this knowledge? I don't think so. But is this knowledge sufficient to design high-quality instruction? I don't think that, either.

The point is that instructional designers and other educators should recognize that there are two major kinds of instructional methods: *basic methods,* which have been scientifically proven to consistently increase the probability of learning under given situations (e.g., for given types of learning and/or learners), such as the use of "tell, show, and do" (generality, examples, and practice with feedback) for teaching a skill, and *variable methods,* which represent alternatives from which you can choose, as vehicles for the basic methods (e.g., PBL versus tutorial versus apprenticeship). Although this greatly oversimplifies the relationships that exist between methods of instruction and the various situations under which they should and should not be used, it is nonetheless an important distinction of which designers should be aware. Traditional instructional-design theories have typically not provided guidance as to when to use each of these variable methods. As you read through Units 2–4, I suggest you try to identify which methods are basic and which are variable.

To provide guidance on when to use these methods, we need a truly new paradigm of instructional-design theory that has evolved from being a "monologue [to] a dialogue, not just between designers and users but also between designs and those who interact with them." (Mitchell, 1997, p. 64). This new paradigm should subsume current theory and should offer flexible guidelines about such things as when and how learners:

- should be given initiative (self-direction);
- should work in teams on authentic, real-world tasks;
- should be allowed to choose from a diversity of sound methods;
- should best utilize the powerful features of advanced technologies; and
- should be allowed to persevere until they reach appropriate standards.

Learning-focused instructional-design theory must offer guidelines for the design of learning environments that provide appropriate combinations of challenge and guidance, empowerment and support, self-direction and structure. And the learning-focused theory must include guidelines for an area that has largely been overlooked in instructional design: deciding among such variable methods of instruction as PBL, project-based learning, simulations, tutorials, and team-based learning. Fig. 1.3 and 1.4 show some of these kinds of approaches that learning-focused theory might encompass. We also need flexible guidelines for the design of each of these and other approaches to instruction.

Furthermore, the old paradigm of instructional-design theory focused on relatively few kinds of learning. But different types of learning require different methods of instruction (see, e.g., the partial list in Fig. 1.5). Attitudes and values and other types of learning in the affective domain are best facilitated in very different ways from cognitive skills and other types of learning in the cognitive domain, even though there are cognitive elements to those affective learnings, and even though cognitive and affective learnings are often highly interrelated. And learning of domain-dependent knowledge (confined to a particular subject area) is facilitated in different ways from that of domain-independent knowledge (which represents higher levels of learning, such as metacognitive skills), even though both types of knowledge are often used together.

In the industrial age, education needed to focus primarily on simple (domain-dependent) cognitive learning. But, as we evolve deeper into the information age, learners need more skills for complex cognitive tasks, such as solving problems in ill-structured domains. And they need more support to develop in noncognitive areas, such as emotional development, character development, and spiritual development. Instructional-design theories to date have focused almost exclusively on the cognitive domain and, within that, largely on simpler procedural tasks and information in well-structured areas. When you consider the full range of types of learning, it is clear that our current theories are not adequate. The new paradigm of instructional-design theory must address how to support learning in all its varieties and forms. This book contains a sampling of the early work being done for most of these important types of learning, but much work remains to be done to develop powerful guidelines for designing ways to facilitate their development.

For instructional-design theory to remain a vibrant and growing field that will help meet the changing needs of our systems of education and training, we desperately need more theorists and researchers working collaboratively to develop and refine this new paradigm of instructional-design theories. I hope that this book will encourage more people to work in this area, more funders to support work in this area, and more practitioners to use the growing knowledge base in this area. Formative research (see chap. 26) represents one possible methodology for developing such theories because it focuses on how to improve existing design theories, rather than on comparing one theory with another (as experimental research does) or on describing what happens when a theory is used (as naturalistic qualitative research does).

Apprenticeship: an experiential learning strategy in which the learner acquires knowledge and skills through direct participation in learning under immediate personal supervision in a situation that approximates the conditions under which the knowledge will be used.

Debate: a formally structured discussion with two teams arguing opposing sides of a topic.

Demonstration: a carefully prepared presentation that shows how to perform an act or use a procedure; accompanied by appropriate oral and visual explanations and illustrations; frequently accompanied by questions.

Field trip: a carefully planned educational tour in which a group visits an object or place of interest for first-hand observation or study.

Game: an instructional activity in which participants follow prescribed rules that differ from those of reality as they strive to attain a challenging goal; is usually competitive.

Group discussion, guided: a purposeful conversation and deliberation about a topic of mutual interest among 6–20 participants under the guidance of a leader.

Group discussion, free/open: a free group discussion of a topic selected by the teacher, who acts only as chairman; learning occurs only through the interchange among group members.

Ancient symposium: a group of 5–29 persons who meet in the home or private room to enjoy good food, entertainment, fellowship, and with the desire to discuss informally a topic of mutual interest.

Interview: a 5- to 30-minute presentation conducted before an audience in which a resource person(s) responds to systematic questioning by the audience about a previously determined topic.

Laboratory: a learning experience in which students interact with raw materials.

Guided laboratory: an instructor-guided learning experience in which students interact with raw materials.

Lecture/Speech: a carefully prepared oral presentation of a subject by a qualified person.

Lecture, guided discovery: a group learning strategy in which the audience responds to questions posed by the instructor selected to guide them toward discovery (also called recitation class).

Panel discussion: a group of 3–6 persons having a purposeful conversation on an assigned topic before an audience of learners; members are selected on the basis of previously demonstrated interests and competency in the subject to be discussed and their ability to verbalize.

Project: an organized task performance or problem solving activity.

Team project: a small group of learners working cooperatively to perform a task or solve a problem.

Seminar: a strategy in which one or several group members carry out a study/project on a topic (usually selected by the teacher) and present their findings to the rest of the group, followed by discussion (usually teacher-led) of the findings to reach a general conclusion.

Quiet meeting: a 15- to 60-minute period of meditation and limited verbal expression by a group of five or more persons; requires a group of people who are not strangers to each other; is used at a point when the leaders or members feel that reflection and contemplation are desirable.

Simulation: an abstraction or simplification of some specific real-life situation, process, or task.

Case study: a type of simulation aimed at giving learners experience in the sort of decision making required later.

Role play: a dramatized case study; a spontaneous portrayal (acting out) of a situation, condition, or circumstance by elected members of a learning group.

Think Tank/Brainstorm: a group effort to generate new ideas for creative problem solving; thoughts of one participant stimulate new direction and thoughts in another.

Tutorial, programmed: one-to-one method of instruction in which decisions to be made by the tutor (live, text, computer, or expert system) are programmed in advance by means of carefully selected, structured instructions; is individually paced, requires active learner response, and provides immediate feedback.

Tutorial, conversational: one-to-one method of instruction in which the tutor presents instruction in an adaptive mode; is individually paced, requires active learner response, and feedback is provided.

Socratic dialogue: a type of conversational tutorial in which the tutor guides the learner to discovery through a series of questions.

Note: There are many variations of these approaches, and different approaches are often used in combination.

FIG. 1.3.   Approaches to instruction. (from Olson, Dorsey, & Reigeluth, 1988)

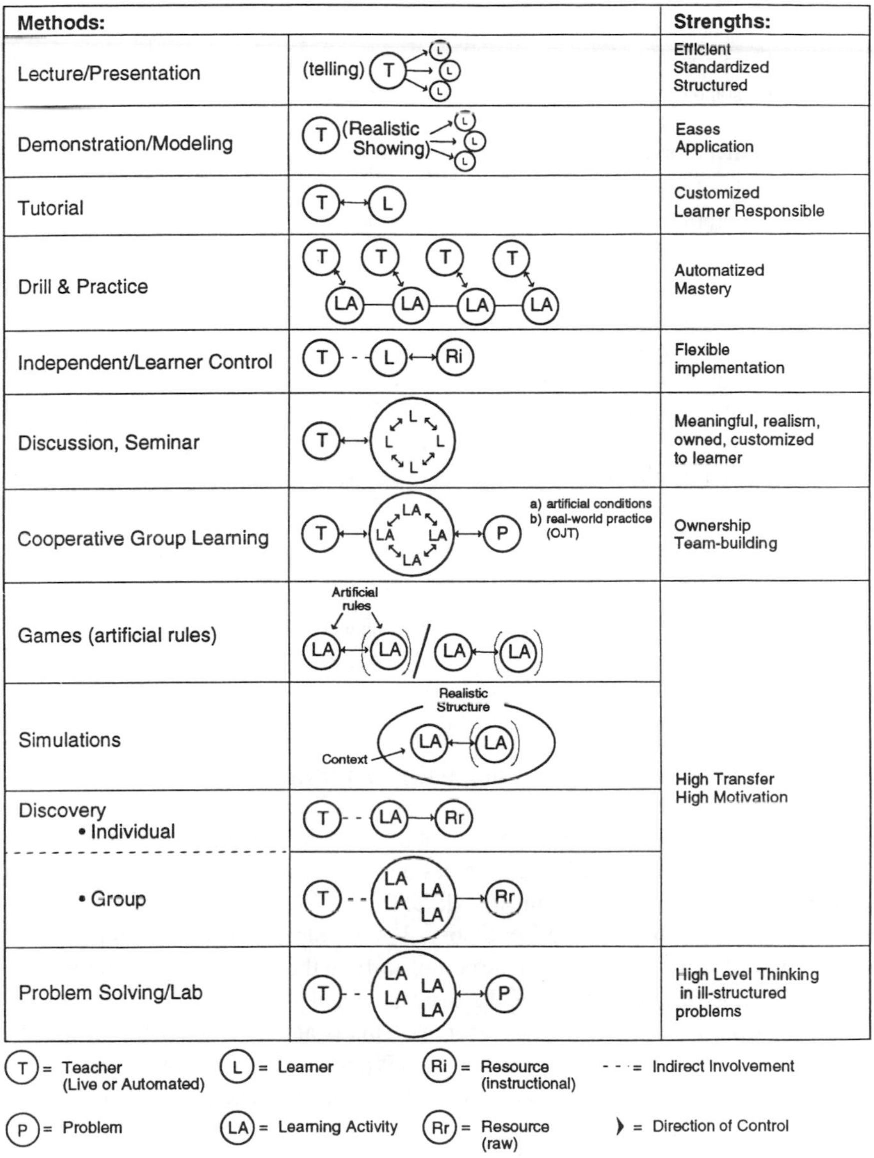

Methods:		Strengths:
Lecture/Presentation	(telling) T →L L L	Efficient Standardized Structured
Demonstration/Modeling	T (Realistic Showing) L L L	Eases Application
Tutorial	T ← L	Customized Learner Responsible
Drill & Practice	T T T T / LA—LA—LA—LA	Automatized Mastery
Independent/Learner Control	T - L ← Ri	Flexible implementation
Discussion, Seminar	T ← (L L L L)	Meaningful, realism, owned, customized to learner
Cooperative Group Learning	T ← (LA LA LA LA) ← P a) artificial conditions b) real-world practice (OJT)	Ownership Team-building
Games (artificial rules)	Artificial rules LA ← LA / LA ← LA	High Transfer High Motivation
Simulations	Realistic Structure Context — (LA ← LA)	
Discovery • Individual	T - - LA → Rr	
• Group	T - - (LA LA LA LA) → Rr	
Problem Solving/Lab	T - (LA LA LA) → P	High Level Thinking in ill-structured problems

T = Teacher (Live or Automated)   L = Learner   Ri = Resource (instructional)   - - - = Indirect Involvement

P = Problem   LA = Learning Activity   Rr = Resource (raw)   ❭ = Direction of Control

FIG. 1.4. Alternative methods for instruction. (Personal communication from M. Molenda, June 16, 1995.)

23

Affective domain
   Emotions and feelings
   Attitudes and values
   Morals and ethics
   Personal development
   ...
Cognitive domain
   (Subject area) domain-dependent
      Information and facts
      Understandings and comprehension
      Skills
   (Subject area) domain-independent
      Learning strategies
      Thinking and problem-solving skills
      Metacognitive skills
   ...
Psychomotor domain
   Reproductive skills
   Productive skills
   ...

FIG. 1.5.   A partial list of different types of learning.

Use of the New Instructional-Design Theories

I expect that the new paradigm of instructional-design theories will be used differently from the way the old paradigm has been used, and that this will place new demands on what the theories must be like.

First, an instructional-design theory should help the stakeholders to develop a vision (or fuzzy image) of the instruction early in the design process, both in terms of ends (how the learners will be different as a result of it) and the means (how those changes in the learners will be fostered). This is an opportunity for all the stakeholders to share their values about both ends and means and to reach some consensus, so that there will be no major disappointments, misunderstandings, or resistance when it comes time for implementation. The practice of thinking about the vision in the ideal often leads to creative approaches that are all too often lacking in instruction. This kind of ideal-visioning activity is advocated by Diamond (1980), who finds a number of practical benefits of this approach, not the least of which is that it gets the design team excited about a solution. Perhaps every instructional theory should come with a prototypical scenario that would help users of the theory to create a "fuzzy" ideal vision of its application to their particular situation.

Second, an instructional-design theory should allow for much greater use of the notion of "user-designers" (Banathy, 1991). This is a natural progression beyond Burkman's (1987) notion of "user-oriented ID" in that it goes beyond measuring and incorporating relevant potential user perceptions—it entails having the users play a major role in designing their own instruction. Users are primarily the learners and facilitators of learning (which should not be confused with the current conceptions of students/trainees and teachers/trainers). But what does an instructional theory need to be like to meet the needs of user-designers? I think the most important issue is the form that the theory takes. Rather than being a printed chapter in a book (to which we are unfortunately constrained in the present work), it might take an electronic form that is more easily used by practitioners. I can imagine two different scenarios that go well beyond the innovation of adding users (students and teachers) to our typical instructional design teams. One of them requires high-tech learning tools, and the other does not.

In one scenario, an instructional-design theory is embodied in a computer system that will help a design team (including all stakeholders) to create flexible, computer-based learning tools, like intelligent tutoring systems. These learning tools, in turn, will allow learners—while they are learning—to create or modify their own instruction. This concept is like adaptive instruction, except that the learners are able to ask the computer system to use certain instructional methods, and the computer is able to give advice or make decisions on some methods based on learner input or information about the learner. As Winn (1989) put it:

> This means that the role of instructional designers will involve less direct instructional decision making and more concentration on the mechanisms by means of which decisions are made (Winn, 1987). ... It follows that the only viable way to make decisions about instructional strategies that meshes with cognitive theory is to do so during instruction using a system that is in constant dialogue with the student and is capable of continuously updating information about the student's progress, attitude, expectations, and so on. (pp. 39–41)

In this scenario instructional-design theories will have to provide guidance on three levels:

- What methods best facilitate learning and human development under different situations?
- What learning-tool features best allow an array of alternative methods to be made available to learners and allow them to make decisions (with varying degrees of guidance) about both content (what to learn) and methods while the instruction is in progress?
- What system features best allow an instructional design team (that preferably includes all stakeholders) to design quality learning tools?

The work of Dave Merrill and associates on "transaction shells" (Li & Merrill, 1990; Merrill, Li, & Jones, 1992; Merrill, chap. 17 of this volume) has produced this type of learning tool and could well lead to this type of system.

To fulfill this scenario, an instructional-design theory must offer guidance for designing a learning tool that can do much of the analysis and decision making during instruction that are now done by a designer for a whole "batch" of learners well ahead of the actual instruction. The learning tool must continuously collect information from an individual learner and/or a small team of learners and use that information to present an array of sound alternatives to the learner(s), about both what to learn next and how to learn it. Also, the instructional-design theory must prescribe that the computer system will afford teachers or trainers the opportunity and mechanisms to easily modify the system in ways they think are important, but with built-in advice to help teachers avoid selecting a weak method. The systems concept of "equifinality" reflects the reality that there are usually several acceptable ways to accomplish the same end. The new paradigm of instructional-design theory will, I believe, prescribe mechanisms to allow for such diversity of means, as well as a diversity of ends, for learners.

In the other scenario of instructional-design theories to implement the concept of user-designers, computers will play a relatively minor role, and teachers will select, adapt, and/or create a wide variety of materials that they can use, frequently in novel ways, during instructional activities. In these situations, the teachers also must (ahead of time) design the framework or support system within which the instruction will occur (though many instructional decisions may be made during the instruction).

For these situations, instructional-design theory will be embodied in electronic performance support systems (EPSSs), which teachers can use to adapt or design their own materials for instruction and the framework of activities in which those materials will be used. Such systems would provide powerful tools for developing a teacher's expertise in design theory if they had the capability for the teacher to query them for their rules or for other logic behind their instructional decisions. With such tools, teachers might gradually acquire all the complexity that the systems "know," and the EPSSs could even be designed to learn from the teacher and students. It could also be designed to help teachers keep track of all the important information about what each of their students has learned and how they learn best. At the same time, I believe that teachers will always have some capabilities that the systems cannot match, so their roles in meeting students' individual needs will likely diverge from (but still overlap to some extent with) the role of the EPSSs.

If this idea of EPSSs for users is construed to also be used by learners, as it should be, it seems likely that the distinction between EPSSs and the kind of computer system discussed in the first scenario may become negligible, as these same systems help learners to make instructional decisions that are instantly implemented by the system. Furthermore, it seems likely that these instructional-design EPSSs will merge with other EPSSs (e.g., a project-management EPSS) to provide simultaneous on-site performance support and instruction—the ultimate case of learning in context. Instructional-design theories will certainly need to change considerably to provide guidance for such integrated systems.

CONCLUSION

In this chapter we began by looking at what an instructional-design theory is. It is design-oriented, offering guidelines about what methods to use in what situations. Its methods are componential, offering varying levels of guidance for educators. The methods are also probabilistic: not always producing the desired results. And we have seen that values play an important role in instructional-design theories in that they underlie both the goals these theories pursue and the methods they offer to attain those goals. We have also explored what an instructional-design theory isn't. It isn't the same as a learning theory, an ISD process model, or a curriculum theory; but it is closely related to all three, and educators should supplement their knowledge of instructional-design theory with all three. In fact, it is often useful to combine instructional-design theory and curriculum theory. Hopefully, these ideas will make it easier for the reader to analyze and understand the theories that follow in Units 2–4.

We have explored the need for a new paradigm of instructional-design theory. We have looked at ISD's supersystems and seen some dramatic changes taking place—changes that have profound implications for what systems of training and education must do to meet the needs of their supersystems. Foremost among those implications is the need for a paradigm of training and education based on learning instead of on sorting students. Other implications include the need to develop initiative, teamwork, thinking skills, and diversity. To help all learners reach their potential, we need to customize, not standardize, the learning process. This, indeed, represents a new paradigm of education and training.

We have also seen that this new paradigm has important implications for instructional-design theory. There is a desperate need for theorists and researchers to generate and refine a new breed of learning-focused instructional-design theories that help educators and trainers to meet those needs, (i.e., that focus on learning and that foster the development of initiative, teamwork, thinking skills, and diversity). The health of instructional-design theory also depends on its ability to involve all stakeholders in the design process. But perhaps the most important of all implications is that much of the designing should be done by the learners (user-designers) while they are learning, with help from a computer system that generates options for the learners based on information collected from the learners. We also need to provide EPSSs to support trainers and teachers in their instructional-design activities. Our theories need to be designed to meet these new needs.

But with all these needs for a new paradigm of instructional-design theory, it is important not to completely reject and discard the old paradigm. In fact, the new paradigm needs to incorporate most of the knowledge generated by previous instructional-design theories, but that knowledge needs to be restructured into substantially different configurations to meet the new needs of those whom we serve.

In order for instructional-design theory to make this transformation to a new paradigm, we desperately need more people working to develop theories such as the ones in this volume—to help take these theories to a higher level of development (guidance and situationality) and to develop theories in other parts of the cognitive, affective, and psychomotor domains that haven't received much attention yet. I think I speak for all the authors in this book in saying that we hope that this book will draw more attention to the need for more work in this new paradigm, that it will encourage more people to contribute to this growing knowledge base for educators, and that it will help others to undertake work in this area by providing easy access to a broad range of work that has already been undertaken.

REFERENCES

Adler, M. (1982). *The paedeia proposal: An educational manifesto.* New York: Macmillan.

Banathy, B. H. (1991). *Systems design of education: A journey to create the future.* Englewood Cliffs, NJ: Educational Technology Publications.

Burkman, E. (1987). Factors affecting utilization. In R. M. Gagné (Ed.), *Instructional technology: Foundations.* Hillsdale, NJ: Lawrence Erlbaum Associates.

Campbell, R., & Monson, D. (1994). Building a goal-based scenario learning environment. *Educational Technology, 34* (9), 9–14.

Cronbach, L., & Suppes, P. (Eds.). (1969). *Research for tomorrow's schools: Disciplined inquiry for education.* New York: Macmillan.

Cuban, L. (1993). The lure of curriculum reform and its pitiful history. *Phi Delta Kappan, 75,* 182–185.

Diamond, R. M. (1980). The Syracuse model for course and curriculum design, implementation, and evaluation. *Journal of Instructional Development, 4*(2), 19–23.

Drucker, P. (1989). *The new realities.* New York: Harper & Row.

Educational Technology. (1994). Special issue on goal-based scenarios, *34*(9).

Ferguson, D. E. (1992). Computers in teaching and learning: An interpretation of current practices and suggestions for future directions. In E. Scanlon & T. O'Shea (Eds.), *New directions in educational technology* (pp. 33–50). Berlin: Springer-Verlag.

Hammer, M., & Champy, J. (1993). *Reengineering the corporation: A manifesto for business revolution.* New York: HarperCollins.

Hequet, M. (1995, November). Not paid enough? You're not alone. *Training, 32*(11), 44–55.

Hutchins, C. L. (1996). *Systemic thinking; Solving complex problems.* Aurora, CO: Professional Development Systems.

Landa, L. N. (1983). Descriptive and prescriptive theories of learning and instruction: An analysis of their relationships and interactions. In C. M. Reigeluth (Ed.), *Instructional-design theories and models: An overview of their current status.* (pp. 55–69). Hillsdale, NJ: Lawrence Erlbaum Associates.

Lee, C., & Zemke, R. (Nov. 1995). No time to train. *Training, 32*(11), 29–37.

Leinhardt, G. (1989). Development of an expert explanation: An analysis of a sequence of subtraction lessons. In L. Resnick (Ed.), *Knowing, learning and instruction: Essays in honor of Robert Glaser.* Hillsdale, NJ: Lawrence Erlbaum Associates.

Leshin, C. B., Pollock, J., & Reigeluth, C. M. (1994). *Instructional design strategies and tactics.* Englewood Cliffs, NJ: Educational Technology Publications.

Li, Z., & Merrill, M. D. (1990). Transaction shells: A new approach to courseware authoring. *Journal of Research on Computing in Education, 23*(1), 72–86.

Merrill, M. D., Li, Z., & Jones, M. K. (1992). Instructional transaction shells: Responsibilities, methods, and parameters. *Educational Technology, 32*(2), 5–26.

Mitchell, C. T. (1997). New thinking in design. *Urban Land, 56*(12), 28–64.

Olson, J., Dorsey, L., & Reigeluth, C. M. (1988). *Instructional theory for mid-level strategies.* Unpublished manuscript.

Osborne, D., & Gaebler, T. (1992). *Reinventing government: How the entrepreneurial spirit is transforming the public sector.* New York: Penguin.

Perkins, D. N. (1992). *Smart schools: Better thinking and learning for every child.* New York: The Free Press.

Pogrow, S. (1996). Reforming the wannabe reformers: Why education reforms almost always end up making things worse. *Phi Delta Kappan, 77,* 656–663.

Reigeluth, C. M. (Ed.). (1983a). *Instructional-design theories and models: An overview of their current status.* Hillsdale, NJ: Lawrence Erlbaum Associates.

Reigeluth, C. M. (1983b). Instructional design: What is it and why is it? In C. M. Reigeluth (Ed.), *Instructional-design theories and models: An overview of their current status* (pp. 3–36). Hillsdale, NJ: Lawrence Erlbaum Associates.

Reigeluth, C. M. (1994). The imperative for systemic change. In C. M. Reigeluth & R. J. Garfinkle (Eds.), *Systemic change in education* (pp. 3–11). Englewood Cliffs, NJ: Educational Technology Publications.

Reigeluth, C. M. (1995). Educational systems development and its relationship to ISD. In G. Anglin (Ed.), *Instructional technology: Past present, and future* (2nd ed., pp. 84–93). Englewood, CO: Libraries Unlimited.

Reigeluth, C. M., & Garfinkle, R. J. (Eds.). (1994). *Systemic change in education.* Englewood Cliffs, NJ: Educational Technology Publications.

Rummelhart, D. E., & Norman, D. A. (1978). Accretion, tuning, and restructuring: Three modes of learning. In J. W. Cotton & R. L. Klatzky (Eds.), *Semantic factors in cognition* (pp. 37–53). Hillsdale, NJ: Lawrence Erlbaum Associates.

Simon, H. A. (1969). *Sciences of the artificial.* Cambridge, MA: MIT Press.

Snelbecker, G. E. (1974). *Learning theory, instructional theory, and psychoeducational design.* New York: McGraw-Hill.

Winn, W. (1989). Toward a rational and theoretical basis for educational technology. *Educational Technology Research & Development, 37* (1), 35–46.

Winn, W. (1997). Advantages of a theory-building curriculum in instructional technology. *Educational Technology, 37*(1), 34–41.

2 Some Thoughts About Theories, Perfection, and Instruction

Glenn E. Snelbecker
Temple University

PRELIMINARIES: THOUGHTS AND ANECDOTES ABOUT THEORIES, GUIDELINES, AND INSTRUCTIONS

Researchers' Versus Practitioners' Views About Theories: Two Anecdotes

After a researcher had discussed current findings with colleagues, the colleagues asked why "other topics" were not also addressed by the researcher and by the theory from which the research plans were developed.

An instructor found a theory to be very interesting, was persuaded that the theory explained many things that occurred with students, and then tried to change almost all aspects of classroom instruction to fit the particular theory; in a sense, the instructor tried to create curriculum and instruction based on the theory.

Theories: Guidelines, Not Perfection

Dewey (1929) writes:

> The third point is that laws and facts, even when they are arrived at in genuinely scientific shape, do not yield *rules of practice*. Their value for educational practice—and *all* education is a mode of practice, intelligent or accidental and routine—is indirect; it consists in provision of *intellectual instrumentalities* to be used by the educator. (p. 28)

Furthermore, Popper (1957) notes that "All theories are trials; they are tentative hypotheses, tried out to see whether they work; and all experimental corroboration is simply the result of tests undertaken in a critical spirit, in an attempt to find out where our theories *err*" [italics added] (p. 87).

One Theory Versus Many Theories: What if No "Complete" Theory Exists?

Hall & Lindzey (1957) strongly recommended "that the student should, once he has surveyed the available theories of personality, adopt an intolerant and affectionate acceptance of a particular theoretical position without reservation, ... wallow in it, revel in it, absorb it, learn it thoroughly, and think that it is the best possible way to conceive of behavior" (pp. 556–557).

In response to the e-mail message "Teacher training colleges and universities must emphasize CL as the primary teaching paradigm," Michael Scriven wrote: "Too bad. I'd buy *allowing* CL, pending more serious evaluation, but as for *establishing* it, that way dogma lies and dogma *always* lies" (AERA-C, Division C: Learning and Instruction listserv, December 8, 1996).

And perhaps the following slogan could be applied, analogously, to theories of instruction: "We don't make a lot of the products you buy. We make a lot of the products you buy better."™ (Trademark of BASF Corporation).

INTRODUCTION

This volume provides an overview of instructional theories and models that are increasing our understanding about instruction and that can help practitioners to design conditions that facilitate learning. Earlier (Paterson, 1977; Snelbecker, 1974, 1983) it was noted that, though the practice of education has been a matter of concern for centuries, formally organized instructional theories were not available until the middle of the 20th century. The two anecdotes and five quotations, above, were selected because collectively they reflect some of the conflicting views and expectations that people have about the nature and value of instructional theories. Although most would agree that instructional theories, compared with learning theories, are closely related to practice, people have different expectations about whether instructional theories "should" (a) give explicit detailed prescriptions for practice or (b) mainly provide general guidelines that practitioners can use to design instruction.

What should we expect from a particular instructional theory, and from theories in general? One goal for this chapter is to provide some ideas that will be useful as you examine the array of instructional theories and models presented in this book. Another goal is to stimulate constructive dialogues among advocates of various theories, even between "competitive" groups, about ways to further our understanding about designing instruction to facilitate learning. A third goal is to propose some ways for "identifying the scope" of a particular theory (or the implications and limitations of research findings). This chapter includes descriptions of "theory integration" ventures regarding psychotherapy theories because they may be applicable to instructional theories, and also explains how an interesting advertising slogan might help readers to clarify what respective theories and research reports do and do not address in a given practical situation.

Before proceeding further, it is important to clarify what is meant, in this chapter, by certain terms. First, *theory* refers to an organized set of propositions that are syntactically and semantically integrated (that is, that follow certain rules by which they can be logically related to one another and to observable data) and that serve as a means of predicting and explaining observable phenomena. Some authors use the term *model* to designate a concretization of a theory, or they use the terms *model* or *miniature model* to refer to theories with a more narrowly defined scope of explanation. In this chapter, theory will be used broadly to refer to all of the examples just noted, including what some authors may call theories and others may call models. Second, *instructor* will be used collectively to refer to both teachers and trainers. Third, for brevity in this chapter, *instructional theory* will be used instead of *instructional-design theory*.

Cultural Differences Among People Interested in Instructional Theories

It is important to recognize the existence of "cultural differences" among people who have an interest in instructional theories. In the first volume of this series, I observed (Snelbecker, 1983) that two groups may be interested in the status of instructional theories: the first group, which includes researchers and theorists, I called *knowledge producers*; the second group, called *knowledge users*, includes instructors (teachers and trainers), instructional designers, curriculum supervisors, administrators, and other practitioners. As the two anecdotal observations at the beginning of this chapter portray, knowledge producers are less likely to expect research findings or theories to provide definitive answers than are knowledge users. Such fundamental differences are at least partly reflective of the different workplace cultures for knowledge producers versus knowledge users.

Instructors, administrators, and other practitioners work in a culture where they must provide, in a timely and cost-effective fashion, the best possible instruction for the students or clients in their care. They do not have the luxury of waiting until tomorrow for new data or research interpretations; they must make decisions now on the basis of whatever information is available. Moreover, they can rarely select the students or clients with whom they would prefer to work or demand better conditions and support. Stated another way, instead of changing their clients and their setting to fit with some theory, instructors and instructional designers must try to envision how various theories and research findings might be relevant for their clients and their setting, including the resources and constraints that actually exist there.

In contrast, the workplace culture of researchers and theorists dictates that they exercise caution in drawing conclusions and that they consider carefully the vari-

ables and conditions involved in their research. To help ensure that research findings are likely to be valid, they have the responsibility of clearly stating research
questions, selecting appropriate people to be studied, identifying which variables to
study and which to exclude, and preparing appropriate conditions under which to
collect data. Otherwise it may not be possible to detect patterns and relationships
relevant to the research questions they are trying to answer. This usually means that
only certain kinds of people will be appropriate for that particular study, and that
many influences and conditions must be excluded or controlled if they are not
clearly relevant for the research questions of interest. Even so-called action research and applied research projects, including studies conducted in classrooms or
in other practical settings, typically involve changes in the "usual, normal" workplace culture in order for the studies to be appropriately conducted. For example, at
a minimum, these studies typically involve extra personnel and extra resources beyond what is customarily available when such studies are not being conducted, and
they may also involve selection or assignment of certain students, rather than trying
to instruct all of the students regularly found in that setting. On a daily basis in their
workplace culture, researchers and theorists typically must offer only tentative
conclusions based on currently available data and specify what additional kinds of
research need to be conducted, as well as what factors and conditions need to be included (and which excluded), to have well-designed studies that can yield sound
information.

The two anecdotes at the beginning of this chapter illustrate how some instructors
and other practitioners tend to have expectations about theories that differ from the
typical expectations of researchers and theorists. Researchers and theorists who are
engrossed in the development and modification of theories tend to be keenly aware of
which topics have been addressed and which have been omitted by a particular theory, especially when they are examining someone else's theory. People who want to
use knowledge about instructional theories are often so involved, almost overwhelmed, with the needs and demands of their practical situations that they may not
be as critical of the omissions or limitations of a particular theory if and when it appears that the theory may help them address an important, pressing practical concern.
Consequently, communication between knowledge producers and knowledge users
is sometimes compromised due to their different work cultures.

Even further compounding the problem, when practitioners express great interest in a researcher's findings or in the apparent practical implications of a theory, it
is not so easy for the researcher or the theorist to emphasize the limitations of their
offerings to the people displaying such great interest in their work. The knowledge
producers, who are quite familiar with academic guidelines (e.g., for journal publications) where one carefully qualifies what is being concluded and identifies what
is being omitted, tend to be less conscious of the widely ranging conditions which
instructors and other practitioners regularly encounter. Although researchers typically are very cautious in stating how findings from one research environment may
be generalized to another research environment, they may not display this cautious

attitude when practitioners ask them for help. They may focus so much on the features addressed in their research that they may not adequately take into account all of the myriad conditions and diverse client characteristics with which instructors and other practitioners must deal on a daily basis, thus they may grossly underestimate the differences between their research context and the practical context.

As a result, the practitioners become frustrated and criticize theorists and researchers when their attempts to apply theories do not work out as desired and expected with their clients; the researchers and theorists become hesitant—perhaps almost totally unwilling—to engage in further discussions, as they feel that their ideas have been misunderstood, distorted, and/or grossly misapplied. While many express the view that it is important for knowledge producers and knowledge users to cooperate with each other to their (potential) mutual benefit, it is also recognized that there are barriers to such cooperation (cf. Casanova, 1989; Leby-Leboyer, 1988; Phillips, 1989).

Contrasting Judgments About the Value of Theories

One particular way in which practitioners and researchers/theorists seem to have a cultural gap concerns the basis for judging the value of theories and research findings, especially about the extent to which theories should tell practitioners what to do. Instructional designers and other practitioners primarily judge the value of a theory or of research findings based on the extent to which some *practical implications* can be derived from them. In contrast, knowledge producers primarily judge the value of a theory or of research findings based on the extent to which they lead to new insights and point to new directions for conducting further studies and constructing theories.

In a sense, the knowledge user is typically looking for help in making practical decisions and wants "final answers" from research findings and theory. The knowledge producer is engaged in an unending attempt to understand particular phenomena and thus views research reports and theory essentially as "progress reports," rather than as final answers. Thus, a teacher or other practitioner may try to modify classroom instruction based on research findings or theory, even though not all aspects of the practical context have been addressed by the theory or research, whereas researchers and theorists are much more likely to discuss what variables and conditions have not been addressed by some study or theory as well as to consider those aspects that have been addressed. However, it should be noted that this close scrutiny may be less likely with their own theories.

Knowledge Users: Value of Theories and Research Findings

As a natural consequence of the work they do, teachers, trainers, instructional designers, and other practitioners tend to be less interested in learning about theories and research findings than in hearing (cookbook?) directions about how they can help their students and other clients. Although many practitioners adamantly say (and mean!) that they want to make their own decisions, other practitioners (including administrators) regularly tell researchers to stop equivocating and simply say which actions are supported by the data.

The practitioners' expectations about the practical value of theory probably evolved at least partly because they were told that John Dewey or someone else has said that there is nothing as practical as a good theory. Dewey often talked about ways in which psychological and educational research might improve practice (cf. Dewey, 1900, 1929). But, as illustrated by Dewey's comment that was quoted at the beginning of this chapter, Dewey was suggesting that a theory can mainly help the practitioner think about practical problems in different ways; he was not contending that the theorist or the theory will tell the practitioner precisely which actions to take and which ones to avoid.

Of course, instructional theories and research findings—because of their focus on the design of instruction—may sometimes point more clearly toward particular decisions and/or actions than would be true, for example, of learning theories or motivation theories. But because it is unlikely that any practical situation will be identical to conditions actually studied, the practitioner generally must make decisions about the learners' characteristics and existing conditions in a given practical situation. Thus, it is likely that the theory will mainly help the practitioner to consider the merits of alternative approaches, including a fuller understanding about likely outcomes of various options, so as to have a better basis for choosing what should be done in a given practical situation.

Thus, readers would be well advised to check each theory to see what it does and does not address of all the conditions and people characteristics found in a practical setting, rather than simply looking for specific directions to follow.

Knowledge Producers: Value of Theories and Research Findings

Knowledge producers' views about the value of theories and research findings seem to be developed, at least to some extent, by what they have heard during their academic training and seen in the professional literature. For example, it is quite common in courses and in scholarly writing to encourage new researchers and new theorists to delimit the scope of their inquiries (e.g., to focus on only a few of the many influences in a learning situation) and also to organize their ideas within some single theory. In a sense, aspiring knowledge producers are being told that they should select some theoretical position and/or research approach and act as if the others do not even exist, as illustrated by the Hall and Lindzey (1957) quotation featured at the beginning of this chapter.

These guidelines make sense for researchers because it is difficult enough to understand thoroughly any given theoretical framework, and it can be distracting and sometimes even counterproductive to try to work with two or more different theoretical frameworks at the same time. From this perspective, it is better to deal with erroneous expectations or predictions and other problems as they occur, rather than to "jump" from one approach to another (sometimes called a "shotgun approach" because of scattered, rather than focused, thinking). Of course, at some point after carefully pursuing some line of research or theoretical position, the psychologist might decide that modifications in the approach are necessary or even that a new theory may be needed. In brief, the recommendation was to focus on whatever approach had been selected and see how it works. However, these otherwise quite constructive recommendations to focus on one theory often seem to have an isolating and possibly even debilitating effect on the advancement of instructional theories, as well as of social science theories more generally.

It appears that somehow this otherwise good advice has often been misinterpreted, i.e., interpreted quite differently from what Hall and Lindzey (and other authors saying similar things) had in mind. Focusing intently, even passionately, on one's theory, to the extent that you act as though the other theories do not exist, may sometimes be useful in conducting research or constructing theory. However, when debating the merits of different theories, sometimes advocates of a given position have not only emphasized how good their approach is, but have also made such strongly critical comments about other positions that they seem to be saying that competing positions have such limitations or even are so wrong that they should not even exist.

Though I can no longer find and thus properly credit the original author(s), early in my career I was profoundly influenced by a comment that went something like this: "Why is it that in the physical and biological sciences, current researchers attempt to advance their views by standing on the shoulders of their predecessors, whereas in the social sciences people seem to try to advance their views by stepping in the faces of their predecessors?" Although I had already developed curiosity about different approaches, this observation caused me to be even more interested in, and appreciative of, a wide range of theories and research approaches: Considering competing theories has often provided me with a wider perspective and given me more "lenses" with which to view various topics and issues, regarding both practical matters and theoretical matters.

There is an important reason why knowledge producers, like knowledge users, should appreciate and benefit from having an array of theories available, even competitors to one's own favored theory: Our understanding about instruction, especially identification of various ways in which we can facilitate learning, can be greatly enhanced by the existence of alternative theories, especially through constructive discussions about the nature, strengths, and weaknesses of respective theories.

In his role as Features Editor of the *Educational Researcher*, Donmoyer (1997) noted that too often there are "adversarial" exchanges between advocates of competing paradigms and approaches, and he proposed that we would all benefit from more constructive exchanges. His comments actually addressed contrasting views about situated cognition and other cognitive views of learning, but they also are relevant for instructional theories. An earlier paper (Anderson, Reder, & Simon, 1996) had critiqued the literature on "situated cognition," and Greeno (1997) challenged the criticisms by Anderson et al. Donmoyer observed:

> Greeno's departure from traditional academic discourse norms, in other words, does not seem to be a product of politeness or result primarily from a desire for civility (although politeness and civility are certainly ancillary consequences of the stance taken). Rather, the stance seems to be motivated by intellectual concerns, and Greeno's intellectual concerns make sense today when paradigm differences are evident even within a single discipline such as educational psychology. (p. 4)

Donmoyer went on to express the view that development of theories in general (I would emphasize: including instructional theories and models) will benefit from constructive exchanges between advocates of alternative positions.

TWO IDEAS TO FACILITATE CONSTRUCTIVE DISCUSSIONS ABOUT COMPETING INSTRUCTIONAL THEORIES

Two general ideas will now be explored that, hopefully, might do two things. First, these ideas may lead to more formal support for constructive exchanges about the contributions of different theories. Second, they also may help clarify, for knowledge producers as well as for knowledge users, what a given theory or research report *does and does not* address. The first general idea comes from work on psychotherapy theories, involving knowledge producers and knowledge users in their attempts to integrate psychotherapy theories. The second general idea comes from industry, involving attempts by companies to state what their products can and cannot do; this idea leads to questions and possible answers about what we can, and cannot, expect from instructional theories.

Progress Regarding Other Applied Psychology Theories: Psychotherapy Theory Integration

The present volume and others in this series represent attempts to foster discussion about instructional theories and models, as have discussions at various conventions, in sections of journals, in other publications, and so forth. Sometimes, however, it is useful to consider how parallel issues and concerns have been addressed in other areas of applied psychology. Thus, some approaches to the use and production of psychotherapy theories will be described. Obviously, the purpose here is not to say that the identical approach would be useful in attempts to improve the use and production of instructional theories; instead, this information is presented as a means to stimulate thinking about whether some aspects of this approach might be of value to improve how we think about, use, and produce instructional theories.

Researchers and practitioners interested in furthering advancement of an empirical and conceptual basis for psychotherapy practice had, over the years, exchanged ideas informally about their satisfaction and concerns about the respective approaches they had been using. But these exchanges across theoretical boundaries (i.e., even between advocates of opposing views) were apparently fostered particularly by Goldfried's (1980) call for action in the article "Toward the Delineation of Therapeutic Change Principles."

The *Journal of Psychotherapy Integration* was established to explore prospects for integrating theory, and other journals documented the growing interest in comparing and exchanging ideas by proponents of various theoretical orientations (Goldfried & Wachtel, 1983). It should be noted that both knowledge users and knowledge producers contributed to these ongoing discussions. For example, Castonguay and Goldfried (1994) proclaimed that psychotherapy integration is "an idea whose time has come"; Jacobson (1994) indicated prospects for contemporary behaviorism; and Mitchell (1994) contended that psychoanalysts were ready to explore interfaces with other psychotherapies. Garfield (1994) pointed to the popularity of eclecticism (i.e., essentially using a number of different views rather than relying almost exclusively on one theoretical orientation) among practitioners as qualified support for psychotherapy integration. While acknowledging the attractiveness of some form of theoretical integration and emphasizing the need for developing guidelines (Beitman, 1994), various authors have also noted that there are issues and complexities that need to be considered (e.g., Fonagy & Target, 1996; Lazarus, 1995, 1996; Lemmens, de Ridder, & van Lieshout, 1994; Norcross, 1995; Steenbarger, Smith, & Budman, 1996; Strupp, 1996).

Is *instructional theory* integration "an idea whose time has come," as Castonguay and Goldfried (1994) suggested for psychotherapy theories? Perhaps only time will tell. But though some aspects of papers cited above are mainly relevant for psychotherapy theories, the general ideas and issues about exploring theory integration seem to be equally relevant for instructional theories. For example, with only slight modification to reflect the contemporary influence of various cognitive psychology approaches and to deemphasize the relevance of psychoanalytic theories, two comments by Goldfried about the status of psychotherapy theories in 1980 seem to be somewhat relevant for the status of instructional theories and models today. Goldfried noted concerns among people with various theoretical orientations concerning limits of their respective approaches, and he expressed some concern that advocates of the respective positions might even be "completely blind to alternative conceptualizations and potentially effective intervention procedures" (Goldfried, 1980, p. 991).

There are at least two general ways in which these theory integration ventures in psychotherapy might be relevant for future development and use of instructional theories. First, as is the case with instructional theories, there has been a strong contemporary influence of cognitive psychology (cf. Alford, 1995) that sometimes moves integration in the direction of reinterpreting other psychotherapy theory positions within a cognitive framework (cf. Persons, 1995). Second, psychotherapy integration has prompted discussion about the extent to which integration efforts should reflect applied versus theoretical emphases. While acknowledging that other authors have emphasized advantages for practitioners, Safran and Messer (1997) focused on some very important advantages for knowledge producers that can result from theory integration ventures: "The greatest value of the psychotherapy integration movement lies in the creative and growth-oriented confrontation with and dialogue about difference, and it is in this process that the payoff lies" (p. 149). Thus, many of the leading psychotherapy researchers and theorists as well as practitioners have been interested in theory integration efforts because they recognize that both knowledge producers and knowledge users can benefit from these efforts.

The present volume, as well as other publications and presentations at professional conventions, has been facilitating discussions about alternative approaches to instructional theory. Whether these collaborative activities lead to the kind of integrative efforts now established for psychotherapy theories remains to be seen (Snelbecker, 1993).

Prospects for "Advertising"/Clarifying What One Should/Should Not Expect of a Theory or Research Report

At the risk of being accused of "naively using a business model or an industrial model," I am suggesting that we must be more precise in our designation of what to expect from a theory, specifically as the result of this interesting advertising theme: "We don't make a lot of the products you buy. We make a lot of the products you buy better"™ (trademark of BASF Corporation). (In case readers are concerned, this is a company in which I have no financial or other involvement!) But before explaining how this particular advertising theme might be helpful with regard to production and use of instructional theories, it is important to provide some background information.

In a sense, this advertising theme led me to the belief that we need the equivalent of "truth in advertising" guidelines so that research reports and instructional theories will more prominently display statements about what they do and do not address. There are three matters in particular that, in my opinion, need to be addressed in a forthright manner: (a) Is any theory perfect? (b) Does any theory include everything about the topic(s) it addresses? (c) Is it, or should it be, the only theory that anyone should consider with regard to the particular topic(s) addressed? I'm proposing that such guidelines are needed by, and can help, not only instructors and other practitioners who otherwise may attempt to "stretch" the applicability of ideas to fit some practical situation, but also researchers and budding theorists who may become so enamored of a theory that they forget its limitations and categorically exclude all competitive views.

Is Any Theory Perfect?

I honestly doubt that you'll find such a claim formally stated by the originator of any scientific theory. Popper (1959), a distinguished philosopher of science, cautioned that

> [E]very scientific statement must remain *tentative for ever.* It may indeed be corroborated, but every corroboration is relative to other statements which, again, are tentative. Only in our subjective experiences of conviction, in our subjective faith, can we be "absolutely certain." (p. 280)

He also suggested:

> Science never pursues the illusory aim of making its answers final, or even probable. Its advance is, rather, towards the infinite yet attainable aim of ever discovering new, deeper, and more general problems, and of subjecting its ever tentative answers to ever renewed and ever more rigorous tests. (p. 281)

In some respects, it is far better to consider even our favorite theories to be "progress reports" rather than final statements about the design of instruction. When instruction based on a theory works as expected, there is certainly reason to be pleased, even to have a certain amount of pride and confidence. But we must also be cautious and restrained in our enthusiasm because future research findings and theories almost inevitably will lead us to consider issues and questions that need further examination and modification of our progress reports.

Does Any Theory Include Everything About the Topic(s) It Addresses?

Think for a moment: How many times have you ever heard a theorist proclaim that his or her theory addresses anything and everything you want to know about a given topic? Although you may find some protégé or self-proclaimed promoter of a theory making pronouncements of this magnitude, it is not likely that the originator, the person who knows the theory best, will make such an unrestricted claim. When we're studying some interesting theoretical issue or trying to identify ways to cope with some practical matter, it is very easy to begin thinking and acting as though anything and everything in that situation will be taken into account. But in contrast, theorists are expected to clarify the scope of phenomena addressed by their theory and to designate limitations that apply to their theory and its proper use. Similarly, competent researchers are expected to recognize (and, often, to state explicitly) delimitations and limitations of their research design in order to address selected factors and to at least temporarily ignore others. Although not as formally codified as are requirements for test and measurement developers and publishers (cf. American Psychological Association, 1985), these delimitations and qualifying comments are routinely expected in professional communications, written and oral, about interpretations of research results and discussions of the scope and applicability of respective theories.

Is, or Should, Any Theory Be the Only Theory With Regard to a Topic?

I'll use the literature on psychotherapy integration as a basis for addressing this question. Saffran and Messer (1997) contend that it is important to have alternative approaches available to facilitate development of theories. In their call for "a more contextually based, pluralistic approach toward psychotherapy integration," they observed: "In the natural sciences it is recognized that multiple, contradictory theories are necessary to capture different aspects of the underlying phenomenon, and that a given theory captures some of these aspects at the expense of others" (p. 149); they cited Nozick (1981) in support of their view. In their conclusion, Safran and Messer then cautioned: "A theoretical system is always in danger of becoming a fossilized remnant of what was once a vital insight, even in the hands of the person who developed it" (p. 149). Thus, knowledge producers as well as knowledge users can benefit from using an array of possible theories, rather than just one approach or point of view.

If There's No Problem Here, Why Discuss These Three Questions?

Logically, then, it might not seem plausible to expect that any given theory will be perfect, will address all facets of a topic, or will be the single, dominant way of viewing some theoretical issue or practical matter. And yet, it is not unusual to find such views being expressed.

For example, while writing the present chapter, I noticed an exchange of e-mail messages on an American Educational Research Association listserv about the merits of *CL*. (Some listserv participants seemed to be focusing on CL as collaborative learning while others considered CL to be mainly cooperative learning. But the specific theory is not what is relevant to the present discussion. Thus, for our purposes here, CL could stand for any theory that one might want to endorse.) After having discussed the merits of CL, one listserv participant wrote: "Teacher training colleges and universities must emphasize CL as the primary teaching paradigm." In response, Michael Scriven wrote: "Too bad. I'd buy *allowing* CL, pending more serious evaluation, but as for *establishing* it, that way dogma lies and dogma *always* lies" (AERA-C Division C: Learning and Instruction listserv, December 8, 1996).

I asked for (and received) permission to use Professor Scriven's comment in this chapter because it concisely summed up the problem I'm discussing here. Dictionaries I consulted indicate that "dogma" essentially refers to major tenets or beliefs that are central to some point of view. I do not believe that Scriven was denying someone the right to identify such key aspects of a view. However, in his objection to establishing one theory or approach, he seems to be cautioning against becoming dogmatic in making claims. My dictionaries indicate that "dogmatic" involves presenting views, incorrectly, as though they are established facts. Using my three questions, I'm suggesting that an overly enthusiastic advocate of a theory may (intentionally or even unintentionally) start acting and implying that the preferred theory is virtually perfect or complete and/or the only theory worthy of consideration.

Theories typically pose significant challenges not only for novices but even for experienced professionals. On the one hand, theories are supposed to be helping us to understand something; on the other hand, they are quite abstract and they have these annoying limitations in the extent to which they are supposed to be providing explanations. To put it mildly, they are far from being easy to learn or to use in that they have so many qualifications and constraints.

When trying to teach students to understand what they should and should not expect from theories and reports of research results, I've often found it necessary to start with some concrete examples with which they are familiar. Because theories and information in general are so abstract, it usually has been easier to first illustrate principles I'm trying to teach by showing how they apply to products and other concrete objects. For example, I suggest that they should think about how they have tried to be better consumers of products as an aid in trying to become better consumers of information. These steps have been pedagogically useful, not only with teachers and other practitioners, but also with aspiring researchers and theorists and with undergraduate and graduate students.

Over the years, I have used various examples and analogies in classes on learning theories and instructional theories. I've often asked students if they have seen "movies." When almost all say that they have, I emphasize that they actually saw a series of *still* pictures, not literally moving pictures, that gave them an impression of seeing people and objects moving. I point out the fact that these so-called movies could differ, even quite dramatically, depending on the location of the camera(s), the lens or lenses used, prevailing conditions, and many other potential influences on the final movie. Moreover, I emphasize that, because the movies are really based on static pictures of dynamic, changing people and objects, the movie is necessarily somewhat obsolete as soon as it is completed. However, the completed movie can give us a very useful representation of the people, objects, and events that were being filmed. Similarly, theories provide us with helpful representations of the phenomena being described, even though the theories are not the phenomena, per se. As with movies, there are many influences on the theories that have been developed about a given topic—influences that may significantly affect the kinds of theory or theories that result from our efforts. As long as we recognize that these theories are only representations of phenonema, they can help us enormously in understanding the phenomena addressed by the respective theories.

I've tried to help students understand how the emergence of new theories can and should be based on previous offerings, much as new products typically represent improvements on, rather than rejections of, earlier versions of the same product. Obviously, there are some exceptions with regard to products and with regard to theories. The computer and high technology industries provide countless examples of ways in which many new products are somewhat obsolete even as we're buying them. We also know that this newly purchased and soon-to-be-obsolete product can nonetheless provide us years of valuable service. Similarly, I try to help students understand how they can gain valuable ideas from research reports and theoretical principles, despite the fact that knowledge producers may be conducting further studies and modifying theories that will change the way that we think about the particular phenomena. Just as we have to make careful decisions about how any upgrades in computer equipment or software may impact how we work with those technologies, we need to think carefully about how we, as knowledge producers as well as knowledge users, should react to new research findings and new modifications in theories that we have been using.

But at this point problems are routinely encountered that puzzled me for a long time: Since early in my own graduate student years, I've been emphasizing this idea: "A slave to a theory is a slave, no matter how good the theory might be." Nonetheless, many people with whom I have discussed theories, whether budding knowledge users or aspiring knowledge producers, graduate or undergraduate students, or even experienced professionals, seem to develop a preference for some particular theory and to have problems in seeing how they may use more than one theory in a given context, no matter whether it involves a research or practical situation. This very strong commitment to some theory (people differ in the particular theory they choose) often leads to a call to get rid of, or at least disenfranchise, any and all competitor theories.

ADVANTAGES OF "ADDED VALUE": WHY CLAIM THAT WE'RE "ONLY" DOING CERTAIN ASPECTS INSTEAD OF "THE WHOLE THING"?

Several years ago, while trying to solve this puzzle, I kept noticing a series of advertisements that had a common theme. "We don't make a lot of the products you buy. We make a lot of the products you buy better"™ (trademark of BASF Corporation). Some of their advertisements were: "At BASF we don't make the skates, we make them smoother"™ and "We don't make the helmet, we make it more comfortable."™ Out of curiosity, I first asked students if they had seen or heard these advertisements. When I learned that many of my students had seen them, I asked what was meant by these commercials, and how they might be relevant for our ongoing discussions of theories and their use. After successfully using this theme to help students think more clearly about what theories do and do not address, I contacted BASF. Through Terrence M. Cooper (personal communication, December 12, 1996) I received permission to cite their themes here; I also received a paper in which von Moltke (1993) provided more background information about the evolution of this advertising theme and its effectiveness that made me even more intrigued with prospects that a parallel approach could be useful in describing the scope and limitations of instructional design research findings and theories.

Perhaps we can learn something from this advertising theme. Perhaps what we need to do in describing theories and research reports is to identify the "added value" that the respective theory or research results provide us. We need not claim that we have all the answers for a theoretical issue or a practical matter, but we properly can claim credit for having addressed at least some aspects of those matters.

As I've already noted above, in principle, such details are already expected for theories and research results. Perhaps it's just that, in our enthusiasm in talking about what has been learned, we sometimes temporarily forget the restrictions of our preferred theories or research findings. This open, candid kind of approach that recognizes contributions that improve some aspect of instruction, instead of pretending that everything must be changed, can be mutually beneficial for knowledge producers and knowledge users. It can help clarify what theorists and researchers are selecting to do, without presenting pressures for them to do more. It can help instructors and other practitioners to know what aspects of a given practical situation have been addressed and which have been intentionally or unintentionally excluded.

WHAT SHOULD WE EXPECT OF THEORIES? SOME THOUGHTS TO CONSIDER IN REVIEWING THESE AND OTHER THEORIES

The fact that authors have agreed to include their theories in this volume represents an important step in helping people—knowledge users and knowledge producers—to be aware of the rich array of approaches to the design of instruction. In a somewhat broader context, it is noteworthy that there is growing support for theory development in psychology (Slife & Williams, 1997), along with some concern about prospects that the gap between theory and practice may be expanding (Stricker, 1997). Whether or not the time is right for organized attempts to integrate instructional theories, which could both foster theory development and strengthen ties between theory and practice, there are some steps that can be taken at an individual level or small group level that also foster more constructive exchanges among advocates of competing theories.

Individual knowledge producers could help by clarifying what their respective theories and research reports address, as well as what each excludes from consideration and what added value is provided for a theoretical issue or practical problem by their particular research findings or theory. Hopefully, that will be one outcome of the present book. Although it might seem that such ideas would primarily help knowledge users, knowledge producers also need to be aware of the scope and limitations of their preferred theory and to recognize that they can benefit from the contributions of other approaches, even closely competing views.

Knowledge users should note carefully what authors "announce" ("advertise"?) they are trying to do with their respective theories. Unfortunately, some instructors try to use theories in ways that the authors had not anticipated or even in a manner that is not consistent with what the theorist proposed—and then sometimes complain that the theory is not working the way it should. To minimize such misuses of theories, practitioners should note the topics covered and the kinds of instruction primarily addressed by the theory, as well as the ways that the theory is supposed to be used (according to the theory authors) in designing instruction. Of course, instructors may opt to use a theory in some new way; but they should then acknowledge that they are going beyond (or, perhaps, even against) what the theory's author(s) had in mind. Whether we elect to exercise our option to rely mainly on one theory to guide our design of instruction or to use some combination of theories for the diverse characteristics of our students and the different facets of our learning situations, our ultimate goal should be to select those principles and ideas that can enhance the quality of instruction provided to our clients.

REFERENCES

Alford, B. A. (1995). [Introduction to the Special Issue] "Psychotherapy integration" and cognitive psychotherapy. *Journal of Cognitive Psychotherapy, 9*, 147–151.

American Psychological Association. (1985). *Standards for educational and psychological testing.* Washington, DC: Author.

Anderson, J. R., Reder, L. M., & Simon, H. A. (1996). Situated learning and education. *Educational Researcher, 25*(5), 5–11.

Beitman, B. D. (1994). Stop exploring. Start defining the principles of psychotherapy integration: Call for a consensus conference. *Journal of Psychotherapy Integration, 4*, 203–228.

Casanova, U. (1989, January). Research and practice: We can integrate them. *National Education Association Today* [Special Edition], 44–49.

Castonguay, L. G., & Goldfried, M. R. (1994). Psychotherapy integration: An idea whose time has come. *Applied & Preventive Psychology, 3*(3), 159–172.

Dewey, J. (1900). Psychology and social practice. *Psychological Review, 7*, 105–124.

Dewey, J. (1929). *The sources of a science of education.* New York: Liveright.

Donmoyer, R. (1997). Introduction: Refocusing on learning. *Educational Researcher, 26*(1), 4–34.

Fonagy, P., & Target, M. (1996). Should we allow psychotherapy research to determine clinical practice? *Clinical Psychology: Science & Practice, 3*, 245–250.

Garfield, S. L. (1994). Eclecticism and integration in psychotherapy: Developments and issues. *Clinical Psychology: Science and Practice, 1*, 123–137.

Goldfried, M. R. (1980). Toward the delineation of therapeutic change principles. *American Psychologist, 35*, 991–999.

Goldfried, M. R., & Wachtel, P. L. (1983). *Results of the questionaire. Society for the Exploration of Psychotherapy Integration Newsletter, 1*(1), 1–3.

Greeno, J. G. (1997). Response: On claims that answer the wrong question. *Educational Researcher, 26*(1), 5–17.

Hall, C. S., & Lindzey, G. (1957). *Theories of personality.* New York: Wiley.

Jacobson, N. S. (1994). Behavior therapy and psychotherapy integration. *Journal of Psychotherapy Integration, 4*, 105–119.

Lazarus, A. A. (1995). Different types of eclecticism and integration: Let's be aware of the dangers. *Journal of Psychotherapy Integration, 5*, 27–39.

Lazarus, A. A. (1996). The utility and futility of combining treatments in psychotherapy. *Clinical Psychology: Science & Practice, 3*, 59–68.

Leby-Leboyer, C. (1988). Success and failure in applying psychology. *American Psychologist, 43,* 779–785.

Lemmens, F., de Ridder, D., & van Lieshout, P. (1994). The integration of psychotherapy: Goal or utopia? *Journal of Contemporary Psychotherapy. 24,* 245–257.

Mitchell, S. A. (1994). Recent developments in psychoanalytic theorizing. *Journal of Psychotherapy Integration, 4,* 93–103.

Norcross, J. C. (1995). A roundtable on psychotherapy integration: Common factors, technical eclecticism, and psychotherapy research. *Journal of Psychotherapy Practice and Research, 4,* 248–271.

Nozick, R. (1981). *Philosophical explanations.* Cambridge, MA: Harvard University Press.

Paterson, C. H. (1977). *Foundations for a theory of instruction.* New York: Harper & Row.

Persons, J. (1995). Are all psychotherapies cognitive? *Journal of Cognitive Psychotherapy. 9,* 185–194.

Phillips, B. N. (1989). Role of the practitioner in applying science to practice. *Professional Psychology, 20,* 3–8.

Popper, K. R. (1957). *The Poverty of historism.* Boston: Beacon Press.

Popper, K. R. (1959). *The logic of scientific discovery.* New York: Basic Books.

Safran, J. D., & Messer, S. B. (1997). Psychotherapy Integration: A Postmodern Critique. *Clinical Psychology: Science and Practice, 4*(N2), 140–152.

Slife, B. D., & Williams, R. N. (1997). Toward a theoretical psychology: Should a subdiscipline be formally recognized? *American Psychologist, 52,* 117–129.

Snelbecker, G. E. (1974). *Learning theory, instructional theory and psychoeducational design.* New York: McGraw-Hill. (Reprinted in 1985 by University Press of America, Lanham, MD.)

Snelbecker, G. E. (1983). Is Instructional Theory Alive and Well? In C.M. Reigeluth (Ed.), *Instructional design theories and models: An overview of their current status* (pp. 437–472). Hillsdale, NJ: Lawrence Erlbaum Associates.

Snelbecker, G. E. (1993). Practical ways for using theories and innovations to improve training: Functional relevance, and Differentiated Instructional Systems Design (DISD). In G. M. Piskurich (Ed.), *The ASTD Instructional Technology Handbook,* (19.3–19.26). New York: McGraw-Hill.

Steenbarger, B. N., Smith, H. B., & Budman, S. H. (1996). Integrating science and practice in outcomes assessment: A bolder model for a managed era. *Psychotherapy, 33,* 246–253.

Stricker, G. (1997). Are science and practice commensurable? *American Psychologist, 52,* 442–448.

Strupp, H. H. (1996). The tripartite model and the *Consumer Reports study. American Psychologist, 51,* 1017–1024.

von Moltke, H. (1993, January). *Measuring the Impact of Your Campaign.* Paper presented at the Fourth Annual Image Conference, New York.

Unit 2 Fostering Cognitive Development

FOREWORD

This unit opens with a chapter that helps the reader analyze and understand the theories in the unit. Chapter 3 presents a framework showing six of the more important dimensions on which instructional-design theories can differ from each other, such as the type(s) of learning each addresses and who controls the learning process. Chapter 3 also provides a framework for thinking about problem-based learning.

It was not easy to decide which theories to include in this unit, for there is much exciting work being done on the new paradigm of instructional theory in the cognitive domain. I was particularly sorry not to be able to get contributions from John Anderson (see e.g., Anderson, 1976; Neves & Anderson, 1981) and Rand Spiro (see, e.g., Spiro, Feltovich, Jacobson, & Coulson, 1992). I was also sorry not to be able to get contributions from outside of North America. Due to the amount of excellent work being done, I intend to begin work immediately on a Volume III, and I encourage anyone who knows of good work that I should include to contact me at reigelut@indiana.edu.

It was also difficult to decide how to group and sequence the chapters in this unit. I have arranged them loosely on the basis of major similarities. Chapters 4–7 are concerned primarily with understanding—ways of fostering it and kinds of understanding worth fostering. Chapters 8–11 focus primarily on problem-based learning. Chapters 11–13 emphasize collaboration and self-regulation in learning. Chapters 14–15 are concerned primarily with higher-order thinking skills. And chapters 16–18 address a variety of other concerns. However, it was difficult to categorize the chapters because most of them deal to some extent with most of the categories.

I encourage you to explore the extent to which these 15 theories are incompatible with each other, or are compatible in the sense of being complementary to each other (addressing areas the others don't address), or are compatible in the sense of offering many of the same methods, albeit perhaps using different terminology. The chapter forewords and editor's notes are intended to help you to think about these issues and to compare and contrast the theories.

The chapter forewords have a section that summarizes the values underlying both the goals that the theory pursues and the methods that it offers to attain those goals. The values are described as a list of things (nouns and gerunds) that are valued (considered important). Alternative formats for describing values include "importance" statements:

- The importance of ... ,

And "should" statements:

- The instruction should ...

As you read through the chapters in this unit, you might find it helpful to periodically review the list of questions on pp. 1–2 (see Unit 1 Foreword).

—C.M.R.

REFERENCES

Anderson, J. R. (1976). *Language, memory and thought*. Hillsdale, NJ: Lawrence Erlbaum Associates.

Neves, D. M., & Anderson, J. R. (1981). Knowledge compilation: Mechanisms for the automatization of cognitive skills. In J. R. Anderson (Ed.), *Cognitive skills and their acquisition*. Hillsdale, NJ: Lawrence Erlbaum Associates.

Spiro, R. J., Feltovich, P. J., Jacobson, M. J., & Coulson, R. L. (1992). Cognitive flexibility, constructivism, and hypertext: Random access instruction for advanced knowledge acquisition in ill-structured domains. In T. Duffy & D. Jonassen (Eds.), *Constructivism and the technology of instruction: A conversation*. Hillsdale, NJ: Lawrence Erlbaum Associates.

3 Cognitive Education and the Cognitive Domain

Charles M. Reigeluth
Julie Moore
Indiana University

INTRODUCTION

In the industrial-age paradigm of instructional-design theory, work focused almost exclusively on the cognitive domain, and within that domain, it focused almost exclusively on remember-level and application-level learning (memorization and procedural-skill development). While information technologies and information-age roles make those levels of learning less important now, they still have an important place. But higher levels of learning are becoming relatively much more important for the vast majority of learners. And there is a greater need for methods of instruction that allow for much greater customization of the learning experience and much greater utilization of information technology, fellow learners, and other resources for learning. This unit of the book describes a variety of emerging instructional-design theories to meet these needs: a new paradigm of instructional theories for the information age.

While it is certainly impossible to include all such instructional theories, the ones found in chapters 4–18 represent a wide array of thinking about what it means to teach and learn, and how we can best facilitate that learning. The influence of constructivism on instructional design since Volume I of *Instructional-Design Theories and Models* (Reigeluth, 1983) is reflected in many of the design theories presented in the present volume. The purpose of this chapter is twofold. First, it serves as an introduction to the theories in this book related to cognitive development. Second, this chapter provides a framework of dimensions with which to compare and contrast the various instructional theories. We offer this framework as a tool to help readers better understand the differences and commonalties among the

disparate theories included in this unit. Finally, due to the promise of problem-based learning (PBL), we offer additional issues for thinking about theories for
the design of PBL.

KINDS OF LEARNING

Before we go any further, it would be helpful to define exactly what we mean by
cognitive domain and cognitive education. While there may be many different
kinds of learning (Gardner, 1983), most theorists (Bloom, 1956; Gagné, 1985) categorize kinds of learning in three domains: cognitive, affective, and motor. For our
purposes we will make a small addition to Bloom's (1956) definition of the *cognitive domain* as the domain that deals with the recall or recognition of knowledge
and the development of understandings and intellectual abilities and skills. Thus,
cognitive education is composed of the set of instructional methods that assist students in learning knowledge to be recalled or recognized, as well as developing students' understandings and intellectual abilities and skills. Since metacognition (the
ability to think about one's own thinking) is an intellectual skill, we consider it to
fall in the cognitive domain.

Bloom and his colleagues (1956) developed a taxonomy that is widely used to
categorize types of educational objectives for the cognitive domain. Their work has
provided a common language for educators and has become the standard for identifying and classifying educational objectives and activities. The main types of learning they identified are shown in Table 3.1.

Much of the focus of the new paradigm of instructional theories seeks to push us
beyond the lower levels of objectives to the higher levels, commonly referred to as
higher order thinking skills. This will be evident in many of the instructional theories in this unit, especially chaps. 14–15.

TABLE 3.1
BLOOM'S TAXONOMY

Knowledge	Students working at this level can remember and recall information ranging from concrete to abstract.
Comprehension	At the comprehension level, students are able to understand and make use of something being communicated. Bloom felt that this level was the major emphasis of schools and colleges. In this level, students can translate, interpret, and extrapolate the communication.
Application	Students can apply appropriate concepts or abstractions to a problem or situation even when not prompted to do so.
Analysis	Students can break down the material into its parts and define the relationship between the parts.
Synthesis	Students create a product, combining parts from previous experience and new material to create a whole.
Evaluation	Students make judgements about the value of materials, ideas, and so forth.

Various instructional theorists have proposed other taxonomies of types of learning in the cognitive domain. Gagné (1985) proposed a taxonomy of learning outcomes with three main categories for the cognitive domain:

- *verbal information*, in which the learner "may learn to *state* or *tell* a fact or set of events by using oral speech or by using writing, typewriting, or even drawing a picture" (p. 48),
- *intellectual skills*, in which the learner "interacts with the environment by *using symbols*" (p. 47); and
- *cognitive strategies*, in which "the individual has learned *skills that manage her own learning, remembering, and thinking*" (p. 48).

Ausubel (1968) distinguished two types of learning:

- *rote learning*, in which "learned materials are discrete and relatively isolated entities which are only relatable to cognitive structure in an arbitrary, verbatim fashion, not permitting the establishment of [significant] relationships" (p. 24); and
- *meaningful learning*, which "takes place if the learning task can be related in a nonarbitrary, substantive fashion to what the learner already knows, and if the learner adopts a corresponding learning set to do so" (p. 18).

Anderson (1983) distinguished between:

- *declarative knowledge*, which "comes in chunks or *cognitive units*.... Cognitive units can be such things as propositions, strings, or spatial images. In each case a cognitive unit encodes a set of elements in a particular relationship. Chunks contain no more than five elements" (p. 23); and
- *procedural knowledge*, which is the "knowledge about how to do things" (p. 215).

Similarly, Merrill (1983) proposed the following taxonomy:

- *remember verbatim*, which is "associated with the literal storing and retrieving of information" (p. 302);
- *remember paraphrased*, which is "associated with the integration of ideas into associative memory" (p. 303);
- *use a generality*, in which the student can "use a general rule to process specific information" (p. 303); and
- *find a generality*, in which "the student is finding a new generality or is finding a higher-level process" (p. 304).

These taxonomies all have many similarities, which leads us to propose a synthesis of them into a form that uses more intuitive language in verb–noun form (see

Table 3.2). The proposed synthesized terms are given in the column headed "Reigeluth." The following paragraphs provide an explanation of each of these new terms.

Memorize information is similar to Bloom's "knowledge," Ausubel's "rote learning," and Merrill's "remember verbatim." Also, combined with the next category, "understand relationships," it is similar to Gagné's "verbal information" and Anderson's "declarative knowledge." We find this refinement of Gagné's and Anderson's distinctions to be important because very different instructional methods are needed to help learners memorize information, compared to understanding relationships. As the simplest, most superficial level of learning, memorization is a type of learning that behaviorists have addressed extensively; but cognitivists have also explored the use of mnemonics and metacognitive skills for helping students to memorize information. This type of learning is greatly overused in schools and other instructional contexts today, perhaps partly because it is the easiest to teach and test.

Understand relationships is similar to Bloom's "comprehension," Ausubel's "meaningful learning," and Merrill's "remember paraphrased." Also, as mentioned in the previous paragraph, it is part of Gagné's "verbal information" and Anderson's "declarative knowledge." Understanding is primarily a matter of learning the relationships among elements of knowledge. Learners' construction of these relationships organizes the knowledge elements into knowledge structures, often called schemata. Behaviorism offered little guidance for this type of learning, and in fact greatly discouraged consideration of understanding as a valid learning outcome. Concern for such internal knowledge structures was one of the major benefits of cognitive learning theory over behaviorist learning theory, and much work has been done over the past two or three decades to advance our understanding of how this type of learning occurs and how to foster it. But it remains more difficult to teach and test than is memorizing information.

Apply skills is similar to Bloom's "application," Gagné's "intellectual skills," Anderson's "procedural knowledge" and Merrill's "use a generality." It requires very different methods of instruction than does either memorize information or understand relationships. Behaviorism contributed much to our understanding

TABLE 3.2
INSTRUCTIONAL TAXONOMIES

Bloom	Gagné	Ausubel	Anderson	Merrill	Reigeluth
Knowledge	Verbal information	Rote learning	Declarative knowledge	Remember verbatim	Memorize information
Comprehension		Meaningful learning		Remember paraphrased	Understand relationships
Application	Intellectual skill		Procedural knowledge	Use a generality	Apply skills
Analysis Synthesis Evaluation	Cognitive strategy			Find a generality	Apply generic skills

of how to teach and test this kind of learning, and cognitive learning theory has added to that base. Applying skills is common in schools and training contexts. Although it is harder to teach and test than is memorizing information, it is still typically easier than is the development of deep understanding of complex phenomena.

Apply generic skills includes Bloom's "analysis," "synthesis," and "evaluation," Gagné's "cognitive strategies," and Merrill's "find a generality." It differs from the previous category in that the skills are domain–independent (usable to varying degrees across different subject areas), rather than domain–dependent (only applicable within one subject area), and it usually takes much longer to acquire generic skills. We feel that Bloom's distinction among analysis, synthesis, and evaluation, while useful for making decisions about what to teach, is not very useful for deciding on methods of instruction, for they are all taught through basically similar methods; hence we have collapsed them into a single category. This type of learning includes higher order thinking skills, learning strategies, and metacognitive skills. Cognitive learning theory has contributed the most to understanding how best to teach and test this type of learning, but it remains among the most difficult to teach and test.

FRAMEWORK FOR COMPARISON

The instructional theories for the cognitive domain that are described in this book are vast and varied. They offer methods that range from organizing print material to encouraging problem solving to creating open learning environments. In many ways, trying to compare the theories is like comparing apples and oranges. Therefore, we offer a comparison framework upon which you can build your understanding of each theory and how each one compares to or differs from other theories of instruction (see Table 3.3 and Figure 3.1).

We do not suggest that each instructional theory can be thought of as a discrete point on each of these comparison elements. Many of the instructional theories

TABLE 3.3
DESCRIPTION OF COMPARISON FRAMEWORK

Comparison Point	Description
Type of Learning	What type(s) of learning do the theory and its methods address?
Control of Learning	Who controls the nature of the learning process: the teacher, the student, the instructional designer?
Focus of Learning	Do the learning activities revolve around specific topics, or problems or something else?
Grouping for Learning	How are learners grouped? Do they work individually or with others?
Interactions for Learning	What is the primary nature of interaction: teacher with student, student with student, student with material?
Support for Learning	What kinds and levels of support are given to the learner? What kinds of cognitive support are given by the teacher or the materials? What kinds of resources are available? What kinds of emotional support are given?

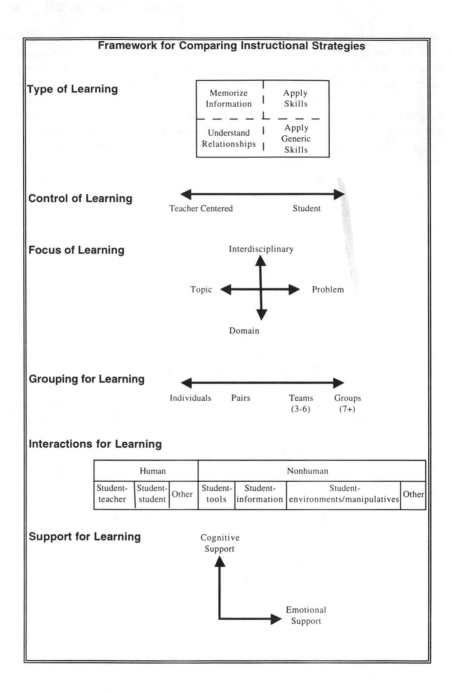

FIG. 3.1. Framework for comparing instructional strategies.

may offer particular attributes for some elements and not for others. Some theories are flexible enough to encompass several aspects across categories, while others promote only one alternative. Let's examine each of these comparison points in more detail.

Type of Learning

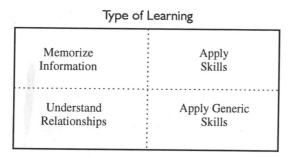

Type of Learning

Memorize Information	Apply Skills
Understand Relationships	Apply Generic Skills

The type of learning relates to the purpose of the learning activity and the type of learning involved. In essence, this comparison point is the application of an instructional taxonomy to the content of instruction (i.e., to the type of learning or cognitive development desired). For our purposes, we will use Reigeluth's synthesis of taxonomies: memorizing information, understanding relationships, applying skills, and applying generic skills. We can visualize Reigeluth's taxonomy as an interconnected categorization scheme. While we see these categories as distinct, they can overlap and constitute a sort of continuum. For instance, it may be necessary for students to have memorized information to apply a skill, but this is not always the case. This interconnectedness is denoted in our framework through the use of dashed lines, showing that while there are categories, they can and do overlap or support one another.

Pogrow's theory (chap. 14 in this volume) discusses lessons learned from action research in teaching higher order thinking skills (HOTSs). The emphasis on students creating stories, predicting actions, and using a variety of sources to respond to questions certainly places his strategy on the "applying generic skills" quadrant (see next page).

While some theories focus specifically on developing higher order skills (chaps. 14 and 15), those instructional theories which align themselves with the constructivist perspective use activities in the higher order thinking skills range (most notably problem solving, which includes analysis, synthesis, and evaluation) to develop the lower levels of learning, while simultaneously developing the higher order skills. An example of this is Schwartz, Lin, Brophy, and Bransford's STAR (Software Technology for Action and Reflection) LEGACY (chap. 9) software shell. The STAR LEGACY uses challenges and problems to stimulate iterative in-

Type of Learning: Pogrow's HOTS

Memorize Information	Apply Skills
Understand Relationships	Apply Generic Skills

quiry cycles. Within this framework, students work with others, use resources, and conduct simulations and hands-on experiments to solve the challenge. Through these problem solving activities, students develop skills, understandings, and to some extent information in several domains.

Type of Learning: Schwartz, Lin, Brophy, and Bransford

Memorize Information	Apply Skills
Understand Relationships	Apply Generic Skills

One area of generic skills that requires special attention is the area of metacognition, which is the ability to think about the way we think. Several instructional theories emphasize the importance of teaching metacognitive strategies explicitly (Corno & Randi, chap. 13; Pogrow, chap. 14; Landa, chap. 15), while others utilize metacognition within their model (Jonassen, chap. 10; Nelson, chap. 11).

Control of Learning

The traditional source of control in the learning process has been the teacher, who chooses educational objectives, selects content, determines the instructional strategies to be used, and evaluates learning. However, a key marker of the new paradigm of instructional theories is the creation of "learner-centered" environments, in which the learner takes more responsibility for defining learning outcomes and choosing the road needed to achieve those outcomes. Most educational situations are not entirely teacher centered or entirely learner centered, but exist on some point along the continuum between the two. One extreme is not always better than the others; different points on the continuum are appropriate for different conditions.

Control of Learning

Teacher centered   Learner centered

There are several questions you should ask while deciding where a particular instructional strategy fits on this continuum. This set of questions can be thought of as a categorization of elements, each of which is also a continuum:

1. Who determines the educational goals?
2. Who determines how the goals are to be accomplished?
3. Who selects the content?
4. Who selects the kinds and levels of support and resources?
5. Who chooses when support and resources are used?
6. Who decides what activities will be done, and in what order?
7. Who evaluates the learning?

Different situations will likely call for quite different positions on the continuum for different questions.

Gardner (chap. 4) provides an example of an instructional strategy whose locus of control is geared towards the teacher-centered end. While Gardner does promote using student interests and strengths to guide the choices that the teacher makes in presenting topics and information, it is the teacher who makes the decisions and guides the learning process. Most of Gardner's points are geared toward teacher behavior. These include telling stories, using analogies and examples, and choosing representations that capture important topic aspects that reach a large number of students. Therefore, the content and instructional decisions lie mainly in the hands of the instructor, not the students.

Control of Learning: Gardner

Teacher centered   Learner centered

In contrast, Hannafin, Land, and Oliver (chap. 6) describe a learning environment in which the students take more control over their learning. The authors identify three different types of enabling contexts, which they describe as "vehicles through which individuals are oriented to a need or problem and interpretive perspectives are situated." The three types of enabling contexts (externally imposed, externally induced, and individually generated) describe a range of control types, from using a problem selected by the instructor with the means to solve it left to the learner, to a more learner-centered strategy of having students select not just the means to solve a problem but also the problem itself.

Control of Learning: Hannafin, Land, and Oliver

Teacher centered   Learner centered

Focus of Learning

The focus of learning can vary widely, from the use of domain-specific topics to interdisciplinary problems. Unlike the previous elements of this framework, we see this point of comparison as a two-dimensional space which allows for comparison of not just the activity, but also the content upon which the activity is based. Again, each of these axes can be thought of as a continuum.

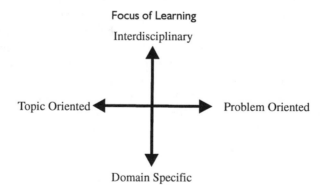

For example, Perkins and Unger, in chapter 5, "Teaching and Learning for Understanding," use generative topics as the basis for the learning activity. These topics are supposed to be "central to the domain," and therefore would be listed in our matrix as topic oriented and domain specific. While the understanding performances that students engage in may very well include problem-solving activity, these are wrapped around the topic, making the topic the primary learning vehicle.

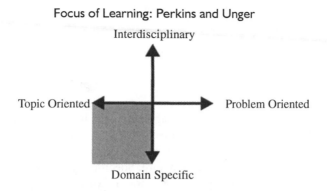

Focus of Learning: Perkins and Unger

Interdisciplinary

Topic Oriented   Problem Oriented

Domain Specific

In some contrast, Shank, Berman, and Macpherson (chap. 8) organize learning around goal-based scenarios. These scenarios have both content and process goals and require that students learn certain content to be able to achieve the mission or goal. While this strategy is flexible, it is primarily problem oriented but could be either domain specific or interdisciplinary depending upon the nature of the goal or mission selected.

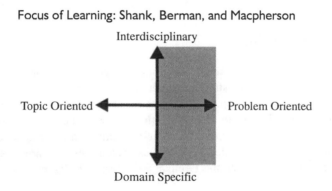

Focus of Learning: Shank, Berman, and Macpherson

Interdisciplinary

Topic Oriented   Problem Oriented

Domain Specific

Grouping for Learning

The next comparison point in our framework is learner grouping. This aspect considers the number of students who are working together. Are students working individually or in groups? For comparison purposes, we suggest the following breakdowns of learner grouping: individuals, pairs, teams (3–6), and groups (7+). Each type of grouping has its own logistical and process concerns that must be considered when planning instruction. Many instructional theories do not dictate using or not using groups. However, several have them as an essential feature.

Grouping for Learning

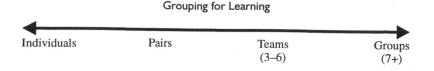

| Individuals | Pairs | Teams
(3–6) | Groups
(7+) |

Nelson's "Collaborative Problem Solving" (chap. 11) is an instructional theory with the use of teams as its center point. Nelson outlines a series of "comprehensive guidelines" that should be carried through the entire experience, as well as "process activities," which are more sequential in nature. Specifically, she suggests that the groups be small, heterogeneous, and together for an extended amount of time. In her model, these group members are not just working together, but collaborating together to determine their own learning issues, needs, and plan.

Grouping for Learning: Nelson

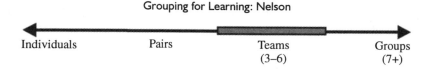

| Individuals | Pairs | Teams
(3–6) | Groups
(7+) |

Interactions for Learning

Another framework comparison revolves around the types of student interactions that result from use of a given instructional theory. While some instructional theories outlined in this book do not specify the types of interactions the instruction will inevitably require (e.g., Reigeluth, chap. 18), others are very specific in the types of interactions recommended. We separate student interactions into two major categories: human and nonhuman. Within each of these categories are various specific types of interactions that students may be engaged in during the learning process:

Interactions for Learning

Human			*Non-human*			
Student– teacher	Student– student	Other	Student– tools	Student– information	Student– environment/ manipulatives	Other

student–teacher: interacting with the teacher or instructor;

student–student: working with or utilizing other students as resources, individually or in a group;

student–other human: interacting with a community member, parent, or other individual (or group);

student–tools: using tools that enable completion of tasks;

student–information: working with, and making sense of, the information that is available or found;

student–environment/manipulatives: utilizing and working with resources and simulations, both within and outside the classroom environment;

student–other nonhuman: working with any other conceivable nonhuman resources.

In "Learning Communities in Classrooms" (chap. 12), Bielaczyc and Collins describe a community whose members work together to expand knowledge. As part of this community, students participate in multiple ways for multiple purposes. The result is that students must interact in a variety of ways. Bielaczyc and Collins describe an environment in which students work with teachers to define goals (student–teacher interaction), go beyond the bounds of the traditional classroom for approaches and challenges (student–environment interaction), and create a dependence on one another and share with one another (student–student). While use of resources and tools aren't specifically mentioned and may not be necessary at all times, students are expected to produce quality products. This product expectation suggests the use of some tools and resources for completion.

Interactions for Learning: Bielaczyc and Collins

Human			Non-human			
Student–teacher	Student–student	Other	Student–tools	Student–information	Student–environment/manipulatives	Other

Landa, in chap. 15, proposes a general method of instruction, focusing on helping students build metacognitive skills. Landa concentrates on student interactions with the teacher as the teacher leads the students to discover a process by which they can recognize and classify knowledge. Therefore, while other interactions may (and most certainly will) occur, student–teacher interactions are the primary kind in this design theory.

Interactions for Learning: Landa

Human			Non-human			
Student–teacher	Student–student	Other	Student–tools	Student–information	Student–environment/manipulatives	Other

Support for Learning

As students learn, support is needed for improvement and growth. This support comes primarily in two varieties: cognitive support and emotional support. Cognitive
support consists of those elements which serve to support the students in building
their understandings of, and competence in, the subject matter. This could be in the
form of print resources, computer resources, human interaction, sequenced access
to information, feedback, evaluation, and so forth. Emotional support consists of
those elements that support learner attitudes, motivation, feelings, and
self-confidence. These are not necessarily distinct items, as the manner in which a
teacher provides feedback to correct a cognitive error certainly plays a role in the
student's attitude, feelings, and confidence level. However, some strategies do explicitly support either the cognitive or the emotional development of the learner.
Again, we use an axis as a means of representing this comparison.

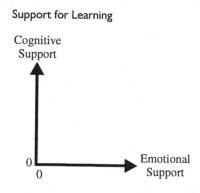

Mayer's SOI (selecting, organizing, and integrating) model (chap. 7) focuses on
strategies for designing instructional messages. Mayer is concerned with providing
strategies for organizing, emphasizing, and utilizing instructional messages that assist students in selecting, organizing, and integrating material to support their learning. As such, the support for learners that he provides rests completely in the
cognitive area.

Support for Learning: Mayer's SOI Model

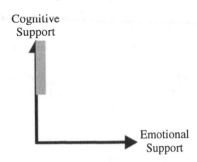

Jonassen's "Designing Constructivist Learning Environments" (chap. 10) focuses on elements of emotional as well as cognitive support. Jonassen uses the images of coaching and scaffolding to suggest strategies that provide emotional support to students. These strategies include emphasizing the importance of the task, boosting confidence levels, and adjusting task sequencing and difficulty. Cognitively, instructors should provide related cases, information resources, knowledge, construction tools, and conversation and collaboration tools. Additionally, the instructor prompts appropriate thinking strategies, consideration of related cases, and feedback on performance.

Support for Learning: Jonassen's Constructivist
Learning Environment

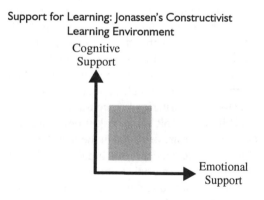

ADDITIONAL ISSUES FOR THEORIES ON PBL

The central premise of PBL is that instruction should begin with a problem that is important and relevant to the learners. Learning, for both lower order and higher order thinking, occurs in the context of solving the problem. *Given this premise, we propose that any theory for the design of PBL should offer guidance for selecting appropriate problems, based on the lower order and higher order "content" that the learner and/or educator feels is important.* An inevitable concern in the selection of appropriate problems is problem complexity. Vygotsky (1978) proposes that instructional experiences should be within the zone of proximal development, or not so far beyond the learners' current capability that they have great difficulty mastering the experiences. *Therefore, a theory for the design of PBL should offer guidance that helps to design a sequence of problems that build appropriately upon each other in complexity (see e.g., the simplifying conditions method in Reigeluth, chap. 18).*

We propose that it is helpful to think of the learners as operating in two "spaces" during the problem-solving/learning process. One is the "problem space," in which the learners work directly on solving the problem. But when the learners encounter a knowledge or skill deficiency related to solving the problem, it is helpful to think of them as jumping out of the problem space and into an "instructional space," in which the learners work on acquiring the necessary knowledge, skills, and attitudes. This instructional space can be designed anywhere on a continuum from a highly constructivist approach, in which the learners are basically on their own to figure out where and how to acquire the knowledge, skills, and attitudes, to a highly directive approach, in which a lot of structure is provided to help the learners acquire the knowledge, skills, and attitudes. Basically, this "structure continuum" reflects the amount of structure and support that is provided to the learners.

This is important for several reasons. First, Anderson's (1976; Neves & Anderson, 1981) work on the acquisition of complex cognitive skills identifies several stages of skill development, including reaching a criterion for accuracy (which requires declarative encoding and proceduralization), followed by the automatization of the skill (composition). He states that this is important for complex cognitive skills, such as problem-solving, because automatization of lower order skills frees up a person's conscious cognitive processing resources to attend to higher order, more strategic concerns. Learning enough to solve one problem seldom offers enough varied practice to reach a criterion for accuracy, let alone automatization of the skill. This makes PBL vulnerable to poor skill development unless sufficient and appropriate types of practice are provided in the instructional space. The same concerns apply to building sufficient depth and breadth of understandings (including causal model development), memorizing important information, and acquiring important attitudes for the problem domain under study, as well as developing appropriate higher order thinking, problem-solving, and metacognitive skills. Different situations call for different degrees of support for each of these kinds of learning. It is not always best for learners to find and use primary sources. Learning requires active engagement by the learner, but active engagement is not always beneficial, for instance, if it is "busy work" or it only encompasses skills and understandings that the learner has already mastered.

Therefore, a theory for the design of PBL should offer guidance as to where you should be on the structure continuum for any given instructional situation; and it should offer guidance as to what methods should be used and when in order to provide each particular degree of support. For example, tutorials (demonstrations, explanations, and divergent practice with immediate feedback) may be beneficial in some situations for skill development; simulations or virtual worlds (e.g., SimCity) may be appropriate in some situations for complex causal model development, and proven mnemonics may be beneficial in some situations for memorizing information.

When the problem is finally solved, learners can learn much by reflecting back on what was learned about both the problem domain and the problem-solving process. What obstacles or difficulties did they encounter? How could they have dealt better with them? What do other problem-solvers or the literature in the field have to say about the issues they addressed? In some situations, learners can learn more from reflecting back on the problem-solving experience than they learned during it. *Therefore, a theory for the design of PBL should offer guidance on the reflection process.*

These additional issues for thinking about theories for the design of PBL are by no means comprehensive; they do not represent all the important issues in PBL. And they do not represent any variable aspects of PBL, such as whether to have learners work in teams or individually. But they do represent some of the most important issues that we believe theories in this area should address. As you study the PBL theories in this book (principally chaps. 8–11), we suggest that you add these issues to the above framework as a lens for understanding those theories, and that you try to identify additional issues that should also be considered.

CONCLUSION

As you examine the various instructional strategies for the cognitive domain described in the rest of this book, it will be helpful to have some means to compare them to one another. This chapter offers a framework that compares the type of learning, control of learning, focus of learning, grouping for learning, interactions for learning, and support of learning as a tool to guide this comparison. We also offer additional issues for thinking about PBL. These issues and the framework are not intended to be all-encompassing but, rather, to provide a starting point from which to begin your own process of analysis and discussion.

REFERENCES

Anderson, J. R. (1976). *Language, memory and thought*. Hillsdale, NJ: Lawrence Erlbaum Associates.
Anderson, J. R. (1983). *The architecture of cognition*. Cambridge, MA: Harvard University Press.
Ausubel, D. P. (1968). *The psychology of meaningful verbal learning*. New York: Grune & Stratton.
Bloom, B. S. (Ed.). (1956). *Taxonomy of educational objectives. Handbook 1: Cognitive domain*. New York: David McKay.

Gagné, R. M. (1985). *The conditions of learning* (4th ed.). New York: Holt, Rinehart, & Winston.

Gardner, H. (1983). *Frames of mind: The theory of multiple intelligences.* New York: Basic Books.

Merrill, M. D. (1983). Component display theory. In C. M. Reigeluth (Ed.), *Instructional-design theories and models: An overview of their current status* (pp. 279–333). Hillsdale, NJ: Lawrence Erlbaum Associates.

Neves, D. M., & Anderson, J. R. (1981). Knowledge compilation: Mechanisms for the automatization of cognitive skills. In J. R. Anderson (Ed.), *Cognitive skills and their acquisition.* Hillsdale, NJ: Lawrence Erlbaum Associates.

Reigeluth, C. M. (1983). *Instructional-design theories and models: An overview of their current status.* Hillsdale, NJ: Lawrence Erlbaum Associates.

Vygotsky, L. S. (1978). *Mind in society: The development of higher psychological processes.* (Edited by M. Cole, V. John-Steiner, S. Scribner, & E. Souberman). Cambridge, MA: Harvard University Press.

4 Multiple Approaches to Understanding©

Howard E. Gardner
*Harvard University Graduate School
of Education*

Howard E. Gardner

Howard E. Gardner is Hobbs Professor of Education and Adjunct Professor of Psychology at Harvard University, and Co-Director of Harvard Project Zero. The recipient of many honors, including a MacArthur Prize Fellowship, he is the author of 18 books including *Frames of Mind*, *Multiple Intelligences*, and *Leading Minds*, and several hundred articles. Gardner is best known in educational circles for his theory of multiple intelligences, a critique of the notion that there exists but a single human intelligence that can be assessed by standard psychometric instruments. His most recent work includes the study of exemplary creators and leaders.

FOREWORD

Goals and preconditions. *The primary goal of this theory is to foster under-standing in ways that capitalize on differences in learners' intelligences. No pre-conditions are identified.*

Values. *Some of the values upon which this theory is based include:*

- *the criticality of "what to teach" and the considerable variability of "how to teach it,"*
- *being able to deploy understanding (performances of understanding),*
- *preparing students for valued adult roles,*
- *helping students to enhance their various intelligences,*
- *tailoring instruction to individual differences in students' intelligences,*
- *an approach to instruction that is not formulaic.*

Methods. *Here are the major methods this theory offers:*

*Select a few **significant topics**—topics that can be reasonably connected to pow-erful themes and disciplinary ideas and approaches.*

- *Select fewer topics, to treat them in greater depth.*
- *Select only topics that can be reasonably connected to some powerful themes.*

*Use **entry points**, to engage the student in the topic, considering multiple intelligences.*

- *Narrational – Tell stories.*
- *Quantitative/numerical – Use statistics and quantitative patterns.*
- *Foundational/existential – State the issue in terms of broad philosophical queries and issues.*
- *Aesthetic – Use works of art, and appeal to the artistic properties of materials and topics.*
- *Hands-on – Provide hands-on activities.*
- *Social – Use group settings, role-play, and collaborative arrangements.*

*Tell **analogies** and **examples**, to inculcate specific modes of understanding.*

- *Use analogies, metaphors, and examples to enhance understanding of new material.*
  - Qualify each analogy as appropriate.

Approach the core, to convey the central understandings of the topic, using multiple representations.

- *Spend significant time on the topic (teach fewer topics in greater depth).*
- *Portray the topic in a number of ways, calling on a range of intelligences, skills, and interests, and an array of symbols and schemes, to build a depth of understanding of the topic.*
  - *Pick representations that capture important aspects of the topic.*
  - *Pick representations that reach a significant number of students.*
  - *Resist the temptation to represent the topic in one "optimal" mode.*
  - *Provide many opportunities for performance of varied types, including:*

short-answer test	*debate*	*interview*
essay question	*experiment*	*discussion*
works of art		*designs*

Major contributions. The focus on understanding as an important kind of learning outcome. The use of several representations that are tailored to students' intelligences as well as to the nature of important aspects of the topic, so that instructors reach more students and also demonstrate the nature of flexible expertise.

—C.M.R.

Multiple Approaches to Understanding

Topics Worth Understanding

Certain topics suffuse the discourse of an era. Hardly a week goes by without some reference in the media to key scientific ideas, like the theory of evolution, or to pivotal historical events, like the Holocaust. Even the culturally illiterate have heard of these topics; all who would presume to be educated should be able to recall central points about evolution or the Holocaust from their education, their casual reading and movie- or television-viewing and their residence in a news-dense culture. Educated persons should also be able to assimilate new information. They should be able to comment on news stories about the disappearance of dinosaurs, the rise of creationism, the apparently punctuated bursts of new species. They should have views about the Swiss hoarding of Nazi gold, a fictional work about a survivor, the collective guilt of the German people.

All too often, however, contemporary discussions of education skirt these hallmarks of the educated person. We find ourselves impaled on questions of methods, for example, should we encourage tracking, cooperative learning, the use of projects in the classroom; or we debate political topics, for example, should we embrace vouchers, choice, national standards? While worth discussion, these issues seem suspended in surreality when they are considered in the absence of consensus, or even debate, about what should be taught and why.*

Issues of curriculum inevitably arouse segments of the community. While texts on evolution or the Holocaust would seem straightforward in most educational contexts, we have seen in our own time fundamentalist efforts to exclude evolution from the textbooks or to denigrate Darwin's work as "just another theory." And while few educators directly question the occurrence of the Holocaust, cultural commentators have attacked Holocaust curricula either because they do not adequately represent the German point of view or because they claim that the treatment of 6 million European Jews was qualitatively different or qualitatively more brutal than that of other groups at other times. Perhaps it is safer simply to memorize a few facts or a few definitions, and then move on swiftly to other theories and to other historical events.

The Goals of Education

A brief essay scarcely allows one to adjudicate purposes of education or to lay out and defend the "ideal curriculum." My purpose is different. I do not think it is possible to talk intelligibly about how to teach unless one has taken a stand on what one should teach and why. And even if one's position on these questions may seem straightforward (particularly in the company of friends), it is salutary to lay one's curricular cards on the table.

Education in our time should provide the basis for enhanced understanding** of our several worlds: the physical world, the biological world, the world of human beings, the world of human artifacts, the world of self.*** Individuals perennially have been interested in these topics: contemporary disciplines have added to and revised insights put forth originally in mythology, art, and folk knowledge. Evolution and the Holocaust are hardly the only topics worth understanding. Yet it is hard to see how an individual could understand the world of biology without some mastery

---

* This pertains to the suggestion in chapter 1, p. 14, that curriculum theory and instructional-design theory are often so interrelated that they should be combined into a single theory.

** As discussed in chapter 3, understanding is an important kind of learning that has traditionally been ignored in instructional theory and practice (and assessment theory and practice).

*** This indicates where this theory falls on the "Focus of Learning" continuum (see chap. 3, p. 58). Can you figure out where it falls on each of the other dimensions?

of evolutionary theory; or attain comprehension of the world of human beings, in the absence of a study of the Holocaust (or another genocidal episode).

Note that this goal does not mention the acquisition of literacy, the learning of basic facts, the cultivation of basic skills, or mastery of the moves of the several disciplines. Though they are important, these achievements should be seen as means, not ends in themselves. One learns to read, write, and compute not so that one can report these milestones (as one would report one's attendance record), nor even so that one can achieve a certain score on an admissions test. Rather, literacies, skills, and disciplines ought to be pursued as tools which allow one to enhance one's understanding of important questions, topics, and themes.

This set of goals may sound quaint or idealistic. After all, aren't the real purposes of education to learn to get along with others, to acquire personal discipline, to become well rounded, and to prepare for the workplace and for the ultimate rewards of success and happiness? Certainly, arguments can be mounted in favor of these and other instrumental ends. Yet, each of these goals ought to be seen as the responsibility of the broader society, ranging from parents and families, on the one hand, to religion, the media, and community institutions, on the other end. I believe that resources invested in formal education, in our and other countries, can best be justified if, at the end of the day, all students can demonstrate enhanced understanding of the important questions and topics of the world.

A Performance View of Understanding

Both folk wisdom and contemporary psychology conspire to convince us that understanding is an event or process that occurs between the ears: in the mind/brain. Certainly, as a psychologist who also honors common sense, I would underscore the importance of the processes of mental representation that occur in the assimilation and transformation of information and knowledge. Yet, from the perspectives of the teacher and the learner, the physical events in the mind/brain are far from transparent and in any event irrelevant to their educational missions.

Instead, when it comes to understanding, the emphasis falls properly on performances that can be observed, critiqued, and improved.* Strictly speaking, we do not care about the elegance of a mental representation if it cannot be activated when needed; and while it is unlikely that performances of quality will emerge in the absence of intricate mental representations, such performances may in fact emanate from a variety of cognitive schemas across situations and individuals.

Accordingly, when it comes to probing a student's understanding of evolution, the shrewd pedagogue looks beyond the mastery of dictionary definitions or the recitation of textbook examples. Students "perform" their understanding when they can examine a range of species found in different ecological niches and speculate about the reasons for their particular ensemble of traits, or when they can point out the similarities and differences among the Malthusian, Darwinian, and social Dar-

---

* Behaviorists will be happy to see this.

winist versions of "survival of the fittest." By the same token, students perform their understanding of the Holocaust when they can interpret the contents of a diary of an SS officer in light of claims about the "good German," or when they can compare the events in a German concentration camp to those that occur in contemporary genocidal efforts, such as those in Bosnia.

Such measures of understanding may well seem demanding, particularly when contrasted with current, often superficial, efforts to measure what students know and are able to do. And indeed, recourse to performing one's manifestations of understanding are likely to stress students, teachers, and parents, all of whom have grown accustomed to traditional ways of doing (or not doing) things.

Nonetheless, embracing a performance approach to understanding is justified. To begin with, the fact that something is new is hardly a justification for avoiding it, though that fact may signal obstacles to its ready implementation. More importantly, the actual decision to focus on performances immediately shifts the emphasis from mastering content to thinking about the reasons why a particular content is being taught and how best to display one's comprehension of that content in a publicly justified manner. When students realize that they will have to apply knowledge and insights in public form, they assume a more active stance vis-a-vis material, seeking to exercise their "muscles of performance" whenever possible.

Let me offer a personal example. Having adopted a performance view of understanding some years ago, I revised my standard graduate student course on "theories of cognitive development." My goal was not just "knowing the theory," but being able to use it productively.* Under the new dispensation, each week students sought to master a particular theory of development, such as the ones put forth by Jean Piaget or Lev Vygotsky. Students were given prompts, for example, a set of data or a story about an educational practice, and asked to illuminate that prompt by invoking "the theory of the week." One day a student approached me and said "Dr. Gardner, how can I apply the theory if I don't understand it?" I thought for a moment and responded, "You'll never understand the theory unless you apply it." An emphasis on performance not only stimulates the student's active consumption of classroom material; frequent opportunities to perform constitute the best way to achieve enhanced understanding of the material.

Understanding: Obstacles and Opportunities

I have yet to mention an important and troubling consideration. There has been a virtual conspiracy to avoid assessment of understanding. Perhaps this avoidance has been innocent: if one assumes that understanding is equivalent to mastery of factual materials, or if one assumes that understanding follows naturally from exposure to materials, then there is no reason to require performances of understand-

---

* This goal highlights the fuzzy boundary between understandings and skills, as discussed in chapter 3, p. 55.

ing. But it is more likely that we have avoided the assessment of understanding because such assessment takes time and because we lacked confidence about what we would find.

Thanks to hundreds of studies carried out in the past few decades by cognitively oriented psychologists and educators, we now know one truth about understanding. Most of the students in most of our schools—indeed, many of the best students in the best schools—are not able to exhibit appreciable understandings. The most dramatic findings are manifest in physics. Students who are awarded top grades in high school and college courses are not only unable to apply their presumably mastered knowledge when asked to invoke it appropriately in a new situation. Even more damning, they also tend to respond much the way young children do: in a manner that has been described as "unschooled" (Gardner, 1991).

Would that the problems surfaced only in physics! Throughout the sciences, researchers find, students are rife with misconceptions.* In the case of the theory of evolution, for example, students gravitate almost ineluctably to a teleological and perfectibility view. That is, despite the fact that evolution consists of random mutations that cannot follow from any kind of a predetermined script, students typically reframe this state of affairs. In their description of evolution, the process is guided by an unseen hand: each species is in some sense more perfect than the previous one, with the height of evolution magically coinciding with our own species in our own time. Similar misconceptions crop up in physics, biology, geology, astronomy, and kindred sciences.

In other areas of the curriculum, analogous "unschooled" difficulties abound. In mathematics, students are at the mercy of rigidly applied algorithms. They learn to use certain formalisms in certain ways, and do so effectively, so long as they pick up a signal that a particular formalism is wanted. If, however, no cue for the formalism is provided, or the students have to derive the formalism afresh, they are stymied; after all, they never really understood the formalism, they just waited for the signal that has reliably invoked it in previous situations.

In social studies and the humanities, the enemies of understanding are scripts and stereotypes. Students readily believe that events occur in typical ways, and evoke these scripts whether or not they are appropriate. Struggles between two parties in a dispute, for example, are readily assimilated to a "good guy/bad guy Star Wars" script, where one roots for the good guy to prevail. Superficial understandings of the Holocaust deny its existence altogether, blame it entirely on the evil Germans, treat the Jewish people as unique, or say that such an event could never happen again. A deeper understanding—that human beings everywhere have the potential to engage in genocide or to become victims of such cruelty—requires more intensive and extensive grappling with the historical, social, and personal worlds.

Obstacles to understanding are ubiquitous: They cannot be readily averted. Moreover, misunderstandings are inevitable so long as individuals succumb to the

---

* This is an important aspect of an information age view of learning and instruction (see chap. 1).

American temptation (shared by other countries) to "cover everything:" to jet from Plato to NATO in a 36 week course on Western history. Nonetheless, in recent years, four promising approaches to understanding have evolved. Each of these recognizes the obstacles to understanding and seeks to inculcate more productive performances of understanding. I will mention three briefly and then turn to the fourth approach, which is my principal focus in this essay.

The first approach involves study of institutions that have successfully inculcated understanding and application of the lessons learned thereby. The traditional institution of the apprenticeship* is one such example. Young apprentices spend much time in the presence of a skilled "understander," have the opportunity to observe this person up close, and are gradually drawn into the daily practices of problem solving and product making. The contemporary institution of the children's museum or the science museum is another exemplary molder of understanding. Students have the opportunity to approach intriguing phenomena in ways that make sense to them. They can take their time, because "no one flunks museum." More important, they may bring issues with them from home to school, to the museum, and back again, gradually constructing sturdier understandings by making use of multiple inputs. In deciphering how these institutions have generated deeper understandings, we receive clues about how best to teach for understanding.

A second approach to enhanced understanding features frontal tackling of the obstacles described above. One comes to grips directly with one's own misconceptions. For example, if one believes in the inheritance of acquired characteristics, one can cut off the tails of generations of salamanders and see whether a shorter tailed salamander gradually (or abruptly) emerges. If one is prone to invoking rigidly applied algorithms,** one can be given the opportunity to construct one's own formula through experimentation with relevant variables. Or if one engages habitually in stereotypical thinking, one can be encouraged to consider each event or work of art from multiple perspectives.

To be sure, none of these approaches constitutes a fool-proof antidote to misunderstandings. Occasional adoption of "multiple perspectives" or occasional challenges to misconceptions will not suffice. Teachers encourage understandings by recognizing and pointing out inadequate conceptualizations. If such challenges are invoked regularly, and their consequences reflected upon, students will gradually learn to apply such ploys on their own. Internalization of these "checks" should facilitate the cultivation of habits of understanding.

A third approach to understanding has been developed in recent years in collaboration with David Perkins, Vito Perrone, Stone Wiske, and others. Called "teaching for understanding," this approach takes an explicitly performing stance. Teachers are asked to state a limited set of explicit understanding goals and to stipulate the

---

* Curiously, apprenticeship was one of the more predominant approaches in the agrarian age, which bears more similarity to the information age than does the industrial age.

** This approach works well for certain kinds of tasks (e.g., in well-structured domains), and it was addressed well by the industrial age paradigm.

correlated performances of understanding. These perspectives are shared with the students. Other key features of the "understanding framework" include a stress on generative topics that are at once central to the discipline and attractive to students; the identification of "through-lines" that percolate a unit or course; and an insistence on assessment that is ongoing   that takes place from the first and regularly involves the student as well as the teacher (Wiske, 1998).

Multiple Intelligences: A Potential Ally for Understanding

Until this point, I have intimated that understanding is a generic problem with a set of generic solutions. It is important for students to understand; the achievement of such understanding is challenging; there exist a variety of means that might aid students. Initially, such a generic approach is justifiable. It is reasonable to approach a problem in terms of its fundamental constituents; certain tacks may in fact prove successful with all, or at least the vast majority of students.

Recent work in cognitive and differential psychology challenges a faith in the generic approach: considerable research suggests that not all human minds work in the same way and that not all human beings exhibit the same profile of cognitive strengths and weaknesses. To the extent that this characterization is true, it ought strongly to influence how we teach students and how we assess what they learn.* In what follows, I introduce this new perspective on cognition. Thereafter, I turn to a hitherto unappreciated aspect of this novel stance; one that might aid us in inculcating and enhancing student understanding.

Traditional psychology and psychometrics have long assumed that human beings possess a single intelligence, that it is relatively fixed, and that psychologists can accurately assess a person's intelligence through the use of simple paper-and-pencil–style measures. On this view, we all represent discrete points on a single "bell curve" (Herrnstein & Murray, 1994). There is no reason to individualize education except by creating tracks composed of students of differing abilities. We all learn pretty much in the same way, and the major difference among us consists in how quickly we can proceed down the single path to enhanced learning, knowledge, and understanding.**

Though research evidence supports certain aspects of the traditional view, this view is no longer a compelling one. Findings from neuroscience, cognitive science, and anthropology converge to call into question each of the building blocks of this view. In other words, many authorities now challenge the hegemony of a single intelligence, the claim that intelligence(s) is (are) fixed at birth, and the adequacy of standard psychometric measures (Sternberg, 1985).

My own work has led to the development of a theory of multiple intelligences (Gardner, 1993a; 1993b, 1998). On this view, all human beings represent the culmi-

---

* This focus on customization is a key marker of the new paradigm of instruction (see chap. 1, p. 18)
** This is an excellent characterization of the industrial age view of learning and instruction.

nation of an evolutionary process that has yielded at least eight relatively discrete information-processing mechanisms. All of us possess linguistic intelligence (epitomized by the poet or orator); logical-mathematical intelligence (the scientist, the logician); musical intelligence (the composer or performer); spatial intelligence (sailor or sculptor); bodily-kinesthetic intelligence (athlete, dancer); naturalist intelligence (hunter, botanist); interpersonal intelligence (clinician, salesman); and intrapersonal intelligence (individual with a keen understanding of himself/herself). There may also be an existential intelligence that reflects humans' propensity to pose and struggle with the enigmas of life, death, the cosmos, and fate.

We all possess this ensemble of intelligences; in one sense, it represents our species' intellectual heritage. Yet, we do not exhibit equal strengths or similar profiles. Some individuals are strong in one intelligence, others, in another. Strength in a particular intelligence does not necessarily predict strength (or weakness) in another intelligence. Directly challenging the standard theory, individuals are able through practice to enhance their particular intelligences or to alter the profile of intellectual strengths and weaknesses. And whereas paper-and-pencil measures can provide limited insights into certain of the intelligences, intelligences are best assessed in an "intelligence-fair" way: by placing individuals in situations where they must use an intelligence directly. As I have sometimes quipped, a fair measure of spatial intelligence is to place a person in downtown Boston (a warren of narrow, curved streets) and see whether he or she can find the way home.

To the surprise of many, including me, the theory of multiple intelligences has become influential in educational circles. It is often assimilated, inappropriately, in my view, into work on cognitive or learning styles. Educators have sought to determine the intellectual strengths (the intelligence profiles) of their students through a variety of informal, jerry-built methods. They have also drawn a multitude of often inconsistent inferences about practice from the theory.* These range from teaching seven or eight different subjects, each centering on a particular intelligence; to organizing groups of students based on their favored intelligences; to building curricula that focus on specific intelligences; to teaching subjects in seven or eight different ways. I have learned a great deal from attempts by others to adapt my theory to educational settings. Yet, it has become clear that, for most educators, the theory is basically a Rorschach test; individuals discern within the theory the educational practices that they already value, rather than deducing educational implications from a sober confrontation of this new psychological theory (Gardner, 1993b).

Many educators see multiple intelligences as an end in itself. That is, a school or program is meritorious to the extent that it extols multiple intelligences, or measures students' intelligences, or features the various intelligences in curriculum or pedagogy. While I do not consider these achievements to be insignificant, they suf-

---

* This is a good example of the difficulty of applying descriptive theory to educational practice and hence of the importance of design theory (see chap. 1, p. 7).

fer from the problem described above; that is, a failure to proceed from, or consider sufficiently, the goals of education.

My own view is that "multiple intelligences" does not in itself constitute a suitable goal of education, any more than a single intelligence or cooperative learning or self-esteem should so qualify. Multiple intelligences is better thought of as a handmaiden to good education, once educational goals have been established on independent grounds. Indeed, I would argue that multiple intelligences is most usefully invoked in the service of two educational goals.

The first goal is the achievement of certain valued adult roles or end states. If one wants every individual, or, at any rate, some individuals, to be able to engage in artistic activities, it makes sense to develop linguistic intelligence (for the poet), spatial intelligence (for the artist), and/or musical intelligence (for the composer or performer). If one wants every individual, or some individuals, to be civil, then it is important to develop the personal intelligences.

The second goal is the mastery of certain curricular or disciplinary materials. Following the line of argument introduced above, one might decide that it is important for students to study biology, so that they can better understand the origins and development of the living world; and to study history, so that they can better understand the good and the evil which human beings have achieved in the past. One could take the position that everyone should study the same thing in the same way, and be assessed in the same way. The standard view of intelligence leads readily, perhaps ineluctably, to that educational course. Yet, if there is validity to multiple intelligences—if individuals indeed harbor different kinds of minds, with different strengths, interests, and strategies—then it is worth considering whether pivotal curricular materials could be taught and assessed in a variety of ways.

UNDERSTANDING: AN APPROACH
THROUGH MULTIPLE INTELLIGENCES

Here, at last, I can introduce the core ideas of the educational approach that I embrace (see Gardner, 1999). I believe that every person ought to master a central body of curricular materials and approaches, though I am not thereby wedded to a specific canon. For this essay I have selected the examples of evolution and the Holocaust, though they are not without controversy, because I think that they lie comfortably within the ensemble of ideas that every educated person should have encountered, grappled with, and mastered. (Elsewhere, I have added to the true [evolution], and the evil [the Holocaust] an example of the beautiful [the music of Mozart].) I depart from traditional educators, and from their allies in psychology, in the assumption that such topics need to be taught or assessed in a single way.

Because of their biological and cultural backgrounds, personal histories, and idiosyncratic experiences, students do not arrive in school as blank slates, nor as individuals who can be aligned unidimensionally along a single axis of intellectual accomplishment. They possess different kinds of minds, with different strengths, interests, and modes of processing information. While this variation (a product of evo-lution!) initially complicates the job of the teacher, it can actually become an ally in effective teaching. For if the teacher is able to use different pedagogical approaches, there exists the possibility of reaching more students in more effective ways.

Differences among students can be described in innumerable ways, and it is a simplification to prioritize any. For my purposes, I will speak of students as high-lighting different intelligences. However, to follow this argument, one need not en-dorse my particular theory of intelligences. Any approach that recognizes and can somehow label or identify differences in intellectual proclivity will suffice.

Assume that our educational goals include an enhanced understanding of the theory of evolution and the events called the Holocaust, topics drawn respectively, from biology and history. Specifically, we want students to appreciate* that evolu-tion, a process of random mutation in the genotype, is the driving force behind the variety of species that have existed historically and contemporaneously. The di-verse phenotypes yielded by genetic variation result in organisms that are differen-tially able to survive in specific ecological contexts. Those that survive to reproduce in abundance have a competitive advantage over those who, for whatever reason, are less prone to adjust adequately to a given ecological niche. If these trends con-tinue over the long run, the survivors prevail while those who cannot compete suc-cessfully are doomed to extinction. The fossil record documents the course and fate of different species historically; one sees the gradual increase in variety of species, as well as the increasing complexity of certain lines of descent. It is possible to study the same processes contemporaneously, with relevant research ranging from the breeding of Drosophila of various strains to experimental investigations of the origin of genes.

Turning to the Holocaust, we want students to appreciate what happened to the Jewish people, and to certain other condemned minorities and political dissidents, during the Nazi Third Reich, from 1933–1945. Efforts to castigate and isolate the Jewish people began with simple verbal attacks and laws of exclusion, gradually evolved to more violent forms of abuse, and ultimately culminated in the devising of camps whose explicit goal was the extinction of European Jewry. The contours of anti-Semitism were laid out in Hitler's early speeches and writings; but the histori-cal course from plans to actualities took several years and involved hundreds of thousands of individuals in various capacities. Genocide, the effort to eliminate a people in its entirety, is hardly a new phenomenon; it dates back to Biblical times. Yet, the systematic way in which an allegedly civilized, modern nation proceeded to eradicate 6 million Jews is without precedent.

In brief form, these understandings would constitute a reasonable goal for a course or unit. Sheer memorization or faithful paraphrase of these paragraphs, of course,

---

* The word "appreciate" connotes that affect is an element of deep understanding. This intersection of cognition and affect is further explored in Unit IV, especially chapters 21 (Lewis, Watson and Schaps) and 22 (Stone-McCown and McCormick), as well as other chapters in this unit, such as chapter 16 (Kovalik and McGeehan).

does not count as understanding. Rather, as noted above, students exhibit understanding to the extent that they can invoke these sets of ideas flexibly and appropriately to carry out specific analyses, interpretations, comparisons, critiques. An "acid test" of such understanding is the students' ability to perform their understandings with respect to material that is new—perhaps as new as today's newspaper.

How to approach these formidable topics? From the vantage point of multiple intelligences, I propose three, increasingly focused lines of attack.

A. Entry Points

One begins by finding a way to engage the students and to place them centrally within the topic. I have identified at least six discrete entry points, which can be roughly aligned with specific intelligences.* In each case, I define the entry point and illustrate it with respect to our two topics:

1. Narrational. The narrational entry point addresses students who enjoy learning about topics through stories. Such vehicles, linguistic or filmic, feature protagonists, conflicts, problems to be solved, goals to be achieved, and tensions aroused and, often, allayed. Evolution invites treatment in terms of the story of Darwin's voyages (as it contrasts with the story of origins told in the Bible) or of the "course" of a particular species. The Holocaust can be introduced through a narrative account of a particular person, or through a year-by-year chronicle of events in the Third Reich.

2. Quantitative/numerical. The quantitative entry point speaks to students who are intrigued by numbers, the patterns that they make, the various operations that can be performed, and the insights into size, ratio, and change. From an evolutionary perspective, one can look at the incidence of different individuals or species in different ecological niches and at how those aggregates change over time. With respect to the Holocaust, one can look at the movement of individuals to various camps, the survival rates at each, the comparisons of the fates of Jews and other victim groups in different cities and nations.

3. Foundational/existential. This entry point appeals to students who are attracted to fundamental "bottom line" kinds of questions. Nearly all youngsters raise such questions, usually through myths or art: the more philosophically oriented come to pose and argue about issues verbally. Evolution addresses the question of who we are and where we come from, and whence all living matter emanates. The

---

*The previous sentence describes a general method. Each of the six entry points is a "component method" that is more precise and detailed. But each also represents an alternative kind of the general method and therefore is situational in that each is used for a different situation—e.g., different kinds of learners or goals (see chap. 1, pp. 8–11).

Holocaust addresses the questions of what kinds of beings humans are, and what are the virtues and vices of which they/we are capable.

4. Aesthetic.   Some individuals are inspired by works of art, or by materials arranged in ways that feature balance, harmony, or a carefully designed composition. The tree of evolution, with its many branches and interstices, may attract such individuals; Darwin himself was intrigued by the metaphor of the "tangled bank" of nature. Many efforts have been undertaken to portray the Holocaust in works of art, literature, and music, both by those who were ultimately killed and by those survivors and observers who have tried to capture its horror.

5. Hands-on.   Many individuals, particularly young persons, find it easiest to approach a topic through an activity in which they become actively engaged: one where they can build something, manipulate materials, carry out experiments. The chance to breed generations of fruit flies (Drosophila) gives one the opportunity to observe the incidence and fate of genetic mutations. Holocaust displays can provide a harrowing introduction to this event. When students receive an alternative "identity" upon their entrance and later ascertain what happened to this person in the course of the Holocaust, the personal identification can be very powerful. Being a subject in a psychological experiment that documents the human proclivity to follow orders can be a jarring experience as well.

6. Social.   The entry points described thus far address the individual as a single person. Many individuals learn more effectively, however, in a group setting, where they have the opportunity to assume different roles, to observe others' perspectives, to interact regularly, and to discuss and debate issues to complement one another. A group of students can be given a problem to solve, for example, what happens to various species in a given environment following a dramatic change in climate, or how would the Germans have reacted had the Allies blown up the train tracks that led to a concentration camp. Or they can be asked to role play, e. g., different species in a shifting ecology or different participants in a rebellion in a ghetto that is under siege.

B. Telling Analogies

An entry point perspective places students directly in the center of a disciplinary topic, arousing their interests and securing cognitive commitment for further exploration. The entry point, however, does not necessarily inculcate specific forms or modes of understanding.

Here the teacher (or the student) is challenged to come up with instructive analogies, drawn from material that is already understood, and that can convey important aspects of the less familiar topic. In the case of evolution, for example, analogies can be drawn from history or from the arts. Societies change over time, sometimes gradually, sometimes apocalyptically. The processes of human social change can be compared with those of biological change within and between species. Evolution can also be observed in works of art. Characters change within the course of a book, and, sometimes, over a series of books. Themes in a fugue evolve and develop in certain ways, and not (ordinarily) in others.

One may search for analogies to the Holocaust. The effort to annihilate a people can be analogized to the eradication of traces of an event or even of an entire civilization. Sometimes these efforts at eradication are deliberate, as when the criminal seeks to hide all evidence of a crime. Sometimes these efforts occur as a result of time, as happens when the traces of an ancient city are virtually destroyed (absent relevant historical records, we do not know, of course, about those cities whose vestiges have altogether disappeared as the result of natural disaster or a vengeful enemy).

Analogies can be powerful, but they can also mislead. Analogies are an excellent way to convey important facets of a topic to individuals who have little familiarity with it. However, each analogy can also suggest parallels that do not hold, for example, the informing intelligence that constructs the theme of a fugue differs from the random nature of biological evolution, and a murderer working in isolation differs from a large sector of society working secretly but in concert. The obligation of the teacher is to qualify each analogy as appropriate and to make sure that the misleading parts of the analogy are not allowed to distort or cripple the students' ultimate understanding.*

C. Approaching the Core

Entry points open up the conversation; telling analogies conveys revealing parts of the concept in question. Yet, the challenge of conveying the central understandings still remains.

We now come to the most vexing part of our analysis. Traditionally, educators have relied on two seemingly opposite approaches. Either they have provided quite explicit instructions, usually didactic, and assessed understanding in terms of linguistic mastery of materials ("Evolution is ... ," " The five central points about the Holocaust are ... "). Or they have supplied copious information to students and hoped that, somehow, the students would forge their own syntheses ("On the basis of your reading, our trip to the museum, and various classroom exercises, what would you do if ... "). Some teachers have pursued both approaches, either simultaneously or successively.

Here we encounter the crucial educational question: Can one use knowledge about individual differences in strengths and modes of representations to create educational approaches that can convey the most important, "core notions" of a topic in a reliable and thorough manner?**

---

* This sentence describes component methods that are more detailed parts of the more general method, "use analogies to foster understanding." No situationality is identified, indicating that these parts should be used whenever the general method is used.

** This is a key question that drives the new paradigm of instructional theories.

First, one must acknowledge that there cannot be a formulaic approach.* Every topic is different, just as every classroom context is different, and so each topic must be considered in terms of its own specific concepts, network of concepts, issues, problems, and susceptibilities to misconception.

A second step recognizes that topics do not exist in isolation;** they come from and are, to some extent, defined by the ensemble of existing and emerging disciplines. Thus, a study of evolution occurs within the domain of biology and, more generally, within the realm of scientific explanation. As such, it involves the search for general principles and for models that will apply to all organisms under all kinds of circumstances (though some idiographically oriented scientists seek to explicate specific events like the disappearance of dinosaurs). In contrast, a study of the Holocaust occurs within history and, sometimes, within literary or artistic efforts to render this historical event. Parts of the Holocaust may resemble other historical events, but a foundational notion of history is that it offers an account of specific events, occurring in specific contexts. One can neither expect general principles to emerge nor build models that can be tested (though some scientifically oriented historians have attempted to construct and test such models).

The third step acknowledges commonly used ways of describing and explaining a concept. Thus evolution is typically described using certain examples (e.g., the disappearance of Neanderthal man, the branching tree of evolution), while the Holocaust is typically presented in terms of certain key events and documents (e.g., Hitler's *Mein*, the formulation at the 1942 Wannsee Conference of the Final Solution, the records kept at Auschwitz, the reports by the first Allied soldiers to liberate the camps, the chilling photographs of the survivors). These familiar examples are not randomly chosen; rather, they have helped scholars to define these topics in the past, and they have proved effective pedagogically with at least a reasonable percentage of students.

But while these examples have their reasons, one must not infer that such examples are uniquely or permanently privileged. One can certainly feature these examples without ensuring understanding; and, by the same token, it is surely possible to enhance understanding of evolution or the Holocaust by using other examples, other materials, differently formulated causal accounts. We know that this ensemble changes, because there are new historical or scientific discoveries, as well as novel pedagogical approaches that have been proved effective. (Thus, for example, the opportunity to simulate evolutionary processes in a computer program, or to create virtual realities, spawns educational possibilities that could not have been anticipated a generation or two ago.)***

---

* I interpret this as a call for situationality and flexibility—adaptability of the methods by teachers—in instructional theories. See especially chapter 1, pp. 8 and 25; chapter 9 (Schwartz, Lin, Brophy & Bransford), p. 189; and chapter 13 (Corno & Randi), pp. 312 and 313.

** The issues of connectedness (among topics/domains) and context (within a broader domain) are key markers of the new paradigm of instruction (see especially chap. 16 by Kovalik & McGeehan, and chap. 22 by Lewis, Watson & Schaps).

*** The new opportunities afforded by information technologies represent yet another aspect of the new paradigm of instructional theories.

For me, the key step to approaching the core is the recognition that a concept can only be well understood—and can only give rise to convincing performances of understanding—if an individual is capable of representing that core in more than one way, indeed, in several ways. Moreover, it is desirable if the multiple modes of representing draw on a number of symbol systems, intelligences, schemas, and frames. Going beyond analogies (indeed, proceeding in the opposite direction), representations seek to be as accurate and comprehensive as possible.

Several implications follow from this assertion. First, it is necessary to spend significant time on a topic.* Second, it is necessary to portray the topic in a number of ways, both to illustrate its intricacies and to reach an ensemble of students. Third, it is highly desirable that the multiple approaches explicitly call upon a range of intelligences, skills, and interests.

It may seem that I am simply calling for the "smorgasbord" approach to education: throw enough of the proverbial matter at students and some of it will hit the mind/brain and stick. Nor do I think that this approach is without merit. However, the theory of multiple intelligences provides an opportunity, so to speak, to transcend mere variation and selection. It is possible to examine a topic in detail, to determine which intelligences, which analogies, and which examples, are most likely both to capture important aspects of the topic and to reach a significant number of students. We must acknowledge here the cottage industry aspect of pedagogy, a craft that cannot now and may never be susceptible to an algorithmic approach. It may also constitute the enjoyable part of teaching: the opportunity continually to revisit one's topic and to consider fresh ways in which to convey its crucial components.

Educators and scholars may continue to believe that there is still an optimal mode for representing the core of a topic. I respond as follows. The history of disciplinary progress makes it inevitable that experts will think about a topic in terms of privileged considerations—perhaps genetic mutations and ecological niches in biology, perhaps human intentions and worldwide forces in the case of history. Such consensual portrayal is reasonable. However, one should never lose sight of the fact that evolution did not occur in biology, and the Holocaust did not occur in history; they are events and processes that happened and became available for observers and scholars to interpret and explicate them as best they could. New discoveries, as well as new disciplinary trends, gradually undermine today's orthodoxy; tomorrow's scholar might remake our understandings. Just as Darwin rewrote Lamarck's view of evolution, the believers in punctuated equilibrium aim to overthrow Darwinian gradualism (Gould, 1993). By the same token, Goldhagen's *Hitler's Willing Executioners* (1996) gives a far more "ordinary Germanic" cast to the Holocaust than had historians of earlier decades.

---

* Depth versus breadth is another consistent theme in the new paradigm of instructional theories.

GENERALIZING THE APPROACH

Even if I have achieved some success in suggesting how best to approach two gritty topics of education, I have evidently left untouched the vast majority of the curriculum. My focus has been on a high school, or perhaps a college, pair of topics; I have drawn from biology and European history, rather than from mathematics, music, or meteorology; and I have focused on topics or issues, rather than, say, specific chemical reactions, or metrical analyses, or geometrical proofs.

I would be remiss were I to imply that the approach sketched here could be applied equivalently to every topic of the syllabus. Indeed, I deliberately selected two topics that are relatively rich and multifaceted and that readily allow consideration from several perspectives. I suspect that no pedagogical approach is going to prove equally effective for the full range of topics and skills that need to be conveyed; teaching French verbs or the techniques of Impressionism is simply not commensurate with covering the Russian Revolution or explicating Newton's laws of mechanics.*

Still, the approach sketched here can have wide utility. First, it raises the question of why one is teaching certain topics and what one hopes that students will retain at some time in the future. Much of what we teach recurs through habit; it makes sense to teach fewer topics and to treat them in greater depth.** Such an approach allows one to relate materials to a few central themes, like evolution in biology or the Holocaust in history (or energy in physics, or character in literature), and to eliminate topics if they cannot be reasonably connected to some powerful themes or throughlines. After all, we cannot conceivably cover everything; we may as well strive to be coherent and synthetic in what we do cover.

Having determined which topics require sustained attention, one can then exploit an ensemble of pedagogical approaches. To recapitulate: one begins by considering which entry points might succeed in attracting the interest and attention of diverse students. One then considers which kinds of analogies and other kinds of comparisons (for example, metaphoric expressions) might convey important parts of the topic in ways that are powerful and not misleading. Finally, one seeks to find a small family of literally appropriate representations that, taken together, provide a rich and differentiated set of representations of the topic under consideration. Such an ensemble conveys to students what it is like to be an expert. And to the extent that the family of representations involves a range of symbols and an array of schemes, it will prove far more robust and useful to students.

Presenting materials that foster multiple representations is one component of effective teaching; the complementary component entails the provision of many opportunities for performance, which can reveal to the student and to others the extent to which the material has been mastered. In stimulating informative performances

---

* This, again, I interpret as a call for situationality in instructional theories, including the notion that we need guidelines (a meta design theory) for deciding which theories to use when.

** See note on p. 85.

of understanding, teachers need to be imaginative and pluralistic. Although it is easy to fall back on the tried-and-true—the short answer test, the essay question—there is no imperative to do so. Performances can be as varied as the different facets of the topic, and the diverse sets of skills of students.* A variety of sanctioned performances not only provides more students with an opportunity to show what they have understood; it also ensures that no single "take" on a topic exerts an inappropriate hegemony on students' (or test-makers'!) understandings of that topic.

With respect to our present examples, then, I encourage teachers to have students engage with one another in debates, for example, on the causes of the Holocaust or the merits of Lamarckianism; to carry out experiments that probe different aspects of the evolutionary process; to interview individuals who have survived the Holocaust or various other of the global conflicts of our time; to create works of art that commemorate heroes of the Resistance; or to design a creature that can survive in an environment that has become highly toxic. Perhaps most challengingly, they might need to be asked to discuss the factors that permitted the Holocaust in terms of what we know about the evolution of behavior in that line called *Homo sapiens sapiens*. Hence, our two topics would at last be joined. Consultation of curricular guides and conversations with other teachers should stimulate the imagination with respect to other kinds of performances for other specimen curricula.

Is this just another call for projects, one of the sins of the Progressive movement, recently castigated by Hirsch (1996)? Quite the contrary. Student projects need to be considered critically in two respects: (a) adequacy as an example of a genre (is it a coherent essay, is it an effective monument, does it qualify as a causal explanation?); (b) adequacy as an occasion for performing one's understandings (does the debater stick to the consensual facts or does she distort what is known? does the newly designed species have a life span that allows reproduction and rearing of offspring?). Far from being a superficial measure of understanding, such projects and performances hold the students to high standards; the key features of the concept should be performed in vehicles that meet the test of cultural viability.

CODA: TECHNOLOGICAL MEANS, HUMAN ENDS

I have restricted myself until now almost entirely to the simplest forms of technology: books, pencils, and papers, perhaps a few art supplies, a simple biochemical laboratory. This is appropriate; fundamental discussions of educational goals and means should not be dependent upon the latest technological advances.

Yet, the approach outlined here promises to be enhanced significantly by current and future technologies. It is no easy matter for teachers to provide individualized curricula and pedagogy for a class of 30 elementary school students, let alone several high school classes totaling more than 100 students. Similarly, it is challenging

---

* This illustrates how the new paradigm doesn't reject or replace the old; rather, it expands or reconfigures it.

to have students present a variety of performances and then provide meaningful feedback on this potpourri.

Happily, we have in our grasp today technology that will allow a quantum leap in the delivery of individualized services for both students and teachers.* It is already possible to create software that addresses the different intelligences; that provides a range of entry points; that allows students to exhibit their own understandings in symbol systems (linguistic, numerical, musical, and graphic, just for starters); and that begins to allow teachers to examine student work flexibly and rapidly. Student work can even be examined from a distance, thanks to e-mail, video conferencing, and the like. The development of "intelligent systems" that will be able to evaluate student work and provide relevant feedback is no longer simply a chapter from science fiction.

In the past, it might have been possible to argue that personalized or individualized instruction, though desirable, was simply not possible. That argument is no longer tenable.** Future reluctance will have to be justified on other grounds. My strong hunch is that such resistance is not likely to persuade students and parents who are not experiencing success "in the usual way" and who might benefit from alternative forms of delivery; neither will such resistance satisfy scholars who have arrived at new ways of conceptualizing materials, nor teachers who are themselves dedicated to a variety of pedagogies and assessments.

Educators have always tinkered with promising technologies, and much of the history of education chronicles the varying fates of paper, books, lecture halls, film strips, television, computers, and other human artifacts. Current technologies seem tailor-made to help bring into reality the kind of multiple intelligences that I have endorsed here. Still, there are no guarantees. Many technologies have faded; many others have been used superficially and unproductively. And we cannot forget that some of the horrible events of human history, such as the Holocaust, featured a perversion of existing technology.

That is why any consideration of education cannot remain merely instrumental. The question is not "computers or not?", but "computers for what?",and more broadly, "education for what?" I have taken here a strong position: that education must ultimately justify itself in terms of enhancing human understanding. But that understanding itself is up for grabs. After all, one can use knowledge of physics to build bridges or bombs; one can use knowledge of human beings to help or to enslave them.

I want my children to understand the world, but not just because the world is fascinating and the human mind is curious. I want them to understand it so that they will be positioned to make it a better place. Knowledge is not the same as morality,

---

* This captures the core idea that information technologies play a critical enabling role for the information-age paradigm of instruction.

** Amen! Although I prefer the term "personalized" over "individualized," because personalized learning doesn't have to occur with students working alone.

but we need to understand if we are to avoid past mistakes and move in productive directions.*

An important part of that understanding is knowing who we are and what we can do. Part of that answer lies in biology—the roots and constraints of our species—and part of it lies in our history—what people have done in the past and what they are capable of doing. Many topics are important, but I would argue that evolution and the Holocaust are especially important. They bear on the possibilities of our species—for good and for evil. A student needs to know about these topics not primarily because they may appear on an examination but rather because they help us to chart human possibilities. Ultimately, we must each synthesize our understandings for ourselves. The performances of understanding that truly matter are the ones that we carry out as human beings in a world that is imperfect but that we can affect—for good or for ill.

ACKNOWLEDGMENTS

For support of this work, I am grateful to the Ross Family Charitable Foundation, the Louise and Claude Rosenberg, Jr. Family Foundation, and Thomas H. Lee. I thank Veronica Boix-Mansilla, David Perkins, and Charles Reigeluth for their helpful critiques of an earlier draft of this paper.

REFERENCES

Gardner, H. (1991). *The unschooled mind: How children think and how schools should teach*. New York: Basic Books.

Gardner, H. (1993a). *Frames of mind: The theory of multiple intelligences*. New York: Basic Books.

Gardner, H. (1993b). *Multiple intelligences: The theory in practice*. New York: Basic Books.

Gardner, H. (1998). Are there additional intelligences? In J. Kane (Ed.), *Education, information, and transformation*. Englewood Cliffs, NJ: Prentice-Hall.

Gardner, H. (1999). *The disciplined mind: What all students should understand*. New York: Simon and Schuster.

Goldhagen, D. (1996). *Hitler's willing executioners*. New York: Knopf.

Gould, S. J. (1993). *Wonderful life*. New York: Norton

Herrnstein, R., & Murray, C. (1994). *The bell curve*. New York: Free Press.

Hirsch, E. D. (1996). *The schools we need*. New York: Doubleday.

Sternberg, R. J. (1985). *Beyond IQ*. New York: Cambridge University Press.

Wiske, M. S. (Ed.). (1988). *Teaching for understanding*. San Francisco: Jossey-Bass.

---

* Again the importance of the affective domain emerges.

5 Teaching and Learning for Understanding

David N. Perkins
Chris Unger

Harvard University Graduate School of Education

David Perkins

Chris Unger

David Perkins is Co-director of Harvard Project Zero and a Senior Research Associate at the Harvard Graduate School of Education. A cognitive scientist with degrees in mathematics and artificial intelligence from MIT, he is the author of *Smart Schools: From Training Memories to Educating Minds, Outsmarting IQ: The New Science of Learnable Intelligence, Knowledge as Design*, and several other books as well as many articles. He has participated in the development of a number of instructional programs and approaches for teaching understanding and thinking, including initiatives in South Africa, Israel, and Latin America. He is a former Guggenheim fellow.

Chris Unger is a Principal Investigator at Project Zero at the Harvard Graduate School of Education. He played an integral role in the development of the Teaching for Understanding framework, and directed research on student understanding. He is currently working with Dr. Perkins and other colleagues at Project Zero on a framework for understanding in organizations (e.g., businesses and communities). His current work is focused on the use of Teaching for Understanding as a framework for supporting and guiding personal and organizational inquiry in schools, businesses, reflective communities, and individuals' personal lives.

FOREWORD

Goals and preconditions. *The primary goal of this theory is the cultivation of understanding as a performance capability. Therefore, it is intended only for situations where understanding is a central concern.*

Values. *Some of the values upon which this theory is based include:*

- *being able to deploy knowledge with understanding.*
- *learning topics that are central to the discipline or domain.*
- *motivation ("genuine involvement, commitment, and emotional response").*
- *active use and transfer of knowledge.*
- *retention of knowledge.*
- *organized, systematic approaches to constructivist teaching.*
- *a broad and flexible range of pedagogical styles, including direct instruction.*
- *students providing feedback to each other.*

Methods. *Here are the major methods this theory offers:*
*Select **generative topics** for study (teacher and student). They should be:*

- *central to the domain or discipline.*
- *accessible and interesting to the students.*
- *interesting to the teacher.*
- *connectable to diverse themes.*
- *typically grander themes of rich and illuminating character.*

*Select and publicly state **understanding goals** (teacher and student). They should be:*

- *nested (with subgoals)*
- *central to the domain or discipline regarding:*
  - *content knowledge in the domain*   *- methods in the domain*
  - *purposes of the domain*   *- forms of expression in the domain*

*Engage in **understanding performances** (students).*
Purposes:

- *advance learners' understanding.*
- *publicly demonstrate learners' understanding so far.*

Criteria:
- *should relate directly to the understanding goals.*

- *should develop understanding through practice.*
  - *reflective engagement in challenging, approachable tasks.*
  - *sequenced to broader and deeper understandings.*
    - *entry performances (exploratory).*
    - *mid-sequence performances (organized; guided inquiry).*
    - *culminating performances (product and/or presentation).*
  - *feedback and revision.*
- *should engage multiple learning styles and forms of expression.*

*Provide **ongoing assessment** (teacher). It should be:*

- *relevant, explicit, and public.*
- *frequent.*
- *from multiple sources.*
- *used to gauge progress and inform planning.*

Major contributions. *The focus on understanding as an important kind of learning outcome. The emphasis on performances as integral to both the development and assessment of understanding. A teaching methodology that makes practical sense to teachers, operationalizing in an accessible way a broadly constructivist approach to teaching and learning.*

—C.M.R.

Teaching and Learning for Understanding

Suppose you were asked: "What is one thing you understand really well? It doesn't necessarily have to be an academic subject." Further questions invited you to explain how you came to understand whatever it was, and how you knew you understood it well.

Responding to the first question, people often mention areas like cooking, driving, sailing, gardening, or running a small business. Addressing the second question, people foreground active involvement, opportunity to receive feedback, episodes of reflection, and the like. Asked the third question, they tend to say something that amounts to: "Because I can function well. I can deal with problems and opportunities effectively, explain things to others, make reasonable decisions." In summary, queried about understanding, people respond with a picture of learning for understanding as an active, involving, thoughtful enterprise. In strong trend, their answers are an intuitive vindication of a broadly constructivist perspective on learning for understanding.

Interestingly, very few respond to the first question with typical academic topics. The trend is a little discouraging but unsurprising on two counts. First, it is easy for educators to forget that formal education only constitutes one thread in the intricate tapestry of living a life, with learning opportunities abundant elsewhere. But the second reason is especially worth pondering. Classrooms from kindergarten to college tend not to offer as involved, dynamic, and feedback-rich a setting for learning as people generally report for their best learning experiences.* A challenge for pedagogical theory is to provide visions and guidelines that help teachers and curriculum designers to foster learning at its best.

This article describes one response to that challenge: a theory of understanding and a framework for the design of instruction that fosters understanding.** This framework was developed by a team at Project Zero of the Harvard University Graduate School of Education over several years, with support from the Spencer Foundation. The process was intensively collaborative and school based, with teachers involved from the start in close working relationships with the university participants. The framework and the results are discussed at length in two books. *Teaching for Understanding* (Wiske, 1998) offers a coherent set of articles for researchers and practitioners by a number of the project participants. *Understanding Up Front* (Blythe and associates, 1998) is a teachers' guide. Earlier treatments in chapter and article form include Gardner (1991), Perkins (1992, 1993), Perkins and Blythe (1994), Simmons (1994), and Unger (1994).

To give the philosophy and framework of teaching for understanding a handy name, we call it TfU.

Purpose and Value

Understanding is widely recognized as an important value of education (Cohen, McLaughlin, & Talbert, 1993; Gardner, 1991; Perkins, 1992; Perkins, Schwartz, Wiske, & West, 1995; Perrone, 1998). While the acquisition and retention of knowledge certainly serve important purposes, knowledge does not come into its own until the learner can deploy it with understanding. It is one thing to be able to execute the algorithms of arithmetic accurately, but quite another to discern what

---

* These are some of the characteristics that help distinguish the new paradigm from the industrial-age paradigm of instruction.

** Understanding is one of the kinds of learning that was largely overlooked by the industrial-age instructional theories (see chap. 3, p. 52).

situations call for what operations. It is one thing to learn a list of the causes of the Civil War, but another to be able to think about a contemporary situation and make illuminating analogies with what one knows about the Civil War. Understanding, one might say, is knowledge in thoughtful action.

This would be no more than a philosophical point if it could be taken for granted that the acquisition of knowledge brought understanding along like the caboose of a train. Unfortunately, a rich history of research during the past three decades has demonstrated over and over again that students often know far more than they understand about subjects that they have studied. Most students suffer from a number of misunderstandings about science concepts that persist in the face of conventional instruction, even instruction at the university level (e.g., Clement, 1982; Gardner, 1991; Gentner & Stevens, 1983; McDermott, 1984; Novak, 1987; Perkins & Simmons, 1988). Students of history display "presentism", the tendency to project on past times' expectations rooted in present times (Carretero, Pozo & Asensio, 1989; Shelmit, 1980). Students have difficulty applying their computational knowledge of arithmetic and algebra to story problems and to mathematical modeling generally (e.g., Lochhead & Mestre, 1988; Resnick, 1987). In sum, the challenge of teaching and learning for understanding is blatant. Organized systematic approaches to a pedagogy of understanding are needed.*

None of this means that understanding is a universal educational value dominant over other considerations in all circumstances. For some kinds of learning, understanding may be less of a central concern. Children acquire their mother tongues with no explicit academic understanding of grammar, although they might be said to have an operational understanding of grammar as exhibited by their linguistic behavior. In everyday life, young children must learn a number of practical lessons about what to avoid that they are too young to understand. Their safety, rather than an ideology of understanding, is the driving factor in parents' sometimes stern "Just do it!" In the classroom, some things are best committed to reliable memory and well-practiced routine (phonetic equivalences of letter combinations, multiplication tables) even though one hopes that surrounding these facts and routines will be larger understandings that make good use of them.

However, if understanding is not the end-all of learning, neither is it the luxury it is sometimes considered. From time to time, someone suggests that the facts and routines need to come first. These basics establish a foundation for deeper learning in later years, at least for those students with the flair and enthusiasm for the venture. However, such a "yes but not now" policy risks making education boring and meaningless for students. For the most part, learning with understanding can be expected to yield higher engagement, more active use and transfer of knowledge, and indeed better retention of knowledge than learning with a rote emphasis (cf. Perkins, 1992).

---

* This is a direct call for more instructional theory in this area (understanding).

In summary, understanding is a fundamental, widely recognized aspiration of education, but one often thought to be readily achieved, deferrable until later, or a luxury to be reserved for the best and the brightest. We argue that none of these is generally the case. Accordingly, to achieve the aspirations of education, pedagogies are needed that deal effectively with the challenge of teaching and learning for understanding (Perrone, 1998).

A Performance View of Understanding and Learning for Understanding

What is understanding? Any approach to a pedagogy of understanding needs to pay heed to such a fundamental question. Research conducted with high school students as part of the aforementioned project revealed that most students identify understanding, especially academic understanding, with knowledge. Understanding a topic is a matter of knowing it well. However, it is clear that knowledge in itself does not guarantee understanding. One may know Newton's laws in the sense of being able to recite them or solve conventional quantitative problems without any real understanding of them. One may know by heart Hamlet's famous "To be or not to be" soliloquy without having a clue as to its possible meanings or any ability to deliver the speech with a personal interpretation.

Other limited meanings of understanding occur imbedded in natural language. Understanding often gets identified with seeing or receiving, as in expressions like, "I see what you mean," "I see the point," "I get it," "I grasp the idea." All these locutions suggest an immediacy of apprehension: The understanding comes all at once, as a kind of gestalt. However, here again the common notion deceives. Plainly, many understandings are hard won by incremental effort, not achieved in sudden epiphanies.

Perhaps the most prominent technical answer in contemporary cognitive science to the question "What is understanding?" focuses on mental models or schemata of some kind (e.g., Gentner & Stevens, 1983; Johnson-Laird, 1983; Rumelhart, 1980; Schank & Abelson, 1977). To have an understanding of anything from Newton's laws to the Peloponnesian Wars is to have a good mental model or set of schemata regarding the subject. Mental models are often "runnable": they enable mental simulations that aid in the generation of predictions and plans of action. Schemata allow reasoning about a topic because they specify default values for "slots" that allow extrapolation in the face of missing information and yield anomalies when expectations are violated, among other reasons.

Research findings support the idea that mental models or schemata are important for many kinds of understandings. For example, Mayer (1989) demonstrated that what he called "conceptual models"—basically, diagrammatic representations of systems such as radar or a computer—enhance understanding in less able learners. Perkins and Unger (1994) argue that mental and physical representations support understanding by providing learners with structured problem spaces that support the kinds of thinking they have to do to display understanding.

However, identification of understanding with the possession of a mental representation goes too far. Possession of a model or schema is not nearly sufficient for understanding. To plan, predict, invent, or otherwise make good use of a mental representation, one must not just have it, but operate with and through it. For example, "running" an imagistic mental model characteristically calls for creating a mental image and putting it through its paces. The representation supports the processing, but does not *do* the processing (Perkins & Unger, 1994). Such facility cannot be taken for granted. Moreover, for at least some kinds of intuitive or internalized understanding, perhaps that of a jazz musician skillfully and flexibly improvising a performance or a carpenter skillfully and flexibly crafting a book case to fit an odd corner, conscious representations may not even be necessary (cf. Perkins, 1998).

With such concerns in mind, the present framework advances as its centerpiece a performance conception of understanding. To put it in a phrase, *understanding a topic is a matter of being able to think and act creatively and competently with what one knows about the topic.* A student understands Newton's laws to the extent that the student can explain them in his or her own words, solve problems of kinds not encountered before, explore what might be done to test the laws, and so on. A student understands the law of supply and demand to the extent that the student can explain particular price fluctuations, ponder what the law might mean in a trade rather than a currency economy, and even extrapolate its significance for energy flow in ecological systems. A student understands a poem to the extent that the student can offer and defend a personal interpretation, elaborate connections with his or her own outer or inner life, discern the strategies the author used to make it compelling, discuss content and stylistic similarities with other works, and so on. The kinds of performances called for are of course context-relative. They reflect the characteristic demands of the discipline or domain. But the ability to perform in a flexible, thought-demanding way is a constant requirement.

Accordingly, we call such thought-demanding activities *understanding performances* or *performances of understanding.* An understanding performance both displays the learner's understanding-so-far and, by asking the learner to solve problems, make decisions, and adapt old ideas to new situations, expands that understanding further. Learning for understanding becomes a progressive process of attempting more and more challenging understanding performances, gradually expanding the flexible performance capability of the learner. This does not mean that traditional tools of pedagogy such as texts and lectures have no place.* Information sources, written and oral, can be invaluable components of a process of learning in

---

* This indicates that the new paradigm should expand or reconfigure, not reject, many of the methods that comprised the industrial-age paradigm of instruction. It needs to reorganize their use into fundamentally different patterns.

this style, depending on the topic and the learners. But the emphasis on performance recenters the learning enterprise on engagement in progressive performances of understanding, supported by whatever information is needed.

A four-part framework develops this basic idea into a practical tool for designing and delivering instruction. The key elements, mentioned here and elaborated later, are *generative topics* (topics chosen for their generativity relative to subject matter, teacher, and learner), *understanding goals* (specifying what is to be understood about a topic), *understanding performances* (the activities that will display and advance learners' understanding), and *ongoing assessment* (assessment practices that provide learners with informative feedback early and often throughout the learning process).

Comparison and Contrast With Other Views

Anyone acquainted with the history of education and psychology over the past several decades will recognize that the framework advanced here is a constructivist pedagogy. However, there are two notable contrasts between the TfU framework and a general constructivist stance. First, many teachers and developers find constructivism confusing as a general philosophy. Just what does it mean for the learner to be active? What kinds of activities constitute making meaning? What is it that learners construct? The performance perspective and the four categories just mentioned provide a particular version of the constructivist story that, for many, is more orienting and supportive than generic constructivist discourse on the challenges of teaching and learning.

Second, the TfU framework allows more flexibility than one particular but rather common version of the constructivist story, which might be called constructivist discovery learning. This story involves commitments to three ideas: (a) some kind of mental model or representation is central to understanding; (b) the learner must construct the mental model personally for it to constitute a good understanding; and (c) once attained, the conception empowers the learner to go on from there and display a range of understandings. Accordingly, a student studying electricity and electrical circuits might examine a range of phenomena and get encouragement and support from a teacher toward constructing and testing models of electrical flow.

Such a learning process is consistent with TfU. However, the TfU model does not treat discovery as the only path to understanding.* Indeed, the present perspective affords more flexibility with respect to all three of the above points. (a) As already mentioned, some understandings may not rest on conscious mental representations in any obvious way (Perkins, 1998). (b) Learner-constructed mental models are not necessarily particularly good, nor are learners always adept at improving them or eager to do so (Collins & Gentner, 1987; Driver, Guesne, &

---

* This supports the theme of diversity of methods, which runs throughout the new paradigm of instructional theory.

Tiberghien, 1985; Gentner & Stevens, 1983; Smith & Unger, 1997); and ones provided by teachers and developers may serve quite well, as in Mayer's (1989) work.* (c) Attaining a reasonable model may not always empower the learner to go on from there to a range of diverse understanding performances. Using the model flexibly and effectively can be a further challenge.

Accordingly, while one might well engage students in an inquiry process to cultivate understanding of a target topic, one might also introduce the concept or principle directly, supporting an explanation with an imagistic mental model, a demonstration, or other such device. One would follow on with a range of activities designed to test and expand the initial understanding. In sum, the TfU framework allows for a greater range of pedagogical styles, including direct instruction, provided that performances of understanding receive ample attention along the way.

Conditions of Application

It is our belief that TfU is a suitable guide to organizing learning in any situation where understanding is a priority. The range of applications of the framework is very broad, including all disciplines at all levels as well as out-of-school kinds of learning and even "organizational learning" (Argyris, 1993; Argyris & Schön, 1996; Garvin, 1993; Senge, 1994). Our practical experiences include working with not only classroom teachers but university professors, curriculum developers, and administrators working on organizational change. The flexibility of the framework occurs because of the freedom to choose generative topics, understanding goals, understanding performances, and means of ongoing assessment adapted to different learners, domains, and contexts.

However, this flexibility inherently brings with it a challenge to the teacher or other designer of learning. Because the guidelines are broad, they require thoughtful interpretation based on a reasonable understanding of what is to be learned.** Sometimes teachers or developers find themselves less well versed in the topic of instruction than would be ideal. The TfU framework tends to highlight limited understanding, and teachers or developers may have scant time, resources, or even inclination to deal with that.

As with any new framework, it takes a while for teachers and developers to get oriented to TfU. Moreover, teaching for understanding requires a significant time investment from learners, whether by way of TfU or other means. Understanding does not come free and often not at all easily. If, for whatever reason, the time and effort cannot realistically be allocated, TfU or any pedagogy of understanding may generate more frustration than it is worth.

---

* See also chapter 7 of this volume.

** This is related to the discussion in chapter 1 (p. 10) about the level of detail or generality of methods of instruction and how methods can be broken down into more detailed component methods. Broader methods offer less guidance and therefore require more "thoughtful interpretation." But more detailed methods are subject to greater situationality, with alternative kinds of methods being most appropriate for different situations.

In our experience, the effort required by TfU varies considerably depending on whether teachers already teach somewhat in the manner recommended (and many do!) and on the adventurousness with which they approach TfU. It is perfectly possible to employ TfU for individual lessons or units of instruction without radically reorganizing the curriculum. With moderate effort, such conservative applications can help students.

THE TEACHING FRAMEWORK IN DETAIL

The core of TfU is the notion of understanding as a performance capability. The essence of learning is learners' engagement in understanding performances. But these principles are too sparse to support the effective planning of instruction.* How should one select topics or adjust established topics to support learning for understanding? What principles govern the choice of understanding performances? How can learners be helped to refine and advance understanding performances? Such questions as these motivated the development of a four-part framework to organize the design and delivery of instruction. The sections below describe the four categories and their use with a small-scale example. A larger scale example appears later, and fully elaborated examples from several disciplines can be found in Wiske (1998) and Blythe and associates (1998).

1. Generative Topics

One challenge of teaching for understanding is that many school topics do not appear to offer rich opportunities for the mission. Such topics as the joints of the body (including hinge joints, fused joints, ball-and-socket joints, and so on) notoriously lead to didactic treatments emphasizing definitions and locations. Poems often become objects of memorization, historical events, the occasion for learning lists of facts and supposed causes.

The theme of generative topics issues an invitation to teachers and curriculum planners to select topics that have a rich and illuminating character** that invite a constructivist approach to understanding or to reframe and redescribe conventional topics in this direction. For example, the topic "joints of the body" can be construed in several ways that make it richer and more inviting: "the joints of the body as wheels, levers, and other simple machines"; "the joints of the body in sports and dance"; or the "joints of the body, injury, and aging."

---

* This is arguing for the need to break down these general methods into more detailed ones that offer more "support [for] the effective planning of instruction."

** Here the focus is on decisions about what to teach, rather than how to teach it. This highlights the increasing interdependence of, and need to integrate, instructional theory and curriculum theory (see chap. 1, p. 14).

More systematically, what makes for a good generative topic? Through a collaborative process with teachers and over time, we developed four basic attributes that serve as criteria for selecting generative topics.

1. *Central to a domain or discipline.* A good generative topic is central to the domain or discipline it serves. For example, joints of the body becomes more central when seen as part of the basic mechanics of the body or key to the body-in-demanding-action as in sports and dance, or as a medical problem.

2. *Accessible and interesting to students.* A good generative topic has appeal and accessibility, so that students can engage it with some enthusiasm and effectiveness. For example, joints of the body becomes a more appealing topic when related by analogy to more familiar devices like wheels, or to activities like sports and dance, or to matters of urgency like health.*

3. *Interesting to the teacher.* This criterion may come as something of a surprise, since teachers' interests rarely figure as significant elements in guides to instructional design. However, in our experience, teachers' interests are crucial. A teacher with a passion for a topic approaches it with more zest and imagination and displays a greater readiness to engage students in deep learning. Concerning joints of the body, any of the three generative versions of the topic mentioned above, as well as others, could serve as a good vehicle for building basic understandings. A teacher might well choose one on the basis of his or her interest, recognizing how this would energize the planning and instruction.

4. *Connectable.* A good generative topic can be connected to diverse themes within and beyond the discipline in question, as well as to students' prior experiences and current lives.** Indeed, good generative topics often have a "bottomless" character. Because of their rich connectedness, one can explore them and their ramifications endlessly, developing deeper and deeper understandings. For example, joints of the body as wheels, levers, and other simple machines provides entryways into such matters as leverage, material strength, the body as a complex machine, how bones, muscles, and tendons together with joints constitute coordinated systems, and much more. The other versions of joints of the body unfold in similarly rich ways. Indeed, the three could be combined.

It might seem absurd to spend so much time on joints of the body. Indeed, more typically, teachers and developers using TfU select grander themes. However, the example serves to illustrate concisely how much can be done even with a seemingly meek and innocuous topic. It can be reframed as a richly connected microcosm with manifold opportunities for learning that touch themes within and beyond the disci-

---

* Methods of motivating students is a key characteristic of most theories in the new paradigm.
** Relevance to students is a major tool for motivating students. This again highlights the interdependence of content and methods (curriculum and instruction).

pline and in students' lives. We will continue to use it as a small-scale example to illustrate the framework.

2. Understanding Goals

Ironically, a focus on generative topics makes TfU harder in one way, by leading into a maze of opportunities. Returning to joints of the body, taking the perspective of sports and dance suggests such themes as how the body's joints enable and limit different kinds of sports and dance, the role of mechanical advantage and similar physics concepts in sports and dance, how force applied to joints in such activities risks injury, what sports and dance might be like if we were equipped with different joints, how animal motion is differently governed (as in horse racing, for instance), how devices such as poles for pole vaulting extend the possibilities for body motion by providing external joints, and so on. Thus, TfU calls for a rigorous selectivity to match the expansiveness of generative topics. Just what is it that learners should strive to understand?

For a short unit of study, teachers characteristically select three to five understanding goals. More become unwieldy, since each goal must be served. For a semester or year of study, the list can be longer.

For example, three understanding goals for the topic "the joints of the body, injury, and aging," might be:

1. Students will understand how different joints of the body are subject to different forces that may injure them, reflecting different kinds of physically stressful activity.
2. Students will understand the effects of wear and aging on the deterioration of different kinds of joints.
3. Students will appreciate the risks of different kinds of joint injury they expose themselves to in various activities and will consider appropriate preventative practices.

As shown above, teachers are encouraged to express understanding goals with sentence stems such as "Students will understand ... " or "Students will appreciate ... ." This strategy keeps understanding goals at a higher level of abstraction than understanding performances. Otherwise, understanding goals and understanding performances tend to get mixed up. Also, the use of the stem verb *appreciate* for one of the goals is notable. Early in the TfU initiative we learned that the term *understand* sometimes connotes too detached a grasp of the topic, not honoring the importance of genuine involvement, commitment, and emotional response.* The term *appreciate* helps teachers and curriculum designers to reflect such concerns.

---

* These are affective concerns. The interdependence of the affective and cognitive domains is also a consistent theme for the new paradigm of instructional theory. This intersection of cognition and affect is further explored in Unit IV, especially chapter 21 by Lewis, Watson, and Schaps and chapter 22 by Stone-McCown & McCormick, as well as other chapters in this unit, such as chapter 16 by Kovalik and McGeehan.

The individual designing the instruction often selects all the understanding goals. However, many teachers engage in an interactive dialog with their students to specify understanding goals.* Usually the teacher has in mind one or two goals that figure centrally in the teacher's sense of the educational mission. Others may be suggested by the students. This helps to build student commitment as well as to enrich the topic.

A more informal way of expressing goals, and perhaps a more user-friendly way for sharing goals with students, takes the form of broad evocative questions. For instance, the first goal mentioned above for *joints of the body* might be rephrased: "How are different joints of the body subject to different forces that may injure them, reflecting different kinds of physically stressful activity?" When understanding goals in this form pervade and organize instruction for a considerable period, several participants in TfU have called them *"throughlines."* The term comes from Stanislavski's school of method acting, referring to a fundamental theme in a play on which an actor can build the portrayal of a character.**

Finally, there are suggested attributes that serve as criteria to help in selecting and using suitable goals.

1. *Explicit and public.* Whatever the phrasing, a key characteristic of understanding goals is their public nature. All too often, students experience learning with little conception of what the goals are except in the broad and vague sense of "master this topic." Public goals (a list on the blackboard, a set of bulleted items on a handout) help students, teachers, parents and administrators to recognize at the outset and keep in focus the instructional agenda, and to make sense of the overall learning process as a coherent enterprise, gauging progress with respect to the goals.

2. *Nested.* When TfU instruction involves not just a unit of a couple of weeks but themes that run for a semester or a year, goals characteristically are nested, with a few higher order goals providing a setting for more specialized goals for subtopics. Thus, for example, several particular understanding goals under joints of the body might sit within a general semester throughline like "How does the human body work as a complex system with strengths and weaknesses?"

3. *Central to the discipline.* Continuing on from generative topics, understanding goals should be central to the discipline or domain. One way of maintaining this focus is to bear in mind four dimensions of disciplinary understanding and to ask whether the understanding goals and the performances that follow upon them keep these at center stage: *content knowledge in the domain*, avoiding misconceptions and superficial conceptions and aim-

---

* This trend toward greater student self-regulation of learning is another common feature in the new paradigm of instructional theories (see especially chap. 13 by Corno & Randi).

** This is similar to the notion of thematic instruction (see e.g., chap. 16 by Kovalik & McGeehan), which represents a more systemic and authentic approach to learning.

ing at well-integrated knowledge structures; *methods in the domain*, aiming at an understanding of how inquiry is conducted and claims are justified; *purposes of the domain*, recognizing the roles the domain and its results play in varied disciplines and in home, professional, and other activities; and *forms of expression in the domain*, aiming at facility with whatever forms of expression (essayistic writing, formal proofs, graphical representations, physical performances, etc.) serve the domain (Boix-Mansilla & Gardner, 1998). These same dimensions were used in a formal analysis of the impact of TfU on students' understanding, to be discussed later.

3. Understanding Performances

A generative topic and understanding goals set the stage for the main events of learning for understanding: learners' engagement in understanding performances. Recall that the key characteristics of an understanding performance are two: An attempted performance both displays learners' understanding-so-far and advances that understanding. The challenge for the planner of instruction is to arrange a sequence of understanding performances that allows learners ready entry into the topic, advances their understanding at a reasonable pace, and brings them to a contextually appropriate level of understanding with respect to the understanding goals.

Teachers and developers have found it useful to sequence instruction broadly as follows.* Understanding performances early in the treatment of a topic have the character of "messing around." Learners, often working in small groups, air initial conceptions, engage in speculative explorations, gain experience with examining and manipulating any physical materials involved (texts, artifacts, works of art) and so on. After this comes a phase of more organized engagement that might be called guided inquiry, systematically advancing on the several fronts defined by the understanding goals. Learners work sometimes in groups and sometimes alone. Finally, there is a culminating performance with a project-like character, which was in preparation for some time, involving individual or small group performances of considerable scope. The performances may take the form of compositions in writing, pictorial form, models, or mixed media of various sorts, or may occasionally consist of actual performance events that students present. If the instructional sequence represents a semester or year of work, often this culminating performance has a substantial audience, for example, other students in the class, beyond the class, parents, and so on.

For example, for a brief unit on joints of the body as wheels, levers, and other simple machines, one entry performance might involve students examining the joints of their body from the outside, trying different motions, feeling the joints, and charting different kinds of flexibility of motion to produce a preliminary taxonomy

---

* This general specification of a method is, in the next few sentences, broken down into more detailed component methods.

and speculative sketches about how the joints worked. A midsequence understanding performance might involve constructing a model of a hinge joint out of simple materials, considering attachment points for muscles, and measuring or calculating stresses to determine where the weak points of the system were likely to be. A culminating performance might involve redesigning three or four joints for more effective performance of an individually chosen activity, say, a sport, to increase flexibility and minimize stress, displaying the results in terms of diagrams or models with a well-elaborated rationale.

As with generative topics and understanding goals, understanding performances have criteria that help to guide their selection.

1. *Relate directly to understanding goals.* Understanding performances should transparently address the understanding goals established for the unit of instruction. They should not just be in the same neighborhood.

2. *Develop and apply understanding through practice.* As already suggested, understanding performances should advance through a number of activities to move from initial introductory understandings to broader, deeper, and more robust understandings. Characteristically, this involves more than one try at a particular kind of performance, as students draft, critique, and revise.

3. *Engage multiple learning styles and forms of expression.* * Understanding performances collectively and even individually should make room for different styles of learning and forms of expression. For instance, during the initial phase, one student may prefer to dive into a particular exploration while another makes a plan and carries it out. One student may prefer to represent conclusions diagrammatically while another uses a list or a narrative.

4. *Promote reflective engagement in challenging, approachable tasks.* ** Understanding performances should demand thinking, not just action, although the thinking can be imbedded in action. Understanding performances are not just approachably challenging, but challenging in ways that invite reflective engagement more than blind trial and error.

5. *Publicly demonstrate understanding.* From a logical standpoint, understanding performances need not be visible. Certainly, many learners undertake mental performances that involve thinking with what they know and advancing their understandings. However, from the standpoint of instructional planning, the principal understanding performances need to be visible at least in their outcomes if not in their process. Learners have to be able to stand back from what they have done and appraise it. Others (fellow students, teachers, parents) have to be in a position to offer feedback.

---

* This again reflects the theme of diversity of methods for the new paradigm.
** Reflection and other kinds of metacognitive skills are also a common concern for instructional theories in the new paradigm.

4. Ongoing Assessment

The final component of the TfU framework is ongoing assessment. This category recognizes that feedback is one of the most fundamental aspects of learning. Learners gain a great deal from the opportunity to receive informative feedback on performances and refine those performances by taking the feedback into account. Unfortunately, in many school settings learners receive feedback principally at the ends of units of instruction, when there is no time to repair misunderstandings and revise products. Also, learners often receive grades such as Xs or OKs, As, Bs or Cs, with not enough indication of what is wrong or what could be done about it to guide effective revision of conceptions or products.

The notion of ongoing assessment is a simple response to this perennial challenge. Ongoing assessment asks teachers and developers to arrange for informative feedback early and often in the learning process. Ongoing assessment does not typically call for extra events that constitute official tests and require separate preparation.* Rather, learners are assessed on many of the very performances that constitute the instructional sequence of understanding performances. These, after all, are the principal learning experiences and therefore the elements where feedback can be most valuable in advancing understanding. To continue the running example of joints of the body, a student constructing a model of a hinge joint, considering muscle attachment points, and examining stresses might receive feedback from the teacher or other students about the clarity and accuracy of the model, the approximate correctness of the calculations or measurements, and the identification of high-stress points. This would allow the student to revise the model and would lead to yet another assessment.

While the term "assessment" conjures images of official responses from the teacher, total reliance on the teacher is neither logistically practical nor good for learners.** From a logistical standpoint, ongoing assessment requires too much day-by-day attention for the teacher to function as the sole source of feedback. From a learning standpoint, students can learn a great deal by providing feedback for others and for themselves. Also, there is an opportunity for parents and other members of the larger academic community to participate from time to time. Accordingly, the plan for ongoing assessment typically involves multiple sources of feedback, with the students often in the role of providing feedback to other students as well as themselves.

Also, while sometimes ongoing assessment is a distinct element in the process—a period of time where students explicitly receive feedback from one or another source—at other moments, ongoing assessment can occur imbedded in the flow of events, as students discuss among themselves a draft of a paper or discuss in whole-class format the findings from an experiment or their interpretation of a

---

* The formative role of assessment in learning is another consistent concern for the new paradigm.
** This is related to the new paradigm's emphasis on more self-regulated and reflective learner roles.

poem. Simply by listening to one another in thoughtful, probing conversations, students receive some implicit feedback.

Planning who gives what feedback when, and ensuring that there is time for the feedback and follow-up rethinking, are prominent challenges in the TfU classroom. Indeed, in our experience, ongoing assessment is the most difficult aspect of the framework to operationalize, and accordingly it is usually the last aspect that teachers master.

None of this implies that administrative requirements for grading by the teacher need to be set aside, nor does the idea of ongoing assessment challenge the notion of grading. Most TfU teachers need to assign grades to students for their projects and coursework in general, and most view the final decisions about grades as their responsibility and prerogative, although a few share the process with students in various ways.

Finally, as with the preceding three categories, several standards help in establishing a supportive pattern of ongoing assessment:

1. *Criteria are relevant, explicit, and public.* It helps students enormously to have advance knowledge of clear and explicit criteria for performances. For many performances, criteria can be rather informal. But for key performances, and especially culminating performances, criteria are usually rather carefully worked out. Often, rubrics are used where the performance gets rated on several dimensions on a 3- to 5-point scale, with each level from "novice" to "expert" characterized in a sentence or two.

2. *Occur frequently.* As already emphasized, ongoing assessment occurs frequently, at least in its informal varieties, although full-scale use of rubrics typically only happens at occasional, more important junctures.

3. *Multiple sources.* As already emphasized, both logistics and good pedagogy call for multiple sources of feedback.

4. *Gauge progress and inform planning.* Finally, ongoing assessment should serve both to gauge progress and to inform planning. Note that this applies not only to students but to teachers. By seeing how well individual students are progressing, a teacher can focus interventions on their particular needs. By seeing how well the class as a whole is doing, the teacher can revise plans to address emergent problems and seize newly perceived opportunities.

Taken together, the four categories and their associated standards offer teachers and developers a focused framework for planning and implementing learning experiences based on a performance conception of learning for understanding. The summary offered in Table 5.1 underscores how the categories and standards work together to provide a clear but flexible vision of an instructional paradigm.

TABLE 5.1

Standards for the Four Elements of Teaching for Understanding

Generative topics	Understanding goals	Understanding performances	Ongoing assessment
1. Central to a domain or discipline.	1. Explicit and public goals.	1. Relate directly to understanding goals.	1. Criteria are relevant, explicit, and public.
2. Accessible and interesting to students.	2. Goals central to the discipline.	2. Develop and apply understanding through practice.	2. Assessment occurs frequently.
3. Interesting to the teacher.	3. Nested goals	3. Engage multiple learning styles and forms of expression.	3. Multiple sources of feedback.
4. Connectable to diverse disciplines and contexts.		4. Promote reflective engagement in challenging, approachable tasks.	4. Assessment gauges progress and informs planning.
		5. Publicly demonstrate understanding.	

The Flexibility of the Framework

The account above may suggest that planners of instruction should march through the four categories in order. Some teachers and curriculum planners do exactly that with good results. However, experience shows that others prefer to organize the quest differently.* One teacher might begin with a vision of final products and ideas about the assessment called for by those products. Another might begin with a favorite rich performance that has proved itself previously, expanding from there to consider the generative topic and understanding goals heretofore implicit in the performance. Even when planners take the categories more or less in order, there is an inevitable dialog among the four. Consideration of standards for ongoing assessment often suggests refinements or substantial revisions in performances. Working out the details of a performance may recommend adding understanding goals not recognized before to the list.

Moreover, it is possible to introduce the framework to teachers indirectly, deferring mention of the four official categories of the framework and instead foregrounding more natural questions that evoke the same thinking but target the same key TfU ideas. For example:

---

* The issue of flexibility—adaptability of the methods by teachers—is an important one in the new paradigm of instructional theories. See e.g., chapter 1, pp. 8, 25; chapter 9 (Schwartz, Lin, Brophy & Bransford), p. 189; and chapter 13 (Corno & Randi), pp. 312 and 313.

- What do you really want your students to understand?
- What can you do to help them build those understandings?
- What actions can they take to help themselves build their own understandings?
- How will we, and they, know that they understand?

Many teachers find these sorts of questions very user-friendly. In fact, they are the kinds of questions that good teachers ask themselves anyway, at least tacitly if not in so many words. They provide a natural bridge into more formal statements of the framework.

While TfU is a valuable framework for enriching such small-scale and traditionally dry topics as joints of the body, it can also be used much more adventurously. Wiske (1998) and Blythe and associates (1998) include several examples; here is another. One of the present authors (Unger) has been working with Wilsonville High School, which is located in the fastest growing suburb of Portland, Oregon. One day, in the midst of discussing the role of tobacco farming in the growth of southern communities, Kevin Guay, a U.S. History teacher at Wilsonville High School, decided to raise the economic and environmental issues of urban growth in their own, once semirural town. A lively discussion soon made it apparent that the growth of their town, like that of Jamestown in the mid-1800s, was being dictated by economics. The threats were clear: traffic, overcrowding, and loss of pasture and natural environments.

Over the next three months, Mr. Guay's class designed, conducted, and independently managed the first Urban Growth conference for their quickly growing community. Students made action plans, formed committees, designed events, carried out the advertising, constructed the banners, and got the food. They created a multimedia presentation providing the differing views of development, with visuals and statistics. In the end, over 300 people participated, including the former Mayor, Metro-Councilor officers, the City Planner, business owners, and a whole host of other community members.

In the midst of these understanding performances, which might be considered "beyond the call of duty" for studying history, Mr. Guay's class continued with others squarely targeted on history, studying the growth of the United States throughout the 1800s. The students analyzed the central events of U.S. history through the lens of economic gain and differing perspectives, including, for example, the Civil War, slavery, and America's expansion into the West. These events were discussed in relationship to their own community's issues, which made the issues and analytical frameworks much more alive for the students.

THE PATTERN OF TEACHER DEVELOPMENT

One principal aim of our research on TfU was to evolve a profile of characteristic patterns of teacher development around the framework (Wiske, Hammerness, &

Wilson, 1998). Two different populations have contributed to this profile. Some of the teachers collaborating in our formal investigation as part of the process of developing TfU became the focus of extensive case studies. Also, during the past 5 years, we have worked with hundreds of teachers in dozens of schools at all levels from elementary to university throughout the United States and in South America, Europe, and Japan. Further insight came from these experiences.

Teachers report waves of new realization regarding the power and nuances of the framework. Many teachers relate an initial sense of understanding of the ideas and a feeling that in many ways they already practice them. However, after further consultation, discussion, and deliberation, teachers begin to see numerous ways in which they fall short of those ideals, and begin to report new insights into their practice regarding the four elements of the framework. When this realization occurs, teachers often become a bit overwhelmed and choose to work for a while on one element of the framework in a targeted unit, rather than advancing all the ideas throughout their practice. During the first year of experience with TfU, teachers typically try three or four units of instruction of increasing scope, while handling much of their curriculum as usual. Only during the second year do some teachers feel prepared to attempt to reorganize most of their instruction according to the TfU framework.

Some teachers turn their back on the framework, considering it as yet another framework flung in their way. However, the majority of teachers with whom we have had an opportunity to work in a sustained way find it an extremely useful lens through which to examine and reconsider their own practice. We have encountered over and over again a lesson commonplace in the literature on school change. We have seen TfU take flight or fail depending on the degree of colleagueship, administrative support, external support, and leadership within the school.* While occasionally innovative and energetic teachers can put TfU to work despite a climate not conducive to it, such cases are exceptional. TfU, like other innovations in educational practice, depends on leadership and community to put its best foot forward.

THE IMPACT OF TfU ON STUDENTS' UNDERSTANDING

To study the effect of TfU on student understanding, we conducted case studies of 8–10 students from each of four classrooms informed by TfU, including a seventh grade history class, and high school physics, english, and geometry classes. Rather than a more traditional pretest, posttest, and treatment-control group methodology,

---

* This highlights the importance of systemic interdependencies between instructional systems and the various other systems that comprise a school system or corporate training system. Systems thinking is particularly useful for recognizing and dealing with such interdependencies for the successful implementation of a new paradigm of instruction within an organization. See e.g., the chapter by Reigeluth (1995) in G. Anglin (Ed.), *Instructional Technology: Past, Present, and Future (2nd. Ed.).* Englewood, CO: Libraries Unlimited.

we chose to build rich portraits of student understanding through collections of their work and multiple interviews.

To assess student understanding, we developed a rubric focusing on four critical dimensions of understanding mentioned earlier: content knowledge in the domain, methods of the domain, purposes of knowledge in the domain, and forms of expression (Boix-Mansilla & Gardner, 1998; Hammerness, Jaramillo, Unger, & Wilson, 1998). The four reflected the literature on understanding, for example, Bloom (1971), Perry (1970), Entwistle & Marton (1994), and Howard (1990), as well as our analysis of preliminary student interviews. For each dimension, we rated each case study as reflecting one of four levels of understanding, with good interrater reliability: naïve, novice, apprentice, and mastery. The naïve level denoted rote practices and sparse, disconnected, and mistaken knowledge; the mastery level denoted extensive knowledge mobilized in a sophisticated, critical and creative way.

We found that the majority of students did achieve a high level of understanding (apprentice or mastery level) across the four classrooms. The scores varied across the classrooms in keeping with our observations and analysis of the degree to which TfU methods were explicitly practiced. The highest scoring group of students came from our seventh grade history class. The greater majority of students (at least 80% in each of the dimensions) scored at the mastery or apprenticeship level. The teacher had been working closely with us for 2 years, meeting weekly with a researcher/practitioner partner, and had begun in her second year to implement the various attributes of TfU very richly. Her practice at the time of the formal assessment included not only the public articulation of unit-level understanding goals, but year-long understanding goals, with assessment clearly linked to both. Her assessments included self and peer feedback against clearly articulated criteria, a process journal, frequent teacher conferences, and several group discussions on product development.

THE IMPACT OF TfU ON STUDENTS' CONCEPTIONS OF UNDERSTANDING

Besides investigating TfU students' attained understanding in the disciplines, we also examined their conceptions of understanding and learning for understanding (Unger, Wilson, Jaramillo, & Dempsey, 1998). This research began with a group of students of similar age who had not participated in TfU instruction, to provide a baseline. An interview featuring questions like those that opened this article disclosed a strong trend: These students equated understanding with knowledge. Only a few students, and then only with reference to out-of-school matters, displayed anything like a performance-oriented conception of understanding.

To examine conceptions of understanding in TfU students, we interviewed the TfU students discussed earlier a second time, probing their conceptions of understanding and their recognition and appreciation of TfU methods that helped them to learn in these targeted classrooms. We found that students in trend recognized the distinctiveness of the TfU style of instruction and valued it. Many students spoke highly of the TfU methods teachers used in their classrooms. They discussed the power of the generative topics as central and personally engaging, the value of publicly shared goals in guiding their learning, the performances as pressing them to think in new and applied ways, and the assessment practices as supporting them throughout instruction, not just at the end.

We also found that the conceptions of understanding expressed by these students were far more performance oriented than those expressed by the non-TfU baseline students (Unger, 1994). For example, many students spontaneously mentioned how what they were learning extended beyond simply referring to the knowledge in the classroom, empowering them to think about and act in the world differently. In addition, many students explicitly discussed how their perspectives of the world had shifted and displayed considerable personal ownership of their newfound knowledge and ability.

Third, we were able to examine formally the relationship between these variables and students' actual achieved understandings, since each student in our population had been scored independently in each area. We discovered a sizeable and statistically significant positive correlation (Spearman Ranked Correlations at least $p < .01$ in every case) between students' attained understanding, their conceptions of understanding, and their appreciation of the TfU methods practiced by their teachers. In other words, the students who revealed a more performance-like conception of understanding and recognized more fully the distinctiveness of TfU methods were also the students who displayed greater understanding in the disciplines as gauged by the rubric.

Correlational data must always be interpreted cautiously. However, this pattern of results suggests that TfU instruction may enhance students' conceptions of understanding (the contrast with the baseline students) and that the shift in conception of understanding may equip the students better for learning for understanding. This in turn suggests possible extensions of the TfU methodology. As presently constituted, TfU does not emphasize, although it certainly allows, making the framework explicit for students or employing it as a learning-to-learn strategy. It may be that more explicit attention to learning for understanding in coordination with TfU would yield stronger interventions yet. As we continue to develop the implications of TfU, we hope to explore this and other possibilities toward a more powerful pedagogy of understanding.

ACKNOWLEDGMENT

The ideas and findings discussed here were developed at the Harvard University Graduate School of Education under a grant from the Spencer Foundation, with principal investigators Howard Gardner, David Perkins, and Vito Perrone. We are grateful for the foundation's support, noting of course that the positions taken do not necessarily reflect its views or policies.

REFERENCES

Argyris, C. (1993). *On organizational learning*. Cambridge, MA: Blackwell.

Argyris, C., & Schön, D. (1996). *Organizational learning II*. Reading, MA: Addison-Wesley.

Bloom, B. (1971). *Handbook on formative and summative evaluation of student learning*. New York: McGraw-Hill.

Blythe, T. and associates. (1998). *The teaching for understanding guide*. San Francisco: Jossey-Bass.

Boix-Mansilla, V., & Gardner, H. (1998). What are the qualities of understanding? In M. S. Wiske, (Ed.), *Teaching for understanding: Linking research with practice* (pp. 161–196). San Francisco: Jossey-Bass.

Carretero, M., Pozo, J. I., & Asensio, M. (Eds.). (1989). *La enseñanza de las ciencias sociales*. Madrid, Spain: Visor.

Clement, J. (1982). Students' preconceptions in introductory mechanics. *American Journal of Physics, 50*, 66–71.

Cohen, D. K., McLaughlin, M. W., & J. E. Talbert (Eds.). (1993). *Teaching for understanding: Challenges for policy and practice*. San Francisco: Jossey-Bass.

Collins, A., & Gentner, D. (1987). How people construct mental models. In D. Holland & N. Quinn (Eds.), *Cultural models in language and thought* (pp. 243–265). Cambridge, England: Cambridge University Press.

Driver, R., Guesne, E., & Tiberghien, A. (Eds.). (1985). *Children's ideas in science*. Philadelphia: Open University Press.

Entwistle, N. J., & Marton, F. (1994). Knowledge objects: Understandings constituted through intensive academic study. *British Journal of Educational Psychology, 64*, 161–178.

Gardner, H. (1991). *The unschooled mind: How children think and how schools should teach*. New York: Basic Books.

Garvin, D. (1993). Building a learning organization. *The Harvard Business Review, 10*, 803–813.

Gentner, D., & Stevens, A. L. (Eds.). (1983). *Mental models*. Hillsdale, NJ: Lawrence Erlbaum Associates.

Hammerness, K., Jaramillo, R., Unger, C., & Wilson, D. (1998). What do students in teaching for understanding classrooms understand? In M. S. Wiske, (Ed.), *Teaching for understanding: Linking research with practice* (pp. 233–265). San Francisco: Jossey-Bass.

Howard, V. (Ed.). (1990). *Varieties of thinking: Essays from Harvard's Philosophy of Education Research Center*. New York: Routledge.

Johnson-Laird, P. N. (1983). *Mental models*. Cambridge, MA: Harvard University Press.

Lochhead, J., & Mestre, J. (1988). From words to algebra: Mending misconceptions. In A. Coxford & A. Schulte (Eds.), *The idea of algebra k–12: National Council of Teachers of Mathematics Yearbook* (pp. 127–136). Reson, VA: National Council of Teachers of Mathematics.

Mayer, R. E. (1989). *Models for understanding. Review of Educational Research, 59*, 43–64.

McDermott, L. C. (1984). Research on conceptual understanding in mechanics. *Physics Today 37*, 24–32.

Novak, J. D. (Ed.). (1987). *The proceedings of the 2nd misconceptions in science and mathematics conference*. Ithaca, NY: Cornell University Press.

Perkins, D. N. (1992). *Smart schools: From training memories to educating minds*. New York: The Free Press.

Perkins, D. N. (1993). An apple for education: Teaching and learning for understanding. *American Educator, 17*(3), 28–35.

Perkins, D. N. (1998). What is understanding? In M. S. Wiske, (Ed.), *Teaching for understanding: Linking research with practice* (pp. 39–57). San Francisco: Jossey-Bass.

Perkins, D. N., & Blythe, T. (1994). Putting understanding up front. *Educational Leadership, 51*(5), 4–7.

Perkins, D. N., & Simmons, R. (1988). Patterns of misunderstanding: An integrative model for science, math, and programming. *Review of Educational Research, 58*(3), 303–326.

Perkins, D. N., Schwartz, J. L., Wiske, M. S., & West, M. M. (Eds.). (1995). *Software goes to school: Teaching for understanding with new technology*. New York: Oxford University Press.

Perkins, D. N., & Unger, C. (1994). A new look in representations for mathematics and science learning. *Instructional Science, 22*(1), 1–37.

Perrone, V. (1998). Why do we need a pedagogy of understanding? In M. S. Wiske, (Ed.), *Teaching for understanding: Linking research with practice* (pp. 13–38). San Francisco: Jossey-Bass.

Perry, W. (1970). *Forms of intellectual and ethical development in the college years: A scheme.* New York: Holt, Rinehart & Winston.

Resnick, L. B. (1987). Constructing knowledge in school. In L. Liben (Ed.), *Development and learning: Conflict or congruence?* (pp. 19–50). Hillsdale, NJ: Lawrence Erlbaum Associates.

Rumelhart, D. E. (1980). Schema: The building block of cognition. In R. J. Spiro, B. C. Bruce, & W. F. Brewer (Eds.), *Theoretical issues in reading comprehension* (pp. 33–58). Hillsdale, NJ: Lawrence Erlbaum Associates.

Schank, R., & Abelson, R. P. (1977). *Scripts, plans, goals and understanding: An inquiry into human knowledge structures.* Hillsdale, NJ: Lawrence Erlbaum Associates.

Senge, P. (1994). *The fifth discipline: The art and practice of the learning organization.* New York: Doubleday.

Shelmit, D. (1980). *History 13–16, evaluation study.* Edinburgh: Holmes McDougall.

Simmons, R. (1994). The horse before the cart: Assessing for understanding. *Educational Leadership, 51*(5), 22–23.

Smith, C., & Unger, C. (1997) Conceptual bootstrapping. *The Journal of the Learning Sciences, 6*(2), 143–182.

Unger, C. (1994). What teaching for understanding looks like. *Educational Leadership, 51*(5), 8–10.

Unger, C., Wilson, D., Jaramillo, R., & Dempsey, R. (1998). What do students think about understanding? In M. S. Wiske, (Ed.), *Teaching for understanding: Linking research with practice* (pp. 266–292). San Francisco: Jossey-Bass.

Wiske, M. S. (Ed.). (1998). *Teaching for understanding: Linking research with practice,* San Francisco: Jossey-Bass.

Wiske, M. S., Hammerness, K., & Wilson, D. (1998). How do teachers learn to teach for understanding? In M. S. Wiske, (Ed.), *Teaching for understanding: Linking research with practice* (pp. 87–121). San Francisco: Jossey-Bass.

Open Learning Environments: Foundations, Methods, and Models

6

Michael Hannafin
University of Georgia

Susan Land
The Pennsylvania State University

Kevin Oliver
University of Georgia

Michael Hannafin

Michael Hannafin is Professor of Instructional Technology and Director of the Learning and Performance Support Laboratory at the University of Georgia. Previously, he was a member of the Instructional Systems faculty at Florida State University, a visiting professor at the U.S. Air Force Academy, and in faculty positions at Penn State University and the University of Colorado. His research focuses on developing and testing frameworks for the design of technology-enhanced, student-centered learning environments.

Susan Land

Kevin Oliver

Susan Land is Assistant Professor of Instructional Systems at Penn State University. Previously, she worked as a postdoctoral fellow at the University of Georgia's Learning and Performance Support Laboratory and held a faculty position at the University of Oklahoma. Her research focuses on the process of conceptual development with learner-centered technology environments. She earned her doctorate in Instructional Systems from Florida State University.

Kevin Oliver currently works at the University of Georgia's Learning and Performance Support Laboratory, developing multimedia products, conducting teacher-training workshops, and managing grants in K–12 schools. His research interests include problem- and case-based learning, web-based learning tools, and the development of computer-mediated learning environments for K–12 schools. He is a Doctoral Candidate in Instructional Technology at the University of Georgia.

FOREWORD

Goals and preconditions. This chapter provides a theory for situations where divergent thinking and multiple perspectives are valued over a single "correct" perspective. It is appropriate for heuristics-based learning and for exploring fuzzy, ill-defined, and ill-structured problems.

Values. Some of the values upon which this theory is based include:

- *personal inquiry.*
- *divergent thinking and multiple perspectives.*
- *self-directed learning and learner autonomy with metacognitive support.*
- *mediating learning through individual experience and personal theories.*
- *hands-on, concrete experiences involving realistic, relevant problems.*
- *providing tools and resources to aid the learner's efforts at learning.*

Methods. These are the major methods this theory offers:

Enabling contexts (to establish the perspectives taken in the environment).
- *Externally-imposed contexts (specifies specific problems for the learner).*
- *Externally-induced contexts (presents problem context, learner generates the problems to be addressed).*
- *Individually-generated contexts (learner generates both the context and problems).*

Resources (to provide the domain of available information sources)
- *Static (do not change through use).*
- *Dynamic (do change through use).*

Tools (to provide the basic means for manipulating information).
(are not specific methods per se; are used in various ways to represent and manipulate concepts under study)
- *Processing tools (to support learners' cognitive processing).*
  - *Seeking tools (to locate and filter needed resources).*
  - *Collecting tools (to gather resources).*
  - *Organizing tools (to represent relationships among ideas).*
  - *Integrating tools (to link new with existing knowledge).*
  - *Generating tools (to create new things or artifacts to think with).*
- *Manipulation tools (to test the validity of, or to explore, beliefs and theories).*
- *Communication tools (to communicate among learners, teachers, and experts).*
  - *Synchronous communication tools (to support real-time interaction).*

- Asynchronous communication tools (to support time-shifted communication).

Scaffolds (to guide and support learning efforts).
- *Domain-specific versus generic scaffolds.*
- *Conceptual scaffolding (guidance on what to consider).*
- *Metacognitive scaffolding (guidance on how to think about the problem under study).*
- *Procedural scaffolding (guidance on how to utilize resources and tools).*
- *Strategic scaffolding (guidance on approaches to solving the problem).*

While this theory does offer some guidelines (conditions under which different methods should be used), much of it is presented here as a taxonomy of methods, where the practitioner needs to figure out when to use each..

Major contributions. *Addresses a difficult kind of learning with a wide variety of methods and a great deal of flexibility.*

—C.M.R.

Open Learning Environments: Foundations, Methods, and Models

Interest in student-centered learning and learner-centered design has grown dramatically. The emergence of varied teaching–learning frameworks, coupled with technological developments such as the World Wide Web, has made possible approaches that were heretofore impossible, infeasible, or unimaginable.* Open learning environments (OLEs) have proven particularly intriguing. Open learning involves " … processes wherein the intents and purposes of the individual are uniquely established and pursued";** OLEs " … support the individual's efforts to understand that which he or she determines to be important" (Hannafin, Hall, Land, & Hill, 1994, p. 48). In this chapter, we provide a brief overview of OLEs, describe their features, and provide examples of open learning designs.

---

* This identifies the emergence of the new paradigm of instructional theory.
** This is the key marker of customization (see chap. 1, p. 18).

OVERVIEW OF OLES

Open-endedness refers to either the learning goal(s), the means through which learning goals are pursued, or both learning goals and means. Learning goals are determined in one of three methods: (a) externally specified by immersing the learner in a particular problem to be solved, such as bringing a virtual satellite into geosynchronous orbit above the equator; (b) externally induced such as by immersing the learner in a problem such as global warming without specifying a particular learning goal or performance task; or (c) generated uniquely, such as by a learner attempting to understand the etiology of a health problem afflicting a family member. In each case, the need to understand is established individually, although the manner in which the goals are framed varies considerably. The individual determines how to proceed based on his or her unique needs, perceptions, and experiences, distinguishes known from unknown, identifies resources available to support learning efforts, and formalizes and tests personal beliefs (Land & Hannafin, 1996).

OLEs may be contrasted with direct instruction. As shown in Table 6.1, direct instruction typically employs clearly articulated external learning objectives. These tend to isolate critical information and concepts, organize to-be-learned concepts into carefully ordered sequences to reflect the presumed hierarchical nature of knowledge, and employ strategies that induce differential allocation of attention and cognitive resources. They feature a great deal of external engineering of both

TABLE 6.1
Distinctions Between Directed and Open-Ended Learning Environments

Directed Learning Environments...	Open-Ended Learning Environments...
Break down content hierarchically and teach incrementally toward externally generated objectives	Situate processes associated with problems, contexts, and content with opportunities to manipulate, interpret, and experiment
Simplify detection and mastery of key concepts by isolating and instructing to-be-learned knowledge and skill; "bottom up," basics first	Employ complex, meaningful problems that link content and concepts to everyday experience where "need to know" is naturally generated
Convey knowledge and skills through structured, engineered teaching–learning approaches	Center heuristic approaches around "wholes" exploring higher order concepts, flexible understanding, and multiple perspectives
Mediate learning externally via explicit activities and practice; promote canonical understanding as a goal	Develop understanding individually as learners evaluate their own needs, make decisions, and modify, test, and revise their knowledge.
Activate internal conditions of learning by carefully engineering external conditions	Link cognition and context inextricably
Achieve mastery by focusing on production of "correct" responses, thereby reducing or eliminating errors	Stress the importance of errors in establishing models of understanding; deep understanding evolves from initial, often flawed, beliefs

Note. Adapted from "Student-centered learning and interactive multimedia: Status, issues, and implications," by M. J. Hannafin, J. Hill, and S. Land (1997), *Contemporary Education, 68,* pp. 94–99. Copyright 1997. Adapted with permission.

to-be-learned knowledge and skill as well as the strategies presumed to promote learning (Hannafin, 1995).

In contrast, open environments emphasize the mediating role of the individual in uniquely defining meaning, establishing learning needs, determining learning goals, and engaging in learning activities. Consistent with learner-centered design principles, individual perspectives are used to interpret, assign relevance and meaning, and otherwise influence how given circumstances and contexts are uniquely understood (Hannafin & Land, 1997). Contexts, which vary from instance to instance and learner to learner, define the meaning of, need for, and utility of knowledge and skill. Therefore, it is often not feasible to impose direct-instruction strategies a priori to promote specific understanding or performance.

OLEs employ tools, resources, and activities that augment or extend thinking. They are engineered in the sense that, to varying degrees, affordances are enabled and scaffolds are provided, but they do not typically impose or restrict the content or interpretations of learning sequences. OLEs embed learning activities in contexts that foster thinking. These originate not from abstract descriptions of phenomena, but from personal, practical experiences. Individual efforts to understand are supported via immersion in problems, metacognitive scaffolding, and tools through which available resources can be located and assessed for relevance according to the unique sense-making skills and needs of the learner.

OLEs tend to be especially important in promoting divergent thinking and in situations where multiple perspectives are valued, rather a single "correct" perspective. They are particularly valuable for heuristics-based learning in that they afford opportunities to "play with" concepts in order to interpret patterns rather than to impart only certain desired interpretations. OLEs also tend to be valued for exploring fuzzy, ill-defined, and ill-structured problems. They promote the discovery and manipulation of underlying beliefs and structures rather than impose particular beliefs. Open environments help to promote autonomy* in that they encourage individuals to generate problems and needs, select among various available information sources, and evaluate their judgments.

In contrast, OLEs are less amenable to convergent learning tasks, where different learners need to develop the same knowledge, procedural skills, or interpretations. Since they encourage personal inquiry, it is unlikely that all individuals will encounter information sources, much less interpret them consistently. Likewise, OLEs tend to be less effective for learning of a strict, accountability-based nature or when efficiency in terms of acquisition time is critical.**

---

* Self-regulation is another key marker of the new paradigm (see especially chap. 13 by Corno & Randi).

** This highlights the need for different approaches to instruction for different situations—that no one approach is best for all situations. It also highlights the importance of expanding and reconfiguring much of the industrial-age paradigm, rather than rejecting it.

Foundations And Values

Grounded learning systems reflect alignment among core foundations: psychological, pedagogical, technological, cultural, and pragmatic. Grounding is reflected in the extent to which learning environments manifest the core tenets of each foundation, as well as how consistently these beliefs are reflected across foundations (Hannafin, Hannafin, Land, & Oliver, 1997). Each foundation encompasses diverse perspectives; as root foundations vary, underlying assumptions change accordingly. Behaviorism, for example, is quite different from situated cognition in its assumptions about knowledge and the evolution of understanding; yet, both represent a psychological foundation. Likewise, while pedagogical foundations include a myriad of alternative methods and strategies, teaching learning approaches rooted in behavioral psychology should be different from those rooted in situated cognition (see, for example, Hannafin & Land, 1997).*

Several core values are reflected in OLEs. One such value is the centrality of individual experience in mediating learning. Experience shapes an individual's interpretive perspective: how or if a problem is perceived, the manner in which existing knowledge, skill, and experience are related, and the nature of personal as well as canonical beliefs. OLEs not only recognize personal theories, but they are considered the basis of initial and ongoing formative understanding which can be examined, tested, and revised through inquiry (Land & Hannafin, 1997).

Likewise, OLEs feature experience-based problem-solving activities as means through which understanding and formative theories evolve. Personal understanding evolves through hands-on, concrete experiences involving realistic, relevant problems posed or induced through OLEs. Tools are provided to enable learners to manipulate physical objects or attributes in a problem as well as their own ideas.

Finally, metacognitive support is valued for several reasons. Individuals continually interpret, evaluate, and respond based on ongoing assessments as to which actions are likely to advance their understanding. Individuals make important judgments related to and based on their perceived state of understanding; OLEs both facilitate the spontaneous metacognitive activities of individuals and scaffold metacognitive inquiry processes when not spontaneously initiated.

The confluence among OLE foundations and values illustrated in Fig. 6.1 suggests several design features and strategies. For example, OLEs share psychological and pedagogical values: situated thinking, prior knowledge and experience, metacognitive monitoring, and the progressive testing and refining of understanding (Hannafin et al., 1994). Associated methods emphasize authentic learning contexts, anchored problem-based approaches, construction, manipulation, and scaffolding. OLE technological foundations are manifested in the form of diverse tools (e.g., spreadsheets, graphing programs, web browsers) and resources (e.g.,

---

*These roots are the underlying descriptive knowledge (learning theory) discussed in chapter 1, pp. 12–13.

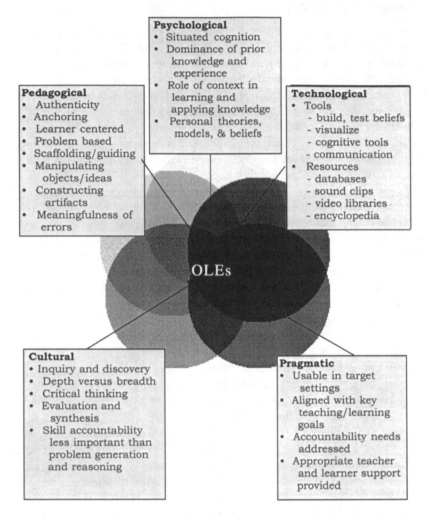

FIG. 6.1.   Relationships among OLE foundations and values. (Adapted from "The Foundations and Assumptions of Technology-Enhanced, Student-Centered Learning Environments," by M. J. Hannafin and S. Land, (1977), *Instructional Science, 25*, pp. 167–202. Copyright 1997. Adapted with permission.

on-line databases, image libraries, source documents) that support varied purposes. The approaches "fit" within the inquiry-oriented, critical thinking teaching-learning culture, which emphasizes processes such as inquiry and discovery over compliance and rote memorization; the environment accommodates relevant situational constraints of the settings in which they are deployed.

COMPONENTS AND METHODS

As shown in Fig. 6.2, OLEs comprise four basic components: enabling contexts, resources, tools, and scaffolds.

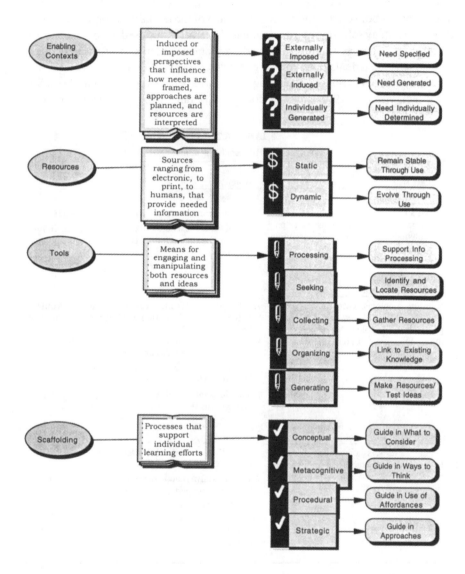

FIG. 6.2.   Overview of OLE components and design heuristics.

Enabling Contexts

Enabling contexts are the vehicles through which individuals are oriented to a need or problem and interpretive perspectives are situated. Enabling contexts guide students in recognizing or generating problems to be addressed and framing learning needs. As summarized in Table 6.2, they take three basic forms.* Externally imposed contexts both clarify the expected product of the learner's efforts and implicitly guide strategy selection and deployment. Externally imposed enabling contexts are often presented as explicitly situated problem statements or organizing questions which aid students in referencing relevant aspects of their experience.

Several externally imposed enabling contexts have been reported. The Great Solar System Rescue's (1992) enabling context, for example, places students in a fan-

TABLE 6.2

Examples of OLE Enabling Contexts

Context Type	*Examples*
Externally Imposed	
Context specifies specific problems and/or performance needs, but the means to pursue solutions are at the learner's discretion	Problem solving, the Great Solar System Rescue (1992) Determine the most cost-effective jet transport aircraft, given a host of performance requirements and cost constraints.
Externally Induced	
Scenarios, problems, cases, analogies, or questions are provided and the learner generates the problems to be solved and means to pursue solutions	Anchored instruction, Jasper Woodbury Problem Solving Series (Cognition and Technology Group at Vanderbilt, 1992) Case-based instruction, The Thematic Investigator (Jacobson, Sugimoto, & Archodidou, 1996) Inquiry-based science, Science Vision (Tobin & Dawson, 1992) Scientific thinking, Knowledge Integration Environment (Linn, 1995)
Individually Generated	
Personal interests, issues, concerns, or problems surface that establish unique learning needs and guide strategies employed	As a graduate student, select a topic and frame a specific problem within existing research and theory. A tropical storm is approaching your newly purchased, beachfront property, and you must ascertain appropriate precautionary measures. Due to recent wave of international terrorism in the Middle East, you decide to learn more about the root causes of the Palestinian uprisings.

---

* This is an example of breaking down a method ("provide an enabling context") into alternative kinds (externally-imposed, externally-induced, and individually-generated enabling contexts).

tasy role (e.g., meteorologist, geologist) in which a space vehicle has crashed on a remote planet. Students are provided clues and challenged to determine on which planet the crash occurred and the precise location of the crash site. The learner's tasks, for the most part, are explicitly delineated. Externally imposed enabling contexts are used widely where knowledge and/or skill accountability requirements are explicitly accepted as well as when concrete progress referents are deemed appropriate or necessary for teachers or students.*

Externally induced contexts introduce the learner to a domain but do not identify specific problems to be addressed. Rather, a domain is encountered in which any number of problems or issues can be generated or studied at the discretion of the learner. Bransford and his colleagues (Cognition and Technology Group at Vanderbilt, 1992)** designed brief video vignettes in *The Jasper Woodbury Problem Solving Series,* featuring a dilemma confronted by the lead character. A situation is introduced in which a problem or problems are apparent. The induced context introduces a circumstance which frames the problems or issues and solicits learner participation. The student interprets the context for meaning, generates subproblems, and devises strategies based on individual interpretations of the enabling context. Jacobson, Sugimoto, and Archodidou's (1996) *Thematic Investigator* employed specific cases of evolutionary biology (e.g., the peppered moth, rabbits in Australia) to provide diverse contexts for the study of complex Darwinian themes. The alternative contexts induced students to "think differently" about scientific concepts that are often complex and ill defined, such as population variety and natural selection. In each of the preceding examples, students are provided perspective-setting or -altering contexts that help to activate relevant prior knowledge, experience, and skill related to the problem and that also help the learner to generate strategies to be potentially deployed.***

In individually-generated enabling contexts, a specific context cannot be designed in advance.**** The learner establishes an enabling context based on needs

---

* Here the theory indicates the situations for which this kind of enabling context (method variable) is likely to be most appropriate. Chapter 1 identified methods and situations as the two major components of an instructional theory (see p. 8).

** See also chapter 9 by Schwartz, Lin, Brophy and Bransford.

*** Here the theory breaks down a method ("provide externally-induced contexts") into *parts* (rather than kinds)—that is, more detailed component methods (as discussed in chap. 1, p. 10)—that are common across situations. However, there certainly are also variations in some component methods across situations, and those variations represent sub-kinds that are recommended for different sub-situations. This illustrates how the complexity of an instructional theory increases geometrically as the theorists attempt to provide more guidance or understanding of the instructional dynamics. See if you can identify additional kinds and parts of methods (and situations for the different kinds) in the remainder of this chapter.

**** This is an important issue for the new paradigm of instructional theory. Sometimes customized instruction cannot be designed in advance. For what aspects of the learning process can and can't an instructional theory offer guidance for such situations? What kinds of support or guidance can an instructional theory offer for such situations? How can technology and/or peers be most effectively used for such situations? This is an extremely important area for additional research and development in the new paradigm of instructional theory.

and circumstances that are unique. For example, a home gardener may wish to determine the cause and treatment of fungus growth in a vegetable patch. A hiker, planning a 3-day trek, may want to better understand how to use various orientation and navigation tools, such as magnetic compasses, landmarks, and sextants. A business executive might need to resolve production deficiencies and inventory control problems. In each case, the individual creates a unique enabling context to frame learning needs. As with induced contexts, the generated context activates relevant knowledge, skill, and experience in order to frame problems and issues and to guide problem-solving strategies.

Resources

Resources are source materials that support learning. Resources range from electronic media (e.g., databases, computer tutorials, video), to print media (e.g., textbooks, original source documents, journal articles), to humans (e.g., experts, parents, teachers, peers). The Web is perhaps the most pervasive repository of available resources. The web enables access, but the potential relevance of the available resources is often difficult for individuals to ascertain (Hill & Hannafin, 1997). While it contains millions of source materials of potential relevance, the utility of web resources for OLEs is often limited due to a lack of clarity of contents, difficulty in accessing or using them, or both. A resource's utility is determined by its relevance to the enabling context and the degree to which it is accessible to the learner. The more relevant a resource is to an individual's learning goals, and the more accessible it is, the greater its utility.

OLEs make extensive use of available resources which provide an extraordinary reserve of source materials across a wide range of OLE applications.* In some cases, available resources are supplemented or augmented with new resources, based on the appropriateness of existing source materials to a given OLE's enabling context. In a simple sense, resources can be either static or dynamic, though increasingly, digital resources reflect both properties.

Static resource contents do not change through use. They may contain information that is stable over time and is not subject to variation, such as photographic images of historical figures. Some resources may only be available through technologies that do not permit their contents to be altered, such as the contents of videodisks, multimedia CD-ROMs, textbooks, and electronic encyclopedias. The *Visible Human* database (National Library of Medicine, 1996) contains thousands of high-resolution photographic slides, graphics, and digital movie clips of the human anatomy, each of which can be used in a theoretically unlimited number of ways. Similar databases have been established by NASA and the National Library

---

* The issue of utilizing available resources versus designing new resources is often an economic decision. But even for situations in which one must utilize available resources, it is helpful to have design criteria for judging the instructional quality of the available resources to help guide either the teacher or the learner in selecting the resources.

of Congress. A learner's interpretations and understanding may evolve considerably through repeated access, but the literal contents of a fixed resource remain unchanged.

In some instances, it is desirable to access resources that change dynamically through time and/or the introduction of new data. This affords the learner the opportunity to repeatedly access the same resource but with different outcomes. For example, dynamic resources such as climatology databases created by the National Weather Service evolve continuously as daily weather data are entered. Dynamic databases can also evolve based on the needs, queries, and intentions of individuals or groups. Smart databases collect data from which they evolve user models to suggest resources. In some systems, users can transform data by adding new entries or annotating existing entries. CSILE (Computer-Supported Intentional Learning Environment), for example, is a social knowledge resource that changes as a function of usage and the ratings of its users (Scardamalia & Bereiter, 1994).

The *Human Body* (Iiyoshi & Hannafin, 1996) provides both static and dynamic resources. *Human Body* is an OLE that contains several thousand multimedia objects, including text, voice narratives, animations, digital movies, and graphic resources. Each resource can be accessed independently or linked according to the ongoing needs of the learner. In addition, individual information can be attached to the resources in the form of personal notes, observations, and elaborations. The core resources remain intact, but dynamic functionality can be attained when users add to, revise, or otherwise customize contents according to the perspectives and needs of individual learners. Likewise, in Honebein's (1996) *Lab Design Project*, students enter a virtual biotechnology research center, identify labs they wish to visit, seek additional details on equipment, and review interviews of the virtual lab inhabitants. These resources are static in their given form, but manipulation is facilitated by providing a pool of research questions and prompting students to generate links among the available resources to address a probing question.

Resources can be identified and selected a priori in cases where enabling contexts are induced externally; judgments as to their potential relevance to the enabling problem or need can be readily made. *Science Vision* resources, for example, include relevant encyclopedia and reference information, on-line domain experts, and libraries of movies and still images (Tobin & Dawson, 1992). Learners are rarely restricted only to the "flagged" resources, but their existence, availability, and potential relevance to the problem context is made apparent. In truly open systems, access is not limited to selected resource pools; the learner can seek and access virtually any resource independent of its designer-perceived relevance to the enabling context. Due to the variable nature of individually created enabling contexts, resource pools cannot be well anticipated. Instead, support for unique enabling contexts is often provided in the form of scaffolding which helps to guide individuals in conceptualizing, seeking, evaluating, and resolving their uniquely defined learning problems and needs.

Tools

Tools provide the overt means through which individuals engage and manipulate both resources and their own ideas. However, tool functions vary according to the OLE's enabling contexts as well as the intents of their users;* the same technological tool can support different functions. Tools do not inherently enhance cognitive activity or skills;** rather, they provide a means through which thinking *can be* enhanced, augmented, and/or extended. Tools provide vehicles for representing and manipulating complex, abstract concepts in tangible, concrete ways. As shown in Table 6.3, three types of tools are commonly used in OLEs: processing tools, manipulation tools, and communication tools.

Processing Tools

Processing tools support the functions typically associated with information-processing models of human cognition (Iiyoshi & Hannafin, 1996).*** Seeking

TABLE 6.3

OLE Tools and Examples

Tool Type	Examples
Processing Tools	Enable and facilitate the cognitive processing tasks associated with open-ended learning.
• seeking	Keyword searches, search engines, indexes
• collecting	Text copying and pasting, file transferring, image grabbing
• organizing	Brainstorming, outlining, flow charting
• integrating	Knowledge representation tools, annotation links, elaborations
• generating	Graphic programs, programming languages
Manipulation Tools	Enable learner to change contents, values, and/or parameters in order to verify, test, extend understanding.
	Plugging in ranges of values into spreadsheet to examine effects
	Programming functions into graphing calculators to visualize effects graphically
Communication Tools	Provide learners, teachers, and experts a means to promote discourse, share ideas, review work, ask questions, and collaborate.
• asynchronous	Messaging centers, e-mail, listservs, video and audio streaming.
• synchronous	Telephone, telementoring, groupware, video conferencing.

---

  * So "enabling context" is a situation variable that influences the selection of tools (a method variable).
  ** In this sense, tools are not inherently methods of instruction. The way they are used, however, can be a method.
  *** Notice the similarity between the following processing tools and Mayer's SOI Model (chap. 7).

tools, for example, support detection and selection of relevant information by helping learners to locate and filter needed resources. Various seeking tools exist, ranging from keyword searches, to topical indexes, to the semantic search engines available on the Web. Each tool supports the user's efforts to search available resources to locate information likely to be relevant to his or her individual learning needs.

Collection tools allow learners to gather resources or pieces of resources for their own purposes. They support learning by aiding in the amassing of potentially important information which can be used to simplify subsequent access, support study in closer detail, or collect subsets of resources appropriate to individual learning needs. Collection tools enable the learner to perform diverse tasks, such as to "grab" text documents or selected text, store copies of graphical images, and create directories of selected Web-site URLs (addresses on the Web).

Organization tools assist learners in representing relationships among ideas. The Highly Interactive Computing Group's Model-It supports learners as they progressively establish and revise their conceptual understanding. Model-It provides a graphical tool with which individuals can create and test qualitative models of scientific understanding (Jackson, Stratford, Krajcik, & Soloway, 1995a). General-purpose organization tools such as Inspiration™ aid the learner in organizing and annotating concept maps depicting complex relationships.

Integration tools help learners to link new with existing knowledge. CONSTRUE, for example, is an Internet shell used to develop dynamic, knowledge-building environments (Lebow, Wager, Marks, & Gilbert, 1996). A typical CONSTRUE environment comprises a variety of options for searching and linking an extensive database of manuscripts and articles. Users can search across documents according to their specifications, and annotate their reactions and interpretations as a permanent resource. The linking and constructing functions assist in both organizing ideas from a variety of perspectives and integrating them with personal knowledge.

Generation tools enable learners to create things. Generation tools have been developed across a wide range of learning environments. Hay, Guzdial, Jackson, Boyle, and Soloway (1994) created the MediaText computer program to simplify the creation of multimedia compositions. Iiyoshi and Hannafin (1996) described a series of tools with which individuals could create their own multimedia lessons using both fixed resources and resources the users develop. Harel and Papert (1991) studied students' generative tool uses of Logo, a high-level and easy-to-use programming language, to develop software designs for teaching peers about fractions. Microworlds Project Builder (1993) can be used to generate objects using given shells as well as to create new shells for use by one or more individuals.*

---

* Note that what we have here is primarily a taxonomy of tools; little guidance is offered as to when to use each. This may be due largely to the complexity of that level of detail of guidance and the space limitations for each chapter of this volume.

Manipulation Tools

Manipulation tools are used to test the validity of, or explore the explanatory power of, beliefs and theories. Vosniadou (1992) noted that in order to promote restructuring of mental models, learners must first be given the opportunity to become aware of their existing beliefs. Rieber (1993) created a microworld within which learners could manipulate Newtonian physics concepts such as mass and velocity while attempting to dock a virtual spacecraft. These manipulations were functionally similar to the Space Shuttle thrust engines used to adjust forward speed, pitch, and yaw. Lewis, Stern, and Linn (1993) described a tool that enables learners to speculate about, then manipulate, the thermodynamic properties of objects. For instance, an individual may believe that increasing the surface area of an object invariably results in additional heat loss independent of insulation properties. Object properties can be altered to test the assumptions and veracity of these beliefs. RasMol (Raster Molecules) is an Internet-based learning environment used to create and display the structure of DNA, proteins, and small molecules (Sayle, 1996). Several RasMol shells can be downloaded and manipulated by learners. Molecules can be displayed as wireframe graphics, cylinder stick bonds, space-filling spheres, macromolecular ribbons, hydrogen bonds, or dot surfaces. These representations may be colored or shaded, and the molecules may be rotated and sized to increase the depth and vividness of the images manipulated.

Communication Tools

Communication tools support efforts to initiate or sustain exchanges among learners, teachers, and experts. They have become especially important in Internet and Web-based OLEs. Communication tools engage participants synchronously or asynchronously depending on their availability, cost, and the nature of the enabling context.

Synchronous communication tools support real-time interaction among participants. For example, telephones are widely available, low-cost tools that support live voice communication among two or more participants. In cases where collaboration is induced through the enabling context, telephone tools may be readily available. However, voice communication is limited to sound, rendering the sharing of other resources via alternate media impossible. Two-way live video teleconferencing, on the other hand, enables both voice and image sharing, thereby increasing the learner's available toolkit; however, it is not widely accessible and can be costly in terms of technology demands and hook-up charges.

Asynchronous communication tools, in contrast, enable communication that is time shifted. They allow for extensive exchanging of ideas and/or resources, but do not rely on the simultaneous availability of all participants. Listservs, for example, provide a vehicle for common discourse among learners and teachers, but do not require their immediate presence.

Examples of synchronous and asynchronous communication tools in practice are widespread. Blieske (1996) involved students in collaboration in the design of floor plans for a new home. Students asynchronously shared their design with other schools, collaborated on the merits of various approaches, and then attempted to build each others' designs. Other projects involved students in different classrooms collaborating in writing different acts for a play (Schubert, 1997a) and writing stories for submission to on-line newsletters for publication (Schubert, 1997b).

Scaffolds

Scaffolding is the process through which learning efforts are supported while engaging an OLE (Jackson, Stratford, Krajcik, & Soloway, 1995b; Linn, 1995). Scaffolding can be differentiated by mechanisms and functions. Mechanisms emphasize the methods through which scaffolding is provided, while functions emphasize the purposes served.

TABLE 6.4

OLE Scaffolding Classifications

Scaffold Types and Functions	*Related Methods & Mechanisms*
Conceptual	
Guides learner in what to consider; considerations when problem task is defined	Recommending the use of certain tools at particular stages of problem solving
	Providing students with explicit hints and prompts as needed (Vygotskian scaffolding, intelligent tutoring)
	Providing structure maps and content trees
Metacognitive	
Guides how to think during learning: ways to think about a problem under study and/or possible strategies to consider; initial role in finding and framing problems, and ongoing role during resolution	Suggesting students plan ahead, evaluate progress, and determine needs
	Modeling cognitive strategies and self-regulatory processes
	Proposing self-regulating milestones and related monitoring
Procedural	
Guides how to utilize the available OLE features; ongoing "help" and advice on feature functions and uses	Tutoring on system functions and features
	Providing "balloon" or "pop-up" help to define and explain system properties
Strategic	
Guides in analyzing and approaching learning tasks or problem; provided initially as macrostrategy or ongoing as needs or requests arise	Enabling intelligent responses to system use, suggesting alternative methods or procedures
	Providing start-up questions to be considered
	Providing advice from experts

Individuals attempt to resolve either a situated problem or a personal learning need reflected in the enabling context. As shown in Table 6.4, OLE scaffolding complexity varies according to the locus of the problem(s) posed and the demands posed in the enabling context.* Scaffolding approaches, therefore, vary accordingly. When enabling contexts and problems are supplied, scaffolding can be closely linked to the domain under study; when enabling contexts are individually generated, scaffolding of a generic nature is generally provided. OLE scaffolding may or may not be faded out as facility is attained. In externally imposed or induced contexts, for example, scaffolding may be faded out since the nature of system needs and learner use can be reasonably established beforehand. For individual uses, where the nature of use and learner needs cannot be established in advance, scaffolding typically remains available but its usage becomes less frequent as the learner's facility increases.

Conceptual Scaffolding

Conceptual scaffolding is provided when the problem under study is defined, that is, for externally imposed or induced enabling contexts. When problem parameters and domains are established externally, it is possible to anticipate methods that are sensitive to the demands of the area under study. Known and widespread science misconceptions, for example, provide a powerful foundation for predicting likely conceptual difficulties and embedding support accordingly. Conceptual scaffolding can be designed to help learners reason through complex or fuzzy problems, as well as for concepts where known misconceptions are prevalent. Hints can guide the learner to available resources, or tool manipulations might be suggested where understanding is typically problematic.

Conceptual scaffolding, then, guides learners regarding *what to consider.* At times, this is accomplished by identifying key conceptual knowledge related to a problem or creating structures that make conceptual organization readily apparent. These structures can be made available through a variety of mechanisms, ranging from the graphical depiction of relationships among concepts, to outlines featuring ordinate–subordinate relationships, to information and hints provided by experts.

In OLEs, conceptual scaffolding provides problem-relevant perspectives related to the concepts under study, not explicit direction as to which resources are considered best. The *Jasper* environment, for example, supplies video clips wherein the thinking of the main characters is presented using think-aloud dubbing. The soundtrack does not isolate the specific concepts or cause–effect relationships, but instead provides examples of things that might be considered.

Metacognitive Scaffolding

Metacognitive scaffolding supports the underlying processes associated with individual learning management. It provides guidance in how to think during learning.

---

* Note the method and situation variables here, albeit on a very general level of description. More detailed guidelines are offered in the next sentences, but there is still room for much more guidance.

Metacognitive scaffolding can be either domain specific, such as where enabling contexts are externally induced, or more generic where the enabling context is not known in advance. Linn's (1995) Knowledge Integration Environment (KIE), for example, provides metacognitive support for externally induced problems as learners attempt to formulate models of scientific phenomena. The processes of scaffolded inquiry help students to consider how or if to initiate, compare, and revise their representations.

Metacognitive scaffolding might also remind learners to reflect on the goal(s) or prompt them to relate a given resource or tool manipulation outcome to the problem or need at hand. When a problem context is known, such as KIE's "How far does light travel?", scaffolded inquiry can be designed to emphasize specific ways to think about the problem under study (e.g., "Would it take more time, less time, or the same amount of time to see light from a candle or a flashlight shown from across a lake?"). In contrast, the scaffolding for generic model-building, though uniform in task, represents a wide array of phenomena to be modeled with very different components and weights. In such a case, the scaffolding focuses on the *processes* of creating models, including finding ways to link models with prior knowledge and experience, linking representational models to current understanding, and enabling learners to manipulate ideas through modeling tools (Jackson, Stratford, Krajcik, & Soloway, 1995b).

Procedural Scaffolding

Procedural scaffolding emphasizes how to utilize available resources and tools. It orients to system features and functions, and otherwise aids the learner while navigating an OLE. For example, some learners become disoriented in OLEs. Procedural scaffolding is frequently provided to clarify how to return to a desired location, how to "flag" or "bookmark" locations or resources for subsequent review, or how to deploy given tools. The *Human Body* (Iiyoshi & Hannafin, 1996), for example, provides several resources and tools with distinct functions. Since the cognitive load associated with remembering all procedures for each tool and resource can be overwhelming, on-demand procedural demonstrations are available. Learners need not develop facility with all procedures until they have established, on an individual basis, the need for a given tool or resource.

Strategic Scaffolding

Strategic scaffolding emphasizes alternative approaches that might prove helpful. It supports analysis, planning, strategy, and tactical decisions during open-ended learning. It focuses on approaches for identifying and selecting needed information, evaluating available resources, and relating new knowledge to existing knowledge and experience. The Great Solar System Rescue (1992), for example, offers a range of alternatives to approach the problem at hand, providing varied degrees of direction. Probe questions can provide an explicit strategic clue for those needing a place to begin, while also helping to trigger a series of related strategies for those who are immersed in, but have not yet reconciled, a problem.

Another type of strategic scaffolding involves alerting the learner to available tools and resources that might prove helpful under given circumstances, and providing guidance in their use. Some OLEs, for example, provide on-demand pools of related questions to consider while evaluating a problem, as well as hints as to which tools and resources might contain the needed information (Litchfield & Mattson, 1989). Expert advice regarding approaches that might be helpful in an OLE can also be embedded.

Finally, strategic scaffolding may take the form of response-sensitive guidance at key decision points. For example, individuals might select a number of resources and "feel comfortable" with their understanding of concepts associated with gravity. Once an intention to exit the environment is indicated, they might be advised to test their understanding. They can make a prediction based on the perceived relationship between or among variables and test the prediction using manipulation tools.

OLES IN PRACTICE: ERGOMOTION

Overview

ErgoMotion is one in a series of interactive multimedia units in the *Science Vision* program. It emphasizes student-centered investigation of the laws of physics and their influence on everyday life (Tobin & Dawson, 1992). *ErgoMotion* is consistent with constructivist epistemology; provides tools with which participants can seek, sort, collect, organize, integrate, and generate knowledge; utilizes a host of multimedia resources; and scaffolds inquiry-based learning to promote understanding based on evolving interpretations (Litchfield & Mattson, 1989).

ErgoMotion combines computer-generated graphics, simulations, video, and print-based materials. Students learn about physics concepts, in part, through the design of a virtual roller coaster. They are given opportunities to select and evaluate various resources related to the underlying concepts, query on-line experts for information or advice, study several physics principles (i.e., energy conversion and acceleration) related to roller coasters, and create and test alternative roller coaster designs.

Enabling Context

ErgoMotion provides externally induced macro- and microcontexts. Macrolevel contexts serve to broaden the frame for understanding as well as to encourage the pursuit of personal interests at more comprehensive levels. The macrocontext for *ErgoMotion* is the learning of physics principles associated with the design of a roller coaster. Learners are oriented to the system with a roller coaster movie accompanied by dubbed-over questions about what makes it interesting and fun.

A variety of perspectives and concepts, designed to encourage learner-centered explorations and interpretations, is provided. Initially, an enabling context is externally induced through a video vignette depicting teenagers boarding a roller coaster; participants observe a brief ride through the eyes of the teenagers. They are then asked to design a roller coaster that is both thrilling and safe using physics principles which, though available in various forms in the environment, are not explicitly cued. Like the *Jasper* series, a problem is introduced which helps to frame the exploration of physics content as well as the complexity of roller coaster design. The nature of the problem vignette stimulates learners to identify hypotheses and plausible explanations and utilize a variety of resources and tools to address the problem.

Similar to microworlds, microcontexts represent skills and concepts within a specific range. They introduce problems that are somewhat narrow in scope and definition, but are open-ended in terms of how they can be addressed. During the coaster challenge, for instance, specific extension problems are externally imposed (e.g., set the size of the hills so that the coaster will come to a rest in the first valley). Three progressively difficult challenges are available which support learners in extending their understanding while demonstrating sophisticated awareness of complex concepts and principles. These problems can only be solved if the student has attained understanding of combinations of related concepts (e.g., friction, mass, horsepower). There is an explicit task to be undertaken, with a specific desired outcome.

Available Resources

Static Resources. *ErgoMotion* features a variety of static resources that provide diverse multimedia examples and explanations of the concepts under study. For instance, learners may view video clips and demonstrations from the "videopedia," an alphabetized listing of physics terms (e.g., Newton's Laws, velocity, friction) which is accessible at all times. Physics information is also available in the form of on-line consultants who explain physics concepts from the perspective of a physicist, motorcyclist, police officer, or roller coaster designer. These resources remain stable throughout and across student referencing, but both the initial inclination to access them and the context for interpretation vary with each individual.

Dynamic Resources. *ErgoMotion* also utilizes resources that are static in initial form but become dynamic based on decisions made by the learner. This is available to enable the student to examine changes in the status of the coaster as different forces are changed. For instance, students collect numeric data on coaster performance based on parameters set in the user-specified designs. As they set the mass of the coaster, curve radius, and hill size, numeric data are generated as to the speed of the coaster, its potential and kinetic energy, acceleration, and g-forces at various points along the track. In effect, new data are generated through user experimentation, which provide resources to support student-centered problem solving. Fig. 6.3 illustrates how resource data, available as data points along the coaster track, vary dynamically as a function of learner-supplied parameters.

Available Tools

Seeking tools are provided in the form of keyword searches and indexes to simplify the task of locating desired information. The program also provides a tool that enables students to mark sections for subsequent review, as well as a tool that allows them to generate original presentations using *ErgoMotion* resources. As shown in Fig. 6.4, one *ErgoMotion* manipulation tool enables learners to define roller coaster parameters and simulate their effects at an experimentation site. These tools allow learners to generate coaster designs or theories and test their viability. For instance, tools can be used to manipulate available design parameters: size of three different hills (three options each), the motor size and mass of the coaster cars (three options each), and the radius of a horizontal curve (small, medium, and large). Parameters are set by simply selecting icons to identify which parameter will be tested.

After setting parameters, learners can simulate a coaster run. The manipulation and simulation tools support both the modeling of the learner's beliefs about how roller coasters function and the real-time simulation of the effects of those beliefs and models. The tools provide a means to *test* ideas and theories, *collect* data on the observed results of decisions, and *integrate* personal beliefs with data that support or contradict them.

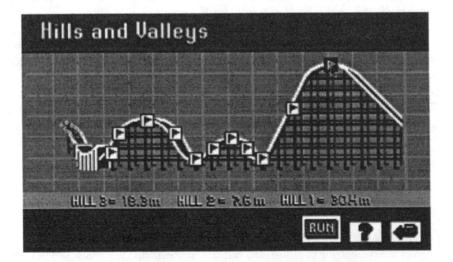

FIG 6.3.   Dynamic resource for identifying data points along the coaster track.

FIG 6.4.   Coaster experimentation site with parameter manipulation tools.

Scaffolding

Procedural scaffolding is provided in the form of a background video tour of the environment accompanied by a demonstration of the system. It introduces learners to the available resources and tools as well as methods for their use. A pull-down menu listing available text resources is also provided. Text files are provided mainly to assist learners in guiding their own explorations, determining where to collect and record data, and generating project ideas.

Conceptual and metacognitive scaffolds include facilitation guidance such as the questions illustrated in Fig. 6.5. These scaffolds provide a set of approaches that *could be* used should assistance be sought in initiating or continuing efforts. *ErgoMotion* also provides divergent questions regarding hills and valleys, energy loading, and the influence of curve radii on coaster performance. Students may investigate one or more questions to gain conceptual understanding of the underlying principles or design task, or may use the probe questions to guide them in the management of their plans and actions.

Additional conceptual scaffolding is provided in the form of opinions and perspectives on given problem areas. For instance, a question such as "What factors affect banking speed?" is posed, and alternative responses are provided. Learners are prompted to evaluate the opinions of the on-line authorities, identify those with which they agree or disagree, and collect evidence to support or refute their positions. Additional conceptual scaffolding is provided in the form of a radio talk show activity, where competing expert opinions are tendered in response to roller coaster design and performance.

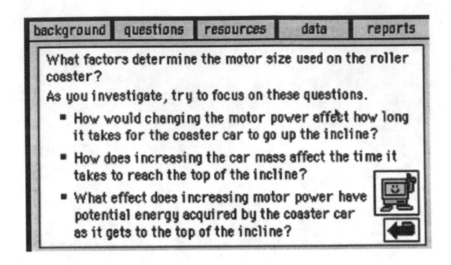

FIG 6.5.   Conceptual scaffolding in the form of guiding questions.

Finally, *ErgoMotion* provides a reports file that contains strategic suggestions for creating artifacts to illustrate what was learned (e.g., concept maps, media clip presentations, games). Another strategic scaffold contains questions to be considered and lists resources available to support students in investigating the key questions. The data file, another text resource, suggests locations in the accompanying student workbook to record data collected at the coaster site.

IMPLICATIONS AND CONCLUSIONS

Alignment among the theoretical foundations and available features is the cornerstone of OLE methods and practices. This chapter has attempted to identify and elaborate the core values, goals, components, and methods of OLEs. This has proven difficult to accomplish in a single chapter. Thus, we have attempted to emphasize fundamental, core-level underpinnings and methods of OLEs, while directing readers to a host of publications and software wherein greater detail is available.

We believe strongly in the importance and utility of OLEs for both current educational practice and emerging resource-based teaching and learning approaches. This is a reflection of our biases toward learner-centered environments. Yet, we do not summarily discount the potential value or viability of competing perspectives. Clearly, there are many ways to learn. Many practical factors must be weighed, and many methods are available that are consistent with both theories of learning and the circumstances within which learning is supported, expected, or required. Indeed, grounded design argues principally for the alignment among the core foundations we described in this chapter, not for the inherent superiority of one approach over others (Hannafin, Hannafin, Land, & Oliver, 1997).*

However, we recognize a need to optimize available resources rather than continually redeveloping and rehosting them. Literally billions of resources in diverse media have been produced during the past two millennia. Growth in both technology and information will only accelerate in the future. This poses a serious dilemma: How can we not only make existing resources more available to support learning, but accommodate future developments in each? It seems unlikely that we will be able to maintain pace using resource-embedded designs.

We need greater utility from the resources we have and those that will emerge in the future. We need systems that utilize resources more flexibly, extensively, and efficiently. We need to accommodate diverse goals and needs involving identical (or similar) resources rather than redeveloping the same resources. The growth of both information and technology require that scaleable models be advanced, along with designs that permit ready access, updating, and inclusion of growing bodies of resources.**

At the same time, learning systems must do more than afford better, dynamic access to rapidly emerging information systems. We need to advance a design technology that optimizes rather than minimizes the reasoning capabilities of learners and that exploits these capabilities to support individual goals and needs. OLEs attempt to address these needs by inducing (or supporting) frames for study, making resources available, providing tools to support and encourage analysis and interpretation, and guiding learners in accomplishing their goals or addressing their needs.

REFERENCES

Blieske, M. (1996). *Collaborative design project for the Internet* [On-line]. Available: gopher://gopher.schoolnet.ca:419/00/grassroots/projects/final.reports/elementary/collaborative

Cognition and Technology Group at Vanderbilt. (1992). The Jasper experiment: An exploration of issues in learning and instructional design. *Educational Technology Research & Development, 40*(1), 65–80.

Great Solar System Rescue [Computer software]. (1992). Watertown, MA: Tom Snyder Productions.

Hannafin, M. J. (1995). Open-ended learning environments: Foundations, assumptions, and implications for automated design. In R. Tennyson (Ed.), *Perspectives on automating instructional design* (pp. 101–129). New York: Springer-Verlag.

Hannafin, M. J., Hall, C., Land, S., & Hill, J. (1994). Learning in open environments: Assumptions, methods, and implications. *Educational Technology, 34*(8), 48–55.

Hannafin, M. J., Hannafin, K. M., Land, S., & Oliver, K. (1997). Grounded practice in the design of learning systems. *Educational Technology Research and Development, 45*(3), 101–117.

Hannafin, M. J., Hill, J., & Land, S. (1997). Student-centered learning and interactive multimedia: Status, issues, and implications. *Contemporary Education, 68*(2), 94–99.

---

* This is an enlightened view that seems to me an essential feature of the new paradigm of instructional theory.

** These last two paragraphs raise many issues that are a consequence of the information age and have great implications for an information-age paradigm of instruction. They are issues that cry out for serious pondering and discussion.

Hannafin, M. J., & Land, S. (1997). The foundations and assumptions of technology-enhanced, student-centered learning environments. *Instructional Science, 25*, 167–202.

Harel, I., & Papert, S. (1991). Software design as a learning environment. In I. Harel & S. Papert (Eds.), *Constructionism* (pp. 41–84). Norwood, NJ: Ablex.

Hay, K. E., Guzdial, M., Jackson, S., Boyle, R. A., & Soloway, E. (1994). Students as multimedia composers. *Computers and Education, 23*, 301–317.

Hill, J., & Hannafin, M. J. (1997). Cognitive strategies and learning from the World-Wide Web. *Educational Technology Research and Development, 45,*(4), 37–64.

Honebein, P. C. (1996). Seven goals for the design of constructivist learning environments. In B. G. Wilson (Ed.), *Constructivist learning environments* (pp. 11–24). Englewood Cliffs, NJ: Educational Technology Publications.

Iiyoshi, T., & Hannafin, M. (1996, February). *Cognitive tools for learning from hypermedia: Empowering learners.* Paper presented at the annual meeting of the Association for Educational Communications and Technology National Convention, Indianapolis, IN.

Jackson, S., Stratford, S. J., Krajcik, J., & Soloway, E. (1995a). Model-It: A case study of learner-centered design software for supporting model building. *Paper presented at the Working Conference on Technology Applications in the Science Classroom.* Columbus, OH: National Center for Science Teaching and Learning, The Ohio State University.

Jackson, S., Stratford, S. J., Krajcik, J., & Soloway, E. (1995b, April). *Making system dynamics modeling accessible to pre-college science students.* Paper presented at the annual meeting of the American Educational Research Association, San Francisco, CA.

Jacobson, M. J., Sugimoto, A., & Archodidou, A. (1996). Evolution, hypermedia learning environments, and conceptual change: A preliminary report. In D. C. Edelson & E. A. Domeshek (Eds.), *Proceedings of ICLS '96* (pp. 151–158). Charlottesville, VA: Association for the Advancement of Computing in Education.

Land, S. M., & Hannafin, M. J. (1996). A conceptual framework for the development of theories-in-action with open-ended learning environments. *Educational Technology Research & Development, 44*(3), 37–53.

Land, S. M., & Hannafin, M. J. (1997). Patterns of understanding with open-ended learning environments: A qualitative study. *Educational Technology Research & Development, 45*(2), 47–73.

Lebow, D., Wager, W., Marks, P., & Gilbert, N. (1996, June). *Construe: Software for Collaborative Learning over the World Wide Web.* Paper presented at the AET Collaboration in Distance Education Conference, Tallahassee, FL.

Linn, M. (1995). Designing computer learning environments for engineering and computer science: The Scaffolded Knowledge Integration Framework. *Journal of Science Education and Technology, 4*(2), 103–126

Lewis, E., Stern, J., & Linn, M. (1993). The effect of computer simulations on introductory thermodynamics understanding. *Educational Technology, 33*(1), 45–58.

Litchfield, B., & Mattson, S. (1989). The IMS Project: An inquiry-based multimedia science curriculum. *Journal of Computers in Mathematics and Science Teaching, 9*(1), 37–43.

Microworlds Project Builder (Version 1.02) [Computer program]. (1993). Highgate Springs, VT: Logo Computer Systems.

National Library of Medicine. (1996). *Visible human project.* Bethesda, MD: Office of Public Information.

Rieber, L. P. (1993). A pragmatic view of instructional technology. In K. Tobin (Ed.), *The practice of constructivism in science education* (pp. 193–212). Hillsdale, NJ: Lawrence Erlbaum Associates.

Sayle, R. (1996). RasMor [Computer program]. Edinburgh, Scotland: University of Edinburgh.

Scardamalia, M., & Bereiter, C. (1994). Computer support for knowledge-building communities. *The Journal of the Learning Sciences, 3*, 265–283.

Schubert, N. (1997a). *Playwriting in the round* [Online]. Available: http://www1.minn.net:80/~schubert/Play.html

Schubert, N. (1997b). *Signs of spring* [Online]. Available: http://www1.minn.net:80/~schubert/spring.html

Tobin, K., & Dawson, G. (1992). Constraints to curriculum reform: Teachers and the myths of schooling. *Educational Technology Research & Development, 40*(1), 64–92.

Vosniadou, S. (1992). Knowledge acquisition and conceptual change. *Applied Psychology: An International Review, 41*(4), 347–357.

7 Designing Instruction for Constructivist Learning

Richard E. Mayer
University of California, Santa Barbara

Richard E. Mayer

Richard E. Mayer is Professor of Psychology at the University of California, Santa Barbara. He serves on the editorial boards of 11 journals, including the *Journal of Educational Psychology and American Educational Research Journal*. He is a former editor of the *Educational Psychologist and Instructional Science*, and a past president of Division 15 (Educational Psychology) of the American Psychological Association. He is the author of more than 200 articles and books mainly in educational psychology, including *The Promise of Educational Psychology: Learning in the Content Areas.* His research interests include cognition and technology, with a focus on multimedia learning.

FOREWORD

Goals and preconditions. *The primary goal of this theory is to foster knowledge construction (understanding) through direct instruction. It is intended primarily for use with textbook-based learning, lectures, and multimedia environments in which behavioral activity (manipulation) is not possible.*

Values. *Some of the values upon which this theory is based include:*
- *instruction that focuses on the process of learning (what goes on inside the learner's head) as well as the product of learning,*
- *transfer (knowledge use), as well as retention,*
- *how to learn, as well as what to learn.*

Methods. *These are the major methods this theory offers:*

Select relevant information
- *Highlight the most important information for the learner, using:*

- Headings	*- Bullets*	*- Margin notes*
- Italics	*- Arrows*	*- Repetition*
- Boldface	*- Icons*	*- White Space*
- Font size	*- Underlining*	*- Captions*

- *Use instructional objectives and/or adjunct questions.*
- *Provide a summary.*
- *Eliminate irrelevant information; be concise.*

Organize information for the learner, using:
- *Structure of the text*
  - *Comparison/contrast structure*
  - *Classification structure*
  - *Enumeration (or parts) structure*
  - *Generalization structure*
  - *Cause-effect structure*
- *Outlines*
- *Headings*
- *Pointer (or signal) words*
- *Graphic representations*

Integrate information
- *Advance organizers*
- *Illustrations (multi-frame) with captions*
- *Animation with narration*
- *Worked-out examples*
- *Elaborative questions*

Major contributions. *Offers a non-discovery, non-manipulation approach to constructivist learning.*

—C.M.R.

Designing Instruction for Constructivist Learning

Constructivist learning occurs when learners actively create their own knowledge by trying to make sense out of material that is presented to them. For example, in reading a textbook lesson on the formation of lightning, a constructivist learner attempts to build a mental model of the cause-and-effect system for lightning formation. The purpose of this chapter is to examine design principles for fostering constructivist learning, such as the learning of scientific explanations in textbooks, lectures, and multimedia environments. An important theme of this chapter is that one does not need discovery learning to have constructivist learning; (i.e., learners can construct meaning from well-designed direct instruction). First, I examine some introductory issues in the design of instruction for constructivist learning. Second, I present and exemplify a general model for describing the cognitive processes involved in constructivist learning. Third, I review instructional methods that are intended to foster constructivist learning. Fourth, I review the goals and values underlying instructional-design principles for constructivist learning.

INTRODUCTION TO CONSTRUCTIVIST LEARNING

Three Views of Learning and Instruction

Mayer (1992) has shown how three views of learning have emerged during the past 100 years of research on learning: learning as response strengthening, learning as knowledge acquisition, and learning as knowledge construction. According to the first view, learning occurs when a learner strengthens or weakens an association between a stimulus and a response. The learning as response strengthening view developed in the first half of the 20th century and was based largely on the study of animal learning in artificial laboratory settings. The role of the learner is to passively receive rewards and punishments, whereas the role of instructor is to administer rewards and punishments, such as in drill-and-practice. The instructional designer's role is to create environments where the learner repeatedly is cued to give a simple response, which is immediately followed by feedback.

The second view, learning as knowledge acquisition, is based on the idea that learning occurs when a learner places new information in long-term memory. This view developed in the 1950s, 1960s, and 1970s and was based largely on the study of human learning in artificial laboratory settings. The role of the learner is to passively acquire information, and the teacher's job is to present information, such as in textbooks and lectures. According to the knowledge acquisition view, information is a commodity that can be transmitted directly from teacher to learner. The instructional designer's role is to create environments in which the learner is exposed to large amounts of information, such as in textbooks, lectures, and computer-based multimedia programs.

The third view, learning as knowledge construction, is based on the idea that learning occurs when a learner actively constructs a knowledge representation in working memory. This view emerged in the 1980s and 1990s and was based largely on the study of human learning in increasingly realistic settings. According to the knowledge construction view, the learner is a sense-maker, whereas the teacher is a cognitive guide who provides guidance and modeling on authentic academic tasks. The instructional designer's role is to create environments in which the learner interacts meaningfully with academic material, including fostering the learner's processes of selecting, organizing, and integrating information. In this chapter, I use the knowledge construction view to guide the discussion of instructional design principles.*

Three Kinds of Learning Outcomes

Consider the following situation. I ask three students, Alice, Belinda, and Carmen, to read a passage on the formation of lightning, such as is partially shown in Table 7.1. Each student reads carefully, making sure she focuses on every word. Then I give students a *retention test* in which I ask them to write down all they can recall from the passage and a *transfer test* in which I ask them to answer questions that require using the information in new ways. Examples of retention and transfer questions are given in Table 7.2.

Alice performs poorly on retention and transfer, indicating that she has not learned much about the formation of lightning. I refer to this learning outcome as *no learning*. In the no-learning scenario, learners may fail to pay attention to relevant incoming information.

Belinda does well on remembering the important information from the passage about the formation of lightning but performs poorly on applying that information to solving new problems. This pattern represents the outcome of *rote learning*. In rote learning, learners attempt to add behaviors or information to their memories. For example, in reading the lightning passage, a rote learner attempts to memorize as many facts as possible, such as "Every year approximately 150 Americans are killed by lightning." The major cognitive process is encoding, (i.e., placing pieces of information into long-term memory). This process is best supported by drill-and-practice methods of instruction.

---

* Perhaps each view represents a different window onto a different aspect of reality. To what extent do you think the new paradigm of instructional theory needs to utilize multiple perspectives as opposed to restricting itself to a single perspective? This relates to the diversity theme of this book.

TABLE 7.1

Portion of Text on the Formation of Lightning

Lightning can be defined as the discharge of electricity resulting from the difference in electrical charges between the cloud and the ground. Every year approximately 150 Americans are killed by lightning. Swimmers are sitting ducks for lighting because water is an excellent conductor of electrical discharge.

When the surface of the earth is warm, moist air near the earth's surface becomes heated and rises rapidly, producing an updraft. When flying through updrafts, an airplane ride can become bumpy. As the air in these updrafts cools, water vapor condenses into water droplets and forms a cloud. The cloud's top extends above the freezing level. At this altitude, the air temperature is well below freezing, so the upper portion of the cloud is composed of tiny crystals.

Eventually, the water droplets and ice crystals in the cloud become too large to be suspended by updrafts. As raindrops and ice crystals fall through the cloud, they drag some of the air from the cloud downward, producing downdrafts. The rising and falling air currents within the cloud may cause hailstones to form. When downdrafts strike the ground, the spread out in all directions, producing gusts of cool wind people feel just before the start of the rain. When lightning strikes the ground, fulgrites may form, as the heat from the lightning fuses sand into the shape of the electricity's path.

Within the cloud, the moving air causes electrical charges to build, although scientists do not fully understand how it occurs. Most believe that the charge results from the collision of cloud's light, rising water droplets and tiny pieces of ice against hail and other heavier, falling particles. In trying to understand these processes, scientists sometimes create lightning by launching tiny rockets into overhead clouds. The negatively charged particles fall to the bottom of the cloud, and most of the positively charged particles rise to the top.

[The next two paragraphs describe the flow of negatively charged particles from the cloud to the ground and the flow of positively charged particles from the ground to the cloud, respectively.]

TABLE 7.2

Retention and Transfer Tests for a Lesson on the Formation of Lightning

Retention Test

Explain how lightning forms.

Transfer Test

Suppose there are clouds in the sky but there is no lightning. Why not?

What could you do to reduce the intensity of a lightning storm?

What causes lightning?

Finally, Carmen performs well on both retention and transfer, a pattern that indicates a *constructivist learning* outcome (i.e., based on constructivist learning). In constructivist learning, learners attempt to make sense out of the presented information. In reading the lightning passage, a constructivist learner tries to build a mental model of the lightning system consisting of a cause-and-effect chain. Constructivist learning is active learning in which the learner possesses and uses a variety of cognitive processes during the learning process. The major cognitive processes include paying attention to relevant information, organizing that information into coherent representations, and integrating these representations with existing knowledge. Instructional methods other than drill-and-practice are required to foster these kinds of processes during learning.

Table 7.3 summarizes these three patterns of learning outcomes in which no learning is indicated by poor retention and transfer, rote learning is indicated by good retention and poor transfer, and constructivist learning is indicated by good retention and good transfer (Mayer, 1984, 1996).

Two Kinds of Active Learning

Consider the following situation. Two students are working at their desks in preparation for an upcoming meteorology test. Rachel engages in hands-on exercises in her workbook in which she must fill in blanks by writing words. For example, one of the activities is: "Each year approximately _____ Americans are killed by lightning." In this case Rachel is behaviorally active, in that she is actively writing in a workbook, but she may not be cognitively active, in that she is not trying to make sense out of the material.

In contrast, Michelle is reading over the text and silently trying to explain it to herself. Where the text is incomplete or unclear, she tries to create what Chi, Bassok, Lewis, Reimann, and Glaser (1989) call a "self-explanation." For example, when the test says that the positive charges come to the surface of the earth, Michelle mentally adds the explanation that opposite charges attract one another. In this case, Michelle is behaviorally inactive, in that she is not writing or talking or doing much of anything, but she is cognitively active, in that she is trying to explain the passage to herself.

Which type of activity leads to constructivist learning? Robins and Mayer (1993) have shown how constructivist learning depends on the learner's cognitive activity rather than the learner's behavioral activity. It follows that instructional de-

TABLE 7.3
Three Kinds of Learning Outcomes for a Lesson on the Formation of Lightning

Performance on Retention Test	Performance on Transfer Test	Learning Outcome
Poor	Poor	No learning
Good	Poor	Rote learning
Good	Good	Constructivist learning

sign should seek to encourage the learner to be cognitively active rather than focusing solely on promoting behavioral activity. The foregoing examples suggest that there can be cases in which a behaviorally active learner does not engage in constructivist learning and there can be cases in which a behaviorally inactive learner does engage in constructivist learning. This chapter focuses on methods for fostering cognitive activity even when behavioral activity is not possible.

Two Kinds of Tests

This example also points to the importance of distinguishing between two classic techniques for evaluating learning: retention tests and transfer tests. Retention tests evaluate how much of the presented material the learner can remember, and include both recall tests, in which students may be asked to write down all they can remember (or fill in a blank), and recognition tests, in which students may be asked to choose which of several possible answers is most appropriate (or match which response goes with which term). Retention tests were the focus of early behaviorist-oriented studies of learning and served to promote drill-and-practice as the most favored instructional method (Thorndike, 1926).

In contrast, transfer tests require that the learner apply what was learned to a novel situation. As can be seen in this example, the characteristic that distinguishes someone who learns by understanding from someone who learns by rote is the ability to engage in *problem-solving transfer*. According to Mayer and Wittrock (1996, p. 47), "problem-solving transfer occurs when a person uses previous problem-solving experience to devise a solution for a new problem." Transfer tests were the focus of early Gestalt-oriented studies of learning and served to promote structural understanding as a valued instructional method (Wertheimer, 1945).

When the goal of instruction is constructivist learning, multiple measures of learning are warranted, including both retention and transfer. Instead of asking solely, "How much was learned?" as measured through retention, the constructivist approach requires also asking, "What was learned?" as measured through transfer tests. For example, in the six levels of Bloom's taxonomy (Bloom, Engelhart, Furst, Hill, & Krathwohl, 1956), the first level involves retention and the remaining five levels suggest different aspects of transfer. Given the importance of transfer tests in distinguishing rote from constructivist learning, the search for transfer is a central mission in designing instruction for constructivist learning.

Three Prerequisites for Problem-Solving Transfer

Mayer (1998) has proposed three major prerequisites for problem-solving transfer: skill, metaskill, and will. Skill refers to component cognitive processes, such as selecting relevant information from a lesson for further processing in working memory, organizing selected information into a coherent mental representation in working memory, and integrating incoming information with existing knowledge from long-term memory. These three mental activities could be called cognitive processes for sense making. Metaskill refers to metacognitive and self-regulatory processes for planning, orchestrating, and monitoring the use of component processes on a learning task. Will refers to the motivational and attitudinal aspects of learning, including the belief that hard work will pay off and that it is possible to understand scientific explanations. Although design of environments for constructivist learning depends on all three prerequisites, I focus mainly on the role of cognitive processes for sense making (i.e., a learning skill) in this chapter.

THE SOI MODEL OF LEARNING: FOSTERING THREE COGNITIVE PROCESSES IN KNOWLEDGE CONSTRUCTION

Constructivist learning depends on the activation of several cognitive processes in the learner during learning, including selecting relevant information, organizing incoming information, and integrating incoming information with existing knowledge. I refer to this analysis as the SOI model to highlight three crucial cognitive processes in constructivist learning: S for selecting, O for organizing, and I for integrating (Mayer, 1996). Unlike earlier theories of learning which emphasized the process by which presented information is encoded into long-term memory, a theory of constructivist learning focuses on the way that knowledge is constructed by the learner in working memory. In this construction process the learner uses both incoming material from the environment and prior knowledge from long-term memory. The SOI model is a theory of learning that can be used to generate instructional implications.

Fig. 7.1 presents the SOI model for instructional messages containing words and pictures.* Following current theories of working memory, the SOI model in Fig. 7.1 distinguishes between visual working memory and auditory working memory (Baddeley, 1992; Sweller, 1994). Visually presented materials, such as pictures and text, are initially retained in visual working memory, although text can be converted to sounds that are retained in auditory working memory. Auditorily presented materials, such as speech, are retained in auditory working memory. Given the limited capacity of visual working memory and auditory working memory, not all of the incoming material may be retained and processed.

For example, consider the lesson on lightning presented in Fig. 7.2. A constructivist learner must mentally select the relevant images and words about lightning formation, must connect them together into respective pictorial and verbal cause-and-effect chains, and must make mental connections between the two chains with prior knowledge.

---

* Note that this is descriptive theory as discussed in chapter 1, p. 7.

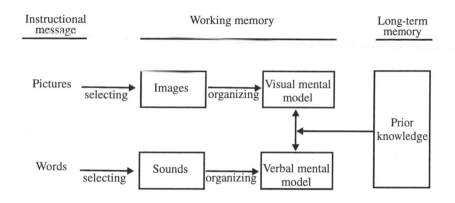

FIG. 7.1.   SOI model of constructivist learning from words and pictures.

Selecting Relevant Information

The first process is the selection of relevant information for further processing. When words and pictures are presented to a learner in an instructional message, the learner represents them briefly in sensory memories. Given the limited capacity of the human information-processing system, only some of these representations can be retained for further processing in working memory. Thus, an important cognitive process is the learner's selection of relevant information to be retained in working memory. This step is represented by the "selecting" arrows in Fig. 7.1, in which incoming images are selected for further processing in visual working memory and incoming words are selected for further processing in auditory working memory.

For example, in reading the lightning passage in Fig. 7.2, a constructivist learner needs to focus on the key steps in the process of lightning such as "negatively charged particles fall to the bottom of the cloud" and on the key images such as a picture of a cloud with pluses on the top half and minuses on the bottom half. The lesson presented in Fig. 7.2 helps to foster the selection process because it emphasizes the relevant words and pictures. Each caption presents a concise statement of a crucial step in the process of lightning formation, and each illustration depicts a crucial step in the process of lightning formation. By providing a summary that pinpoints the major steps, the reader is encouraged to select the relevant information.

Organizing Incoming Information

The next process involves organizing the selected auditory representations into a coherent verbal representation and organizing the selected images into a coherent pictorial representation. Kintsch (1988) refers to this activity as building a situation model from the presented information. This step is represented by the "organizing"

The Process of Lightning

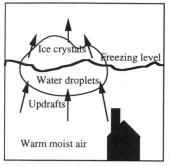

1. Warm moist air rises, water vapor condenses and forms cloud.

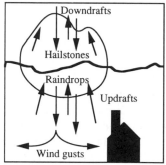

2. Raindrops and ice crystals drag air downward.

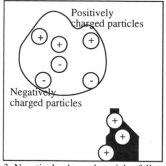

3. Negatively charged particles fall to bottom of cloud.

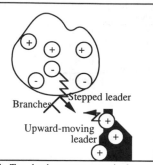

4. Two leaders meet, negatively charged particles rush from cloud to ground.

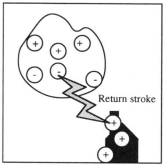

5. Positively charged particles from the ground rush upward along the same path.

FIG. 7.2. Portion of revised lesson on the formation of lightning. Copyright 1996 by the American Psychological Association. Preprinted by permission.

arrows in Fig. 7.1, in which retained visual images are connected by appropriate links (such as cause-and-effect) and retained verbal representations are connected by appropriate links (such as cause-and-effect). This activity takes place in working memory, which is constrained by a limited amount of resources for processing. The outcome of this process is the construction of a coherent pictorial representation (or pictorial mental model) and a coherent verbal representation (or verbal mental model).

For example, in reading the lightning passage presented in Fig. 7.2, a constructivist learner needs to infer the cause-and-effect relations between steps in the process of lightning formation. In reading, "negatively charged particles fall to the bottom of the cloud" followed by "negatively charged particles rush from cloud to ground," the reader must construct a causal link from the former to the latter event. Similarly, in seeing an illustration depicting negatively charged particles in the bottom half of the cloud followed by an illustration showing negatively charged particles moving downward toward the positively-charged particles on the earth's surface, the reader must construct a causal link from the former to the latter. By clearly ordering the events in the illustrations and captions and signaling them as "step 1," "step 2," etc., the instructional message may prime appropriate organizational processing in the reader.

Integrating Incoming Information

In the third process, students make one-to-one connections between corresponding elements of the pictorial and verbal representations they have constructed using prior knowledge. This step is represented in Fig. 7.1 by the arrows labeled "integrating." The outcome is an integrated representation of the presented material.

For example, students reading the lightning passage must make a connection between the words "negatively charged particles fall to the bottom of the cloud" and the illustration of the cloud with minuses in the bottom. This connection may be easier to make when the corresponding words and illustrations are near one another on the page or when corresponding narration and animation are presented simultaneously (Mayer, 1997). Similarly, constructivist learners may use their prior knowledge about friction causing particles to separate as a possible explanation for why negatively charged particles fall to the bottom of the cloud.

A final step in the learning process is encoding, in which the mental representations constructed in working memory are stored in long-term memory for permanent retention. Although this phase is the focus of earlier conceptions of learning, constructivist views of learning emphasize the role of cognitive processes used to build knowledge in working memory, such as selecting, organizing, and integrating. In addition, the construction process requires orchestration and coordination of these component processes, which can be labeled as metacognition or executive control.

INSTRUCTIONAL METHODS SUGGESTED
BY THE SOI MODEL

What are the instructional design implications of the SOI model for improving textbook, lecture, and multimedia messages? When the goal is to encourage the learner to become cognitively involved in learning, instruction should be designed to help the reader identify useful information, understand how the material fits together, and see how the material relates to prior knowledge.

An important instructional-design issue concerns the role of social interaction in constructivist learning. Many of the popular instructional methods for promoting constructivist learning depend on interpersonal learning environments that enable discussion, modeling, guided discovery, and scaffolding. For example, cognitive apprenticeship techniques require that a student and mentor work together on an authentic task (Collins, Brown, & Newman, 1989). Other forms of socially mediated learning, such as cooperative learning (Slavin, 1990) and fostering communities of learners (Campione, Shapiro, & Brown, 1995), require that a student learn as part of a group. Although social contexts of learning provide many opportunities for constructivist learning, not all social contexts promote constructivist learning, and more importantly, not all constructivist learning depends on social contexts.

In contrast, this chapter focuses on the design of instructional messages* (Fleming & Levie, 1993), such as textbook passages, lectures, and multimedia programs. These venues have become handy, albeit unwarranted, targets of the constructivist revolution on the grounds that they are based on an outmoded view of learning as rote transmission of information. However, these environments can support constructivist learning to the extent that they can be designed to promote active cognitive processing in learners. For the past 20 years, my colleagues and I at Santa Barbara have been exploring techniques for promoting constructivist learning from textbooks, lectures, and multimedia programs. The primary design issue is how to prime cognitive processes in learners that are needed for sense making, such as selecting, organizing, and integrating.

Techniques for Encouraging Students to Select Material

How can we encourage students to focus on the most relevant pieces of information in a textbook lesson, lecture, or multimedia presentation? Mayer (1993) has demonstrated how the following techniques can be incorporated into text-based messages: (a) using headings, italics, boldface, larger font, bullets, arrows, icons, underlining, margin notes, repetition, and/or white space to highlight relevant information; and (b) using adjunct questions and statements of instructional objectives to emphasize relevant information.**

---

* This is a precondition for use of the theory.
** Here the method, "encourage students to select material," has been broken down into kinds of methods, but no situations have been identified here to guide their selection.

For example, in order to help students select relevant material from the lightning passage in Table 7.1, we could underline or italicize each major step in the process of lightning formation, such as, "Warm moist air rises, water vapor condenses and forms a cloud," in the second paragraph. Similarly, this summary could be used as a heading for the second paragraph or could be placed in the margin next to it as a note. Another way to direct the reader's attention towards the relevant material is to include adjunct questions or instructional objectives about each major step in the process of lightning formation such as, "What happens when warm moist air rises?" or "You should be able to tell what happens when warm moist air rises," respectively, for paragraph 2. Finally, the reader's attention can be drawn towards the relevant material by providing a summary, such as in Fig. 7.2.

More recently, Mayer, Bove, Bryman, Mars, and Tapangco (1996) tested the idea that providing a summary would help students focus on the relevant information. Consistent with expectations, students who read a summary of the key steps in the formation of lightning performed better on remembering the key steps in the formation of lightning and on solving transfer problems than did students who read the entire lesson. Apparently, "less is more" because the summary encouraged students to focus on the relevant information.

Harp and Mayer (1997) tested the idea that removing interesting but irrelevant information from a passage would help students focus on the relevant information. Some students read a standard passage about the formation of lightning, whereas others read the same passage with interesting text and illustrations interspersed, such as a picture and story of a boy who had been struck by lightning. Consistent with expectations, students who read the standard booklet remembered more of the key steps in lightning formation and performed better on solving transfer problems than did students who read the version of the passage that contained interesting details. This study provides additional evidence that "less is more" because the interesting details result in the reader paying less attention to the relevant information.

These studies point to conciseness as a key factor in encouraging students to select relevant information. This recommendation conflicts with a growing trend for American textbooks to become longer and longer with a tendency to cover many topics superficially (Mayer, Sims, & Tajika, 1995). In contrast, research on textbook design suggests that books should become more concise, covering fewer topics.

Techniques for Encouraging Students to Organize Material

How can we help students to organize incoming information into a coherent representation? Mayer (1993) has shown how to use outlines, headings, and pointer words to signal the organization of the passage. It is also important to use text that has an understandable structure (Cook & Mayer, 1988), such as the cause-and-effect chain in the lightning passage.

For example, in order to help students organize the lightning passage in Table 7.1, we could add an outline in the first paragraph that says: "There are five major steps in the formation of lightning: 1. cloud formation, 2. downward air, 3. cloud charge, 4. leaders meet, and 5. return stroke." In addition, we could add headings to each paragraph, corresponding to each of the five steps, such as listed in the captions in Fig. 7.2. Finally, we can make the organization clearer to the reader by referring to the steps in the text by number, such as "step 1," "step 2," "step 3," and so on. Pointer words such as "because of this" or "as a result" can make the causal links between steps clearer to the learner.

In a research study, Loman and Mayer (1983) asked students to read a passage about the formation of red tides that was either signaled or not signaled. The signaled version included a brief outline of the three steps in the formation of red tides, headings corresponding to each step, and pointer words such as "because of this." Students who read the signaled version performed better than those reading the nonsignaled version on remembering the key steps in the process of red tide formation and on solving transfer problems. These results suggest that making the structure clearer to readers helps them construct coherent representations that can be used to support creative problem solving.

Organized graphic representations can be used in conjunction with signaling to help learners construct coherent mental representations of the structure of texts. For example, Mayer, Dyck, and Cook (1984) asked students to read a passage explaining the nitrogen cycle taken from a science textbook or a signaled version of the passage. In contrast to the original version, the signaled version included an outline at the beginning naming the five main steps in the nitrogen cycle, headings based on the five steps, a reordering of the sentences so that the each step was described in succession, and a figure summarizing the relations among the five steps as a flow diagram. Students who read the signaled version recalled more of the important information and generated more solutions on transfer problems than did students who read the original version.

The process of building a coherent mental representation from text depends on the learners' ability to recognize the structure of the text. For example, Cook and Mayer (1988) have shown that students are often unaware that text can be organized in several common structures, such as compare/contrast (i.e., a comparison of two or more items along several dimensions), classification (i.e., a hierarchical network), enumeration (i.e., a list of parts or features of a topic), generalization (i.e., a general assertion followed by supporting evidence), and cause-and-effect (i.e., a chain of events in a causal system). When text is disorganized, or its structure is not seen by the learner, the learner is likely to engage in rote learning of the text as an arbitrary list of unrelated facts. Outlines coordinated with headings and signal words encourage learners to detect the rhetorical structure of text and to build coherent mental representations.

Techniques for Encouraging Students to Integrate Material

How can we help students to activate and use prior knowledge and to activate and coordinate multiple representations of the material? Mayer (1993) has demonstrated how to use advance organizers, illustrations, worked-out examples, and elaborative questions to foster knowledge integration.

For example, one way to help the reader connect the text to his or her existing knowledge is to present line drawings corresponding to each step, as shown in Fig. 7.2. By representing each step in a concrete way, the reader may be better able to connect the incoming words to his or her existing knowledge. For example, the third frame in Fig. 7.2 shows how the negative particles fall to the bottom of the cloud and the positive particles move to the top. Overall, the summary presented in Fig. 7.2 is consistent with each of the three techniques suggested in this section: the captions help focus students' attention on the relevant material, breaking the message into five steps helps signal the organization of the material to the reader, and coordinating the text with illustrations helps foster the integration of the words with prior knowledge.

Research by Mayer (1989a) has shown how an advance organizer can prime appropriate prior knowledge in learners. In one set of studies, students read a passage explaining how radar works (Mayer, 1983). For some students, the passage began by comparing radar to a ball bouncing off a wall (advance organizer group), whereas the passage contained no analogy for other students (no advance organizer). Consistent with predictions, the advance organizer group performed better than the no advance organizer group on tests of retention and transfer. Mayer (1989a) concluded that the analogy provided in the advance organizer primed familiar prior knowledge in the learner that could be used to make sense out of the rest of the passage.

Inserting elaborative questions in a text can also encourage readers to connect the new information with their existing knowledge. For example, Mayer (1980) asked students to read a text explaining how to use a database system. For some students the text included elaborative questions in which they had to describe the system in familiar terms, such as a worker sorting files into different baskets. These students performed better on recall of important information and on a problem-solving test than did students who received no elaborative questions. The questions encouraged learners to relate the presented information to their existing knowledge about how data can be sorted.

More recently, Mayer (1997) proposed that the use of multiframe illustrations promotes knowledge integration when the illustration frames contain captions that correspond to the explanation depicted in the frames. In a series of studies (Mayer, 1989b; Mayer, Steinhoff, Bower, & Mars, 1995; Mayer & Gallini, 1990), students read passages containing illustrations with coordinated captions (integrated group) or containing illustrations on different pages from captions (separated group). Students in the integrated group performed better than students in the separated group on tests of retention and transfer. Similar results were obtained in a multimedia environment. Students who viewed animation along with concurrent narration outperformed students who viewed the animation and narration successively (Mayer & Anderson, 1991, 1992; Mayer & Sims, 1994). In these cases, coordinated presentation of words and pictures allows students to build and coordinate multiple representations of the same explanation.

In addition to instructional techniques for promoting active cognitive processing, constructivist learning depends on the learner's beliefs, such as the idea that the material is potentially understandable. Researchers have demonstrated how the learner's self-efficacy (Schunk, 1991) and attributions of success and failure (Weiner, 1986) influence their persistence in trying to learn new material.*

VALUES UNDERLYING INSTRUCTIONAL GOALS OF THE KNOWLEDGE CONSTRUCTION APPROACH

The knowledge construction approach to instructional design is based on several underlying values about the appropriate goals of instruction, including a focus on process as well as product, on transfer as well as retention, and on how to learn as well as what to learn.

Focusing on Process as Well as Product. The constructivist approach is based on the idea that there is value in considering what goes on inside the learner's head rather than considering only what is presented. This is an enduring value in education, dating back to Dewey's (1902) classic distinction between child-centered and curriculum-centered education. In a child-centered approach, the focus is on how to promote cognitive change in learners, whereas in a curriculum-centered approach, the focus is on covering material. This value is also reflected in the classic call to focus on the process of learning as well as the product of learning (Bloom & Broder, 1950). The focus on the process of learning is a central value of the constructivist approach.

Enabling Transfer as Well as Retention. The constructivist approach is also based on the premise that students should be able to use what they have learned rather than simply to be able to remember it. One of the motivating values of the constructivist approach is that meaningful learning is often preferable to rote learning, and deep understanding is better than senseless memorization. The case for meaningful learning has a long history in psychology and education, but perhaps was best articulated by the Gestalt psychologists such as Wertheimer (1945). The hallmark of deep understanding is the ability to transfer what was learned to novel situations, so the constructivist approach highlights measures of learning that go beyond retention.

Promoting How to Learn as Well as What Is Learned. Finally, the constructivist approach values knowing how to learn (and think and remember) as well what to learn (and think and remember). An important part of learning involves

---

* This paragraph presents descriptive theory, rather than design theory.

learning strategies in which students develop component processes, such as selecting, organizing, and integrating information, as well as techniques for coordinating and monitoring these processes (Pressley, 1990; Weinstein & Mayer, 1985). In addition to learning subject matter content, students need to know basic learning and thinking skills.

These values underlie the vision of instructional design for constructivist learning that I present in this chapter.

CONCLUSION

The thesis of this chapter is that it is possible to design instruction that promotes constructivist learning, even when the learner is not engaged in a behaviorally active learning episode. In particular, constructivist learning can result from the seemingly passive task of reading a text if the text is designed to foster appropriate cognitive processing in the learner. According to the SOI model of learning, constructivist learning can occur when a learner engages in three cognitive processes: attending to relevant information (i.e., selecting), mentally organizing the information into a coherent mental representation (i.e., organizing), and integrating the information with existing knowledge (i.e., integrating). Instructional methods for fostering the process of selecting information from text include use of headings, italics, boldface, font size, bullets, arrows, icons, underlining, margin notes, repetition, white space, and captions. Instruction methods for fostering the process of organizing information from text include using outlines, signaling headings, pointer words, structured illustrations, and coherent text structures. Instructional methods for fostering the process of integrating presented information and prior knowledge include using advance organizers, captioned multiframe illustrations, narrated animation, worked-out examples, and elaborative questions.

The constructivist revolution offers a new vision of the learner as an active sense-maker and suggests new methods of instruction emphasizing hands-on activity and discussion. In light of the fact that book-based instruction continues to play a major role in education (Britton, Woodward, & Binkley, 1993), it is useful to explore ways of promoting constructivist learning from textbooks. This chapter offers a vision of how to accomplish this goal.

REFERENCES

Baddeley, A. (1992). Working memory. *Science, 255*, 556–559.
Bloom, B. S. & Broder, L. J. (1950). *Problem-solving processes of college students.* Chicago: University of Chicago Press.
Bloom, B. S., Engelhart, M. D., Furst, E. J., Hill, W. H., & Krathwohl, D. R. (1956). *Taxonomy of educational objectives: Classification of educational goals. Handbook I: Cognitive domain.* New York: McKay.
Britton, B. K., Woodward, A., & Binkley, M. (Eds.). (1993). *Learning from textbooks: Theory and practice.* Hillsdale, NJ: Lawrence Erlbaum Associates.

Campione, J. C., Shapiro, A. M., & Brown, A. L. (1995). Forms of transfer in communities of learners: Flexible learning and understanding. In A. McKeough, J. Lupart, & A. Marini (Eds.), *Teaching for transfer* (pp. 35–68). Hillsdale, NJ: Lawrence Erlbaum Associates.

Chi, M. T. H., Bassok, M., Lewis, M., Reimann, P., & Glaser, R. (1989). Self-explanations: How students study and use examples in learning to solve problems. *Cognitive Science, 13*, 145–182.

Collins, A., Brown, J. S., & Newman, S. E. (1989). Cognitive apprenticeship: Teaching the crafts of reading, writing, and mathematics. In L. B. Resnick (Ed.), *Knowing, learning, and instruction: Essays in honor of Robert Glaser* (pp. 453–494). Hillsdale, NJ: Lawrence Erlbaum Associates.

Cook, L. K., & Mayer, R. E. (1988). Teaching readers about the structure of scientific text. *Journal of Educational Psychology, 80*, 448–456.

Dewey, J. (1902). *The child and the curriculum.* Chicago: University of Chicago Press.

Fleming, M., & Levie, W. H. (Eds.). (1993). *Instructional message design: Principles from the behavioral and cognitive sciences* (2nd ed). Englewood Cliffs, NJ: Educational Technology Publications.

Harp, S. F., & Mayer, R. E. (1997). The role of interest in learning from scientific text and illustrations: On the distinction between emotional interest and cognitive interest. *Journal of Educational Psychology, 89*, 92–102.

Kintsch, W. (1988). The use of knowledge in discourse processing: A construction-integration model. *Psychological Review, 95*, 163–182.

Loman, N. L., & Mayer, R. E. (1983). Signaling techniques that increase the understandability of expository prose. *Journal of Educational Psychology, 75*, 402–412.

Mayer, R. E. (1980). Elaboration techniques that increase the meaningfulness of technical text: An experimental test of the learning strategy hypothesis. *Journal of Educational Psychology, 72*, 770–784.

Mayer, R. E. (1983). Can you repeat that? Qualitative and quantitative effects of repitition and advance organizers on learning from science prose. *Journal of Educational Psychology, 75*, 40–49.

Mayer, R. E. (1984). Aids to text comprehension. *Educational Psychologist, 19*, 30–42.

Mayer, R. E. (1989a). Models for understanding. *Review of Educational Research, 59*, 43–64.

Mayer, R. E. (1989b). Systematic thinking fostered by illustrations in scientific text. *Journal of Educational Psychology, 81*, 240–246.

Mayer, R. E. (1992). Cognition and instruction: On their historic meeting within educational psychology. *Journal of Educational Psychology, 84*, 405–412.

Mayer, R. E. (1993). Problem-solving principles. In M. Fleming & W. H. Levie (Eds.), *Instructional message design: Principles from the behavioral and cognitive sciences* (2nd ed., pp. 253–282). Englewood Cliffs, NJ: Educational Technology Publications.

Mayer, R. E. (1996). Learning strategies for making sense out of expository text: The SOI model for guiding three cognitive processes in knowledge construction. *Educational Psychology Review, 8*, 357–371.

Mayer, R. E. (1997). Mulimedia learning: Are we asking the right questions? *Educational Psychologist, 32*, 1–19.

Mayer, R. E. (1998). Cognitive, metacognitive, and motivational aspects of problem solving. *Instructional Science, 26*, 49–63.

Mayer, R. E., & Anderson, A. B. (1991). Animations need narrations: An experimental test of a dual-coding hypothesis. *Journal of Educational Psychology, 83*, 484–490.

Mayer, R. E., & Anderson, A. B. (1992). The instructive animation: Helping students build connections between words and pictures in multimedia learning. *Journal of Educational Psychology, 84*, 444–452.

Mayer, R. E., Bove, W., Bryman, A., Mars, R., & Tapangco, L. (1996). When less is more: Meaningful learning from visual and verbal summaries of science textbook lessons. *Journal of Educational Psychology, 88*, 64–73.

Mayer, R. E., Dyck, J. L., & Cook, L. K. (1984). Techniques that help readers build mental models from scientific text: Definitions pretraining and signaling. *Journal of Educational Psychology, 76*, 1089–1105.

Mayer, R. E., & Gallini, J. (1990). When is an illustration worth ten thousand words? *Journal of Educational Psychology, 82*, 715–727.

Mayer, R. E., & Sims, V. (1994). For whom is a picture worth a thousand words? Extensions of a dual-coding theory of multimedia learning? *Journal of Educational Psychology, 86*, 389–401.

Mayer, R. E., Sims, V., & Tajika, H. (1995). A comparison of how textbooks teach mathematical problem solving in Japan and the United States. *American Educational Research Journal, 32*, 443–460.

Mayer, R. E., Steinhoff, K., Bower, G., & Mars, R. (1995). A generative theory of textbook design: Using annotated illustrations to foster meaningful learning of science text. *Educational Technology Research and Development, 43*, 31–43.

Mayer, R. E., & Wittrock, M. C. (1996). Problem-solving transfer. In D. Berliner & R. Calfee (Eds.), *Handbook of educational psychology* (pp. 47–62). New York: Macmillan.

Pressley, M. (1990). *Cognitive strategy instruction that really improves children's academic performance.* Cambridge, MA: Brookline.

Robins, S., & Mayer, R. E. (1993). Schema training in analogical reasoning. *Journal of Educational Psychology, 85*, 529–538.

Schunk, D. H. (1991). Self-efficacy and academic motivation. *Educational Psychologist, 26*, 207–231.

Slavin, R. (1990). *Cooperative learning.* Englewood Cliffs, NJ: Prentice-Hall.

Sweller, J. (1994). Cognitive load theory, learning difficulty, and instructional design. *Learning and Instruction, 4*, 295–312.

Thorndike, E. L. (1926). *Educational psychology: Vol. 2, The psychology of learning.* Syracuse, NY: Mason.

Weiner, B. (1986). *An attributional theory of motivation and emotion.* New York: Springer-Verlag.

Weinstein, C. E., & Mayer, R. E. (1985). The teaching of learning strategies. In M. C. Wittrock (Ed.), *Handbook of research on teaching, Third edition* (pp. 315–327). New York: Macmillan.

Wertheimer, M. (1945). *Productive thinking.* New York: Harper & Row.

8 Learning by Doing

Roger C. Schank
Tamara R. Berman
Kimberli A. Macpherson
Institute for the Learning Sciences at Northwestern University

Roger C. Schank

Roger C. Schank has been director of the Institute for the Learning Sciences (ILS) at Northwestern University since its founding in 1989. He is a leader in the field of artificial intelligence and multimedia-based interactive training. His work stresses the value of learning from experts, developing skills rather than perfecting routines, and applying the benefits of "just-in-time" training. He holds three faculty appointments at Northwestern University and serves as the Chairman and Chief Technology Officer of Cognitive Arts Corp., formerly Learning Sciences Corporation, a corporate solutions developer born out of the R & D efforts at ILS.

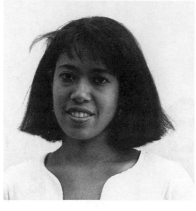

Tamara R. Berman

Kimberli A. Macpherson

Tamara R. Berman is a graduate student in the Learning Sciences PhD program at Northwestern University. She has worked on the design and implementation of several live Goal-based Scenario training courses for working professionals and has done preliminary work on some computer-based training programs. She is currently engaged in dissertation research pertaining to adoption of the Goal-based Scenario training method.

Kimberli A. Macpherson is a graduate student in the Learning Sciences PhD program at Northwestern University. She has worked on the design and implementation of several Goal-based Scenarios (GBS), including computer-based programs for children and live GBS environments for working professionals. Her dissertation research focuses on the methodology of designing live GBSs.

FOREWORD

Goals and preconditions. *The primary goal of this theory is to foster skill development and the learning of factual information in the context of how it will be used. No preconditions are identified.*

Values. *Some of the values upon which this theory is based include:*

- *learning to do (skills), not just to know (factual knowledge),*
- *learning that occurs in the context of a goal that is relevant, meaningful, and interesting to the student,*
- *content knowledge that is learned in the context of relevant tasks closely related to how students will use it outside the learning environment.*

Methods. *Here are the seven essential components of a goal-based scenario:*

1. Goals
- *Process knowledge goals.*
- *Content knowledge goals.*

2. Mission
- *Must be motivational.*
- *Must be somewhat realistic.*

3. Cover story (background story line).
- *Must create the need for the mission.*
- *Must allow enough opportunities to practice the skills & seek the knowledge.*
- *Must be motivating.*

4. Role (who the student will play).
- *Must be one who uses the necessary skills and knowledge.*
- *Must be motivating.*

5. Scenario operations (activities the student does).
- *Must be closely related to both the mission and the goals.*
- *Must have decision points with consequences that become evident.*
  - *The consequences must indicate progress toward completing the mission.*
  - *A negative consequence must be understood as an expectation failure.*
- *Must be plenty of operations for the student to do (to spend most of their time practicing the skills).*
- *Should not require more than what the goals call for.*

6. Resources

- *Must provide the information the students need to succeed in the mission.*

  - *The information must be well organized and readily accessible.*

  - *The information is often best provided in the form of stories. (so knowledge and skills are indexed properly)*

    + *Stories should be understandable as extensions of stories the student knows*

7. Feedback

- *Must be situated, so it is indexed properly as an expectation failure..*

- *Must be just in time, so the student will use it.*

- *Can be given in three ways:*

  - *Consequence of actions*

  - *Coaches*

  - *Domain experts' stories about similar experiences*

Major contribution. *Provides guidelines for all major aspects of project-based learning. Has proven methods developed through formative research.*

—C.M.R.

Learning by Doing

Schools are currently in need of radical change. We exist in a culture in which fact-based knowledge dominates traditional instruction.* People who are good at "knowledge games" like Trivial Pursuit and Jeopardy are considered smart. But, life requires us to *do*, more than it requires us to *know*, in order to function.** It makes more sense to teach students how to perform useful tasks. There is only one effective way to teach someone how to do anything, and that is to let them do it.

Over the years, in our efforts to develop intelligent computers, we have learned much about how human memory works and how people learn. In an effort to em-

---

* This is a feature of the sorting-focused (industrial age) paradigm of education (see chap. 1, pp. 17–19), because it is easier to test objectively.

** In the industrial age, schools didn't need to teach this, because repetitive, assembly-line tasks could be taught in a matter of minutes with on-the-job training.

ploy these lessons and to address the aforementioned problems with traditional learning environments, we developed a structure for teaching and learning called *goal-based scenarios* (GBSs).

A GBS is a learn-by-doing simulation in which students pursue a goal by practicing target skills and using relevant content knowledge to help them achieve their goal. During the simulation, students are provided with coaching just in time for them to use the information. Giving feedback in this manner allows learners to remember what they are taught. GBSs can be either software environments or live role-plays, as long as they contain a rich amount of content, support interesting and complex activities, and are inherently motivating to the student.

In this chapter, we will first discuss problems inherent in traditional instruction. We will then explain our theory of memory and learning, called *case-based reasoning* (CBR), as the basis and support for teaching through goal-based scenarios. Then, we will describe the components of GBS design in more detail. We present GBSs as the ideal method of instruction, appropriate for any subject and any student age, and for both school and business.

THE PROBLEM WITH TRADITIONAL INSTRUCTION AND THE VALUES BEHIND THE GBS METHOD

There are several problems with traditional methods of instruction, which we discuss below. We will then explain how we address these shortcomings within the GBS design. The GBS teaching method is based on specific learning and teaching values that maximize the effectiveness of the GBS learning environment.

The most important problem with traditional teaching methods is that children are not learning skills; teaching is more concentrated on imparting factual knowledge to students. This is evident in the learning goals that are set in school curricula. When school institutions approach us to help them design educational programs, they regularly describe the learning goals in the "know that" format. For instance, a biology department might want students to know that animals have a liver and a spleen. But, unless students know what to do with that knowledge—know why they should care about knowing it—they quickly forget what they were taught.

One of the values the GBS emphasizes is creating a model in which learning goals aim for students to learn "how to" rather than "know that." So, biology students would be better served if they learned how to identify a healthy versus damaged liver in order to diagnose a patient with cirrhosis of the liver. When students learn how, they inevitably learn content knowledge in the service of accomplishing their task. Then, they know why they need to know something, and they know how to use the knowledge (Schank, 1994b).

The second problem is that students are not given the opportunity to pursue new knowledge in the service of achieving intrinsically motivating goals.* In other

---

* Motivation is a common element in the new paradigm of instructional theory.

words, often students need to learn facts, or even skills, for the purpose of finishing a set of homework problems or in order to pass a test. There is nothing about their new knowledge that helps them to achieve a goal that is both relevant and meaningful to them.

The GBS method reflects our theory that students should learn content and skills in order to achieve goals that they find interesting and important* and that relate to the subject matter. For instance, learning that animals have livers, and learning where they are located in order to get a good grade on a test, does not constitute an intrinsically motivating goal. Grades, or even money, are extrinsic motivation (Malone, 1981). On the other hand, if a student needed to learn more about a liver in order to save the life of a sick puppy (assuming the student cares at all about puppies), that would be an intrinsically motivating reason to learn about livers.

A third shortcoming is that children are learning in a decontextualized fashion. Lessons are taught in a way in which use of the knowledge or skills is divorced from how they would be used in real life. Instead, they are contained in textbooks, and they are practiced on paper in preparation for passing exams. The problem is that memory functions in a way that makes it difficult for students to retrieve and use such knowledge.

GBSs emphasize teaching students the desired content knowledge in relevant tasks. The only way we remember what we learned is by having similar experiences that trigger our memories. Taking a test might trigger memories of other tests we have taken. Similarly, diagnosing a problem will trigger memories of other diagnoses we have made. Furthermore, we are more likely to remember our experiences than isolated information. Therefore, it makes sense to teach students by providing them with rich experiences in which they desire to perform skills in order to accomplish motivating goals. The way in which they practice the skills should closely relate to how they will use the skills outside the learning environment.

CASE-BASED REASONING

CBR is our theory of how we remember and how we use our memories in order to solve new problems.** We use CBR regularly in daily life; it constitutes how we learn from the time we are infants through our adulthood. In order to explain how it works, we will give an example of how one might use CBR to learn.

Let us suppose that one wants to learn how to bake chocolate chip cookies. What could baking chocolate chip cookies have to do with learning? When you bake anything, you have an image of how you would like it to turn out. In the end, either it does or does not turn out the way you planned. If it does not, you will have an opportunity to learn what went wrong, so that you might improve upon your baking skills the next time you try. Also, by learning in this manner, you will remember the problems that arose when you baked the first time, so you will know how to improve the

---

* This is related to self-regulated learning (see especially chap. 13 by Corno & Randi).
** Note that this is descriptive theory, not design theory.

second time. You are learning from your prior experiences, or CBR. This form of learning is not only effective in the domain of baking. CBR is an effective way to learn or improve upon any skill. CBR is, generally, how people become experts and how experts often reason about problems in their domains of expertise (Riesbeck & Schank, 1989).

We cannot claim, however, that CBR is the only way people reason. For instance, a problem might be so new and different that you cannot remember any similar prior experiences from which to make an analogy. In such a situation, you will have to begin the reasoning process from first principles. Other times you might simply guess to solve a problem, which is not reasoning at all. Most often, however, we are able to liken our problems to problems we have had in the past, and we are able to use CBR effectively.

The most powerful aspect of CBR is that you are not confined to using memories that are similar according to contextual features, such as baking. You might reason across contexts, where the similarity of the memories is based on themes. For instance, there is a saying which goes, "If at first you don't succeed, try try again." This probably was coined by someone who had many experiences in which he or she failed the first time trying something new, but was successful upon future attempts.

If this is your experience as well, you might have stored some cases from your past in which you failed in some of your first endeavors: the first time you tried a cartwheel, the first time you rode a bicycle, the first time you solved a long division problem, etc. Now you are prepared to reason using those cases to help you. So, you will know that if you are having difficulty baking great cookies, it might be because it is your first time.

Now, notice that the memory of the time you failed to ride a bike well does not seem similar to baking as far as surface features go, but you can draw analogies (or case-based reason) using deeper similarities, such as the theme, "the first time I tend to fail, but later I improve." This will help you to explain why you are a poor baker, and give you the impetus to keep trying. This is how we use CBR across contexts to help solve problems, but in order to keep things simple and clear, we will stick to the baking context as much as possible to explain the learning process.

When we teach we are essentially trying to help novices become experts. This is true for adult training as well as for children in school. When we say "experts," we do not necessarily mean experts in the professional sense. For our purposes, experts are people who can use knowledge and perform skills in a functional manner to achieve their goals.

For instance, in the cookie baking example, as a learner you want to be able to bake good cookies for yourself and perhaps your close friends and family. You may even want to learn something about baking in general. You probably do not intend to become a professional baker for restaurants and bakeries; you just want to be able to bake on occasion. On the other hand, if you wanted to learn to be a professional baker, you would need to learn many more elements of baking. Your goal would be different, so what you would learn would be different. The learning process, however, remains the same. That is, you need to learn by baking, rather than by being told about baking.

So, what constitutes an expert? In terms of CBR, experts are those who have in their minds, rich "libraries" of memories relevant to the domains within which they are working. In other words, experts have lots of experience in their areas of expertise. The expert can retrieve just the right memory, or case, when it is needed to help solve a new problem.

A case is a memory of a particular instance of something that happened. For example, although you are unfamiliar with baking cookies, you may have baked many cakes in your life. All of the times that you baked cakes comprise a part of your case library that pertains to baking. Within that, there is a subsection that holds memories pertaining to cakes. For instance, perhaps there was one time that you put too much flour in your cake batter, and the cake was too dense and heavy. That memory alone is one case. If you have many such memories, and you have learned from lots of different kinds of mistakes, you probably bake pretty good cakes by now, and you are an expert (Schank, 1982).

As we mentioned, experts must have many experiences in their domains of expertise. These collections of experiences become the mental case libraries from which they will retrieve important memories to help them solve new problems. For instance, experiences in cake baking will also help you in baking cookies. When you see that you must add flour to your cookie batter, you are likely to remember that adding more flour than called for could result in overly dense cookies. Therefore, the lessons we learn from one case can be transferred to new cases, as long as they are closely related.

Experts must be able to organize their experiences such that they know where they can find relevant information when needed. We call this *indexing*. In order to store and retrieve memories in a useful way, we must know, though not necessarily on a conscious level, how our experiences are relevant to us right when we have the experience.

Using the library metaphor, indexing consists of "labeling" an experience with the appropriate "title" and then "filing" it in the right place in memory. For example, we should store all cooking memories as a group. Within this group, there should be a section designated for baking memories. Within the baking group, we should have a section all about cakes, and so on. Finally, in order for the memory to really be useful, it must be retrieved at the right time. There are multiple ways that we index our experiences. We use sights, sounds, smells, occurrences, etc. to categorize that which we see and do. We do not choose how we will index; it is a nonconscious[1] process.

---

[1]The term "nonconscious knowledge" refers to knowledge that lies at the heart of what we know about everything. Experts in a subject are not necessarily conscious of what they know about that subject. Similarly, we do not consciously know just how we perform basic mental processes (i. e., how we construct a sentence or how we understand one).

Our memories are retrieved by cues that our current experience provides. Often these cues are related to the context of the experience, the goal of the experience, or the lesson learned from the experience (Schank, 1982). So, when you begin to bake your first cookies, cues such as the experience of taking out the ingredients you intend to use, glancing at the recipe, and your goal of baking good cookies help you to access your general memory structure relating to baking in general, and it might trigger your specific memory of the time that you put too much flour into your cake.

When we learn a scientific fact through traditional educational methods and then use it on a multiple choice test with the goal of passing, we index the information with other memories about school tests, and perhaps with the subcategory of science tests. What helps us to achieve our goal of passing is studying, flash cards, and whatever other tricks we use. The cues for retrieval of the science memory are organized around the test-taking procedure. So, the structure of tests and memories of prior tests lead us to develop study habits. The content of the test itself, however, does not have relevance to a goal we care to achieve. As far as we know, we will never need to know it again, so we do not index it in a way that will allow us to retrieve it.

On the other hand, if we need the content to help us solve an interesting problem, similar problems would be more likely to cue our memories to retrieve the information. For instance, imagine this is a biology class, and we are playing the role of a doctor. We might be presented with a patient who comes to visit us complaining of fever and exhaustion over a long period of time. We are told to draw some blood to examine and determine the cause of the person's illness. Now, when we learn about different types of blood cells and how certain configurations are associated with certain diseases, we will index the content with our desire to cure our patient. We will also be likely to remember the types of illnesses associated with different blood cell problems. So, in the future, when issues pertaining to illnesses or blood cells arise, we are likely to access the case of our ill patient, and we will remember more about the relevant content.

That is why it is so important in GBS design to create a motivating and sensible context in which the learner will practice the target skills. The role and the goal given to learners in the GBS aid their understanding of the relevance of the skill they are learning.* This is where traditional forms of teaching fail. Commonly, learners do not understand the relevance of what they learn, and the lessons do not apply to an intrinsically motivating goal. The effect of these shortcomings is that the learners do not index the lessons learned effectively, and thus cannot retrieve them when they need them.

In order to better explain the steps that go into building well-indexed case libraries that are organized for appropriate retrieval, we shall walk through the process of learning to make good chocolate chip cookies for the first time. In the

---

* This is providing a descriptive-theory rationale for a design-theory guideline (give an appropriate role and goal to learners).

following example, we will discuss the elements that are involved in case-based reasoning and learning, including: goals, plans, expectations, expectation failures, and explanations.

Goals, Plans, and Expectations

Every endeavor begins with a *goal*, and learning results from what happens on the way to achieving our goals. You already know that your goal is to make delicious cookies. With this goal in mind, you will likely develop some *expectations*.* Expectations are a necessary part of our understanding of the world around us. We are unlikely to know if cookies are good or bad if we have no idea what is standard. As we grow and learn, we develop expectations about nearly everything. Sometimes they turn out to be correct, and sometimes they do not. In this case, your expectation might be that you will make great cookies if you follow the recipe.

How do you go about achieving this goal? You will have to make a *plan* to achieve your goal. But do you really have to learn how to make this plan from scratch? Probably not. Often, when you have a goal you wish to achieve, you will be able to use an old plan and adapt it to accommodate a variation of an old goal. In this case you had a goal in the past of baking cakes. Your old plan (the means by which you achieved your goal in the past) was to consult a cake recipe and follow it fairly accurately, making some allowances to accommodate your particular tastes. Note that this plan is a generalization of the many memories of baking you have stored. Can you use the exact same plan to make chocolate chip cookies? The ingredients are different, and some of the steps involved are different, but certainly many things are the same. You should be able to adapt your old, generalized plan to suit the specific needs of your new plan. It is in the adaptation process that learning will occur.

According to the recipe, when you bake chocolate chip cookies you first cream together the butter, sugar, and vanilla, and then you add eggs. In a separate bowl you mix the dry ingredients, like flour, baking soda, and salt. Finally, you blend the contents of both bowls together. Perhaps this time, however, you only have one clean mixing bowl to use for the batter. So, "no big deal," you figure. You just add all of the ingredients to one bowl and blend them all at once. The consistency of the dough does not appear to be quite right, but you put the cookie dough into appropriate sized balls on a baking sheet, and bake as usual. When the timer rings, you open the oven to find very flat, unappealing cookies. They quickly become too crunchy. No one will be impressed by these cookies, especially you. What might you learn from this experience?

---

* This section is still descriptive theory, describing natural human behavior. At best, it would be design theory for human performance, not for instruction. Clearly, it is also probabilistic rather than deterministic theory (see chap. 1, p. 11).

Expectation Failure

This is an important part of the learning process. You had an expectation that when your cookies were finished baking, they would look and taste a certain way. Now you see that they did not turn out as planned. We call this an *expectation failure*. You made a mistake, and now you have the chance to learn from it. If you really do not care about the cookies and you never plan to make them again, it is highly possible that you will not learn anything at all from your mistake. Remember the scientific content that you learned for the test? This is the same thing. If you do not care about the information and you do not know what you need it for, you are likely to forget it altogether. Information gained from an expectation failure must be indexed properly if it is to be used again. If, on the other hand, your mouth still waters at the very suggestion of cookies and milk, or you made the cookies as an expression of love and gratitude to your best friend, or you felt some amount of shame in your culinary failure, you are likely to demand an *explanation* for your flat cookies. Now, you are in prime condition for learning.

Explanations

Once you experience an expectation failure, explanations become important. They form the lesson that you learn from the expectation failure. When something does not happen the way you planned, you need to figure out why that is. The reason will help you to abstract a lesson that you can apply to your expectations in the future. For instance, from the case above, you might review the recipe and think back to what you did that did not match the recipe's requirements. Perhaps you see that you added less sugar, but you generally add less sugar to recipes, which never affects the rising of what you bake. Everything else seems normal, except that you mixed the recipe in only one bowl!

Now you must construct an explanation for why that would cause a problem. Perhaps the flour and baking soda did not get distributed evenly, and maybe most of the baking soda did not get mixed in well with the moist parts of the batter. Now that you have an explanation for the failure, you will connect your explanation to your expectation failure when you index the memory in your case library. So, if you bake again, you will assume that you have to mix things in separate bowls if so specified in the recipe. Otherwise the consistency could come out all wrong. The explanation that you indexed with the failure will help you to do the right thing the next time. This type of learning is also flexible, so you can adapt it to new situations. You probably do not think separate bowls only matter for cookies; you assume that rule is important no matter what you bake. That means that you can achieve "transfer" of your knowledge to other problems.

When you retrieve a case to help you solve new problems, you are using CBR. This is how we learn from experience. We cannot really learn how to do things when we are just being told what we should know. We must learn during our attempts to achieve our goals. When we make mistakes we learn how to prevent them in the future. Or perhaps, before we make a mistake, we ask important questions just in time to prevent us from making the mistake. We remember what we learned because the content is important to us in the service of achieving our goals. The most memorable way to learn is through experience: learning by doing.

TEACHING

Now that we have traced how we learn through our experiences, the next question becomes how we teach someone else.* Unfortunately, according to our theory of memory and learning, you cannot really teach anyone anything unless they are ready to receive the new information. Sometimes people just want to know something because they are curious. If people are driven by their own internal motivations, they are already prepared to learn. Generally, teachers are not so fortunate with the majority of their students.

Teachers have to create motivation and situate students such that they become ready to learn. As we discussed previously, difficulty in achieving a goal is the best primer for our minds to assimilate new information. Therefore, the best way to teach is to place students in situations in which the goals they wish to achieve require the acquisition of the knowledge and skills you wish to impart. This is the essence of the GBS.

GBS Design

At the beginning of this chapter we presented the basic outline of a GBS. Now we will go into further detail to explain the elements that comprise a GBS. In order to do so, we will examine an existing GBS called "Advise the President" (Schank & Korcuska, 1996). The Institute for the Learning Sciences (ILS) created this computer-based GBS in which the student is asked to prepare a report to help the President decide what to do about a civil war in a foreign country called Krasnovia. The GBS is structured so that the student uses a menu system to choose an argument to make, how strong to make it, and upon which evidence or case to base it. Because the student constructs a report based upon the choices within the menu system, the program "knows" how and about what to critique and evaluate the student. The program also contains a video database through which it disseminates relevant historical cases (e.g., video clips of newscasts of historical events) and critiques by advisors and domain experts (e.g., a video clip of a role play advisor criticizing the student for what she has failed to observe). The story of "Advise the President" goes as follows.

---

* This is a great cue for the transition from descriptive (learning) theory to design (instructional) theory.

It is the middle of the night and you are sound asleep. Suddenly the telephone loudly rings and awakens you. You answer it to find you are speaking with the top assistant to the President of the United States. She anxiously implores you to turn on CNN, as they are reporting on a crisis that requires your immediate attention. You are the President's advisor and he needs to meet with you as soon as you hear the full report. There will be a limo waiting outside your door to take you to the White House. You turn on your television and learn that one side of an island called Krasnovia invaded the other side and plans to overthrow the government and control power. You leave to discuss the crisis with the President. In the oval office, the President explains that he is holding a press conference later in the day. By that time he needs your recommendation as to if and how the United States should intervene. He would like you to recommend a strategy in a clear report that you will present to him. Your suggestions must be based on evidence that you collect by getting information from experts.

Now that you know the general premise, we will break down the components that comprise the goal-based scenario. There are seven essential components of a GBS: the *learning goals*, the *mission*, the *cover story*, the *role*, the *scenario operations*, the *resources*, and the *feedback*, including coaches and experts (Schank, R., Fano, A., Jona, M., & Bell, B., 1993). We will examine them from the perspective that you are the educator who intends to teach something to your students. If you plan to design your own GBS, you need to consider each component, although not necessarily in the order listed. Keep in mind that your GBSs do not need to be made into computer programs. We will discuss live GBSs at the end of this chapter.

1. The Learning Goals

We begin GBS design with a very clear idea of what we want our students to learn. Generally, the learning goals fall under two different categories: process knowledge and content knowledge. Process knowledge is the knowledge of how to practice skills that contribute to goal achievement, while content knowledge is the information that achievement of a goal requires.*

The design of the "Advise the President" GBS appeals to both process and content knowledge. In terms of process knowledge, the designers' goal was to teach students to make good arguments by backing up claims with evidence obtained through research. Therefore, in order to achieve success in this design, the student has to practice the aforementioned skills satisfactorily. As far as content knowledge, "Advise the President" requires students to learn factual, historical, and strategic information pertaining to international interference in civil wars. This is the information that serves as the evidence the student provides to the President to support or speak against a claim. In constructing this GBS, the designers began their

---

* Is this first element of a GBS a part of an instructional theory or a part of the ISD process? The statement, "We begin GBS design with... " seems to indicate it is ISD process. To be a part of instructional theory, it would need to emphasize presenting the learning goals to the learner. That would make it a part of the instructional process, rather than a part of the ISD process. From statements elsewhere, I believe the authors intended this as an element in the instructional process and therefore as a part of their instructional theory. But it also seems to be part of their ISD process.

approach by focusing in on the skill set they wanted students to practice, as well as the content knowledge they wanted students to find.

2. The Mission

As we discussed previously, learning begins with a goal and a plan. Therefore, the first step in creating a GBS is determining a goal or mission that will be motivational for the student to pursue.* With this in mind, you should choose a goal that you know the student will relate to, either in that it is something they would already like to do or because it is something that she would think was fun to do upon suggestion. It needs to be somewhat realistic in nature, though.** If it is a wild idea, like "You are E.T. and you need to figure out a way to phone home," the student will not readily understand the real-life application of the skills he or she is practicing. Rather, it should take the form of a goal that a real person would plausibly need to achieve for an important reason. The mission should also be something that requires the skills and knowledge that you wish to impart, in order to achieve the goal successfully.

In "Advise the President," the mission is for the student to prepare a report to present to the President of the United States, as a recommendation for the best strategic approach to resolving a crisis in a foreign country. This is accomplished by gathering information that supports conflicting opinions, and finally making a recommendation based on the information collected.

3. The Cover Story

The cover story is the background story line that creates the need for the mission to be accomplished. When deciding upon a cover story, the most important thing to consider is whether the story will allow enough opportunities for the student to practice the skills and seek the knowledge you wish to teach. At the same time, like the mission, the cover story should be interesting and motivating to the student.

A common problem for new designers is that they will choose a potentially interesting domain in which to situate their mission and cover story, but the skill set they want to teach only occurs during the boring elements of operating in such a domain. Therefore, the student may become quickly unmotivated to complete the task. For instance, if you think flying is a fun activity and students would want to learn in such an environment, you had better want to teach skills and content that are necessary while in flight, so that the student can have the reward of seeing the sky and experiencing the elements of flight that are exciting. If the student is

---

* Again, the authors mention "the first step in creating a GBS... ," but I think they are also calling for presenting the mission to the learner. Also, note the difference between the term "goal" as used in this sentence and the term "learning goals" as used in the previous section. This is a performance goal, as opposed to a learning goal.

** Here (and in subsequent methods) we find criteria being offered for the design of the method (the mission in this case). Is this instructional theory or ISD process? The criteria are guidelines that present a fuzzy image as to what the instruction should be like, so they are part of an instructional theory.

going to practice skills that more often take place at the airport, or in the control tower, you will be challenged to find a compelling cover story that will excite the student enough to care about learning the skills so he or she can successfully complete the mission.

In "Advise the President," the cover story is a scenario in which a country named Krasnovia breaks out into a civil war. The President of the United States needs to figure out what role the United States should play regarding the crisis, so he asks his aid (the student) to advise him with a well-supported report. This cover story serves as a channel through which the student is required to practice the skills and learn the content that comprise the learning goals of the designers. In addition, the cover story itself is a realistic and intense story that is motivating to many potential students. The relevance and importance of the issue draws the student in, and provides the basis for him or her to desire to take on the role presented and to accomplish the goal given.

4. The Role

The role defines who the student will play within the cover story. When defining the student's role, it is important to think about what role is the best in the scenario to practice the necessary skills. For example, the ILS developed a software GBS for the Museum of Science and Industry. The museum wanted to teach users about genes using the example of the illness, sickle cell anemia. Their initial idea was for the student to play the role of a patient who wanted to know if he or she had sickle cell anemia. The problem is that patients do not necessarily need to understand how their illnesses function or how they are transferred. They only need to be diagnosed and to learn to care for themselves. ILS decided that a better role for the user would be that of a counselor whom potential parents would consult in order to decide whether or not they should give birth. In that role, the user would need to understand what put a couple at risk for transferring the sickle cell gene to a fetus. Students would have a reason to learn about the difference between dominant and recessive genes and the transfer of traits to the next generation.

The other important element of the role is that it be truly motivating to a student. As we mentioned earlier, the role should be somewhat realistic and exciting. In "Advise the President," the role of the student is to serve as an advisor to the President of the United States, and to play a major role in helping the President to choose an appropriate military strategy for an international crisis. This is clearly a realistic role in a high-profile case, and it is one that is familiar to all American citizens. It does not matter that the student would not be likely to be in that position in the near future, only that someday, theoretically, he or she could.

5. The Scenario Operations

The scenario operations comprise all of the activities the student does in order to work toward the mission goal. In "Advise the President," some scenario operations are: asking experts for opinions on topics relevant to completing the report, compiling information for future reference, making claims about strategies, and backing up claims with selections from the information the student compiled. Scenario operations should be closely related to both the mission and the learning goals. In the example scenario, the student performs actions that apply to the scenario goals: to make a report that is backed by evidence which support the claims within the report. In addition, the student practices skills such as weighing opposing viewpoints and supporting claims with evidence. These comprise the learning goals.

The scenario operations should also be constructed such that they have consequences that become evident at various points throughout the student interaction.* Generally, that means that there are decision points that arise periodically during the role-play. The effects of the decisions that are made signify success or failure of progress toward successful completion of the mission. If the student is successful, presumably he or she gained the needed information through the avenues provided in the GBS, or the required skills were practiced properly. If information was not clearly understood, or the skill was not mastered, the GBS should provide a negative consequence that the student will understand as an expectation failure. This, as we discussed above, will prime the student to be ready to learn how to accomplish his or her goal more successfully, and thus how to practice the target skill better or learn more content.

A note about complexity: scenario operations are the part of the GBS in which the student participates in his or her own learning. It is important that, within the GBS, little time be spent talking to the student about the scenario, and much more time be spent with the student practicing the skills and learning the information that comprise the learning goals. With this in mind, there must be plenty of operations for the student to do in order to achieve the mission goal, and the scenario must be rich with information to manipulate. On the other hand, students should not need to do more than is necessary for the learning goals to be addressed.

For example, if you want to teach a student to practice reasoning about factors that affect the environment, you might put the student in the role of a scientist who is attempting to propose changes that need to occur in order to save an area of swamp lands. Presumably, in reality, there would be a variety of elements that should be tracked over a number of years, using complex measuring procedures. In this case, however, we only care that the student be able to see how a change in one element effects change in other elements. Therefore, it is not necessary that the student learn to do the real procedures that are used to take the measurements, only that the results of the measurements be available for interpretation. If the student should become interested and invested in the cover story and how his or her role would be accomplished in real life, he or she could learn that information outside the GBS environment. Certainly, an educator should encourage such independent investigation.

---

* Scenario operations should "have consequences." This could be viewed as one of the criteria for the design of scenario operations, or it could be viewed as a more detailed part of the scenario operations (see chap. 1, p. 10). Either way, they are submethods—more detailed guidelines for the instruction.

6. Resources

Resources provide the information the students need to achieve the goal of the mission. There must be plenty of readily accessible and well-organized information for the student to use to help him or her complete the mission successfully. We are not trying to trick students into failing. Rather, we always allow students to ask for information to help them make well-informed decisions. It is only when the student fails to find the pertinent information, and impatiently leaps to making quick decisions, that he or she fails and requires remediation.

Generally, we provide information to the students in the form of stories.* The reason for this brings us back to our discussion of memory and learning. Remember that we form cases via numerous experiences. The memories that contribute to our library of cases are of specific events in the form of stories. When there is a story that looks different from the stories we have experienced in the past, we adjust our memory structures to account for the new memory and to learn a lesson from the explanation we used to make sense of it. Similarly, when we hear the stories of others, we listen to them in the context of our own experiences, and we index them as expectation failures of our own. (Schank, 1994a)

With this in mind, it follows that the best way to convey information is not to teach decontextualized facts, but rather to embed lessons in stories that the learner can understand as an extension of the stories he or she already knows. So, the resources we provide are usually experts telling stories about the information the student needs.

In "Advise the President," the user has access to resources such as expert political analysts who tell stories about how military strategies were applied to political violence in the past. The student listens to the stories and relates them to the current story regarding the United States and Krasnovia. The student will also listen to the stories and use them to better understand his or her own potential claims, based on the stories heard earlier in the GBS. So, for instance, the student may begin to form an opinion (based on a story he or she hears) about something that happened in Vietnam. Then, another story heard about World War II may conflict with the first story, and thus should cause an expectation failure about the initial opinion. The student will now adjust the earlier opinion (understanding of Krasnovia situation and what should be done about it) based on a new story about a strategy used at a different time. Later, when the student thinks about strategies, he or she will remember the story heard about Vietnam, rather than having difficulty remembering decontextualized information about strategies in general.

7. Feedback

Earlier, we discussed expectation failure as information that must be properly indexed in order to be retrieved and used again in the right context. GBSs provide

---

* This seems like a kind of resources (breaking the method into kinds). It would be nice if guidance were offered as to when to use the story form versus other forms of resources, but unfortunately space limitations may have precluded this. Nevertheless, it is such situationalities that elevate this from being an instructional model to being an instructional theory.

feedback in a way that allows learners to properly index information as it is given. It is situated in an appropriate context and provided just in time for the student to use. Feedback is presented when students are primed to learn the target domain content and skills.

The feedback can be given in any of three ways.* The first is through the consequence of actions. That is, when a student is performing a task in a GBS environment and makes a mistake in the process, the GBS can simulate negative consequences as a direct result of the mistake. Another method of feedback is through coaches. As a student performs tasks within a GBS, an online coach following his or her progress can offer advice when needed, providing a just-in-time source to scaffold the student through tasks. Finally, the GBS can offer feedback through domain experts who tell stories that pertain to similar experiences. The expert relays a story and the lesson learned from that story, and students can index the experience almost as if they went through it themselves.

In "Advise the President," the student might hear a story about how the United States used force to stop Hitler's armies in World War II. The student then could use this evidence to support the argument that force is a good way to stop the violence in Krasnovia. However, if the student submits this recommendation to the President, he or she will receive immediate feedback from one of the Presidential advisors criticizing the student for not considering the fact that the two groups in conflict are on an island and that such force as the United States used against Hitler's armies is not necessary in this case, since Hitler's armies were much larger and more aggressive, posing a greater threat to surrounding nations. It is highly unlikely that the aggression from either side of this nation will spread beyond the small island that they inhabit.

Now, the student is primed to learn relevant content and skills. In order to successfully complete the scenario, the student will need to know about strategies utilized to resolve conflicts between smaller armies. He or she will also learn to better scrutinize evidence, to consider varied angles and opposing points of view, and to successfully back up claims and support an argument.

The structure of GBSs provides the necessary constraints to combat problems with traditional instruction, as they leverage off what we know about human mem-

---

* This is clearly a case of breaking the method into kinds, but again no situationalities are offered for helping to decide when to use each kind. This raises the issue of how much detail should a theory provide, and does a theory insult the intelligence of teachers by trying to tell them what to do? Pogrow (1996) states:

> The performing arts have survived and flourished because they have been able to systematize the delivery of highly creative performances by striking an appropriate balance between directive components—e.g., scripts and choreography—and individual interpretation. The same thing can be done in education. The success of HOTS and other creative programs, such as *Reading Recovery* and *Junior Great Books*, suggests that it is possible to develop programs that combine the best of educational research and pedagogy into specified systems that consistently generate high levels of learning and also stimulate highly creative forms of interaction between students and teachers on a large scale (p. 660). (Full reference for Pogrow is in chapter 1.)

But perhaps different audiences of teachers under different circumstances would benefit from different levels of detail.

ory and learning. Students engage in tasks that allow them to practice important skills they can transfer to contexts outside the learning environment. They also learn valuable content that is situated to serve their needs as they work to accomplish their goals.

The Live GBS

Of course, computer-based GBSs are not the only type of simulation that can teach target skills. We also use scripted role-playing simulations or "live" GBSs to teach target skills that are best learned through real human interaction or group interactions.

Some of the most important skills we must learn to function successfully in society are: communications, human relations, and reasoning. As with other target skills, we often learn to communicate, get along with others, and solve problems through our day-to-day interactions with others. We often learn these lessons implicitly when they are done in the service of accomplishing a goal. Since, in our everyday lives, we are constantly practicing, refining, and discovering more about these skills through real human interaction, as teachers we must provide rich, realistic human interaction to teach the skills. There are times when computer technology cannot handle such a demand. In these cases, the most effective way to structure such learning is through "live" GBSs.

These aforementioned skills do not necessarily have to be taught explicitly as part of the scenario; rather, the students can learn them implicitly as they work within the GBS. For example, if students collaborate in a "live" GBS environment, communications and human relations issues inherent to working in groups tend to come up naturally, forcing students to practice these skills.* Similarly, if the scenario contains any unresolved problems or issues, the student will have to exercise reasoning strategies. The nature of the GBS environment allows the students to experience the processes in a realistic way, enabling them to learn what we want them to learn implicitly. Also, because it is a simulation, we can provide coaches to observe student practice and interrupt the process to give instruction just in time.

To illustrate this approach, we will describe an example of a live GBS designed for a midsized business consulting firm that successfully taught all levels of consultants how to analyze business processes and propose reengineering plans for clients. The live GBS course was structured around the case of a fictional client company. Trainees worked together in teams representative of those in their real field practice. Each team worked with client staff, role-played by course designers and personnel from the consulting firm. There were communications and team dynamics coaches on hand to provide guidance and feedback and course operators who worked behind the scenes, monitoring activities and making sure the simulation ran smoothly and realistically.

---

* This emphasis on collaborative skills is dealt with similarly by other theories in the new paradigm, such as chapter 11 by Nelson and chapter 12 by Bielaczyc and Collins.

The course design process contained five steps,* similar to those for a computer-based GBS. The first was to define the learning goals to be taught in the course. We built a model of typical tasks that consultants performed, and we identified four target areas for the training course: domain content (information about the field in which trainees would work), communication (e.g., interviewing and presentation skills), analytical skills (i.e., quantitative business analyses), and technical skills (e.g., software applications). Second, we sought a prototypical real-world case, in which problem solving would require use of the knowledge listed above. We used this case as a base upon which to build our fictitious case. In the third step, we analyzed the case for those issues that arose in reality which would require our students to use the target knowledge and skills.

The fourth step in the methodology was to establish which activities we would require our trainees to do so that they would encounter the target knowledge and skills. For instance, in the real-world case, the consultants had to interview members of the client company to find out about particular problems. We had the choice to give the trainees that information, or to make them conduct similar interviews with role-players to find it out for themselves. We decided that interviewing skills were important to teach in this context, so we planned to have interviewing activities.

Coaches and expert consultants supervised each set of skills the trainees practiced in context. So, when the consultants performed an interview, a communications coach was there to give them feedback on what they did well, and in which areas they could improve. When they gave presentations (another scheduled activity), role-play executives who were experts in the field gave them feedback both in character and, later, out of character. This allowed them to experience "real-world" reactions, as well as explicit instruction from a single activity.

What comes from this are memorable cases that the trainee can index appropriately and apply to future work in the field. In addition, we were able to structure the environment such that trainee assessment was conducted privately, subjectively, and qualitatively, rather than as a public, quantitative measure. The final step in the design was to build an overall infrastructure that supported the pedagogical objectives and enriched the scenario to create a more authentic environment. Such elements included the hierarchical team composition; role-play clients, course staff, scripts for role-players, and data resources for the consultants, as well as support for the culminating activities the trainees performed.

Overall, the trainees found the course to be authentic and engaging. Trainees that were new to consulting expressed the value of practicing basic skills in a realistic, yet safe, context. The more experienced trainees were very pleased by the complexity of the course, as it matched their real-world experience (Macpherson, Berman, & Joseph, 1996). Live GBSs are a great way for teachers to use the GBS methodology without any use of computers.

---

* Although the surface focus is on the ISD process here again, try to look for the instructional methods, which give you an image of what the instruction should be like.

CONCLUSION

In this chapter, we explained how an effective learning environment is one that teaches students to think like "experts" do. That is, experts have had many experiences in their areas of expertise. They use their mental libraries of experience-based cases to retrieve examples that help them solve problems. GBS environments enable students to build case libraries by providing rich experiences through which the students can learn. The GBS framework is geared to leverage off of how people remember.

One can maximize the effectiveness of GBS learning environments when the domain and scenario are interesting to the student. When students are pursuing goals in a topic that they care about, they are motivated to pay attention to the information that is required to accomplish that goal. They are unlikely to forget what they learn, because the lessons will be indexed with other memories of experiences in the domain. When they work within the domain again, they are likely to retrieve the relevant memories. GBSs allow students to learn to do target skills by doing them. Each experience provided within the GBS environment helps the learner to build a domain-relevant case library, complete with many lessons learned. This is how novices become experts.

REFERENCES

Macpherson K., Berman, T., & Joseph, D., (1996) Cases to courses: Mentored case-base training courses, In *International conference on the learning sciences: Conference proceedings (1996);* (pp. 211–218). Charlottesville, VA: Association for the Advancement of Computing in Education.

Malone, T. W. (1981). Toward a theory of intrinsically motivating instruction. *Cognitive Science, 4,* 333–369.

Riesbeck, C., & Schank R. (1989). *Inside case-based reasoning.* Hillsdale, NJ: Lawrence Erlbaum Associates.

Schank, R. (1982). *Dynamic memory.* New York: Cambridge University Press.

Schank, R., Fano, A., Jona, M., & Bell, B. (1993). *The design of goal-based scenarios.* Evanston, IL: Northwestern University Press.

Schank, R. (1994a). *Tell me a story.* Evanston, IL: Northwestern University Press.

Schank, R. (1994b). *What we learn when we learn by doing.* Evanston, IL: Northwestern University Press.

Schank, R., & Korcuska, M. (1996). *Eight goal-based scenario tools.* Evanston, IL: Northwestern University Press.

9 Toward the Development of Flexibly Adaptive Instructional Designs

Daniel L. Schwartz
Xiaodong Lin
Sean Brophy
John D. Bransford
Learning Technology Center, Vanderbilt University

Daniel L. Schwartz

Xiaodong Lin

Daniel L. Schwartz is an assistant professor of Psychology and Human Development at Vanderbilt University and a member of the Learning Technology Center at Peabody College. He received an MA in Computers and Education and a PhD in Human Cognition and Learning from Teachers College, Columbia University. He examines the nonverbal mental models and the social interactions that support more formal and verbal understanding. He is currently designing and investigating instructional methods for creating tighter links between intuitive, symbolic, and theoretical understanding.

Xiaodong Lin is an assistant professor of Education and Technology at Peabody College, Vanderbilt University and a member of the Learning Technology Center. She examines issues related to designing classroom learning activities and evaluating their impact on students' ability to understand and problem solve in complex subject domains. She is currently investigating how to design technology-rich environments that make within- and cross-cultural wisdom accessible to both teachers and students in a way that supports self-assessment and domain learning.

Sean Brophy

John D. Bransford

Sean Brophy has a background in engineering, computer science, and education. He completed a masters in computer science specializing in artificial intelligence. He recently completed his PhD at Vanderbilt. He has developed various computer-based tools to foster young children's literacy skills, support problem solving, and author instructional materials. Currently, he is working for the Center for Innovative Learning Technologies, exploring methods of assessment using technology, including the use of simulations to help students reflect on their understanding.

John D. Bransford is Centennial Professor of Psychology and Education and Co-Director, Learning Technology Center at Vanderbilt University. Author of seven books and hundreds of articles and presentations, Bransford is an internationally renowned scholar in cognition and technology. He and his colleagues have developed and tested innovative computer, videodisc, CD-ROM and Internet programs, including the *Jasper Woodbury Problem Solving Series in Mathematics*, the *Scientists in Action Series,* and the *Little Planet Literacy Series.* The programs have received many awards.

FOREWORD

Goals and preconditions. *The primary goal of this theory is to teach a deep understanding of disciplines—while simultaneously fostering the skills of problem solving, collaboration, and communication—through the use of problem-based learning, followed by more open-ended project-based learning. No preconditions are identified for use of the theory.*

Values. *Some of the values on which this theory is based include:*

- *Helping learners and teachers to understand the point of an instructional design feature to facilitate effective adaptation of the instruction.*
- *Customizing instruction based on learners' initial domain knowledge.*
- *Instruction that provides several models for how to think about things.*
- *Methods used by teachers and learners that are constrained enough to be consistent with important principles of learning and instruction, but that are also flexible enough for teachers to be creative in tailoring instruction to their own strengths and their learners' and community's needs.*
- *Increasing learners' tolerance for ambiguity.*
- *Instruction that is anchored in meaningful, if not authentic, tasks.*
- *Goal setting, student-directed exploration, and revision in learning and instruction.*
- *Motivating learners by stimulating curiosity and aspirations, and motivating them to revise and improve their work.*
- *Helping students to see how much they have learned and to reflect on their growth.*
- *Methods that evolve over time.*
- *Instructional methods that are based on learning functions served, rather than on media utilized.*
- *Each team of students developing a shared, initial mental model of what they are trying to learn about.*
- *Students making their own thinking explicit.*
- *Instructional design as a collaborative effort involving all stakeholders.*

Methods. *These are the major methods this theory offers:*

1. ***Look Ahead and Reflect Back Binoculars***
   - *Provides an understanding of the goals, context, and challenges they will face.*
   - *Provides an opportunity to try it right now (pretest).*
   - *Provides a benchmark for reflection and self-assessment.*
   - *Consists of a motivational series of images, narrative, and questions to be answered.*
   - *Helps students represent a specific problem as an example of a larger set of issues.*

———— *Beginning of inquiry cycle* ————

2. *The initial challenge (beginning of the first inquiry cycle)*
   * *Helps students develop a shared, initial mental model of what's to be learned.*
   * *Challenge selection: Motivating/interesting, invites student-generated ideas.*

3. *Generate ideas (about issues and answers)*
   * *Students store them in an electronic notebook.*
   * *Use a classroom notebook as a focal point for discussion.*
   Purposes:
   * *Helps students make their own thinking explicit.*
   * *Helps students see what other students are thinking.*
   * *Encourages sharing of ideas in a class.*
   * *Helps teacher assess current state of student knowledge.*
   * *Provides students with a baseline to more easily see how much they learn.*

4. *Multiple perspectives (Present models representing ...)*
   * *Provide a way to introduce students to vocabulary and perspectives of experts.*
   * *Allow students to compare their ideas to experts' ideas.*
   * *Provide guidance on what students need to learn about.*
   * *Provide expertise, guidance, models of social practice in the domain.*
   * *Provide realistic standards of performance.*
   * *Indicate that multiple perspectives exist in the domain.*

5. *Research and revise (to help students explore a challenge)*
   * *Consult resources.*
   * *Collaborate with other students.*
   * *Listen to "just-in-time" lectures.*
   * *Complete skill-building lessons.*
   * *Look at legacies left by other students.*
   * *Conduct simulations and hands-on experiments.*
   * *Most resources are outside the STAR shell.*

6. *Test your mettle (formative assessment)*
   * *When students feel ready for it.*
   * *Wide variety of forms.*
     - *Multiple-choice tests, essays, opportunity to test their designs, etc.*
   * *Feedback suggests which resources to consult to reach target level of understanding.*
     - *Check-list to evaluate their own essays and direct students to sections of Research & Revise.*
   * *Feedback is motivational.*

7. Go public

Two ways:
- *Present their best solutions (electronic posting, multimedia presentation, oral presentation).*
- *Leave a Legacy of tips and ideas for future students (new multiple perspectives, resources, test your mettles).*

Criteria:
- *Makes their thinking visible.*
- *Helps students learn to assess others and themselves.*
- *Helps set standards for achievement.*
- *Helps students learn from each other.*
- *Motivates students to do well (high stakes).*

Guidelines:
- *Help students understand why going public is valuable to them.*
- *Have students reflect on the entire inquiry cycle.*

——— *End of inquiry cycle* ———

8. Progressive deepening
- *Thematically related cycles of challenges that build on each other.*
- *Build to a more formal and general level of understanding (of big ideas).*
- *Problem-based (decision) challenges before project-based (design) challenges.*

9. General reflection and decisions about legacies
- *At the end of the third cycle.*
   - *Return to the Look Ahead & Reflect Back to see how much they hav learned.*
   - *Especially important for situations that were confusing or frustrating.*
   - *Shows the payoff of perseverance.*
   - *Focuses on process and content learnings.*
   - *Helps them decide what legacies will be most useful for others.*
   - *Make a CD that contains their solutions and legacies, provides a review.*
- *Teachers should also leave legacies.*

10. Assessment
Provide Rationale Tips for each instructional design feature.

Provide each learning event with a caption and description, to focus attention on instructional goals, emphasize the learning function. Conceptualize instructional design in terms of learning goals and events.

Major contributions. The development of a simple framework to support flexibly adaptive design. Much guidance for designing new programs. Proven methods developed through formative research.

—C.M.R.

Toward the Development of Flexibly Adaptive Instructional Designs

This chapter describes an approach to the design of instruction that has evolved from our work in classroom, corporate, and training settings (e.g., Cognition and Technology Group at Vanderbilt [CTGV], 1990; 1996; 1997). The approach falls midway between two extremes on a continuum that represents the amount of guidance provided to instructors or to students. One extreme leaves all instructional decisions to the designer rather than the teacher or learner. Its assumption is that designers are empowered by theory and research to suggest instructional sequences that approximate the ideal. The other extreme leaves all instructional decisions to the teacher or learner with no guidance provided by the designer. Its assumption is that effective strategies for learning depend on the knowledge, skills, and interests of individual learners and teachers, hence they are in the best position to decide what to do.

As many have noted, there are problems with both extreme positions (e.g., CTGV, 1997; Greenbaum & Kyng, 1991; Hannafin, 1992; Lin et al., 1995). In the discussion below we explore our attempts to strike a balance between these extremes.* Our goal is to develop and test designs for instruction that are flexibly adaptive rather than totally prescriptive or totally unstructured. Our discussion is divided into three major sections:

1. The need for flexibly adaptive designs.
2. A software program, STAR LEGACY, that is designed to promote research on the design of flexibly adaptive instruction.
3. Initial evaluations of STAR LEGACY and plans for future tests.

THE NEED FOR FLEXIBLY ADAPTIVE DESIGNS

Our belief in the need for flexibly adaptive designs stems from our experiences with the concept of anchored instruction. Several years ago we introduced the *Jasper Adventure Series* to teachers in nine different states (CTGV, 1994; 1997). The classroom implementations revealed both good and bad news. The good news was that most teachers adapted *Jasper* with demonstrably positive consequences for student

---

* Avoiding such extreme positions is an important characteristic of the new paradigm of instructional theory. It reflects both the diversity theme and the multiple perspectives theme.

achievement. The bad news arose when a few teachers maladapted Jasper to old ways of doing things. These experiences helped us appreciate the need to provide guidance. But other experiences remind us that our guidance should not prevent teachers from tailoring instruction to their own strengths and their students' and community needs. For example, as any teacher will testify, classes from different years have significantly different complexions. This variability is a natural state of affairs, and teachers try to adapt to these differences to optimize learning. We believe it is important to provide instructional designs that are consistent with important principles of learning yet encourage flexibility as well.

Many curriculum guides for schools and business training try to supply everything from the exact content to the exact sequence of instruction to the exact teaching techniques. In contrast, we view design as a collaborative and emerging process involving "initial designers," teachers, community members, and even students themselves.* The ideas of the initial designers are still very important in this model, but the designs should allow for flexibility within a set of boundary conditions. This is the type of design that we are attempting to develop. One of our approaches is organized around our STAR LEGACY software.

STAR LEGACY:
A SOFTWARE SHELL FOR STUDYING FLEXIBLY
ADAPTIVE DESIGN

STAR LEGACY encourages research and development relevant to flexibly adaptive design. The main menu screen for STAR LEGACY is illustrated in Fig. 9.1. It features learning cycles organized around successive challenges. The challenges are represented as increasingly high mountains that learners are encouraged to "climb." As learners climb each mountain, they progressively deepen their expertise.**

STAR stands for "Software Technology for Action and Reflection," where one of the actions is to leave a legacy. Participants can leave legacies that help the next group that explores a particular topic. These legacies support flexible instructional design because teachers, students, and others adapt particular content to their unique strengths, needs, and interests. In this way, STAR LEGACY evolves over time. Our discussion in this section focuses on four aspects of STAR LEGACY (or just LEGACY for short): (a) general features, (b) the LEGACY learning cycle, (c) multiple learning cycles that help people progressively deepen their understanding, and (d) the importance of reflecting on the overall learning process and creating LEGACY products for others to use.

---

* I believe these are important characteristics for the new paradigm of the process of ISD (see chap. 1 of this volume, p. 25, and the Reigeluth article in the May 1996 issue of *Educational Technology*).

** The Simplifying Conditions Method in chapter 18 by Reigeluth offers some additional guidance for this process.

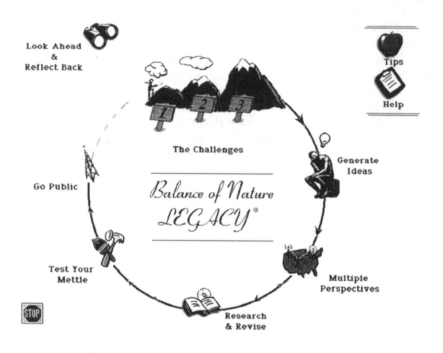

Look Ahead
&
Reflect Back

Tips

Help

The Challenges

Generate
Ideas

Go Public

Balance of Nature
LEGACY®

Test Your
Mettle

STOP

Multiple
Perspectives

Research
& Revise

FIG. 9.1.   Main screen and learning cycle of STAR LEGACY.

General features of STAR LEGACY

LEGACY has grown out of collaborations with teachers, trainers, students, curriculum designers, and researchers. Teachers, in particular, have been instrumental in helping us make explicit the different components of an instructional event and connecting those events with learning theory. LEGACY tries to formalize such components and their rationale within a learning cycle.

Making the Learning Cycle Explicit

A major goal of LEGACY is to help teachers and learners "see where they are" in a complex sequence of learning. The importance of this feature became apparent during the implementation of an integrated model of instruction and assessment called SMART, which stands for "Scientific and Mathematical Arenas for Refining Thinking" (Barron et al., 1995; 1998; CTGV, 1997). Under this model, classrooms progress from problem-based learning that develops a solid knowledge foundation to more open-ended project-based learning where remote instructional designers cannot guarantee the available data and issues. In one unit, for example, students begin with a video-based problem called "The Stones River Mystery" (Vye et al., 1998). The mystery is to decide whether there is pollution in a river, and if so, what kind and from where. To solve the mystery, students learn about sampling for pollution, indirect causal effects, ecosystems, and the role of oxygen in water pollution. To learn these and other concepts, there are many opportunities for consulting knowledge resources, for sharing ideas, and for assessing and revising understanding. Then, after completing The Stones River Mystery, the students plan and conduct a river monitoring project at a local river. By moving through cycles of learning and revision in the context of related problem and project challenges, students progressively deepen their understanding (Vye et al., 1998).

An important element of the SMART sequence turned out to be a visual representation that helped students and teachers to see where they were in the SMART cycle. Fig. 9.2 shows an example of the learning map that was posted in the SMART classrooms. We knew from earlier implementations that students, and often times teachers, felt lost (Barron et al., 1995). They did not know how particular activities fit together or how the activities would contribute to their overall understanding of the problem or their ability to complete the project. Fig. 9.2 was instrumental in helping students develop a map of their own learning. Among other things, it let them know that revision was a natural component of learning, rather than a punishment for not learning. Fig. 9.3 shows that over the course of a SMART sequence implemented in five classrooms, children began to realize that revision is an authentic activity common to adult practices, not just to children in classrooms.

LEGACY provides a visual representation for learning cycles (Fig. 9.1) that is more general than the representation used for SMART. Like the SMART map, the LEGACY representation is designed to help both students and teachers understand where they are in the learning cycle. In addition, it is designed to help teachers and students transfer inquiry practices from one topic to another because they can see similarities across the inquiry activities.*

The components for the learning cycle were chosen because they have repeatedly appeared as important, yet often implicit, components of learning. However, the LEGACY cycle should not be seen as a rigid prescription such that one can only use elements in the order shown in the cycle. Teachers and students may want to return to multiple perspectives after consulting resources, return to resources after attempting to "test their mettle," and so forth. To help them understand these options, context-sensitive "rationale tips" provide important suggestions and explanations. Fig. 9.4 shows the rationale that appears for the main screen. Hopefully, such explanations help people understand the point of an instructional-design feature, and this understanding can, in turn, help them adapt instruction to their own ends.**

---

* This is somewhat similar to Landa's idea of "general methods of thinking" (chap. 15). Higher-order thinking skills are an important goal for most theories in the new paradigm.

** This is similar to Corno and Randi's idea of self-regulated learning for both students and teachers (chap. 13).

River Mystery Challenge

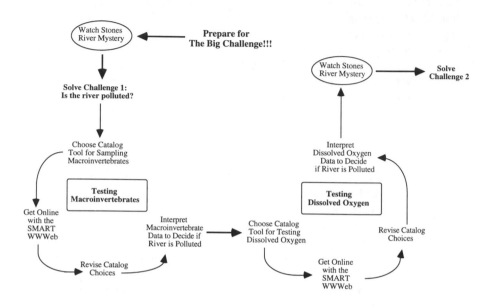

FIG. 9.2.   An earlier learning cycle posted in SMART classrooms.

Traversing an Initial STAR LEGACY Cycle

Our goal in this section is to take a first pass through the LEGACY learning cycle. To contextualize our discussion, we focus primarily on one LEGACY that is organized around a video anchor called "Border Blues." Border Blues is part of our *Scientists In Action* video series that has been developed by Bob Sherwood and his colleagues (CTGV, 1997; Sherwood, Petrosino, Lin, Lamon, & CTGV, 1995). It is about ecosystems and the balance of nature and focuses on plants. As our discussion unfolds, we supplement the Border Blues LEGACY with examples of other LEGACY programs that help clarify particular points.

1. Look Ahead

An important feature of LEGACY is represented by the "Look Ahead & Reflect Back" binoculars (see Fig. 9.1). This brings people to a screen that is designed to help them understand the learning context and learning goals.

Nearly all models of learning and instruction emphasize the importance of goal setting (e.g., Newell & Simon, 1972). Often, goals for learning are presented as spe-

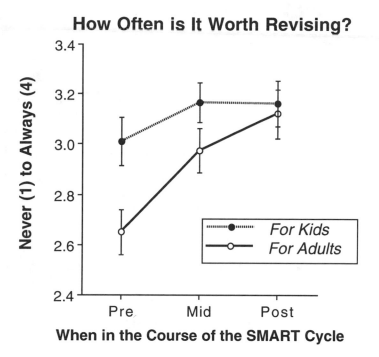

FIG. 9.3.   Changes in students' beliefs about the usefulness of revision for children and adults.

cific objectives, primarily for the teacher's eyes. For Border Blues these might include, "students will understand the interdependencies required to maintain a balance of nature," "students will understand the need to control nonnative species of plants," etc. Our work with teachers and students has helped us see that many attempts to list specific objectives fall short of the ideal because they are frequently perceived as a discrete list of statements that often seem vague and unrelated. Our preference is to help teachers and students develop a more concrete vision of the context and challenges that they will face as they proceed on their LEGACY journey.

The Look Ahead & Reflect Back that accompanies Border Blues illustrates our attempts to help students and teachers develop a more coherent vision of their journey. Teachers and students see a series of images that show, among other things, a field of Kudzu, fruit flies, customs agents, population growth curves, cigarettes, weevils, a food web, a school garden, and a fire. They also hear a narrative that explains that, when they are finished with the Border Blues LEGACY, they will be able to discuss

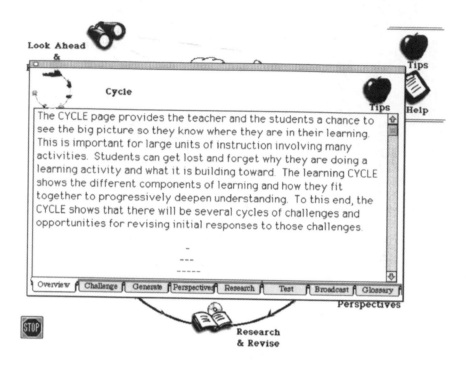

Look Ahead
&

Cycle

The CYCLE page provides the teacher and the students a chance to
see the big picture so they know where they are in their learning.
This is important for large units of instruction involving many
activities. Students can get lost and forget why they are doing a
learning activity and what it is building toward. The learning CYCLE
shows the different components of learning and how they fit
together to progressively deepen understanding. To this end, the
CYCLE shows that there will be several cycles of challenges and
opportunities for revising initial responses to those challenges.

Tips

Tips   Help

Overview   Challenge   Generate   Perspectives   Research   Test   Broadcast   Glossary

Perspectives

STOP

Research
& Revise

FIG. 9.4.   An example of a rationale tip provided with the STAR LEGACY shell.

each of the images as they relate to one another and as they relate to maintaining the
balance of ecosystems. The narrator suggests they try it right now so they may assess
what they already know and where they need to go in their learning.

The Look Ahead & Reflect Back component can take many forms besides the
one just described. Which forms are most useful for particular purposes is an important research question. Currently we envision four potential advantages for the
Look Ahead feature of LEGACY. It should:

- Provide a chance for learners to see where they are going in their learning and
  to see the sorts of things they will come to understand.
- Provide an opportunity for a learner- or teacher-based assessment. Learners
  can identify what things they need to learn more about. For teachers, this activity can occur at a classroom level so that teachers can appraise their class's
  initial domain knowledge. This can help teachers anticipate learning needs,
  as well as help them design and tailor their use of LEGACY and other classroom resources.

- Serve as a motivational teaser that raises both curiosity and aspirations.* Students may, for example, become curious about the relationship between cigarettes and ecosystem balance.
- Serve as a benchmark for reflection and self-assessment. In particular, after completing the LEGACY cycles, students and teachers can return to Reflect Back on what they have learned compared to their first try during the Look Ahead. As we discuss later in the section on "Progressive Deepening," this can be a powerful experience.

2. The Initial Challenge

After completing the Look Ahead, the student or teacher clicks on the first mountain. This brings learners to the challenge that kicks off the first learning cycle. The Border Blues challenge is presented through the video of a young man, Chris, who describes an event that has left him puzzled. Chris explains that on an overseas vacation he bought a plant that was supposed to repel mosquitoes. In the video, we see him briefly detained at a border, while in voice-over he explains that the plant was confiscated. His family was in a rush, so he never had a chance to find out why. Chris then states his challenge. "So now I am left with two questions. First, can a plant really repel mosquitoes? And, second, why did they confiscate my plant at the border?"

The challenges in LEGACY can take many forms, ranging from designing a real-world project to answering sample items from an important test. In any form, the challenges should let students develop a shared, initial mental model of what they are trying to learn about.** The shared challenge facilitates discourse among classmates (CTGV, 1990), and their initial models of the challenge provide the seed of meaning from which knowledge can grow (Bransford, Sherwood, Hasselbring, Kinzer, & Williams, 1990). Effectively designed challenges should also promote learning in the context of problem solving so that learning will be more likely to be used for subsequent problem solving and less likely to remain inert (Bransford, Franks, Vye, & Sherwood, 1989; Morris, Bransford, & Franks, 1979).

As described above, LEGACY is intended to make research issues about flexibly adaptive design explicit. An example can be found by considering the relationship between the initial challenge and the Look Ahead. The juxtaposition of the Look Ahead and the challenge is intended to invite people to consider the relationship between these two components of instruction. Our hypothesis is that students' and teachers' interpretations of the initial challenge will be affected by the information presented in the Look Ahead feature of LEGACY. For example, when viewed

---

* Again, motivation is an important part of many theories in the new paradigm. It is also a key rationale for the "initial challenge" (the next section) and many other features of this theory. See if you can identify all the methods that enhance motivation as you read on.

** Collaboration is also important in many theories in the new paradigm (see especially chaps. 11, by Nelson; 12, by Bielaczyc & Collins; and 13, by Corno & Randi).

as an isolated challenge, Chris' questions in Border Blues do not necessarily invite thoughts about ecosystems and the interdependence of living things. The design of particular Look Ahead experiences can help students begin their learning by representing a specific problem as an example of a larger set of issues. An important body of research shows that people's representations of problems have powerful effects on how they approach the problems and how they transfer to new situations (e.g., Bransford & Stein, 1993; Gick & Holyoak, 1983; Hayes & Simon, 1977; Newell & Simon, 1972). This literature highlights the importance of future research that examines relationships between different combinations of initial challenges and Look Ahead.

3. Generate Ideas

After viewing the challenge, students take an initial pass at generating issues and answers. Fig. 9.5 shows a "Generate Ideas" screen for Border Blues, as well as a student's electronic notebook. Students use the notebook to store the initial ideas that they will subsequently revise and improve. They also use the notebook to collect resources, including video clips, Web-based information, audio notes, computations, and text.

In a computer-rich classroom, one way to use the notebook feature is to have each student generate ideas in a separate notebook. In a classroom with fewer resources, the challenge can be watched as a whole class, and students might generate their initial ideas on paper. In either case, the teacher might eventually combine ideas into a collective notebook that can be projected to the entire class. The classroom notebook may be used as a focal point for a discussion.

There are several reasons why we include Generate Ideas in LEGACY. One reason is that it encourages teachers and students to share ideas in a class; everyone gets an opportunity to see what others think. For the teacher, this complements Look Ahead by providing a more specific assessment of what students understand about the challenge topic. For the students, it allows them to develop an idea about what other students think about a situation. All too often, students have little idea about their peers' knowledge, and teachers' have little idea of their students' knowledge. As a consequence, it becomes difficult to take advantage of the knowledge distributed throughout a typical classroom.

A second reason for asking students to generate their own ideas is that it can help students make their own thinking explicit rather than allow it to remain vague and tacit. The act of specifically recording their own views about a topic helps students discover what they think and know. This can be facilitated by allowing students to contrast their ideas with other ideas. Appropriate contrasts, much like seeing one's ideas juxtaposed with others' ideas, can help students notice important distinctions (Bransford & Nitsch, 1978; Gibson & Gibson, 1955; Schwartz & Bransford, in press). One advantage of asking students to generate ideas is that it can help prevent students from thinking subsequent information is obvious and therefore not notewor-

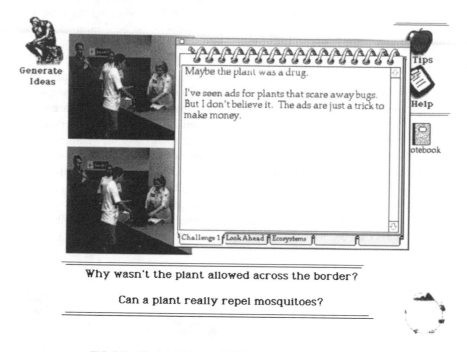

FIG. 9.5.   The use of the notebook in the Generate Ideas phase.

thy. Most instructors in the behavioral sciences have experienced the frustration of students claiming that such and such a point is boring or just common sense, when in fact the students would never have applied the "common sense" on their own. By asking students to generate ideas first, they become more appreciative of the contrast between their initial observation and the ensuing observations that they had originally overlooked. This appreciation can help them accommodate new ideas rather than only assimilate them into old ideas and gloss over what is new and important.

4. Multiple Perspectives

After generating their ideas, students move to "Multiple Perspectives." Fig. 9.6 shows three perspectives for Chris' challenge that help students define issues about a plant and its ecosystem. The fourth image, at the top of the figure, helps introduce the Multiple Perspective section to students.

There are many learning situations where multiple perspectives are a natural, albeit implicit, component of instruction (e.g., a conference panel, different voices in a novel, alternative strategies for solving mathematics problems, jigsawed cooperative groups). LEGACY includes multiple perspectives because they provide a way to introduce students to vocabulary and perspectives that are quite different from

theirs and that often characterize expert approaches to the topic. By focusing attention on contrasts between what the students generated and what the "experts" generated, students are helped to grasp the significance of new information and
understand its relevance for helping them think differently (Schwartz & Bransford,
in press).*

Consider the multiple perspectives for Border Blues. One perspective comes from
a group of students who report on their research about toxins in plants. The students
representing this perspective point out that many plants produce natural insecticides
as protection from pests. They explain that nicotine, for example, is a powerful insec-
ticide. After further considerations, they conclude their report by stating that they
know that some plants can repel bugs, but they do not know if Chris had that type of
plant. They also suggest that maybe the plant was toxic, but they do not really know if
that would be a reason why a plant would not be allowed across the border.

A second group representing another perspective wonders whether the plant
might have been confiscated because it could have been harboring unwanted pests.
They discuss the concern in California over the Mediterranean fruit fly. They do a

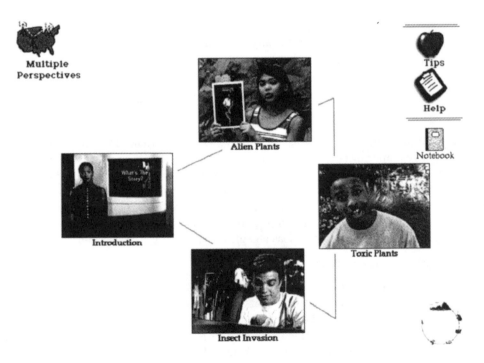

FIG. 9.6.   The Multiple Perspectives screen for Challenge 1.

* How does this instructional method differ from the more common notion of an "example" of the
expert's thinking? What are its advantages and disadvantages?

small experiment showing the rate at which fruit flies can reproduce. And, they develop a model of population growth depending on the level of predation. They conclude with their belief that the plant was confiscated because it could have been carrying insects not found in the local ecosystem, but they do not really know if the plant could repel mosquitoes.

The third perspective is presented by a pair of students in a field of Kudzu. They explain that the government once paid farmers to plant Kudzu. But, as the camera pans back and shows the two girls amidst trees and hedges completely engulfed by a Kudzu vine, they explain that it grew too well in the South. They also describe another "exotic" called Witchweed that does not simply cover plants, it taps directly into their root systems to steal nutrients. They conclude that Chris's plant was probably confiscated at the border because it may have been an exotic that could grow too well in a new habitat.

These multiple perspectives serve a number of purposes. First and foremost, they provide guidance into the topics that students should explore to learn about the domain. The perspectives do not give away solutions; instead they point toward relevant domains of inquiry.

A second purpose for the perspectives is to present models of social practice in the domain. In Border Blues, we have child actors present good-quality reports on Chris' original challenge. These reports help set realistic standards of performance and indicate what progress the presenters have made toward the solution and what problems need to be solved. These models also explicitly indicate that a given situation usually has multiple vantage points and that this is acceptable. This is different from much instruction that provides only one model for how to think about things. Learning multiple entry points into a given topic increases the flexibility of future problem solving (Spiro & Jehng, 1990).

In addition to presenting models of practice and different domains of inquiry, Multiple Perspectives can draw together and make available distributed expertise and practices among people who cannot easily be brought together. For example, a LEGACY on child development uses local faculty in its Multiple Perspectives. The initial challenge shows a 6-month-old infant who encounters her first voice-activated mobile. During the two minutes of video, the infant apparently learns that her voice turns on the mobile for a few seconds. The challenge for students (and faculty) is to generate ideas about what important things they noticed. Students usually notice that "the baby learned," or that "she was preoccupied with the cameraman at first." Afterwards, when students move to Multiple Perspectives, they hear the observations of different university faculty. Among other things, the experts comment on the mastery smile that often appears in infants after learning, on the question of how we can know whether the infant has really learned the contingency between her voice and mobile activation, and on the repertoire of innate behaviors the infant used to stir up an environmental response from which she could learn. By comparing faculty observations to their own, students invariably realize that their observation that "the baby learned" was not sufficiently differentiated. Quite often they state, with some amazement, "I hadn't even noticed that!"

5. Research & Revise

In "Research & Revise" students may complete many different activities, including collaborating with one another, consulting resources, listening to "just-in-time" lectures, completing skill-building lessons, looking at legacies left by students from previous years, and conducting simulations and hands-on experiments.* This component of LEGACY is the broadest and most inclusive. Both traditional and avant garde approaches to instruction can find a home here.** The key criterion is that the instructional materials should help students in their goals of exploring a challenge. In the case of Border Blues, the resources are primarily designed to help students learn and apply relevant empirical content and scientific principles. For a different challenge, such as preparing for the SAT, it may be more appropriate to have students learn about strategies for effective test taking.

There are several resources in Border Blues that have been organized to mirror the Multiple Perspectives. These resources include activities and issues that can be tailored to local knowledge needs and research opportunities. One activity suggests going to garden supply stores to see if they sell exotic plants that are invading the local ecology. As a resource, LEGACY opens a government web site on invasive foreign plants. Another resource launches a simulation that allows students to explore growth curves of plants and insects under different levels of predation, food supply, and reproduction. Another suggests possible hands-on experiments to show that "the fittest" in the survival of the fittest depends on the ecosystem. And yet another provides access to a library of different physical, chemical, and imitative mechanisms that plants use to protect themselves.

The resources that are available for Chris' challenge are mostly outside of the LEGACY shell itself. LEGACY is more of an organizational "launch pad" than a place to program large amounts of content.*** Among other things, it launches video and audio as in the case of the Multiple Perspectives; it launches applications like a Web browser or a simulation; and it suggests activities that can be completed in the classroom. Students have access to their electronic notebook (see Fig. 9.5) throughout their work and can use this workspace to take notes and organize their thoughts.

6. Test Your Mettle

When students feel that they have developed their understanding of the original challenge, they are asked to complete "Test Your Mettle" before they can "Go Public" with their solution to the challenge. This can take a number of different forms, from multiple choice tests with feedback to rubrics for evaluating initial essays to

---

* Again, the theme of diversity of methods is characteristic of the new paradigm.

** This reinforces the notion that the new paradigm reconfigures rather than replaces many elements of the industrial-age paradigm.

*** This launch pad notion may prove to be particularly powerful.

"near transfer" problems. Test Your Mettle is meant as a formative instructional event, not a final exam. It is a chance for students to bump up against the world to see if their knowledge is up to the task.*

One Test Your Mettle option for Border Blues is a close analog of Chris's original challenge that asked whether plants could possibly repel mosquitoes. Students see an advertisement that claims a miracle marigold plant can repel aphids. They are asked whether this is feasible for use in a rose garden. LEGACY contains a number of textual resources that include information about marigold's repelling properties, their likelihood of choking out nearby plants, and so forth. The basic principles that underlie the answer to this test are consistent with the principles needed to evaluate the alleged mosquito-repelling abilities of Chris' plant.

Students write a short essay about their feasibility study on marigolds for pest control in a rose garden. After writing the essay they receive a checklist that asks whether they included such points as the quantity of marigolds needed, the likelihood the marigolds will spread out of control, and so forth. For each point that is not discussed in the essay, there is a suggestion to consult a section from the original Research & Revise that indicates why this point is an important consideration.

In Test Your Mettle students and teachers have a chance to coalesce their knowledge and assess whether understanding is adequate and coverage complete. It is also a chance for students who may have been working in groups to see how they do when working alone.** Test Your Mettle ideally provides focused feedback that suggests which resources the students might consult to reach the needed level of understanding. Alternatively, it can be designed to make thinking sufficiently visible that a teacher or knowledgeable peer can suggest resources for further learning. Test Your Mettle, like other components of LEGACY, is meant to be adaptable. But in all cases, the feedback from Test Your Mettle should suggest how to achieve the needed learning and should motivate students to revise and improve their work.

Additional designs for Test Your Mettle appear in other LEGACY curricula. For example, in a pre-algebra curriculum, students receive a challenge to make "Smart Tools" like graphs and tables that can help them solve recurrent forms of rate problems (Bransford et al., in press). Prior to publishing these tools for other students to see, they get a chance to test their designs.*** They receive different types of rate problems under time pressure. If their tools succeed on all the types of problems, then the students can be sure they are ready to present their designs publicly. If there are problems with which the students have trouble, they receive feedback to consult resources that can help them revise their tools for that form of rate problem. As illus-

---

* Again, the formative role of testing is a key marker of the new paradigm of instructional theories. How to customize it in a cost-effective manner is an issue of great concern—one where information technologies may play a crucial role, as well as feedback from peers.

** This issue of individual accountability is important not to overlook in a group-based learning context.

*** Self-assessment in one form or another is an important aspect of self-regulated learning in the new paradigm.

trated by Fig. 9.7, opportunities to test their mettle have a strong effect on the quality of smart tools that students construct. More generally, we have found that formative assessment coupled with revision opportunities will significantly increase student achievement (e.g., Barron et al., 1995; CTGV, 1997; Vye et al., 1998).

In a different LEGACY, Test Your Mettle involves choices among a set of catalog items such as the one in Fig. 9.8. It is a Web-based assessment that comes from a learning cycle on river pollution and ecology (Vye et al., 1998). Students receive a catalog of different companies that claim they are the ones to help clean grease pollution from a river. The students' task is to select the company they would hire to

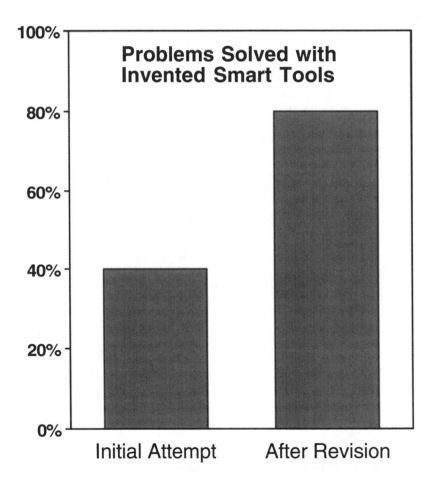

FIG. 9.7.   The positive effects of formative assessment and revision opportunities: Questions answered correctly with a SmartTool on initial attempt and after revision.

clean grease pollution, justify their choice, and justify why they rejected the other companies. Some of the companies reflect common misconceptions. "Recycle Kings," shown in Fig. 9.8, catches the common confusion that a healthy river is as clean as a swimming pool. Fig. 9.9 shows an example of the feedback that is made available upon one choice from Fig. 9.8.

7. Go Public

After completing Test Your Mettle, students are prepared to "go public" with their thinking. There are two ways to do this. One is to present their best solutions to Chris' original challenge and make them available to others. A second is to leave a legacy that includes tips and ideas for future students who will use the program.

There are several reasons we ask students to go public with their knowledge. It makes their thinking visible, so other students and teachers can assess and identify high-quality elements of understanding. This helps students learn to assess others and themselves,* and it also helps set standards for achievement. Sharing results helps students learn to learn from one another, and it shows that there are usually many different facets and problem-solving approaches to any challenge. The public nature of the presentation creates a high-stakes component to the learning cycle that motivates students to do well. Finally, the resulting product is a motivating testimony to the students' work.

What constitutes "public" can vary. Public may mean posting on the Internet, copying one's solution into a collective notebook, designing a multimedia presentation, giving an oral presentation to the class, or presenting to an outside audience such as another class or a panel of experts. Regardless of the most appropriate approach for the local situation, it is important to help students understand why and how various public performances can serve as valuable learning experiences. For this reason, students are asked to reflect on their experiences after they traverse a cycle in LEGACY and before they move on to the next cycle.

Asking students to leave a legacy for future students can further encourage reflection. Rather than leaving a solution (which others could simply copy), students are asked to leave resources and suggestions for how others might proceed with the challenge. Students in a class might provide words of encouragement (e.g., "we found this really hard at first, but it was worth it, keep trying"), ideas for new resources and references, ideas for experiments, and so forth. Legacies can be left as new Multiple Perspectives, as resources, and as new Test Your Mettles.

Progressive Deepening

The preceding section focused on the first LEGACY challenge and its learning cycle. As illustrated in Fig. 9.1, LEGACY encourages multiple challenges, repre-

---

* Such higher-levels of learning (especially metacognitive skills) are important goals of many methods in this theory and the other theories in the new paradigm. Reflection is such a method that is used by many of the new theories. See if you can spot others.

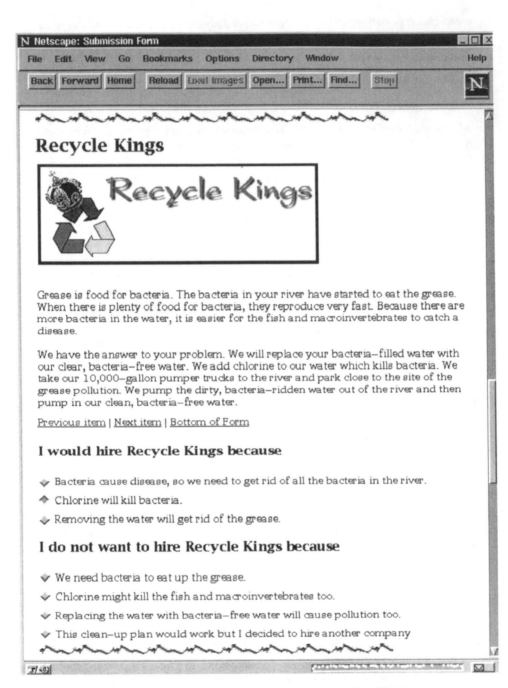

File   Edit   View   Go   Bookmarks   Options   Directory   Window   Help

Back | Forward | Home | Reload | Load Images | Open... | Print... | Find... | Stop   N

Recycle Kings

Grease is food for bacteria. The bacteria in your river have started to eat the grease. When there is plenty of food for bacteria, they reproduce very fast. Because there are more bacteria in the water, it is easier for the fish and macroinvertebrates to catch a disease.

We have the answer to your problem. We will replace your bacteria–filled water with our clear, bacteria–free water. We add chlorine to our water which kills bacteria. We take our 10,000–gallon pumper trucks to the river and park close to the site of the grease pollution. We pump the dirty, bacteria–ridden water out of the river and then pump in our clean, bacteria–free water.

Previous item | Next item | Bottom of Form

I would hire Recycle Kings because

- Bacteria cause disease, so we need to get rid of all the bacteria in the river.
- Chlorine will kill bacteria.
- Removing the water will get rid of the grease.

I do not want to hire Recycle Kings because

- We need bacteria to eat up the grease.
- Chlorine might kill the fish and macroinvertebrates too.
- Replacing the water with bacteria–free water will cause pollution too.
- This clean–up plan would work but I decided to hire another company

FIG. 9.8.   A Web-based catalog that students use for Test Your Mettle.

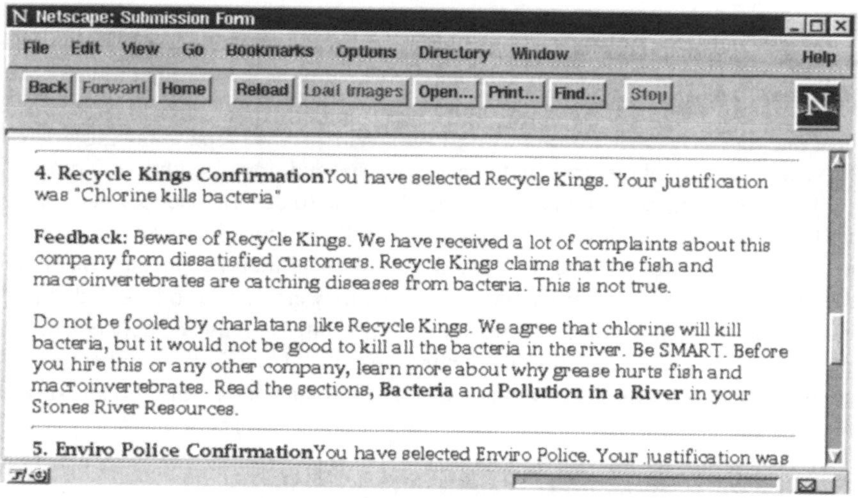

> **4. Recycle Kings Confirmation** You have selected Recycle Kings. Your justification was "Chlorine kills bacteria"
>
> **Feedback:** Beware of Recycle Kings. We have received a lot of complaints about this company from dissatisfied customers. Recycle Kings claims that the fish and macroinvertebrates are catching diseases from bacteria. This is not true.
>
> Do not be fooled by charlatans like Recycle Kings. We agree that chlorine will kill bacteria, but it would not be good to kill all the bacteria in the river. Be SMART. Before you hire this or any other company, learn more about why grease hurts fish and macroinvertebrates. Read the sections, **Bacteria** and **Pollution in a River** in your Stones River Resources.
>
> **5. Enviro Police Confirmation** You have selected Enviro Police. Your justification was

FIG. 9.9.   An example of feedback from the Web-based catalog.

sented as increasingly tall mountains. These challenges provide opportunities for students to progressively deepen their knowledge of the topic being explored.

For Border Blues, we use three challenges, where each provides a slightly different entry point into the issue of balanced ecosystems. Whereas the first challenge emphasizes factors that can throw an ecosystem out of balance (e.g., lack of natural enemies), the second challenge considers how people can put an ecosystem back into balance.

By clicking on the second mountain, students are introduced to the authentic problem of the musk thistle. Musk thistle, an exotic plant to North America, has grown out of control in several states since "invading" America. This has reduced the available grazing land because livestock avoid fields with the thorny plants. The challenge for the students is to develop a plan for managing the musk thistle problem.

As usual, the students begin by generating ideas. Afterwards, they view four perspectives on the problem. One perspective is to burn the fields, although there is concern that the thistle may grow back like some other plants. Another perspective suggests tilling the plants under the soil, although this may be a problem because this actually helps the reproduction of the Canadian thistle. A third perspective suggests poisoning the plants. Finally, a fourth perspective proposes unleashing thistle weevils on the plants as a natural mechanism of control. In the musk thistle's natural ecosystem, thistle weevils help keep the balance. However, this raises some concern about whether the thistle weevils, if introduced into North America, have local predators to keep their population down, and whether they will eat other things.

After exploring the second challenge, students move to the third challenge. In this case, the third challenge is a project. For most students, this particular project is too ambitious and open-ended to have undertaken prior to completing the first two challenges. Our research supports the advantages of beginning with problem-based challenges (like Challenges 1 and 2 in Border Blues) before moving to project-based challenges (CTGV, 1997; Barron et al., 1998). With proper preparation, projects can serve as an excellent opportunity to deepen, apply, and organize understanding.*

The project-based challenge in Border Blues is to design a school garden that will not require pesticides and for which there will be minimal concern about plants or insects upsetting the local ecology. To complement their design and to help the students develop a more formal understanding, they create a "food web" that indicates the attracting, feeding, and repelling relationships among and between the expected insects and the plants. By having completed the initial challenges, the students' understanding should make the project manageable and the abstraction meaningful.

General Reflection and Decisions About Legacies

We noted earlier that STAR stands for "software technology for action and reflection," and that students reflect on their progress after completing each learning cycle. At the end of the third cycle, there are special opportunities for important reflections that involve returning to the Look Ahead & Reflect Back component to reexamine their notebook and their initial thoughts. This gives the students a chance to see how much they have learned and to further extend their knowledge about the domain and their own learning processes. For example, when they revisit the image of a cigarette for Border Blues, they should be able to relate tobacco to ecosystems by understanding that it has nicotine to protect itself from insect predators. Perhaps they will wonder whether tobacco is a general poison or whether it only interacts with specific types of organisms, much like the thistle weevil only attacks thistle plants (and artichokes).

Reflect Back is important because it gives students an opportunity to appreciate their own learning. Often, students do not have a chance to see just how much they have learned. Consider graduate education. Grades do not give students a chance to perceive their own knowledge growth in any direct way. Comparisons to peers do not work well because one and one's peers could both move forward, and therefore one might never know there was change.** Furthermore, comparing oneself against a mentor such as a professor does not work very well because the contrast can be too great. Often times, it is a self-comparison that makes students realize how much they

---

* It seems that the distinction between problem-based learning and project-based learning is one of solving something versus creating something.

** This helps to highlight the role of grades in a sorting-focused instructional system and the nature of alternatives to grades that are needed in a learning-focused system.

have learned. For example, by rereading an article after some time, most students are heartened by their discovery of how much more they can see in the article.

With respect to developing habits of learning, we also believe it is important for students to reflect on their own growth and to recognize that they have been successful learners. We especially encourage reflection on occasions that initially seem confusing and perhaps frustrating. We want our students to develop a "tolerance for ambiguity" (Kuhn, 1962) and "healthy courage spans" (Wertime, 1979). Seeing perseverance pay off in knowledge terms is important to this end (Dweck, 1989).

Reflections on their own learning processes can also be useful for helping students decide on the legacies they want to leave for others. For example, students who have a chance to look back at how much they have learned by traversing all three LEGACY cycles may leave a resource for future generations of students indicating that perseverance through a particularly tough section of LEGACY is difficult but worth it.

One of the nicer anticipated technological changes is the ease of creating CD-ROMS. This makes it possible for students to leave a class with a CD that includes their solutions to the challenges plus the legacies they have left for the next group of students. The CDs provide an excellent review of the course content, and they can be very motivating for students by helping them to realize that their insights are valuable for the next generation of students. Similarly, teachers may also leave legacies for future classes and teachers.

ASSESSMENT OF FLEXIBLY ADAPTIVE INSTRUCTIONAL DESIGN

As noted earlier, a major goal of LEGACY is to promote research on issues of flexibly adaptive design and learning. There are many issues to be explored for a variety of audiences including teachers, designers, and students. Because LEGACY is only about six months old at the time of writing, we have just begun to explore its strengths and limitations. Some examples of our efforts are discussed below.

STAR LEGACY and Teachers

Earlier in this chapter we noted that a major goal of LEGACY is to help students, teachers, and designers see where they are with respect to learning goals. During the past several months we had the opportunity to introduce the LEGACY framework to a number of K–12 teachers who had been using various non-LEGACY curriculum units such as *Jasper* and *Scientists in Action* (e.g., CTGV, 1997). We showed them how these units looked when placed in a LEGACY framework and asked for their reactions. The response was extremely positive. Teachers felt that they could instantly "see" the learning cycles, especially the idea of progressive deepening. Teachers also found it easier to talk with team partners who teach other disciplines, because they shared a common structure of inquiry. As they worked with LEGACY, it became easier to decide on multiple perspectives and resources that they might use. It also became clear that different teachers wanted to add their own touches. Some added their own comments to multiple perspective and to resources. Some wanted to reword challenges so that they better fit the needs and interests of their students. Teachers also felt that their students would be highly motivated by the idea of leaving legacies for other students to appreciate.

A number of teachers also used the LEGACY framework as they developed new curricula for the coming year. The teachers found it particularly useful to think first about the Look Ahead components of a unit as well as the initial challenge, and then to think carefully about Test Your Mettle in order to clarify what students should be learning. Designing multiple challenges, as opposed to a single challenge, also helped in this regard. After that, it became easier for them to decide on perspectives and resources.*

STAR LEGACY and Corporate Instructional Designers

We have also used elements of LEGACY in a graduate course that was composed of professional instructional designers and corporate trainers who had returned to school. The course began with a video that showed an employee who was hindering his team because he was not meeting his quota. The students' initial challenge was to design instruction to handle this type of business-setting conflict. After the designers generated their initial ideas, they heard multiple perspectives from other designers, employees, and academics. They consulted resources on different models of design and revised their initial designs.

On the second cycle the students created a design that would actually be tried with undergraduates. For this cycle, special emphasis was placed on Test Your Mettle, where they tried their designs with undergraduates and reflected on the experience.

The progressive deepening of the multiple cycles seemed especially important for the designers. On the first go-around, the designs were based on the "traditional models" of instructional design they had employed elsewhere. This occurred even though the students acknowledged and studied different perspectives and resources in the classroom discussions and assignments. It was not until the second cycle that the students began to take the elements of LEGACY to heart and included things like Multiple Perspectives in their own designs (something that one would think is especially important in designing lessons about conflict resolution).

In addition to the value of the multiple cycles, the students commented on the positive effects of hearing multiple perspectives, of explicitly questioning the learning goals behind a particular piece of instruction, and of seeing the variability of the context in which their designs were applied. The following quote provides one example:

> I have been an instructional designer for years, and I have done training in many different settings. However, most of the training was similar in format, activities and in-

---

* This represents ISD process, as opposed to instructional theory.

structional strategies. This experience with undergraduates made me feel how dangerous it was not to examine how the nature of the learning context affected the effectiveness of the strategies and other design features. In our second group, most of our students came from other countries, and they were not as talkative as American students in the first group. This made a huge impact on how our instructional strategy was working. What we had planned did not work. We were lucky that we [had] prepared some alternatives.

Designers at the Learning Technology Center

A third knowledgeable group to whom we have introduced LEGACY is our Learning Technology Center (LTC). This group allows us to see how readily the framework can help people rethink their current work by placing it in a LEGACY format. It also allows us to see whether LEGACY is flexible enough to work for different designers in a variety of content areas with a variety of resources.

Thus far, opportunities to work with LTC designers have taught us a great deal. For example, we have noted an important potential drawback that arises from the formalization of the LEGACY learning cycle. There is a tendency to assume that any given learning component can only be used in its particular place within a cycle. This is not an intended implication of the interface. For example, we do not wish to imply that the only place students should generate ideas is after a challenge. Learning is fundamentally generative and should be encouraged throughout. In fact, many of the resources in Research & Revise create minichallenges that encourage generative thinking. The learning components have been placed in the shown sequence because we have found this to be a useful sequence of instruction. Ideally, however, our goal is to help learners, teachers, and designers recognize the importance of each of the different elements of learning so they can use them flexibly in their own instructional designs.

Another interesting outcome of the development efforts within the LTC is the diversity of the designs being produced. Different people have often come up with very different ways to use the same basic curriculum in a LEGACY context. The strength of this diversity is that there is a lot of room in LEGACY for creativity. A weakness is that the current implementation of LEGACY is still underconstrained with respect to principles for effective design. We hope to handle some of this through the "rationale tips" provided with LEGACY. At present, however, we are trying to maximize creativity in design rather than prematurely constrain people's designs.

We are experimenting with ways to provide more guidance for design decisions during the authoring process.* For example, as we began to test the LEGACY shell within the LTC, people tended to organize the different learning materials according to the types of media. They organized the learning resources according to useful Internet locations, suggestions for hands-on activities, textual resources, video

---

* Perhaps the amount of guidance for design decisions should vary from one situation to another. Identifying such situationalities and the ways the guidance should differ for each would be a useful contribution.

segments, simulations, and so forth. Although this creates a fine organizational scheme for a merchandise catalog, one would ideally like instructional materials to be organized according to the learning function or concept they serve rather than the media they utilize.* Consequently, we have developed software tools that encourage people to "justify" the learning function for a particular instructional activity. Fig. 9.10 shows an example of the main "programming tool" that encourages this justification.

Designers can add a "learning event" to LEGACY by clicking on a design tool that opens the dialog box shown in Fig. 9.10.** This box asks the designer to define various features of this "learning event object" including physical appearance, its pedagogical description, and its action. The action defines what type of interactive event occurs when a student or teacher clicks on the object. These events include playing a movie or sound, opening a Web browser to a specific page, showing text, simulations, etc. To encourage attention to instructional goals, designers are expected to provide each learning event with a caption (the "action name" shown in Fig. 9.10) and a learning description. The caption is meant to tell students what topic or problem space is covered by that particular learning event as in "How Plants Turn into Pests." Notice that the caption is about learning content rather than about the media or activity.

The description associated with a learning event helps designers think explicitly about why they included a particular activity as it relates to the overall structure of the learning cycle. This provides the dual function of helping the learners to recognize the intent of the learning event and to see how it will fit into the larger goal of solving the challenge. This descriptive box next to the caption in Fig. 9.10 shows an example that fits these goals.

STAR LEGACY and Students

We are especially interested in conducting studies on the degree to which LEGACY can help students, including preservice teachers, think about learning and instructional design. We also plan to study how the LEGACY framework helps different teachers, schools, and communities adapt particular curriculum units to their unique needs and interests.

Overall, it has been instructive to introduce LEGACY to four different audiences (teachers, business designers, LTC designers, and students). First, the experience has sensitized us to the strong need for flexibility even when attempting to teach the same basic content. Second, it has helped us appreciate the need to help each of these

---

* This notion of basing the selection of instructional methods on the kinds of learning functions they should serve at different points in time during the learning process seems very powerful to me. This illustrates how knowledge of learning theory can be helpful in developing instructional theory.

** I find this very exciting as a tool for practitioners to contribute to the development of instructional theory. This bears some relevance to Corno and Randi's role for teachers (chap. 13) and to Reigeluth and Frick's formative research methodology (chap. 26).

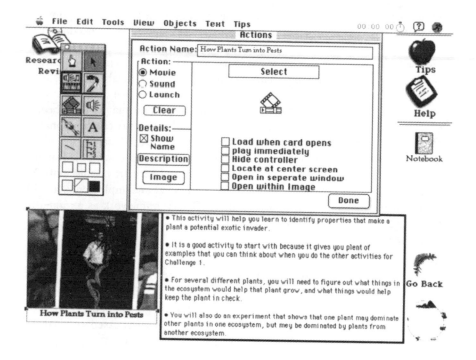

FIG. 9.10.   STAR LEGACY in Authoring mode.

groups understand the reasons for various instructional procedures from the perspective of modern theories of learning. Rather than simply attempting to follow a set of procedures, people working with LEGACY have found themselves asking how to create sequences of "assessable challenges" that are guided by questions of learning. As different groups use LEGACY, we hope to develop a "user-friendly" theory of instruction that can guide them in their instructional designs.

SUMMARY AND CONCLUSIONS

Our discussion in this chapter follows from a basic assumption: in order to optimize the effectiveness of an instructional design, it is important to make the design conform to important principles of learning and assessment, yet also fit the needs, skills, and resources of teachers, learners, and their community. One approach to this challenge has been to make instructional settings and students' prior knowledge as homogeneous as possible. Instructional designers can then assume that they are aiming for a fixed target: a classroom will be a classroom, a student will be a student, and a trainee will be a trainee. These assumptions about student and classroom homogeneity, however, are analogous to the common but faulty assumption that the people from a particular foreign culture are all the same. Culture provides ways for organizing the diversity inherent within its population.*

Rather than assuming that diversity is the exception, we assume that learning settings and learners exhibit important variability in terms of local practices, learning resources, and prior knowledge. Moreover, we believe that powerful understanding incorporates the diversity of perspectives that people may bring to bear on any given situation. Therefore, we are working towards a theory of instructional design that can be optimally adapted to fit diverse communities of learners, plus help people involved with learning to know enough about the processes of learning to make sound instructional decisions and adaptations of instructional materials. We have created LEGACY as one example of how to organize and implement a flexibly adaptive instructional design. By using the LEGACY framework as a model for evaluating and improving itself, we hope to provide at least one way to promote flexibly adaptive design.

ACKNOWLEDGMENTS

The work reported in this paper was conducted through the support of USDOE grant 305F60090, and NSF grant ESI-9618248. The ideas expressed in this paper, however, do not necessarily reflect those of the granting agencies.

REFERENCES

Barron, B. J., Vye, N. J., Zech, L., Schwartz, D., Bransford, J. D., Goldman, S. R., Pellegrino, J., Morris, J., Garrison, S., & Kantor, R. (1995). Creating contexts for community-based problem solving: The Jasper challenge series. In C. N. Hedley, P. Atonacci, & M. Rabinowitz (Eds.), *Thinking and literacy: The mind at work* (pp. 47–71). Hillsdale, NJ: Lawrence Erlbaum Associates.

Barron, B. J., Schwartz, D. L., Vye, N. J., Moore, A., Petrosino, A., Zech, L., Bransford, J. D., & Cognition and Technology Group at Vanderbilt. (1998). Doing with understanding: Lessons from research on problem- and project-based learning. *Journal of the Learning Sciences, 7,* 271–312.

Bransford, J. D., Franks, J. J., Vye, N. J., & Sherwood, R. D. (1989). New approaches to instruction: Because wisdom can't be told. In S. Vosniadou & A. Ortony (Eds.), *Similarity and analogical reasoning* (pp. 470–497). New York: Cambridge University Press.

Bransford, J. D., & Nitsch, K. E. (1978). Coming to understand things we could not previously understand. In J. F. Kavanagh & W. Strange (Eds.), *Speech and language in the laboratory, school and clinic* (pp. 267–307). Cambridge, MA: MIT Press.

Bransford, J. D., Sherwood, R. D., Hasselbring, T. S., Kinzer, C. K., & Williams, S. M. (1990). Anchored instruction: Why we need it and how technology can help. In D. Nix & R. Spiro (Eds.), *Cognition, education, and multi-media: Exploring ideas in high technology* (pp. 115–141). Hillsdale, NJ: Lawrence Erlbaum Associates.

Bransford, J. D., & Stein, B. (1993). *The IDEAL problem solver* (2nd ed.). New York: Freeman.

Bransford, J. D., Zech, L., Schwartz, D. L., Barron, B. J., Vye, N. J., & Cognition and Technology Group at Vanderbilt. (in press). Designs for environments that invite and sustain mathematical thinking. In

---

* This addresses the issue of uniformity (massification) versus diversity (customization), a key marker of the difference between the industrial age paradigm and the new paradigm.

P. Cobb (Ed.), *Symbolizing, communicating, and mathematizing: Perspectives on discourse, tools, and instructional design*. Mahwah, NJ: Lawrence Erlbaum Associates.

Cognition and Technology Group at Vanderbilt. (1990). Anchored instruction and its relationship to situated cognition. *Educational Researcher, 19*, 2–10.

Cognition and Technology Group at Vanderbilt. (1994). Generative learning and anchored instruction: Design, research and implementation issues. In B. P. M. Creemers & G. J. Reezigt (Eds.), *New directions in educational research: Contributions from an international perspective* (pp. 33–62). Groningen, The Netherlands: ICO.

Cognition and Technology Group at Vanderbilt. (1996). Looking at technology in context: A framework for understanding technology and education research. In D. C. Berliner & R. C. Calfee (Eds.), *The handbook of educational psychology* (pp. 807–840). New York: Macmillan.

Cognition and Technology Group at Vanderbilt. (1997). *The Jasper project: Lessons in curriculum, instruction, assessment, and professional development*. Mahwah, NJ: Lawrence Erlbaum Associates.

Dweck, C. S. (1989). Motivation. In A. Lesgold & R. Glaser (Eds.), *Foundations for a psychology of education* (pp. 87–136). Hillsdale, NJ: Lawrence Erlbaum Associates.

Gibson, J. J., & Gibson, E. J. (1955). Perceptual learning: Differentiation or enrichment. *Psychological Review, 62*, 32–51.

Gick, M. L., & Holyoak, K. J. (1983). Schema induction and analogical transfer. *Cognitive Psychology, 15*, 1–38.

Greenbaum, J., & Kyng, M. (1991). Introduction: Situated design. In J. Greenbaum & M. Kyng (Eds.), *Design at work: Cooperative design of computer systems* (pp. 1–24). Hillsdale, NJ: Lawrence Erlbaum Associates.

Hannafin, M. I. (1992). Emerging technologies, ISD, and learn environments: Critical perspectives. *Educational Technology Research and Development, 40*, 49–63.

Hayes, J. R., & Simon, H. H. (1977). Psychological differences among problem isomorphs. In N. J. Castelan, D. B. Pisoni, & C. F. Potts (Ed.), *Cognitive theory* (Vol. 2, pp. 21–42). Hillsdale, NJ: Lawrence Erlbaum Associates.

Lin, X. D., Bransford, J. D., Kantor, R., Hmelo, C., Hickey, D., Secules, T., Goldman, S. R., Petrosino, T., & Cognition and Technology Group at Vanderbilt. (1995). Instructional design and the development of learning communities: An invitation to a dialogue. *Educational Technology, 35*, 53–63.

Kuhn, T. S. (1962). *The structure of scientific revolutions*. Chicago: University of Chicago Press.

Morris, C. D., Bransford, J. D., & Franks, J. J. (1979). Levels of processing versus transfer appropriate processing. *Journal of Verbal Learning and Verbal Behavior, 16*, 519–533.

Newell, A., & Simon, H. (1972). *Human problem solving*. Englewood Cliffs, NJ: Prentice-Hall.

Schwartz, D. L., & Bransford, J. D. (in press). A time for telling. *Cognition & Instruction*.

Sherwood, R. D., Petrosino, A. J., Lin, X., Lamon, M., & Cognition and Technology Group at Vanderbilt. (1995). Problem-based macro-contexts in science instruction: Theoretical basis, design issues, and the development of applications. In D. Lavoie (Ed.), *Towards a cognitive-science perspective for scientific problem solving* (pp. 191–214). Manhattan, KS: National Association for Research in Science Teaching.

Spiro, R. J., & Jehng, J. C. (1990). Cognitive flexibility and hypertext: Theory and technology for the nonlinear and multidimensional traversal of complex subject matter. In D. Nix and R. J. Spiro (Eds.), *Cognition, education, and multimedia: Exploring ideas in high technology* (pp. 163–205). Hillsdale, NJ: Lawrence Erlbaum Associates.

Vye, N. J., Schwartz, D. L., Bransford, J. D., Barron, B., Zech, L., & Cognition and Technology Group at Vanderbilt. (1998). SMART environments that support monitoring, reflection, and revision. In D. Hacker, J. Dunlosky, & A. Graesser (Eds.), *Metacognition in Educational Theory and Practice* (pp. 305–346). Mahwah, NJ: Lawrence Erlbaum Associates.

Wertime, R. (1979). Students' problems and "courage spans." In J. Lockhead & J. Clements (Eds.), *Cognitive process instruction*. Philadelphia: The Franklin Institute Press.

10 Designing Constructivist Learning Environments[1]

David Jonassen
Pennsylvania State University

David Jonassen

David Jonassen is Professor of Instructional Systems at Pennsylvania State University. He previously taught at the University of Colorado, the University of Twente, the University of North Carolina at Greensboro, Syracuse University, and Temple University, and has consulted with businesses, universities, and other institutions around the world. He is working on his twentieth book and has written numerous articles, papers, and technical reports. His current research focuses on designing constructivist learning environments, cognitive tools for learning, knowledge representation formalisms, problem solving, computer-supported collaborative argumentation, and individual differences and learning.

---

[1]In order to conform to the structure of this book, the design of constructivist learning environments (CLEs) is described conceptually in an objectivist way in this chapter. That is not my preference. In my classes, students define or accept a problem first and learn how to design CLEs in the context of that problem. However, any competent objectivist instruction (including this chapter) is obligated to provide examples. Page limitations prevent this, as well as a full elaboration of the model and its theoretical foundations. So CLE prototypes and environments can be examined elsewhere (http://www.ed.psu.edu/~jonassen/CLE/CLE.html).

FOREWORD

Goals and preconditions. *The primary goal of this theory is to foster problem solving and conceptual development. It is intended for ill-defined or ill-structured domains.*

Values. *Some of the values on which this theory is based include:*
- *learning that is driven by an ill-defined or ill-structured problem (or question, case, project),*
- *a problem or learning goal that is "owned" by the learner,*
- *instruction that consists of experiences which facilitate knowledge construction (meaning making),*
- *learning that is active and authentic.*

Methods. *Here are the major methods this theory offers:*
1. *Select an appropriate problem (or question, case, project) for the learning to focus on.*
   - *The problem should be interesting, relevant and engaging, to foster learner ownership.*
   - *The problem should be ill-defined or ill-structured.*
   - *The problem should be authentic (what practitioners do).*
   - *The problem design should address its context, representation, and manipulation space.*
2. *Provide related cases or worked examples to enable case-based reasoning and enhance cognitive flexibility.*
3. *Provide learner-selectable information just-in-time.*
   - *Available information should be relevant and easily accessible.*
4. *Provide cognitive tools that scaffold required skills, including problem-representation tools, knowledge-modeling tools, performance-support tools, and information-gathering tools.*
5. *Provide conversation and collaboration tools to support discourse communities, knowledge-building communities, and/or communities of learners.*
6. *Provide social/contextual support for the learning environment.*

This theory also offers the following instructional activities to support learning:
   A. *Model the performance and the covert cognitive processes.*
   B. *Coach the learner by providing motivational prompts, monitoring and regulating the learner's performance, provoking reflection, and/or perturbing learners' models.*
   C. *Scaffold the learner by adjusting task difficulty, restructuring the task, and/or providing alternative assessments.*

Major contribution. *The integration of much work in the constructivist arena into a coherent instructional framework.*

—C.M.R.

Designing Constructivist Learning Environments

INTRODUCTION

Objectivist conceptions of learning assume that knowledge can be transferred from teachers or transmitted by technologies and acquired by learners. Objectivist conceptions of instructional design include the analysis, representation, and resequencing of content and tasks in order to make them more predictably and reliably transmissible.

Constructivist conceptions of learning, on the other hand, assume that knowledge is individually constructed and socially coconstructed by learners based on their interpretations of experiences in the world. Since knowledge cannot be transmitted, instruction should consist of experiences that facilitate knowledge construction. This chapter presents a model for designing constructivist learning environments (CLEs) that engage learners in meaning making (knowledge construction). For an elaboration of the assumptions and beliefs on which CLEs are based, see Duffy and Jonassen (1992); Jonassen (1991, 1995a, 1995b, 1996a); Jonassen, Campbell, and Davidson (1994); Jonassen, Peck, and Wilson (1998); and Savery and Duffy (1996).

While objectivism and constructivism are usually conveyed as incompatible and mutually exclusive, that is not an assumption of this chapter. Rather, I believe that objectivism and constructivism offer different perspectives on the learning process from which we can make inferences about how we ought to engender learning. The goal of my writing and teaching is not to reject or replace objectivism. To impose a single belief or perspective is decidedly nonconstructivist. Rather, I prefer to think of them as complementary design tools (some of the best environments use combinations of methods) to be applied in different contexts.*

MODEL FOR DESIGNING CONSTRUCTIVIST LEARNING ENVIRONMENTS

The model for designing CLEs (Fig. 10.1) illustrates their essential components. The model conceives of a problem, question, or project as the focus of the environment, with various interpretative and intellectual support systems surrounding it. The goal of the learner is to interpret and solve the problem or complete the project.

---

* This diversity of perspectives and methods is an important aspect of the new paradigm of instructional theories.

Related cases and information resources support understanding of the problem and suggest possible solutions; cognitive tools help learners to interpret and manipulate aspects of the problem; conversation/collaboration tools enable communities of learners to negotiate and coconstruct meaning for the problem; and social/contextual support systems help users to implement the CLE.

1. Question/Case/Problem/Project

The focus of any CLE is the question or issue, the case, the problem, or the project that learners attempt to solve or resolve. It constitutes a learning goal that learners may accept or adapt. The fundamental difference between CLEs and objectivist instruction is that the problem drives the learning, rather than acting as an example of the concepts and principles previously taught. Students learn domain content in order to solve the problem, rather than solving the problem as an application of learning.

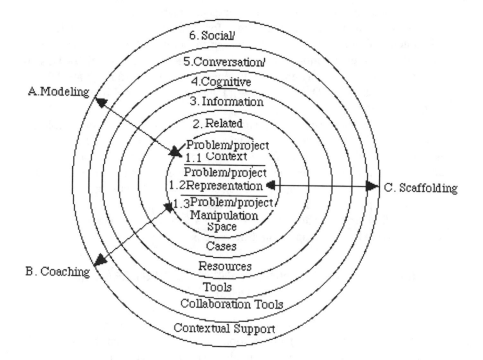

FIG. 10.1.   Model for designing CLEs

CLEs can be constructed to support question-based, issue-based, case-based, project-based, or problem-based learning. Question- or issue-based learning begins with a question with uncertain or controversial answers (e.g., Should welfare recipients be required to work? Should environmental protection seek to eliminate pollution or regulate according to location-sustainable standards?). In case-based learning, students acquire knowledge and requisite thinking skills by studying cases (e.g., legal, medical, social work) and preparing case summaries or diagnoses. Case learning is anchored in authentic contexts; learners must manage complexity and think like practitioners (Williams, 1992). Project-based learning focuses on relatively long-term, integrated units of instruction where learners focus on complex projects consisting of multiple cases. They debate ideas, plan and conduct experiments, and communicate their findings (Krajcik, Blumenfeld, Marx, & Soloway, 1994). Problem-based learning (Barrows & Tamblyn, 1980) integrates courses at a curricular level, requiring learners to self-direct their learning while solving numerous cases across a curriculum. Case-, project-, and problem-based learning represent an approximate continuum of complexity,* but all share the same assumptions about active, constructive, and authentic learning. CLEs can be developed to support each of these, so for purposes of this chapter, which seeks to present a generic design model, I will refer to the focus of the CLEs generically as a problem.

Since the key to meaningful learning is ownership of the problem or learning goal, you must provide interesting, relevant, and engaging problems to solve.** The problem should not be overly circumscribed. Rather, it should be ill defined or ill structured, so that some aspects of the problem are emergent and definable by the learners. Why? Without ownership of the problem, learners are less motivated to solve or resolve it. Contrast ill-structured problems with most textbook problems, which require practice of a limited number of skills to find the correct answer without helping to shape or define the problem. Ill-structured problems, on the other hand:

- have unstated goals and constraints,
- possess multiple solutions, solution paths, or no solutions at all,
- possess multiple criteria for evaluating solutions,
- present uncertainty about which concepts, rules, and principles are necessary for the solution or how they are organized,
- offer no general rules or principles for describing or predicting the outcome of most cases, and
- require learners to make judgments about the problem and to defend their judgments by expressing personal opinions or beliefs (Jonassen, 1997).

---

* Interestingly, Schwartz, Lin, Brophy, and Bransford (chap. 9) viewed project-based learning as more complex than problem-based learning (p. 206). See if you can figure out why. Clearly, there can be a great range of complexity within each.

** The issues of motivation and ownership are consistent themes in the new paradigm.

How Can You Identify Problems for CLEs?   Examine the field of study, not for its topics (as in a textbook) but for what practitioners do. You need only ask experienced practitioners to describe cases, situations, or problems that they have solved. Newspapers and magazines are replete with problems and issues that need resolution. Ask yourself, "What do practitioners in this field do?" In political science, students may construct a viable constitution for an emerging third world democracy that can accommodate the social, cultural, political, and historical characteristics of the population and their relationship with other countries in the region. In philosophy, render judgments on ethical dilemmas, such as right-to-die cases or same-sex marriages. In science, decide whether a local stream can accommodate a new sewage treatment plant. You need to evaluate all suggested problems for their suitability. Do your students possess prerequisite knowledge or capabilities for working on this problem? Do not assume that they will produce solutions as elegant or efficient as experienced practitioners. That is not the goal. Rather, the goal is to learn about the field by thinking like a member of that practice community.

Problems in CLEs need to include three integrated components: the problem context, the problem representation or simulation, and the problem manipulation space.* In order to develop a CLE, you should try to represent each in the environment.

1.1. Problem Context

An essential part of the problem representation is a description of the context in which it occurs. Tessmer and Richey (1997) have developed a conceptual model and set of processes for analyzing and mapping the physical, organizational, and sociocultural context in which problems occur. The same problem in different social or work contexts is different. CLEs must describe in the problem statement all of the contextual factors that surround a problem.

Performance Environment.   You should describe the physical, socio-cultural, and organizational climate surrounding the problem. Where and in what time frame does it occur? What physical resources surround the problem? What is the nature of the business, agency, or institution in which the problem occurs? What do they produce? Provide annual reports, mission statements, balance sheets, and profit-and-loss statements if they appropriately describe the situation. What is the history of the setting? This information should be made available to learners in order to understand the problem.**

Community of Practitioners/Performers/Stakeholders.   What are the values, beliefs, sociocultural expectations, and customs of the people involved? Who sets policy? What sense of social or political efficacy do the members of the setting or organization feel? What are the skills and performance backgrounds of performers?

---

* Here a general method is being broken down into three more detailed component methods.
** Here the component method is being further broken down into sub-components.

Provide resumes for key players that describe not only their experience, but also their hobbies, traits, and beliefs. You can also convey this information in stories or interviews with key personnel in the form of audio or video clips. It is the community of participants who define what learning occurs in a context. Learning is not an isolated event. Rather it is an incidental by-product of participation in that community (Lave & Wenger, 1991), so knowing what that community believes is important.

1.2. Problem Representation/Simulation

The representation of the problem is critical to learner buy-in. It must be interesting, appealing, and engaging. It must perturb the learner. The Cognition and Technology Group at Vanderbilt (1992)* insists on high-quality video scenarios for introducing the problem and engaging learners. Virtual reality may become the default method for representing problems soon. An effective, low-tech method for representing problems is narrative.** The problem context and problem representation become a story about a set of events that leads up to the problem that needs to be resolved. The narrative may be presented in text, audio, or video. Effective examples of narrative forms of problem representations are the instructional-design cases by Lindeman et al., (1996; see also http://curry.edschool.virginia.edu/go/ITCases/). In these cases, characters are developed who interact in realistic ways to introduce the case problem. Stories are also the primary means of problem representation and coaching in goal-based scenarios (Schank, Berman, & Macpherson, chap. 8 of this volume). The problem presentation simulates the problem in a natural context. Stories are a natural means for conveying them.

Authentic.   Nearly every conception of constructivist learning recommends engaging learners in solving authentic problems.*** What is authentic? Some designers insist that authentic refers to supporting the performance of specific real-world tasks. This restrictive conception of authenticity will render learning environments that are authentic in a narrow context. Most educators believe that "authentic" means that learners should engage in activities which present the same type of cognitive challenges as those in the real world (Honebein, Duffy, & Fishman, 1993; Savery & Duffy, 1996), that is, tasks which replicate the particular activity structures of a context.

Activity structures rely on the socio-historical context of Activity Theory (Leontev, 1979), which focuses on the activities in which community members engage, the goals of those activities, the physical setting that constrains and affords

---

* See also chapter 9 by Schwartz, Lin, Brophy and Bransford in this volume.

** Notice that here the component method (problem representation) is being broken down into kinds, rather than parts. Presumably, different kinds of representations will be preferable for different situations, and it is those situationalities that make this a theory rather than just a model of instruction (see chap. 1, p. 21, in Volume 1).

*** Here it is more helpful to think of a guideline as a criterion for the design of a method than to think of it as either a part or kind of that method.

certain actions, and the tools that mediate activity. Activity Theory provides an effective lens for analyzing tasks and settings and provides a framework for designing CLEs (Jonassen & Rohrer-Murphy,).1999

Another method for isolating required activity structures is cognitive task analysis using the PARI approach (Hall, Gott, & Pokorny, 1994). The PARI (precursor/action/result/interpretation) method uses pairs of experts to pose questions and think aloud while solving complex problems. It identifies not only the activities that are engaged in while solving a problem, but also the domain knowledge and strategic knowledge that enable solution of the problem. Activity structures can be evaluated within any community context for their relevance and importance to that community.

Authentic can also simply mean personally relevant or interesting to the learner. The *Jasper* series, for instance, provides engaging problems, conveyed in high-quality video, that middle school students identify with, even though most students have never experienced the kind of problem or context presented. Authentic problems, for purposes of designing CLEs, engage learners; they represent a meaningful challenge to them. See Petraglia (1998) for a fascinating discussion of authenticity in learning environments.

1.3. Problem Manipulation Space

A critical characteristic of meaningful learning is mindful activity. In order for learners to be active, they must manipulate something (construct a product, manipulate parameters, make decisions) and affect the environment in some way. Activity theory describes the transformational interactions among the learner, the object that the learner is acting on, and the signs and tools which mediate that interaction. The problem manipulation space provides the objects, signs, and tools* required for the learner to manipulate the environment. Why? Students cannot assume any ownership of the problem unless they know that they can affect the problem situation in some meaningful way.

The form of the problem manipulation space will depend on the nature of the activity structures the CLE is engaging.** However, it should provide a physical simulation of the real-world task environment, that is, a phenomenaria (Perkins, 1991). Phenomenaria, or microworlds, present a simplified model, along with observation and manipulation tools necessary for testing learners' hypotheses about their problems (Jonassen, 1996a). Learners are directly engaged by the world they explore, because they can experiment and immediately see the results of their experiment. If constructing a constitution, show the social, political, and military results of each of the articles included. Ethical judgments might be tested with briefs from real court cases. Stream models can be created to graphically illustrate the effects of contaminants and clean-up activities.

---

* Are these parts, kinds, or criteria for the problem manipulation space?
** Here is a clear indication of a situationality (see chap. 1, p. 8).

Problem manipulation spaces are causal models that enable students to test the effects of their manipulations, receiving feedback through changes in the appearance of the physical objects they are manipulating or in the representations of their actions, such as charts, graphs, and numerical output. They should be manipulable (allow learners to manipulate objects or activities), sensitive (ensure the environment responds in realistic ways to learner manipulations), realistic (have high fidelity of simulation), and informative (provide relevant feedback).* Later, I will describe dynamic modeling tools (a combination of problem manipulation space and cognitive modeling tools) that enable learners to construct and test their own models of task worlds.

In creating problem manipulation spaces, it is not always necessary for learners to manipulate physical objects or simulations of those objects. It may be sufficient merely to generate a hypothesis or intention to act and then to argue for it.** When engaging learners in solving ill-structured problems, requiring learners to articulate their solutions to problems and then to develop a coherent argument to support that solution is often sufficient (Jonassen, 1997). The argument is an excellent indicator of the quality of domain knowledge possessed by the learner. However, argumentation skills in most learners are underdeveloped, so it will be necessary to scaffold or coach the development of cogent arguments, perhaps using argument templates or checklists (described later under conversation tools).

2. Related Cases

Understanding any problem requires experiencing it and constructing mental models of it. What novice learners lack most are experiences. This lack is especially critical when trying to solve problems. So, it is important that CLEs provide access to a set of related experiences to which novice students can refer. The primary purpose of describing related cases is to assist learners in understanding the issues implicit in the problem representation. Related cases in CLEs support learning in at least two ways: by scaffolding student memory and by enhancing cognitive flexibility.***

Scaffold Student Memory: Case-Based Reasoning

The lessons that we understand the best are those in which we have been most involved and have invested the greatest amount of effort. Related cases can scaffold (or supplant) memory by providing representations of experiences that learners have not had. They cannot replace learners' involvement, but they can provide referents for comparison. When humans first encounter a situation or problem, they naturally first check their memories for similar cases that they may have solved previously (Polya, 1957). If they can recall a similar case, they try to map the previous

---

* Are these parts, kinds, or criteria for the problem manipulation space?

** This is an alternative kind of the method, manipulation space, and what follows is a general indication of the situation that calls for its use.

*** Are these parts, kinds, criteria, or something else (for the method, related cases)?

experience and its lessons onto the current problem. If the goals or conditions* match, they apply their previous case. By presenting related cases in learning environments, you are providing the learners with a set of experiences to compare to the current problem or issue.

Case-based reasoning argues that human knowledge is encoded as stories about experiences and events (Schank, 1990).** So, when people experience a problem or situation that they do not understand, they should be told stories about similar situations that function as lessons for the current problem. Learners retrieve from related cases advice on how to succeed, on pitfalls that may cause failure, and on what worked or didn't work and why (Kolodner, 1993). They adapt the explanation to fit the current problem.

In order to provide a rich set of related cases that will help learners to solve the current one, it is necessary to collect a set of cases that are representative of the current one (those with similar contexts, solutions, or results), identify the lessons that each can teach, characterize the situations in which each case can teach its lesson, and develop an index and represent its features in a way that allows cases to be recalled (Kolodner, 1993). If constructing a constitution, provide examples of constitutions from other emerging democracies, along with descriptions of social and political consequences (e.g., newspaper or magazine clippings, video footage). In a case-based learning environment in transfusion medicine, we provided a set of related cases that could be accessed by medical students who were involved in solving new cases in transfusion medicine (Jonassen, Ambruso, & Olesen, 1992). Case reviews were indexed to each of the practice cases based on the similarities in symptomatology, pathophysiology, and so on. Learners were provided the opportunity in every case to review related cases. Developing a story index, representing those stories, and providing access to them at appropriate times is difficult but very effective.

Another way of scaffolding (or supplanting) memory for novices is to provide worked examples of problems (described later).

Enhance Cognitive Flexibility

Related cases also help to represent complexity in CLEs by providing multiple perspectives, themes, or interpretations on the problems or issues being examined by the learners. Instruction often filters out the complexity that exists in most applied knowledge domains, causing shallow understanding of domain knowledge to develop.

An important model for designing related cases in CLEs, cognitive flexibility theory, provides multiple representations of content in order to convey the complexity that is inherent in the knowledge domain (Jonassen, 1993; Spiro, Vispoel,

---

* These are situationalities, but for the task (content) rather than for the instructional theory (method).
** See also chapter 8 by Schank, Berman, and Macpherson.

Schmitz, Samarapungavan, & Boerger, 1987). Stress the conceptual interrelatedness of ideas and their interconnectedness by providing multiple interpretations of content. Use multiple, related cases to convey the multiple perspectives on most problems. To enhance cognitive flexibility, it is important that related cases provide a variety of viewpoints and perspectives on the case or project being solved. For instance, if resolving ethical dilemmas, provide divergent personal interpretations of the dilemma as well as interpretations of similar ethical conundrums, in order to convey thematic perspectives. By contrasting the cases, learners construct their own interpretations.

3. Information Resources

In order to investigate problems, learners need information with which to construct their mental models and formulate hypotheses that drive the manipulation of the problem space. So, when designing CLEs, you should determine what kinds of information the learner will need in order to understand the problem. Rich sources of information are an essential part of CLEs. CLEs should provide learner-selectable information just-in-time. CLEs assume that information makes the most sense in the context of a problem or application. So, determine what information learners need in order to interpret the problem. Some of it is naturally included in the problem representation. Other relevant information banks and repositories should be linked to the environment. These may include text documents, graphics, sound resources, video, and animations that are appropriate for helping learners comprehend the problem and its principles.

The World Wide Web is the default storage medium, as powerful new plug-ins enable users to access multimedia resources from the net. Too many learning environments, however, embed hypertext links to Web sites based on the surface features of the site. Since learners do not possess sophisticated literacy skills for evaluating the quality of and filtering the information provided, information resources included in or linked to a CLE should be evaluated for their relevance and organized for ready access in ways that support the kind of thinking that you want the learners to do. Based on the activity structures that support the problem solution, information needed to perform each of the tasks should be linked to those activities. With learners who are new to CLEs, simply pointing to Web resources may provide serious distractions to thinking necessary for solving the problem.

4. Cognitive (Knowledge-Construction) Tools

If CLEs present complex, novel, and authentic tasks, you will need to support learners' performance of those tasks. To do that, you must identify the activity structures that are required to solve the problem. Which of the required skills are likely to be possessed by the learners? For those that are not, you should provide cognitive tools that scaffold the learners' abilities to perform those tasks.

Cognitive tools are generalizable computer tools that are intended to engage and facilitate specific kinds of cognitive processing (Kommers, Jonassen, & Mayes, 1992). They are intellectual devices that are used to visualize (represent), organize, automate, or supplant thinking skills. Some cognitive tools replace thinking, while others engage learners in generative processing of information that would not occur without the tool.*

Cognitive tools fulfill a number of intellectual functions in helping learners interact with CLEs. They may help the learners to better represent the problem or task they are performing (e.g., visualization tools). They may help the learners to represent what they know or what they are learning (static and dynamic knowledge modeling tools), or they may offload some of the cognitive activity by automating low-level tasks or supplanting some tasks (performance support). Finally, cognitive tools may help learners to gather important information needed to solve the problem. Each kind of cognitive tool engages or replaces different cognitive activity, so cognitive tools must be selected carefully to support the kind of processing that needs to be performed.

Problem/Task Representation Tools

Learners' mental models of objects, systems, or other phenomena possess visual-spatial components (Jonassen & Henning, 1996). In order to understand a phenomenon, it is necessary for most humans to generate a mental image of it. Visualization tools help learners to construct those mental images and visualize activities. For example, graphical user interfaces visually represent files and applications to be manipulated.

Numerous visualization tools provide reasoning-congruent representations that enable learners to reason about objects that behave and interact (Merrill, Reiser, Bekkalaar, & Hamid, 1992). Examples include the graphical proof tree representation in the Geometry Tutor (Anderson, Boyle, & Yost, 1986); the Weather Visualizer (colorizes climatological patterns); and the Climate Watcher (colorizes climatological variables; (Edelson, Pea, & Gomez 1996). Programs such as MATHEMATICA and MATHLAB are often used to visually represent mathematical relationships in problems so that learners can *see* the effects of any problem manipulation.

Visualization tools tend to be task- and domain-specific. There are no general-purpose visualization tools. Rather, these tools must closely mimic the nature of images required to understand the ideas. As a CLE designer, you should analyze the activity structures required to solve the problems and identify processes that need to be represented visually and how the learner needs to manipulate those images to test their models of the phenomena.

---

* Are these parts, kinds, or criteria for cognitive tools?

4.2. Static and Dynamic Knowledge Modeling Tools

Jonassen (1996a) describes the critical thinking and knowledge representation activities involved in articulating knowledge domains using different static knowledge representation tools, such as databases, spreadsheets, semantic networks, expert systems, and hypermedia construction. As students study phenomena, it is important that they articulate their understanding of the phenomena. Modeling tools provide knowledge representation formalisms that constrain the ways learners think about, analyze, and organize phenomena, and they provide an environment for encoding their understanding of those phenomena. For example, creating a knowledge database or a semantic network requires learners to articulate the range of semantic relationships among the concepts that comprise the knowledge domain. Expert systems engage learners in articulating the causal reasoning between objects or factors that predict outcomes in a domain. Modeling tools help learners to answer "what do I know?" and "what does it mean?" questions.* As a CLE designer, you must decide when learners need to articulate what they know and which formalism will best support their understanding.

Complex systems contain interactive and interdependent components. In order to represent the dynamic relationships in a system, learners can use dynamic modeling tools for building simulations of those systems and processes and for testing them. Programs like Stella and PowerSim use a simple set of building blocks to construct a map of a process. Learners supply equations that represent causal, contingent, and variable relationships among the variables identified on the map. Having modeled the system, simulation modeling tools enable learners to test the model and observe the output of the system in graphs, tables, or animations. At the run level, students can change the variable values to test the effects of parts of a system on the others.

Building models of real-world phenomena is at the heart of scientific thinking and requires diverse mental activities such as planning, data collecting, accessing information, data visualizing, modeling, and reporting (Soloway, Krajcik, & Finkel, 1995). The process for developing the ability to model phenomena requires defining the model, using the model to understand some phenomena, creating a model by representing real-world phenomena and making connections among its parts, and finally analyzing the model for its ability to represent the world (Spitulnik, Studer, Finkel, Gustafson, & Soloway, 1995). They have developed a user-friendly dynamic modeling tool (Model-It) which scaffolds the use of mathematics by providing a range of qualitative relationships that describe the quantitative relationships among the factors or by allowing them to enter a table of values

---

* Is a modeling tool an instructional method? If not, what relationship does it have to an instructional method, and what is that method? What about performance support tools and information gathering tools (see next two subsections)?

that they have collected. Young learners create and then test models that represent real-world phenomena.

Performance Support Tools

In many environments, performing repetitive, algorithmic tasks can rob cognitive resources from more intensive, higher order cognitive tasks that need to be performed. Therefore, CLEs should automate algorithmic tasks in order to offload the cognitive responsibility for their performance. For example, in business problem-solving environments, we have provided spreadsheet templates of problems for learners to test their hypotheses about levels of production, inventory, and sales. Most forms of testing in CLEs should be automated so that learners can simply call for test results. Generic tools such as calculators or database shells may be embedded to help learners organize the information they collect. Most CLEs provide notetaking facilities to offload memorization tasks. Identify in the activity structures those tasks that are facile for learners and those that may distract reasoning processes, and try to find a tool which supports that performance.

Information Gathering Tools

As stated before, information resources are important to understanding phenomena. Library research has shown that most learners are not skilled information seekers. The process of seeking information may distract learners from their primary goal of problem solving. So, embedding search tools may facilitate learning. Sophisticated search engines (many with graphical interfaces) and intelligent agents are in common use for seeking out and filtering information sources on the Web and selecting information that may be relevant to the user. Consider embedding information gathering tools like these in CLEs.

5. Conversation and Collaboration Tools

Contemporary conceptions of technology-supported learning environments assume the use of a variety of computer-mediated communications to support collaboration among communities of learners (Scardamalia, Bereiter, & Lamon, 1994). Why? Learning most naturally occurs not in isolation but by teams of people working together to solve problems. CLEs should provide access to shared information and shared knowledge-building tools to help learners to collaboratively construct socially shared knowledge. Problems are solved when a group works toward developing a common conception of the problem, so their energies can be focused on solving it. Conversations may be supported by discourse communities, knowledge-building communities, and communities of learners.

People who share common interests enjoy discussing their interests. In order to expand the community of discussants, people talk with each other through newsletters, magazines, and television shows. Recently, computer networks have evolved to support discourse *communities* through different forms of computer conferences (listservs, electronic mail, bulletin boards, NetNews services, chats, MUDs (multiuser dimensions) and MOOs (MUDs object oriented). These technologies support discourse on a wide range of topics.

Scardamalia and Bereiter (1996) argue that schools inhibit, rather than support, knowledge building by focusing on individual student abilities and learning. In *knowledge-building communities*, the goal is to support students to "actively and strategically pursue learning as a goal" (Scardamalia et al., 1994, p. 201).* To enable students to focus on knowledge construction as a primary goal, Computer-Supported Intentional Learning Environments (CSILEs) help students to produce knowledge databases so that their knowledge can "be objectified, represented in an overt form so that it could be evaluated, examined for gaps and inadequacies, added to, revised, and reformulated" (p. 201). CSILEs provide a medium for storing, organizing, and reformulating the ideas that are contributed by each of the members of the community. The knowledge base represents the synthesis of their thinking, something they own and of which they can be proud.

CLEs can also foster and support *communities of learners* (COLs). COLs are social organizations of learners who share knowledge, values, and goals (see, e.g., Bielaczyc & Collins, chap. 12 of this volume). COLs emerge when students share knowledge about common learning interests. Newcomers adopt the discourse structure, values, goals, and beliefs of the community (Brown, 1994). COLs can be fostered by having the participants conduct research (reading, studying, viewing, consulting experts) and share information in the pursuit of a meaningful, consequential task (Brown & Campione, 1996). Many of these learning community environments support reflection on the knowledge constructed and the processes used to construct it by the learners.** Scaffolded environments that support COLs include the Collaboratory Notebook (Edelson, Pea, & Gomez, 1996); CaMILE (Guzdial, Turns, Rappin, & Carlson, 1995), and the Knowledge Integration Environment (Bell, Davis, & Linn, 1995). Their common belief is that learning revolves around learners' conversations about what they are learning, not teacher interpretations.

In order to support collaboration within a group of learners, who may be either co-located or at a distance, CLEs should provide for and encourage conversations about the problems and projects the students are working on. Students write notes to the teacher and to each other about questions, topics, or problems that arise. Textualizing discourse among students makes their ideas appear to be as important as each other's and the instructor's comments (Slatin, 1992). When learners collaborate, they share the same goal: to solve the problem or reach some scientific consensus about an issue.

CLEs should support collaboration within a group of participants, shared decision making about how to manipulate the environment, alternative interpretations of top-

---

* See also chapter 12 by Bielaczyc and Collins.
** Reflection is a common feature in many theories in the new paradigm.

ics and problems, articulation of learners' ideas, and reflection on the processes they used.* Collaboration on solving a problem requires shared decision making, which proceeds through consensus-building activities to socially shared construction of knowledge and understanding about the problem. Reflection through computer conferences also engenders metaknowledge, the knowledge that participants have of the process in which the class is operating as well as the knowledge of themselves as participants in an evolving, ongoing conversation (Slatin, 1992).

6. Social/Contextual Support

Throughout the history of instructional design and technology, projects have failed most often because of poor implementation. Why? Because the designers or technology innovators failed to accommodate environmental and contextual factors affecting implementation. Frequently they tried to implement their innovation without considering important physical, organizational, and cultural aspects of the environment in which the innovation was being implemented.** For instance, many implementations of film and video failed because the physical environment couldn't be darkened sufficiently, adequate equipment wasn't available, or the content of the film or video was inimical or culturally insensitive to the audience. So the message was rejected by the learners.

In designing and implementing CLEs, accommodating contextual factors is important to successful implementation. It is also necessary to train the teachers and personnel who will be supporting the learning and to train the students who will be learning from the environments. The CoVis project (Edelson et al., 1996) supports teachers by sponsoring workshops and conferences in which teachers can seek help from and establish a consensus with the researchers. Questions can be posed by teachers, which are answered by peer teachers or technical staff. Social and contextual support of teachers and users is essential to successful implementation of CLEs.

SUPPORTING LEARNING IN CLEs

Table 10.1 lists learning activities that students perform in CLEs and instructional activities the CLE provides to support them. In most CLEs, learners need to explore; articulate what they know and have learned; speculate (conjecture, hypothesize, test); manipulate the environment in order to construct and test their theories and models; and reflect on what they did, why it did or didn't work, and what they have learned from the activities.

---

* Are these parts, kinds, or criteria?

** This highlights the importance of systemic thinking for recognizing and dealing with interdependencies between an instructional system and its environment, for the successful implementation of a new paradigm of instruction. See, e.g., the chapter by Reigeluth (1995) in G. Anglin (Ed.), *Instructional Technology: Past, Present, and Future (2nd Ed.).* Englewood, CO: Libraries Unlimited. Perkins and Unger (chap. 5) also raised this concern.

Learning Activities	Instructional Activities
Exploration	Modeling
Articulation	Coaching
Reflection	Scaffolding

Exploring attributes of the problem includes investigating related cases for similarities, and perusing information resources to find evidence to support solution of the problem or completion of the project that focuses the CLE. The most important cognitive components of exploration are goal-setting and managing the pursuit of those goals (Collins, 1991). What are the cognitive entailments of exploration?

The cognitive activities engaged while exploring CLEs include speculating and conjecturing about effects, manipulating the environment, observing and gathering evidence, and drawing conclusions about those effects. Most of these activities require reflection-in-action (Schon, 1982). Skilled practitioners often articulate their thoughts while performing, that is, they reflect-in-action.

CLEs also require articulating and reflecting on one's learning performance. Reflecting-on-action—standing outside yourself and analyzing your performance—is essential to learning. Requiring learners to articulate what they are doing in the environment and the reasons for their actions and to explain the strategies they use supports knowledge construction and metacognition.* Collins and Brown (1988) when learners imitate and practice the performance that is modeled for them, and the teachers replays learners' performances (using videotape, audit trails, think alouds, etc.), for they engage learners in reflection-on-action.

These learning activities indicate the goals for providing instructional supports in CLEs, such as modeling, coaching, and scaffolding (illustrated in Fig. 10.1).

A. Modeling

Modeling is the easiest implemented instructional strategy in CLEs. Two types of modeling exist: behavioral modeling of the overt performance and cognitive modeling of the covert cognitive processes. Behavioral modeling in CLEs demonstrates how to perform the activities identified in the activity structure. Cognitive modeling articulates the reasoning (reflection-in-action) that learners should use while engaged in the activities.

Model Performance

Carefully demonstrate each of the activities involved in a performance by a skilled (but not an expert) performer. When learners need help in a CLE, they might press a "Show Me" or a "How Do I Do This?" button. Modeling provides learners with an example of the desired performance. It is important to point out each of the discrete

---

* Such higher-order thinking skills are an important kind of learning (goal) that received little attention in the industrial-age paradigm of instruction.

actions and decisions involved in the performance, so that the learner is not required to infer missing steps. A widely recognized method for modeling problem solving is worked examples.

Worked examples include a description of how problems are solved by an experienced problem solver (Sweller & Cooper, 1985). Worked examples enhance the development of problem schemas and the recognition of different types of problems based on them. Using worked examples redirects the learner's attention away from the problem solution and toward problem-state configurations and their associated moves. Worked examples should be augmented by articulation of the reasoning (reflection-in-action) by the performer.

Articulate Reasoning

As an experienced performer models problem-solving or project skills, he or she should also articulate the reasoning and decision making involved in each step of the process, that is, model the covert as well as the overt performance. For example, record the performer thinking aloud while performing. Analyze the protocol in order to provide cues to the learners about important actions and processes, perhaps even elaborating on, or providing alternative representations of, those activities. You might also record the performer conducting a postmortem analysis or abstracted replays, where you discuss the performer's actions and decisions.

In solving the ill-structured problems that characterize most CLEs, learners need to know how to develop arguments to support their solutions to the problem. In these cases, performers should overtly model the kinds of argumentation necessary to solve the problem. You might also consider providing reasoning-congruent visual representations (described before) generated by the skilled performer. These visual models of the objects of expert reasoning may provide rich alternative representations to help learners perceive the structure of reasoning. You might also have performers use some of the cognitive tools to represent their understanding of, or reasoning through of the problem. The purpose in all of these is to make the covert overt, so that it can be analyzed and understood and so that learners know why they should perform, as well as how to perform.

B. Coaching

Modeling strategies focus on how expert performers function. The assumption of most instruction is that, in order to learn, learners will attempt to perform like the model, first through crude imitation, advancing through articulating and habituating performance, to the creation of skilled, original performances. At each of these stages, learners' performances will likely improve with coaching. The role of coach is complex and inexact. A good coach motivates learners, analyzes their performances, provides feedback and advice on the performances and how to learn about how to perform, and provokes reflection on and articulation of what was learned.

Coaching may be solicited by the learner. Students seeking help might press a "How Am I Doing?" button. Or coaching may be unsolicited, when the coach observes the performance and provides encouragement, diagnosis, directions, and feedback. Coaching naturally and necessarily involves responses that are situated in the learner's task performance (Laffey, Tupper, Musser, & Wedman, 1997). You can include the following kinds of coaching in CLEs.

Provide Motivational Prompts

A good coach relates the importance of the learning task to the learner. In case the learners are not immediately engaged by the problem, then the CLE coach needs to provide learners a good reason for becoming engaged. Once started, the coach should boost the learners' confidence levels, especially during the early stages of the problem or project. Motivational prompts can usually be faded quickly once learners become engaged by the problem. It may be necessary to provide additional, intermittent prompts during the performance of particularly difficult tasks.

Monitor and Regulate the Learner's Performance

The most important role of the coach is to monitor, analyze, and regulate the learners' development of important skills. Coaching may:

- provide *hints* and *helps*, such as directing learners to particular aspects of the tasks or reminding learners of parts of the task they may have overlooked;
- prompt appropriate kinds of thinking, such as suggestions to generate images, make inferences, generalize another idea, use an analogy, make up a story, generate questions, summarize results, or draw an implication;
- prompt the use of collaborative activities;
- prompt consideration of related cases or particular information resources that may help learners interpret or understand ideas;
- prompt the use of specific cognitive tools that may assist articulation and understanding of underlying concepts or their interrelationships;
- provide feedback that not only informs the learners about the effectiveness and accuracy of their performance, but also analyzes their actions and thinking.

Provoke Reflection

A good coach becomes the conscience of the learner. So, a good coach provokes learners to reflect on (monitor and analyze) their performance. Engaging the monitoring of comprehension and the selection of appropriate cognitive strategies can be implemented in CLEs by inserting provoking questions that:

- ask the learners to reflect on what they have done,
- ask the learners to reflect on what assumptions they made,
- ask the learners to reflect on what strategies they used,

- ask the learners to explain why they made a particular response or tool an action,
- ask learners to confirm an intended response,
- ask learners to state how certain they are in a response,
- require learners to argue with the coach,
- provide puzzles that learners need to solve which will lead to appropriate performance.

Perturb Learners' Models

The mental models that naive learners build to represent problems are often flawed. They often misattribute components of the problem or incorrectly connect them, so they are trying to solve the wrong kind of problem. So it is necessary to perturb the learner's model.* When learners see that their models do not adequately explain the environment they are trying to manipulate, they adjust or adapt the model to explain the discrepancies.

Perturbing learners' understanding can be accomplished by embedding provoking questions (Have you thought about … ?, What will happen if … ?, Does your model explain … ?). It is also useful to require learners to reflect on actions they have taken (Why did you … ?, What results did you expect … ?, What would have happened if … ?). A simpler approach is to ask learners to confirm or clarify what did happen (Why did that reaction occur … ?). Along with eliciting responses, the coach should ascertain the learner's response certainty. That is, when a learner makes a response (keys a response into the computer), a simple probe (On a scale of 1 to 10, how sure are you of that response?) will cause the learner to reflect on how much he or she knows about the subject. This tactic will likely not work for every response due to learner fatigue, so reserve it for the important interactions. Another approach to perturbing learner models is to provide dissonant views or interpretations in response to student actions or interpretations.

Most of the coaching processes, especially the monitoring and regulation of learner performance, require some form of intelligence in the CLE system in order to judge the performance. That normally entails some form of expert model of the performance and thinking to be used as the benchmark for analyzing and comparing the student's performance, thinking, and resulting mental model.

C. Scaffolding

Modeling is focused on the expert's performance. Coaching is focused on the learner's performance. Scaffolding is a more systemic approach to supporting the learner, focusing on the task, the environment, the teacher, and the learner. Scaf-

---

* The development of learners' mental models is a kind of learning that was not often addressed in the industrial-age paradigm, but is a common feature of most theories in the new paradigm (see chap. 3, p. 54, "Understand relationships").

folding provides temporary frameworks to support learning and student performance beyond the learners' capacities.

The concept of scaffolding represents any kind of support for cognitive activity that is provided by an adult when the child and adult are performing the task together (Wood & Middleton, 1975). Wood, Bruner, and Ross (1976) describe scaffolding during problem solving as recruiting the child's interest, simplifying the task, motivating the child, and demonstrating the correct performance. Resnick (1988) proposes that record keeping and other tools, especially representational devices commonly found in computer microworlds, can serve as instructional scaffolds. Lehrer (1993) also suggests scaffolding with computer tools, as well as scaffolding through alternative assessments. It is obvious from these descriptions that the concept of scaffolding is fuzzy and indistinct as it relates to modeling and coaching.

For purposes of CLEs, I believe that scaffolding represents some manipulation of the task itself by the system. When scaffolding performance, the system performs part of the task for the student, supplants the student's ability to perform some part of the task by changing the nature of the task or imposing the use of cognitive tools that help the learner perform, or adjusts the nature or difficulty of the task. Whereas coaching focuses on an individual task performance, scaffolding focuses on the inherent nature of the task being performed. A learner's request for scaffolding might take the form of a "Help Me Do This" button.

Learners experiencing difficulties in performing a task possess insufficient prior knowledge or readiness to perform. This suggests three separate approaches to scaffolding of learning: adjust the difficulty of the task to accommodate the learner, restructure the task to supplant a lack of prior knowledge, or provide alternative assessments. Designing scaffolds requires explication of the activity structure required to complete a job (using activity theory or cognitive task analysis, as described before). From the list of tasks or activities, identify those that are not currently possessed by the learners or for which the learners are not ready (defining the learner's zone of proximal development).

Adjust Task Difficulty

Scaffolding may provide an easier task. Start the learners with the tasks they know how to perform and gradually add task difficulty until they are unable to perform alone. This will be their zone of proximal development. This form of task regulation is an example of black-box scaffolding (Hmelo & Guzdial, 1996), that which facilitates student performance but which will not be faded out while learners are using the environment. This is the kind of scaffolding that learners cannot see; the adult supporter is invisible.

Restructure a Task to Supplant Knowledge

Another approach to scaffolding learners' performance is to redesign the task in a way that supports learning, that is, supplanting task performance (Salomon, 1979).

Task performance may also be supplanted by suggesting or imposing the use of cognitive tools to help learners represent or manipulate the problem. These forms of scaffolding are examples of glass-box scaffolding (Hmelo & Guzdial, 1996) because they are faded after a number of cases. Otherwise they become intellectual crutches. Learners need to be helped to perform that which they cannot do alone. Having performed desired skills, they must learn to perform without the scaffolds that support their performance.

Provide Alternative Assessments

Learning is, to a large degree, assessment-driven. Learners develop fairly sophisticated strategies for identifying the expected performance and studying accordingly. More often than not, that performance is reproductive, so learners develop strategies for identifying what the teacher will believe is important and memorizing that. Test pools and notetaking services scaffold this kind of learning. However, when learners apply these reproductive strategies in problem-oriented CLEs, they often fail.* Learners must be aware of the complex nature of the learning task and understand what the task means, so that they metacognitively adjust their attention, effort, and thinking strategies to accommodate the task. In CLEs, it is important that the project or problem requirements are clearly communicated, so that learners understand what will be required of them. This may be done through worked examples of sample problems or sample questions, as well as understanding the nature of the problem. The problem representation and decomposition process cannot begin until learners understand what the solution will be like (Jonassen, 1997).

CONCLUSION

This chapter has cursorily described a model for designing CLEs. It has conceptually described the components of a CLE and the strategies for supporting learners' performances in them. Because of page limitations, I was unable to articulate the philosophical assumptions behind CLEs, impediments to learning from CLEs, how to evaluate learning in CLEs, and alternative approaches to using technology to support constructive learning. Those topics will be addressed in other publications.

It is important to note that this model is intended to provide guidelines for designing learning environments to support constructive learning. Constructive learning emphasizes personal meaning making and so intentionally seeks to relate new ideas to experiences and prior learning. Constructive learning therefore engages conceptual and strategic thinking, in contrast to reproductive learning. CLEs are not appropriate for all learning outcomes. If you want to design learning environments to engage learners in personal and/or collaborative knowledge construction and problem solving outcomes, then consider designing CLEs.

---

* This helps identify ways that the new paradigm differs from the industrial-age paradigm of instruction.

REFERENCES

Anderson, J. R., Boyle, C. F., & Yost, G. (1986). The geometry tutor. *Journal of Mathematical Behavior, 5,* 5–19.

Barrows, H. S. (1985). *How to design a problem-based curriculum for the pre-clinical years.* New York: Springer-Verlag.

Barrows, H. S., & Tamblyn, R. M. (1980). *Problem-based learning: An approach to medical education.* New York: Springer-Verlag.

Bell, P., Davis, E. A., & Linn, M. C. (1995). The knowledge integration environment: Theory and design. In J. L. Schnase & E. L. Cunnius (Eds.), *Proceedings of CSCL '95: The first international conference on computer support for collaborative learning* (pp. 157–160). Hillsdale, NJ: Lawrence Erlbaum Associates.

Brown, A. L. (1994). The advancement of learning. *Educational Researcher, 23*(8), 4–12.

Brown, A. L, & Campione, J. C. (1996). Psychological theory and the design of innovative learning environments: On procedures, principles and systems. In L. Schanble & R. Glaser (Eds.), *Innovations in learning: New environments for education* (pp. 289–325). Hillsdale, NJ: Lawrence Erlbaum Associates.

Bruner, J. (1990). *Acts of meaning.* Cambridge, MA: Harvard University Press.

Cognition and Technology Group at Vanderbilt (1992). Anchored instruction in science and mathematics: Theoretical bases, developmental projects, and initial research findings. In R. A. Duschl & R. J. Hamilton (Eds.), *Philosophy of science, cognitive psychology, and educational theory and practice* (pp. 244–273). New York: State University of New York Press.

Cooper, G., & Sweller, J. (1987). The effects of schema acquisition and rule automation of mathematical problem-solving transfer. *Journal of Educational Psychology, 79,* 347–362.

Duffy, T. M. & Jonassen, D. (Eds.). (1992). *Constructivism and the technology of instruction: A conversation.* Hillsdale, NJ: Lawrence Erlbaum Associates.

Edelson, D. C., Pea, R. D., & Gomez, L. (1996). Constructivism in the collaboratory. In B. G. Wilson (Ed.), *Constructivist learning environments: Case studies in instructional design* (pp. 151–164). Englewood Cliffs, NJ: Educational Technology Publications.

Guzdial, M., Turns, J., Rappin, N., & Carlson, D. (1995). Collaborative support for learning in complex domains. In J. L. Schnase & E. L. Cunnius (Eds.), *Proceedings of CSCL '95: The first international conference on computer support for collaborative learning* (pp. 157–160). Hillsdale, NJ: Lawrence Erlbaum Associates.

Hall, E. P., Gott, S. P, & Pokorny, R. A.(1994). *A procedural guide to cognitive task analysis: The PARI methodology* (AL/HR-TR-1995-0108). Brooks Air Force Base, TX: Armstrong Laboratory.

Hmelo, C. E., & Guzdial, M. (1996). Of black and glass boxes: Scaffolding for doing and learning. In *Proceedings of the Second International Conference on the Learning Sciences* (pp. 128–133). Charlottesville, VA: Association for the Advancement of Computers in Education.

Honebein, P., Duffy, T. M., & Fishman, B. (1993). Constructivism and the design of learning environments: Context and authentic activities for learning. In T.M. Duffy, J. Lowyck, & D. Jonassen (Eds.), *Designing environments for constructivist learning* (pp. 87–108). Heidelberg, Germany: Springer-Verlag.

Jonassen, D. H. (1991). Objectivism vs. constructivism: Do we need a new philosophical paradigm? *Educational Technology: Research and Development, 39*(3), 5–14.

Jonassen, D. H. (1993). Cognitive flexibility theory and its implications for designing CBI. In S. Dijkstra, H. P. Krammer, & J. V. Merrienboer (Eds.), *Instructional models in computer based learning environments.* Heidelberg, Germany: Springer-Verlag.

Jonassen, D. H. (1995a). Supporting communities of learners with technology: A vision for integrating technology with learning in schools. *Educational Technology, 35*(4), 60–63.

Jonassen, D. H. (1995b). An instructional design model for designing constructivist learning environments. In H. Maurer (Ed.), *Proceedings of the World Conference on Educational Media.* Charlottesville, VA: Association for the Advancement of Computers in Education.

Jonassen, D. H. (1996a). *Computers in the classroom: Mindtools for critical thinking.* Columbus, OH: Prentice-Hall.

Jonassen, D. H. (1996b). Scaffolding diagnostic reasoning in case-based learning environments. *Journal of Computing in Higher Education, 8*(1), 48–68.

Jonassen, D. H. (1997). Instructional design model for well-structured and ill-structured problem-solving learning outcomes. Educational Technology: Research and *Development 45*(1), 65–94.

Jonassen, D. H., Ambruso, D. R., & Olesen, J. (1992). Designing a hypertext on transfusion medicine using cognitive flexibility theory. *Journal of Educational Hypermedia and Multimedia, 1*(3), 309–322.

Jonassen, D. H., Campbell, J. P., & Davidson, M. E. (1994). Learning with media: Restructuring the debate. *Educational Technology: Research and Development, 42*(2), 31–39.

Jonassen, D. H., & Henning, P. H. (1996). Mental models: Knowledge in the head and knowledge in the world. In Proceedings of the 2nd International Conference on the *Learning Sciences*. Evanston, IL, Northwestern University Press.

Jonassen, D. H., Peck, K., & Wilson, B. G. (1998). *Learning WITH technology: A constructivist perspective*. Columbus, OH: Merrill/Prentice-Hall.

Jonassen, D. H., & Rohrer-Murphy, L. (1999). Activity theory as a framework for designing constructivist learning environments. *Educational Technology: Research and Development, 46*(1).

Kolodner, J. (1993). *Case-based reasoning*. San Mateo, CA: Kaufmann Development.

Kommers, P., Jonassen, D. H., & Mayes, T. (1992). *Cognitive tools for learning*. Heidelberg, Germany: Springer-Verlag

Krajcik, J. S., Blumenfeld, P. C., Marx, R. W., & Soloway, E. (1994). A collaborative model for helping middle grade science teachers learn project-based instruction. *The Elementary School Journal, 94*(5), 483–497.

Laffey, J., Tupper, T., Musser, D., & Wedman, J. (1997). *A computer-mediated support system for project-based learning*. Paper presented at the annual conference of The American Educational Research Association, Chicago, IL.

Lave, J., & Wenger, E. (1991). *Situated learning: Legitimate peripheral participation*. New York: Cambridge University Press.

Lehrer, R. (1993). Authors of knowledge: Patterns of hypermedia design. In S. P. LaJoie & S. J. Derry (Eds.), *Computers as cognitive tools*. Hillsdale, NJ: Lawrence Erlbaum Associates.

Leont'ev, A. N. (1979). The problem of activity in psychology. In J. V. Wertsch (Ed.), *The concept of activity in Soviet psychology* (pp. 37–71). Armonk, NY: Sharpe.

Lindeman, B., Kent, T., Kinzie, M., Larsen, V., Ashmore, L., & Becker, F. (1995). Exploring cases online with virtual environments. In J. Schnase & E. Cunnius (Eds.), *Proceedings of the First International Conference on Computer-Supported Collaborative learning*. Hillsdale, NJ: Lawrence Erlbaum Associates.

Merrill, D. C., Reiser, B. J., Bekkelaar, R., & Hamid, A. (1992). Making processes visible: Scaffolding learning with reasoning-congruent representations. In C. Frasson, C. Gauthier, & G. I. McCall (Eds.), *Intelligent tutoring systems: Proceedings of the Second International Conference, ITS '92* (Lecture Notes in Computer Science No. 608, pp. 103–110). Berlin: Springer-Verlag.

Perkins, D. (1991). Technology meets constructivism: Do they make a marriage? *Educational Technology, 31*(5), 18–23.

Polya, M. (1957). *How to solve it* (2nd Ed.). New York: Doubleday.

Petraglia, J. (1998). *Reality by design: The rhetoric and technology of authenticity in education*. Hillsdale, NJ: Lawrence Erlbaum Associates.

Resnick, L. B. (1988). *Treating mathematics as a ill-structured discipline*. Pittsburgh, PA: University of Pittsburgh, Learning Research & Development Center, (ED 299133).

Salomon, G. (1979). *The interaction of media, cognition, and learning*. San Francisco: Josey-Bass.

Savery, J., & Duffy, T. M. (1996). Problem based learning: An instructional model and its constructivist framework. In B. G. Wilson (Ed.), *Designing constructivist learning environments* (pp. 135–148). Englewood Cliffs, NJ: Educational Technology Publications.

Scardamalia, M., & Bereiter, C. (1996). Adaptation and understanding: A case for new cultures of schooling. In S. Vosniadou, E. De Corte, R. Glaser, & H. Mandl (Eds.), *International perspectives on the design of technology-supported learning environments* (149–163). Hillsdale, NJ: Lawrence Erlbaum Associates.

Scardamalia, M., Bereiter, C., & Lamon P. (1994). The CSILE Project: Trying to bring the classroom into World 3. In K. McGilly (Ed.), *Classroom lessons: Integrating cognitive theory and classroom practice* (pp. 201–228). Cambridge MA: MIT Press.

Schank, R. C. (1990). *Tell me a story: Narrative and intelligence*. Evanston, IL: Northwestern University Press.

Schank, R. C., Kass, A., & Riesbeck, C. K. (1994). *Inside case-based explanation*. Hillsdale, NJ: Lawrence Erlbaum Associates.

Schon, D. A. (1982). *The "reflective practitioner" How professionals think in action*. New York: Basic Books.

Slatin, J. M. (1992). Is there a class in this text? Creating knowledge in the electronic classroom. In E. Barett (Ed.), *Sociomedia: Multimedia, hypermedia, and the social construction of knowledge*. Cambridge, MA: MIT Press.

Soloway, E., Krajcik, J., & Finkel, E. A. (1995, April). *The ScienceWare project: Supporting science modeling and inquiry via computational media & technology*. Paper presented at the annual meeting of the America Educational Research Association, San Franciso, CA.

Spiro, R. J., Vispoel, W., Schmitz, J., Samarapungavan, A., & Boerger, A. (1987). Knowledge acquisition for application: Cognitive flexibility and transfer in complex content domains. In B. C. Britton (Ed.), *Executive control processes*. Hillsdale, NJ: Lawrence Erlbaum Associates.

Spitulnik, J., Studer, S, Finkel, E. A. Gustafson, E., Laczko, J., & Soloway, E. (1995). The RiverMUD design rationale: Scaffolding for scientific inquiry through modeling, discourse, and decision making in community based issues. In J. L. Schnase & E. L. Cunnius (Eds.), *Proceedings of CSCL 95: The first international conference on computer support for collaborative learning*. Hillsdale, NJ: Lawrence Erlbaum Associates.

Sweller, J., & Cooper, G. (1985) The use of worked examples as a substitute for problem solving in learning algebra. *Cognition and Instruction, 2*, 59–89.

Tessmer, M., & Richey, R. C. (1997). The role of context in learning and instructional design. *Educational* Technology: Research and Development, 45(3).

Whitehead, A. N (1929). *The aims of education and other essays*. New York: Macmillan.

Williams, S. (1992). Putting case-based instruction into context: Examples from legal and medical education. *Journal of the Learning Sciences, 2*(4), 367–427.

Wood, D. J., Bruner, J. S., & Ross, G. (1976). The role of tutoring in problem solving. *Journal of Child Psychology and Psychiatry, 17*, 89–100.

Wood, D. J., & Middleton, R. (1975). A study of assisted problem solving. *British Journal of Psychology, 66*(2), 181–191.

11 Collaborative Problem Solving

Laurie Miller Nelson
Brigham Young University

Laurie Miller Nelson

Laurie Miller Nelson is Assistant Professor of Instructional Psychology and Technology at Brigham Young University. She received her PhD in Instructional Systems Technology from Indiana University. She teaches undergraduate courses in educational psychology and graduate courses in instructional theory and research. Her current interests are in instructional theory building, formative research on collaborative problem solving, and development of online collaborative tools and pedagogy.

FOREWORD

Goals and preconditions. *The primary goals of this theory are to develop content knowledge in complex domains, problem-solving and critical thinking skills, and collaboration skills. It should only be used when those types of learning are paramount and when the students and instructor are receptive to this approach to learning, with its shift in roles and power relationships.*

Values. *Some of the values upon which this theory is based include:*
- *learning to use naturally effective collaborative processes,*
- *critical-thinking and problem-solving skills,*
- *rich social contexts and multiple perspectives for learning,*
- *learning environments that are situated, learner-centered, integrated, and collaborative,*
- *authenticity, ownership, and relevance of the learning experience for students,*
- *cultivating supportive, respectful relationships among learners, as well as between learners and the instructor,*
- *developing a desire for life-long learning and the skills to sustain it.*

Methods. *Here are the major methods this theory offers:*

Comprehensive guidelines
Instructor-Implemented Methods
- *Act as a resource and tutor.*
- *Create learning environments that allow learners to work in a variety of small groups, each for an extended period of time.*
- *Formulate questions to focus the learner on important aspects of content and learning processes.*
- *Provide just-in-time instruction when requested by learners.*

Learner-Implemented Methods
- *Determine how the acquired knowledge and resources will be used to resolve the problem.*
- *Determine and account for individual and group time on project activities.*

Instructor- and Learner-Implemented Methods
- *Collaborate to determine learning issues and objectives.*
- *Conduct group progress meetings.*
- *Collect needed resources.*
- *Evaluate learners in multiple ways; provide group and individual evaluations/grades.*

Interactive Methods
- *Learn and purposefully use appropriate social skills and team-building activities.*

- *Promote investigation, interaction, interpretation, and intrinsic motivation.*
- *Encourage simultaneous interaction and face-to-face promotive interaction.*
- *Promote equal participation, positive interdependence, and individual accountability.*

Process activities

1. Build Readiness
  - *Overview the collaborative problem-solving process.*
  - *Develop an authentic problem or project scenario to anchor instructional and learning activities.*
  - *Provide instruction and practice in group process skills.*

2. Form and Norm Groups
  - *Form small, heterogeneous work groups.*
  - *Encourage groups to establish operational guidelines.*

3. Determine a Preliminary Problem Definition
  - *Negotiate a common understanding of the problem.*
  - *Identify learning issues and goals.*
  - *Brainstorm preliminary solutions or project plans.*
  - *Select and develop initial design plan.*
  - *Identify sources of needed resources.*
  - *Gather preliminary information to validate the design plan.*

4. Define and Assign Roles
  - *Identify the principal roles needed to complete the design plan.*
  - *Negotiate the assignment of roles.*

5. Engage in an Iterative Collaborative Problem-Solving Process
  - *Refine and evolve the design plan.*
  - *Identify and assign tasks.*
  - *Acquire needed information, resources, and expertise.*
  - *Collaborate with instructor to acquire additional resources and skills needed.*
  - *Disseminate acquired information, resources, and expertise to the other group members.*
  - *Engage in solution- or project-development work.*
  - *Report regularly on individual contributions and group activities.*
  - *Participate in intergroup collaborations and evaluations.*
  - *Conduct formative evaluations of the solution or project.*

6. Finalize the Solution or Project
  - *Draft the final version of the solution or project.*
  - *Conduct final evaluation or usability test of the solution or project.*
  - *Revise and complete the final version of the solution or project.*

7. Synthesize and Reflect
  - *Identify learning gains.*

• *Debrief experiences and feelings about the process.*
• *Reflect on group and individual learning processes.*

8. *Assess Products and Processes*
   • *Evaluate the products and artifact created.*
   • *Evaluate the processes used.*

9. *Provide Closure*
   • *Formalize group adjournment through a closure activity.*

Major contributions. *The synthesis of problem-solving and collaborative methods of instruction. The comprehensive yet detailed nature of the guidance offered.*

—*C.M.R.*

Collaborative Problem Solving

INTRODUCTION

Often in our daily lives we find ourselves working in small groups, whether it be in the context of a work project, a civic group, a classroom, or a family. Group problem solving is one of the most common and natural situations in which we accomplish the work of society.* As a result, education and business have come to recognize the significant learning gains and increased creativity which develop from learning and working collaboratively in groups or teams (Johnson & Johnson, 1990). In recognition of these benefits, educators are realizing the need for better instructional theories and methods for assisting learners in engaging in efficient, effective, collaborative problem-solving processes.

In response to the need to work and learn collaboratively, a number of instructional approaches have been developed. One of the principal approaches has been *cooperative learning*. Forms of this approach have been used for a number of years (Sharan, 1994), becoming a major force in encouraging the use of collaboration in the classroom. A more recent approach is *problem-based learning*, which grew out of the need in medical education for richer, more realistic learning experiences for

---

* This was rare in the industrial age but is becoming very common as we evolve deeper into the information age. This is one of the forces driving the need for a new paradigm of instruction.

young medical students (Albanese & Mitchell, 1993). Each approach focuses on different aspects of the collaborative learning process. Cooperative learning provides guidelines on how to organize learning groups and suggests specific activities to structure their learning experiences, such as the jigsaw method (Aronson, Blaney, Stephan, Sikes, and Snapp, 1978), think-pair-share (Kagan & Kagan, 1994), and Student Teams-Achievement Divisions (Slavin, 1995). In contrast, problem-based learning emphasizes the development of a carefully constructed problem scenario, which collaborative groups, with assistance from faculty tutors, then work to solve (Savery & Duffy, 1995).

Both of these approaches provide valuable instructional guidelines for creating collaborative learning environments, but neither is comprehensive. That is, cooperative learning is not usually conceived in the context of a problem-based learning environment, and problem-based learning doesn't always require collaboration. And difficulties can arise in both approaches when not enough guidance is provided about the actual collaborative problem-solving process in which the students are to engage. Thus there is a need for a more comprehensive approach, which not only adapts and integrates the best strategies from both of the earlier approaches, but also provides additional guidelines on how to support learners through the actual problem-solving process. This chapter presents guidelines for a theory of collaborative problem solving (CPS) that address the whole of the collaborative learning process, including building a readiness in students to learn collaboratively, developing group skills, forming groups, engaging in collaborative problem solving, and finalizing the process through appropriate synthesis, assessment, and closure activities.

In addition to its comprehensive nature, another important feature of the CPS instructional theory is that it supports the most powerful types of problem-solving activity that learners can engage in—those that are based on their own natural collaborative processes. I believe that, to the extent possible, it is important to design learning environments which support and augment those naturally effective collaborative processes which learners develop intuitively through their own life experiences. When we impose unnatural structures, we may, in fact, hinder the flow of interaction and learning and curtail effective, efficient problem solving.

Maximizing the natural collaborative processes of learners is only one of the pedagogical values emphasized in the CPS approach. Other values evident in this approach include the following:

- creating learning environments which are situated, learner-centered, integrated, and collaborative, versus ones which are decontextualized, isolated, and competitive;
- honoring the importance of authenticity, ownership, and relevance of the learning experience for students in relation to the content to be learned and the process by which it is learned;
- allowing students to learn by doing as active participants in their own learning processes;

- fostering the development of critical thinking and problem-solving skills;
- encouraging the exploration and analysis of content from multiple perspectives;
- acknowledging the importance of rich social contexts for learning;
- cultivating supportive, respectful relationships among learners, as well as between learners and the instructor;
- developing a desire for life-long learning and the skills to sustain it.

These values are the basis for framing appropriate methods and guidelines for the CPS instructional theory. These guidelines evolved from a synthesis of the research literature on small-group problem-solving processes, collaborative-learning theory, and cooperative and problem-based instructional theories, along with my practical experience as a learner, educator, and researcher. The intent of this approach is to provide instructors and learners with an integrated set of guidelines which they can use to design and participate in authentic learning environments which invoke critical thinking, creativity, and complex problem solving while developing important social interaction skills.

The CPS guidelines described in this chapter are of two general types: *comprehensive guidelines* and *process activities.* Comprehensive guidelines underlie and are applied throughout the entire process. In contrast, process activities are limited to specific phases of the problem-solving process. It is intended that these two types of guidelines will act in concert to provide instructors and learners with a wholistic approach to collaborative problem solving, offering a rich learning experience in which students not only learn salient content knowledge and skills, but also develop problem-solving skills.

This chapter will begin by discussing the conditions under which the CPS approach should be used and ways in which it should be implemented. This will be followed by a description of the CPS instructional theory itself.

CONDITIONS FOR USING CPS

Because not every instructional approach is effective in every learning context, it is necessary to determine *when* a particular approach is the best possible match for the learner's needs, the instructor's teaching style, the learning environment, and the instructional goals. It is also important to determine *how* an instructional approach should be used in a given context. Does the whole approach need to be implemented to maintain its integrity or can certain parts or strategies be used in isolation? This section will consider conditions related to when the CPS approach is most appropriate and how it is best implemented.

When to Use the CPS Approach

When using CPS, a number of conditions should be considered, including the type of content and the learning environment, in addition to the characteristics of the learner and the instructor.

Type of Content. The CPS approach is most appropriate with heuristic tasks, as opposed to procedural tasks (Nelson & Reigeluth, 1997). Heuristic tasks are made up of a complex system of knowledge and skills which can be combined in a variety of ways to complete the task successfully (Reigeluth, chap. 18 of this volume). For instance, the type of knowledge and skills that a psychologist must draw upon when counseling clients would require an understanding of a wide range of principles of human behavior, different ones of which would be required for different cases. In contrast, procedural tasks, like assembling a bicycle, generally have a more stable and predictable pattern.

In addition to heuristic tasks, other types of learning appropriate for CPS include developing conceptual understandings and cognitive strategies.* Developing conceptual understandings includes either developing schemas for new knowledge or assimilating the content into existing schemas. Cognitive strategies include critical thinking skills, learning strategies, and metacognitive skills. When any of these are the primary types of learning desired, then CPS can be an extremely effective instructional approach.

The CPS approach is not usually suitable if the content to be learned is either factual information which needs to be memorized or a procedural task which is best accomplished by a fixed series of steps. Under these conditions, CPS would not only waste precious instructional time, but could be frustrating for both the learners and the instructor as the learning groups struggle to invent a procedure when a highly developed and tested procedure already exists and can be taught more effectively with a direct approach.

Thus CPS is most appropriate when there is not a single answer to a question or best way of doing something, but rather when the nature of the task varies considerably from one situation to another, or when a depth of understanding is desired.

Learning Environment. The learning environment which is most effective for CPS is one conducive to collaboration, experimentation, and inquiry, an environment which encourages an open exchange of ideas and information.** Learners should feel free to voice their opinions, explore new ideas, and try out a variety of approaches in their work. This type of collaborative climate needs to be fostered and protected not only by the instructor, but also by the learners themselves.

---

* These three kinds of learning are ones that were seldom addressed by industrial-age theories but are commonly addressed by the new paradigm (see especially chap. 14 by Pogrow and chap. 15 by Landa).

** This is also typical of the new paradigm of instructional theories (see especially chap. 12 by Bielaczyc & Collins).

It is important that the learning environment reflect the values inherent in collaboration. This may require reconceptualizing the curriculum and adapting the physical surroundings and the classroom climate to support small-group work. Adequate time, space, and resources must be available. CPS can often be very time intensive for both learners and instructors. Careful planning is required to provide enough time for groups to meet and to complete the project. Adequate space must also be made available for group meetings and project work. Furthermore, a variety of information, materials, and human resources should be reasonably available to learners.

It is also important that CPS be based on a well-conceived problem or project scenario. These scenarios can vary on a continuum from those which are entirely designed by the instructor prior to instruction to those which are real-world and ill defined, identified by the instructor and/or students once the learning experience has begun and the parameters of the problem or project have been determined. Conditions which influence the types of problems or project scenarios that are appropriate include the type of content to be learned, the time allocation for each assignment, and the degree of access to real-world problems and subject-matter experts.

Learner Characteristics.   The types of learners who will engage in CPS and their capabilities are additional critical factors influencing when the CPS approach can be successfully used. It is essential that students using CPS are, or can become, self-directed learners who are comfortable with, and willing to take responsibility for, their own learning.* Often the instructor will need to cultivate these characteristics in learners, especially if the learners' experiences have been primarily with traditional educational approaches. Otherwise, learners will feel so uncomfortable with the new roles they and the instructor are asked to take that their learning will be significantly inhibited. Not only must they come to trust that the instructor is truly willing to *allow* them ownership over their learning; they must also *accept* this ownership. When presented with this alternative student–teacher relationship,** learners often try to maintain the previous status quo, where the instructor is responsible for directing all classroom activities and providing all necessary information and resources. Consequently, learners often need coaching on how to operate in this new environment, including what new roles, expectations, and responsibilities will be required.

This shift in roles highlights how learner characteristics and instructor characteristics are inextricably linked. The more autonomous the learner, the less need there is for structure from the instructor. But both need to become comfortable with making changes in typical classroom power and control structures, creating a more open, collaborative learning environment.

---

* This, too, is typical of the new paradigm (see especially chap. 13 by Corno & Randi).

** Significant changes in roles and relationships are a major distinction between the new and old paradigms of instruction. This depicts the nature of some of those changes. It also highlights the need for changes in mindsets of teachers and students for the new paradigm to be successfully implemented. These are all aspects of systemic change in education. See e.g., Banathy, 1991 (full reference is in chap. 1); Schlechty, P. C. (1990). *Schools for the 21st century: Leadership imperatives for educational reform.* Josey-Bass.

Instructor Characteristics. As discussed above, instructors must also be comfortable with less direct control of the students and instruction. They must be willing to encourage self-directed learning by students and to operate more as facilitators than as micromanagers. This requires that instructors be flexible and tolerant of a certain degree of ambiguity in what exactly is to be learned and how this will take place. Instructors must also be prepared to use a wide range of teaching approaches as needed, such as large- and small-group discussion, direct instruction, active learning, and just-in-time instruction.

How CPS Should Be Implemented

Because of its comprehensive nature, the CPS instructional theory, as outlined below, should be implemented in its entirety in order for the collaborative problem-solving process to have integrity and coherence. Otherwise, the theory may not provide the rich, wholistic experience in collaboration and problem solving for which it was designed. However, flexibility is built into the theory so that it can be adapted to a variety of learning situations.* For example, the type of problem or project used, the level of support provided by the instructor, and the composition of the learning groups can all be customized to the unique requirements of a given learning context.

INSTRUCTIONAL THEORY FOR COLLABORATIVE PROBLEM SOLVING

This instructional theory describes the guidelines and instructional strategies used during collaborative problem solving and explains their organization. As indicated earlier, guidance is grouped into two general categories, (a) *comprehensive guidelines,* which are applied to and support the entire process, and (b) *process activities,* which are used during specific phases of the process. As the theory was being developed, the guidelines that best addressed the process as a whole, the comprehensive guidelines, were synthesized from cooperative learning and problem-based learning approaches. In contrast, the process activities for use during an actual instructional event were formulated from research on group problem-solving processes. When used in concert, the comprehensive guidelines and the process activities provide a coherent instructional approach which supports a naturally efficient, "expert" collaborative learning environment. What follows is a description of the comprehensive guidelines and the process activities.

COMPREHENSIVE GUIDELINES

The comprehensive guidelines collectively form a mindset from which the instructor and learners operate during instruction. The basic assumption characterizing

---

* Flexibility is a common feature for many theories in the new paradigm (see especially chap. 9 by Schwartz, Lin, Brophy & Bransford, and chap. 13 by Corno & Randi).

these methods is that the learning environment is cooperative and collaborative, with the instructor and learners engaging in activities that not only solve a problem or lead to the completion of a project, but also encourage the development of problem-solving, critical-thinking, and team-building skills.

To facilitate explanation, these comprehensive guidelines have been grouped into categories which reflect their commonalities and instructional intent. The first three categories are concerned with who will implement the method: instructor, learner, or instructor and learner together. The fourth category includes methods that help provide a framework for the types of interactions which should be taking place in the learning groups. These interactive methods also contribute to a collaborative mindset, which is critical for engaging in this type of learning.

It is important to remember that, even though the comprehensive guidelines are grouped into categories, the interrelated, iterative, and dynamic way in which these guidelines interact with each other and with the process activities should be emphasized. At any given time during the process, any number of the guidelines can and should be used.

Table 11.1 provides an outline of the comprehensive guidelines. As stated earlier, many of these comprehensive guidelines draw from a variety of approaches related to problem-based learning and cooperative learning. For those guidelines which are unique to a particular approach, references to the literature are included. Following Table 11.1, a detailed description of each guideline is given.

Instructor-Implemented Methods

Teaching in a collaborative environment is quite different from traditional approaches, and the teacher can use the methods described below to reconceptualize her role.

Act as a resource and tutor/facilitator rather than as a dispenser of knowledge (Barrows, 1996; Bridges, 1992; Stinson & Milter, 1996). When an instructor takes the role of a tutor or facilitator, the climate and power structure in the classroom change dramatically in a number of ways. The most significant change is that the primary responsibility for managing learning is shifted to the students.* The students determine what information and resources they need and how to obtain them, with the instructor available to provide guidance, feedback, and skill development as needed.

Create learning environments that allow learners to work in a variety of small groups, each for an extended period of time (Barrows, 1996). If the time allowed each group is too brief, the experience for the learners is often superficial and doesn't allow them to learn the content in-depth or to experience the full impact of the

---

* This shift is often a gradual one, depending on the learner's readiness and ability for self-regulated learning (see chap. 13 by Corno & Randi). The focus on developing self-regulated learners is often characterized as developing life-long learners, and is common to most theories in the new paradigm.

TABLE 11.1

Types of Comprehensive Guidelines

Instructor-Implemented Methods	*Interactive Methods*
• Act as a resource and tutor (Barrows, 1996; Bridges, 1992; Stinson & Milter, 1996).	• Learn and purposely use appropriate social skills (Johnson & Johnson, 1994; Kagan & Kagan, 1994).
• Create learning environments that allow learners to work in a variety of small groups, each for an extended period of time (Barrows, 1996).	• Engage in team-building activities (Kagan & Kagan, 1994).
• Formulate questions to focus learner on important aspects of content and learning processes (Barrows, 1996; Savery & Duffy, 1995).	• Promote notions of investigation, interaction, interpretation, and intrinsic motivation (Sharan & Sharan, 1994).
• Provide just-in-time instruction when requested by learners (Johnson & Johnson, 1994).	• Encourage simultaneous interaction (Kagan & Kagan, 1994).
	• Ensure equal participation (Kagan & Kagan, 1994; Slavin, 1995).
Learner Implemented Methods	• Promote positive interdependence (Johnsonn & Johnson, 1994; Kagan & Kagan, 1994).
• Determine how the acquired knowledge and resources will be used to resolve the problem (Bridges, 1992; Sharan & Sharan, 1994).	• Advocate face-to-face promotive interaction (Johnson & Johnson, 1994).
• Determine and account for individual and group time spent on project activities (Barrows, 1996; Bridges, 1992; Savery & Duffy, 1995).	
Instructor- and Learner-Implemented Methods	
• Collaborate to determine learning issues and objectives (Bridges, 1992).	
• Conduct group progress meetings.	
• Collect needed resources (Bridges, 1992; Stinson & Milter, 1996; West, 1992).	
• Evaluate learners in multiple ways (Bridges, 1992; Johnson & Johnson, 1994).	
• Provide group and individual evaluations and grades (Bridges, 1992).	

group problem-solving process.* While it is often appropriate for a class to start out with shorter assignments or projects that only take a few days to complete, the goal is to build in complexity to experiences that may take a few weeks.

Formulate questions to focus the learners on the important aspects of the content and their own learning processes (Barrows, 1996; Savery & Duffy, 1995). This is one way the instructor can facilitate the learning of the students without taking control of their learning. The instructor acts as a cognitive coach, asking the students probing questions to focus learners on the most important aspects of the content and to encourage them to investigate certain aspects more deeply or to rethink their approach to the problem.

---

* Time for in-depth study is emphasized by many theories in the new paradigm (especially chap. 4 by Gardner and chap. 5 by Perkins & Unger).

Provide just-in-time instruction when requested by learners (Johnson & Johnson, 1994). As the students progress with their problem solving and project development, they often discover that they do not possess the knowledge or skills necessary to complete their work. As specific deficiencies are identified, the instructor can provide just-in-time instruction in the form of miniworkshops, demonstrations, or lectures that allow learners to acquire the needed knowledge or skills.* Often these deficits can be anticipated; learning activities can then be prepared in advance and delivered either to the entire class or to specific groups, as needed.

Learner-Implemented Methods

With guidance from the instructor, learners use these methods to assist themselves in forming their groups and managing group activities. When appropriate, these methods should be implemented directly by the learners.

Determine how the acquired knowledge and resources will be used to resolve the problem (Bridges, 1992; Sharan & Sharan, 1994). As each group begins problem-solving work, a variety of information and resources will need to be gathered for use by the group. How the information and resources will be used should be determined by the group. This complex problem-solving experience includes having the learners evaluate the various resources they find and decide what is relevant and how it will be used to further their work.**

Determine and account for individual and group time spent on project activities. (Barrows, 1996; Bridges, 1992; Savery & Duffy, 1995). Each group should be allowed to determine how their time can best be used in accomplishing the tasks they identify for themselves. They also need to account for both individual and collective contributions. This can be achieved by having each individual in the group report regularly on what he or she is contributing, what others in the group seem to be contributing, and how the project work and group processes are going. This keeps each group member accountable and allows the instructor to identify and mitigate problems early on.

Instructor- and Learner-Implemented Methods

These methods are intended to be implemented collaboratively as the instructor and learners work in concert. How much guidance is provided by the instructor and how much freedom is given to the learners will vary depending on the comfort level of the instructor and the capacity of the learners to direct their own learning.***

---

* These supports for learning can be designed anywhere on the continuum from highly structured to highly unstructured that I discussed in chapter 3, p. 66.

** What other theories have proposed this method?

*** This is a clear case of the selection of alternative methods governed by situationalities, as discussed in chapter 1, p. 8. Such variability identifies this as a theory rather than a model of instruction.

Collaborate to determine learning issues and objectives (Bridges, 1992). Early on in this process, the instructor and learners should define together what learning issues will be explored and what goals and objectives will be chosen for the learning experience. How much is determined by the instructor and how much by the learners varies, with the instructor making most decisions at one end of the continuum and the learners determining most aspects on the other. The extent to which learners are allowed to determine the learning issues and objectives will directly affect the level of ownership and relevance that the learners tend to feel towards the assignment and towards their work.* When possible, they should be encouraged to participate fully in this process.

Conduct group progress meetings with the instructor. Throughout the entire CPS learning process, meetings of each group with the instructor should be scheduled regularly. These can be initiated by either the group or the instructor, as needed. During these meetings, a group can discuss their progress, questions, and problems. In this way the instructor can provide customized feedback to each group while tracking their progress.

In addition to these group meetings, the instructor should also be readily available to discuss problems or concerns on an individual basis. Guidance should be provided with the intent of assisting learners in developing better skills with which to go back and work through their interpersonal and work-related problems directly within the group. The instructor needs to be careful not to fragment or divide a group, or to make it overly dependent on instructor mediation.

Collect needed resources (Bridges, 1992; Stinson & Milter, 1996; West, 1992)). As described above, many types of information and resources should be collected as the groups work through their problem or project. The instructor and learners should work together to identify and acquire needed resources. Also, groups should be encouraged to share with each other the resources and information that they are acquiring. Collaboration should be taking place both within groups and among groups. This intra- and intergroup collaboration should be a hallmark of this type of learning experience.

Evaluate learners in multiple ways (Bridges, 1992; Johnson & Johnson, 1994). Evaluation of learners should be taking place during the entire learning experience, taking a variety of forms, both informal and formal. These forms can include informal conversations and meetings with groups by the instructor, observations of the groups at work, assessment of students' individual progress reports, and reports from each group's formative evaluations and usability tests. Learners should also be continuously reflecting on and evaluating both their products and their processes. Then the formal assessment of the final product should be done by both the

---

* This is a descriptive principle, but it helps the reader to understand the rationale for the guideline (design principle) that is offered in this paragraph. It is often helpful to intersperse descriptive theory with design theory.

instructor and the learners as they evaluate and discuss together the product's quality and its effectiveness in addressing the original problem or project scenario.*

Provide group and individual evaluations and grades (Bridges, 1992). The final grade should be a combination of assessments of the group project and individual contributions. This can be done by having a portion of the final grade reflect evaluations of individual products created during the project, such as the weekly progress reports or a culminating individual reflection paper. Part of the final grade can also reflect an evaluation of an individual by fellow group members, as well as a self-assessment of specific contributions to the project work and the group process.

Interactive Methods

These methods provide guidance for the interactions which take place during CPS. These interactions and processes are crucial because they provide the context in which the instruction and the learning occur. Such guidelines should (a) assist the instructor in supporting the work of the learners and in dealing with problems and concerns as they arise, and (b) help the learners engage in powerful, meaningful, and effective collaborative processes that allow them to learn the content and develop better group problem-solving skills.**

Learn and purposefully use appropriate social skills, such as leadership, decision making, trust building, communication, and conflict management (Johnson & Johnson, 1994; Kagan & Kagan, 1994). Many of these social skills are the bedrock of effective group processes; their deficiency can spell disaster for a team. Thus it is important for the instructor to provide instruction and resources related to these social skills, appropriate to the level of experience and ability of the learners.

Engage in team-building activities (Kagan & Kagan, 1994). Team-building activities help develop collaborative skills and group identity. The instructor should design a series of short activities for new groups to engage in to build trust and cohesiveness. These activities can include ice-breakers and time set aside early on for group members to interact with each other, cooperative puzzles or games for the groups to work through, or a structured activity that encourages group participation and cooperation, such as a ropes course.

Promote notions of investigation, interaction, interpretation, and intrinsic motivation (Sharan & Sharan, 1994). These four concepts capture several of the most important elements constituting the learning environment necessary for CPS. *Investigation* entails creating a classroom climate in which the learners and instructor are seen as a "community of inquirers" (Thelen, 1981). This mindset is essential for CPS. A primary goal of this approach is for learners to come to view themselves as investigators who are posing hypotheses; exploring possible solutions and design

---

*Diversity and multiplicity are as important for evaluation as for instruction in the new paradigm.

**Much of what follows in this section has significant affective elements, such as those discussed in Unit 4. This illustrates the highly integrated nature of the affective and cognitive domains.

plans; acquiring necessary information, resources, and skills; and formulating salient solutions and robust products which adequately address the original learning issues learners identified for themselves.

Interaction is also key, since collaboration is the hallmark of this theory. Learners need a supportive social context in which they can freely interact with one another as they engage in their problem-solving groups. It is through these interactions that they accomplish their work and hone important social and critical thinking skills.

Learners also need to develop the skill to correctly *interpret* and evaluate the various types and sources of information they gather. They need to be able to make meaning of what they are learning and to understand how it fits into their learning goals and project work. Learners should have abundant opportunities to organize, analyze, and synthesize their findings as they begin to integrate them into their solutions or projects.

It is also hoped that collaborative problem solving will provide learners with experiences that build an *intrinsic motivation** to learn, inquire, collaborate, and problem solve. This can often be promoted by building the relevance and ownership that learners feel over their learning. It is essential to nurture attitudes and skills that will encourage students to be life-long learners.

Encourage simultaneous interaction where there are multiple active participants engaged in problem-solving tasks (Kagan & Kagan, 1994). This is the essence of CPS. It is accomplished when each group member is responsible for a task essential to the project and when the group must work in concert to succeed. This type of interaction promotes the development of a number of critical thinking and problem-solving skills and provides rich experience in working as a cohesive team.

Ensure equal participation so that all learners have an opportunity to contribute (Kagan & Kagan, 1994; Slavin, 1995). A problem that small learning groups often have is that one or more students may begin to dominate the group, controlling the outcome of decisions and the division of labor for group members. This can destroy the true collaborative spirit which should reside in these groups. Thus it is important that instructors directly address the likelihood of imbalance with learners and encourage groups, when they are first forming, to discuss ways of dealing with this problem, should it arise. The instructor should also monitor group interactions and assist groups or individuals who may be struggling in this area. The goal is to foster an environment where each group member feels safe to share ideas and make contributions in an atmosphere of acceptance and respect.

Promote positive interdependence, in that each group member is positively linked with others in such a way that the individual cannot succeed unless the group does (Johnson & Johnson, 1994; Kagan & Kagan, 1994). When group members feel this positive interdependence with the other group members, they are more willing to work collaboratively for the progression of the group rather than compet-

---

* This is a consistent concern for theories in the new paradigm.

itively for individual gains. The instructor can promote positive interdependence by clearly communicating to learners that their individual success is based primarily on the success of their group. Learners soon begin to understand this intuitively as they work collaboratively and gain experience through their collective successes and failures.

Advocate face-to-face promotive interaction in which the students promote each other's success by praising, encouraging, helping, and supporting each other's efforts to learn (Johnson & Johnson, 1994). Not only do group members need to realize their interdependence, but they also need to actually promote each other's success. There should be a true regard for the success of their teammates' efforts, manifested through encouragement and a willingness to help and assist each other.*

Require individual accountability where students are held responsible for doing their share of the work (Johnson & Johnson, 1994; Kagan & Kagan, 1994; Slavin, 1995). Individual accountability is important in maintaining a sense of fairness about the contributions that each group member makes. As described previously, this can be accomplished externally through reports written to the instructor. But the sense of accountability should also exist as an intrinsic quality of each individual's work, as each learner honestly contributes a fair share of the work. Again, this should be advocated directly by the instructor and established as an expectation for learners.

Now that the comprehensive guidelines have been discussed (see Table 11.1 for a summary), the next section will describe the process activities that guide the primary learning activities. This will include an outline and discussion of each of the phases of the collaborative problem-solving process in which the learners engage, along with related instructional guidelines.

PROCESS ACTIVITIES

In contrast to the comprehensive guidelines, which are used throughout the entire learning event, process activities are instructional strategies and methods which apply to particular phases and processes during the learning event. The purpose of these guidelines is to provide a general blueprint to learning groups about the types of activities in which they should engage as they collaborate on their solution or project. These learning activities will likely take place over a number of weeks and are often iterative and/or concurrent.

The guidelines for the process activities have been developed to support, as much as possible, a naturally effective, problem-solving process. They are primarily based on research and theory on best practices for group interaction and learning. The result is a comprehensive instructional theory that addresses each of the process activities related to collaborative problem solving. Table 11.2 provides an

---

* This is a key feature that distinguishes the new paradigm from the industrial-age paradigm of instructional theory.

outline of these nine process activities and their related guidelines. Next is a detailed description of each of the specific guidelines.

As a whole, each of the major phases is designed to interact with all the others in an iterative and flexible fashion. This means that, while there is an inherent order to the phases, conditions will likely arise during the learning event which necessitate the instructor or learners revisiting an earlier phase. For instance, as groups work on their problem solution or project, a need may arise to renegotiate and redefine the group's common understanding of the initial assignment. Phases may also occur concurrently. For example, during the primary collaborative problem-solving process, the activities of engaging in development work, reporting progress, and participating in intergroup collaborations usually take place simultaneously. The overarching principle is that the process is dynamic and flexible. It needs to be customized to each learning experience, based on the needs of the learners, as well as the instructional content and skills to be learned. The instructional guidelines for each of the process activities are described next.

1. Instructor and Learners Establish and Build Their Readiness to Engage in Collaborative Group Work

The instructor begins with an overview of the basic ideas and values related to this type of teaching/learning process (Johnson & Johnson, 1994; Stinson & Milter, 1996). This review should include addressing the benefits and pitfalls of group work, outlining how the process tends to progress and what the learners might experience in their groups, and discussing how they and their products will be evaluated. Then the instructor should allow the students to ask questions and discuss concerns about the process. It is important that the instructor respond to these concerns by making appropriate adjustments or by providing instruction or resources to the students. The primary goal of this phase is to help the learners to understand what they will be engaging in and why.

Next, an authentic problem or project assignment is formulated by the instructor (Barrows, 1996; Savery & Duffy, 1995; Stinson & Milter, 1996). When appropriate, this can be done in collaboration with the students. Considerations in determining the amount of learner involvement to be included in formulating the assignment include the age and abilities of the learners, time constraints, instructional goals, and course or classroom structure. The intent here is to create a scenario which will frame the problem or project the learners will be working on. There is a continuum of how structured the scenario can be. At one extreme, the assignment might be highly structured by the teacher before instruction begins. At the other, the learners may identify their own real-life problem to work on, based on the learning issues and objectives identified at the beginning of the instruction. The primary goal of this activity is to develop a scenario or find a prob-

TABLE 11.2
Outline of Process Activities

1. Build Readiness

- Overview the collaborative problem-solving process (Johnson & Johnson, 1994; Stinson & Milter, 1996).
- Develop an authentic problem or project scenario to anchor instruction and learning activities (Barrows, 1996; Savery & Duffy, 1995; Stinson & Milter, 1996).
- Provide instruction and practice in group process skills (Johnson & Johnson, 1997; Kagan & Kagan, 1994).

2. Form and Norm Groups

- Form small, heterogeneous work groups (Bridges, 1992; Johnson & Johnson, 1997; Slavin, 1995).
- Encourage groups to establish operational guidelines.

3. Determine a Preliminary Problem Definition

- Negotiate a common understanding of the problem (Barrows & Tamblyn, 1980; Schmidt, 1989).
- Identify learning issues and goals (Barrows & Tambly, 1980; Bridges, 1992).
- Brainstorm preliminary solutions or project plans (Bransford & Stein, 1993).
- Select and develop initial design plan.
- Identify sources of needed resources (Bridges, 1992; Stinson &n Milter, 1996).
- Gather preliminary information to validate the design plan.

4. Define and Assign Roles

- Identify the principle roles needed to complete design plan (Bridges, 1992; Johnson & Johnson, 1997; West, 1992).
- Negotiate the assignment of roles (West, 1992).

5. Engage in an Iterative Collaborative Problem-Solving Process

- Refine and evolve the design plan.
- Identify and assign tasks.
- Acquire needed information, resources, and expertise (Schmidt, 1989).
- Collaborate with instructor to acquire additional resources and skills needed (West, 1992).
- Disseminate acquired information, resources, and expertise to the other group members (Barrows & Tamblyn, 1980; Sharan & Sharan, 1994; West, 1992).
- Engage in solution- or project-development work (West, 1992).
- Report regularly on individual contributions and group activities.
- Participate in intergroup collaborations and evaluations.
- Conduct formative evaluations of the solution or project (Schmidt, 1989).

6. Finalize the Solution or Project

- Draft the preliminary final version of the solution or project.
- Conduct the final evaluation or usability test of the solution or project.
- Revise and complete the final version of the solution or project.

7. Synthesize and Reflect

- Identify learning gains (Barrows & Tamblyn, 1980; Bransford & Stein, 1993; West, 1992).
- Debrief experiences and feelings about the process (Johnson & Johnson, 1994).
- Reflect on group and individual learning processes (Barrows & Tamblyn, 1980; Johnson & Johnson, 1994; Savery & Duffy, 1995).

8. Assess Products and Processes

- Evaluate the products and artifacts created (Bridges, 1992).
- Evaluate the processes used (Bridges, 1992).

9. Provide Closure

- Formalize group adjournment through a closure activity.

lem that is authentic and at the right level of complexity for the learners.* Some general guidelines for developing a problem or project scenario include:

- develop problems that are ill-defined and appropriately complex to encourage development of critical thinking and problem-solving skills;
- incorporate issues and problems that are authentic and relevant to users;
- create problems that epitomize professional practice in the domain being studied;
- use novel problems or ones that address sigificant, current problems.

Another important activity in building readiness is for learners to identify and develop skills crucial for creating successful learning groups. Learners should engage in group- or team-building activities under the guidance of the instructor (Johnson & Johnson, 1997; Kagan & Kagan, 1994). This can be accomplished either by providing an instructor-led workshop or by distributing self-instructional materials to learners. The primary purpose is to build competency in such areas as interpersonal interactions, group leadership, process management, interdependence, and consensus building. Time should be allowed for learners to practice some of these skills in temporary groups before they go into their primary groups for the first project, unless their development of such skills is already fairly high.

2. Either the Instructor or the Learners Form Small, Heterogeneous Work Groups, and then the Groups Engage in Norming Processes

Forming these groups is one of the most important activities related to the success of a collaborative problem-solving experience (Bridges, 1992; Slavin, 1995). Small learning groups of at least three and not more than six members have been shown to be the most effective (Johnson & Johnson, 1997; Putnam, 1997). Such groups are small enough to be manageable for group meetings and to encourage the greatest amount of participation from each group member. Groups formed for project work do best when they consist of three or four members, while decision-making groups can be slightly larger (Bruffee, 1993).

The composition of the groups is also important. A richer experience is generally provided for the students when the groups are heterogeneous. Criteria for forming groups can include gender, ethnicity, relevant pre-existing knowledge or skills, and previous experience with working on a team. When possible, students should be allowed to form their own teams based on the criteria chosen by the instructor. For instance, a set of group-formation criteria might include that both sexes be represented, that at least one person be an international or ESL student (where applica-

---

* This instructional decision is a difficult one that could benefit from a whole chapter's worth of guidance.

ble), and that each person on the team should work with at least one person who is not already known. These types of guidelines help prevent cliques or "power" teams of only the most capable students from forming repeatedly. If there is a likelihood of this being a problem, then the instructor may form the groups based on information gathered from the students.

While teams should be heterogeneous in relation to the criteria described above, there are some learner characteristics that should be *generally* homogenous. Learners not of adult age should be of the same general age, and group members should possess compatible levels of learning ability and sophistication. They should also share a common interest in the topic. The intent is that the learners not be so disparate that they don't share similar interests or learning capabilities. Often these parameters result naturally from the structures of formal education, such as grade levels.

Once the groups have been formed, they need to begin the norming process: development of a sense of group identity and agreement on their own operational guidelines. These guidelines could include ground rules for group interactions, division of labor, and procedure for reaching consensus. Generally the instructor will need to be available to facilitate groups as they negotiate this often rocky norming process.

3. Groups Engage in a Preliminary Process to Define the Problem They Will Work On

After the groups have been formed and normed, they need to begin defining, for themselves, the task that lies ahead. First the group negotiates a common understanding of the assignment (Barrows & Tamblyn, 1980; Schmidt, 1989). This is important because each person in the group will initially have a slightly different interpretation of the problem or project scenario, along with ideas for approaching it. This process of defining the assignment is a critical step in CPS. Yet often this process is overlooked or rushed. It then becomes difficult for the group to progress, since each member is working from a different understanding of the assignment. Thus, for the group to be effective, the members need to come to consensus on what the assignment means. This also allows group members to identify which learning issues and goals are most important for them to focus on as they work through their solution or project.

Once a common understanding of the problem is reached, the group begins brainstorming a number of possible solutions or project plans (Bransford & Stein, 1993). It is important for the instructor to encourage the group to come up with a wide range of possibilities. From these possibilities, the group can then choose one to develop into an initial design plan. Next, the group identifies resources, expertise, knowledge, and information needed to begin working on the design plan, tentatively identifying sources where they can be obtained, both within and outside the group itself (Bridges, 1992; Stinson & Milter, 1996). Then the group is ready to initiate a preliminary fact-finding mission in which group members explore which resources and information are readily available to them and which they will need to obtain with assistance from the instructor. This information is then brought back to the group and used to determine whether the initial design plan is valid or whether it needs to be refined or even dropped in favor of a new one.

4. Each Group Defines What Roles are Necessary to Accomplish the Design Plan and Then Assigns Them

By defining roles for each group member, learners analyze what needs to be done and who will be responsible for doing it. Particularly when students are new to collaborative processes, this helps them organize and structure their group's activities. First, the principal roles that must be filled to complete the design plan should be identified (Bridges, 1992; Johnson & Johnson, 1997; West, 1992). The instructor can assist this process by making sure each group has identified all necessary positions. These might include project coordinator, process facilitator, designer, developer, or recorder. Once all the roles are identified, their respective responsibilities should be determined.

Then assignment of these roles can be negotiated by the group, with the instructor facilitating the process, when necessary, to insure that each learner has an opportunity to try different roles while working in various groups (West, 1992). While attention should be paid to an individual's present interests and abilities, it is also important that each learner has the opportunity to expand knowledge and skills in important areas where he or she may not be strong. Thus the best practice is not always to allow the person most suited to a role to fill it, but rather to allow someone who needs the learning experience to fill it.* Learners should also keep in mind that, as the project progresses, roles will shift as needs change, and that role definitions need to stay flexible enough to allow group members to help one another, take on different responsibilities, and even redefine a role.

5. The Group Engages in the Primary, Iterative CPS Process

Once a design plan has been decided upon and roles assigned, the group is ready to engage in the primary CPS process. This phase is the heart of this instructional theory. This is where the learners will invest the majority of their time as they design and develop their solution or project through the following activities:**

- refine and evolve the design plan;

---

* Thus, a strong focus on accomplishing the task can actually hinder learning! This is an important concern for theories that promote collaboration.

** Are these parts, kinds, or criteria for the method, "engage in the collaborative problem-solving process?" In the following elaboration on each of these 9 sub-methods, you are likely to find all three of these. Try to identify which is which, and for kinds, try to identify the situationalities for their use.

- identify and assign tasks;
- acquire needed information, resources, and expertise;
- collaborate with the instructor to acquire additional resources and skills needed;
- disseminate acquired information, resources, and expertise to the other group members;
- engage in solution- or project-development work;
- report regularly on individual contributions and group activities;
- participate in intergroup collaborations and evaluations;
- conduct formative evaluation of the solution or project.

The iterative nature of this process should be emphasized. It is anticipated that learners will engage in this process multiple times as they evolve their solution or project towards its final form. This iterative process is similar to rapid collaborative prototyping (Dorsey, Goodrum, & Schwen, 1995), in which each successive version incorporates newly acquired understandings and resources, as well as information gained from formative evaluations. Because of the importance of this phase of activity, each of the subprocesses is discussed in detail.

Refine and evolve the design plan. If this is the first iteration of the process, the group uses information gained from its initial fact-finding mission to refine and evolve the design plan. If this is a subsequent iteration, then information from the formative evaluation that has just been conducted on the current version of the project or solution is used. Either way, this refining is done by comparing the newly acquired information with the current version of the solution or project. As discrepancies or corroborations are noted between the new information and the current version, the design plan is developed and refined from its initial fuzzy version (Bruner, 1966; Reigeluth & Nelson, 1997) into one that will result in a more refined and detailed project or solution. During this activity, the role of the instructor is to assist groups in effectively using the information they are accumulating to advance their design plans.

Identify and assign tasks. As the design plan progresses, new tasks tend to emerge as well, in order to incorporate what has been learned into the project. Once these tasks have been identified, team members need to negotiate who will be responsible for the completion of each task. Typically, these tasks are either actual work on the project or the need to acquire and disseminate new information or resources. Tasks can be done either by an individual or by the group as a whole. Usually a task will build upon ongoing work a group member is already doing in an assigned role. However, at other times unique tasks will emerge and need to be assimilated into a role. What is important is that each task is identified and responsibility taken for its completion. How these tasks are to be accomplished is addressed in the next four activities, which typically take place concurrently.

Acquire needed information, resources, and expertise (Schmidt, 1989). During CPS there is a continuous and ever-changing need for information, resources, and expertise. Often these needs are identified during the preceding task-identification stage. Once identified, the group must locate appropriate sources and then acquire the information, resources, and expertise needed to address them. This can be accomplished through such activities as library searches, field investigations, or meetings with subject-matter experts. While it appears simple, this can be a daunting and formidable undertaking for a group. Often there are false leads and time wasted in irrelevant activities, or the group erroneously assumes that it already possesses the critical information or skill. A vigilant instructor can facilitate the acquisition process by pointing out possible sources of information, assisting learners in judging the value and accuracy of the information or the applicability of the resource, or providing instruction on much-needed skills and knowledge, which is described in the next guideline.

Collaborate with the instructor to acquire additional resources and skills needed (West, 1992). It is critical that each group be able to communicate to the instructor which resources, information, or expertise they need assistance in obtaining. The instructor then provides assistance on how to acquire these needed resources. She also designs appropriate just-in-time instruction on knowledge and skills needed to complete the solution or project. This interaction between the instructor and the groups will be ongoing as learners identify new gaps in their understandings and abilities. Thus the instructor must be especially astute in monitoring the progress of each group and in keeping the lines of communication open so that needs are communicated and addressed. This process of allowing learners to identify and communicate their own learning needs increases their ownership of the learning process and builds a feeling of relevance for the instruction provided.

Disseminate acquired information, resources, and expertise to other group members (Barrows & Tamblyn, 1980; Sharan & Sharan, 1994; West, 1992). Once acquired, the information, resources, understandings, and skills should be appropriately disseminated throughout the group, particularly to those team members for whom these are crucial to their work or responsibilities within the group. Consequently, competency in communicating the findings to other group members during the frequent work meetings is essential. It is critical that what has been learned or acquired is communicated accurately and effectively so it can be used by the team to develop the design plan and refine the solution or project during the next phase of the process.

Engage in solution- or project-development work (West, 1992). A new round of solution-building or project-development work occurs each time new information and resources are assimilated by the group into the current version of the product. However, for this to occur, all members of the group need to understand what their roles or assignments are and feel competent to accomplish them. Therefore, it is important that the instructor continue to interact with the groups both as an organizational facilitator and as a resource for skill building. The instructor must solicit and receive adequate feedback and reflection from the groups on their progress in order to anticipate and address their needs.

Report regularly on individual contributions and group activities. One highly effective feedback and assessment method is to have each group member submit a confidential weekly or biweekly report to the instructor that describes (a) what the individual's contributions were to the project and to the group's processes, (b) what each of the other team members' contributions were, (c) what project work has been accomplished, and (d) how the team's group processes are going. Through these reports (and regular meetings with each group) the instructor can stay in touch with how each person perceives his or her own contributions, as well as those of the teammates. Group members also help the instructor identify problems, either with the project work or with the group's processes, and assist in mediating these on an individual or group basis.

Participate in intergroup collaborations and evaluations. One of the most powerful experiences that can occur during CPS is when the groups begin to collaborate with each other. This collaboration allows groups to exchange ideas, discuss successes and concerns, and give feedback to one another. It can be accomplished by setting aside class time for larger groups of three to four teams to meet together. During these meetings, each small group should present its work thus far and ask for feedback from the other groups. Since each group is working on its own but similar project, groups can share valuable insights with other groups on what works and what doesn't work in relation to the project, as well as in relation to group processes. These intergroup collaborations and feedback sessions are catalysts for new ideas or new interpretations of the assignment. In addition, these meetings help prevent competitive feelings from forming between groups, which can be an unintentional and destructive outcome of multiple groups working on the same assignment.

Conduct formative evaluations of the solution or project (Schmidt, 1989). In addition to the feedback received from the instructor and from other groups, each group needs to periodically conduct formative evaluations of the current version of the product.* This often occurs in parallel with the cycles of collecting and disseminating resources and with development work. Essential to this activity is that the group understand the role and processes related to effective formative evaluation. Also, this evaluation should only be done when a new version of the solution or project has progressed enough to warrant a new evaluation. As each version of the project emerges, the team should organize formative evaluation activities, such as field tests, usability tests, and expert reviews. These might be done informally at first, becoming more structured over time as the solution or project nears its final version. The role of the instructor during these activities is, again, to be a guide, informing the teams of the importance, purpose, and processes of formative evaluation.

This completes the primary collaborative problem-solving process. What follows are the activities during which the solution or project is finalized, the results evaluated, and closure given to the learning experience (see Table 11.2).

---

* This is a form of self-evaluation whereby the learners test out their designs or solutions to see if they are of high quality and revise them as needed. It is an important part of self-regulated learning.

6. Groups begin to finalize their solutions or projects

After engaging in adequate iterations of the primary CPS process, the groups begin to formulate a final version of their product. Once a preliminary final draft of the product has been made, the groups then go on to conduct a final usability test or summative evaluation of the product. This should be done in as realistic a setting as possible. For example, each group will want to test its proposed solution or product with subjects from the target audience in a setting and under conditions as close to real-world as possible. With the results from this final evaluation, the group does a final revision and completes the solution or project for submission to the instructor for assessment.

7. The instructor and learners engage in activities to help them reflect and synthesize their experiences*

Another critical phase of the learning event is for those involved to have a chance to engage in a debriefing or postmortem evaluation of the experience (Barrows & Tamblyn, 1980; Bransford & Stein, 1993; West, 1992). The purpose of this final reflection is for students to identify and discuss their learning gains in the areas of (a) content knowledge and skills, (b) group-process skills, and (c) metacognitive strategies. It is also important for the learners to have a chance to share their feelings about the process they have just experienced (Johnson & Johnson, 1994). Culminating activities for this phase could be small-group and whole-class debriefings followed by individual reflection papers in which learners describe what they learned and experienced (Barrows & Tamblyn, 1980; Johnson & Johnson, 1994; Savery & Duffy, 1995).

8. The instructor, and, when appropriate, the learners assess their products and processes

Once learners have had an opportunity to debrief their experiences, authentic assessment of their learning gains, products, and processes is done (Bridges, 1992). First, the three areas for learning gains identified in phase 7 are evaluated: (a) content knowledge and skills, (b) group-process skills, and (c) metacognitive strategies. Next, the solutions or projects developed by each group are evaluated for their design, quality, and workability in the real world. Finally, the group processes of each team are discussed and assessed. Evaluations can be done in numerous ways. One approach is for the learners, with assistance from the instructor, to help develop the criteria for evaluating the final outcomes. Groups can also write up their own evaluations of their work and processes. These can then be considered along with the instructor's final evaluation.

---

* Reflection, again, is an important aspect of many theories in the new paradigm.

9. The instructor and learners develop an activity to bring closure to the learning event

Closure is an important but often-neglected aspect of any social activity, including group-based learning. During this phase, an activity is planned and then engaged in to celebrate the work of the participants and the adjournment of the groups. The intent of these activities should be to help learners honor their experiences and commemorate their accomplishments.

CONCLUSION

In conclusion, the interrelatedness and interdependence of the elements of the CPS instructional theory should be highlighted. Often the completion of one activity is a precursor for the next. Or the success of one is dependent on the concurrent application of and integration with another. Also, the significance of the integration of the comprehensive guidelines and the process activities should be emphasized. For instance, the comprehensive guideline "collect needed resources" is actualized in the specific process activities "gather preliminary information to validate the design plan" in phase 3 and "acquire needed information, resources, and expertise" in phase 5. These relationships underscore the systemic nature of good instructional theory. Each general guideline or method is part of a larger, cohesive instructional system.*

This chapter outlined the current status of the CPS instructional theory. However, future research and development on this theory is planned through a series of qualitative case studies, which will be used to conduct formative research on the theory. These case studies are of two types: designed case studies and naturalistic case studies (Reigeluth & Frick, chap. 6 of this volume). The designed case studies will analyze implementations of the CPS theory and will then be used to evaluate and improve the current version of the theory. The naturalistic case studies will be on naturally occurring learning groups (not using any formal collaborative approaches) and will be used to develop grounded theory related to collaborative processes. Through these case studies, I hope to identify weaknesses and strengths in the CPS theory which result from discrepancies or corroborations between the theory and the formative research findings. These will then be synthesized and integrated into future versions of the CPS theory.

ACKNOWLEDGMENTS

Special thanks is given to Charles Reigeluth and Joseph South for their comments on earlier versions of this chapter.

---

* To what extent can you see this in the other theories in this volume?

REFERENCES

Albanese, M. A., & Mitchell, S. (1993). Problem-based learning: A review of literature on its outcomes and implementation issues. *Academic Medicine, 68,* 52–81.

Aronson, E., Blaney, N., Stephan, C., Sikes, J., & Snapp, M. (1978). *The Jigsaw classroom* Beverly Hills, CA: Sage.

Barrows, H. S. (1996). Problem-based learning in medicine and beyond: A brief overview. *New Directions for Teaching and Learning, 68,* 3–12.

Barrows, H. S., & Tamblyn, R. M. (1980). *Problem-based learning: An approach to medical education.* New York: Springer-Verlag.

Bransford, J. D., & Stein, B. S. (1993). *The ideal problem solver: A guide for improving thinking, learning, and creativity* (2nd ed.). New York: W. H. Freeman.

Bridges, E. M. (1992). *Problem-based learning for administrators.* Eugene, OR: ERIC Clearinghouse on Educational Management. (ERIC/CEM Accession No: EA 023 722)

Bruffee, K. A. (1993). *Collaborative learning: Higher education, interdependence, and the authority of knowledge.* Baltimore: Johns Hopkins University Press.

Bruner, J. S. (1966). *Toward a theory of instruction.* Cambridge, MA: Belknap Press.

Dorsey, L. T, Goodrum, D. A., & Schwen T. M. (1995). *Rapid collaborative prototyping as an instructional development paradigm.* Unpublished manuscript, Indiana University.

Johnson, D. W., & Johnson, R. T. (1990). Cooperative learning and achievement. In S. Sharan (Ed.), *Cooperative learning: Theory and research* (pp. 23–37). New York: Praeger.

Johnson, D. W., & Johnson, R. T. (1994). Learning together. In S. Sharan (Ed.), *Handbook of cooperative learning methods* (pp. 51–65). Westport, CT: Greenwood Press.

Johnson, D. W., & Johnson, R. T. (1997). *Joining together: Group theory and group skills* (6th ed.). Boston: Allyn & Bacon.

Kagan, S., & Kagan, M. (1994). The structural approach: Six keys to cooperative learning. In S. Sharan (Ed.), *Handbook of cooperative learning methods* (pp. 115–133). Westport, CT: Greenwood Press.

Nelson, L. M., & Reigeluth, C. M. (1997, March). *Guidelines for using a problem-based learning approach for teaching heuristic tasks.* Presentation at the annual meeting of the American Educational Research Association, Chicago, IL.

Putnam, J. (1997). *Cooperative learning in diverse classrooms.* Upper Saddle River, NJ: Merrill/Prentice Hall.

Reigeluth, C. M., & Nelson, L. M. (1997). A new paradigm of ISD? In R. C. Branch & B. B. Minor (Eds.), *Educational media and technology yearbook* (Vol. 22, pp. 24–35). Englewood, CO: Libraries Unlimited.

Savery, J. R., & Duffy, T. M. (1995). Problem-based learning: An instructional model and its constructivist framework. In B. Wilson (Ed.), *Constructivist learning environments: Case studies in instructional design.* Englewood Cliffs, NJ: Educational Technology Publications.

Schmidt, H. G. (1989). The rationale behind problem-based learning. In H. G. Schmidt, M. Lipkin, M. W. de Vries, & J. M. Greep (Eds.), *New directions for medical education: Problem-based learning and community-oriented medical education* (pp. 105–111). New York: Springer-Verlag.

Sharan, S. (1994). *Handbook of cooperative learning methods.* Westport, CT: Greenwood Press.

Sharan, Y., & Sharan, S. (1994). Group investigation in the cooperative classroom. In S. Sharan (Ed.), *Handbook of cooperative learning methods* (pp. 97–114). Westport, CT: Greenwood Press.

Slavin, R. E. (1995). *Cooperative learning: Theory, research, and practice.* Needham Heights, MA: Allyn & Bacon.

Stinson, J. E., & Milter, R. G. (1996). Problem-based learning in business education: Curriculum design and implementation issues. *New Directions for Teaching and Learning, 68,* 33–42.

Thelen, H. (1981). *The classroom society: The construction of educational experience.* London: Croom Helm.

West, S. A. (1992). Problem-based learning—a viable addition for secondary school science. *School Science Review, 73,* 47– 55.

Learning Communities in Classrooms: A Reconceptualization of Educational Practice

12

Katerine Bielaczyc
Ontario Institute for Studies in Education and Boston College

Allan Collins
Northwestern University and Boston College

Katerine Bielaczyc

Allan Collins

Katerine Bielaczyc is a Research Scientist at Boston College (formerly Senior Scientist at Bolt, Beranek and Newman). She received a PhD from the Education in Math, Science, and Technology Program at U.C. Berkeley and an honors BSc in computer science from the University of Edinburgh, Scotland. She was a Spencer Doctoral fellow. Currently, she is Director of Research on the NSF Vanguard for Learning project. A McDonnell post-doctoral fellow, she is also researching metacognitive processes in CSILE classrooms. Her research intersets include metacognition, affordances of media and symbol systems, and CSCL.

Allan Collins is Professor of Education and Social Policy at Northwestern University, and Research Professor of Education at Boston College. He is a member of the National Academy of Education, a fellow of the American Association for Artificial Intelligence, and served as first chair of the Cognitive Science Society. He is best known in psychology for his work on semantic memory and mental models, in artificial intelligence for his work on plausible reasoning and intelligent tutoring systems, and in education for his work on inquiry teaching, cognitive apprenticeship, situated learning, epistemic games, and systemic validity in educational testing.

FOREWORD

Goals and preconditions. *The primary goal of this theory is to advance the collective knowledge and skills and thereby to support the growth of individual knowledge and skills. Preconditions include a diversity of expertise among the members of the learning community and an emphasis on learning how to learn.*

Values. *Some of the values upon which this theory is based include:*

- *learning how to learn,*
- *learning how to direct one's own learning,*
- *learning how to deal with complex issues,*
- *learning how to work with people,*
- *a culture of learning as a collective effort and sharing of knowledge,*
- *a respect and appreciation for differences within the community,*
- *a respect and appreciation for all members of the community.*

Methods. *These are the major methods this theory offers:*

- *Community growth: Overall goal is to expand the community's knowledge and skills.*
- *Emergent goals: Goals should be co-constructed with the students and emerge from their activities.*
- *Articulation of goals: Teacher and students must articulate their goals and criteria for judging success.*
- *Metacognition: The community should keep asking itself what its goals are and whether it is progressing to meet them. It should also reflect back on what was learned and the processes that were used.*
- *Beyond the bounds: The community should try to go beyond the knowledge in the community and seek out new approaches and ideas that challenge what they believe.*
- *Respect for others: Students need to learn respect for other students' contributions and differences. Clearly articulate and enforce the rules for respect.*
- *Failure-safe: The community should accept failures and not try to assess blame. There must be a sense that failure is O.K. and that taking risks fosters learning.*
- *Structural dependence: The community should be organized such that students are dependent on other students. This fosters respect for others and self-esteem.*
- *Depth over breadth: Students should have sufficient time to investigate topics in enough depth to gain real expertise on important, generative ideas.*
- *Diverse expertise: Students should develop the areas in which they are most interested and capable, with the responsibility to share their expertise with*

the community so that they not only learn by doing, but also learn from what others do.

- *Multiple ways to participate: Students should have a range of activities—such as formulating questions, gathering knowledge, and sharing knowledge—and a variety of roles—such as researcher, expert, and moderator—and the community should value all roles.*
- *Sharing: There should be a mechanism for sharing individuals' knowledge throughout the community, so that every student can give and receive.*
- *Negotiation: Ideas are improved by an argumentation process based on logic and evidence, and there should be modeling and coaching on how to depersonalize critiques of others' ideas.*
- *Quality of products: The quality of the knowledge and products should be valued by the individuals, the community, and outsiders, based on community standards.*

Major contributions. *The notion of a group as the focus for learning, rather than an individual. Methods to develop respect for, and understanding of, fellow students. Methods to encourage students to pursue their interests. The importance of the culture of the learning environment.*

—C.M.R.

Learning Communities in Classrooms: A Reconceptualization of Educational Practice

INTRODUCTION

In recent years in America there has developed a "learning-communities" approach to education. In a learning community the goal is to advance the collective knowledge and in that way to support the growth of individual knowledge (Scardamalia & Bereiter, 1994). The defining quality of a learning community is that there is a culture of learning in which everyone is involved in a collective effort of understanding.

There are four characteristics that such a culture* must have: (a) diversity of expertise among its members, who are valued for their contributions and given support to develop, (b) a shared objective of continually advancing the collective knowledge and skills, (c) an emphasis on learning how to learn, and (d) mechanisms for sharing what is learned. If a learning community is presented with a problem, then the learning community can bring its collective knowledge to bear on the problem. It is not necessary that each member assimilate everything that the community knows, but each should know who within the community has relevant expertise to address any problem. This is a radical departure from the traditional view of schooling, with its emphasis on individual knowledge and performance, and the expectation that students will acquire the same body of knowledge at the same time.**

Why Learning Communities?

As the world becomes more complex, students find themselves unprepared for its challenges, both personal and social. The new demands that society is placing on young people are reflected in a wide variety of reports on education, such as the U.S. Department of Labor's SCANS Commission report (1991) and a recent book by Murnane and Levy (1996), which address the question of what skills and knowledge will be needed for work in the 21st century. These sources, in summary, report that, students need to be able to direct their own learning, work with and listen to others, and develop ways of dealing with complex issues and problems that require different kinds of expertise. These, for the most part, are not skills that are currently taught in schools.***

So why should we redesign education around learning communities? There are at least three arguments as to why it would be good to do so.

Social-Constructivist Argument. The "social-constructivist" view of education, characteristic of Dewey and Vygotsky, holds that the theory of individual learning, which pervades schools, is flawed. The constructivist view is that people learn best not by assimilating what they are told, but rather by a knowledge-construction process. In order for individuals to learn how to construct knowledge, it is necessary that the process be modeled and supported in the surrounding community. This is what occurs in a learning community.

Learning-to-Learn Argument. Smith (1988) argues that children will learn to read and write if the people they admire read and write. That is, they will want to join the "literacy club" and will work hard to become members. Brown, Ellery, and Campione (1998) argue that there has been a change in the demand on schools, to-

---

* The notion of culture as a method of instruction is an explicit part of a growing number of theories in the new paradigm.

** This (and similar contrasts over the next five pages or so) helps to further clarify the differences between the new paradigm and the industrial-age paradigm of instruction.

*** This helps to show how the new paradigm of instruction is being driven by powerful societal changes outside of schools. See chapter 1, pp. 16–21, for more on this topic.

ward a goal of producing expert learners or "intelligent novices." This change has been brought on by (a) increasing knowledge, such that no one can absorb in school everything they will need to know in life, and (b) the changing demands of work, where technology can carry out low-level tasks, requiring workers who can think abstractly and learn new skills. So, given that we want people who know how to learn, it follows from Smith's argument that children will learn to be learners by joining a "learning club."

Multicultural Argument.   The world is becoming more closely integrated through the advent of new communication technologies, and societies are becoming increasingly diverse through mixing of people from different cultures. This requires people to interact and work with people from different backgrounds. To prepare people to live and work amid such cultural diversity, schools need to construct a learning environment that fosters students' abilities to work and learn with other people. Each person's contributions must be respected, and the community must synthesize diverse views. This is the type of learning environment that a learning-communities approach promotes.*

In summary, the learning-communities approach addresses the needs for students to deal with complex issues, figure things out for themselves, communicate and work with people from diverse backgrounds and views, and share what they learn with others. Therefore, educational researchers in America have begun to experiment with different models of learning communities to determine which ways of organizing learning communities are most effective (Brown & Campione, 1994; Collins & Bielaczyc, 1997; Lampert, Rittenhouse, & Crumbaugh, 1996; Rogoff, 1994; Scardamalia & Bereiter, 1994; Wineburg & Grossman, 1998).

A Framework for Viewing Learning Communities

The learning-communities approach raises a number of issues about the design of learning environments. We treat each issue as a dimension, along which we will contrast a learning-communities approach with an approach emphasizing the individual mind and how it develops. Classrooms have changed over the years to involve more social interaction, but classrooms organized as learning communities still differ from most classrooms along these dimensions. These eight dimensions provide a framework we will use to examine three examples of classroom-based learning communities described in the next section.

Goals of the Community.   In a learning-communities approach the goal is to foster a culture of learning, where both individuals and the community as a whole are learning how to learn.** Further, members of the community share their individual efforts towards a deeper understanding of the subject matter under study.

---

* In other words, the information-age work environment requires a new kind of "hidden curriculum," which requires fundamental changes in our approach to instruction.
** This focus on higher-order thinking is typical of the new paradigm.

Students learn to synthesize multiple perspectives, to solve problems in a variety of ways, and to use each other's diverse knowledge and skills as resources to collaboratively solve problems and advance their understanding. The intent is for members to come to respect and value differences within the community. In contrast, most classrooms tend to foster a culture in which students are expected to acquire the same body of knowledge at the same time. Rather than an emphasis on diverse expertise and problem solving, there tends to be an emphasis on conformity and on learning particular subjects.

Learning Activities.   Because the goals focus on fostering a culture of learning, the activities of learning communities must provide a means for (a) both individual development and collaborative construction of knowledge,* (b) sharing knowledge and skills among members of the community, and (c) making learning processes visible and articulated. A learning-communities approach tends to use a variety of learning activities, including individual and group research; class discussions; cross-age tutoring; working together to create artifacts or presentations that make public both what is learned and ways of learning; and collaborative problem solving where students take on particular roles toward a common end.

It should be noted that the learning activities described in a learning-communities approach and those found in most classrooms may share some similarities. However, because the learning activities are used toward different ends, differences arise. For instance, social learning techniques such as cooperative learning and collaborative learning (Cohen, 1986; Damon & Phelps, 1989; Slavin, 1986) can be used to support a learning community's goals, but they can equally well support more traditional learning aimed at inculcating particular knowledge among students. Brown and Campione (1996) contrast the learning activities in most classrooms with those of learning communities in terms of two other factors: that the activities in a learning community operate as a system,** and that their underlying objectives are articulated. They write:

> There are by now many procedures available that were designed to foster thinking. These procedures are part of the teacher's tool box. But the procedures are understood as unrelated tools, not as systems of interdependent activities.... Teachers may, for example, decide to include forms of cooperative learning, the use of long-term projects, a writer's workbench approach, etc. The problem we see is that such an approach ignores the potential power of creating a classroom system of activities that mutually influence and reinforce each other.... There is a purpose for every activity, and nothing exists without a purpose. All members of the community—students, teachers, parents, and researchers alike—should be aware of this. (Pp. 292, 314)

---

* This transcendence of extremist, ideological, "either-or" thinking is also typical of the new paradigm.

** A systems view of the instructional and learning processes is advocated by several theories in the new paradigm (see e.g., chap. 5 by Perkins & Unger, chap. 10 by Jonassen, chap. 11 by Nelson, and chap. 13 by Corno & Randi).

Teacher Roles and Power Relationships.   In a learning-communities approach, the teacher takes on roles of organizing and facilitating student-directed activities,* whereas in most classrooms the teacher tends to direct the activities. The power relationships shift as students become responsible for their own learning and the learning of others. Students also develop ways to assess their own progress and work with others to assess the community's progress.** In contrast, in most classrooms the teacher is the authority, determining what is studied and assessing the quality of students' work.

Centrality/Peripherality and Identity.   The degree to which people play a central role and are respected by other members of a community determines their sense of identity (Lave & Wenger, 1991). In a learning-communities approach the central roles are those that most directly contribute to the collective activities and knowledge of the community. However, opportunities exist for all community members to participate to whatever extent is possible, and students working in peripheral roles are also valued for their contributions.*** Centrality and peripherality are context dependent. Certain students may have more to contribute at a given time, so a student's centrality can change over time. As members of a learning community take on different roles and pursue individual interests toward common goals, students develop individual expertise and identities. Because diversity is important, an atmosphere in which students respect each other's differences needs to develop.

In contrast, in most classrooms students work on the same things and are all expected to reach a base level of understanding. Students tend to form their identity through being measured or by measuring themselves against this base level. Centrality tends to mean those who meet and exceed this base level: those who "get it." Schofield (1995) notes the benefits of such centrality in that teachers typically spend most of their time interacting with the better students. Students on the periphery are then those students needing remediation and extra help: those that "aren't quite there yet," which diminishes their value to others in the classroom.

In a learning-communities approach there is also the notion of a *community identity.* By working toward common goals and developing a collective awareness of the expertise available among the members of the community, a sense of "who we are" develops. In the absence of a learning culture that builds a collective understanding and views its members as learning resources, most classrooms fail to develop a strong sense of community identity.

Resources.   Both a learning-communities approach and many classrooms use resources outside of the classroom, including disciplinary experts, telementors,

---

* The notion of new roles for teachers and students (and technology) is a key marker of the new paradigm and a basic aspect of systemic change.

** Self-regulation is an important dimension of the new roles and is common to most theories in the new paradigm (see especially chap. 13 by Corno & Randi).

*** Continuing the theme of diversity of methods, here is advocated a diversity of roles for students.

the World Wide Web. However, in learning communities, both the content learned and the processes of learning from outside resources are shared more among members of the community and become part of the collective understanding. A further distinction between learning communities and most classrooms is that in learning communities, both the members themselves and the collective knowledge and skills of the community are viewed as important resources.

Discourse.   In the learning-communities approach the language for describing ideas and practices in the community emerges through interaction with different knowledge sources and through co-construction and negotiation among the members of the community. Also, learning communities develop a common language for more than just content knowledge and skills. The community develops ways to articulate learning processes, plans, goals, assumptions, etc. In contrast, in most classrooms the teacher and texts tend to promulgate the formal language to be learned.

Discourse functions in a learning community as a medium for formulating and exchanging ideas. It serves to motivate the research and reflection in the community by raising new questions and hypotheses, which give rise to further research and understanding (Bereiter & Scardamalia, 1993). Students are expected to provide feedback to each other and are supported in doing so. In contrast, in most classrooms communication occurs principally between the teacher and students. The discourse functions as a medium for conveying knowledge to students and asking students questions to test their knowledge (Schofield, 1995).

Knowledge.   In learning communities the development of both diverse individual expertise and collective knowledge is emphasized. In order for students to develop expertise, they must develop an in-depth understanding about the topics that they investigate. Rich subject matter is important. The topics are not randomly chosen, but rather the depth centers on key principles or ideas in a domain that are generative for understanding a broad array of topics.* There is also a circular growth of knowledge, wherein discussion within the community about what individuals have learned leads individuals to seek out further knowledge that they then share with the community. Thus, there is an interplay between the growth of collective knowledge and of individual knowledge, with each supporting the other. In most classrooms the goals tend towards covering all the topics in the curriculum (emphasizing breadth over depth) and for everyone to learn the same thing.

Products.   Dweck (1986) has shown how students who adopt performance goals put their energy into looking good and tend to give up when they fail. But

---

* This focus on depth of understanding is typical of the broadening of kinds of learning that characterizes the new paradigm (see especially chap. 4 by Gardner, chap. 5 by Perkins & Unger, and chap. 6 by Hannafin, Land & Oliver). This also illustrates the considerable overlap and compatibility among the "understanding" theories and the "community of learners" theories.

those students who adopt learning goals learn more from their mistakes and pursue learning in the face of failure. One concern is that an emphasis on products may lead students to adopt performance goals and to focus on production values rather than meaningful learning.* But, as Bruner (1996) points out, a culminating event or product can act to focus the energy of the entire class on a joint effort, which helps to build community.

In a learning-communities approach, members work together to produce artifacts or performances that can be used by the community to further their understanding. There is sustained inquiry and development of products over months.** In contrast, most classrooms tend toward individual or small group assignments with little sharing or collective products. Usually work is produced in short periods of time.

ANALYSIS OF LEARNING-COMMUNITY CLASSROOMS

To give a picture of what a learning-communities approach implies for schooling, we describe three exemplary cases of learning communities that have been set up in American classrooms. After briefly describing each of the three cases, we will compare them with respect to the eight issues raised in the "Introduction." Then we will attempt to extract general principles for the design of learning communities.

Scardamalia and Bereiter's Knowledge-Building Classrooms

Scardamalia and Bereiter (1991, 1994) have developed a model they call Knowledge-Building Communities. CSILE (Computer Supported Intentional Learning Environment) is the name commonly applied to this model, although strictly speaking it is the name of the computer software they developed, which is used in classrooms that may or may not have adopted the pedagogical model. The essential idea is that students work together to make sense of the world around them and work towards advancing their own state of knowledge and that of the class.

The model involves students investigating problems in different subject areas over a period of weeks or months. As students work, they enter their ideas and research findings as notes in an on-line knowledge base. The software (originally called CSILE, now in a new version called Knowledge Forum) supports students in constructing their notes through features such as theory-building scaffolds (e.g., "My Theory," "I Need to Understand") or debate scaffolds (e.g., "Evidence For"). Students can read through the knowledge base adding text, graphics, questions, links to other notes, and comments on each other's work. When someone has commented on another students' work, the system automatically notifies them about it.

The central activity of the community is contributing to the communal knowledge base. Contributions to CSILE can take the form of (a) *individual notes*, in which stu-

---

* This is similar to the concern raised by Nelson on p. 261.
** This issue of time, or depth versus breadth of learning, is a consistent theme in the new paradigm.

dents state problems, advance initial theories, summarize what needs to be understood in order to progress on a problem or to improve their theories, provide a drawing or diagram, etc., (b) *views*, in which students or teachers create graphical organizations of related notes, (c) *build-ons*, which allow students to connect new notes to existing notes, and (d) *"Rise Above It" notes*, which synthesize notes in the knowledge base. Any of these kinds of contributions can be jointly authored.

When students feel a note makes an important contribution to the collective knowledge base, they can propose the note for publication. An editorial group and the teacher then decide whether to publish the note. At the end of the school year the class may decide on a selection of notes to retain in the knowledge base for classes that come after them. The goal is to engage students in progressive knowledge building, where they continually develop their understanding through problem identification, research, and community discourse. The emphasis is on progress toward collective goals of understanding, rather than individual learning and performance.

Brown and Campione's FCL Classrooms

Brown and Campione (1994, 1996; Brown, 1992) have developed a model they call Fostering a Community of Learners (FCL) for Grades 1–8. The model provides what is termed a "developmental corridor," where the learning community extends not only horizontally across a classroom, but vertically across grades. This makes it possible for learning topics to be revisited at increasing levels of disciplinary sophistication.* We will focus here on communities in classrooms, rather than across grades.

The FCL approach promotes a diversity of interests and talents,** in order to enrich the knowledge base of the classroom community as a whole. The current focus of FCL classrooms is on the subject areas of biology and ecology, with central topics such as endangered species and food chains and webs. There is an overall structure of students (a) carrying out research on the central topics in small groups where each student specializes in a particular subtopic area, (b) sharing what they learn with other students in their research group and in other groups, and (c) preparing for and participating in some "consequential task" (Scardamalia, Bereiter, & Fillion, 1981) that requires students to combine their individual learning, so that all members in the group come to a deeper understanding of the main topic and subtopics. Teachers orchestrate students' work and support students when they need help.

There are roughly three research cycles per year.*** A cycle begins with a set of shared materials meant to build a common knowledge base. Students then break into research groups that focus on a specific research topic related to the central topic. For example, if the class is studying food chains, then the class may break

---

* This bears some similarity to Reigeluth's elaboration theory (chap. 18).

** This idea of helping each child to develop his or her unique talents is typical of the learner-focused paradigm as opposed to the standardization typical of the sorting-focused paradigm.

*** The idea of research cycles is similar to the idea of learning (or inquiry) cycles presented by Schwartz, Lin, Brophy, and Bransford in chapter 9.

into five or six research groups that each focuses on a specific aspect of food chains, such as photosynthesis, consumers, energy exchange, etc. Students research their subtopic as a group and individually, with individuals "majoring" by following their own research agendas within the subtopic. Students also engage in "crosstalk," talking across subtopic groups to explain, ask questions, and refine their understanding. The research activities include reciprocal teaching (Palincsar & Brown, 1984), guided writing and composing, consultation with subject matter experts outside the classroom, and cross-age tutoring. In the final part of the cycle, a member from each of the subtopic groups come together to form a "jigsaw" group (Aronson, 1978) in order to share learning on the various subtopics and to work together on some consequential task. Thus, in the jigsaw, all pieces of the puzzle come together to form a complete understanding.

The consequential task requires the different subtopics to be used together to form a common product or common understanding. The choice of consequential tasks is ideally made by the teacher and students together. In some cases the consequential task might be a bulletin board display, the design of a bio-park to protect an endangered species, a presentation to the community at large, or in some cases a test of their knowledge. These tasks "bring the research cycle to an end, force students to share knowledge across groups, and act as occasions for exhibition and reflection" (Brown & Campione, 1996, p. 303).

Lampert's Mathematics Classroom

Lampert (1986, 1990; Lampert et al., 1996) taught mathematics to fifth-grade students for a number of years, where she developed an approach to teaching that reflected her view of an idealized mathematics community. The class usually starts with a problem posed to the students,* which they work on alone or in groups, developing their solutions in notebooks that retain all their work during the year. After 15–20 minutes of work the class as a whole discusses the problem and various possible solutions. Lampert encourages students to discuss different ideas and solutions, so that they develop a deep understanding of the mathematical principles underlying their work.

Lampert chooses problems that foster deep inquiry and mathematical argumentation by students. Students are encouraged to present different ideas and methods, and to discuss which are correct and why. There is an emphasis on how to resolve mathematical arguments by appeal to logic and evidence. Participating in the mathematical discussions, learning how to make mathematical arguments, and learning the language of mathematics (terms such as "conjectures" and "commutativity") are the central activities in the classroom.

---

* It seems that the scope of these problems is considerably smaller than for the problems in chapters 8 (Schank, Berman, & Macpherson), 9 (Schwartz, Lin, Brophy, & Bransford), 10 (Jonassen), and 11 (Nelson). But this theory still seems to qualify as problem-based learning (PBL), which shows the considerable overlap and compatibility among the PBL theories and the "community of learners" theories.

Lampert orchestrates the discussion and picks up on certain ideas, revoicing them so that everybody can understand. She opportunistically follows the ideas the students suggest in order to relate them to important mathematical ideas. The students are on an equal footing in the discussions, offering their ideas and discussing other students' ideas and arguments. She carefully orchestrates the discussion to maximize the participation among the students. Her technique of asking students to explain other student's ideas is particularly effective in making them listen to and respect other students. The discussion involves students in a way that fosters understanding of the ideas and principles that the class is developing.

COMPARISON OF THE THREE CASES

We will compare the three cases in terms of the eight issues outlined in the "Introduction." By looking at the similarities and differences between these exemplary cases of classroom learning communities, we can more clearly see the essential characteristics of learning communities.

Goals

All three cases foster a culture of learning, where students come to see themselves as contributors to their own learning and that of the community. The goals in all three cases are consonant with the learning-community goals described in the "Introduction." This includes the goals of students learning how to (a) learn and reflect on their learning, (b) become critical thinkers who know how to frame questions and develop a deep understanding of the issues they investigate, and (c) share their learning and work with others in the community as resources.

Learning Activities

While the three cases share the same goals, they involve different learning activities and types of support. In CSILE, students investigate problems and develop theories, contribute written and graphic descriptions about what they are learning to the collective knowledge base, and comment on and respond to other students' contributions. This tends to be accompanied by oral discussion. These learning activities are guided by the software through the different scaffolds (e.g., "My Theory," "What I Learned") and by interactions with other students around their ideas. In FCL, the learning activities center on research, sharing knowledge, and producing joint products. The different activities (e.g., reciprocal teaching, guided writing, cross-age tutoring) each have a structure, which serves to guide the students. Lampert's classroom focuses on problem solving and mathematical argumentation as learning activities. Lampert provides guidance throughout the process, by posing provocative problems and directing discussion toward important mathematical issues.

Teacher Roles and Power Relationships

In all three classrooms, the teacher takes the role of a facilitator. The learning activities and lines of inquiry tend to be driven by student questions and interests. In Lampert's classroom, by comparison with CSILE and FCL, the teacher is much more in control of what students are doing. By leading students in whole-class discussion, Lampert supports students in coming to reason and argue mathematically in the ways that she has mastered. The teacher's role in CSILE is not prescribed and can vary widely, depending on the teacher's knowledge and orientation toward a particular unit. As Scardamalia, Bereiter, and Lamon (1994, p. 209) point out, "CSILE opens up a significant channel for communication in the classroom that is not mediated through the teacher." FCL falls somewhere in between. Certain activities, such as the benchmark lessons, are closely guided by the teacher or by guest experts. However, students also direct the community's learning, as in one case where students became interested in the question of whether mosquitoes could transmit AIDS (Brown & Campione, 1994).*

In both CSILE and FCL classrooms, a student may have more expertise in a particular area than the teacher, changing the typical student–teacher power relationship that exists in most classrooms. Ideally, students benefit from the knowledge of their teachers and available experts, but at the same time go beyond such knowledge whenever feasible (Scardamalia & Bereiter, 1991).

Centrality/Peripherality and Identity

As stated earlier, the central roles are those that directly contribute to the collective activities and knowledge of the community. All three cases also provide a means for all community members to participate in peripheral roles to whatever extent is possible. In CSILE, students can still participate in the community while engaging in peripheral activities, such as reading notes in the knowledge base and making comments on other students' notes. Students' roles begin to shift as they create notes of their own, either as individuals or in a group. Students begin to play more central roles as they have their notes published or linked to other students' notes. Centrality increases further when a student's notes are chosen to be saved for future generations of CSILE users.** In FCL classrooms, students move into central roles when their expertise is required within their jigsaw group, when creating products, or when their individual expertise is called on by the whole community. In Lampert's

---

* Self-regulated learning was not characteristic of the industrial-age paradigm and therefore represents a significant departure for the new paradigm. Nevertheless, the diversity in "control of learning" illustrated here (and discussed in chap. 3 on pp. 58–60) shows that the new paradigm still can utilize teacher-centered control when appropriate. This illustrates how the new paradigm incorporates many aspects of the industrial-age paradigm, rather than replacing them.

** This seems similar to the idea of "legacies" in chapter 9 by Schwartz, Lin, Brophy, and Bransford.

classrooms, students move into central roles when they contribute to the mathematical discoveries and arguments that the class is engaged in.

Individual identity is developed in CSILE when one's contribution is recognized: other students read, comment, or make links to one's note; one's note is published, or the whole class identifies one's note as worthy of being saved for later generations. In FCL classrooms, individual identity is developed through being responsible for others' learning in contexts such as jigsaw groups or cross-age teaching. Identity is also developed in contributing one's individual expertise and skills to the public, collective understanding. In Lampert's classroom, individual identity is developed as one's contributions to the class discussions are commented on or built upon, and from the teacher revoicing what one has said.

A major effort in these classrooms goes into ensuring that all students are making contributions to the community and that their contributions are valued by other students. This is accomplished in different ways. CSILE encourages students to investigate issues they care about, and so they develop diverse expertise, which serves to make their contributions valuable to other students. In addition, students are taught how to make effective comments on each other's notes, so that their criticism is constructive (Woodruff & Brett, 1993). By setting up jigsaw and reciprocal teaching groups and jointly produced consequential tasks, FCL fosters diverse expertise and interdependence, which encourages students to rely on and value other students' work. Students also learn how to give helpful guidance to each other. For example, before students work with each other in cross-age teaching, tutors are trained in tutoring methods (Brown & Campione, 1996). Lampert also uses a variety of stratagems to build a community where all the students respect each other. This includes revoicing what students say so that their ideas are understood by other students, and asking students to explain what other students are saying before they disagree, so that they must listen carefully to other students during the discussion. In addition, she gives feedback to students when they do not listen to and respect other students.

In all three cases, a community identity is also developed. In CSILE this comes from all students building a common knowledge base and from students working together to examine their collective knowledge base and to decide what should be passed on to future generations. In FCL classrooms, community identity comes from participating in the creation of joint products and through experiencing how the subgroups of the class work together. In Lampert's classroom this comes from the whole class working together in depth on math problems, engaging in mathematical argumentation with each other, and coming to a common understanding of mathematical principles.

Resources

In all three cases, the students come to view each other as legitimate resources for learning. Another resource that is common to all three cases is the collective knowledge and skills that the community is developing. The teacher is also a resource, although in Lampert's classroom the teacher is a more central resource than in the CSILE and FCL classrooms. Lampert provides a deep understanding of mathematical issues and skills in mathematical argumentation, which she uses in selecting problems and guiding students' discussion.

FCL and CSILE classrooms bring in resources from outside the classroom in whatever ways possible. Because students are investigating questions in depth, they often come upon issues that are beyond the classroom community's expertise to answer. Therefore, FCL encourages students to find resource people that can help with the questions they are investigating, to learn from students in cross-age tutoring interactions, to communicate with telementors about issues, and to find information on the Web. FCL's benchmark lessons often bring in experts from the community. This resource contributes not only to the students' learning, but also to the teacher's professional development. "With increasing exposure to the visitor's lessons, the classroom teachers learn more about the content area and increasingly come to take over responsibility for benchmark lessons" (Brown & Campione, 1996, p. 299).

Scardamalia and Bereiter (1994, 1996) have begun to develop a new type of relationship between students and outside resources in the CSILE model. They envision a knowledge-building society where both adults and students work in a common knowledge base. To illustrate how they see such a society functioning, suppose that fifth and sixth graders are working on the problem of "How does electricity work?" and that museum curators are working on an exhibit about electricity. The curators might investigate the students' knowledge base to see what interests them or confuses them about electricity. Similarly, the students might follow the ongoing development of the exhibit discussions in the knowledge base, making comments on what they find interesting and what they don't understand. Further, scientists involved in the exhibit might contribute to knowledge building by providing useful comments on or links between students' notes. Students might also learn from observing the thinking processes exhibited in adult discourse in the knowledge base.

Discourse

All three cases encourage public discussion of issues among students. This is one of the central ways that a learning community expands its knowledge.

The CSILE system emphasizes a discourse of formulating problems, constructing theories, and bringing questions, comments, and new information to bear on them. The labels on the notes guide the students in making contributions (e.g., "My Theory," "I Need to Know"). In producing notes about what they have learned, students are encouraged to use both written and graphical discourse. Communication in CSILE is asynchronous, which may allow students to express themselves more clearly, since they are not able to rely on immediate context in making their points clear (Bereiter & Scardamalia, 1993). An interesting aspect about the use of written discourse in CSILE is that the basis for determining a student's status tends to be different from that in face-to-face settings. Because a great deal of classroom interchange in CSILE is in written form, qualities such as clarity, persuasiveness, and inventiveness come to dominate over forcefulness, looks, and popularity, which usually determine status in face-to-face settings. In CSILE, students are also encouraged to critique each other's work by reading and commenting on their notes. Students are taught how to use these different genres effectively. For example, in order to get students not to make superficial comments, students are taught to identify both the strengths and weaknesses in other students' work.

Similarly, FCL emphasizes students engaging in questioning, explaining, and constructive discussion of issues, both in written and oral modes. Students work in groups to formulate questions that they pursue in their research. They write up their findings for the other students, and these writings form the basis for reciprocal teaching sessions with the other students in the class. In the crosstalk and jigsaw sessions, students discuss what they have learned and make comparisons with what others have learned. Brown and Campione (1996) claim that

> dialogue provides the format for novices to adopt the discourse structure, goals, values, and belief systems of scientific practice. Over time the community of learners adopts a common voice and common knowledge base, a shared system of meaning, beliefs, and activity that is as often implicit as it is explicit.... Ideas are seeded in discussion and migrate throughout the community. (pp. 305, 319)

Lampert emphasizes mathematical argumentation in her classroom in order to teach students how to reason mathematically. One challenge to this approach is that students find this emphasis on argumentation at odds with their desire to get along with other students and not to criticize them (Lampert et al., 1996). As Lampert and her colleagues point out, it is very difficult for adults to separate criticism of ideas from criticism of the person, so it is not surprising that students find argumentation uncomfortable. With the teacher's guidance and with experience and modeling by other students over time, students learn how to argue about ideas effectively without personalizing the criticisms.

Knowledge

The three cases differ as to how much they encourage people to develop common knowledge as opposed to diverse knowledge. Lampert strives for common knowledge among all participants. Lampert encourages students to help each other in their groups, and in the group discussion of problems she works toward the goal of everyone understanding the ideas discussed. With CSILE, on the other hand, students are encouraged to go off in depth in their own direction to develop expertise. Some students may focus on one aspect of a topic, and other students on another aspect. Through reading each other's notes and producing a database for which they are collectively responsible, they form a common understanding.

FCL supports diverse expertise in that it has each research group study a different topic and each member of the group become expert in a different aspect of the topic. But FCL also strives for common knowledge through different mechanisms, such as crosstalk, classroom discussions, consequential tasks, and students sharing their expertise. The activities are also structured to ensure that students know who has what expertise. So, if a question arises with respect to a problem they are working on, they know who to ask for help.

All three cases help students to develop metaknowledge about both the subject matter and the learning processes they are engaged in. In CSILE the development of higher-order views of the community's work, together with the "What We Have Learned" notes and "Rise Above It" notes, encourages students to engage in a type of "meta-discourse." That is, students engage in discourse about the discourse in the knowledge base where they reflect on their own and on the community's progress in understanding. FCL grows out of a long line of research on metacognition and the development of activities that foster reflective learning practices (see Brown & Campione, 1996). The learning activities in FCL classrooms are meant to create an atmosphere of reflection on learning and to encourage articulation of learning processes.* For example, in completing a public performance, students reflect on what they have learned and set priorities: "What is important to know? What is important to teach? What of our new found knowledge do we display?" (Brown & Campione, 1996, p. 295). In Lampert's classrooms, students are frequently asked to explain what another student is thinking or to articulate the idea one is arguing against, prior to making a proposal of one's own. Such activities require students to examine the ideas of the community, to compare proposals, and to talk about knowledge and understanding.

Products

As mentioned earlier, a concern with students developing products is that such an activity may lead students to adopt performance goals and focus on production values rather than on meaningful learning. Scardamalia and Bereiter (1991) have always been concerned with keeping students focused on learning goals, but they have incorporated into CSILE the publishing of notes and the handing on of the published notes to future classes. This acts as a kind of culminating product that can serve to focus the community's work. FCL emphasizes consequential tasks, where students work on a project that requires all the diverse expertise that different students have acquired. FCL also has students give presentations and exhibitions for a wide variety of audiences, such as parents, community members, and younger students. So there is an emphasis on products that bring together different strands of the students' work and that reach outside the classroom. In Lampert's classes, stu-

---

* Reflection is a common feature in most theories in the new paradigm.

dents produce a journal with their individual work; however, the class does not produce any physical collective products.

One final point concerns the idea of the collective knowledge of the community as a product. While in all three cases the members of the community share a certain level of common understanding, differences exist between the three cases in terms of the level to which the collective knowledge is objectified. In CSILE, there is a complete written database, which embodies the community's knowledge and forms a repository that can be inspected and reflected upon. In FCL, the collective knowledge is expressed orally, which produces no repository, and also through artifacts and public performances, which provide records of the collective knowledge. In Lampert's classes, all discussions are oral, leaving no tangible record of the shared, collective knowledge. The only written record of what was learned is in the individual students' journals, which do not reflect the collective understanding and are not shared resources.

PRINCIPLES FOR THE DESIGN OF EFFECTIVE LEARNING COMMUNITIES

In considering these different cases, we have tried to encapsulate what we have learned from them into a set of principles for the design of effective learning communities.*

Community Growth Principle

The overall goal of the community should be to expand the community's knowledge and skills. To maximize its learning, the community needs to take advantage of the knowledge of all its members. The goal is for individuals to constantly gain new knowledge and to share among themselves. By pooling knowledge from all individuals, the community can expand its collective knowledge.

Emergent Goals Principle

The learning goals of the community should be co-constructed with the students and come out of the activities and questions that arise, as students carry out their investigations. The teacher must be sensitive to the needs, interests, and abilities of the individual students.** The goals therefore should reflect what the students know and help them build on both their strengths and weaknesses. The students spawn goals of their own as the learning community evolves and they take over more of the work of the community. In this way collective goals are emergent.

---

* Try to see which of these principles are exhibited in each of the other theories in this volume.

** This customization of instruction is perhaps the most important of all the key markers of the new paradigm (see chap. 1, p. 18).

Articulation-of-Goals Principle

The teacher and students should articulate the goals they are pursuing and the terms by which they will judge their success. This allows all members of the community to have a clear idea of the goals and of the criteria by which they can tell if they have reached their goals. All the students should develop the ability to judge if the goals have been met.

Metacognitive Principle

Metacognition involves (a) monitoring one's thinking processes, (b) being aware of what one knows and doesn't know, and (c) reflecting on what one has learned (Brown, Bransford, Ferrara, & Campione, 1983). In terms of monitoring, the community should keep asking itself what its goals are and if what it is doing will help it reach them. The community should also try to identify at regular intervals what it knows and does not know. Finally, in terms of reflection, the class can look back at what it has done (for example, at its products and performances) and evaluate what was learned and how well they did.

Beyond-the-Bounds Principle

The community should attempt to go beyond the knowledge and skills within the community and the resources easily available to them. They should try to make sense of things for themselves and welcome new approaches and challenges. They do not want simply to regurgitate what they find in their resources. They should seek ideas that challenge what they believe by soliciting diverse opinions and views on a topic. They should not just try to find support for their current beliefs.

Respect-for-Others Principle

Students need to learn to respect other students' contributions and differences, and to feel safe in speaking up and giving their own ideas. The more everyone is heard, the more sources of knowledge there are for expanding the community's knowledge. When only one or two students are heard, then the learning of the community is limited to what those few students provide and develop. The rules for respect should be clearly enforced and articulated.

Failure-Safe Principle

We often learn from failures, so that to the degree a learning community accepts failures and does not try to assess blame, then it fosters a more experimental approach that allows failures to occur as the community learns. Often the failures will be collective failures. There must be a sense that failure is okay, and that taking risks and an experimental approach will lead to more learning. Reflection without blame can help to ensure that the community learns from its mistakes.

Structural-Dependence Principle

The community should be organized such that students are dependent on other students' contributions in some way. It is important to have a valid reason for students to work together that makes sense to the students, such as a common task that requires their joint effort. If students are working on a task and they need another student's help, it makes that student important to them. This fosters both respect for the other student and that student's self-esteem.* This validation of differences is lost in traditional schooling, because it tries to ensure that everyone is always learning the same thing.

Depth-Over-Breadth Principle

The students have sufficient time to investigate topics in enough depth that they gain real expertise in the topics. This is necessary to foster a sense of their own expertise and to support meaningful discourse among the students. Ideally the depth should center on important ideas that are generative for understanding a broad array of topics. It is critical for students to get beyond memorizing knowledge and procedures, in order for students to care about what they are learning and to develop a sense of how to learn.

Diverse-Expertise Principle

Students develop the areas in which they are most interested and capable, with the responsibility that they share their expertise with the other students and the teacher. By developing diverse expertise, the community can deal with problems and issues that are too difficult for any individual to handle. A learning community continually discusses ideas and examines its progress in understanding, so that what an individual learns is not just from the activities that they themselves carry out, but from all the activities that different members of the learning community engage in. This is fundamentally different from "learning by doing," as it is commonly understood. To most people, the phrase implies that individuals learn from what they themselves do. What occurs in a learning community is "collective learning by doing," where participants also learn from what others do. What is learned by individuals is what "gets into the air" of the community.

Multiple-Ways-to-Participate Principle

In order to advance its collective understanding, a learning community has a variety of jobs it needs done. Students may be more or less interested and adept at different

---

* The attention to affective outcomes is a common feature for most of the theories in the new paradigm. Theories with an emphasis on affective outcomes are found in Unit 4.

activities, so that there should be a range of activities in which they participate. The different activities should support the multiple learning goals of the community, such as formulating questions, gathering knowledge, sharing knowledge within the community, presenting their knowledge to the outside world, and reflecting on what they have learned. Students will take on different roles in the various activities, such as researcher, expert, co-investigator, monitor, interpreter, moderator, etc. The community needs to value all roles and their contributions and not regard some roles as inferior.

Sharing Principle

There needs to be a mechanism whereby knowledge and skills gained by different individuals is shared throughout the community, so that each student is both a learner and a contributor to the community knowledge. Unless something enters into the collective knowledge of the community, it does not serve the common good. Many communities lack adequate ways of sharing knowledge and practices, so that members often end up doing a poor job, because they did not know that some other member had the expertise they could benefit from. So it is important to share knowledge, not simply so that everyone profits from what each individual learns, but also so individuals know who to go to when a difficult problem arises.

Negotiation Principle

Ideas, theories, procedures, etc. are constructed by a negotiation process among members of the community and arguments among them are resolved by logic and evidence (Collins, 1998). Argumentation is necessary for finding better solutions or understandings because the learning community needs to identify errors and misconceptions that inevitably arise. But students usually do not like to participate in argumentation, since it makes them uncomfortable to criticize others (Lampert et al., 1996). There needs to be ways to model and to coach participants on how to critique other people's ideas without personalizing the critique, by trying to separate the ideas from the person. There is a variety of stratagems for depersonalizing critiques (e.g., focusing on the strong aspects of work as well as the weak aspects; couching comments in terms of what to change, rather than what is wrong, etc.) that students need to develop to make interactions in a learning community effective.

Quality-of-Products Principle

The quality of the products produced by the community should be valued both by the community itself and by outsiders to the community. In particular the students need to think highly of the goals they are pursuing and the knowledge and products they are producing. There must be standards that the community agrees upon as to what makes for good quality work, and these standards must be tested against the outside world. One way to do that is to bring in different audiences to judge the work, such as parents, community members, and other students.

CONCLUSION

The idea of learning communities in classrooms will grow as we try to address the needs of being able to reason through complex issues and problems, direct one's own learning, communicate and work with people from diverse backgrounds and views, and share what one learns with others.

A key idea in the learning-communities approach is to advance the collective knowledge of the community, and in that way to help individual students learn. This is directly opposed to the approaches found in most schools, where learning is viewed as an individual pursuit and the goal is to transmit the textbook's and teacher's knowledge to students. The culture of schools all too often discourages sharing of knowledge, by inhibiting students' talking, working on problems or projects together, and sharing or discussing their ideas. Testing and grading are administered individually. When taking tests, students are prevented from relying on other resources, such as students, books, or computers. The approach is aimed at ensuring that students have all the knowledge in their heads that is included in the curriculum. Thus the learning-community approach is a radical departure from the theory of learning and knowledge underlying schooling.

The development of the learning-communities approach reflects a more widespread change in our understanding of education. Educational thinking in America has long been dominated by the psychologist's point of view, starting with Thorndike and coming down to us through behaviorists, such as Skinner and Gagné, and more recently cognitive psychologists, such as Bruner and John Anderson. This dominance is beginning to change as anthropological and Vygotskian influences have begun to "enculturate" educational thinking. The cultural view emphasizes that learning is a social and cultural enterprise, expressed in Frank Smith's (1988) terms as, "We learn from the company we keep." Learning in this view is coming to belong to a community of practice (Brown, Collins, & Duguid, 1989; Lave & Wenger, 1991). The idea of learning communities is the culmination of this view as applied to schooling.

The learning-communities approach also fits with the growing emphasis on lifelong learning. While in this paper we have emphasized the role of learning communities in classrooms, this view of learning can naturally be extended beyond the classroom walls. In addition to children, there is every reason for a learning community to include parents and members of the wider society. With the addition of computer networks it becomes possible to include scientists and other professionals, as well as students around the globe, in communities that are trying to understand and deal with social and political ideas and issues (Collins & Bielaczyc, 1997; Scardamalia & Bereiter, 1996). Children will benefit greatly from interacting with more adults in learning situations. Thus, the learning-communities approach offers a way to end the isolation of children in schools and integrate their learning with that of the wider society.

ACKNOWLEDGMENTS

This paper was partially funded by a fellowship from the McDonnell Foundation to the first author. We thank Marlene Scardamalia, Carl Bereiter, Magdalene Lampert, Nick Haddad, Ann Koufman, Michael Reynolds, and Charles Reigeluth for their suggested revisions to a previous draft.

REFERENCES

Aronson, E. (1978). *The jigsaw classroom.* Beverly Hills, CA: Sage.

Bereiter, C., & Scardamalia, M. (1993). Surpassing ourselves: An inquiry into the nature and implications of expertise. La Salle, IL: Open Court.

Brown, A. L. (1992). Design experiments: Theoretical and methodological challenges in creating complex interventions. *Journal of the Learning Sciences, 2,* 141–178.

Brown, A. L., Bransford, J. D., Ferrara, R. A., & Campione, J. C. (1983). Learning, remembering and understanding. In J. H. Flavell & E. M. Markman (Eds.), *Handbook of child psychology: Vol. 3. Cognitive development* (4th ed., pp. 77–166). New York: Wiley.

Brown, A. L., & Campione, J. C. (1994). Guided discovery in a community of learners. In K. McGilly (Ed.), *Classroom lessons: Integrating cognitive theory and classroom practice* (pp. 229–270). Cambridge, MA: MIT Press/Bradford Books.

Brown, A., & Campione, J. (1996). Psychological theory and the design of innovative learning environments: On procedures, principles, and systems. In L. Schauble & R. Glaser (Eds.) *Innovations in learning: New environments for education* (pp. 289–325). Hillsdale, NJ: Lawrence Erlbaum Associates.

Brown, J. S., Collins, A., & Duguid, P. (1989). Situated cognition and the culture of learning. *Educational Researcher, 18,* 32–42.

Brown, A., Ellery, S., & Campione, J. (1998). Creating zones of proximal development electronically. In J. G. Greeno & S. Goldman (Eds.), *Thinking practices.* Hillsdale, NJ: Lawrence Erlbaum Associates.

Bruner, J. S. (1996). *The culture of education.* Cambridge, MA: Harvard University Press.

Cohen, E.G. (1986). *Designing groupwork: Strategies for the heterogeneous classroom.* New York: Teachers College Press.

Collins, A. (1998). Learning communities: Comments on papers by Brown, Campione and Ellery and by Riel. In J. G. Greeno and S. Goldman (Eds.), *Thinking practices.* Hillsdale, NJ: Lawrence Erlbaum Associates.

Collins, A., & Bielaczyc, K. (1997). Dreams of technology-supported learning communities. In *Proceedings of the Sixth International Conference on Computer-Assisted Instruction* (pp. 3–10). Taipei, Taiwan.

Damon, W., & Phelps, E. (1989). Critical distinctions among three forms of peer leaning. *International Journal of Educational Research, 13,* 9–19.

Dweck, C. (1986). Motivational processes affecting leaning. *American Psychologist, 41,* 1040–1048.

Lampert, M. (1986). Knowing, doing, and teaching multiplication. *Cognition and Instruction, 3,* 305–342.

Lampert M. (1990). When the problem is not the question and the solution is not the answer: Mathematical knowing and teaching. *American Educational Research Journal, 27,* 29–63.

Lampert, M., Rittenhouse, P., & Crumbaugh, C. (1996). Agreeing to disagree: Developing sociable mathematical discourse. In D. Olson & N. Torrance (Eds.), (pp. 731–764). *Handbook of education and human development.* Oxford, England: Blackwell's Press.

Lave, J., & Wenger, E. (1991). *Situated learning: Legitimate peripheral participation.* New York: Cambridge University Press.

Murnane, R. J., & Levy, F. (1996). *Teaching the new basic skills.* New York: Free Press.

Palincsar, A. S., & Brown, A. L. (1984). Reciprocal teaching of comprehension-fostering and monitoring activities. *Cognition and Instruction, 1,* 117–175.

Rogoff, B. (1994). Developing understanding of the idea of communities of learners. *Mind, Culture, and Activity, 1,* 209–229.

SCANS Commission. (1991). *What work requires of schools: A SCANS Report for America 2000.* Washington, DC: The Secretary's Commission on Achieving Necessary Skills, U.S. Department of Labor.

Scardamalia, M., & Bereiter, C. (1991). Higher levels of agency for children in knowledge building: A challenge for the design of new knowledge media. *Journal of the Learning Sciences, 1,* 37–68.

Scardamalia, M., & Bereiter, C. (1994). Computer support for knowledge-building communities. *Journal of the Learning Sciences, 3,* 265–283.

Scardamalia, M., & Bereiter, C. (1996). Engaging students in a knowledge society. *Educational Leadership, 54*(3), 6–10.

Scardamalia, M., Bereiter, C., & Lamon, M. (1994). CSILE: Trying to bring students into world 3. In K. McGilley (Ed.), *Classroom lessons: Integrating cognitive theory and classroom practice* (pp. 201–228). Cambridge MA: MIT Press.

Scardamalia, M., Bereiter, C., & Fillion, B. (1981). *Writing for results: A sourcebook of consequential composition activities.* Toronto: OISE Press & La Salle, IL: Open Court.

Schofield, J. W. (1995). *Computers and classroom culture.* Cambridge, England: Cambridge University Press.

Slavin, R. (1986, Summer). Learning together. *American Educator, 12,* 6–13.

Smith, F. (1988). *Joining the literacy club.* Portsmouth NH: Heinemann.

Wineburg, S., & Grossman, P. (1998). Creating a community of learners among high school teachers. *Phi Delta Kappan, 79,* 350–353.

Woodruff, E., & Brett, C. (1993, November). Fostering scholarly collaboration in young children through the development of electronic commenting. *Research in Education, 50,* 83–95.

13 A Design Theory for Classroom Instruction in Self-Regulated Learning?

Lyn Corno
Judi Randi
Teacher's College, Columbia University

Lyn Corno

Judi Randi

Lyn Corno has been on the faculty at Teachers College, Columbia University, since 1982. Her research specialties are student learning and motivation, classroom teaching, and teacher development. Dr. Corno has been an editor of the Teaching, Learning, and Human Development section of the American Educational Research Journal (1992-1995), Secretary for AERA's Division C, and Member-at-Large for Division 15 of the APA. She is a Fellow of APA, APS, and AAAS, and serves on editorial boards for the NSSE, Educational Psychologist, and Contemporary Educational Psychology. Her publications include contributions to more than 20 books and more than 30 journal articles.

Judi Randi received her doctorate in Curriculum and Teaching from Teachers College, Columbia University. She is currently teaching secondary humanities and is Adjunct Assistant Professor of Education at Teachers College, Columbia University. She has conducted research and development activities with classroom teacher–researchers. Her research focuses on teacher professional learning, collaborative research, and the research–practice connection. She has co-authored several book chapters on teacher–researcher collaboration.

293

FOREWORD

Goals and preconditions. The primary goal of this theory is to foster self-regulated learning among students and teachers. This includes developing teachers' potential as innovators, problem solvers, and experiential learners. The major preconditions are a situation where self-regulated learning is an important goal and there is sufficient time to develop self-regulatory skills in the learners.

Values. Some of the values upon which this theory is based include:

* student self-regulated learning, both as an end and as a means to support improved subject-matter competence,
* supporting students' pursuit of learning goals,
* teacher self-regulation, to develop their own models for teaching self-regulated learning to their students,
* contextualized professional development that focuses on teachers' skills for inquiry and inventing new instructional practices,
* linking research and practice.

Methods. Here are the major methods this theory offers:

For a teacher:

Collaborate with a researcher to generate appropriate methods and foster your own self-regulated learning.

Structure the classroom for self-regulated learning.
* Refocus the evaluation system to emphasize qualitative aspects of student work, rather than ranking students by "grades," especially in the early stages of learning new skills.
* Encourage students to set criteria and select assignments.

Prime the students.
* Prepare the students for reflective self-evaluations and peer evaluations.
* Provide explicit instruction in planning, self-monitoring, and resource management.
* Teach them how to seek help when they need it.

Provide ample opportunities for students to engage in self-regulated learning and to feel successful.
* For students who need it, provide explicit instruction and labeling of self-regulatory strategies from the beginning. For all other students, model and label self-regulatory learning strategies only in response to students' own efforts.

- *Have students inductively identify self-regulatory strategies in meaningful literature and students' own life experiences (through group discussion and class presentation).*
- *Have students experience SRL vicariously, and suggest SRL strategies for others, before they articulate and develop their own SRL strategies (e.g., invent self-regulatory strategies for characters in literature before they write about personal experiences).*
- *Have students write essays about their own self-regulatory experiences, then analyze their own essays for evidence of strategy use.*
- *Encourage students to select homework partners who share perspectives and practice articulating SRL habits.*
- *Provide qualitative feedback on students' work that models SRL strategies.*
- *Continually assess students' readiness and adjust instruction to support students who need it and stretch others.*
- *Design the culminating assignment in a way that allows each student to incorporate something s/he is dealing with in life.*

For a researcher:

Encourage teachers to engage in self-regulated learning about their teaching methods.

- *Use the cycle of planning, enacting, and reflecting on their lessons.*
- *Expose teachers to various teaching methods (models of instruction).*
- *Help teachers adapt those methods to their classrooms.*
- *Help teachers invent new instructional methods.*
- *Help teachers evaluate their new instructional methods, with students as the focus.*
- *Encourage teachers to articulate what they learned and how, to bring teachers' own self-regulatory strategy use to a conscious level.*
- *Help teachers to reconcile their new teaching methods with "old" ones.*
- *Encourage trust, experimentation, and problem-solving.*

Approach research with teachers as an opportunity for collaboration and shared expertise

- *Use work with teachers to develop new modes of data collection and new ways of evaluating instructional effects.*
- *Use collaborative research and new modes of data collection to contribute to the knowledge base on SRL.*

See also the principles on pp. 24-27.

Major contributions. *The emphasis on self-regulated learning and how to foster it. The attention to ways of fostering appropriate teacher development to use the approach effectively with students.*

—C.M.R.

A Design Theory for Classroom Instruction in Self-Regulated Learning?

Our title is intended to call into question the appropriateness of design theory for classroom instruction in self-regulated learning. More than a decade of research has stressed that self-regulation—the strategic, personal management of schoolwork—can be promoted through explicit teaching. However, our own work has led us to the position that the specification necessary for creating a good design theory of self-regulated learning may undermine the ultimate accomplishment of this goal. Our contribution here may thus be somewhat unconventional, but our position is consistent with the new paradigm for instructional theory Reigeluth described in chapter 1 of this volume.

We first characterize self-regulated learning, and briefly note some research history. Our primary focus in this chapter is a description of our current research with practicing teachers. This research has led us to emphasize the importance of teachers' own regulatory efforts in the process of classroom instruction. Rather than maintaining traditional distinctions between instructional-design theory and process, our work suggests the importance of a *collaborative innovation* process in the actual formation of theory in this domain. If teachers are to help students become self-regulated learners, their own self-regulation has to be unleashed as well. Traditional design theories of instruction run the risk of interfering with rather than supporting this goal.*

A Brief Overview of Related Research on Student Self-regulated Learning

One way to support students' goal pursuit is to teach specific strategies they can call upon to assist in completing academic tasks. Asking oneself questions when reading such as "What is the main idea here?," or in problem solving such as "Have I used all the information given?," are examples. To reach goals students also need to learn to manage time and reward themselves for work well-done. The habitual use of identifiable learning and self-management strategies is enabling because ultimately learning becomes less of a cognitive and behavioral burden (Corno & Mandinach, 1983). Although there are several different definitions of student self-regulated learning, all of these involve bringing learning-related knowledge

---

* This is similar to the call for flexibly adaptive instruction in chapter 9 by Schwartz, Lin, Brophy, and Bransford.

and self-management strategies into tasks, and emphasize the inclination to use them appropriately (Zimmerman & Schunk, 1989). Self-regulated learning has also come to be understood as a dimension on which students differ reliably; some students are more prone to use self-regulated learning than others. It is important that self-regulated learning becomes more widespread, however, because it functions, in principle to lead students toward various forms of educational accomplishment, under the kinds of conditions that typically exist in schools.

Much previous research on student self-regulated learning has been conducted following the objective, scientific methods associated with a positivistic world view. For example, predictive research programs led by Pintrich (Pintrich & DeGroot, 1990; Pintrich & Garcia, 1991), C. Weinstein (Weinstein & Meyer, 1991), and Zimmerman (Zimmerman & Martinez-Pons, 1986; 1988) have focussed on expressed strategy use in academic situations and correlated students' self-reports with educational outcomes such as grades and achievement tests. These types of studies find self-regulated learning to be (a) measured reliably by self-report, (b) distinct from measures of general cognitive ability and other aspects of motivation such as anxiety, and (c) to predict important educational attainments in adolescence and beyond.

Other research has moved away from analytic and predictive studies of self-regulated learning in coursework towards the design and evaluation of instructional procedures and models (see, e.g., Harris & Graham, 1985; 1992 regarding special education; and Bereiter, 1990 and Bereiter & Scardamalia, 1987 regarding writing instruction). These investigators have focused on the development of instructional models for teaching self-regulatory principles and strategies to students who need to learn them to support their subject matter acquisition. In general, instruction such as this is successful. Even learning disabled students can learn to self-regulate on school tasks with the right kind of instructional prompts.

Efforts such as these complement the prominent strategy instruction research in reading by Palincsar and Brown (1984; Palincsar, 1986), Pressley and his colleagues (Pressley, Forrest-Pressley, Elliott-Faust, & Miller, 1985; Pressley, Goodchild, Fleet, Zajchowski, & Evans, 1989; Borkowski, Carr, Rellinger, & Pressley, 1990; Brown & Pressley, 1994), and others (Dole, Duffy, Roehler, & Pearson, 1991). Much of that technical work has been summarized by Pressley in numerous books and articles on the "good strategy user model" (Brown & Pressley, 1994). Again, strategy instruction benefits many students in reading, even if some studies have failed to obtain transfer of strategy use to other tasks.

Qualitative-interpretive and ethnographic studies, conducted more recently, offer a different form of evidence and an alternative research paradigm for supporting the practical value of explicitly teaching self-regulation strategies in subject matter contexts. Qualitative research also spotlights the numerous teaching and teacher education challenges these efforts entail (Trawick & Corno, 1995), some of which are noted in Table 13.1.

TABLE 13.1

Teacher Education Obstacles to Instruction in Good Strategy Use

- Teachers have not been educated about information processing.
- The strategy-instructional perspective puts great responsibility on the teacher.
- Strategy instruction requires demanding methods of teaching.
- Durable strategy use often does not follow from strategy instruction.
- Lack of evaluation data makes it difficult for educators to select effective strategy-instructional materials.
- Educators have limited access to information about strategies.

Note. From "The Challenges of Classroom Strategy Instruction," by M. Pressley, F. Goodchild, J. Fleet, R. Zajchowski, and E. Evans, 1989, *The Elementary School Journal, 89,* pp. 309–322.

Teacher Professional Learning

This brief overview of the self-regulated learning research informs new approaches we shall describe in which both the theoretical perspective and situations for investigating questions about students' self-regulated learning are broadened. Nonetheless, attention remains to be given to teachers' own self-regulation, especially in the face of challenging teaching situations. Traditional staff development has afforded teachers few opportunities for self-regulated learning about teaching. The history of staff development research and practice provides the context for our current thinking about teachers as self-regulated learners.

Historically, teachers have been asked to implement innovations developed outside their own classrooms (Corno, 1977). In traditional staff development, teachers are viewed as passive learners carrying out these mandates assisted by skill training, "coaching," and implementation support (McLaughlin & Marsh, 1978). Few staff development programs promote the idea of teachers becoming innovators themselves. In short, little attention has been paid to developing self-regulation in teachers. More recently, calls for teachers to become "reflective" and "teacher researchers" (Cochran-Smith & Lytle, 1992; Schon, 1983) have ushered in new forms of teacher professional development that view teachers as active learners (Lieberman, 1995).*

New understandings about how teachers learn, together with the research on student self-regulated learning, provide a foundation for investigating self-regulated learning in teachers. Qualitative-interpretive studies, for example, can disclose teachers' own self-regulatory efforts as well as strategies teachers use to promote self-regulation in students (see, e.g., Gudmundsdottir, 1997). In our current work, we struggle with a different kind of case-based, qualitative data. One objective is to

---

* These new forms of teacher professional development are examples of the new paradigm of instruction.

open up new ways of seeing and assessing the construct of self-regulated learning beyond extant psychometric scales or statistical combinations derived from questionnaire items. We also move beyond previous research that sought to gauge the advantages of explicit teaching by reducing the incidence of implicit prompts through controlled delivery of instruction. Rather than designing systematic instructional treatments to be "implemented faithfully" by teachers in our studies, our approach has been to work with teachers to develop their own models for teaching self-regulated learning to their particular students.*

Although traditional staff development has encouraged the implementation of innovations, it has not encouraged innovation itself. The widespread use of measures of implementation to evaluate the impact of staff development reveals inconsistencies inherent in the "old" model. Although they touted innovation as a means for improving instruction, staff developers actually taught and tested imitation. New approaches to teacher professional development value inquiry and invention over implementation and unreflective imitation, and strive for consistency between medium and message, method and content, and what is valued and what is evaluated (see, e.g., Lewis, 1997).

Efforts such as these have led us gradually to the philosophical position that it is almost an oxymoron to "provide guidelines for teaching self-regulated learning." The goal of self-regulated learning in students needs a different form of work with teachers. Our work is intended to complement earlier instructional interventions at the same time that it offers an alternative form of instructional theory.** Depending on the side of the psychological fence on which one sits, our theory may or may not be "design theory."

Although it is antithetical to our position to provide specific guidelines for teaching self-regulated learning, we describe the collaborative process we have used in our work with practicing teachers. During this process, we have observed teachers' own self-regulatory efforts being unleashed.*** The ongoing collaborative nature of our work has enabled us to record the process of self-regulation during teachers' own learning and problem solving as they strive to provide enhanced learning experiences for their own students.

In the remainder of this paper we describe this collaborative process,**** which is at once a new form of research and a new form of teacher professional learning. After a long history of implementation research and practice, this form of teacher professional learning, which we have termed *collaborative innovation,* seems long overdue, especially for the kind of teacher who, as Reigeluth (1996) says, "tends to

---

* This appears to be a form of problem-based learning for teacher professional development.

** This captures the theme that the new paradigm incorporates many aspects of the previous paradigm.

*** So the issue becomes, can we provide guidelines that will help those involved with professional development to enhance teachers' self-regulatory capability? If so, then is that not instructional-design theory, albeit in the new paradigm?

**** Collaboration is a common feature in most theories in the new paradigm.

take pre-constructed instructional products, deconstruct them, and then use the resulting resources in unique ways during instruction." That is, consistent with the kind of teacher professional learning called for in recent reform literature (Lieberman, 1995), collaborative innovation supports teacher invention, rather than the implementation of others' ideas (Randi, 1996; Corno & Randi, 1997).*

Definition and Goals of Collaborative Innovation

Collaborative innovation supports teacher invention at the same time that it links research with practice through teacher–researcher collaboration. It defines a process whereby teachers work together within a larger school community that includes researchers to construct, assess, and describe new classroom practices consistent with the changing needs of their particular students. Rather than providing teachers with materials and instructional models for implementing others' ideas, rather than coaching teachers in how to use these models or how to "install these programs," and rather than assessing the degree of conformance or "fidelity" to a model, collaborative innovation encourages teacher invention of fresh practices. That is, collaborative innovation encourages teachers to move beyond the models provided them to adapt and invent new instructional practices consistent with modern psychological theory yet personally attuned to the individual differences** of both the teachers and students involved. Teachers' innovations are thus highly situated in the contexts of their own classrooms. And so the collaborative innovation model not only addresses constituents of teachers' own motivation but also leads to the development of new instructional practices crafted to accommodate students' individual differences.

Collaborative innovation is grounded in the dynamics of practice. Today's schools and classrooms are continually changing (McLaughlin, 1993). Schools, classrooms, and increasingly diverse student populations present ever unique challenges for today's educators. Waiting for research and policy to invent solutions to these problems would be inefficient and foolish. Today's teachers need the tools of invention not the skills of technicians (Olson, 1997). Thus one important goal of collaborative innovation is to develop teachers' potential as innovators and problem solvers. Another goal is to promote the development of self-regulated learning in students, which may be best done by means other than direct instruction. For example, the collaborative innovation process enables teachers to experience the learning process as students. In this process, teachers are guided by researchers to articulate what they have learned so that they, in turn, may guide their students in similar learning experiences. Finally, collaborative innovation aims to enhance teachers' experiential learning. Teachers often say they learn best from experience

---

   * As will be seen shortly, others' ideas are not totally ignored in this theory. So in fact the authors avoid the either-or trap and reconcile opposites into a more powerful alternative that is a synthesis of both. This is typical of theories in the new paradigm.
   ** Again, customization is manifest as a key marker of the new paradigm.

with clear models (Hargreaves, 1984; Olson, 1997). Experiential learning is thought to serve an important role in adult learning (Brookfield, 1996). Collaborative innovation supports teachers' attempts to learn from their own teaching context, encouraging them to articulate their knowledge.

AN ILLUSTRATION OF COLLABORATIVE INNOVATION

We have used collaborative innovation in our own research on self-regulated learning, but a growing number of other researchers have done so as well (see e.g., Perry, 1997). We do not have space in this chapter to describe others' related investigations, but readers should see Corno and Randi (1997) and Guthrie & Wigfield (1997) for more details. An example from one of our studies serves to illustrate the dilemma with respect to systematic instructional theory and self-regulated learning. In this example, we focus on students as learners and on what teachers might do to create classroom environments supporting students as self-regulated learners. The collaborative research process we used traced the invention of instructional practices developed by teachers with individual students in mind. Following the description of classroom practice is a summary of the instructional components used to create a classroom structure supportive of self-regulated learning.

Teaching Self-Regulated Learning Through Literature

Our own collaborative exploration of self-regulated learning instruction began when one of us (Randi) was teaching advanced Latin at a suburban public high school.

Convinced that student self-regulated learning might be promoted through modeling and multiple opportunities for independent learning, we started to discuss the different ways that Randi's high school Humanities curriculum might be structured to afford such opportunities for learning self-regulation more or less implicitly. We explored enduring themes of self-reliance and independence that mark the Humanities literature and film, such as quests, persistence, resiliency, and courage. We began to see how the Humanities curriculum itself might provide a model for implicit instruction in self-regulated learning.

Beyond the curriculum itself, our intent was to provide a classroom structure offering many ways for students to engage in self-regulated learning. Students might then experience self-regulated learning vicariously through literature at the same time that they learned self-management strategies inductively. Their inductive learning would involve literary analysis of characters exemplifying personal traits characteristic of self-directed learners.* Always at the center of attention was the thought that it would be Randi, the teacher, intervening in her own classroom—with her own materials, developed specifically for this purpose.

---

* This is reminiscent of the use of stories as cases in chapter 8 by Schank, Berman, and Macpherson.

The Students

The 10 advanced Latin students in this particular class were actually aver-age-to-below-average students. Although Latin was an elective in this school, some low-performing students were counseled into this course. Parents in this community perceived that taking advanced courses would enhance students' chances for college admissions. Typically, these students valued "good grades" as admission tickets to prestigious colleges.

Creating a Classroom That Enables Self-Regulated Learning

To help students learn how to be students and how to strive after learning as self-regulated learners are expected to do, it seemed important to set the stage by creating a classroom structure that enabled self-regulated learning to take place. If they felt sufficiently supported, we believed, the students would enjoy taking on new and increasingly difficult challenges. To this end, we provided students explicit instruction in how to be successful as learners. They were taught planning as well as how to monitor their own learning;* students were also carefully scaffolded to experience success in increasingly challenging learning situations.

One element that contributed to students' feelings of success was the way in which evaluation was used to provide feedback and assist students in aspiring to increasingly challenges. For example, these students had been previously taught how to evaluate their own work by comparing their work with exemplars and preestablished criteria. Students' own responses as well as hypothetical examples of responses that completely addressed a target assignment were discussed with the class until students understood how to evaluate their work against preestablished criteria. Thus, students were encouraged to evaluate their work objectively and candidly. They were also allowed to revise their work after self-evaluations, or were awarded extra credit when their explanations and evaluations were consistent with the teacher's feedback.**

Students were provided specific, qualitative feedback on their work. The feedback identified both strengths and weaknesses and contained information to help the students improve. The importance of grades was minimized intentionally. Although students always received written feedback, they only occasionally received a grade. To encourage effort in all tasks, students were not forewarned when assignments were to be graded. Most often, grades were avoided when students struggled with new skills. Thus, negative affect associated with new learning and delayed gratification were minimized.

As another element for success, students were encouraged to negotiate criteria and assignments to make any assigned tasks more pleasurable. One student, for example, was permitted to write a narrative account of a personal experience in the

---

* Again, elements of the industrial-age paradigm are utilized in the new paradigm.
** Self-evaluation and opportunity to revise one's work are both common in the new paradigm of instructional theory.

third person because he expressed some discomfort about writing about himself in a personal way. Streamlining or embellishing tasks is one motivational control strategy self-regulated learners can draw upon to maintain effort toward goals (Corno, 1993).

To encourage independent learning, promote goal orientation, and minimize students' frustration in tackling difficult tasks, students were provided with explicit instruction in planning and resource management such as how to seek help from friends, ways to brainstorm lists of possible resources, and alternatives for planning a course of action or follow-through. Students were assigned "homework partners" and required to check with partners whenever they missed an assignment or needed help. The classroom structure, along with inductive instruction in strategy use, reinforced the message that the responsibility for learning rested with students themselves.

It is important to note that this classroom was purposefully structured to enable self-regulated learning from the start of the course, not expressly for this particular research project. Students, for example, were taught how to evaluate their own work in a series of instructional activities throughout the course. Students (and their parents) were informed about the "always feedback, sometimes grading" policy as well as the intent behind the policy.

Lessons Embedded in the Curriculum

It was within the context of this purposefully structured classroom environment that we began to explore the possibility of teaching specific self-regulation strategies implicitly through the curriculum. Thus we embarked upon a plan that would mingle structure and content, medium and message, and, as Cronbach (1989) wrote, "performance and process." Not surprisingly, our attempt to teach self-regulated learning strategies implicitly through curriculum content rendered the teacher's goal of fostering independent learning more explicit and more understandable to the students

Convinced that embedded within this particular Humanities curriculum was a different means for developing an intellectual understanding of self-regulated learning, we directed our attention to the curriculum of this 12th-grade Latin class. The classical literature, and in particular, the quest literature, seemed to provide a natural framework for inferring self-regulatory strategies and teaching them. Universal themes in the quest literature actually paralleled the self-management and learning strategies employed by self-regulated learners: maintaining effort in difficult tasks, focusing attention on the task at hand, remembering prior successes in similar situations, managing time and resources, juggling priorities, and imagining the feeling of accomplishment at the quest's end.

An analysis of this literature within the context of experiences designed to evoke self-regulatory efforts in students proved especially useful. In one such activity, students were asked to create an imaginary character who embodied three Roman qualities exemplified by the hero, Aeneas, in Virgil's *Aeneid*. The Roman qualities of loyalty, seriousness of purpose, and perseverance were targeted by the teacher for this assignment because they were thought to be especially indicative of self-regulatory effort.*

One instructional activity focusing on these qualities was a small group activity, in which the students invented "Fred," the volunteering judge and dedicated family man to five adopted children, who regularly gave to charities, performed community service, and taught karate weekly. The students were led by the teacher to consider and resolve conflicts that arose when Fred attempted to give equal weight to conflicting obligations (e.g., what Fred might do should his wife become ill on the night he taught karate). As students described the strategies that Fred might use, they were learning to think about ways to juggle priorities and manage time and resources. They argued, for example, that Fred might relocate the karate class to his own home so that he could simultaneously tend to his family's needs and his students' instruction. If they could solve Fred's problems, it seemed likely that these students could invent similar strategies to solve their own problems under similarly challenging personal conditions. This activity is an example of instruction designed as part of the stream of ongoing classroom events and student responses. It was only when one small group of students invented Fred that these and other students were able to construct other characters that embodied such qualities. Only then could the teacher continue to build upon students' work and lead them to resolve conflicts other than just Fred's.

In a follow-up activity, students articulated self-regulatory strategies in analyzing how quest heroes overcame multiple obstacles without losing sight of their goal. Specifically, students were asked to enumerate, categorize, and label the various strategies that Odysseus used in his quest for homecoming in *The Odyssey*. The categories and labels that students themselves identified and constructed were remarkably similar to metacognitive, motivation, and emotion-control strategies** described in the literature on self-regulated learning (see Table 13.3).

Finally, students were asked to identify a quest in their own lives, to evaluate their decision to follow it, and to describe how they overcame obstacles encountered en route to their goals. Table 13.4 presents written excerpts from these students' personal quests. Our strategy codes are italicized.

Although the real test of these students' independence as learners will come when they are confronted with new academic challenges in future learning, we found that every student in this class demonstrated the use of self-management strategies in their written essays. Planning, emotion control, and self-evaluation were especially in evidence. Nine of ten students wrote papers with at least eight examples of self-management strategies.

---

* Note the overlap into the affective domain here. This is typical in the new paradigm.
** The interrelatedness of the affective and cognitive domains is evident in many theories in the new paradigm.

TABLE 13.2

Self-Regulation Strategies Exemplified by Students[a]		Parallel Strategies Exemplified by Quest Heroes[b]	
Strategy	*Student*	*Strategy*	*Quest Hero*
		Covert	
Metacognitive control	Think of the first steps to take and get started right away.	Planning	Odysseus thought of what he needed to do to trick Polyphemus and escape from the cave.
	Set some reachable goals.	Monitoring/ setting benchmarks	Odysseus had to kill the suitors before he could reclaim his place as king of Ithaca.
			Odysseus took on one obstacle at a time.
	Check work as you go; look for feedback.	Evaluating goals/progress	Odysseus was forced to reconsider the importance of his goal when Calypso offered him a chance for immortality.
Motivation control	Imagine doing this work well.	Focusing/ positive thinking	Odysseus imagined being home with his wife Penelope and his son, Telemachus.
	Give myself instruction and orders about timeliness; reward myself for hard work.	Endurance/ self-reliance	Odysseus talked to himself while he was alone on the raft; he told himself to stay on the raft until he could swim to shore safely.
Emotion control	Remember: I've done this kind of thing before.	Visualization/ mental imagery	On Calypso's raft, Odysseus remembered the many hardships he had endured before.
	Imagine being good at this.		After Athena showed Odysseus a vision of his success, Odysseus was ready to take on the suitors.
		Overt	
Control the task situation	Gather materials and people to get the work started.	Resource use/sorcery	Odysseus used a magical herb to counteract the spell of Circe.
	Streamline the task so it's easier and takes less work; add challenge or embellishment to task to make it more fun.	Use of own cleverness/ trickery	Odysseus allowed himself to hear Sirens' song but did not give up his quest for home; his men tied him to the ship's mast so he would not be tempted to jump overboard.
Control others in the task setting	Ask for help from teacher.	Getting help from confidants	Odysseus had help from Athena.
	Ask kids to be quiet if they're bothering me; move to a quiet place.	Controlling his men	Odysseus tried to keep his men from eating the sacred cattle and incurring the anger of Helios, the sun god.

[a]see also Corno and Kanfer (1993).

[b]Strategies were identified by students in an analysis of the literature; labels were coconstructed by teacher and students in an activity that led students to categorize the strategies and assign labels to the categories.

TABLE 13.3

Excerpts from Students' Personal Quests

I took a deep breath and tried to start again (emotion control) when I froze. I couldn't remember what I was writing and didn't know where to begin. I had encountered my second obstacle, writer's block.... I could quit and give up on college or I could go back to the desk and tackle that horrible monster of a computer (metacognitive: evaluating). I thought pensively about what to do when I decided how important this one essay was to my future and I was going to defeat this (motivation control).

I had dreams of driving down the open road headed for nowhere. I never imagined the many hardships that eventually came up during my quest to complete driver's ed and ultimately get my license.... Nevertheless, I trudged on and began my classes (metacognitive: planning/setting reachable goals). Looking back, I am glad that I pushed myself and succeeded at my goal because now I have greater independence and more self-confidence. Everything I had to give up and all the time I had to invest eventually rewarded me (metacognitive: evaluating).

Since my freshman year, I have done everything I could do to get into West Point. This has been a dream of mine ever since I could remember (motivation control).... A few weeks ago, I received a letter stating that I was fully qualified for admission to West Point. Just knowing that I have made it this far has made this process worth it (metacognitive: monitoring and evaluating).

This is not the end of my journey because I still have some remaining months of schooling to finish (metacognitive: monitoring). After writing down my ideas and mapping out my options (metacognitive: planning), I have gained a better understanding of myself and the goals I have to achieve within the next few months of my life (metacognitive: evaluating).

The students were also asked to evaluate their own essays for evidence of strategy use. Specifically, Randi had them identify strategies they used to overcome obstacles in their personal written quests. These strategies included motivation and emotion control modeled by the quest heroes (e.g., endurance, positive thinking, self-reinforcement, and mental visualization). Students also identified where they had used metacognitive strategies such as planning, monitoring their progress, or evaluating goals as well as their own ways of managing resources. Students were asked to quote from their essays and show how they planned a course of action, evaluated their goals, set benchmarks along the way, looked for and found resources, and relied on a confidant (the full assignment is presented in the Appendix). These learning experiences were designed by the teacher (Randi) to instruct and scaffold students in the use of self-management and learning strategies, as well as to assess students' progress toward independent learning (e.g., recognition of strategy use in literary characters, invention of strategies to help any and all characters accomplish goals, and self-evaluation of strategy use in students' personal essays).

The Teacher's Role

Throughout this instructional unit, the teacher served as facilitator. Consistent with our intent to teach self-regulation "implicitly," students were led by the teacher to identify the qualities exemplified by quest heroes and to make connections between the heroes' efforts and their own goal-oriented efforts. Thus students first identified and described self-regulatory strategies in their own words.* Students' own discoveries were then labeled and reinforced by the teacher through modeling** and subsequent activities focused on articulating self-regulated learning strategies, such as the students' strategy identification in their own essays.

Although our evidence shows that these students were guided by the teacher to learn self-regulatory strategies implicitly through the curriculum, we caution that not all students may benefit from this inductive learning process. Randi's journal recorded this observation:

> Might it be helpful for teachers to have conditional knowledge about the use of implicit and explicit teaching of self regulatory learning? It seems to me that there are times when it is more effective to teach self-regulatory learning implicitly and other times when explicit instruction is more effective*** ... I think back to one student who was especially sensitive and perceptive. Implicit instruction and modeling would eventually bring her around. But some students need explicit instruction and labeling from the beginning because they ... are unaware of their own thinking, insensitive to feedback, etc.

This excerpt articulates the need for instruction tailored to individual differences among students (Cronbach & Snow, 1977). Typically, the observations in Randi's journal had a dual emphasis on: (a) data collected on student progress toward self-regulated learning, and (b) the ways that she (the teacher) analyzed and used that data to focus students on what she felt needed to change. This excerpt also highlights the teacher's critical role in context-sensitive curriculum making. This type of curriculum development is not likely to have come about in traditional instructional design.

Summary of Instructional Components for This Project

Our project provides an example of how what is currently known about instructional conditions for self-regulated learning might be embedded by one practicing teacher into particularly suitable curriculum content in meaningful ways. We can summarize the elements of this "instructional theory" as follows:

- First, the classroom was deliberately structured to enable self-regulated learning to occur, and to facilitate the learning of new cognitive and self-management strategies. For example, the importance of grades was in-

---

* This method could be characterized as a recognize-produce sequence (identify self-regulatory strategies, then use them yourself), a strategy offered by Gropper in his behavioral instructional theory in chapter 5 of Volume I (which was actually recognize-edit-produce).

** In Volume I, Merrill identified tell, show, and do (generality, example, and practice) as three primary instructional methods (not necessarily in that order). It appears that self-regulation is fostered by beginning with "do" and following it up with "show" (modeling) and "tell" (labeling and coaching)—an inductive learning process.

***Again we see diversity of methods, rejecting an "either-or" mentality.

tentionally minimized and students were encouraged to set criteria and select assignments they themselves deemed meaningful. Thus, through the distribution of rewards as well as the nature of assignments and policies on student choice, students were able to take risks with their learning that they might not otherwise have taken.

- Second, the students were primed by the teacher to partake in the challenges this unit entailed. Although all students of "average" ability participated, each was prepared in advance for the kinds of self-evaluations and peer evaluations about to take place.
- Third, evaluation was used to move students toward goal attainment of goals rather than as judgment of students' performance.* For example, students were provided specific, qualitative feedback on their work more often than they received a grade.
- Fourth, to insure success and minimize frustration in learning, students were provided explicit instruction in planning and resource management. For example, although students were encouraged to become independent learners, they were taught how to seek help when they needed it, whether from the teacher, a homework partner, or some other resource.
- Fifth, the instructional unit provided ample opportunity for students to learn and demonstrate self-regulated learning. For example, students' own attempts to identify self-regulated learning strategies exemplified by quest heroes were acknowledged and validated before formal labels were eventually provided by the teacher as another way of describing self-regulated learning.
- Sixth, the culminating assignment was homework used in what Hill (1992) calls the prospective rather than the retrospective sense, that is, bringing into the classroom something each student is dealing with in life.** Adolescence is a time of many quests (seeking a college or some other future direction).
- Seventh, the teacher-developed unit was sensitive to students' individual differences and patterns of response. Curriculum was fluid in the sense that students' readiness was continually assessed and instruction regularly adjusted to stretch students to their full potential.***
- Eighth, the Humanities curriculum itself provided meaningful literature and themes for use as a basis for discussion and learning about self-regulation (see Table 13.3). We do not think these themes are unique to Humanities curricula; however, they were a critical element of our particular perspective. Other literature, including biography, as well as students' own life experi-

---

* This formative rather than summative role of student evaluation is a common feature of the new paradigm of instructional theories.

** This seems like a powerful way to customize learning.

*** Such customization—of both goals and instructional methods—is probably the most important indicator of the new paradigm.

ences, can provide opportunities for leading students to articulate self-regulatory strategies as we did in this particular Humanities curriculum.

• And finally, our collaborative work together generated both multimethod and comprehensive assessments of the self-regulated learning construct in students that might not have come about otherwise.* Our evidence suggests that our project succeeded in combining the types of diagnostic assessments used by classroom teachers in daily instructional interactions with the types of measures traditionally employed by qualitative researchers, such as coding student essays for evidence of self-management strategies.

How Collaborative Innovation Supports Self-regulated Learning

Earlier, we argued that teachers' own self-regulation must be unleashed if they are to support students' self-regulatory efforts. As we have demonstrated, teaching in context-sensitive ways requires dynamic curriculum making. Teachers' own innovations are an integral part of teaching but they have seldom been acknowledged, much less encouraged. Working as we did, acknowledging the integrity of teaching and instructional design, we found we were able to design instruction tailored to students' individual differences and to maximize each student's potential as a self-regulated learner.

Equally important, we found that the experience of working together to embed research findings into curriculum and instruction in this classroom afforded both of us opportunities for learning implicitly—opportunities that are seldom available to researchers in traditional case studies of classroom events and seldom afforded to classroom teachers in traditional forms of professional development. We found that new instructional strategies were generated from the ongoing interaction of research and practice.** Our research also suggests that the introduction of any novel perspective in classrooms will probably benefit from collaborative innovation (Corno & Randi, 1997; Olson, 1997; Randi, 1996).

Moreover, collaborative innovation, as we practiced it in this particular project, provides an alternative model for validating the effectiveness of other innovative teaching strategies developed by other classroom teachers. Notably, the combination of data generated from this one classroom case involved precisely the sort of multimethod assessment, multievent sampling, and comprehensiveness of measures that have long been promoted by measurement specialists concerned with construct validity (Snow, Corno, & Jackson, 1996). But it would not have come about if we had not worked as we did.

Self-regulated learning strategies are important for students to learn. But knowing how to learn is as valuable in the workplace as it is in the classroom (Corno &

---

* In other words, teachers, in their professional development, can benefit more from having a "guide on the side" than a "sage on the stage," just as students can so benefit.

** The use of collaborative innovation to generate better instructional strategies bears some resemblance to the use of formative research (see chap. 26 by Reigeluth & Frick).

Kanfer, 1993). Teachers, like students, have often been left to acquire "tacit knowledge" (Schon, 1983) or knowledge of how to succeed in the workplace with little help from others (Sternberg, 1995). This ability to acquire tacit knowledge may be critical to exceptional performance (Sternberg & Wagner, 1993). Although few staff development programs assist teachers in learning to innovate, and historically, teachers have been encouraged to implement others' innovations, there is some evidence that some teachers have learned to innovate implicitly by adapting models provided to them (Randi & Corno, 1997).

In traditionally structured classrooms, as in traditional staff development, there may be few opportunities for students to learn self-regulation. And yet, some students (and some teachers) clearly have acquired self-regulated learning strategies. Teachers and parents (Xu, 1994) model self-regulatory strategies but may not label these strategies for learners. Thus some students may be disadvantaged in acquiring the strategies typically used by "good" students. Left to learn from experience without guidance, some teachers too may be disadvantaged as professionals (Olson, 1997). Collaborative innovation assists teachers in learning from their own teaching by encouraging teacher invention arising from unique classroom situations, as well as the articulation of what they have learned.* Thus collaborative innovation brings teachers' own strategy use to a conscious level and enables teachers to label strategies for students.

Finally, the collaborative process allows teachers to participate in learning experiences similar to those we hope teachers design for their students. Working collaboratively, as we did, we observed multifaceted problem solving replace simple solutions, probing inquiry replace cursory judgment, and context-sensitive invention replace imitation of imported ideas. In short, teachers and students seem to benefit from learning self-regulated learning strategies implicitly through the contexts of their own experience. In the next section, we discuss teachers as self-regulated learners and explore collaborative innovation as one means for supporting self-regulated learning in teachers.

TEACHER INNOVATION AND SELF-REGULATED LEARNING

Teachers as Self-Regulated Learners

Collaborative innovation may have been practiced by some teachers long before researchers "discovered" the process and labeled it.** In the long tradition of externally generated, research-based innovations, practitioners have been recipients of numerous models of innovative instruction. Teachers encouraged to replicate these

---

*Again, we see reflection, including articulation of what one has learned and how one has learned it, as a key feature of the new paradigm.

** This is true for all methods of instruction, except those that are only possible with new technologies.

practices have been characterized as imitators or consumers more than innovators. But even when fidelity was expected, teachers have been more often observed adapting than replicating instructional innovations (McLaughlin & Marsh, 1978). Researchers have observed teachers inventing their own instructional practices, abstracting principles from the models they were encouraged to imitate (Connelly & Clandinin, 1988; Randi, 1996), and some research has described teachers as self-regulated learners (Gallimore, Dalton, & Tharp, 1986; Manning & Payne,1993).

One way teachers may become self-regulated is through interaction with the instructional innovations in their teaching repertoires or learning environments. Brown et al. (1993) purposefully structured a similar learning environment for students to include both human resources and artifacts as agents of *proximal development* for students (Vygotsky, 1978), a collaborative process that guides learners in working toward their full potential. So, too, teachers may learn to invent new practices from instructional models provided them (Randi, 1996). But because invention has not been the goal of staff development, teachers are likely to learn the process without articulating their knowledge and without formal labels for what they do. That is, they learn implicitly, acquiring "tacit" knowledge about the design of the innovations they have been expected to implement.

Creating an Environment for Teachers as Learners

Convinced that teachers, like students, might benefit from an enriched learning environment that provides challenges at the same time that it supports risk-taking, we set out to structure such learning opportunities for teachers. Capitalizing on teachers' tendency to learn from practice, we began to think how to promote learning-in-context, as Cronbach (1955) suggested, by providing "more experiences of a certain type than nature might offer ... and by helping the person to draw his conclusion more rapidly" (p. 79).

The opportunity came when one of us (Randi, 1996) had an occasion to study the practices of eight secondary school teachers implementing a program designed to teach higher order thinking skills in the content areas. Struck by this contrast between the creativity the program intended to foster in students and the prescription the program required of teachers, we wondered what might happen if these teachers were "given permission" to deviate from the prescribed program. Thus these teachers were invited to plan, enact, and reflect upon lessons of their own choosing. Unlike in traditional staff development, these teachers were not asked to implement a particular innovation. Instead, these teachers experienced interviews and classroom observations and reflected on the lessons they themselves designed. Interpretive narratives were then coconstructed by the researcher with the teachers. These narratives traced the development of teachers' lessons from the sources of their ideas to enactment in the classroom.

Rather than implement their staff development program as prescribed, these teachers adapted models provided them or invented their own instructional strategies responsive to the contexts of their own classrooms. We found that their adaptations and inventions were deliberate; teachers clearly identified differences between their instructional practices and the models they identified as sources of their ideas. Given choices themselves, these teachers allowed their students choices too (see Randi, 1996, for more details). One social studies teacher, for example, encouraged her students to ask a guest student from Ghana questions that interested them. Another teacher, an English teacher, allowed her students to choose the contemporary plays they wished to read. Just as opportunities for choice encouraged the previously described students to take risks with the challenges of their Humanities curriculum, so too, we observed these teachers taking risks and experimenting with new instructional practices when invited to design lessons of their own choosing.

We found the collaborative research process supported teacher invention in several ways important for our theory. First, the research process followed the instructional planning process that teachers typically use. For example, the interviews and observations in which teachers engaged collaboratively captured the temporal cycle of deliberation, enactment, and reflection-on-action that has been thought to characterize teachers' individual curriculum making (Connelly & Clandinin, 1988). Thus, in this cyclical process, teachers continually evaluated and revised their work. Second, teachers were invited to characterize their own lessons and describe how they differed from the models they identified as sources of their ideas. Thus, teachers' own inventions were acknowledged as a legitimate form of knowledge. Finally, the collaborative process supported teachers in solving problems in context, constructing new knowledge about teaching and learning, and reconciling their new teaching practices with "old" ideas that continued to dominate outside their own classrooms.

Instructional Components for Teacher Professional Learning

Ten principles of teacher professional learning have emerged from our collaborative work with teachers. The collaborative process we used provides some examples of how teachers learn in their own teaching context, including how teachers' learning might be enhanced by providing learning-rich environments and guiding teachers to articulate their knowledge. Below, we summarize the instructional components and move toward a more formal "theory" of collaborative innovation as a form of teacher professional learning:*

Principle 1: Teacher Invention. Consistent with current conceptions of teachers as knowledge workers, collaborative innovation encourages teacher invention. For example, rather than evaluate teachers' instructional practices by assessing the degree of "conformance" to particular models, teachers were invited to

---

* Try to see how many of these principles are exhibited in each of the other theories in this volume.

characterize their own lessons as innovations, describing how they differed from the clear models provided.

Principle 2: Teacher Choice. Collaborative innovation affords teachers opportunities for making choices about instruction. For example, we invited teachers to plan lessons of their own choosing; we did not ask them to implement a particular model. Teachers also were encouraged to discuss advantages and disadvantages of models they identified as sources of their ideas. Unlike other forms of teacher professional development, there was no attempt to change teachers' beliefs or practices to conform to others' ideas. Rather than encourage teachers to conform to a particular philosophical orientation, collaborative innovation encourages critical inquiry and choice. Thus, teachers' own motivation is addressed, and teachers retain the flexibility to meet students' differing needs in a variety of ways.

Principle 3: Evaluating New Practices. Collaborative innovation focuses teachers' attention on the evaluation of new instructional practices. In the collaborative process, teachers had to label their new practices and evaluate their effects on students. More like research and development and less like traditional staff development, teacher evaluation, or even coaching models, the yardstick is placed on the instructional innovation, rather than the teacher's use of the innovation.

Principle 4: Cyclical Curriculum Making. Collaborative innovation follows the process teachers typically use to design instruction. That is, in practice, curriculum making is nonlinear. The collaborative research process thus engages teachers in a cyclical process of planning, enacting, and reflecting on lessons they themselves design.

Principle 5: Problem Solving. Collaborative innovation presents teachers with opportunities for problem solving as they attempt to merge new and exisiting instructional practices. Resolving dissonance between the new and the old is one way of acquiring new knowledge (Pribram, 1964). Teachers' learning is not limited to skill acquisition. Thus teachers' access to knowledge can be richer and deeper than in traditional staff development programs.

Principle 6: Learning-in-Context. Collaborative innovation affords opportunities for learning-in-context by encouraging teachers to invent fresh new practices. Encouraged to adapt and invent, teachers continually tested and revised their instruction as they "discovered" new teaching strategies. In contrast with traditional staff development, where externally generated ideas are imposed on teachers, the collaborative innovation process acknowledges teachers' own ideas.

Principle 7: Students as Focus. Collaborative innovation places students at the center of curriculum making. Perhaps because they were encouraged to invent in context, teachers evaluated particular instructional practices in different contexts. They then modified instruction based on students' reactions. Thus they invented and reinvented, adapting even their own inventions from class to class.

Principle 8: Knowledge Construction. The collaborative innovation process assists teachers in articulating their knowledge. For example, teachers had to articulate what they learned, bringing to a conscious level knowledge that had been implicit in their practices. In this inductive process, tacit understanding often preceded language acquisition. As Sarason said, quoting Dewey, "knowledge is external; knowing is internal" (Dewey in Sarason, 1996, p. 320). Collaborative innovation helps teachers internally construct personal knowledge that is then labeled, situated in a larger body of knowledge, and shared through the collaborative research process.

Principle 9: Collaborative Apprenticeship. The collaboration inherent in this form of teacher professional learning serves to scaffold teachers to higher levels of thinking and performance—levels they may not otherwise reach by themselves. Unlike in traditional coaching, however, teachers are not guided in the imitation of models or acquisition of specific behaviors. Consistent with sociocultural theory (Vygotsky, 1986), collaborative innovation assigns more collaborative roles to teacher and researcher.

Principle 10: Low Risk and High Challenge. Teacher professional learning is supported in a low-risk, high-challenge environment. That is, by allowing for adaptation and invention, we encouraged trust, experimentation, and problem solving. Understanding that there is no "one best way," teachers are less at risk of "making a mistake." Just as students are motivated by challenging tasks that are difficult but not impossible to achieve, so too, teachers become self-regulated learners when they are afforded opportunities for problem solving in context along with the flexibility to adapt instruction to solve the problems that challenge their teaching practice. Put another way, teachers (and students) are more likely to succeed when there are many ways to achieve success.

Collaborative Innovation as Teacher Professional Learning

Although collaborative innovation incorporates new forms of teacher professional learning called for in recent staff development literature (Lieberman, 1995), collaborative innovation is not appropriate in all situations. Some teachers, like some students, may benefit from more direct forms of instruction. Further, not all teachers may desire to work as we did; it would be antithetical to our position to impose collaborative innovation on teachers. But unfortunately, many teachers who might otherwise benefit from the kind of collaboration we described do not have opportunities to form partnerships with researchers, although such collaborations are increasingly common.

There certainly may be other ways to promote self-regulated learning in teachers as well. We offer collaborative innovation as one way of structuring an enriched learning environment for teachers—one in which teachers are offered the same types of meaningful learning experiences we hope they design for students. Ironically, asked to accompany others as learners, teachers have rarely themselves been afforded such guidance.

SUMMARY AND CONCLUSIONS

We began by suggesting that traditional instructional design may be inconsistent with the kinds of classroom instruction teachers typically use to move students toward desired outcomes while maintaining attention to individual differences among students. We found, as we worked collaboratively with teachers, that instructional design as practiced by teachers was a dynamic process. This process appeared highly dependent on moment-by-moment as well as larger units of teacher–student interaction. Thus we argue that instruction responsive to individual differences among students may be best invented by teachers in classrooms. We propose collaborative innovation as a means for bringing about teacher invention, for supporting teacher professional learning, and for documenting teachers' own self-regulatory processes and innovations.

Collaborative innovation, as a form of invention, offers an alternative to traditional instructional-design theory. Our work with practicing teachers has led us to believe that prescribed curricular and instructional practices may undermine teachers' efforts to provide students with enriched curriculum experiences. Other researchers have also noted a conflict between what is encouraged for students and what is required of teachers. Cohn and Kottkamp (1993) argued, "Teachers who are not free to construct their own activities, inquire, engage in meaningful learning, take risks, make decisions and assess their own competence will be unable to create those possibilities for students" (p. 223).

As a form of teacher professional learning, collaborative innovation affords teachers opportunities to learn from their practice. Collaborative innovation capitalizes on teachers' expressed preference for learning from experience while the researcher plays a personal role in melding research and practice by situating teachers' discoveries in a larger body of systematic knowledge.

As a form of research on practice, *collaborative innovation* serves to document teachers' learning. Instead of the careful triangulation and constant comparison seen in more traditional case studies, collaborative innovation offers a more "systemic" (Salomon, 1991) view of classroom practice.* This form of research is typically undertaken by the teacher to improve classroom practice; as a collaborator, the researcher is invited to experience classroom events as teachers do. We believe that

---

* Thus, systemic thinking is also integral to this theory.

a collaborative model has the potential to inform both research and practice as well as to provide opportunities for life-long learning in the educational workplace.

Thus collaborative innovation promises to enhance learning for students, teachers, and researchers. Further, our research provides some evidence that both teachers and students learn a great deal implicitly. If teachers, like students, learn self-regulation implicitly through models, then the collaborative research process provides teachers with an implicit model for reflective teaching and self-regulated learning. Having experienced problem solving, authentic learning, and "discovery" themselves, teachers may be more likely to provide those experiences for students.

REFERENCES

Beauchamp, G. A. (1981). *Curriculum theory.* Itaska, IL: Peacock.

Bereiter, C. (1990). Aspects of an educational learning theory. *Review of Educational Research, 60,* 603–624.

Bereiter, C., & Scardamalia, M. (1987). *The psychology of written composition.* Hillsdale, NJ: Lawrence Erlbaum Associates.

Borkowski, J., Carr, G., Rellinger, E., & Pressley, M. (1990). Selfregulated cognition: Interdependence of metacognition, attributions, and self-esteem. In B. F. Jones & L. Idol (Eds.), *Dimensions of thinking and cognitive instruction* (pp. 53–86). Hillsdale, NJ: Lawrence Erlbaum Associates.

Brookfield, S. (1996). Experiential pedagogy: Grounding teaching in students' learning. *Journal of Experiential Education, 19*(2), 62–68.

Brown, A. L., Ash, D., Rutherford, M., Nakagawa, K., Gordeon, A., & Campione, J. C. (1993). Distributed expertise in the classroom. In G. Salomon (Ed.), *Distributed cognitions: Psychological and educational considerations* (pp. 188–228). New York: Cambridge University Press.

Brown, R., & Pressley, M. (1994). Self-regulated reading and getting meaning from text: The transactional strategies model and its ongoing validation. In D. H. Schunk & B. J. Zimmerman (Eds.), *Self-regulation of learning and performance* (pp. 155–180). Hillsdale, NJ: Lawrence Erlbaum Associates.

Cochran-Smith, M., & Lytle, S. L. (Eds.). (1992). *Inside/outside: Teacher research and knowledge.* New York: Teachers College Press.

Cohn, M. M., & Kottkamp, R. B. (1993). *Teachers: The missing voice in education.* Albany, NY: State University of New York Press.

Connelly, F. M., & Clandinin, D. J. (1988). *Teachers as curriculum planners.* New York: Teachers College Press.

Corno, L. (1977). Teacher autonomy and instructional systems. In L. Rubin (Ed.), *Curriculum handbook: Administration and theory* (pp. 234–248). Rockleigh, NJ: Allyn & Bacon.

Corno, L. (1993). The best-laid plans: Modern conceptions of volition and educational research. *Educational Researcher, 22*(2), 14–22.

Corno, L., & Kanfer, R. (1993). The role of volition in learning and performance. In L. Darling-Hammond (Ed.), *Review of research in education* (Vol. 19, pp. 301–341). Washington, DC: American Education Research Association.

Corno, L., & Mandinach, E. B. (1983). Using existing classroom data to explore relationships in a theoretical model of academic motivation. *Journal of Educational Research, 77*(1), 33–42.

Corno, L., & Randi, J. (1997). Motivation, volition, and collaborative innovation in classroom literacy. In J. Guthrie & A. Wigfield (Eds.), *Reading engagement: Motivating readers through integrated instruction* (pp. 14–31). Newark, DE: International Reading Association.

Cronbach, L. J. (1955). The learning process and text specification. In L. J. Cronbach (Ed.), *Text materials in modern education* (pp. 59–95). Urbana, IL: University of Illinois Press.

Cronbach, L. J. (1989). Construct validation after thirty years. In R. L. Linn (Ed.), *Intelligence* (pp. 147–171). Urbana, IL: University of Illinois Press.

Cronbach, L. J., & Snow, R. E. (1977). *Aptitudes and instructional methods.* New York: Irvington/Naiburg.

Dole, J., Duffy, G., Roehler, L., & Pearson, P. D. (1991). Moving from the old to the new: Research on reading comprehension instruction. *Review of Educational Research, 61*, 239–264.

Gallimore, R., Dalton, S., & Tharp, R. G. (1986). Self-regulation and interactive teaching: The effects of teaching conditions on teachers' cognitive activity. *The Elementary School Journal, 86*, 613–631.

Gudmundsdottir, S. (Ed.). (1997) Narrative perspectives on research on teaching and teacher education [Theme issue]. *Teaching and Teacher Education, 13*

Guthrie, J., & Wigfield, A. (Eds.). (1997). *Reading engagement: Motivating readers through integrated instruction.* Newark, DE: International Reading Association.

Hargreaves, A. (1984). Experience counts; theory doesn't. How teachers talk about their work. *Sociology of Education, 57*, 244–254.

Harris, K. R., & Graham, S. (1985). Improving learning disabled students' composition skills: Self-control strategy training. *Learning Disability Quarterly, 8*, 27–36.

Harris, K. R., & Graham, S. (1992). *Helping young writers master the craft: Strategy instruction and self-regulation in the writing process.* Cambridge, MA: Brookline.

Hill, C. (1992). *Testing and assessment: An ecological approach.* Inaugural lecture as A. I. Gates Professor in Language and Education. Teachers College, Columbia University, New York. (Published as a pamphlet.)

Lewis, A. C. (1997). A new consensus emerges on the characteristics of good professional development. *The Harvard Education Letter, 13*(3), 1–4.

Lieberman, A. (1995). Practices that support teacher development: Transforming conceptions of professional learning. *Phi Delta Kappan, 76*, 591–596.

Manning, B. H., & Payne, B. D. (1993). A Vygotskian-based theory of teacher cognition: Toward the acquisitions of mental reflection and self-regulation. *Teaching and Teacher Education, 9*, 361–371.

McLaughlin, M. W. (1993). What matters most in teachers' workplace context? In J. W. Little & M. W. McLaughlin (Eds.), *Teachers' work: Individuals, colleagues, and contexts* (pp. 79–103). New York: Teachers College Press.

McLaughlin, M. W., & Marsh, D. (1978). Staff development and school change. *Teachers College Record, 80*, 69–94.

Olson, L. (1997, April 30). Teachers need nuts, bolts of reforms, experts say. *Education Week, 1*, 37.

Palincsar, A. (1986). The role of dialogue in providing scaffolded instruction. *Educational Psychologist, 2*, 73–98.

Palincsar, A. M., & Brown, A. L. (1984). Reciprocal teaching of comprehension-fostering and comprehension-monitoring activities. *Cognition and Instruction, 1*, 117–175.

Perry, N. E. (1997). *Examining the relationships between classroom writing environments and students' self-regulated learning*: Research proposal submitted to the Social Sciences and Humanities Research Council of Canada.

Pintrich, P. R., & DeGroot, E. V. (1990). Motivational and self-regulated learning components of classroom academic performance. *Journal of Educational Psychology, 82*, 33–40.

Pintrich, P. R., & Garcia, T. (1991). Student goal orientation and self-regulation in the college classroom. In M. Maehr & P. R. Pintrich (Eds.), *Advances in motivation and achievement: Goals and selfregulatory processes* (Vol. 7, pp. 371–402). Greenwich, CT: JAI.

Pressley, M., Forrest-Pressley, D., Elliott-Faust, D., & Miller, G. (1985). Children's use of cognitive strategies, how to teach strategies, and what to do if they can't be taught. In M. Pressley & C. J. Brainerd (Eds.), *Cognitive learning and memory in children* (pp. 1–47). New York: Springer-Verlag.

Pressley, M., Goodchild, F., Fleet, J., Zajchowski, R., & Evans, E. (1989). The challenges of classroom strategy instruction. *The Elementary School Journal, 89*, 301–342.

Pribram, K. H. (1964). Neurological notes on the art of educating. In E. Hilgard & H. G. Richey (Eds.), *Theories of learning and instruction: The sixty-third yearbook of the National Society for the Study of Education, Part I* (pp.78–110). Chicago: University of Chicago Press.

Randi, J. (1996). *From imitation to invention: The nature of innovation in teachers' classrooms.* Unpublished doctoral dissertation, Teachers College, Columbia University, New York.

Randi, J., & Corno, L. (1997). Teachers as innovators. In B. Biddle, T. Good, & I. Goodson (Eds), *The international handbook of teachers and teaching, Vol 1*, (pp. 1163–1221). New York: Kluwer.

Reigeluth, C. M. (1996). A new paradigm of ISD? *Educational Technology, 36*(3), 13–20.

Richardson, V. (1990). Significant and worthwhile change in education. *Educational Researcher, 23*(5), 5–10.

Sarason, S. (1996). *Revisiting "The Culture of School and the Problem of Change"*. New York: Teachers College Press.

Salomon, G. (1991). Transcending the qualitative-quantitative debate: The analytic and systemic approaches to educational research. *Educational Researcher, 20*(6), 10–18.

Schon, D. A. (1983). *The reflective practitioner: How professionals think in action.* New York: Basic Books.

Snow, R., Corno, L., & Jackson, D. III (1996). Individual differences in affective and conative functions. In D. Berliner & R. Calfee (Eds.), *Handbook of Educational Psychology* (pp. 243–310). New York: Macmillan.

Sternberg, R. J. (1995). Testing common sense. *American Psychologist, 50*(11), 912–925.

Sternberg, R. J., & Wagner, R. K. (1993). The geocentric view of intelligence and job performance is wrong. *Current Directions in Psychological Science, 2,* 1–4.

Trawick, L., & Corno, L. (1995). Expanding the volitional resources of urban community college students. *New Directions for Teaching and Learning, 63,* 57–70.

Vygotsky, L. S. (1978). *Mind in society: The development of higher psychological processes.* Cambridge, MA: Harvard University Press.

Vygotsky, L. S. (1986). *Thought and language.* Cambridge, MA: MIT Press.

Weinstein, C. E., & Meyer, D. K. (1991). Cognitive learning strategies and college teaching. *New Directions for Teaching and Learning, 45,* 15–26.

Xu, J. (1994). *Doing homework: A study of possibilities.* Unpublished doctoral dissertation. Teachers College, Columbia University, New York.

Zimmerman, B. J., & Martinez-Pons, M. (1986). Development of a structured interview for assessing student use of self-regulated learning strategies. *American Educational Research Journal, 23,* 614–628.

Zimmerman, B. J., & Martinez-Pons, M. (1988). Construct validation of a strategy model of student self-regulated learning. *Journal of Educational Psychology, 80,* 284–290.

Zimmerman, B. J. & Schunk, D. (1989) (Eds.). *Self-regulated learning and academic achievement.* New York: Springer-Verlag.

APPENDIX A

Quest Essay Assignments, Humanities Curriculum

1. Write your own "Odyssey" or saga of a quest you followed in your own life.

    - Explain your decisions for undertaking it, obstacles along the way, decisions made, and results or consequences of decisions.

    - Consider and discuss: Did you reach your goal? Was it worth it? Why? Keep in mind the motifs we identified in the quest literature. You will be asked to identify these motifs in your saga, or in someone else's saga. Feel free to parody any ancient author we read!

2. Based on what you learned from characteristics in literature and media, describe the next quest you will undertake and what strategies you will use to accomplish your goal.

    - Map out, in detail, your plan for a successful quest.

We will negotiate criteria for grading these essays before you write.

Systematically Using Powerful Learning Environments to Accelerate the Learning of Disadvantaged Students in Grades 4–8

14

Dr. Stanley Pogrow

University of Arizona

Stanley Pogrow

Stanley Pogrow has a PhD in Education from Stanford University, and is currently an Associate Professor of Educational Administration at the University of Arizona. He specializes in the design, implementation, and dissemination of more powerful learning environments for educationally disadvantaged students, and the role such environments play in school improvement/restructuring for all students. He has also worked at the National Science Foundation, the California State Department of Education, and was a public school teacher in New York City for six years. He is the author of 4 books and more than 80 articles, has made over 240 presentations around the country, and has obtained over $3 million in research and development grants.

FOREWORD

Goals and preconditions. *The primary goal of this theory is to foster the development of thinking skills. The theory was developed specifically for educationally disadvantaged students in Grades 4–8.*

Values. *Some of the values upon which this theory is based include:*
- *instruction that is targeted to learning needs,*
- *for educationally disadvantaged students in Grades 4–8, learning such thinking skills as*
  - *metacognitive strategies,*
  - *inferencing from context,*
  - *generalizing (decontextualizing) ideas,*
  - *synthesizing and selecting information,*
- *acculturating an internal sense of understanding and abstraction,*
- *sophisticated forms of student-teacher interactions (conversations), which requires pull-out or after school programs,*
- *using computer experiences as a basis for rich conversations (i.e., computer as a metaphor for life),*
- *affective arousal (motivation),*
- *using computers and fantasy situations to motivate students to think deeply.*

Methods. *These are the major methods this theory offers:*

Organize disadvantaged students in Grades 4–8 into homogeneous groupings of 5-13 students, 35-40 minutes a day, 5 days a week, for 1.5-2 years.

Have students read interesting, dramatic stories (containing unknown words and culturally familial visuals) on the computer.

Use such sophisticated forms of teacher-student interactions as conversations and Socratic dialogue to have students
- *infer words' meanings from context,*
- *predict what will happen next in the story,*
- *synthesize and select important information,*
- *generalize (decontextualize) concepts to new contexts,*
- *think about what strategy they used to infer or predict or synthesize/ select or generalize.*

Then, after 1-2 years, place the student in "thinking-in-content" situations with a heterogeneous group of peers.

Major contributions. *The identification of specific learning needs of disadvantaged students in Grades 4–8—namely, deep cognitive skills which can over-*

come a variety of learning deficits. The identification of some robust, consistent, and systematic techniques for developing those skills and motivating those students, within the present time and fiscal parameters of schools. It also describes the conditions under which the proper mix of learning environments tied to cognitive needs can dramatically increase learning on a large scale.

—C.M.R.

Systematically Using Powerful Learning Environments to Accelerate the Learning of Disadvantaged Students in Grades 4–8

INTRODUCTION

The biggest problem in American education is the decline of educational performance that educationally disadvantaged students experience in Grades 4–8. Even when such students make gains in Grades 1–3, their performance tends to stabilize in the fourth grade and then start to decline, leading all too often to dropping out. School reform efforts have been of little help, and may even have made the problems worse (Pogrow, 1996). As this chapter was being written, another national study was released that once again shows that Title I is having little effect in closing learning gaps (Hoff, 1997). Indeed, few educational practices have been validated with educationally disadvantaged students after the third grade. As a result, whenever the government periodically decides to make education a priority, it focuses on "getting students off to a good start" in Grades 1–2. Yet such efforts never seem to lead to sustained improvements later on.

Most excuses for the failure of reforms to have much affect after the third grade are philosophical and sociological in nature, (e.g., hormones, peer pressure, etc). However, my experience has led me to believe that there is something much more systematic and cognitively based that causes educational failure after the third grade.

My own approach to trying to increase learning on a large scale after the third grade has been to design and test more powerful learning environments. Over the past 18 years I have developed and experimented with: a) the Higher Order Thinking Skills (HOTS) program that replaces all the supplemental remedial work provided to Title I and Learning Disabled (LD) students with challenging thinking development activities, and b) SuperMath, a new two year pre-algebra curriculum. HOTS develops the general thinking skills of Title I and LD students, (i.e., enables them to internalize a fundamental sense of how to work with any idea as opposed to thinking about formal classroom content). SuperMath, on the other hand, is a thinking in content curriculum that uses a constructivist, problem solving approach to learning math.

Over the course of 18 years the HOTS program has expanded to 2,000 sites. It has been successful in producing high levels of a wide variety of learning outcomes in Grades 4–8. (Research with SuperMath is just beginning.) Some of the results will be described later.

Once we knew that HOTS worked, we began to try to understand why it worked and with whom it worked. Over time we tapped our teachers' and administrators' experiences, impressions, and data on a large scale to develop a deeper understanding. We looked for patterns in what we were finding from reports from teachers and administrators around the country. I refer to this approach to research as "pattern sense making," (i.e., trying to find the patterns in massive information inflows). This form of research can also be described as large-scale anthropological research.

We learned from this research, to our pleasant surprise, that the program worked with Native American students and most LD students. We began to wonder why a program designed for Title I students also worked for LD students. At the same time, we began to realize that HOTS did not work for about 15% to 20% of the students served and began to wonder why. Out of this learning and wondering, a clear pattern began to emerge. As the hypotheses were sustained, this research began to generate fundamental knowledge about the hidden learning needs of students that led to a new explanation about the reasons for reform failure and that provided insight into how to do substantially better.

This chapter presents things in a backwards fashion. Part I describes the conclusions reached from the pattern sense-making research that unlock the puzzle of how to produce learning in educationally disadvantaged students in Grades 4–8, and explains why current reforms are not working. Part II briefly describes the rationale behind the HOTS program and how the learning environments that produced these conclusions were designed.

PART I. THE SITUATIONAL MECHANISMS FOR PRODUCING LEARNING IN GRADES 4–8

The most important factor in the decline of academic performance of educationally disadvantaged students after the third grade is the growing sophistication of the school's curriculum. Learning strategies that are successful earlier are no longer sufficient and may even impede learning after the third grade. Producing learning after the third grade requires much more sophisticated interventions than are generally available, and it requires applying such interventions in a systematic and intensive way that focuses on specific learning needs. The current fashionable approach to reform, which is everyone doing their own thing and treating all students the same in the name of site-based management, collaborative participation, learning communities, full inclusion, equity, etc., are not likely to work after the third grade.

Producing learning after the third grade requires the use of sophisticated learning environments. A quality learning environment is a system that provides sophisticated forms of student-teacher interactions over a significant period of time. Contrast this with what is seen in the typical classroom with a substantial number of educationally disadvantaged students. A teacher either asks simple questions to bored students, or when an occasional difficult question is asked, the same few students participate. Interaction is minimal for most students

A powerful learning environment requires a creative, yet detailed, curriculum that incorporates some form of conversational system and a very good teacher who is trained to teach differently. Few existing curricula or programs can meet this standard. At the same time, it appears that to be effective, even sophisticated learning environments have to be applied in a focused, situational way that is targeted to learning needs. Research on the use of the HOTS learning environment found the following key situational effectiveness parameters.

Finding 1

The key learning problems of educationally disadvantaged students are very different in Grades K–3 than they are in Grades 4–8 and require totally different approaches.* Continuing the same approach that has been effective in Grades K–3 to the later grades will actually cause scores to drop.

The biggest learning problem in K–3 is content knowledge deficit; (i.e., students do not know letters, numbers, etc). The biggest learning problem after the third grade is that students do not understand understanding; (i.e., they do not begin to understand how to deal with ideas, generalizations, or abstractions).

This finding suggests that helping students in Grades K–3 is not enough. An additional type of non content-based help is needed after the third grade. Indeed, many of the seeming content learning problems after the third grade are not really content learning problems but a symptom of the understanding deficit. For example, if a *fifth grade* Title I student is having trouble with reading and doing a variety of math problems, the conventional approach is to provide extra help in reading and math. However, a content reinforcement approach does not help much after the

---

* This is certainly a strong argument for the situationality of instructional theory, as discussed in chapter 1, p. 8.

third grade because the content learning problems are probably a manifestation of the deeper problem that students lacks a sense of how to organize and understand ideas. As such, students are unable to apply content which is force fed to them to problem solving situations or test items. (Indeed, claims by vendors of major gains after the third grade from direct content instruction approaches usually turn out to be true only for the specific test items that students have been taught to take. Change the test and scores drop dramatically since students cannot apply the rote information to an unfamiliar context.)

At this point it is important to step back from specific content help and spend the available time first developing a sense of understanding. A sense of understanding will generally enable students to learn content the first time it is taught.

Finding 2

Until a sense of understanding is developed, educationally disadvantaged students in Grades 4–8 cannot succeed in thinking-in-content curricula. (This is the theory of cognitive underpinnings.)

Full development of the intellectual potential of educationally disadvantaged students requires a two-stage process. The first stage is the development of a general sense of understanding. This is the catalyst that enables them to learn everything else at a more sophisticated level. The second stage is to then place students into exemplary thinking-in-content curricula in a heterogeneous environment. The internalization of a sense of understanding enables the students to subsequently understand academic content.* Eliminating the first step, and following the natural progressive urge to immediately place educationally disadvantaged students into thinking-in-content in the name of equity, does not work. This is probably the primary reason why the nobly intentioned discovery math and science movements of the mid-1960s and early 1970s did not work.

At the same time, a sense of understanding cannot be produced via casual effort.

Finding 3

In stage 1 of intellectual development, it takes 1.5-2 years to develop a sense of understanding through small group (5-13 students) sophisticated Socratic conversations provided in a homogeneous setting for 35-40 minutes a day.

The reason why such conversations have to be provided in a self-contained homogeneous environment (which at the elementary level means pullout) is that such conversation cannot be provided with sufficient intensity in a regular-sized classroom to overcome the understanding deficit. However, once students develop a sense of understanding, they are able to benefit equally with other students from the more limited conversation in the regular classroom.

---

* This represents descriptive theory that provides a rationale for the design theory that follows.

The natural reaction of educators to the news that the right learning environment can produce a sense of understanding with just 35–40 minutes of intensive sophisticated discussions a day is that, if such activities provide so much benefit, then all learning should be done this way. There are two problems with this perspective. First, while additional conversation does not hurt, providing more conversation does not seem to reduce the time it takes to develop a sense of understanding. Second, actually producing the needed activities is extremely difficult, and few schools have the resources and expertise to provide such activities throughout the school day. Actually, the fact that producing understanding requires so little time in the school day is good news. It can be done in a practical way using existing federal funds. In addition, it is important to use traditional approaches to teaching and learning part of the school day.

Finding 4a

Developing a sense of understanding in a program such as HOTS simultaneously generates substantial improvement both in standardized tests scores and on a wide variety of other alternative measures of cognitive development.

Research has found that HOTS students do better on both traditional and alternative forms of assessment than control groups of Title I students. Close to 50 studies done over the years by schools and districts generally find HOTS students achieving twice the national average gains on both standardized reading and math tests (spring to spring testing) and three times the gains as control groups on the comprehension sections of standardized tests. In addition to basic skill gains, almost 15% of HOTS students nationally make honor role, suggesting that students are transferring the cognitive development to the learning of content.

Darmer (1995) confirms the apparent transfer effects. Darmer measured the development of HOTS students in terms of gains in: (a) reading comprehension, (b) metacognition, (c) writing, (d) components of IQ, (e) transfer to novel problem-solving tasks, and (f) grade-point average (GPA). Of the 12 measures used in the study, HOTS students went up substantially in all, and overwhelmingly outperformed a control group of students in the same school in all the comparisons. Indeed, the fifth-grade control Title I students in the same school declined in reading comprehension and GPA.

This research suggests that the effects of developing a sense of understanding were so powerful that they produced transfer to gains in both content learning and problem solving, and the effects showed up on both traditional standardized tests as well as on alternative assessment. Particularly significant is the transfer to gains in GPA. HOTS students improved a whole letter grade on classroom content, even though there was almost no linkage between HOTS and classroom content.*

---

* This provides a strong rationale for the common emphasis on higher order thinking skills in the new paradigm of instructional theories, while the increased need for such skills in the workplace is another strong rationale.

Counterintuitively, the control students declined in GPA despite being pulled out half as much and receiving help in the classroom. In other words, the more time that students spent in the classroom the worse they did in classroom academic performance. This disparity in classroom performance is a testament to the power of developing a sense of understanding.

The declines in reading scores and GPA for the control students confirm the typical research finding that the longer students are in Title I the worse they tend to do. Some have argued that this decline is because students either become dependent on the service or become stigmatized, particularly by pullouts, or that the tests are inappropriate. None of these excuses are valid. The fact that the HOTS students from the same classrooms increased so dramatically in so many ways refutes those explanations. The simple truth is that students increase or decrease after the third grade as a function of the type of learning environment that is provided, and with the right type of learning environment, both traditional and nontraditional measures increase. Such effects are true regardless of race or ethnicity.

That is not to say that HOTS students are guaranteed future success. What HOTS does is get students to the point where they have the skills to be successful players in the game of school and are able communicators and thinkers. They still need to maintain a desire to succeed.

Finding 4b

Most educationally disadvantaged students have high levels of intellectual ability.

Finding 5

Once students have either completed two years of HOTS, or are in their second year, a core of such students should be grouped heterogeneously in at least one exemplary thinking-in-content course. (This is stage 2 of the intellectual development process.)

In a pilot test of the two-stage model in a Denver school, Title I students were placed in HOTS in the sixth grade and were then placed into the second year of HOTS as seventh graders, along with a heterogeneously grouped class of SuperMath. Some of the students had pre-test math scores in the 90th percentile, and some of the HOTS students were below the 12th percentile. The HOTS students held their own in SuperMath and made substantial test score gains. As one of the students noted, "It was neat to see how our thinking strategies could help in math." The high-performing students stayed high. What was especially important was the bonding that occurred between the low-performing students who had a weak math background but who had more experience in explaining ideas and representing them on the computer and the high-performing students who had a good math background but did not feel comfortable representing their ideas.

The above findings demonstrate that it is possible to accelerate the intellectual abilities of educationally disadvantaged students on a large scale. However, the conditions for producing such gains are highly situational. Good intentions or occasional access to good stuff is not sufficient. Developing the intellectual ability of educationally disadvantaged students requires a commitment to providing exemplary learning environments, sequenced as described, for a 3- 4-year period. Global approaches to reform are too diffuse to meet this need. More systematic approaches are needed.*

Why Reforms Fail After the Third Grade

While developing a sense of understanding has proved to be very effective under the situated conditions of use, it is not successful with 15% to 20% of Title I and LD students. Why not?

The pattern-sense-making approach to research revealed that these populations are very heterogeneous in terms of their learning needs. Title I appears to have three distinct learning-need populations. The majority, 75% to 85%, are high-potential students who suffer from metacognition deficits (i.e., do not understand understanding). The second category (about 5% to 10%) is students who are borderline educationally mentally handicapped (EMH). These students are truly significantly below average intelligence. They are in Title I only because Special Education will not, or cannot afford to, serve them. The final category (about 5% to 10%) are students with physiological problems, mostly undiagnosed severe dyslexia and severe behavioral disorders. Many/most in this category are high-potential students.**

LD also consists of the same three distinct learning-needs populations. The situation is depicted in Fig. 14.1.

Not only have the patterns of large-scale effects from HOTS revealed a more detailed picture of distinct learning needs, but this method of research also provides a relatively precise way of predicting what students' needs are and how to help different students. For example, once LD students are lower than 80 verbal IQ they cross the boundary for benefiting from developing a sense of understanding, and the metacognition development approach of HOTS stops having an effect.

This research clearly shows that the labels "Title I" and "LD" are merely legal contrivances that have nothing to do with students' learning needs. Clearly, common sense would say that if we were truly interested in meeting students' needs, special services should be organized and funded according to the categories of: (a) metacognition development, (b) borderline EMH, and (c) physiologically challenged. In other words, the Title I and LD students whose primary learning need is to develop a sense of understanding should be grouped together and provided with the same service. This is illustrated in Fig. 14.2.

---

* So the issue is not whether structure is needed in instruction; it is how much and what kinds.

** This highlights the importance of customizing instruction, which requires instructional theories to pursue different goals and use different methods depending on such situationalities as the nature of the learner and the nature of the kind of learning desired. In a personal response to this note, Pogrow suggested that "such customization should be focused on a *few* specific categories of needs as opposed to the advocacy of the sixties and seventies which was to treat *all* students differently."

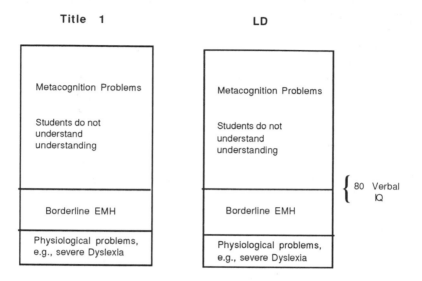

FIG. 14.1. Categories of fundamental learning problems (Grades 4–8).

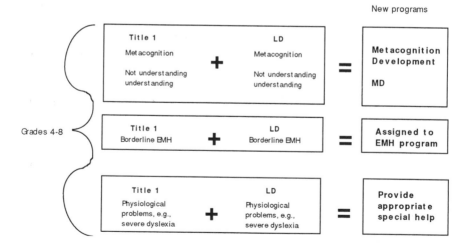

FIG. 14.2. Organizing programs according to student learning needs in Grades 4–8.

The reason why HOTS only helps 80% to 85% of the students is that developing a sense of understanding will help both those Title I and LD students who need metacognition development help, but will be of little benefit to those who are borderline EMH or physiologically challenged. Reorganizing federal help efforts as indicated in Fig. 14.2 would enable all the special needs to be served, probably even within the same funding levels.

If the above findings are correct, then it is not surprising that most reforms have had little effect beyond the third grade. Schools/districts currently plan separately for Title I and LD with little or no coordination. In addition, they tend to implement a uniform approach to Title I across the grade levels. The uniform approach invariably is dominated by a content reinforcement strategy (regardless of whether in-class or pullout approaches are used), and that is the crux of the problem.

A uniform content reinforcement approach works very well for the needs of K–3 students, and their scores increase. But, *after the third grade* the content reinforcement at best meets the needs of only one category of the three categories learning needs—that of borderline EMH students. However, these represent a very small percentage of the overall Title I and LD population. At the same time, the content reinforcement approach retards the progress of those in the category of needing metacognition development help—which is the vast majority of students. As a result, current approaches after the third grade help 10% of the Title I and LD students and unintentionally retard the progress of 80%. Hence, overall scores increase K–3 and decline 4–8. In other words, the uniform content reinforcement approach to providing services does not meet the real learning needs of the majority of Title I or LD students in Grades 4–8, hence scores decline.* (Note! This explanation shows that contrary to popular opinion, the failure of early gains to be sustained is not a function of problems in K–3, but in shifting and varying needs in Grades 4–8.)

Of course, when the field becomes disillusioned with uniform content approaches it shifts to uniform progressive reforms such as multi-disciplinary integration, schoolwide restructuring, pure whole language, etc. These reforms tend not to help because they are not situated enough and do not insure the actual delivery of a powerful learning environment under the conditions where they tend to be needed and effective. They are amorphous reforms that rely on good intentions, philosophy, advocacy and hope and therefore do not develop metacognition skills in the majority of Title I and LD students who need such skills. Indeed, idealogical progressive reforms tend to make things worse by not only failing students in Grades 4–8, but also tend to produce a decline in K–3 as a result of their deemphasis on formally teaching basic content.

Instead of uniform approaches, of either traditional or progressive approaches, we need more precise targeting and mixing approaches in a more scientific way.

---

* Uniform (standardized) approaches represent the industrial-age mentality and its attendant paradigm of instruction. The information-age mentality emphasizes customization based on needs, as discussed in chapter 1.

The combination of some basic skill intervention early and a situated carefully specified progressive approach such as HOTS later on appears to be the best combination for most students.

This explanation for why interventions tend not to work after the third grade has nothing to do with empowering parents, schoolwide restructuring, site-based management, organizational renewal, multi-disciplinary curricula, authentic assessment, student hormones, inappropriate tests, or any of the other recently touted reforms or cop-outs. Rather, the policy failure after the third grade is a result of not meeting student needs due to a misunderstanding of, and a lack of concern for, what those needs are.

PART II   THE HOTS PROGRAM

HOTS got started 18 years ago. That period was the height of the drill and kill era, (i.e., the belief that the best way to help educationally disadvantaged students was to drill them in basics until they got it right). That was also the time when education started to become highly conscious about technology and incorporating microcomputers into the curriculum. The big technology debates of that era were whether schools should teach the Basic, Pascal, or Logo programming languages, and whether schools should buy Apple II, Pet Commodore, or Radio Shack TRS-80 computers. Schools largely responded to the new technology push by creating computer literacy curricula, (i.e., the thousand facts that students needed to know about computers in Grades K–8). The push was to prepare kids for the future by making them computer literate.

I was an opponent of computer literacy. My argument was that computers were going to become increasingly people literate, (i.e., easier to use and requiring little technical knowledge). Therefore, teaching all this technical knowledge would be a waste of time. In addition, I felt that the primary impact of the computer was that it was going to obsolesce routine work. Given the growing ubiquitousness of ever more powerful computers, the only reason employers would hire people was that an individual could perform uniquely human functions at high levels. These functions would be creative and innovative reasoning, human interaction skills, and artistic capabilities. Such jobs would require the manipulation of information and ideas in new ways. In other words, the challenge of technology was not to make everyone "computer literate," but to make everyone "highly literate" in the traditional sense. Anyone who was not highly literate and creative would be relegated to low-level jobs which it did not pay to automate, (e.g., flipping burgers).

In a world in which technology raised the importance of literacy and its creative application, the equity issue to me was not equal access to the use of computers, but equal access to the development of thinking literacy. (I still retain this belief.) This access would determine who would have a chance to achieve the fruits of this society.

The beginning of the 1980s was a heady time for anyone with technology experience. I was invited to speak at lots of conferences, mostly conferences on defining computer literacy. I was the one who said: "Don't do it." While my speeches would get applause, my views were totally ignored, until one day when I was approached after a speech by several individuals from a school outside of Los Angeles. They indicated that they were impressed with my ideas and that the drill approach was not working with their Title I students. But, given my remarks, they realized that even if the drilling did work, the students would not be prepared to compete for the high paying jobs, which would be a tragedy, since they felt that most of their students were bright. They felt that most of their students could work at high levels if somehow the school could find a way to reach them. They then asked me to design a Title I program for them based around thinking and computers, in which all drill was eliminated.

I agreed. We sat down in a room, and everyone had a blank sheet of paper. The goal was to create a learning environment that could accelerate the intellectual development of Title I students by treating them as gifted students. Instead of designing a Title I program, we would treat the students as though they were attending a fancy private school and would design the best possible educational experience that could be provided—even if they would obtain such an education for only a small part of the day.

We then tried to figure out what to do. No one really knew how to pull it off. Thus the origin of HOTS was good intention informed by ignorance. However, as the program evolved, the initial ignorance turned out to be a strength, because we did not get locked into clichés or rely on research, most of which I would come to discover in the later years was completely wrong. Rather, we relied on our own creativity, instincts, luck, metaphors (see the next section), and careful observation of the students to look for patterns in what seemed to work and what didn't.

Amazingly, the data from the first year were very positive. I began to wonder that if we could produce these kinds of results when we did not know what we were doing, what would happen if we knew what we were doing. (Fortunately, I didn't realize at the time that it would take at least another 10 years to really learn how to do it, because I then might have given up.) Equally amazingly, other schools began to call, wanting to try this approach. When I explained to them that I did not know what I was doing, their reply invariably was: "It has got to work better than what we are now doing." It was a shock to me to discover that noone seemed to know how to help these students, even though the government was spending $5–6 billion a year to try to help.

Over the years helping the disadvantaged students through a higher order thinking development approach became a mission. The 18 years went by fast, and the program has spread to almost 2,000 schools. The thrill of discovery and the stories about student successes that arrive almost daily have been the big rewards.

In the early days of HOTS, people argued either that a thinking development approach was illegal or that it could not work. Yet, we could clearly see that these students were bright and that capitalizing on this intelligence by challenging them intellectually in ways that interested them was the best way to not only prepare them for a nonroutine world of work, but also to produce substantially higher levels of basic skills in grades 4–8. Today, the law has been changed to require that Title I services challenge students at high levels and be based on the best possible pedagogical practice. Unfortunately, while this has legitimized what we did in HOTS, current reformers have underestimated the need for a highly systematized approach to converting such good intentions into actual learning gains. As a result, HOTS remains unique in the systematization of state-of-the-art pedagogy and a novel approach to using computers on a large scale.

The Design of the HOTS and SuperMath Learning Environments

Stage 1: Understanding Understanding

In the absence of knowledge about how to design a program that intellectually challenged educationally disadvantaged students in a way that translated into overall academic gains, the design process relied heavily on metaphors. The first key metaphor for the design of the HOTS curriculum was dinner table conversation. Conversation was selected because of the beliefs that early conversational experiences in the home develop a cultural sense of how adults in a given culture expect you to think and that such conversation is critical to general cognitive development. It was also believed that the absence of such conversation in the home and regular classroom was the primary cause for most of the learning problems.

HOTS was therefore designed to combine the use of Socratic conversation with computers. Computers were selected in order to design an interactive learning environment in which students could test their ideas as they thought of them, as well as to build upon their prior experience in learning through largely visual experiences. The curriculum would combine the familiar visual form of learning with the unfamiliar auditory and textual forms of learning.

The dinner table conversation metaphor led to two major decisions. The first was that HOTS would be a general thinking program. In other words, the thinking would not be tied to the school's content, much as dinner table conversation in the home is ad hoc, (i.e., taking advantage of whatever a given day's experience provided the opportunity or incentive to talk about). The second key decision was not to use the computer as a tool or a content presentation mechanism, but rather as a "metaphor for life." In other words, the importance of software would not be what its explicit goal was, but rather whether experience with learning to use it would provide the opportunities to construct the types of systematic discussions that would promote cognitive growth—just as experiencing everyday life provides the basis for dinner table conversation in the home. Much as in the home, the daily similar form of conversation would produce the general cognitive growth. (In this approach technology is not integrated into the curriculum but becomes one basis for designing the curriculum to begin with, and this is made possible by conceiving and implementing a more appropriate approach to using technology.)

Much as the power of dinner table conversation derives from its consistency and appropriateness, the same characteristics were needed for HOTS conversations. Key elements of cognitive psychology were used to create a consistent form for the conversations that would model those thinking skills that appear to underlie all learning. The thinking skills chosen were:*

- metacognition: consciously applying strategies to solve problems;
- inference from context: figuring out unknown words and information from the surrounding information;
- decontextualization: generalizing ideas from one context to another;
- information synthesis: combining information from a variety of sources and identifying the key pieces of information needed to solve a problem.

A detailed curriculum was developed that provided model conversations over a 2 year period to operationalize these skills. Metacognition had the biggest influence on the nature of the daily conversations that were mapped into the curriculum, while decontextualization had the biggest impact on the structure of the curriculum and is what makes the HOTS curriculum unique. The focus on decontextualization came from our observations of student conversation in which they almost never seemed to generalize across contexts.

The second guiding metaphor behind the development of the HOTS curriculum was to think of the brain as a muscle. The way one improves the functioning of a muscle is to repeatedly use it in the way that it is designed to operate. How does the brain operate to store and use information? It creates linkages among related concepts. It was therefore decided to have the HOTS conversations mimic this process and have students constantly link ideas and discuss these linkages. The external conversations would model the internal operation of the brain "muscle." This metaphor inspired us to place even more emphasis on decontextualization.

The curriculum contained conversations that operationalized the above thinking skills as follows.

Metacognition is produced by constantly asking students what strategy they used for solving a problem, how they knew the strategy is a good one, what strategies they found did not work, how they could tell the strategy did not work, and to predict what a better strategy might be and to try it, etc.

Inference from context is initiated in two ways. The first technique is to have students read interesting stories on the computer which combine text with graphics.** Teachers previously heighten student involvement by introducing the setting of the

---

* Note how the consideration of both what to teach and how to teach it are intertwined so as to offer a hybrid of curriculum theory and instructional theory. This more integrated, more systemic view of instruction is an important aspect of the new paradigm.

** Note that stories are used in several other theories, including chapters 8 (Schank, Berman & Macpherson), 13 (Corno & Randi), and 21 (Lewis, Watson & Schaps). How does the use of stories differ for each of those theories?

story in a dramatic fashion, such as warning the students that they will encounter many dangers in the story. The dramatic element builds high levels of engagement, a prerequisite for thinking to take place.

The story chosen must also have words in key places that students do not understand. (It does not matter which words, or whether the words are in the students' regular curriculum.) Students are then told that every time they come to a word they do not understand they should: (a) write down the sentence in which it appears, (b) circle the word, and (c) call the teacher over and make a guess about what the word means. They are also told to make a prediction of what will happen next in the story. (Twist-a-Plot stories are best.) The next day the teacher lists the sentences on the board and asks students to explain what they think the circled words mean from the reading and pictures, and why they think that. The conversations begin and student answers are probed. These rich conversations model prediction comprehension processes that good readers spontaneously engage in, and provide experience in information synthesis and metacognition, as well as in inference from context.

The second technique for "inference from context" is to build inference questions around unknown or ambiguous words in the instructions. Teachers constantly ask students to figure out what the unknown words mean, along with the strategy they used for figuring it out. The visual clues make it easier initially for students to build up confidence in their inference skills. Inference then becomes a normal part of learning how to use any piece of software.

Decontextualization occurs in two ways. The first is by using words in the software that students are familiar with from their everyday experience and having them make predictions about what they are likely to do in the context of that program. For example, the graphics program DAZZLE DRAW has a menu choice called "flood fill." Students are asked to predict what will happen if they make that choice based on what they know about the word "flood." Students then go to the computers to test their predictions. ("Flood Fill" fills an area of the screen with the color they chose.)

The second, and more powerful, decontextualization technique is the use of a series of concepts that are discussed across many different contexts (software programs). For example, perspective is discussed when flying a hot-air balloon, writing a story from the perspective of an object using a word processor, and discussing the perspective from which a character in a story is viewing a given situation. Students are then asked about how the use of the linkage concept in the current piece of software is the same and different than in the prior program(s).

Information synthesis is done by creating a situation where students have to use information from a variety of sources, or several different types of information, to answer a question.

The curriculum was developed by taking a piece of software that would be of interest to students (games and adventure stories are always good) and inventing a series of questions that provided practice in all of the above thinking skills and that link to the key linkage concepts discussed regarding other pieces of software. For example, in the popular simulation OREGON TRAIL, the explicit goal is for students to reach Oregon using the old Oregon trail. They have to budget food and supplies appropriately in order to make it safely through a variety of problems, such as attacks, bad weather, and floods.

The curriculum then asks questions such as: "From what perspective are you looking at the wagon?" (decontextualization of the use of "perspective" as a key linkage concept), "What could the 'yoke' of an ox be?" (inference from context), "What strategy did you use to reach Oregon?" (Metacognition), and "Is anyone who traveled the trail alive today?" (information synthesis.) These questions are incidental to the goal of reaching Oregon. They are based on words or phrases in the instructions. The questions are asked to initiate discussions which provide practice in the four key thinking skills. The quality, intensity, and consistency of discussions about the answers to these questions are far more important to the learning process than the quality of the software or successful use of the software.

It is this focus on conversations about tangential questions that consistently model key thinking processes that distinguishes the HOTS approach to using computers from computer-assisted instruction (CAI) or integrated learning systems (ILS).* The HOTS and SuperMath curricula represent clean-sheet designs that explore how technology enables one to rethink the nature of curriculum, which in turn inspires new conceptions of how to use technology.**

The HOTS program evolved as a 35–40 minute self-contained period, 4–5 days a week for 1–2 years. The first half of the period is used for conversation; then the students are given a challenge to figure out on the computer. The key questions that need to be asked during the conversation portion are specified in the curriculum, along with the hoped-for answer(s). However, merely asking questions and getting answers does not produce sophisticated conversation. A Socratic system was developed based on extensive observation of student–teacher interactions. The observations revealed the interaction situations where ambiguity broke down and teachers reverted to being dogmatic and directive instead of questioning. The HOTS Socratic system specifies key events and situations in conversations, and specifics strategies for the teacher to invent appropriate follow-up questioning probes that continue to place the student in a reflection mode that hopefully leads to self-generated understanding.

The key to making this work is a terrific teacher who is trained to teach differently. Metaphors from the theater were used to design the training. Prospective HOTS teachers go through an intensive small-group 5-day training workshop. Dur-

---

* It seems that the major instructional methods are exercising and modeling the "key thinking processes." These represent two of the three primary instructional methods described by Merrill in Volume I: practice and example. These were identified as "basic" methods in chapter 1 (p. 20), but they are used as building blocks in broader methods (e.g., conversation), which were identified as "variable" methods in chapter 1 (p. 20).

** This is a key consideration in the development of the new paradigm of instructional theory. Technology is enabling us to design new conceptions of instruction that were not possible in the industrial age. We have only begun to scratch the surface of what will be possible.

ing the training they are not presented with theory. Rather, they slowly internalize the Socratic system via practicing, teaching lessons to the other participants who act as students. As a result of the practice teaching, they learn new reflexes for talking and listening to students and develop expertise in the improvisation of follow-up probes to students' initial answers. They learn how to analyze everything that students say from an understanding point of view and learn how to develop appropriate and creative follow-up questions that enable students to construct meaning. As such, the teachers learn how to teach differently within a curriculum that is designed from the ground up to support Socratic interactions.*

Finally, all of this will not produce thinking unless students decide to exert mental energy. HOTS intrigues students through the use of the visual and culturally familiar stimulation of the computer's visuals and through the incorporation of drama. Each unit has a storyline, much like a play. Students are drawn into the activities through a variety of theatrical techniques. For example, some days the teachers are dressed in strange costumes.**

All the above elements—drama, cognitive psychology, Socratic conversation, and computers—are systematically blended into a curriculum that has been tweaked over an extended period of time to produce a powerful, intensive, systematic learning environment. Students cannot hide from the small-group conversation process, anymore than a child can hide at the dinner table. The system pushes students into increasingly sophisticated forms of verbalization and strategizing around the use of textual information. The tasks are difficult, way beyond their developmental level. However, through the combined processes of experimentation and increasingly sophisticated reflection strategies, students develop confidence in their problem solving and communication skills.

Stage 2: Thinking-in-Content

The SuperMath program is a two-year pre-algebra program that is a new approach to designing a thinking-in-content curriculum, designed from the ground up around the capabilities of computers and Socratic dialogue. It uses a thinking-in-content, problem-solving, constructivist approach to teaching traditional mathematics as well as some of the newer topics. Given the goal of creating a student-centered curriculum, the problem-solving activities are not built around real-world applications but around fantasy environments that will be culturally familiar and interesting to students.*** Fantasy environments are used because there are precious few real-world mathematical applications that are relevant to middle school students,

---

* Because the teacher's role is so different and unfamiliar, training is essential. To what extent is the Corno and Randi approach to teacher training compatible with Pogrow's theory?

** Here, motivation appears as an integral feature of this theory, as it does for most theories in the new paradigm.

*** This is an important issue. Should instruction always use authentic, real-world tasks, as some have advocated, or is this a case of "either-or" thinking that we should transcend? See chapter 19 by Romiszowski for further discussion of this issue (pp. 476–477).

and drawing examples from the adult world are a turn-off. Examples of fantasy environments include: (a) going to Mars and then ordering burgers and trying to figure out how or if the Martians are ripping them off, (b) trying to track down the arch villain, Carmen San Decimal, one of the most crooked decimals in the world, who is hiding in the "hood," (c) driving a car in San Francisco while trying not to get lost or arrested, and (d) trying to communicate with a lonesome space creature stuck inside the student's computer. The latter is used to enable students to construct a sense of the relationship between language and math to help them solve word problems. A simple form of artificial intelligence enables the creature to process the students' English and then react in its mathematics language.

Space permits only a brief description of the design of the HOTS and SuperMath Learning Environments. I have described them in more detail elsewhere (Pogrow, 1990, 1997).* However, I would like to provide just a few more insights into the design.

The basic design technique, which I call "learning dramas," requires users to purchase software, use it in unintended ways, develop a curriculum around such unintended uses, and then train teachers in advanced pedagogical techniques. This is a lot of work. In addition, ignoring the explicit goal of software and using it to create a setting around which to invent conversations seems counterintuitive. However, the success of using technology in a nonexplicit way has also been demonstrated by Bransford et al. (1989).** He used laser disk technology to show a segment of Indiana Jones jumping across a pit (i.e., to set an interesting visual context that was familiar to students), followed by a discussion of the physical forces and mathematics that makes such an act possible. He found that using technology to provide visual settings to set a context for a follow-up discussion was a more effective way to teach math than using the technology to present the math, or even one-on-one instruction.

The design of learning dramas, however, is becoming more difficult due to the declining quality of software. As technology has gotten more powerful, developers are doing with software today what textbook publishers did in the 1980s: dumbing down the language. In new software you point to icons and click, and then get more pictures, all of which is useless for promoting literacy. Indeed, where commercial software is used in HOTS, we usually use older versions and resist the newer, glossier, dumbed-down versions. Unfortunately, as the older titles or versions are discontinued, we need to develop our own versions wherever possible.

---

* Clearly, the level of description of the instructional methods here is not sufficiently detailed for a reader to be able to go out and use this theory without a tremendous amount of invention and trial-and-error. More detailed guidelines are offered in this cited chapter, and even more detailed guidance is surely provided in the five-day training program mentioned earlier. A challenge for instructional theorists is how to provide sufficient guidance for successful use of the theory without constraining its flexible and creative application to unique situations. Perhaps users of a theory also bear some responsibility for applying it flexibly and creatively, as opposed to viewing it as a formula that must be followed precisely.

** See also chapter 9.

Finally, the idea of creating HOTS and SuperMath as powerful learning environments involving the use of technology was inspired by Papert's work (1980). Unfortunately, he thought that the use of sophisticated software such as Logo would produce a learning environment. That is not true. Both HOTS and SuperMath combine and systematize the many additional elements to construct a true learning environment, along with the use of technology not as a tool or as a deliverer of content or instruction, but rather as a setting that is a metaphor for life.

The Role of Research in Program Design

Despite all the brave talk by academicians about the role of theory and research in program design, I found them to be of only marginal value. Theory is simply someone's best guess about something. Many theories abound. Which one is right? Indeed, even if you know that a theory is right, there could be 100 different ways to operationalize it in a program, and perhaps only 5 would work.* The odds are against theory being of any major value. In addition, you quickly find that almost none of the theory that you might be interested in has any supporting data at all, let alone on a reasonable scale with the population that you are interested in.

Indeed, I would later discover that if I had initially made greater use of theory I would have gone down the wrong track. For example, I would have designed HOTS to be more linked to classroom/content work and would have tried to incorporate thinking into specific classroom content since virtually all cognitive theory believed that thinking development should evolve in content rather than as general thinking skills. HOTS has demonstrated that this theory is clearly wrong for educationally disadvantaged students. (It is probably true for the college students on whom most of the research was conducted.)

The most important step in design is selecting metaphors, which is largely a matter of instinct and luck. Once the metaphors have been selected, you can make some judicious use of theory. Once we had decided to use the metaphor of the brain as a muscle, it became clear that the information-processing branch of psychology had the most relevant information, and within that branch there were a few ideas that had sufficient data to be credible. The only other literature which seemed to have a base in success with educationally disadvantaged students was the work in metacognition, even though it had generally not been used with Grades 4–8. Within these areas of research a few selected studies were used to help flesh out some of the design details of how the metaphors would be implemented—a limited but valuable contribution.

---

* This is precisely why instructional theorists must elaborate their theories to greater levels of detail—component methods (parts, kinds, and criteria) and the situationalities that guide the selection of alternative ways of operationalizing them. But when does the amount of detailed guidance unduly constrain the flexibility and creativity of its application (see note on p. 337)? And will different people need different levels of detail? Perhaps electronic performance support systems offer a solution to this problem. Maybe all instructional theories should be published in the form of an EPSS.

Rather than using theory as the basis of design, it was fun to discover along the way which of the theorists had come to the same conclusions that the HOTS program was coming to, and then incorporate some of their ideas as modifications to the program. The work of L.S. Vygotsky was a notable example.*

The irony is that a successful innovative learning environment has more value for generating theory (as indicated by the results in Part I) than theory has for its initial design.**

CONCLUSIONS

HOTS has demonstrated that it is possible to design a highly creative yet directive learning environment that is consistently effective for educationally disadvantaged students on a large scale in Grades 4–8, regardless of race, culture, and geographic location. It also demonstrated that it is possible to design learning environments that, when provided for a small part of the school day, produce transfer to a wide variety of academic, social, and cognitive gains. However, producing such a consistently powerful learning environment takes a great deal of time and luck in selecting the right metaphors and then implementing them the right way. In addition, to be effective the learning environment must match a powerful curriculum with a very good teacher who is trained to teach differently.

The HOTS curriculum worked because it set new standards for: (a) blending creativity and directedness; (b) conceptualizing how to use technology; (c) providing a consistent and focused framework for enhancing general cognitive development, (i.e., it successfully developed a small set of the most important thinking skills that have the greatest impact on literacy development as opposed to trying to cover a wide range of skills more superficially); (d) combining good teaching with the use of technology; and (e) combining curricula with innovative training; and (f) blending a disparate group of powerful metaphors.

HOTS has also demonstrated that it is possible to use an innovative program as a large-scale research tool to generate: (a) basic knowledge of learning needs, and (b) knowledge of situational effectiveness. The former is valuable for trying to influence policy, while the latter knowledge is incorporated into the program's dissemination process, which further increases its effectiveness. For example, administrators are told which students are not helped by HOTS so that they can consider a more appropriate alternative approach for them.*** Indeed, research-based

---

* This is an advocacy of using an inductive approach to instructional theory development (developing it from practice and trial-and-error) rather than a deductive approach (deriving it from learning theory), or, more accurately (avoid that either-or thinking!) an advocacy of a combination approach that is weighted on the inductive side of the continuum.

** This testifies to the power of formative research (see chap. 26). In fact, the theory–construction approach that Pogrow used has much in common with formative research.

*** Indeed, more theorists should explicitly state the preconditions for use of their theories.

integrity in the dissemination process is as important to the ultimate success of a program on a large scale as is the quality of the program's design!

The HOTS experience indicates that, while it is possible to accelerate the learning of educationally disadvantaged students in Grades 4–8 in a systematic way on a large scale, there are situational parameters that guide the effectiveness of even powerful learning environments. Violate the key situational parameters, and even the best learning environments will have little effect.

Unfortunately, current reforms violate all the parameters identified in Part I. There are cognitively based reasons why current reforms, including the new Title I legislation, have little effect. The learning problems identified within the Title I and LD populations are very real and represent substantial deficits that need to be addressed in specific ways. Effectively addressing these needs can only be done with targeted help based on appropriate situational knowledge—knowledge which I believe can only be generated from large-scale experience.

This chapter has shown how to help the vast majority of the educationally disadvantaged population in Grades 4–8. It has provided key guidelines for what needs to be done at the local and federal levels. We need to provide sustained, powerful learning environments for metacognition-deficient students for a 3–4 year period between Grades 4 and 8 for a small part of the day. We also need to reorganize Federal and state supplemental funding so that it is targeted to the three different learning needs that have been identified.

While this article provides specific guidelines for policy and practice, I doubt that any of its recommendations will be considered by policy makers and practitioners in the foreseeable future. Under current conceptions of site-based management, every school does its own thing, which makes sustaining a developmental approach for a targeted group of students almost impossible. At the federal level, powerful interest groups want to protect their turf and funding and maintain the current legal and funding categories. As such, we may be destined to underserve yet another generation of educationally disadvantaged students who will never discover how bright they really are. We could be doing so much better.

REFERENCES

Bransford, J. et al. (1989). Mathematical thinking. In R. Charles & E. Silver (Eds.) *Teaching for evaluating mathematical problem-solving*. City: National Council of Teachers of Mathematics.

Darmer, M. A. (1995). Developing transfer and metacognition in educationally disadvantaged students: Effects of the higher order thinking skills (HOTS) program. Unpublished dissertation, University of Arizona, Tucson.

Hoff, D. (1997, April, 2). Chap. 1 aid failed to close learning gap, study finds. *Education Week*, pp. 1–29.

Papert, S. (1980). *Mindstorms: Children, computers and powerful ideas.* New York: Basic Books.

Pogrow, S. (1990). *HOTS (higher order thinking skills): A validated thinking skills approach to using computers with students who are at-risk.* New York: Scholastic.

Pogrow, S. (1996). Reforming the wannabee reformers: Why education reforms almost always end up making things worse. *Phi Delta Kappan*, 656–663, Vol. 77.

Pogrow, S. (1997). Using Technology to combine process and content. In A. Costa & R. Liebman, (Eds.), *When process is content: Towards renaissance learning* (pp. 98–116). Corwin Press.

15

Landamatics Instructional Design Theory and Methodology for Teaching General Methods of Thinking

Lev N. Landa
Landamatics International, New York

Lev N. Landa

Lev N. Landa was a resident of the USSR until 1976. He received doctoral and postdoctoral degrees in psychology in Moscow and Leningrad, and a life-long title of Professor was granted to him by the Ministry of Higher Education of the USSR. In the USSR, he was Professor and Director of a department at the Institute of General and Educational Psychology, Moscow, as well as a professor at the Institute for Advanced Training of University and Pedagogical College Teachers at the USSR Academy of Pedagogical Sciences, Moscow. Since 1976, he has been a visiting professor at the universities of Utrecht (Holland), Iowa (USA), and Columbia University in New York. He is president of Landamatics International, New York, a management and education consulting firm. He has more than 100 publications, 27 of which have been translated into 15 languages.

FOREWORD

Goals and preconditions. *The primary goal of this theory is to teach general methods of thinking (the highest-order thinking skills). It is intended for all situations which, though different in content, have similar general logical structures (often hidden) that allow one to mentally handle them in the same way by employing the same general mental operations.*

Values. *Some of the values upon which this theory is based include:*
- *general methods of thinking (for success in education, industry, and today's information society),*
- *identification of general logical structures of various subject matters which determine methods of handling those structures.*

Methods. *Here are the major methods (or strategies) this theory offers:*

Strategy 1: Guided Discovery

1. Guide the students to discover a system of mental operations underlying a general method of thinking.
- *Give them a task or problem and have them perform it.*

2. Help the student to become aware of what they did in their minds when performing the task and then to formulate a method that corresponds to it.
- *Ask them to formulate a detailed set of instructions (a method) so that other people will be able to follow them to perform the task.*
- *If they have difficulty, explain how to formulate the method.*
- *Identify an overt or hidden (implicit) logical structure of the task's or problem's content and explicitly describe it.*
- *Show how the content's logical structure determines the method of handling it.*
- *Use a flowchart when it will help the students to graphically represent the method.*

3. Help the students to learn to apply the discovered method.
- *Have them practice using the discovered method (instructions), in a step-by-step manner, on new cases.*

4. Help the students to internalize the method.
- *Have them practice the method on new cases without looking at instructions and using only self-instructions.*

5. Help the students to automatize the method.

• *Require them to perform the task on new cases very quickly, without using even self-instructions.*

6. *Repeat steps 1-5 to gradually increase the degree of generality of the method the student have discovered.*

  • *In step 1, give the students tasks (or problems) that are just outside the subject-matter domain where the method was initially discovered and used, and that require a modification of the discovered method.*

  • *In step 2, help the students formulate a single more general method that works in both domains.*

  • *Steps 3-5 are unchanged.*

Strategy 2: Expository Teaching
  The same six steps occur, but the first two are provided to the students in ready-made form (with appropriate demonstrations).

Strategy 3: Combination Approach
  Some steps are taught through discovery and some through expository methods, depending on the teacher's objectives.

Major contributions. *The focus on general methods of thinking—the highest-order thinking skills—as an important kind of teaching objective and learning outcome. An instructional method based on stages of mental skill development. Options for discovery and/or expository instruction.*

—C.M.R.

Landamatics Instructional Design Theory and Methodology for Teaching General Methods of Thinking

INTRODUCTION

Landamatics is not a theory of learning and instruction that indicates how to teach one or another specific topic, concept, or skill. It is not a collection of effective lesson plans. Rather, it is a *general method (or methodology) of approaching* the *design* of any effective course of instruction or any lesson plan, whether the task is to teach knowledge of certain phenomena, or a process of visual analysis of an object, or a strategy of thinking, or anything else. The method formulates general, but at the same time sufficiently detailed, procedures—algorithmic or nonalgorithmic—which can be applied to designing and teaching any specific knowledge and any cognitive process (on the difference between algorithmic and non-algorithmic procedures or methods, see Landa, 1983, 1997.)

The intent of this chapter is to formulate and describe, by example, a Landamatics method of teaching general methods of thinking. To achieve the challenging learning results we have called for, what to teach and how to teach are equally important aspects of Landamatics.*

For the purpose of illustration, we chose for this chapter a particular method of thinking-the method of identification of objects as belonging to or not belonging to a certain class on the basis of concepts of those classes and their respective definitions. Later in the chapter, the method will be extended to the method for drawing conclusions about objects' attributes and their relationships to other objects. Because the process of identification is used only to illustrate how to teach any methods of applying knowledge, we will often use a broader term, "a method of knowledge application" rather than the more narrow term, "a method of knowledge application for the purpose of identification." This will be done to underscore that what is being said with regard to a method of identification is true for all other methods of thinking and, often, even for all methods of cognitive activity.**

Teaching General Cognitive Processes as One of the Most Important Goals of Education

In our modern, information-based society, knowledge is changing so rapidly that what we learn today may become outdated and obsolete a few years from now.[1] But does that mean that the cognitive mechanisms of acquiring and applying knowledge change as well? Or, to be more precise, do they change as rapidly as the knowledge being acquired by mankind? The answer is no.

Experts in any field of scientific or practical activity, who have already learned how to effectively acquire and apply knowledge, use essentially the same cognitive operations and processes (out of some repertoire) to learn and manipulate various

---

* Again, the integration of instructional theory and curriculum theory is important here.

** This relates to the "focus of learning" continuum from domain-specific to interdisciplinary, presented in chapter 3, p. 60. Some theorists have argued that an instructional theory must be domain-specific. Clearly, Landa takes a different view. See what you think of Landa's view as you proceed. Decide if this might or might not be another situation where extreme, "either-or" positions should be avoided.

[1] One has, of course, to keep in mind that not all knowledge is changing with time and becomes obsolete. For example, fundamental knowledge like the knowledge about basic laws of mathematics or mechanics, historical facts and events, many geographical phenomena, and some others are very stable and, in fact, "eternal."

kinds of knowledge. These processes may be different for different kinds of knowledge (for example, knowledge about facts versus knowledge about laws of nature) and/or with regard to different kinds of problems to be solved, but these processes are the same with regard to the same kinds of knowledge and problems. Therefore, we can say that these mechanisms are *content-independent* and therefore general.

If we accept the point that learning how to acquire and apply knowledge is as important as learning the fundamental knowledge (and perhaps more important than learning specific knowledge that can soon become obsolete), then teaching students general cognitive processes and their corresponding methods becomes one of the critical goals of education.* (Obviously, this can be carried out only through teaching specific knowledge.)

An Odd Situation in Education

An odd situation takes place in schools: students are requested to identify objects, explain things, draw conclusions, prove statements, and so on, but are not taught—and don't know—what an identification is, what an explanation is, what it means to draw a conclusion, to prove a statement, etc. At issue is not a lack of formal definitions of those processes (a definition would not teach much) but a lack of knowledge of the mental operations, and their systems, engaged in those processes (what, for example, one should mentally do with something to be explained to make it clear).

Numerous interviews we conducted with teachers showed that, in the overwhelming majority of cases, they themselves didn't know on an operational level what is involved in the processes they try to teach students and request them to perform. In other words, they don't know appropriate methods of thinking to teach their students.

Not surprising, therefore, are the recent findings of the National Assessment of Educational Progress which were summarized by Peter Applebome of the New York Times (1997) as follows: "American students have some understanding of basic scientific facts and principles, but their ability to apply scientific knowledge, design an experiment or clearly explain their reasoning is 'disappointing', according to the latest national test of science education" (p. 36).

Methods

Meanings of the Term "Method"

Many definitions of the term "method" exist in philosophical and scientific literature which often create confusion and hamper communication among scientists. To clarify the issue, let s look at the use of the term "method" in everyday language.

---

* This is an important tenet of the new paradigm.

A semantic analysis of the word "method" shows that it has two meanings: (a) *actions* leading to solving problems or performing tasks, and (b) *prescriptions* pointing out the actions to be performed. To distinguish the two meanings of the term "method," we will designate a method as a system of *a*ctions as M_a, and a method as a system of instructions—a *p*rescription—as M_p. Normally, in searching for ways to solve new problems or perform new tasks, people first discover M_a's and then convert them into M_p's.*

We define "method" as a structured system of instructions and/or actions for achieving some goal.** This definition delineates the following essential characteristics of a method:

1. A method is always a *system* of instructions and/or actions, not just a single one. Only in extreme cases does the system consist of just one single instruction or action.
2. A method is always a *structured* entity which consists of basic instructions and/or actions connected in a certain manner (for example, organized in a certain sequence or hierarchy).
3. A method is always a *goal-oriented* phenomenon which is geared to achieving some goal (to perform a task, to solve a problem, etc.).

In everyday language and science, the notion of a method is often conveyed by a number of full or partial synonyms, such as "process," "procedure," "guide," "technique," "strategy," and some others. The problem is that some of them (like strategy) are much more polysemantic and ambiguous than method.

Once concepts, propositions, and methods are developed in social practice and science, they become social phenomena objectivized (materialized) in language. Once learned, these phenomena become subjective psychological phenomena that are *counterparts* to the objectivized social phenomena. Subjective methods may or may not conform to the objectivized methods. For example, explanations given by many people are often faulty (incorrect, superficial, inconsistent, etc.). Hence, one of the important objectives of education entails teaching methods in such a way that the subjective methods formed in students' minds conform to the effective objectivized methods developed in social practice and science.

The Relationships Between Methods and Skills

Although partially related, methods and skills are not the same, for they reflect different psychological phenomena.

As far as M_p's are concerned, it is obvious that the knowledge of actions to be performed to achieve some goal is not the same as the actual execution of actions. For example, one can know what actions to perform to swim, but not be able to

---

* This is an inductive approach to knowledge acquisition.
** In chapter 1, methods of instruction were defined in a way that is consistent with this definition.

swim. A clear distinction must also be made between the notion of M_a as a system of actions and the notion of a skill. Skills are *not* systems of actions; they are physiological processes in the brain which represent a *potential* for performing systems of actions, M_a.

Obviously, there is a direct connection between the systems of actions making up M_a's and skills: the performance of actions leads to the formation of physiological processes and associations in the brain by leaving "traces" after the actions cease to be executed. These traces *are* skills. The fact that skills are formed only through performance of certain actions and their systems makes it clear that in order to develop good, effective skills in students, it is necessary to teach them good, effective methods.

This highlights the distinction between the knowledge of, and the command of, a method. To *know* a method means to know its instructions, which manifests itself in the ability to *verbally formulate* them. *To have command* of a method means to be able to *perform operations* (physical and/or mental) making up a method. The following situations may, and do, take place in schools and real life:

1. A person knows a method and has command of it.
2. A person knows a method but does not have command of it.
   Example: A person knows how to swim (has knowledge of the actions to be performed) but is unable to swim.
3. A person doesn't know a method but has command of it.
   Example: A person is able to swim, but is unable to describe the actions or formulate a system of corresponding instructions.
4. A person neither knows a method nor has command of it.

Failure to Teach General Methods of Thinking in Conventional Instruction

One of the problems encountered by practically all teachers is this: many students are able to solve problems similar to those they were taught to solve, but are unable to solve problems of the same class or type which don't have enough outward similarity to the taught ones, or they make errors in solving such problems. Why?

Our analysis has shown that it is because they were taught solution processes which, in the demonstrations provided, were applied to some selected content-specific problems only, but they were not taught the general mental operations that can be used and applied to *any* content. This kind of instruction is typical and widespread. As a result of such instruction, a system of actions (M_a) is associated in the students minds only with the content that was used in the demonstration.*

Our former colleague at the Institute of General and Educational Psychology in Moscow, Dr. Zykova, was present at a geometry lesson in one of the Moscow

---

* This is related to the notion of "learning in context."

schools. The topic was right triangles. This is what the teacher and the students were doing at the lesson:

Pedagogical action 1. The teacher explained that there are several types of triangles and that each type has specific characteristics. She said that today they would be studying right triangles and gave a definition ("a right triangle is a triangle which has a 90° angle").

Pedagogical action 2. She then demonstrated right triangles by giving several illustrations of this concept.

Pedagogical action 3. She then provided practice for the students to learn the concept (definition) of a right triangle and how to apply it:

Action 3a.   She asked students to formulate the definition of a right triangle. A few students did it correctly.

Action 3b.   She then asked students to give examples of right triangles by drawing them on the blackboard. Two students did it correctly.

Action 3c.   Afterwards, she displayed several geometric figures on the blackboard, among which were right and non-right triangles, and asked students to point out (identify) the right triangles. Several students did it correctly.

Action 3d.   She then asked students if they had any questions or if everything was clear. The students enthusiastically responded—in chorus—that everything was clear.

Everything went very well and both the teacher and the students were sure that they had perfectly mastered the concept and learned how to apply it.

After the classes, Zykova asked one of the students, who was very active during the lesson and had correctly answered the teacher's questions, to participate in a small experiment. In it, she asked the student to give the definition of a right triangle. The student gave the correct definition, saying that a right triangle is a triangle which has a 90° angle.

Then she offered him four triangles (see Fig. 15.1) and asked him to indicate which of them were right triangles. He chose (1) and (3). The student was asked: "What about triangle 2? It also has a right angle! Isn't it a right triangle?"

He responded: "No, for a triangle to be right, the right angle should be at the bottom of the triangle, either on the left- or right-hand side."

How did the student's erroneous concept form in his mind when the instruction was seemingly well conducted (examples and counterexamples of the concept were given, practice provided, etc.)? Despite the correct definition the student knew and gave, his actual concept reflected an *empirical generalization* of the examples (geometric figures) he encountered in the course of instruction—the spatial positions of the right angles in the triangles which were given as illustrations of the concept.

Zykova says that the students were shown triangles only in the "standard" positions (triangles 1 and 3 in Fig. 15.1). The pedagogical cure offered by Zykova (1963)

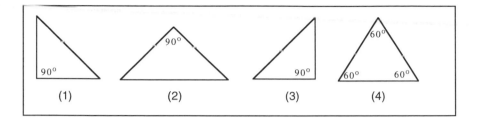

FIG. 15.1. Triangles shown to the student.

and her colleagues was: a teacher who introduces a new concept should vary, as widely as possible, the irrelevant features of the objects which illustrate the concept.

Certainly, limited variations of objects' irrelevant features is one of the causes of students' wrong concepts and errors in concepts' application. But the major, deep-rooted cause of the problem is, in our view, different.

Why It Is Impossible to Provide High-Quality Instruction on the Basis of Empirical Generalizations

Empirical generalizations formed by varying irrelevant objects' characteristics are good when the number of irrelevant variables and their related attributes is very small. But when it is greater than "very small," then the number of necessary variations gets so large that it becomes practically impossible to provide all of them in the course of instruction.

The greater the discrepancy between the objectively required number of variations and those actually provided, the greater the probability that (a) the generalizations formed in the students' minds will be inadequate and, as a result, (b) the rate of inaccurate concepts based on those generalizations will be very high.

The true cause of the problem of faulty concept formation and faulty concept application is, according to Landamatics, that students are not taught general methods of concept acquisition and application. And if this is the true cause, then the preventive medicine and cure would be not the exhaustive variation of objects' irrelevant features, but the teaching and learning of general methods of thinking.

LANDAMATICS APPROACH TO INSTRUCTION

Landamatics has developed and advocates a radically different approach to forming generalizations, concepts, and thought processes via purposefully and explicitly teaching methods of thinking (both M_a's and M_p's).

This approach:

- Makes a great number of variations unnecessary.
- Guarantees* the formation of proper, adequate generalizations.
- Guarantees the formation, on the basis of adequate generalizations, of accurate concepts and propositions.
- Guarantees the formation, within students, of effective methods of acquisition and application of knowledge (images, concepts, and propositions).
- Guarantees the broadest and most accurate transfer, not limited by experience, of both knowledge and mental operations to new situations and problems.
- Guarantees a dramatic reduction in errors and difficulties of learning.
- Guarantees the development of the ability to self-manage, self-regulate, and self-control one's own mental operations.**
- Makes it possible to achieve all of the above reliably and relatively fast.

In contrast to the empirical generalizations formed in the minds of students who have had conventional instruction, the Landamatics approach forms *r*eliable, *s*cientific, *c*oncept-*c*ongruous (RSCC) generalizations. To show, in a simple and contrasting way, the difference between the formation of a concept on the basis of an empirical generalization, on the one hand, and of the RSCC generalization, on the other hand, we will use the same example of teaching students the concept of a right triangle. As in teaching everything, two basic strategies can be used in teaching right triangles: (a) get students to make an independent discovery of what is to be learned by properly guiding them, and (b) teach them ready-made knowledge and methods.*** Or one can combine both strategies in a certain proportion.

Strategy 1: Guided Discovery

Here are the instructional objectives and activities which guided discovery involves:

1. The students' independent discovery of the concept of a right triangle.
2. Figuring out the triangle's name (the term used in science to designate the concept).
3. Framing the concept's logically correct definition.
4. The independent discovery of a system of mental operations (M_a) for applying the concept.
5. Formulation of the discovered method (M_p).
6. Learning, through practicing, how to apply the method.
7. Internalization of the method's instructions (M_p).

---

* In this chapter Landa discusses deterministic instructional methods, rather than probabilistic ones, as described in chapter 1, p. 11. However, this does not mean that his methods are only deterministic.

** Self-regulated learning is closely tied to higher-order thinking skills.

*** This represents the "control of learning" continuum described in chapter 3, p. 58.

8. Automatization of the method's operations (M_a) and, thus, ensuring its complete mastery and command.*

Out of the eight instructional objectives and activities listed above, we will describe here the last five, which are particular to the Landamatics method.

Instructional objective 4: Get students to discover and consciously realize the system of mental operations (M_a) involved in the application of the learned concept, and its definition, to the task of identifying objects as belonging or not belonging to the defined class (in this case, the class of right triangles).

Pedagogical action: Ask the students what they should do in their heads in order to determine, on the basis of the definition, whether a triangle is a right triangle.** In the example we are using, the students say that they have to check whether a triangle has a right angle.

Instructional objective 5: Get students to explicitly formulate the corresponding system of instructions (M_p).

Pedagogical actions:

1. Ask the students to formulate a detailed set of instructions, or commands, (i.e., a method, of what a person, who does not know how to use the definition of a right triangle, should do in his or her mind in order to determine whether some given triangle is a right triangle or not).

2. If the students formulate the method correctly, proceed to the next instructional objective; if not, then explain to them (the explanation is not given here for lack of space) how to formulate the method (M_p) of actions in order to recognize whether a triangle is right or not right.

Students formulate, with the teacher's help, if needed, the following method:

1. Refer to the definition of a right triangle and isolate its characteristic feature—the presence of a 90° angle.

2. Mentally superimpose this feature on the given triangle, and check to see if it has a 90° angle.

3. Draw a conclusion according to the following rules:

   (a) If a triangle has a 90° angle, then it is a right triangle.

   (b) If it does not have a 90° angle, then it is not a right triangle.

4. Write down the formulated method (algorithm) on the blackboard or display it by any other medium (if prepared beforehand).

---

* These phases of instruction clearly correspond to phases in a theory of learning.

** I don't think I would characterize this as *independent* discovery. This does not in any way lessen the credibility of the instructional strategy; rather it indicates that the strategy is not all the way on the learner extreme of the "control of learning" continuum.

Instructional objective 6: Provide practice in the application of the formulated method (M_p).
Pedagogical actions:
1. Tell the students that the task now is to practice applying the formulated method for recognizing right triangles among other triangles.*
2. Show them various triangles and have them determine, following the method, which of them are right triangles and which are not.
3. Explain that they should use the method in a step-by-step manner: look at the first instruction and do what it says, then look at the second instruction and do what it says, etc. In our example, following this method, the students easily identify right triangles regardless of the position of the right angle.

Instructional objective 7: Provide for the method's internalization, through special exercises, and thus ensure its full mastery.
Pedagogical actions:
1. Tell the students that they seem to no longer need the instructions on the blackboard and seem to be able to replace them by *self-instructions (self-commands).*
2. Tell them that you will now erase the instructions on the blackboard and show a few more triangles. They should determine which of them are right triangles by giving themselves self-instructions as to what to do instead of by following the instructions on the blackboard. Our students easily perform all the necessary mental actions (M_a) by giving themselves self-instructions.

Instructional objective 8: Effect automatization of the mental operations of the method (M_a).
Pedagogical actions:
1. Tell the students that they don't seem to further need even self-instructions, for they now know what to do in order to recognize a right triangle.
2. Show them the last set of triangles among which they have to find the right triangles. Ask them to find them as quickly as possible without giving themselves any self-instructions. Our students easily perform the assignment and find the right triangles instantaneously.

This completes the full circle of Landamatics-designed instruction based on Strategy 1.

Although this description of the Landamatics methodology of teaching and learning the concept of a right triangle and the method of its application was fairly long, in reality the entire lesson takes no more than 15 to 20 minutes.

---

* This is obviously not self-regulated learning at this point, but notice that Corno and Randi (chap. 13) advocated "explicit instruction in how to be successful as learners" (p. 302).

THE PSYCHOLOGICAL MECHANISMS OF A METHOD'S INTERNALIZATION AND AUTOMATIZATION

What does it mean to internalize the *instructions* of the method (M_p) and automatize the *operations* of the method (M_a)? What happens in the mind during the processes of internalization and automatization?

According to the Landamatics theory, gradual internalization and automatization of a method is nothing other than a *gradual shift*, in the process of learning and practicing, from one kind of an operations' actuator to another.

1. *At the first stage* of learning a method, operations are actuated *externally* (from the outside) by the *method's instructions*, which exist in some tangible, material form (printed or electronic).
2. *At the second stage*, operations become actuated *internally* (from the inside) by the *self-instructions*. This is the stage of the method's (M_p's) internalization.
3. *At the third stage*, a need for any instructions (external or internal) disappears and the operations start to get actuated by the goals and problem conditions themselves. This is the stage of the operations (M_a's) automatization.

In the course of moving from stage to stage, internal psychological mechanisms of mental processes undergo, according to Landamatics, one critical change: executed *successively* (in a step-by-step manner) at stages 1 and 2, mental operations start to be performed *simultaneously* (or partially simultaneously) at stage 3. Simultanization of mental operations makes possible the following:*

* *Simultaneous* processing of information instead of initial sequential processing;
* Recognition of objects as *patterns*, as *gestalts*;
* Carrying out mental operations (processes) very *fast, instantaneously* or almost instantaneously;
* Carrying out mental operations (processes) *without effort* (they proceed as if by themselves).

These characteristics of mental processes are signs of their mastery and automatization.

In conventional instruction these characteristics are formed (if formed) in a spontaneous, haphazard and often ineffective way. Landamatics makes their formation a well planned and instructionally well managed process, thus guaranteeing the high quality of mental abilities developed as a result of simultanization.

---

* Note that this is descriptive theory here.

Strategy 2: Expository Teaching

With Strategy 2, instead of having the students discover the concept of a right triangle, figure out its term, and frame its definition (as was the case with Strategy 1), the teacher simply teaches all this knowledge to the students in ready-made form (with appropriate illustrations and exercises).

Conditions for Choosing Between Strategies 1 and 2*

It is obvious that Strategy 1 is educationally more valuable, advantageous, and beneficial than Strategy 2. But Strategy 1 takes more time. Often there is not enough time for using the full-fledged Strategy 1 but more time available than needed for using Strategy 2. For this situation, Landamatics suggests using both strategies in a certain proportion. We call this a mixed, or combination, strategy.

Strategy 3: A Combination Strategy

With this strategy, certain things within a topic are taught using the discovery strategy, and certain other things are taught by providing knowledge in ready-made form. Which topics should be taught by one or the other strategy is determined by the teacher's objectives at the given moment and by the relative benefits that each of the methods would provide.*

INCREASING THE DEGREE OF GENERALITY OF A METHOD

The method of thinking formulated for identifying right triangles was *general* in the sense that it could be applied to *any* right triangle, but it was, at the same time, *very specific*, for it could be applied *only* to the identification of right triangles. Is it possible to modify this method so that it will be applicable to other contents as well? In other words, is it possible to make it more general? The answer is yes.

As an example and a departure point, we will use the method of identifying a right triangle formulated earlier. Let us designate the lowest *d*egree of generality as d_1, the next (higher) degree of generality as d_2, and so on. Because the degree of generality of the method for identifying a right triangle is the lowest, this method will have index d_1. It is placed in the left column of Fig. 15.2. The method having the next higher degree of generality is placed in the right column of the figure. This makes the comparison of the methods' degrees of generality easier. The differing elements in the two methods are delineated by italics.

---

* Hopefully, you recognized this right away as a situationality for deciding between two alternative instructional methods.

We suggest that the reader apply Method 2, following its instructions in a step-by-step manner, to each of a number of geometric figures given in Fig. 15.3. The task is to identify which of them is a rhombus. Here is a definition of a rhombus that can be used: "A rhombus is a parallelogram whose four sides have the same length."

Now please apply this method to the task of identifying a right triangle (using examples of triangles given in Fig. 15.1). The reader will see that Method 2 is applicable to the identification of both a right triangle and a rhombus. This means that it is more general than Method 1, which is applicable only to identifying right triangle.*

Method 1 (d₁)	Method 2 (d₂)
In order to identify a *right triangle*:	In order to identify *an object* as belonging or not belonging to a certain class:
1. Refer to the definition of the *right triangle* and isolate its characteristic feature—*the presence of a 90° angle.*	1. Refer to the definition of the *class* and isolate its characteristic feature(s).
2. Mentally superimpose this feature on any given *triangle* and check to see if it has a *90° angle.*	2. Mentally superimpose this feature(s) on any given object and check to see if it has *all* of the features.
3. Draw a conclusion according to the following rules:	3. Draw a conclusion according to the following rules:
(a) If a *triangle* has a *90° angle*, then it is a *right triangle.*	(a) If an *object* has *all* of the *features* indicated in the definition, then it belongs *to the class of objects* defined in the definition.
(b) If it does *not* have a *90° angle*, it is *not a right triangle.*	(b) If it does not have *at least one* of the *features*, it *does not belong to this class of objects.*

FIG. 15.2.   Generalization 1: From d₁ to d₂

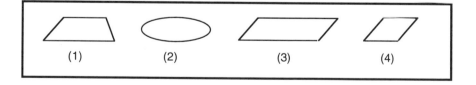

(1)   (2)   (3)   (4)

FIG. 15.3.   Which geometric figure is a rhombus?

---

* Note that "more general" is not any less detailed. This is different from the discussion in chapter 1 about a component method being more detailed than the general method of which it is a kind or part. It seems we have two kinds of generality: generality of scope (the breadth of kinds of cases to which the method can be applied) and generality of description (the amount of detail or guidance in the description of the method). This is an important distinction for both producers and consumers of theories to be aware of.

To appreciate the degree of generality of Method 2, we suggest that the reader apply it to solving the grammatical task of identifying a clause within the following groups of words: (a) "My God!"; (b)"Please, forgive me"; (c) "When Peter entered the room"; and (d) "I really like this book." The following definition of a clause can be used: "A clause is a group of words with a subject and a predicate" (Hirsch, 1993).

How General Is Method 2?

Browsing through a math text, we stumble upon the following rule: "A number is divisible by 5 if it ends in 5 or 0." In order to test Method 2 for its degree of generality, let us select a few test numbers (for example, 15, 17, 20, and 23) and determine, following Method 2, whether they are divisible by 5. We suggest you go through this exercise.

If you did, you should have come to a few erroneous conclusions. Why? Because Method 2 is not general enough.

How do you find a more general method? In order to do so, it is necessary to find out why Method 2 worked successfully when applied to some concepts and definitions and didn t work on some others.

Why Didn't Method 2 Always Work?

To diagnose the problem, let us compare the definitions of those concepts for which the method worked and the rule for which it didn't. How do they differ from each other? The difference is almost obvious: the characteristic features of both a rhombus and a clause are connected by the logical conjunction *and* (i.e., conjunctively), whereas the characteristic features of divisibility by 5 are connected by the logical conjunction *or* (disjunctively). Apparently, Method 2 works only for conjunctive concepts and propositions and does not work for disjunctive ones. The task now is to devise a method, Method 3, for disjunctive structures of characteristic features.

Fig. 15.4 shows Method 3 as compared to Method 2.

The reader can easily test Method 3 by finding definitions whose characteristic features are connected by the logical conjunction *or.* Here are some of them from various textbooks: "A change in the size or shape of something is a physical change"; "The indirect object answers the question, 'To whom?' or 'To what?'"; "Adjectives are the words we use to describe *how* something looks or feels or tastes or sounds."

Method 2 (d_2) *(for conjunctive concepts)*	*Method 3 (d_3)* *(for disjunctive concepts)*
In order to identify an object as belonging or not belonging to a certain class:	In order to identify an object as belonging or not belonging to a certain class:
1. Refer to the definition of the class and isolate its characteristic feature(s).	1. Refer to the definition of the object and isolate its characteristic feature(s).

2. Mentally superimpose this feature(s) on any given object and check to see if it has *all of the features*.	2. Mentally superimpose this feature(s) on any given object and check to see if it has *at least one of the features*.
3. Draw a conclusion according to the following rules:	3. Draw a conclusion according to the following rules:
(a) If an object has *all* of the features indicated in the definition, then it belongs to the class of objects defined in the definition.	(a) If an object has *at least one* of the features indicated in the definition, then it belongs to the class of objects defined in the definition.
(b) If it does not have *at least one* of the features, it does not belong to this class of objects.	(b) If it does not have *all* of the features (i.e., it has none of the features), it does not belong to that class of objects.

FIG. 15.4.   Comparison with a method for disjunctive concepts.

Is Method 3 more general than Method 2? The answer is no. If Method 3 had subsumed Method 2, then it would have been more general than Method 2. But it is not; it just *complements* Method 2. This means that it has the same degree of generality.

An effective way of describing, in detail, the system of actions involved in executing a method is to represent it graphically in flowchart form (see Fig. 15.5).[2]

Is a Combination of Methods 2 and 3 General Enough?

When testing Methods 2 and 3 for their generality to handle any logical structure of characteristic features, we have encountered the following two propositions:

1. A provision of the Social Security Administration: "Only unmarried mothers who have one dependent child and whose income does not exceed $12,000, or married mothers who have two dependent children and whose household income does not exceed $16,500, are eligible for this benefit."
2. A grammatical definition: "A verb is a word that is characteristically the grammatical center of a predicate and expresses an act, occurrence, or mode of being" (*Webster's Guide to Business Correspondence*, 1988, p. 217).

How do you determine whether or not a specific woman is eligible for the benefit in question? How should you reason? Similarly, how do you determine whether or not a specific word is a verb? How should you reason?

Those propositions contain both the conjunction *and* and the disjunction *or*. But Methods 2 and 3 are designed, respectively, for purely conjunctive or purely disjunctive logical structures and do not say anything about how to handle mixed structures. Therefore, they are not general enough, and a more general method is needed.

---

[2]Graphic representations that organize mental and other processes have recently been labeled "graphic organizers" (see, for example, Parks & Black, 1990, 1992).

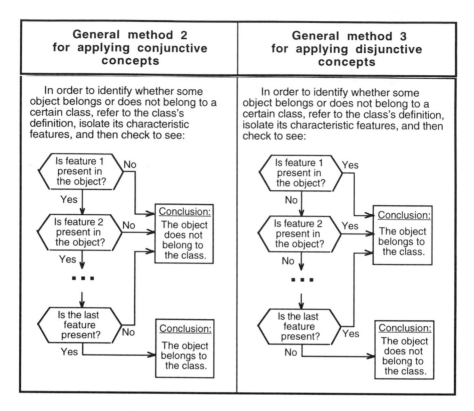

FIG. 15.5.   A flowchart of general Methods 2 and 3.

A Method for Discerning the Inner Logical Design of Mixed Logical Structures

Let us demonstrate the method offered by Landamatics by the example of the Social Security Administration provision cited in the previous section:

Operation 1. Convert a proposition stated in the categorical form into the conditional "if ... , then" form.

> If an unmarried mother has one dependent child and her income does not exceed $12,000 or a married mother has two dependent children and her household income does not exceed $16,500, **then**, and only then, is she eligible for the benefit in question.

Operation 2. To reveal the converted proposition's inner logical structure, describe it using the parentheses.

> If (an unmarried mother has one dependent child and her income does not exceed $12,000) OR (a married mother has two dependent children and her household in-

come does not exceed $16,500), **then**, and only then, she is eligible for the benefit in question.

Operation 3. Present the revealed logical structure in the graphic form that we called a "logic diagram" to make the structure more transparent and distinct.

Logic diagram

IF

I.

(a) an unmarried mother has one dependent child

and

(b) her income does not exceed $12,000

OR

II.

(a) a married mother has two dependent children

and

(b) her household income does not exceed $16,500,

THEN, and only then, is she eligible for the benefit in question.

Operation 4. Express the proposition (in its sentence or diagram form) in a formula of propositional logic which describes its logical structure succinctly in the most generalized form.

Let us designate condition I(a) by the letter *a*, condition I(b) by *b*, condition II(a) by *c*, condition II(b) by *d*, and the conclusion "she is eligible for the benefits in question" by *E*. We will further designate the logical conjunction *and* by &, the logical conjunction *or* by ∨, the *"if … , then"* connection in one direction as →, and the *"if … , then"* connection in both directions as ↔. Then, in the language of propositional logic, our formula will look like this:

$$(a \ \& \ b) \ v \ (c \ \& \ d) \leftrightarrow E.$$

The formula reads as follows: *If* there are conditions *a* and *b* OR conditions *c* and *d*, *then*, and only then, draw conclusion *E*.

We suggest that the reader apply the method for discerning the inner logical design of mixed logical structures just described to the definition of a verb and then compare the logical structures of both propositions. Once done, it will become obvious that, while the first proposition is a *disjunction of conjunctions,* the second proposition is a *conjunction of disjunctions.*

Now we suggest that the reader independently figure out a method for applying the disjunctive–conjunctive propositions (Method 4) and a method for applying conjunctive–disjunctive propositions (Method 5). These methods will have a greater degree of generality (d_3) than Methods 2 and 3, whose level of generality was d_2.

A Still More General Method Is Needed

Now we need a unifying, more general method 6 (d_4) that will subsume and bring together in a single system all the methods developed so far. Fig. 15.6 shows how it can look.

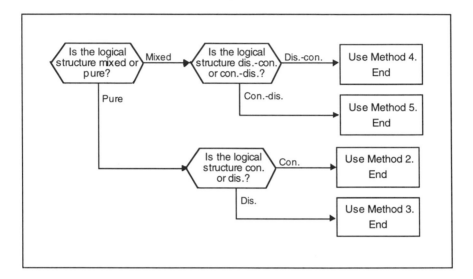

FIG. 15.6.   Method 6 (d_4).

Is Method 6, Finally, the Most General Method?

The methods formulated above were developed for the application of concepts with different logical structures of characteristic features, which were reflected in the concepts' definitions. But definitions are just one kind of proposition. Other kinds of propositions are rules, axioms, theorems, laws of nature (of physics, chemistry, biology, etc.), statements about attributes of objects and their relationships, and some others. Students encounter all of them in their studies at school, and they are supposed to learn them and know how to apply them.

In order for the formulated Method 6 to be the *most general* method for applying knowledge, it must work on *any* knowledge, including rules, laws, and other kinds of propositions. Let's test Method 6 by considering a simple geometric proposition (theorem) about one of the attributes of squares: "The diagonals of a square are perpendicular."

In the conditional "if … , then" form: "If a geometric figure is a square (S), then its diagonals are perpendicular (dp)." In the language of propositional logic: $S \rightarrow dp$. This is obviously a true statement.

Now let's invert it: "If the diagonals in a geometric figure are perpendicular, then this figure is a square: $dp \rightarrow S$." This statement is not true, for a figure that has perpendicular diagonals may also be a rhombus, not just a square.

Thus, statement $S \rightarrow dp$ in our example is true, but the inverse statement $dp \rightarrow S$ is not true.

Only one kind of proposition exists which is always true in both directions: definitions. Other propositions that are true in one direction may or may not be true in the other direction. Their truth or falsity in the other direction must be determined in each particular instance.

The methods described so far were general only with regard to definitions and other two-directional propositions. But these methods are not applicable, or not completely applicable, to one-directional propositions. This means that the described method 6 is still not the most general.

In Fig. 15.7 we will describe methods for pure conjunctive (Method 2a) and pure disjunctive (Method 3a) structures within *one-directional* propositions. We suggest that you compare them with their corresponding Methods 2 and 3 for *two-directional* propositions (Fig. 15.4) to see the difference. Obviously, the need for Methods 2a and 3a creates a need for Methods 4a and 5a, which the reader can easily create by modifying Methods 4 and 5.

Methods for Pure Conjunctive and Disjunctive Structures Within One-Directional Propositional Knowledge

Fig. 15.7 shows the methods for one-directional propositions.

Method 2a (d_2) *(for conjunctive concepts and conditions expressed in one-directional propositions)*	*Method 3a (d_2)* *(for disjunctive concepts and conditions expressed in one-directional propositions)*
In order to identify an object as belonging or not belonging to a certain class or to determine whether to perform an action indicated in the right part of an if ..., then proposition:	In order to identify an object as belonging or not belonging to a certain class or to determine whether to perform an action indicated in the right part of an if ..., then proposition:
1. Refer to the proposition and isolate the characteristic feature(s) or condition(s) indicated in its left part.	1. Refer to the proposition and isolate the characteristic feature(s) or condition(s) indicated in its left part.
2. Mentally superimpose the feature(s) or condition(s) on any given object or situation and check to see if it has *all* of the feature(s) or the condition(s).	2. Mentally superimpose the feature(s) or condition(s) on any given object or situation, and check to see if it has *at least one* of the feature(s) or the condition(s).
3. Draw a conclusion according to the following rules:	3. Draw a conclusion according to the following rules:
(a) If an object or situation has *all* of the features or conditions, indicated in the left part of the proposition, then it belongs to the class of objects specified in the proposition's right part. If the proposition's right part indicates an action to be performed, this is the action to execute.	(a) If the object or situation has *at least one* of the features or conditions, indicated in the left part of the proposition, then it belongs to the class of objects specified in the proposition's right part. If the proposition's right part indicates an action to be performed, this is the action to execute.

(b) If an object or situation does not have *at least one* of the features or conditions, **then no conclusion can be drawn. If an action is indicated in the right part of the proposition, it is not known whether this is the action to be performed.**	(b) If the object or situation does not have *all* of the features or conditions, then **no conclusion can be drawn. If an action is indicated in the right part of the proposition, it is not known whether this is the action to be performed.**

FIG. 15.7.   A comparison of Methods 2a and 3a.

An example explaining instruction 3b of Method 2a. Let us suppose that someone has formulated the following "if ... , then" rule with an action indicated in its right part: "If it is raining, take an umbrella when leaving home." Now suppose that it is *not* raining. Must I *not* perform the action (i.e., *not* take an umbrella)? Not necessarily. I still may take the umbrella if I *expect* rain later in the day. The rule says what to do if the condition is *present* but does not say what to do if it is *not* present. The rule offers no conclusion about what to do if it is *not* raining. It leaves the decision open.

An example explaining instruction 3b of Method 3a. Let us suppose that someone has formulated the following "if ... , then" rule with an action indicated in its right part: "If it is raining or you expect it to rain later in the day, take an umbrella when leaving home." Now suppose that it is not raining nor is it expected to rain. Must I *not* perform the action (i.e., *not* take an umbrella with me)? Not necessarily. I still may take the umbrella for some other reason. The rule says what to do if at least one of the conditions is present, but it does not say what to do if neither of them is present. It leaves the decision open.

It is obvious that the modifications made to Methods 2 and 3 to turn them into Methods 2a and 3a (to fit one-directional propositions) should be made in all the other methods (4–6) because they are also based on Methods 2a and 3a. We suggest that the readers make these modifications and develop Methods 4a–6a on their own.

Method 7: The Most General One (d$_s$)

Now we have arrived—at last!—at the most general method for learning and applying *any* conceptual knowledge expressed in *any* kind of proposition (definitions, rules, theorems, laws, etc.). These propositions may have *any* logical structure in the left part of the "if ... , then" statement, and they may have *any* of the two kinds of connections between the left and right parts (two-directional or one-directional).

Fig. 15.8 shows the prescriptions that should precede Methods 6 and 6a in order to make Method 7 the most general

Note. In propositions covered by the methods described in this chapter, the connection between the antecedent and the consequent is deterministic. There are also propositions which have a probabilistic connection, where the consequent follows from the antecedent with some probability rather than certainty. That is why Method 7 is the most general with respect to deterministic propositions only.

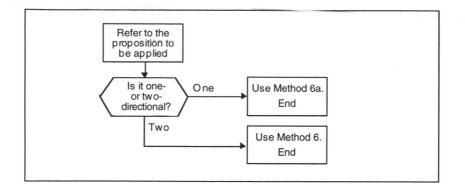

FIG. 15.8.   Method 7 (d,).*

How Difficult Is It to Teach Students the Most General Method?

From the description of the most general Method 7, and the way we have arrived at it, an impression may have arisen that teaching and learning general methods of thinking is a difficult and lengthy process. In fact, it is an easy and relatively fast process that students greatly enjoy. Moreover, it is possible to teach even junior high school students how to independently discover both the basic logical structures of propositions and the methods of handling them. Some preliminary experiments with primary school students showed that younger children, too, can be taught the basic logical structures and methods of handling them. It takes more time to teach students some auxiliary methods, which are discussed in the next section.

In chapter 15 of Landa (1974), a detailed lesson on how to teach general methods of thinking, even to small children, is described. We strongly suggest that readers familiarize themselves with that lesson, as it almost gives a script on how to conduct it.

The Explicit and Implicit Logical Structures of Propositions

In the majority of examples which we used to build the most general method of applying knowledge, the logical conjunctions *and, or, not,* and *"if ... , then"* were present in the propositions, and, thus, were explicit. This made discerning the logical structures, and their representation in the logic diagram form, relatively easy. However, in many propositions in both science and everyday language the logical conjunctions are expressed by grammatical conjunctions or are not present at all, which makes them, and their related logical structures, hidden or implicit.

---

* Note that a method is more complex than a method that is a part of it.

Landamatics (Landa, 1990) has developed methods for "explicitating" hidden or implicit logical structures, which cannot be discussed here for lack of space. We call the translation of grammatical conjunctions into the logical conjunctions *and, or, not,* and *"if ... , then"* the reduction of propositions to their *standard logical form,* or *logical standardization.* Figure 15.9 shows an example just to give an idea of the nature of the problem. Only a reduction of this kind clearly brings to light the logical structures of characteristic features and conditions and makes it possible for a person to correctly and effectively use the methods of applying knowledge described above.

Implicit logical structure	*Standard (explicit) logical structure*
1. "A participial phrase is a group of related words containing a participle." (Warriner & Griffith, 1957, p. 37)	1. **If,** and only if, the words in a group are (a) related **and** (b) contain a participle, **then** this group of words is a participial phrase.

FIG. 15.9.   Example of logical standardization of an implicit logical structure.

We suggest that the reader select or make up a number of sentences with various grammatical conjunctions (for example, *therefore, rather than, otherwise, neither ... nor, provided,* and others) and translate them into standard logical form (see Fig. 15.10).

Grammatical conjunctions	*Translation into logical conjunctions*
1. He is smart **but** lazy.	1. He is smart **and** lazy.
2. I will **not** forgive him **unless** he apologizes.	2. **If** he **does not** apologize, **then** I will **not** forgive him. Also: **If** he apologizes, **then** I will forgive him.
3. The bank robber said to the tellers, "Keep quiet **and** you will be OK."	3. The bank robber said to the tellers, "**If** you keep quiet, **then** you will be OK."

FIG. 15.10.   Examples of translation of grammatical conjunctions into logical conjunctions.

We also suggest that the reader select a number of propositions with implicit logical structures and then "explicitate" them. An example of such a proposition may be the following definition:

An adverb is a word or a combination of words typically serving as a modifier of a verb, an adjective, another adverb, a preposition, a phrase, a clause, or a sentence and expressing some relation of manner or quality, place, time, degree, number, cause, opposition, affirmation, or denial. (*Webster's Guide to Business Correspondence,* 1988, p. 197)

ISSUES RELATED TO TEACHING GENERAL METHODS OF THINKING

The Educational Value of General Methods of Thinking

Teaching and learning general methods of thinking have the following important educational benefits:*

- It equips students with uniform and ubiquitous mental *tools* to acquire, manipulate, and apply knowledge of *any* content across all disciplines.
- It requires teaching and learning each of the methods just *once*, making it unnecessary to teach and learn how to acquire, manipulate, and apply each *particular* knowledge.
- It *saves an enormous amount of time*, and thus vastly increases the *productivity* of both teaching and learning.
- It enormously *increases the quality* of acquired knowledge, skills, and abilities.
- It dramatically *reduces difficulties* in teaching and learning.
- It *prevents many errors* or immensely *reduces their rate*.
- It *creates expert-level learners and performers* out of almost everyone—and does this reliably and relatively quickly.

Here are some additional, but extremely important, educational benefits derived from teaching general methods of thinking:

- Students begin to understand the *general makeup* and *structure* of knowledge—*any* knowledge regardless of its specific domain and contents, which leads to the development of *interdisciplinary thinking*.
- Students acquire a powerful tool for *structural analysis* and comparison of knowledge regardless of its contents and domain specificity.
- They acquire a tool and develop the ability to *see the common* (*general*) in the *particular* (*specific*).
- They begin to more easily *transfer* knowledge, mental operations, and their systems (general and more specific methods) from one content to another, both within the same subject matter and between different subject-matter domains; the range of transfer becomes incomparably broader.
- They become *conscious* of their own thinking processes and acquire the tools and the ability to *self-manage*, *self-regulate*, and *self-control* these processes. Their thinking becomes truly *self-sufficient* and *independent*.
- They develop *general approaches* to *attacking different problems* within the same or different domains of knowledge.

---

* This is a curriculum theory issue, for it is a rationale for what to teach.

Why Are General Methods of Thinking Not Commonly Taught in Schools Today?

There are several reason for this:

1. The insufficient maturity of educational science, which has yet to realize the critical importance of teaching students of all ages general methods of thinking.
2. The underdevelopment of general methods of thinking in pedagogy and psychology, which results in a lack of scientific knowledge of the makeup and structure of different methods of thinking.
3. The underdevelopment in pedagogy and psychology of instructional methods for teaching general methods of thinking.
4. The focus, in instructional practice, on teaching and learning specific knowledge and skills rather than general methods of knowledge acquisition, manipulation, and application, on whose basis, from Landamatics point of view, specific knowledge and skills should be taught and learned.
5. The unawareness or insufficient awareness that most teachers have, and that many professionals and expert performers in all areas of activity have, of their own mental processes and methods of thinking, which makes the communication of these methods and their transfer to students practically impossible.
6. The flaws in teacher preparation and training that result in the fact that student teachers and practicing teachers do not learn either general methods of thinking (and other methods of cognitive activity) or general methods of teaching general methods of thinking.

Problems Resulting From Not Teaching General Methods of Thinking

Here is a brief summary of problems in learning and thinking which develop when students are taught neither general methods of thinking nor how to discover them on their own:

1. If general methods of thinking are not taught, students are forced to try to discover them on their own.
2. If methods for the discovery of general methods of thinking are not taught, then students can use the only method available to them: trial and error.
3. Discovering general methods of thinking by trial and error is a difficult process (hence, the difficulties and problems in learning and thinking).
4. Discovering general methods of thinking by trial and error is a long process (hence, the duration of instruction and learning in each particular topic is too long).

5. Discovering general methods of thinking by trial and error is, as a rule, an unsystematic and haphazard process.
6. The discovered methods are, very often, based on empirical generalizations and are not general enough (they enable only limited transferability and limited areas of application).
7. Very often, not all the component mental actions are discovered and, as a result, the discovered methods are defective in one or several respects (incomplete, ineffective, etc.).
8. In cases where the discovered methods are correct and general enough, they are often inefficient (not economical).
9. Students who discover the operations of a method (M_a) through trial and error are, as a rule, unaware of them, for the operations don't reach the level of consciousness (M_p). As a result, students are unable to self-manage, self-regulate, and self-control their mental processes.
10. Because of the unawareness of mental operations, students cannot communicate their mental processes and their systems (M_a's) to other people.

Are General Methods of Thinking Content-Free?

The answer is yes if one understands content to be, for example, the features that make a triangle different from a rhombus or a noun. But the answer is no if one includes the logical structures of those features in the notion of content. *The logical structure of content is also content*, although of a radically different nature. Methods are not determined by content of the first kind, but are determined by, and reflect, the content of the second kind.

The power of general methods of thinking consists of the fact that they allow one to isolate content of the second kind and mentally separate it from the content of the first kind. This makes it possible to apply mental operations to *any* content of the first kind, even to that which was never encountered in past experience. Thereby, general methods of thinking enable people to overstep the limits of their past experiences and effectively think about things with which they have had no prior personal experience.*

General Methods of Thinking and Intelligence

Cognitive psychology in the United States and some other countries has finally come to the thesis that intelligence is teachable and learnable (see, for example, Wimbey & Wimbey, 1975; Sternberg, 1983; Perkins, 1995). (This thesis, incidentally, was put forward in Soviet cognitive and educational psychology several

---

* This brings us back to the issue I raised at the beginning of this chapter as to whether instructional theory must be domain-specific, whether it should be general or cross-disciplinary, or whether it should transcend this particular "either-or" issue by having theories of both kinds or by defining a continuum between the two extremes whereby theories can be at any point on the continuum.

dozen years ago.) What, however, is specifically teachable? Until there is a clear and precise answer to this question, the thesis about teachability and learnability of intelligence hangs in the air. In order to know how to teach (i.e., to produce intelligence), it is necessary to know precisely what intelligence is).

According to Landamatics, general intelligence is nothing other than a command of (not just knowledge of) a system of the most general methods of thinking applicable to any content-specific knowledge.

What does it mean to teach and learn intelligence then?

It means, according to Landamatics, teaching and learning general methods of thinking that *lead* to the development of general intelligence. One note is necessary here. Intelligence is *not* the performance of operations which make up methods (M_a's). Intelligence is what is *left* in the brain as a *result* of performing the methods' operations. Intelligence is the "traces" of previously performed systems of operations, their aftereffects.

This can be expressed in another way: intelligence cannot be taught or learned, only methods can. Intelligence can only be formed as a result of performing and internalizing methods' operations.

CONCLUSION

We have been dealing, in this chapter, with only *deterministic* methods of knowledge application, which are based on full information about the objects to which knowledge is applied. There are, however, *probabilistic* general methods of cognitive activity and thinking that lie at the foundation of probabilistic intuitive judgments. The discussion of the probabilistic methods of cognitive activity and the instructional methods of teaching them is a separate topic.

REFERENCES

Applebome, Peter (1997). U.S. pupils score high on science facts but fault on reasoning. *The New York Times*, May 4, 1997.

Hirsch, Jr., E. D. (Ed.). (1993). *What your 6th grader needs to know. Fundamentals of a good sixth-grade education*. New York: Delta.

Landa, L. N. (1974). *Algorithmization in learning and instruction*. Englewood Cliffs, NJ: Educational Technology Publications.

Landa, L. N. (1983). The algo-heuristic theory of instruction. In C. M. Reigeluth (Ed.), *Instructional-design theories and models: An overview of their current status*. Hillsdale, NJ: Lawrence Erlbaum Associates.

Landa, L. N. (1990). *Logic foundations of Landamatics and derivation of algorithms from propositions and rules: A Training Course*. New York: Landamatics International.

Landa, L. N. (1997). The algo-heuristic theory and methodology of learning, performance, and instruction as a paradigm. In C. R. Dills & A. J. Romiszowski (Eds.), *Instructional development paradigms* (pp. 661–693). Englewood Cliffs, NJ: Educational Technology Publications.

Parks, S. & Black, H. (1990, 1992). *Organizing thinking. Graphic organizers.* Pacific Grove, CA: Critical Thinking Press and Software.

Perkins, D. (1995). *Outsmarting IQ: The emerging science of learnable intelligence.* New York: Free Press.

Sternberg, R. (1983). *How can we teach intelligence.* Philadelphia: Research For Better Schools.

Warriner, J. E., & Griffith, F. (1957). *English grammar and composition.* New York: Harcourt, Brace & World.

Webster's guide to business correspondence (1998). Springfield, MA: Merriam-Webster.

Whimbey, A., & Whimbey, L. S. (1975). *Intelligence can be taught.* New York: Dutton.

Zykova, V. I. (1963). Formirovaniye prakticheskikh umeny na urokakh geometrii. (in Russian). (*The formation of practical skills at geometry lessons.*) Moscow: APS Publishing House.

16 Integrated Thematic Instruction: From Brain Research to Application

Susan Jafferies Kovalik
President, Susan Kovalik & Associates

with Jane Rasp McGeehan
CEO, Susan Kovalik & Associates

Susan J. Kovalik

Jane R. McGeehan

Susan J. Kovalik is creator of Integrated Thematic Instruction (ITI), a systemic instructional model for applying research about the biology of learning to classrooms and schools to improve learning. An experienced teacher and long-time education consultant, she is president of Susan Kovalik & Associates and Books for Educators—providing staff development and resources to support those implementing the ITI model. She is in demand as a keynote speaker for national and international education gatherings. She is author of *ITI: The Model* and *Kids' Eye View of Science*, as well as producer of numerous video tapes about ITI.

Jane R. McGeehan is a life-long public school educator having taught Grades 3–9, been principal of both an elementary and a high school, and served as Assistant Superintendent for Curriculum and Instruction. Currently Chief Executive Officer of Susan Kovalik & Associates; she draws on her extensive practical experience to help others learn about and implement Integrated Thematic Instruction (ITI) with success. She is contributing editor of *Transformations: Leadership for Brain-Compatible Learning*.

FOREWORD

Goals and preconditions. The primary goal of this theory is to foster the complete, well-rounded development of children in a way that is consistent with the biology of human learning, as well as learners' and communities' needs. The only precondition is K–12 education.

Values. Some of the values upon which this theory is based include:
- responsible citizenship to perpetuate a democratic society—students learning that they can make a difference,
- learning that is organized around a yearlong theme that integrates the disciplines and fosters systemic thinking,
- caring, respect, and collaboration,
- trustworthiness, truthfulness, active listening, no put-downs, and personal best ("Lifelong Guidelines"),
- intelligence as something that can be cultivated, acquired,
- every student is important,
- student mastery versus covering material,
- some choice for students over what they study and how,
- involvement of students in political/social (community) action,
- basing instructional methods on the biology of human learning (brain research findings),
- learning that is meaningful for students—"for real purposes and audiences,"
- emotions as strongly influencing learning,
- "being there" (real-world) experiences as the most important sensory input.

Methods. These are the major methods this theory offers:

Absence of threat. Help students feel free from anxieties and associate positive emotions with learning.

Meaningful content. Select topics that interest students and have power to help them understand and influence their world. The yearlong theme should have (approx. monthly) components, each of which has (approx. weekly) topics, each of which has key points (conceptual, significant knowledge, and skill).

Choices. Provide options as to how learning will occur, considering multiple intelligences and personality preferences.

Adequate time. Provide enough time for students to thoroughly explore, understand, and use information and skills.

Enriched environment. Provide an inviting setting with many resources, emphasizing real places, people, and objects. Use job shadowing, mentorships, etc. "to re-establish the connection between what students do in schools and what adults do in life."

Collaboration. Have students work together to solve problems, explore, create.

Immediate feedback. Provide coaching to promote correct initial learning and sustain motivation to learn.

Mastery/application. Ensure a curriculum focus so that students acquire mental programs to use learnings in real-life situations. Key points are learned through inquiries (practice activities) that are done to reach mastery.

ITI sequence. Start with "being there" (real-world) experiences, then conceptual development, then language development, and finally application to the real world.

Major contributions. Bridging the gap between research on the biology of learning and classroom practice. Organizing instruction around themes. Importance of responsible citizenship and community action. Focus on the whole child. Offering choices.

—C.M.R.

Integrated Thematic Instruction: From Brain Research to Application

Citizenship: The state of being vested with the rights, privileges and duties of a citizen; the character of an individual viewed as a member of society; behavior in terms of the duties, obligations and functions of a citizen.
Webster's Unabridged Dictionary

Responsible: Answerable or accountable, as for something within one's power, control, or management.
Webster's Unabridged Dictionary

The Challenge: The democratic problem in education is not primarily a problem of training children; it is the problem of making a community within which children cannot help growing up to be democratic, intelligent, disciplined to freedom, reverent of the good of life, and eager to share in the tasks of the age.
Joseph K. Hart
Founder of Community Schools Movement

The most striking difference between the world when I began teaching in 1961 and today's world is size. The world is dramatically smaller in ways that make the global village a reality. Today we receive minute-by-minute accounts of news events. Personal messages are sent and received from across the globe in an instant. Computers invite us to travel an information highway that affords access to a knowledge base unimaginable just a decade ago. Knowledge from all over the world can be shared by many—not just a chosen few in universities.

We open the doors of our country and our homes to unprecedented numbers of refugees and immigrants. We witness the growing group of expatriates who move from country to country, lacking strong loyalty to any, following their desired employment. We see that one country's economic development produces a neighboring country's pollution problems. Our children come to school from homes that represent 50 or more languages and as many or more cultural orientations. Together on this small planet, with a common goal of the survival of our children and our children's children, we confront astounding diversity and its implications.

The Integrated Thematic Instruction (ITI) model for curriculum and instruction reflects my optimistic belief that humans will use the strengths inherent in their diversity to discover and address common needs and goals. Thus, *responsible citizenship* is a critical need common to countries across our global village.* Responsible citizens understand rights, privileges, and duties. They are accountable for their behavior and understand their vested role in the productive functioning of the town, village, city, state, nation, and world. They see that leaders must work in harmony to benefit the majority of the citizens.

But responsible citizenship in the sense that I describe here is frequently not what today's schools teach our young. The needed transformation of the educational system is much broader and deeper than the usual proposals for curricular reform, instructional improvement, or innovative management structures.** Common sense enhanced by our personal experiences suggests that dramatic global changes demand correspondingly dramatic school changes. The needed changes in schools go beyond the small arc of the pendulum swings that have preoccupied us in the past. If we sincerely intend to achieve such significant change, we must commit ourselves to creating a public system of education expressly designed to perpetuate a democratic society within a global village using teaching and learning strategies that are based on the biology of human learning.

To support such overarching goals, a viable curriculum model must be able to answer pivotal questions:***

1. What do you want students to understand? (What must students understand in order to carry out their roles as responsible citizens?) ITI educators express

---

* This is a curriculum theory issue, which of course is intertwined with this instructional theory.
** This is a call for a new paradigm of education, which was discussed in chapter 1, pp. 19–21.
*** Which of the following address instructional theory and which address curriculum theory?

learning goals as key points and believe that student mastery is more valuable than "covering" material.

2. What do you want them to do with it? (What governmental, political, and/or social arenas must students access in order to responsibly apply such understandings to benefit society?) ITI students prepare for "doing" through inquiries (learning activities).
3. What experiences are most likely to produce those results? ITI teachers place strong emphasis on real experiences outside the school followed by direct instruction and adequate time for practice within the school.
4. How will you and your students know that they have the requisite understandings and the ability to apply them beneficially?* ITI schools create meaningful situations in which students demonstrate mastery for real purposes and audiences, with political/social action at the top of the list of possibilities.

While the questions are not new, the answers suggested by the ITI model call for fresh approaches. With the focus on responsible citizenship, ITI is a comprehensive model that translates the biology of learning into practical classroom and school strategies.

UNDERLYING VALUES MADE EXPLICIT

Stating the values that are implicit in the ITI model lets readers assess the extent to which these values align with their personal values. The ITI model values:

- each human life and interdependence among all living things;
- caring, respectful communities working collaboratively at all levels;
- responsible, global citizens;
- earth as a habitat for a sustainable future; and
- the capacity of humans to make a positive contribution to their world.**

The ITI model is an educator's vehicle for acting on these values through teaching and learning.

OVERVIEW OF THE ITI MODEL
AND THE BIOLOGY OF LEARNING

It was clear to me upon my first reading of Hart's *Human Brain and Human Learning* in 1983 that discoveries revealing the mysteries of our brains would change forever the definition of quality education and schooling. Research by

---

* You may have noticed in other theories you have read so far that evaluation theory is also closely (inextricably) related to instructional theory in the new paradigm.

** Note that these are values underlying the curriculum theory presented here, not the instructional theory.

neuroscientists and others is revealing how our "bodybrain partnership" learns. Such research* provides a window on learning never before available in the history of civilization. It must become the basis for all decisions educators make to improve student and teacher performance. Just as the river will ultimately make its own course in spite of human plans, so too will the biology of learning prevail. (Note: "bodybrain" is a coined word to reflect the collaborative activity of both brain and body for learning.)

The ITI model marries research about the biology of learning with appropriate teaching strategies and curriculum development as presented in Fig. 16.1. The result is practical application of theory that rings true with human intuitions and experiences.

The biology of learning explains what we know to date about how, when, and why we remember and are able to use information effectively. From this growing body of research, I have selected six powerful concepts I call the "bodybrain basics." They are:

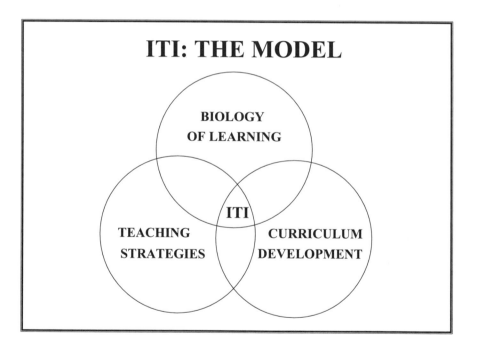

FIG. 16.1.   Overview of ITI.

---

* Do you think this body of work is descriptive theory or design theory?

1. Emotions are the gatekeeper to learning* and performance (Goleman, 1995; LeDoux, 1996; MacLean, 1990; Pert, 1997; Sylwester, 1995).
2. Intelligence is a function of experience (Begley, 1997; Diamond, 1998; Perkins, 1995).
3. Humans in all cultures use multiple intelligences to solve problems and to create products (Gardner, 1983).
4. The brain's search for meaning is a search for meaningful patterns (Calvin, 1996; Hart, 1983).**
5. Learning is the acquisition of useful mental programs (Hart, 1983; Perkins, 1995; Sylwester, 1995).
6. Personality—one's basic temperament—affects how a learner takes in information, organizes and uses it, makes decisions about it, and orients him/herself with respect to the world and other learners (Jung, 1976; Keirsey & Bates, 1984; Myers, 1956).

A brief look at each of these basic concepts introduces the foundation for the entire ITI model.

Bodybrain Basic 1: Emotions Are the Gatekeeper to Learning and Performance

Sylwester (1995) states the situation clearly in his book, *A Celebration of Neurons:* "We know emotion is very important to the educative process because it drives attention, which drives learning and memory" (p. 72). All sensory data entering the brain from cells throughout the body are screened by brain structures designed to detect imminent dangers. LeDoux (1996) explains that such possible threats to safety or even survival are detected unconsciously. A brain triggered by the amygdala, a structure within the brain's limbic system, has the power to override rational thought and orchestrate a rapid, reflexive response. Sylwester (1995) suggests that we consider the amygdala our brain's "911" system. In cases of less severe threat, stress hormones are released that can also have a negative impact on learning.

The main point for educators to understand is that events in classrooms or schools judged to pose a threat, whether psychological or physical, risk triggering an emotional take-over that prevents or diminishes the possibility of new learning. The environment that consistently promotes new learning allows learners to feel relaxed, alert, and safe.***

---

* Note the close relationship between the affective domain and the cognitive domain.
** Again, understanding is an important kind of learning in the new paradigm.
*** This is a theme common to many theories in the new paradigm—see especially chapters 21 (Lewis, Watson & Schaps) and 22 (Stone-McCown & McCormick).

Bodybrain Basic 2: Intelligence Is a Function of Experience

One of the most surprising revelations of the research about the biology of learning is that nature and nurture are truly partners.* A newborn arrives with basic neural wiring to handle necessary reflexes such as sucking; Chugani and other researchers are using newly available technology and procedures, as reported by Begley (1997), to demonstrate that experiences in the world after birth literally hardwire the brain in preparation for most of life's tasks. This stunning finding applies most strongly to a child's first 3 years and accounts for the brain's plasticity, or flexibility, to learn new things throughout life. At any age, when confronted with new experiences, the brain begins the process of recruiting neurons and sprouting dendrites to communicate among neurons in various locations in the brain.

Stimulated by an enriched environment, connections among neurons increase, as described by Diamond (1998). The brain literally becomes denser and heavier. This burgeoning growth enables the learner to "connect" ideas, to have fuller understandings, to be more intelligent. Perkins (1995) suggests we are witnessing a revolution in our understanding of intelligence and that " ... this revolution has a restorative character. It says that we are not so boxed in by our genetic heritage. On the contrary, intelligence is something that can be cultivated and acquired. People can learn to think and act more intelligently" (p. 18).**

Bodybrain Basic 3: Humans in All Cultures Use Multiple Intelligences to Solve Problems and to Create Products

Gardner's (1983) breakthrough theory of multiple intelligences is a gift for students whose strengths do not match what schools traditionally do. He establishes a useful definition of human intelligence as

> a set of skills of problem solving—enabling the individual to resolve genuine problems or difficulties that he or she encounters and, when appropriate, to create an effective product—and must also entail the potential for finding or creating problems—thereby laying the groundwork for the acquisition of new knowledge. (pp. 60–61)

Across cultures, he identifies eight intelligences: linguistic, musical, logical-mathematical, spatial, bodily-kinesthetic, naturalist, intrapersonal, and interpersonal (see chap. 4 of this volume).

Bodybrain Basic 4: The Brain's Search for Meaning Is a Search for Meaningful Patterns

---

* Transcending "either-or" thinking.
** Gardner (chap. 4), Pogrow (chap. 14), and Landa (chap. 15) all make similar arguments.

Bodybrain Basic 5: Learning Is the Acquisition of Useful Mental Programs

Hart (1983) describes learning as a two-part process that involves extraction from confusion of meaningful patterns and the acquisition of useful mental programs.* To recognize a pattern, one must be able to detect its attributes: characteristics that distinguish one object or action from another. What is the difference between running and walking? How do you know? Every verb and noun in the English language represents a pattern, a collection of attributes captured symbolically. Recalling the earlier discussion about the vital role of sensory input from experiences, it is clear that pattern recognition depends on the experiences one brings to the situation.

It is one thing to recognize a pattern and another to be able to use it. At some point you recognized the difference between running and walking, but weren't yet able to produce the action of running. It would take more practice at walking fast, observing, trying a few things, and finally having neurons attached to the right muscle groups in the right way before you could take off on a run.

In the same way, students need practice in order to develop mental programs enabling them to use new information beyond the walls of the school in real-world contexts. The new setting may resemble something at school where the mental program was first practiced but may require application in a creative or novel way. When the program is thoroughly mastered, flexibility to adjust its use in unique settings is possible.

Bodybrain Basic 6: Personality (One's Basic Temperament) Affects Learning

Beyond varieties of intelligence, personality or temperament differences have a profound impact on learning. Keirsey and Bates (1984) describe a useful framework for looking at the impact of personality preferences. Starting with the work of Jung, Kiersey and Bates identify four broad types of orientations to new information and other people, some of which are a better match than others for traditional school settings. The four are represented as four ranges of possible characteristics with extremes at each end, as shown in Fig. 16.2. Humans can learn behaviors at many points on each continuum, but have strong preferences that they call on in new situations or when dealing with learning new information.

Critical for educators is the understanding that teachers tend to teach as they like to learn: based on their own personal temperament. Kiersey and Bates report that approximately 56% of teachers have sensing/judging (SJ) temperaments and that SJ students have just a 25% chance of becoming school dropouts. It is revealing that from 75% to 90% of our schools' at-risk students have sensing/perceiving (SP) personalities. "The system is simply too structured, too rigid, too boring, too

---

* This is similar to Landa's focus on mental operations in chapter 15.

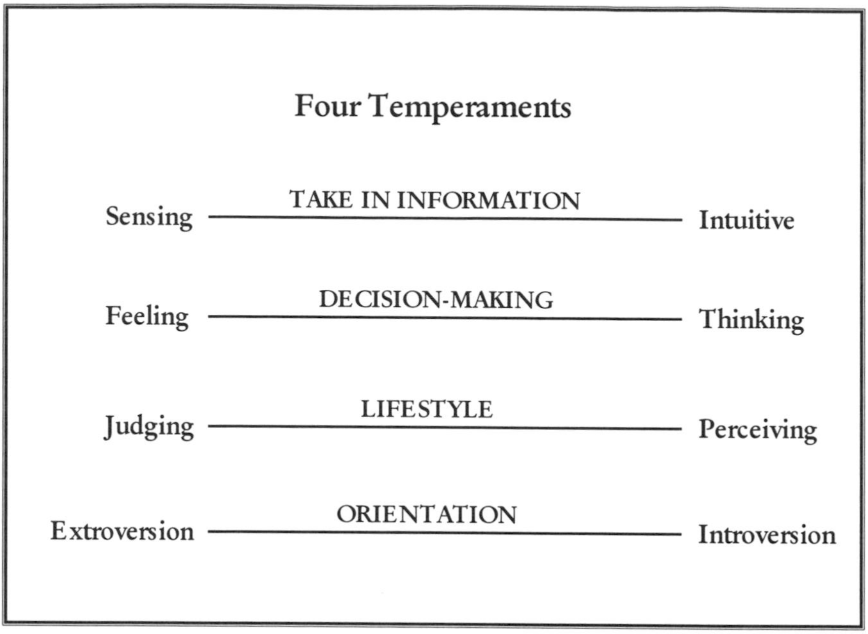

FIG. 16.2.   Four temperaments (Ross & Olsen, 1995, after Keirsey and Bates).

oppressive" (Ross & Olsen, 1995, pp. 1–41). Many become "pushouts." In ITI classrooms, these preferences are considered so that there are opportunities for students of all temperaments to succeed as learners.*

To move from research to application and to guide practice, I created the list of eight bodybrain-compatible elements of instruction explained in the following section. Following also from the research about the biology of learning, my associates and I selected teaching strategies and created a method for writing curricula that enable educators to orchestrate learning in classrooms, schools, and school districts that works with the bodybrain partnership.

THE ITI BODYBRAIN-COMPATIBLE ELEMENTS

Each of the bodybrain basics relates to one or more of the elements created as guidelines to help teachers translate research and theory about the biology of learning into practice. They are:**

---

* Hopefully, you recognized this as a situationality for deciding on different methods of instruction.

** These are similar in nature to the principles that were offered by Bielaczyc and Collins (chap. 12) and Corno and Randi (chap.13). How many of these "elements" are manifest in each of the other theories in this volume?

absence of threat:	being free from fears or anxiety about physical or mental safety, experiencing a general sense of well-being and positive emotions with respect to learning experiences;
meaningful content:	selecting topics that interest students and have power to help them understand and influence their world;
choices:	providing options as to the what and how of learning, with attention to multiple intelligences, higher level thinking, and personality preferences;
adequate time:	having enough time to thoroughly explore, understand, and use ideas, information and skills;
enriched environment:	providing a healthful, inviting, homey setting with many resources from which the students can learn, with special emphasis on real places, people, and objects;
collaboration:	acting on the belief that two heads are better than one to solve problems, explore, and create;
immediate feedback:	providing coaching to promote correct initial learning and sustain motivation toward more learning;
mastery/application:	ensuring a curriculum focus so that students acquire mental programs stored in long-term memory to use what is learned in real-life situations.

I invite you to go with me to several ITI classrooms to glimpse the ways in which the bodybrain-compatible elements work together to inform a teacher's choice of teaching strategies.

In practice the bodybrain-compatible elements overlap as teachers orchestrate the learning opportunities for their students. Since I can't actually take you to an ITI classroom, I'll present instead several descriptions of visits I've made.

ITI Classroom 1

The teacher greets each student personally as students enter the classroom to begin their day. Students check the "Morning Procedures" that the teacher posted, and carry them out in a business-like manner. One procedure is the reminder to greet one another with a smile, so the emotional climate quickly becomes friendly and inviting. Students move to tables designed for four-person learning teams, each one taking their three-ring binder used to collect and organize materials. While three students begin copying the daily agenda posted at the front of the room into the appropriate section of their binder, one delays long enough to water the green plant in the center of their table. Students seem to enjoy Vivaldi's "Four Seasons," a musical selection typical of the music frequently used in classrooms to create a calm, relaxed, but alert mood. The soft hum of voices and frequent, easy smiles indicate that students are happy to be there. One student is writing a target talk statement noting how a classmate used a particular "LIFESKILL" (see below). The full agenda creates a sense of anticipation about what is to come: aerobic warm-up, community circle, guest speaker, learning club posters summarizing new information from the speaker, review of skills for writing a thank-you note, drafting thank-you notes to speaker, inquiry work, and journal reflection about the day.

Strategies That Work With the Bodybrain Partnership

This vignette illustrates strategies that directly support *absence of threat* (personal greetings, morning procedures, daily agenda, baroque music, classroom meetings),* *collaboration* (students seated at four-person tables, shared classroom jobs, target talk), and the need for an *enriched environment* (plants on student tables, baroque music, plans for guest speaker). Knowing the central role of emotions in the learning process, ITI teachers use many strategies to provide the needed emotional climate for learning.

Experienced ITI teachers know how each teaching strategy they choose supports the biology of learning research.** In this case, the daily agenda provides the security of knowing what is coming throughout the day, and written procedures and directions make expectations clear. Classroom meetings and other positive classroom management strategies both prevent discipline problems and teach students to accept responsibility for their own behavior.*** Students are held to a very high standard of behavior that in turn allows them to relax and focus on learning. Students feel confident in the face of new challenges, knowing that they can often collaborate with peers to understand and to solve problems.

Of all the tools used to create a positive and productive classroom and school climate, the ITI "Lifelong Guidelines" and "LIFESKILLS" carry the most power for building community. They nourish respectful, caring teacher–student and student–student relationships that not only diminish classroom management distractions, but also open the door to long-term learning. The teacher of the 21st century must fully understand that teaching the personal and social skills necessary for successful collaboration in the classroom and beyond is not a luxury.**** It is critical to in-depth learning in the classroom and for citizenship and relationships as an adult.

Agreement about how individuals expect to be treated and treat others is a fundamental part of "growing" responsible citizens. The ITI Lifelong Guidelines and LIFESKILLS are guideposts for respectful human relationships. While we can only imagine the future our children and grandchildren will meet, we can prepare them with skills that transcend time and are a part of great human achievements.

---

* Here a general method (absence of threat) is being broken down into alternative kinds, each of which in turn could be done in very different ways. It is also possible, of course, to use more than one of the alternative kinds. What we don't see here is the specification of any situationalities for deciding which ones to use when. You can imagine the additional space needed to provide a detailed set of guidelines that would cover even just the major alternatives and the major considerations for their selection! An electronic performance support system might be able to provide an appropriate level of detail for different teachers and circumstances.

** Knowledge of such descriptive theory may help teachers decide which alternative methods to use when.

*** Hopefully, you noticed this as self-regulation. What other common features that I have pointed out in other chapters can you find here?

**** This concern for the whole child, including affective development, is a growing concern in the new paradigm, see especially chapters 21 (Lewis, Watson & Schaps) and 22 (Stone-McCown & McCormick).

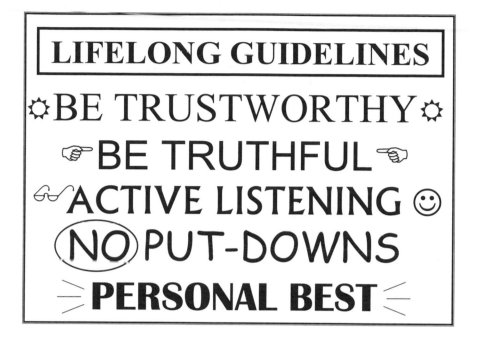

FIG. 16.3.   Lifelong guidelines.

Creating the ITI model has brought me much joy over the years, especially when collaborating with associates—bright and caring professionals. On one such occasion, I posed the question, "How do you wish to be treated by your spouse, other family members, and closest friends?" After brainstorming, categorizing, and paring down the list, the Lifelong Guidelines emerged; Fig. 16.3. Who wouldn't want to be in a relationship or work at a school where everyone agreed to such standards for interacting with one another? Consider how you feel when someone else listens with eyes, ears, heart, and undivided attention (the literal translation of the Chinese character for the verb "to listen"). Consider how you feel when you know that someone will not deliver a put-down. Consider how you feel when someone is always truthful and trustworthy. Finally, consider how you feel when you know that someone gives his or her personal best to an endeavor. Such feelings promote the positive emotional state that is essential for learning.

As time passed by, people asked me just what I meant by the term "personal best." To generate a more specific description, I worked with my associates to list the characteristics of people they respect and admire. The resulting LIFESKILLS (see Fig. 16.4) are the definition of "personal best."

LIFESKILLS

- **INTEGRITY:** To act according to what's right and wrong
- **INITIATIVE:** To do something because it needs to be done
- **FLEXIBILITY:** The ability to alter plans when necessary
- **PERSEVERANCE:** To keep at it
- **ORGANIZATION:** To work in an orderly way
- **SENSE OF HUMOR:** To laugh and be playful without hurting others
- **EFFORT:** To do your best
- **COMMON SENSE:** To think it through
- **PROBLEM-SOLVING:** To seek solutions
- **RESPONSIBILITY:** To do what's right
- **PATIENCE:** To wait calmly
- **FRIENDSHIP:** To make and keep a friend through mutual trust and caring
- **CURIOSITY:** To investigate and seek understanding
- **COOPERATION:** To work together toward a common goal (purpose)
- **CARING:** To show/feel concern
- **COURAGE:** To act according to one's beliefs
- **PRIDE:** Satisfaction from doing your personal best

FIG. 16.4.   ITI LIFESKILLS.

The Lifelong Guidelines and LIFESKILLS are essential ITI tools* leading to a bodybrain-compatible learning environment, but they also play another important role in ITI schools. They create the framework within which adults can describe for one another their personal and professional expectations. Based on agreements resulting from dialogue about the Lifelong Guidelines and LIFESKILLS, behaviors that undermine both respect and community disappear. Gone are behind-the-back conversations. Gone is the need to tone down one's performance to remain a part of the social group. Gone are side conversations and grading papers during dialogue at the faculty meeting. Gone are remarks that indicate to students that the work of some adults has more importance than the work of others as in, "Mrs. Smith is *only* a secretary."

Adults are the examples for students as they all work to create a bodybrain-compatible school. School becomes a joyful place for adults and youth when all agree to use the Lifelong Guidelines and LIFESKILLS as the standards for behavior. ITI is about personal respect.

ITI Classroom 2

It is a special day for these rural Virginia high school biology students: the day for exploring the nearby river and historic remains of a long-abandoned canal system. The teacher, the county extension agent, a member of the local historical society, and adult chaperones will join the teens as resources. The ITI teacher uses the trip to initiate a new unit of study, rather than the more traditional use for closure. Students are absorbed as they wear hip-waders, collect and analyze aquatic larvae and insects as clues to water quality, participate in a simulation to illustrate ecosystem dynamics, and hear stories about earlier human uses of the river and canal system. Even as I watch the videotape of these experiences, I can sense the curiosity and enthusiasm of the students. Cooperation and respect among all are very evident as nearly 100 students, who reflect a variety of ethnic and economic backgrounds, are making responsible behavior choices.

Strategies That Work With the Bodybrain Partnership

In this slice of life we see strategies that provide for *meaningful content* (selection of a nearby location for exploration, focus on field test to determine water quality, ecosystem simulation, stories by a local historian whom many students already know), *enriched environment* (situated in the outdoors where the richest sensory input is available, use of expert resource people, actual use of hip-waders), and *immediate feedback* (responsible choices lead to a safe experience, procedures for collecting aquatic life yield adequate numbers of specimen for water quality analysis, cooperating makes this an enjoyable experience). The decision to spend time in the river is the key here.

---

* Are the "Lifelong Guidelines" and "LIFESKILLS" curriculum theory or instructional theory?

Acting on the biology of learning means providing sensory input so that students understand and apply concepts. Being out in the world to explore is such a powerful strategy for enhancing all subsequent learning that it merits extra emphasis.

ITI INSTRUCTIONAL SEQUENCE

BEING THERE ⇒ CONCEPT ⇒ LANGUAGE ⇒ APPLICATION TO THE REAL WORLD

ITI curriculum begins with the real world: a nearby location or event that students can experience first-hand. This starting point offers significant advantages from the standpoint of the biology of learning. First, the human brain is designed to make sense of information coming into it through all 19 senses as identified by Rivlin and Gravelle (1984). Pattern recognition and conceptual development are based on sensory input. In the enriched environment of the park, the grocery, the city hall, or the river, the bodybrain pays attention and absorbs the setting as it processes thousands of bits of sensory data per minute. Out of each such experience for students come the conceptual capacity, language development, and possibility for application that we seek.

The teacher who launches a unit of study with a field trip and extends the learning through immersion experiences such as simulation and role play, reaps the rewards of watching students succeed. As ITI teachers consider ways to provide further input, they know that "being there" has the most power and that symbolic input, such as lecture without illustration, has the least. This hierarchy is illustrated in Fig. 16.5. They also know that reading about something after being there gives the words on the page added power.

Remember, intelligence is a function of experience. With limited relevant experiences to provide the neural "hooks," students whose only tools are textbooks and videotapes are left to memorize, take the test, and forget. Those who come to school with a rich set of experiences that relate to material in books and videos thus have a built-in advantage over those with limited experiences.

"Being there" experiences not only provide essential sensory input, they also are the beginning point for natural curriculum integration. Any location or event embodies all subject areas. For example, no location is devoid of math, science, or a sense of history. All have an element of aesthetics, and so on.

Think about everyday locations in the home. Say the bathroom needs new wallpaper. We may start with the family budget to establish project boundaries. We use mathematical principles when we measure and determine how many rolls to order. We rely on principles of design and color to make the best paper selection. And so it goes, from our idea through project completion, as each part of our prior knowledge plays a role when appropriate.

Another invaluable result of "being there" experiences is that they tend to build in immediate feedback as a natural part of the learning process. Students don't have

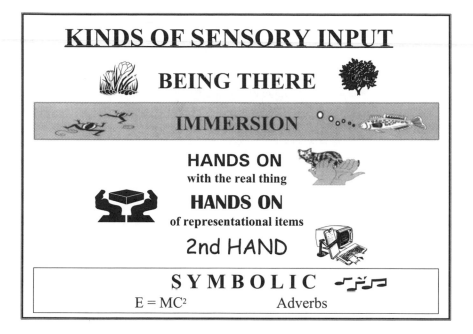

FIG. 16.5.   Kinds of sensory input.

to ask, "Teacher, is this right?" Exploring tidal pools as part of a yearlong theme featuring interdependence, a student asks if the bright-colored starfish he sees feels hard or soft to touch. The answer is immediate as the student reaches cautiously into the pool. Students conducting a population study in a mountain stream wonder if they will get the same kinds of aquatic insect life under rocks near the edge as in the swiftly running center. After collecting several samples from each location and documenting results, the answer emerges.

ITI students learn to trust their own observations. They become less dependent on teachers, textbooks, and quizzes to know that they are learning something worthwhile. Experience-rich students see connections, build confidence in their ability to solve problems, and make sensible predictions about what may happen next.

CURRICULUM DEVELOPMENT THAT WORKS
WITH THE BODYBRAIN PARTNERSHIP

ITI teachers begin with a location or event and the question most natural for their students, "What's going on here?" Many questions follow, varying with the age and prior experiences of both teacher and students.* Consider the local building supply

---

* Did you identify this as another situationality?

store. Where does the lumber come from? What kinds of lumber do people buy most? Who are the biggest customers and why? How does this business contribute to the local economy? How many people are employed here? Are most of the available products made in America? If some products are imported, from where? In what ways are computers used in this business? Who founded this business and when?

Locations that lead to essential learning goals as defined by district and state are favored, and teachers find that any setting when explored in depth requires knowledge from mathematics, the sciences, language arts, social studies, and other disciplines as they naturally arise. Teachers select those locations that best illustrate key concepts from the curriculum. The more adept the teacher and students become at posing and seeking answers to questions that reveal a rich understanding of the place, the more integrated the curriculum becomes. The inevitable "connectedness" of things is exposed in memorable ways.*

ITI Classroom 3

A fourth- and fifth-grade, multiage classroom accepts responsibility for running the school bank. They visit a nearby bank and invite bank employees fulfilling different roles to come to their class for follow-up questions. Students gather additional data about banking functions, practice writing checks and maintaining a balance, design a system for all students to establish savings accounts to accrue interest, learn how to obtain capital investment, find out how to reinvest deposited money, and set up a weekly schedule for classes to visit the school bank. Once they all recognize and understand the new patterns related to banking, they open a "practice" bank just for their own class using the forms and procedures they created. Finally, they are ready to apply their mental programs about banking and they open the school bank. Profits at the end of the year go to a local food bank, which extends the learning to include political/social action.

YEARLONG THEME (ORGANIZING CONCEPT)

Traditional teacher preparation too often doesn't include training in curriculum development. Thus, ITI implementation depends on substantial training, practice, and coaching with feedback.** Outstanding curriculum also depends on clear articulation of the important concepts and skills (patterns) students need to understand and apply (programs.)

The yearlong theme is a giant pattern with the power to serve as a mental organizer for everything studied during the year.*** It provides an "address" in the brain for processing and retaining the content of the entire year. Creating curriculum is a some-

---

* Exposing connectedness is a way of fostering systemic thinking. This is an important feature for the information-age paradigm. Is this instructional theory or curriculum theory?

** Again, we see that the new paradigm calls for new roles for teachers that require considerable professional development.

*** Themes may be serving a similar function to Schank, Berman & Macpherson's case (chap. 8).

what messy, nonlinear process consisting of four main activities: (a) select a physical location or event; (b) identify key points; (c) write inquiries and assessment strategies; and (d) create the yearlong theme.*

The organizing structures for the curriculum are the yearlong theme, monthly components, and weekly topics. Teachers understand, however, that components may take longer than a month and topics may take longer than a week when the goal is to ensure acquisition of new mental programs.** The theme is the core idea—the organizing concept for the year. Teachers must provide a solid rationale to explain why the theme is important and merits a year of study. Examples of such organizing concepts include change, interdependence, community, and the like. Topics are explored as students master the specified key points.

A key point is a clear, concise statement of a concept, significant knowledge, or skill that the teacher wants students to know and to be able to apply (Kovalik, 1997). It is a pattern critical for a full understanding of the selected physical location. *Conceptual key points* focus on big ideas that allow students to transfer their understanding to other locations or situations and make reasonable predictions. *Significant knowledge key points* provide specific information vital for a full understanding of the patterns embedded within the conceptual key point.*** Finally, *skill key points* ensure student mastery of requisite skills for applying the concepts.

Powerful key points are conceptual and bristle with pattern detection possibilities. In contrast, factoids (statements of fact with little or no context to give them meaning or a sense of usefulness) that have too often been the focus of textbook-driven curriculum offer little potential for detecting patterns because they are too narrow.

An example of each kind of key point illustrates the intent of each.

Conceptual key point: A system is a collection of parts and processes that interact to perform some function. To study a system, one must define its boundaries and parts.

Significant knowledge key point: A watershed is an example of a system that includes both living and nonliving parts. Its boundaries are the whole region from which a river receives its supply of water.

Skill key point: (To collect and share observations about the watershed.) There are various kinds of graphs that allow you to record data in ways that make it easier to interpret. Choose the form of graph that would best assist the reader to perceive and interpret the data that you most want him/her to analyze and understand.

---

* Note how different this is from the traditional ISD process (e.g., the Dick & Carey process).

** "Ensuring acquisition" is one of the most important aspects of the learning-focused instructional system (see chap. 1, pp. 19–21).

*** These are the kinds of learning that Gardner (chap. 4) and Perkins and Unger (chap. 5) focus on.

Common choices of graphs include: bar graphs, circle graphs, Venn circles, the simple column chart, and mindmaps.

ITI emphasizes creating in-depth understanding as opposed to "covering" material, so the curriculum includes fewer topics. "Less is more," I remind teachers, as they struggle with the need for *adequate time.** In our ethnically diverse country, a curriculum grounded in concepts identifies common themes, or so-called common ground, that we all need to understand as responsible citizens. It allows students to relate new knowledge to important ideas that are the bridges among the disciplines.

I can picture ITI students as adults making government and corporate policy. I strongly believe that the years of practice thinking about concepts and connections will lead them to decisions that consider both the part and the whole.** Our students need a broad understanding, not just cursory knowing. It gives me great hope to think that decisions grounded in a fuller understanding will in turn lead to a country that operates harmoniously at social, political, and economic levels. Now that is a goal that sustains my motivation as a teacher.

ITI Classroom 4

The teacher completes direct instruction about the habits of birds that students observed in a nearby sanctuary the previous week. Her instruction presents the content using musical, bodily-kinesthetic, spatial, and naturalist capacities as well as the usual linguistic. These fifth graders now eagerly examine an array of five different learning activities, or "inquiries," related to the new information. Each chooses an activity to do alone, with a partner, or with two others that will provide practice understanding and applying the new information. Students know about Gardner's eight intelligences, and recognize that their teacher created inquiries that represent four of them. All inquiries provide practice in applying the key concepts, information, or skills being learned. Students may select the inquiries that interest them most. They also know that choosing to work outside a strong area of intelligence can help to develop their ability to use that intelligence. Within about five minutes, students make their choices and the room has the busy sound of engaged learners.

Choices and Inquiries

Although teachers, with help from local, state, and national policymakers, are responsible for establishing what concepts, information, and skills students need to learn, students have latitude within those boundaries for significant choice about the specific examples they study and how the learning takes place.*** They can also choose to pursue as much learning beyond expectations as they wish. Giving learners choices is essential in a brain-compatible classroom and school; it provides

---

* Which other theories emphasize these points?

** Here, systemic thinking is viewed as an important goal (what to teach) in curriculum theory.

*** The element of choice about what to learn is related to self-regulated learning and is an important feature of many theories in the new paradigm.

students with practice directing their own learning, increases success, reduces frustration and boredom, applies and extends problem-solving and product-creating capacities, and enables students to handle new information according to their temperament.

Let's say that the curriculum in a high school class focuses on integrity. In ITI's "being there" environment, students can choose the areas that most spark their interest. For example, they could consider integrity issues faced by the mayor or city manager, by teachers, or by lawyers or doctors. Whatever their choices, the students are still studying integrity, and their work as individuals contributes simultaneously to the richness of their own and the community's understanding. Students and their teachers come together as a group to share what this concept means. Such dialogue enhances the capacity to understand the issue in the present and provides a meaningful perspective from which to view historical events.

Gardner's theory of multiple intelligences plays a key role in offering choice to ITI students as it strengthens mutual respect and provides additional rationale for frequent learner collaboration. Using Gardner's descriptions, we teach ITI students that humans display intelligent behavior in a variety of ways. They learn that each person has more and less developed intelligences that are not fixed, but flexible. Students thrive because they can choose how to get to the learning goal through several pathways.

Gone is the overused admonition to "read the chapter and answer the questions." Gone is the idea that a student will attain a new mental program after hearing "teacher talk" and doing just one related activity. Students may choose to do several inquiries that all focus on the same key point, and do so using different intelligences. Students from third grade on are frequently involved in developing inquiries for themselves and for classmates. Then the learning really gets exciting.

Inquiries are what students do to practice until they achieve mastery (mental program). They are the footbridge between the "what" of curriculum and demonstrations of mastery. They are the vehicle that carries learning from short- to long-term memory. Teachers write inquiries that sample Gardner's eight intelligences and use action verbs from all levels of Bloom's Taxonomy of Cognitive Objectives.

Returning to our watershed example, the following inquiries illustrate some of the possibilities for engaging the learner with the material presented in key points.

1. Using the topological map of our area, determine the boundaries of our watershed. Draw an 8.5" by 11" map to scale. Include our school, major roads, and a dozen other well-known reference points.
2. Working with a partner, walk at least 1 mile along the watershed. Observe carefully for examples of each part of the living system: fungi, bacteria, algae (or protista), plants, and animals. Tally the most commonly observed examples of each. Create at least one graph to represent your findings. Compare your graph(s) with those of two other partnership groups. Bring any differences of perspective back to the entire group for discussion.

3. With a partner, listen closely to the sounds around you. Identify rhythmic patterns and create a way to represent them for others. Be prepared to perform your sound patterns from the watershed for classmates and to identify if the sounds were produced by living or nonliving sources.

Once we accept, openly and without making judgments, that students possess differing strengths, we also realize that diverse groups have extraordinary strengths and advantages. For example, the learning group that prefers drawing to talking struggles to find its spokesperson while the group whose members represent strengths in linguistic, spatial, and musical intelligence revel in preparing a classroom presentation. Using the skills of the "artists" and the "talkers," old boundaries separating students fade away. Each group appreciates the other's special talents. The result is a strong, cohesive classroom community.*

OUTREACH: POLITICAL ACTION AND COMMUNITY SERVICE

Recently, a seventh-grade ITI teacher happily reported to me her students' mastery of persuasive writing. I smiled appreciatively, and then said, "Where are you taking it now? What is your outreach? What if your students created persuasive essays about why all seventh grades in America should use ITI? Put it on your Web page. Do the next step: use political/social action." She was eager to return to her students with a new and meaningful challenge.

It is commitment to community that makes a nation strong and the world safe. Discovering and developing strengths and talents brings huge rewards. But responsible educators know that beyond such development, teaching the commitment to give back what one has received must be learned at an early age. Each part of the curriculum must connect back to something bigger, something in the community. Ask yourself: "Where are you taking it?" and "How does it connect meaningfully to these important goals outside the school?"

For me, everything is about making the world a better place to live in. Each person's immediate world is the one where he or she lives each day: home, school, community, state. When we volunteer or serve on committees, we're making time to give back to the community. We must teach youngsters to do those things by providing examples in school. With ITI's being there experiences, our students literally see that they can make a difference, both now and in the future.

Have you ever participated in 4-H, Scouting programs, Indian Guides, Boys' and Girls' Clubs, or Bluebirds? In such organizations, knowledgeable adults share their understanding of how something in the immediate environment works. Before organizations such as these existed, the knowledgeable adult was the parent, grandparent, or extended family member. The younger generation learned what adults

---

* The idea of creating a community of learners is emphasized by a number of theories, including those in chapters 12 (Bielaczyc & Collins), 21 (Lewis, Watson & Schaps), and 22 (Stone-McCown & McCormick).

did by watching them and working side-by-side. In small towns and on farms the family's survival depended on each member's contribution, and that included the youngest as soon as they could do their part.

Today the work of adults is most often out of the view of children. We have even created a special day to take our children to work so that they begin to glimpse productive adult contributions. Once a year is not enough. In response, many schools design on-going job shadowing, mentorships, and apprentice experiences to try to re-establish the connection between what students do in schools and what adults do in life.*

Our children are cut off from the sense that their work has meaning for the family and the community. Too often they are left with the frivolous and the unimportant. However, we can do something about that through the school's curriculum.

I believe strongly that young people have to realize at an early age that their actions make a difference now and that, based on the decisions they make, the difference can be positive or negative. ITI schools embrace positive social/political action and community service projects so that students learn they can make a difference right now and that it is rewarding to do so. We must "hook" them young on responsible citizenship by providing appropriate being there experiences.

In most cases, political/social action and community service provide the student with both a context and a real audience. They provide multiple ways to apply new knowledge and skills, demonstrating mastery and significance.

Examples from ITI classes include:

- An elementary class studying ecosystems and waste management designed and implemented a school-based recycling plan.
- A middle school class held successful fundraisers to benefit their counterparts in Slovakia, and another provided funds for a refugee family from Bosnia now in their community.
- A high school class adopted a section of highway which they proudly kept free of litter.
- A middle school class adopted the residents of a nearby retirement home as grandparents.
- A high school geometry class redesigned a dangerous interstate ramp, shared their ideas with local decisionmakers, and witnessed construction based on their ideas.
- Sixth grade students read with and provided tutoring for younger students, and helped them to write and illustrate original books to delight their fancy.

Our schools and communities face endless challenges, and the younger generation is full of ideas, creativity, and energy to help address them. When they do, our

---

* This is an increasingly common focus for instructional theory as well. In fact, design theories (guidelines) are needed for how to design these kinds of experiences to be optimally effective.

students learn that they have the personal power to make a difference now, a critical disposition of the responsible citizens we need.

The skills and attitudes of responsible citizenship do not spring forth magically at one's 18th birthday; rather, they require years of meaningful practice. School is about meaning for today, and preparation for the future.

ASSESSMENT IN ITI

There are two levels of documenting mastery: the teacher's mastery of the ITI model and the student's mastery of the curriculum. In the case of the teacher, we know that appropriate training must be followed by coaching and feedback. ITI teachers select their own goals and assess progress within the ITI model based on the ITI classroom rubric. Stage 1 of the rubric (Fig. 16.6) is provided to illustrate the many choices teachers have. Stage 1 may take one year or several to master, depending on the teacher's prior experience and the context in which he or she is working.

For students mastering the curriculum, ITI educators design strategies through which students show that they have mastered a new mental program.* The teacher's best inquiry can also be the best assessment instrument. Beyond the limits of paper-and-pencil tests, such activities require students to apply the knowledge they have gained in a real-world setting. Sometimes such a demonstration becomes a form of political or social action, as previously discussed.

CONCLUSION

Bodybrain-compatible curriculum and instructional strategies match our human biology and thus our personal learning experiences. At the heart of the matter, we must have the courage to ask and answer:

1. What kinds of people do we want to be?
2. What kinds of people do we want our neighbors to be?
3. What kinds of people do we want our children to be?
4. What specific commitment by parents, schools, and community does it take for our children to become such people?

Remember, great work is its own reward. Students must "get hooked" on a sense of how important their lives are and how important their participation is. Our children must see their community, including their school, as a home base. I want them to walk down the street or the hallway saying, "I belong here and I feel safe. I know

---

* Student evaluation in the new paradigm is focused on ensuring and documenting mastery, rather than comparing students with each other, for example, by grading on a curve, which tells you nothing about what they actually know and can do.

ITI Rubric Stage 1

Stage 1—Entry level for making the learning environment brain-compatible

CURRICULUM	INSTRUCTIONAL STRATEGIES	EXPECTATIONS	INDICATIONS
The elements of absence of threat are taught as an important and on-going part of the curriculum: Lifelong Guidelines, including the LIFESKILLS, the triune brain, problem solving and product-producing using the seven intelligences, and collaboration.	The teacher's classroom leadership and management is based upon modeling the lifelong Guidelines and LIFESKILLS. "Discipline" is based upon helping students develop personal skills and behaviors needed to successfully practice the Lifelong Guidelines rather than upon a system of externally imposed rewards and punishments.	Absence of threat has been established in the classroom.	Post-lesson processing about academic or collaborative experiences occurs daily.
		Students are beginning to take responsibility for their own behavior through the use of LIFESKILLS.	Decline in classroom and schoolwide discipline problems
	The calmness of the teacher's voice contributes to a settled classroom environment.	An atmosphere of mutual respect and genuine caring is obvious among and between students and adults. Students do not put each other down; their behaviors with each other support absence of threat.	Differences in student engagement when real life experiences are provided are obvious to teacher and parents.
	The classroom is healthful (clean, well lighted, and pleasant smelling), aesthetically pleasing (calming colors and music, living plants, well laid out for multiple uses), and uncluttered yet reflects what is being learned.	Students demonstrate collaborative skills, e.g., active listening, taking turns, and respect for other's opinions.	
	Written procedures and agendas provide consistency and security for students.		Teacher includes student input when selecting work for the student's portfolio folder.
Time frames for activities and areas of study are no longer rigid and students are given adequate time to complete their work.	Students sit in clusters with easy access to work tools; collaborative learning is a frequently used learning strategy.	Students focus their attention on learning as soon as they enter the classroom.	
	Teacher is developing a variety of instructional strategies to supplement direct instruction.	Lack of self-directedness and responsibility for learning has been replaced by a student focus on school as a safe and pleasant place to learn and grow; there is a growing sense of calm and openness.	
	Teacher includes real life experiences—being there, immersion, and hands-on experiences—to supplement classroom instruction; resource people are invited to the classroom.	Parents understand the purpose and research behind brain-compatible education and are supportive of the teacher's efforts.	
	Limited choices are introduced through student selection of supplies, time allocations, mediums used for completing projects, etc.	Parents notice evidence of LIFESKILLS at home.	
	Teacher meets frequently with a professional or peer coach who supports the implementation of a brain-compatible learning environment for students.	Teacher confidence and enjoyment in teaching increases.	

FIG. 16.6. ITI Rubric Stage 1.

and I am known. I am proud to be the person I am known to be." They must see that they can make a contribution and that their contribution is needed and valued.

REFERENCES

Begley, S. (1997, Spring/Summer). How to build a baby's brain. *Newsweek,* 28–32.

Calvin, W. (1996). *How brains think.* New York: Basic Books.

Diamond, M. (1998). *Magic trees of the mind.* New York: Dutton.

Gardner, H. (1983). *Frames of mind: Theory of multiple intelligences.* New York: Basic Books.

Goleman, D. (1995). *Emotional intelligence.* New York: Bantam Books.

Hart, L. A. (1983). *Human brain and human learning.* Kent, WA: Books for Educators.

Jung, C. (1976). Psychological Types. In R. F. C. Hull (Ed.), *Collected works of C. G. Jung, Vol. 6.,* Princeton, NJ: Princeton University Press.

Keirsey, D., & Bates, M. (1984). *Please understand Me: Character and temperament types.* Del Mar, CA: Prometheus Nemesis Books.

Kovalik, S., with Olsen, K. (1997). *ITI: The model* (3rd ed.). Kent, WA: Susan Kovalik & Associates.

LeDoux, J. (1996). *The emotional brain: The mysterious underpinnings of emotional life.* New York: Simon and Schuster.

MacLean, P. (1990). *The triune brain in evolution.* New York: Plenum.

Myers, I. (1956). *The Myers-Briggs type indicator.* Palo Alto, CA: Consulting Psychologists Press.

Perkins, D. (1995). *Outsmarting I.Q.: The emerging science of learnable intelligence.* New York: The Free Press.

Pert, C. (1997). *Molecules of emotion.* New York: Scribner.

Rivlin, R., & Gravelle, K. (1984). *Deciphering your senses.* New York: Simon and Schuster.

Ross, A., & Olsen, K. (1995). *The way we were ... The way we can be. A vision for the middle school through integrated thematic instruction.* Kent, WA: Susan Kovalik & Associates.

Sylwester, R. (1995). *A celebration of neurons.* Alexandria, VA: Association for Supervision and Curriculum Development (ASCD).

17

Instructional Transaction Theory (ITT): Instructional Design Based on Knowledge Objects

M. David Merrill
Utah State University

M. David Merrill

M. David Merrill is a professor in the Department of Instructional Technology at Utah State University and director of the ID$_2$ Research Group. He also served on the faculty of George Peabody College, Brigham Young University, Stanford University, and University of Southern California. He was a founder and principal of Anderson Consulting Courseware, Inc. (1972-1980), MicroTeacher, Inc. (1981-1985), and River Park Instructional Technologies, L.L.C. (1996-1997). He is author or co-author of 12 books, 20 book chapters, more than 200 articles and technical reports, and more than 25 instructional products. He has been a major contributor to the TICCIT authoring system in the 1970s, component display theory and elaboration theory in the 1980s, and instructional transaction theory and ID based on knowledge objects in the 1990s.

FOREWORD

Goals and preconditions. *ITT is intended to foster almost any kind of learning in the cognitive domain, though this chapter focuses on just a few kinds of learning. No preconditions are identified.*

Values. *Some of the values upon which this theory is based include:*
- *efficient learning process (via carefully defined learning strategies),*
- *efficient instructional design process through automation,*
- *efficient simulation design through automation,*
- *combining simulations with tutorial instruction,*
- *the power of exploration with guidance,*
- *adapting instruction to individual students in real time as their needs change during learning.*

Methods. *Here are the major methods this theory offers:*
Present the goal of the instruction
Provide an open-ended learning environment
- *Simulation*
  - *Diagram*
  - *Learner can perform any action possible in the real-world environment*
  - Learner can reverse any action
"Identify" transaction: for learning the name, location, and function of parts of a device:
- *Presentation*
  - *Explore the names, Explore the functions,*
  - *Tell me about the parts (name, location, function)*
- *Practice*
  - *Let me locate the parts, Let me name the parts,*
  - *Let me identify the functions of the parts*
- *Immediate feedback*
- *Score*
- *Sampling with replacement*
"Execute" transaction: for learning to perform a procedure:
- *Hands-off demonstration (action - consequence)*
- *Practice*
  - *Simon says (direction - consequence), Do the next step (consequence),*
  - *You do it (consequence)*
- *Feedback*
- *Guidance*
  - *Progression of practice from highly guided to unguided*
  - *Provide explanations (what happened, why)*

"Interpret" transaction: for learning to explain, predict, trouble-shoot:
- *Presentation*
  - *Exploration: explain (what happened, why it happened)*
- *Practice*
  - *Predict (what happens next, why), Trouble-shoot (fault, what happened, why)*
- *Control panel (set conditions to attain a consequence)*
- *Guidance*
- *Explanation (what caused the consequence)*

(The above represent but three of the 13 kinds of instructional transactions identified so far by this theory)
Adapt the instruction to the learner and allow learner choices during instruction

Major contributions. *Greatly reduces the time it takes to design and develop instruction. Is based on proven principles of instruction. Deals with many kinds of learning (in addition to the ones describe in this chapter).*

—C.M.R.

Instructional Transaction Theory (ITT): Instructional Design Based on Knowledge Objects

INTRODUCTION

Purpose

Component Display Theory (CDT, see Merrill, 1983, 1987; Merrill with Twitchell, 1994) provides a list of prescriptions for designing instruction for different kinds of instructional outcomes. As we moved toward trying to automate the instructional-design process, we found that CDT was not precise enough to allow computer implementation of expert system technology that would prescribe instruction. Instructional Transaction Theory (ITT) is an attempt to provide more precision to CDT, thereby making automated instructional design a possibility. This increased precision also has value for instructional-designers in that it provides a more precise way to describe knowledge representation, instructional strategies, and instructional design prescriptions.

CDT was an attempt to identify the components from which instructional strategies could be constructed. CDT describes instructional strategy in terms of strategy components: *primary presentation forms* (PPFs), *secondary presentation forms* (SFPs), and *interdisplay relationships* (IDRs). CDT identifies strategy prescriptions for different kinds of learning outcomes. Each of these prescriptions identifies a best-case combination of PPFs, SFPs, and IDRs for a particular kind of learning outcome. CDT was analysis oriented, emphasizing the components of instructional strategies for different kinds of instructional goals.

ITT is synthesis oriented, emphasizing the integration of these components into instructional transactions.* An instructional transaction is all of the interactions necessary for a student to acquire a particular kind of knowledge or skill.

The presentation of ITT in this chapter emphasizes what Reigeluth calls *component methods.*** In this paper we will introduce a methodology for representing knowledge in the form of knowledge objects and elements (slots) of knowledge objects. Knowledge objects and their elements provide the components of subject-matter content (knowledge). ITT describes instructional strategy as methods (algorithms) for manipulating the elements of knowledge objects.

Instructional Theory

Instructional theory is concerned with two primary considerations: What to teach and how to teach.

What to teach has two considerations: selection and representation. ITT is not concerned with the curriculum selection question of what should be taught, but rather, having selected what should be taught, what are the knowledge components required for a given type of instruction? And how should these knowledge components be represented to facilitate instructional design?

How to teach specifies the way that these knowledge components are presented to the student in order to engage the student in an interaction which is appropriate for promoting the acquisition of the knowledge or skill that is the goal of the instruction. Instructional strategies include the presentation of the appropriate knowledge components, practice with or student activities involving these knowledge components, and learner guidance to facilitate the student's appropriate interaction with these knowledge components.

The Computer Program Assumption

Authoring systems for computer-based instruction are based on a database model of computing. The student is presented with a record containing subject-matter

---

* This more holistic orientation is one change that moves this theory more squarely into the new paradigm. But another more important one is discussed later (p. 404).

** See chapter 1, p. 10.

content (a program frame). The program then presents the student with one of several options: press a key to see the next record; select an item from a menu to see the next record; or respond to a question and the next record will be determined based on the answer given. This model of instructional computing has one serious limitation: except for the branching strategy, all other instructional strategies are hidden in the record (frame) and therefore transparent (not available) to the instructional system for additional processing. The instructional strategies to be used must be determined by the designer of the system and incorporated within the records of the database.

Outside of instruction many computer programs are based on an algorithmic model. In this model data are manipulated by one or more sets of instructions for processing (displaying, transforming) these data. If the knowledge to be taught is thought to be data, and the strategies for teaching this knowledge are thought to be instructional algorithms, then an algorithmic model of computing can also be applied to instruction. However, an algorithmic instructional system requires that the knowledge be accessible in a form that lends itself to processing by the instructional algorithms. A primary focus of ITT is to describe such a knowledge representation system.

ITT is an algorithmic instructional system. Knowledge is represented as data. The components of this knowledge are processed (displayed, transformed) by the instructional algorithms built into an instructional system. While this representation was specifically designed to facilitate the design of computer-based instruction, this form of representation also has value for designing instruction for other modes of delivery.

The Gagné Assumption

Gagné (1965, 1985) stated as a primary assumption of instructional theory that there are different kinds of learning outcomes (learning goals) and that each of these different kinds of learning outcomes requires unique conditions for learning. An appropriate instructional strategy incorporates all of the necessary conditions for presenting the knowledge or demonstrating the skill, providing practice with feedback, and providing learner guidance for a given type of learning outcome. Gagné indicated nine events of instruction which include these three phases of instruction. Appropriate conditions for learning always require all of these activities. Information that does not include presentation, practice, and learner guidance is information but not instruction. Different instructional outcomes (objectives) require different types of presentation, different types of practice, and different kinds of learner guidance.* It is this difference in the required conditions for learning that distinguishes different kinds of learning outcomes.

---

* The situationality here is a kind of instructional outcome.

In previous papers we have called an instructional strategy that incorporates all of the conditions for teaching a given type of learning an instructional transaction.[1] We previously identified 13 classes of instructional transactions (Merrill, Jones, & Li, 1992). In this paper we shall describe only three of these classes in terms of instructional algorithms for processing the elements of knowledge objects. These instructional transactions include: IDENTIFY[2] (component or naming or parts-of ..., also related to "facts" in CDT); EXECUTE (activity or procedures or how-to ... , "procedures" in CDT), and INTERPRET (process or what-happens ... , "principles" in CDT).*

Instructional Transactions

In ITT an instructional transaction is all of the learning interactions necessary for a student to acquire a particular kind of knowledge or skill (learning goal). The instructional algorithm (called an instructional transaction shell) required to promote an appropriate instructional transaction operates on a set of knowledge objects that are related in a particular way (knowledge structure) and that contain all of the knowledge that is required for a student to acquire the instructional goal. An instructional transaction algorithm includes the presentation strategies, the practice strategies, and the learner guidance strategies that are required and appropriate to promote acquisition of the instructional goal.

In ITT, instructional strategies represent various ways to show, or request the student to provide, the elements of knowledge objects. Hence, an instructional strategy is an algorithm for processing the knowledge data (elements) of knowledge objects.

Knowledge Objects

Knowledge objects are containers consisting of compartments (slots) for different related elements of knowledge. The framework of a knowledge object is the same for a wide variety of different topics within a subject domain, or for different subject domains. The contents of a given compartment differ, but the nature of the knowledge element in a given compartment is the same.

All knowledge objects have a set of information slots including: name, portrayal, and description. The name contains one or more symbols or terms that reference the knowledge. The portrayal is one or more multimedia objects (text, audio, video, graphic, animation) that will show or represent the knowledge object to the

---

[1]Previous papers on ITT describe some of the ideas presented in this paper. (See Li & Merrill, 1990; Merrill, Li, & Jones, 1991, 1992; Merrill, Jones, & Li, 1992; Merrill and ID$_2$ Research Team, 1993, 1996). In ITT our focus has shifted from an emphasis on displays (expository and inquisitory instances, expository and inquisitory generalities) to an emphasis on knowledge representation via the elements of knowledge objects.

[2]We used the terms IDENTIFY, EXECUTE, and INTERPRET in order to relate these transactions to our previous paper (Merrill, Jones, & Li, 1992).

* How might these be similar to the kinds of mental operations that Landa talks about in chapter 15?

student. The description slot is an open compartment into which an author can place any desired information about the knowledge object. It is possible for the description slot to be subdivided into several subslots. These might include function, purpose, etc., and may be defined by a given user.

We have identified four types of knowledge objects: entities, properties, activities, and processes.[3] (See Jones, Li, & Merrill, 1990.) Entities represent objects in the world and can include devices, persons, creatures, places, symbols, etc. Properties represent quantitative or qualitative attributes of entities. Activities represent actions that the learner can take to act on objects in the world. Processes represent events that occur in the world that change the values of properties of an entity. Processes are triggered by activities or by other processes.

A knowledge object may also have links to other knowledge objects. The nature of these links will be described in more detail in later sections of this paper.

Goals of ITT

Effective instruction.   First, we are concerned with the current emphasis on information and the lack of emphasis on appropriate instructional strategies. By describing instructional strategies as algorithms (transactions) for manipulating data structures (knowledge objects), we have provided a much more precise description of the different kinds of instructional transactions required for different kinds of instructional outcomes (goals or objectives). Our hope is that this formulation will enable instructional designers to design more effective and appealing instructional products. Furthermore, by building these transactions into instructional development tools, there is an increased probability that the resulting instructional interactions will be based on sound principles of instructional design.*

Efficient instructional development.   Second, our intent was to derive theory and methodology which would facilitate the automation of much of the instructional-design process. Instructional development is a labor-intensive industry. If we are to obtain efficiencies in the development of large amounts of computer-based, interactive, multimedia instruction then we must significantly increase our design and development efficiency. We believe that building appropriate instructional transactions into instructional development tools will enable automat-

---

[3]There is not a one-to-one relationship between the content categories of CDT (facts, concepts, procedures, and principles) and the types of knowledge objects in ITT (entities, activities, processess, and properties). There is not a one-to -one relationship between the performance categories of CDT and the transaction types of ITT. *Remember fact* from CDT is related, but not the same, as the IDENTIFY transaction in ITT. *Remember procedure* and *use procedure* from CDT is related to the EXECUTE transaction of ITT. *Remember principle* and *use principle* from CDT are related to the INTERPRET transaction of ITT.

* This is perhaps the ultimate form of electronic performance support system for applying an instructional theory.

ing portions of the instructional-design process and will enable us to realize this efficiency.*

Instructional learning environments.   Third, the development of interactive learning environments (instructional simulations and microworlds) is extremely labor intensive and hence very expensive to develop using existing technologies. Representing knowledge as knowledge objects enables the building of a general-purpose simulation engine. This makes possible a learning environment builder that enables the efficient development of these more effective instructional interactions. Furthermore, since tutorial instruction and learning environments are based on the same knowledge representation, this architecture enables effective learner guidance to overlay instructional learning environments.

Adaptive instruction.   Fourth, ambiguous representation of knowledge and imprecise specification of instructional strategies has hindered the development of truly adaptive instruction. The precise representation of knowledge in the form of knowledge objects and the representation of instructional transactions as algorithms for manipulating this knowledge makes possible instructional strategies that can be adapted to individual learners in real time as they interact with the instructional materials.**

Scope of ITT

The component methods of ITT can be used to describe any instructional strategy, whether tutorial or experiential. The component methods of ITT have been used to implement technical training as well as *soft skill* training. These methods lend themselves easily to instruction in *well/structured domains*. However, these same methods can be applied to *ill/structured domains.*[4] A detailed explanation of how these methods are applied to soft skills and ill/structured domains is beyond the scope of this chapter.

We previously identified 13 classes of instructional transactions (Merrill, Jones, & Li, 1992). These instructional transactions are listed in Table 17.1. ITT has been used to implement the component transactions: IDENTIFY, EXECUTE, and INTERPRET. An instance of this implementation is described in this chapter. We

---

* By analogy, this may be the equivalent of the first electronic spreadsheet program.

** This ability to, in essence, design instruction for individual learners "in real time as they interact with the instructional materials," is the feature that not only places this theory within the new paradigm, but also makes it one of the most exciting lines of work currently under development.

[4]The Instructional Simulator was used to develop an anthropology study of an African village ("Life in a Mende Village"). This learning environment enabled the student to go to different locations in the village and to converse with villagers in order to gather information about their agriculture and lifestyle. At the conclusion of the study the student submitted a report to the Humanitarian Council. The simulation engine, PEAnet architecture, and learner guidance described later in this chapter for the "Valve Simulation" were all used in this simulation of an ill-structured domain.

designed implementations for some of the abstraction transactions, but only demonstration systems have been implemented. We believe we can also implement the association transactions with knowledge objects and ITT methods.

The transactions for IDENTIFY, EXECUTE, and INTERPRET are building blocks for abstraction and association transactions. All instruction involves acquisition of the knowledge and skills promoted by these fundamental transactions. These transactions account for the instructional strategies found in most of the existing instruction in training.

REFERENCE EXAMPLE[5]

In this presentation we will emphasize instructional goals for IDENTIFY, EXECUTE, and INTERPRET transactions. The example presented for illustration has as a primary goal learning a procedure. In support of this goal the learning environment includes guidance for learning the function and location of the parts of a device. Also in support of the procedural goal, the learning environment includes guidance for learning to predict consequences and trouble-shooting unexpected

TABLE 17.1

Thirteen Classes of Instructional Transactions

Component Transactions	
IDENTIFY:	name and remember information about parts of an entity
EXECUTE:	remember and do steps in an activity
INTERPRET:	remember events and predit causes in a process
Abstraction Transactions	
JUDGE:	order instances
CLASSIFY:	sort instances
GENERALIZE:	group instances
DECIDE:	select among alternatives
TRANSFER:	apply steps or events to a new situation
Association Transactions	
PROPAGATE:	acquire one set of skills in the context of another set of skills
ANALOGIZE:	acquire steps of an activity, or events of a process, by likening to a different activity or process
SUBSTITUTE:	extend one activity to learn another activity
DESIGN:	invent a new activity
DISCOVER:	discover a new process

---

[5]The learning environment described was developed using the Instructional Simulator™ an instructional development tool developed by Drake, the present author, and other members of the ID₂ Research Group at Utah State University. (See Merrill & ID₂ Research Team, 1993; Merrill, 1997). More information about this instructional development tool is available from the ID₂ Research Team World Wide Web site: www.id2.usu.edu.

consequences by identifying the underlying conditions which must be satisfied before a given consequence can occur.

Fig. 17.1 illustrates a learning environment designed to teach the learner how to install or remove a double seat valve. This instruction was prepared to train technicians who must maintain valves in dairies and breweries.

Prior to entering the learning environment, the learner is given the following goal: "This work task involves properly disconnecting all hoses and wires from the valve and correctly unbolting and removing the valve insert from the pipeline."

The learning environment consists of a diagram of the valve showing all of the hoses and wires connected to the valve. The learning environment is an "open-ended learning environment".[6]* Clicking on a given part of the diagram brings up an action menu. For example, clicking on the switch brings up a menu with the action *flip*. Selecting this action causes the switch to change positions

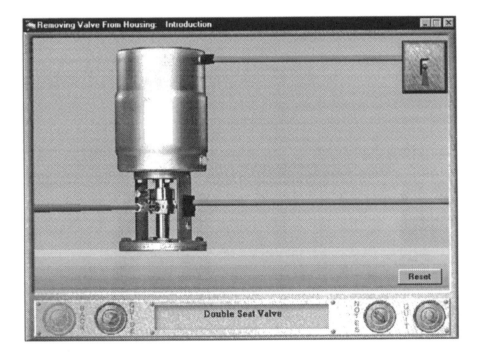

FIG. 17.1.   Learning environment for valve removal simulation.

---

[6]An open-ended learning environment is one in which the learner can perform any of a number of actions in any order and see their consequence. A constrained learning environment often enables the learner to perform only a single action at any moment in time.

*How does the meaning of this term differ from that of Hannafin, Land, and Oliver in chapter 6?

(down to up) and produces an audible click. This action also has the consequence of setting a property of the compressor to *off*. Clicking on the connector for the air hose brings up the action *undo*, which when selected disconnects the air hose from the valve. Hoses and wires can be connected and disconnected at will except as constrained by the conditions of the system. An example of a constraint is that you cannot disconnect the air hose until the compressor is off. By exploring the system, most learners can eventually figure out how to disconnect the valve and remove it from the pipe.

The learning environment is supported by learner guidance of various types. This learner guidance implements various instructional strategies designed to teach the student knowledge about the valve and the skill of removing the valve from the pipe.

Part Location, Function, and Naming

The goal of this learner guidance function is to teach the student the name, location, and function of the various parts of the valve. As the student moves the cursor about the learning environment, the name of the part under the cursor is shown in the window at the bottom of the screen. The window currently shows the name "Double Seat Valve." Thus, by moving the cursor around the screen the student can "explore" the names of the various parts of the valve.

Clicking on the right button of the mouse causes a functional description to appear in a pop-up window near the part under the cursor. For example, right clicking on the air connection brings up the illustration and scrolling description illustrated in Fig. 17.2. Note that the functional description in this system could be any medium including graphic, video, audio, text, or a combination. The authors chose to use a picture and text caption. The student can thus "explore" the function of each part of the device.

Clicking on the "Guide" button on the control panel at the bottom of the screen pops up a menu of guidance options. One option is "Tell me about some of the parts." Selecting this guidance causes a "lecture" to be provided about the parts of the system. The guide presents the same type of information as shown in Fig. 17.2 for each part in turn. The student has control over the pace of the lecture by indicating when they are ready for the next part to be presented.

Another guide option is, "Let me locate the parts." The guide then presents a name of a part and the student is required to point to (click when the cursor is over) the part. Another guide option is, "Let me name the parts." The guide highlights a part and the learner is required to select the correct name from a list. Another guide option is, "Let me identify the functions." The guide presents a description of a part and the student must click on the corresponding part. Right/wrong/correct answer feedback is provided after each response. These practice activities incorporate sampling with replacement such that when a student misses an item, it is put back into the list and presented to the student again until the student has correctly responded

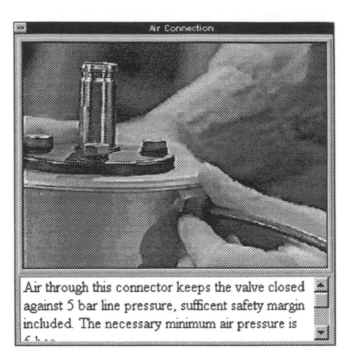

FIG. 17.2.   Functional description of a part of the valve.

to each part. At the end of a practice exercise the student is given a score indicating how many tries were required to correctly name, locate, or identify the function of each part.*

One of the goals of ITT is to enable an instructional development system to automatically generate appropriate instruction. In the Instructional Simulator the instructional strategies (presentation and practice) are built into the system. The designer merely describes the knowledge objects, and the system automatically generates these presentation and practice strategies.

Procedure Learning

Given enough time, most students can eventually discover the procedure for removing the valve from the pipe. However, "raw discover" is inefficient and often results in a trial-and-error approach to the performance in the real world. Procedure learn-

---

* Clearly, the learner has much control over the kinds of instructional methods (i.e., the learner can customize the instruction to their particular needs and preferences). But how can you ensure the learner will make wise decisions? This is addressed later in this chapter.

ing is more efficient when appropriate learner guidance is provided. The goal of procedure learning in this learning environment is to learn the necessary and sufficient steps for removing and replacing the valve in the pipe.

The guide provides four levels of procedure practice. Level 1 is a "hands-off" demonstration. In this demonstration the guide performs each of the steps in turn. The cursor moves to the appropriate part, the appropriate action is indicated, the guide then performs the appropriate action, and the system illustrates the consequence of this action. Level 2 is a "Simon Says" demonstration/simulation. In this demonstration the guide tells the student the step to perform. For example, "Flip the air compressor switch." If the student attempts to do any other action the guide presents a message such as, "That is not the air compressor switch." Thus the student can only perform the step requested by the guide. After the student has selected the action, the system illustrates the consequence of that action.

Level 3 is a "Do the next step" simulation. In this practice the guide presents the message, "Do the next step." If the student attempts to do a different step, the guide presents a hint such as "That is not the air compressor switch." After the student has selected the action, the system illustrates the consequence of that action.

Level 4 is "performance" or "You-do-it" simulation. In this practice the student can perform any of the steps in the procedure and see the consequence of this step subject to the constraints of the system (that is, some steps cannot be performed until a prior step has been completed. For example, you cannot remove the valve until you have removed the flange bolts, inserted a bolt in the tap hole to break the seal, and removed the bolt from the tap hole). When the student believes the procedure has been completed, he or she clicks a "finished" button. The guide then shows the steps required for the shortest path to the goal and also shows the steps taken by the student. Unnecessary or incorrect steps in the student's path are highlighted in red. The number of steps required by the student to accomplish the goal is recorded in the student record.

ITT knowledge objects enable all of these levels of practice to be built into the system. The designer merely provides the elements of the knowledge objects required by the simulation, and the system automatically creates the various levels of practice available in the system. The designer or learner can select some or all of these levels of practice for a given learning environment.

Explanation, Prediction, and Trouble-Shooting

It is one thing to learn the steps in a performance and to be able to carry them out in order to accomplish some goal (such as removing a valve from a pipe). However, when learners have an explanation of each step in the procedure that identifies what happened and why it happened, their ability to retain the procedural skill is enhanced. In addition, knowing what happened and why is necessary to problem solving or trouble-shooting a device or system. What happened indicates the consequence of a given action. Often, what happened can be observed by the student in changes in the appearance of the system. In some cases what happened may change a condition of the system which does not show up in the physical appearance of the system. Why indicates the conditions which must be met for a given consequence to occur. When a student performs an action and nothing happens or something unexpected happens, then an explanation indicates what conditions were not met or what conditions led to the unexpected consequence. The goal of explanation is to enable the learner to "predict" what will happen under specified conditions, or to "explain" (identify the conditions which were not met, often called trouble-shooting) when a consequence fails to occur or when an unexpected consequence occurs.

The guide provides three levels of explanation. One guidance option is "Explain." During free exploration of the system the student can request an explanation after any action. The guide presents a description of what just happened and why it happened. For example, the student attempts to remove the valve. Nothing happens. The student requests an explanation. The guide provides the following message: "When you attempt to remove the valve from the pipe nothing happens. This is because the flange bolt is still in the tap hole." The "Explain" function can also be turned on during any of the practice levels. The "Explain" display is updated after each action by the student.

A second guidance option is "Predict." The guide configures the system and asks the student to select from a list "What happens next?" and "Why?" The student can then confirm his or her prediction by executing the next step(s) in the procedure and observing what happens. The student's accuracy in prediction is recorded by the system.

A third guidance option is "Trouble-Shoot." The guide configures the system, sometimes introducing a fault. The student is requested to carry out the next step(s) in the procedure and to explain "what happened" and "why." In this situation the student, rather than the guide, provides the explanation. The student selects what happened and why from a list of consequences and conditions.

ITT knowledge objects make it possible for the designer of a learning environment which includes an explanation system to instantiate (provide information for) the elements of the knowledge objects required for the simulation, and the system will automatically generate the various levels of explanation.*

INSTRUCTIONAL TRANSACTIONS

In the following paragraphs we first describe a learning environment. A learning environment is described in terms of (a) the instructional goal it is designed to promote; (b) the knowledge structure required by the learning environment; (c) the

---

* Again, these options can be used in such a way that the learner chooses the methods, or the system could make the choices for the learner based on certain learner characteristics or the learner's history of performance. This allows truly customized instruction in a very cost-effective manner.

general simulation engine which operates on this knowledge structure to represent activities and processes that occur in the world; and (d) the learning activity of exploration by which the student interacts with the learning environment.

In each of the subsequent sections we define the instructional transactions of IDENTIFY, EXECUTE, and INTERPRET. In each of these sections we describe (a) the instructional goal promoted by the instructional transaction; (b) the knowledge structure required by this kind of transaction; (c) the presentation of information to the student; (d) the practice with feedback required by the transaction; and (e) learner guidance that facilitates learning from the transaction.

Learning Environment

Goal

The goal of a learning environment is to enable the student to explore some device or setting. The objects in the environment behave in a way similar to their behavior in the real world. Students are able to act on objects in the environment and see the consequences of their actions. An open-ended learning environment allows free exploration within the constraints of the learning environment. So-called simulations that allow only a single action and are constrained as to the path that the student must take are merely interactive demonstrations, not learning environments.

Knowledge Structure

For learning environments a knowledge object for an entity is expanded to include slots that point to one or more property knowledge objects. A property knowledge object, in addition to a name and a description, has a set of possible values. Each of these possible values is associated with a portrayal or indicator; thus a property knowledge object has a portrayal or indicator for each of the values that the property can assume. Thus, when the value of a property knowledge changes, its portrayal also changes.

In the example, a property of the switch is *position* with two values: *on* and *off*. When the value of the switch property, *position*, is *on*, then the portrayal is a graphic of the toggle in the up position. When the value of the switch property, *position*, is *off*, then the portrayal of this value is a graphic of the toggle in the down position.

A *process* is defined as a change in the value of some property of some entity. We say that this change in property value is the *consequence* of the process. Processes are also conditional, that is, a given process will not execute unless its conditions are met. A *condition* for a process is defined as a value on some property of some entity. A condition for a process is thus a value of a property. If in a given situation the value of the property is the same as the value specified for the condition for the process, the process executes; if the value of the property is not the same as the value specified for the condition for the process, the process does not execute. Finally a process can *trigger* another process. This provides for a chain of events (processes), each one triggered by the previous event (process). When a process is triggered, it evaluates its conditions; if they are true, it executes; if the condition is false, it does not execute; it then triggers the next process in the chain whether or not it executed its own consequence.

In the example, one process is *disconnect air line*. It is triggered by the activity *undo air line*. The air line (an entity) has a property, *connection,* with two values: *connected* and *disconnected*. The portrayal for the value *connected* is a graphic of the air hose connected to the double seat valve; the portrayal for the value *disconnected* is a graphic of the air hose disconnected from the double seat valve. This process, *disconnect air line*, has two conditions: (a) the value of the property *connection* of the entity *air line* is *connected* and (b) the value of the property *position* of the entity *air compressor switch* is *off*. If the actual value of the air compressor switch is *on*, then the process, *disconnect air line*, will not execute and nothing happens when the student executes the activity, *undo air line*.

The relationship among processes, entities, and activities enables the construction of learning environments from knowledge objects. In ITT this set of interrelationships is called a PEAnet (process, entity, activity network). Fig. 17.3 illustrates these PEAnet relationships. The learner executes some activity on a controller (itself an entity or part of some other entity). This action triggers a process. If the con-

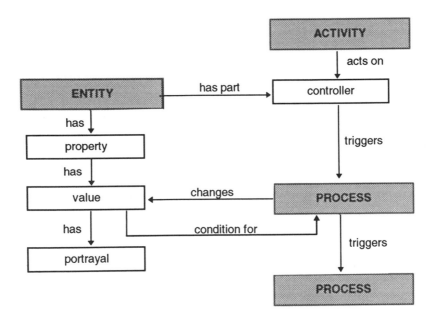

FIG. 17.3.   PEAnet relationships among processes, entities, and activities.

ditions of the process are true, then the process changes the value of a property. When the value of the property changes, the portrayal of this value changes, thus causing a consequence for the process to be indicated to the learner.

Fig. 17.4 lists the entities, properties and property values involved in the Valve Removal learning environment.

ENTITY	PROPERTY	PROPERTY VALUES
AC Switch	position	on/off
Air line	connection	connected/disconnected
Cleaning line	connection	connected/disconnected
Valve indicator line	connection	connected/disconnected
Flange	flange bolts	inserted/removed
Tap hole	flange bolt	inserted/removed
Valve	installation	inserted/removed
	seal	seated/unseated

FIG. 17.4.   Entities, properties, and property values for Valve Removal learning environment

Fig. 17.5 illustrates the PEAnet relationships involved in the "Removing Valve from Housing" learning environment. The sequence of activities required for the student to remove or install the valve from the housing is indicated down the left side of the diagram; the processes triggered by these actions are shown in the center column; and the consequences (changes of value of properties) are shown in the third column. The actions include: flip the air compressor switch, undo/connect the air line, undo/connect the cleaning connection, undo/connect the valve indicator line, remove/insert the flange bolts, insert a flange bolt into the tap hole, remove the flange bolt from the tap hole, pull out/insert the double seat valve.

Some processes have more than one consequence. For example, there are two consequences for the process *toggle*. When the process *toggle* executes, it changes the value of *switch position* to *off* if it is *on*, or to *on* if it is *off*. The letters on the right side of the diagram indicate conditions (property values) for a consequence to execute. If the conditions are not met, the process does not change the value of the property. For many processes, there are alternative consequences. When the value of some property has one value, one consequence is executed; when the same property has a different value, another consequence is executed. For example, there are two consequences for the process *disconnect air line*. The first consequence, *set connection of air line to the value disconnected*, is executed when the value of the switch position is *off* and the second consequence, *show an accident message*, is executed when the value of the switch position is on.

Simulation Engine

PEAnet representation makes it possible to write a general simulation algorithm (sometimes called a simulation engine) which runs any learning environment con-

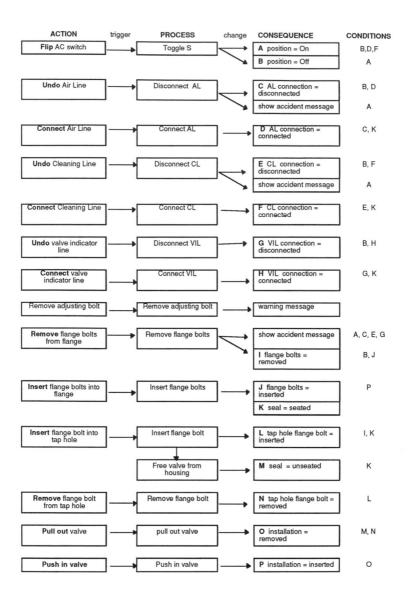

ACTION	trigger	PROCESS	change	CONSEQUENCE	CONDITIONS
Flip AC switch	→	Toggle S	→	**A** position = On	B,D,F
				B position = Off	A
Undo Air Line	→	Disconnect AL	→	**C** AL connection = disconnected	B, D
				show accident message	A
Connect Air Line	→	Connect AL	→	**D** AL connection = connected	C, K
Undo Cleaning Line	→	Disconnect CL	→	**E** CL connection = disconnected	B, F
				show accident message	A
Connect Cleaning Line	→	Connect CL	→	**F** CL connection = connected	E, K
Undo valve indicator line	→	Disconnect VIL	→	**G** VIL connection = disconnected	B, H
Connect valve indicator line	→	Connect VIL	→	**H** VIL connection = connected	G, K
Remove adjusting bolt	→	Remove adjusting bolt	→	warning message	
Remove flange bolts from flange	→	Remove flange bolts	→	show accident message	A, C, E, G
				I flange bolts = removed	B, J
Insert flange bolts into flange	→	Insert flange bolts	→	**J** flange bolts = inserted	P
				K seal = seated	
Insert flange bolt into tap hole	→	Insert flange bolt	→	**L** tap hole flange bolt = inserted	I, K
		Free valve from housing	→	**M** seal = unseated	K
Remove flange bolt from tap hole	→	Remove flange bolt	→	**N** tap hole flange bolt = removed	L
Pull out valve	→	pull out valve	→	**O** installation = removed	M, N
Push in valve	→	Push in valve	→	**P** installation = inserted	O

FIG. 17.5. PEAnet knowledge structure for Valve Removal learning environment.

414

structed on PEAnet architecture. This algorithm monitors for an action (usually some mouse action on the screen); it interprets this action, meaning that it determines from the location of the mouse action which action has occurred; it then checks the conditions of the process triggered by this action; if the conditions are true, it executes the process (changes the value of the property specified by the consequence) and displays the portrayal corresponding to the new value of the property; and if a process-to-process trigger is specified, it triggers the next process in the sequence. This instructional algorithm is written once and used over and over for different learning environments. Any situation, device, or phenomenon which can be represented by properties and their values can be represented in PEAnet architecture and run by the simulation engine.

The set of actions down the left side of Fig. 17.5 does not represent a linear sequence. For example, if the position of the air compressor switch is *off*, then the air line, cleaning line, or valve indicator line can be safely disconnected in any order. The learning environment allows the student to attempt to disconnect any of the lines even if the position of the air compressor switch is *on*; however, the system then displays an accident message, indicating danger to the technician or damage to the valve as a result of this action.

The student can also reverse any action. For example, the student can toggle the switch, reconnect a line, or reinsert the flange bolts at any time. Thus any action which the student could do in the real-world environment is also possible to do in the learning environment, with some representation of the consequence of this action.

Exploration and Guidance

Without instructional overlay, exploration is the only learning activity enabled by this learning environment. The student can operate the device or explore the environment, experiencing consequences representative of those that would occur in the real world. Exploration represents a presentation alternative for a procedural or execute transaction.

It has been found that exploration without guidance is often insufficient for adequate learning. Exploration alone is inefficient. The student engages in trial-and-error behavior and makes many wrong moves before coming across the appropriate sequence of actions to solve a problem. Often the student is unable, from exploration alone, to discover the most efficient sequence of actions to accomplish a given goal in the environment. From unguided practice alone most students are unable to discover the underlying conditions which would prepare them for prediction or trouble-shooting tasks. Hence, a learning environment without instructional overlay is only part of an instructional transaction and is therefore incomplete.

In order for a learning environment to be effective, it is necessary to provide different forms of learner guidance. One type of guidance is propaedeudic[7] instruc-

---

[7]*Propaedeutic* means to teach beforehand or to teach in preparation for some other learning activity.

tion, such as learning the names, functions, and locations of the parts of the situation or device. Learning a procedure is more efficient if learner guidance takes the form of a demonstration in the learning environment itself, followed by scaffolded[8] practice. To acquire prediction or troubleshooting skills, the system must provide guidance in the form of explanations in the context of the student exploration. An explanation indicates those conditions which were met or not met when a given process executes or fails to execute. Finally, prediction and trouble-shooting skills are developed when the student is required to predict the consequence of a given action or set of actions, or to find the conditions which prevented a given consequence or set of consequences from occurring (troubleshooting). In the following sections we will describe each of these instructional transactions as they are implemented using knowledge objects in a learning environment.

Identify (Component) Transaction

Goal

The student will be able to identify the name and location (with regard to some whole) of a given part of an entity (artifact, device, system, location, communication, etc.)

Knowledge Structure

In addition to the information slots (name, description, and portrayal), knowledge objects for component transactions require three additional slots: *location, part-of,* and *has-parts*. The *location* slot indicates the location of the portrayal with regard to some referent (the object to which the part belongs) knowledge object. The *part-of* slot contains a pointer to the referent knowledge object. The *has-parts* slots contain pointers to knowledge objects representing each of the component parts of the referent knowledge object.

The location slot has a parameter of mode with two values (graphical, temporal). If the portrayal of the knowledge object is text or graphic, then the location mode is graphical (which means that it can be located on a computer screen). If the portrayal is audio or video, then the location mode is temporal, meaning that the portrayal of the parts is some time segment of the portrayal of the referent knowledge object, for example, a segment of a video or a segment of a musical rendition.

In the example, each part of the valve is represented by a knowledge object that consists of a name (air hose connection), a description (see Fig. 17.2), and a portrayal (that part of the graphic[9] in Fig. 17.1 where the hose connects to the valve). The learning environment is a composite graphic. Each part of the valve is represented by its own picture (portrayal). Since each part of the system is its own por-

---

[8]Scaffolded practice is guided practice in doing a sequence of events where each successive trial withdraws the support until the student is performing the task in a completely unguided environment.

[9]The Learning Environment is composed of a composite graphic. Each part is represented by its own graphic. The entire set of graphics makes up the picture of the system seen by the student.

trayal (graphic), it also knows where it is on the screen. Hence each graphic contains information about its own location on the screen and can therefore highlight itself even if it is moved to a new location. The background of the learning environment is also a knowledge object. It contains pointers to all of the knowledge objects for each of the parts. Each part of the valve also has a pointer indicating that it is part of the learning environment representing the pump.

Presentation

The presentation mode for the IDENTIFY transaction is as follows: (a) Show the name and portrayal of the referent knowledge object. In our example, the name is in the title bar and the background for the valve including the pipe, the bottom plate of the valve, and the switch plate is the portrayal of the referent knowledge object. (b) Show the portrayal of each part of the referent knowledge object. In our example the illustration of each part is the portrayal. For example, the valve itself, the flange bolts, the air hose connection, the air hose, etc. (c) If explore mode is enabled: on mouse-enter show the name of each part; on right click show the description of each part. (d) If lecture mode is requested "Tell me about some of the parts": highlight each part in the selected item list, show its name, show its description. For temporal portrayals (video or audio) some graphic portrayal usually accompanies the temporal portrayal to identify the parts in time.

Practice

The practice mode for the IDENTIFY transaction is as follows: If "locate parts" is selected: present a part name, the student clicks on the part, provide right/wrong with correct answer feedback. If wrong, retain item in the list. If "name parts" is selected: highlight a part, present a list of part names, the student clicks on the name of the part, provide right/wrong with correct answer feedback. If wrong, retain item in the list. If "identify function" is selected: present a function description, the student clicks on the part, provide right/wrong with correct answer feedback. If wrong, retain item in the list.

Learner Guidance

During practice, if a student points to an incorrect part, the correct part is highlighted for the student. During practice, if a student selects or types the wrong name for a given part, the correct name is given.

Parameters[10]

Presentation and practice strategies can be controlled by a number of parameters. In a given transaction these parameters can produce a variety of different presentation or practice combinations. Some of the parameters for an IDENTIFY transaction in-

---

[10]A complete list of parameters for each of the transactions and all of their implications is considerably beyond the scope of this paper; see Merrill, Li, and Jones (1992) for more details.

clude the following: show name (yes/no) and name mode (text/audio); show portrayal (yes/no) and portrayal mode (text, audio, graphic, video, combination); show description (yes/no), and description mode (text/audio). By employing these parameters, a given part may be represented to the student in any of over 128 different combinations. In our example, the description was a combination graphic and description.

Execute (Activity) Transaction

Goal

The student is able to execute a series of actions which lead to some goal.

Knowledge Structure

The PEAnet structure for a learning environment enables the student to execute the activity. The PEAnet consists of a set of activities, each of which triggers a process which leads to some consequence (change in property value of some entity in the system). In the example, the PEAnet structure of Fig. 17.4 is the knowledge structure for the activity of valve removal.

Inference Engine

PEAnet knowledge representation makes it possible to write an inference algorithm (inference engine) which can determine an appropriate path to a goal from any set of initial conditions (values of properties). The author or student indicates a goal for a procedure. A goal is a value for one or more properties in the system. The inference engine then determines which process sets the goal property to the goal value. It then determines the action (trigger) for this process. If a condition for the process is true, the inference engine goes to the next condition. If a condition is false, the inference engine determines the process that will make this condition true. It then determines the action (trigger) for this second process. If a condition for this second process is true, the inference engine determines a third process that will make this condition true. This backward chaining continues until all the necessary processes and actions (triggers) have been identified. A list of the actions thus determined, in reverse order, is a correct path to the goal.

Presentation

One type of presentation is a hands-off demonstration. In this type of demonstration the guide does the first action by automatically moving the cursor to the appropriate entity part and simulating a click, enabling the system to show the consequence; the guide then does the next action, etc., until the goal has been reached. Since it is passive, we feel that this type of presentation is less appropriate than the Simon Says demonstration described in the following paragraph. Simon Says requires the student to be actively involved in the demonstration, focusing the student's attention on the action to be taken and the consequence of this action.

An appropriate presentation for teaching a procedure (sequence of actions) is a demonstration or Simon Says simulation. The inference engine determines a path (sequence of actions) from the initial state of the system to the goal. The guide then directs the student to execute each of these actions in turn with the direction "Do <action name>." If the student does this action, its consequence is executed and the guide directs the student to do the next action. If the student does some other action, the guide presents a message; "That is not the <entity part on which the action should have been taken>. Try again." This guided demonstration is continued until the goal has been reached.

A Simon Says demonstration is sometimes called "guided practice." We feel that this is a misnomer: that this type of learning experience is not practice but "active presentation." In our view a presentation need not be passive. Requiring the student to carry out each step by following directions focuses the student's attention on the part and action involved in the step.

Practice

We identified two additional levels of practice. Next step practice is the same as Simon Says demonstration, except the guide does not indicate the action to be taken but merely gives the direction: "Do the next step." The student must remember which step is next and then do the action. If the student does a different action, the same reminder is given as with the Simon Says demonstration, that is, "That is not the <name of part on which the action should have been taken>."

In You-do-it practice, the system is put in open-ended mode, enabling the system to execute any consequence to any process trigged by any action within the limitations of the system. However, the guide indicates the goal of the performance and directs the student to take those actions necessary to accomplish the goal. The guide also directs students to click on a "finished" button when they believe they have accomplished the goal. When students click on the finished button, they are told whether or not they have correctly finished the task (accomplished the goal). The guide then shows the student the path (sequence of actions) that the inference determined and shows the student's path (actual actions taken by the student). Unnecessary actions on the part of the student are highlighted to facilitate the student's comparison of his or her path with the guide's path. In systems where there are multiple paths to the goal, the student's path may not be the same as the guide's but may still accomplish the goal. The system recognizes that the goal has been correctly accomplished. The system records the student's actual path and the number of steps required for the student to accomplish the goal.

For complex systems additional practice is desirable. A number of different problems can be defined. A problem is a different set of starting conditions. Selecting a different problem resets the starting conditions to some predetermined values. Such divergent practice facilitates transfer to configurations of the system not encountered as part of the instruction. Additional practice is also desirable when a procedure can be executed with a variety of different, but similar, systems. Practice with a number of these divergent systems will facilitate transfer of the activity to yet other systems not encountered by the student during the instruction.

Learner Guidance

The scaffolding nature of the practice from a Simon Says demonstration to a You-do-it practice is one form of learner guidance. This successive progression from highly guided interaction to unguided interaction has been recommended by a number of different instructional-design theorists and has been supported by empirical investigations to facilitate the learning of procedural skills.*

Providing an explanation to students as they learn a sequence of actions has also been recommended and shown to facilitate the acquisition of procedural skill. PEAnet knowledge structure makes it possible to build a system that can automatically provide explanations under a variety of circumstances. In an explore mode the student can request an explanation from the guide. In a Simon Says demonstration mode or Next Step practice mode, the learner can turn on the explanation, which is then displayed as each step in the procedure is executed. In a You-do-it or performance practice mode, the explanation can be turned on and displayed as the student executes each action.

An explanation has two parts: what happened? and why? In terms of the elements of knowledge objects, what happens is the consequence or change of property value caused by the process. An explanation template enables the guide to provide this what-happened explanation. One template is as follows: When the student requests an explanation, the guide presents this message when the process executes: "When you <action name> the <property> of <entity who owns property> is changed to <value>," and this message when the process does not execute: "when you <action name> nothing happens." A system may have different explanation templates for different kinds of values and different operations for changing those values, but these details are beyond the scope of this chapter.

The why part of the explanation is implemented by presenting the condition(s) that had to be satisfied in order for the process to execute. The why part of the explanation presents a text template of the following form when the process executes: "This happens because the <value> of <property> is <value>," or the following when the process does not execute: "This happens because the <value> of <property> is not <value>."

In the example, suppose the student attempts to remove the valve before removing the flange bolt from the tap hole. The explanation presented by the guide reads as follows: "When you <pull out double seat valve> nothing happens. This happens because the <location> of the <flange bolt> is not <removed from tape hole>."

---

* What other theories in this volume utilize such scaffolding?

Interpret (Process) Transaction

Goal

Given a set of conditions, the student is able to predict the consequence of an event. Or given a consequence (expected or unexpected) the student is able to identify the conditions which were present in order for this consequence to occur. When an unexpected consequence occurs (an error), then finding the precipitating conditions is called trouble shooting.

Knowledge Structure

The knowledge structure required for an interpret transaction is a set of process rules consisting of conditions and consequences, a goal to be accomplished (value for some property or set of properties), and a set of specific problems (initial conditions). Some of the problems may contain faults. A fault is an incorrect condition. That is, when a faulted process executes, an unexpected consequence occurs because of the incorrect condition. An incorrect condition can represent a damaged component, a missing component, or a control set to an inappropriate value.

The same PEAnet knowledge structure described for the explore interaction is required for an INTERPRET transaction. It may be necessary to include additional conditions representing faults. Selecting a problem is an action which triggers a process which changes the initial conditions of the system to some predetermined values.

Presentation

The student is allowed to play with or explore the learning environment to "see what happens if.... " An explanation (a form of learner guidance) is available that indicates the consequence of each action ("what happened") and the conditions that were satisfied or unsatisfied ("why"). If the process applies to a number of different situations, then a number of different scenarios (variations on the learning environment) are provided to the student, and the student is allowed to "play with" these variations. In some situations the student is provided with a "control panel" that allows them to set the values of some of the properties of the system. In this way the student can perform experiments by observing the consequences of different conditions (property values) and receiving the explanation for these consequences. One advantage of a learning environment is that there need not be a distinction between conditions that students can change as a result of their actions (action triggers process, which changes a condition or consequence) and conditions which cannot be changed by student actions. We can always give a student some control action (an action not available in the real world) that allows them to experiment with the system. (An example is a gravity control that increases or decreases gravity.)

Practice

The student is presented with a specific problem in the learning environment. The student is asked to observe the conditions of the device or system and to predict one or more consequences. In the system described, the student is provided a list of properties and allowed to select the value for each property that constitutes the consequence of a given action. One or more of the conditions given may represent a faulted condition. A variation is to provide the student with a control panel and direct them to set the conditions (property values) which will lead to a specified consequence. The consequence may be one that would result from a faulted condition. The prediction is confirmed by allowing the system to execute and showing the consequence of the execution. In complex systems the student may have to trace the execution back through several events to find the condition(s) which caused the observed consequence. Or the student may need to execute several events of the system to see the consequence that results from the conditions.

Learner Guidance

During the presentation or exploration the conditions necessary for a consequence of a given event are made clear to the student. Often the best guidance is to allow students to ask for an explanation of an unexpected consequence during their exploration of the system. This explanation identifies the conditions that caused the consequence. During practice the student's predictions or trouble-shooting are confirmed by executing the system with explanations of what occurred during each step of the process and why.

Adaptive Instruction

Perhaps one of the most exciting possibilities for the use of knowledge object architecture for instructional design is the possibility for truly adaptive instruction. An instructional strategy is an algorithm. An algorithm can be prespecified and preprogrammed. In addition an instructional algorithm can include a number of parameters, the different values of which control the way the strategy promotes interaction with the student. Changing a strategy parameter value changes the nature of the interaction. An adaptive system would include a set of expert system rules relating student parameters to instructional strategy parameters. When a student parameter changes, the expert system would then change the parameter of the strategies, and the subsequent interaction with the student would change. An adaptive system would include a system for monitoring student parameters (level of motivation, level of interest, performance, and other parameters). When the values on these student parameters change, then the system dynamically changes the values of the strategy parameters, thus adapting the system to the individual student.*

The knowledge object architecture together with its simulation engine and inference engine makes it possible to build a learning environment in which students themselves are objects in the learning environment. Like other objects in the learn-

---

* This seems to be a highly cost-effective way to provide powerful types of customization of instruction.

ing environment, the "student entity" has properties and property values. These property values are changed by processes triggered by actions or other processes just like all other entities in the system. Thus, when the properties of the student entity change, the actions that are available to the student change. The learning environment thus adapts to the student or interacts with the student in a dynamic way.

There is not space here to elaborate on adaptive systems. A subsequent paper will describe a theoretical model for adaptive instruction.

SUMMARY

In this chapter we have concentrated on the component methods of ITT. We have suggested that a more precise representation of the knowledge to be taught in the form of knowledge objects increases the precision with which instructional strategies can be described. We have indicated that instructional strategies can be described as methods for manipulating the elements of knowledge objects. This architecture enables the specification of executable knowledge, making possible tutorial and experiential instruction from the same knowledge representation .

In this chapter we have described knowledge objects. We have described how knowledge objects are used to define a number of instructional strategies including: learning environments (exploration), IDENTIFY transactions, EXECUTE transactions, and INTERPRET transactions. We have illustrated one implementation of these strategies in an instructional learning environment.

In our previous presentations of CDT we have provided prescriptions for best-case strategies for different kinds of instructional outcomes. In this chapter we could have recast these prescriptions in terms of strategy algorithms based on knowledge objects, but we chose instead to present the architecture of the system rather than the prescriptions. This chapter is a presentation of the foundation for instructional design based on knowledge objects but is not a complete presentation of the theory* and does not include all of the items that were suggested by the editor of this volume.

REFERENCES

Gagné, R. M. (1965). *The conditions of learning.* New York: Holt, Rinehart & Winston.
Gagné , R. M. (1985). *The conditions of learning and theory of instruction* (4th ed.). New York: Holt, Rinehart & Winston.
Jones, M. K., Li, Z., & Merrill, M. D. (1990). Domain knowledge representation for instructional analysis. *Educational Technology, 30*(10), 7–32.
Li, Z., & Merrill, M. D. (1990). Transaction shells: a new approach to courseware authoring. *Journal of Research on Computing in Education, 23*(1), 72–86.

* In particular, it leaves out 10 of the 13 classes of instructional transactions.

Merrill, M. D. (1983). Component display theory. In Charles M. Reigeluth (Ed.), *Instructional-design theories and models: An overview of their current status* (pp. 279–334). Hillsdale, NJ: Lawrence Erlbaum Associates.

Merrill, M. D. (1987). A lesson based on component display theory. In Charles M. Reigeluth (Ed.), *Instructional Design Theories in Action* (pp. 201–244). Hillsdale, NJ: Lawrence Erlbaum Associates.

Merrill, M. D., with Twitchell, D. G., (Ed.). (1994). *Instructional design theory.* Englewood Cliffs, NJ: Educational Technology Publications.

Merrill, M. D. (1997). Learning-oriented instructional development tools. *Performance Improvement, 36*(3), 51–55.

Merrill, M. D. & ID$_2$ Research Team (1993). Instructional transaction theory: Knowledge relationships among processes, entities, and activities. *Educational Technology, 33*(4), 5–16.

Merrill, M. D. & ID$_2$ Research Team (1996). Instructional transaction theory: Instructional design based on knowledge objects. *Educational Technology, 36*(3), 30–37.

Merrill, M. D., Jones, M. K., & Li, Zhongmin. (1992). Instructional transaction theory: Classes of transactions. *Educational Technology, 32*(6), 12–26.

Merrill, M. D., Li, Z. & Jones, M.K. (1991). Instructional transaction theory: An introduction. *Educational Technology, 31*(6), 7–12.

Merrill, M. D., Li, Z., & Jones, M. K. (1992). Instructional transaction shells: Responsibilities, methods, and parameters. *Educational Technology, 32*(2), 5–27.

18

The Elaboration Theory: Guidance for Scope and Sequence Decisions

Charles M. Reigeluth
Indiana University

Charles M. Reigeluth

Charles M. Reigeluth received a BA in Economics from Harvard University and a PhD in Instructional Psychology from Brigham Young University. He taught science at the secondary level for three years and spent ten years on the faculty of the Instructional Design program at Syracuse University, culminating as chair of the program. He has been a Professor in the Instructional Systems Technology Department at Indiana University since 1988, and served as chairman of the department from 1990-1992. His interests include reinventing public education and designing high quality educational resources. He has published six books and over sixty articles and chapters on those subjects. He is the major developer of several instructional design theories, including the elaboration theory and simulation theory. Two of his books received an "outstanding book of the year" award from the Association for Educational Communications and Technology.

FOREWORD

Goals and preconditions. *The primary goal of this theory is to help select and sequence content in a way that will optimize attainment of learning goals. It is intended for medium to complex kinds of cognitive and psychomotor learning, but does not currently deal with content that is primarily in the affective domain.*

Values. *Some of the values upon which this theory is based include:*
- *a sequence that is as holistic as possible, to foster meaning-making and motivation,*
- *allowing learners to make many scope and sequence decisions on their own, during the learning process,*
- *an approach that facilitates rapid prototyping in the instructional development process,*
- *the integration of viable approaches to scope and sequence into a coherent design theory.*

Methods. *Here are the major methods this theory offers:*
1. *Conceptual elaboration sequence*
   - *Use this approach when the goals call for learning many related concepts.*
   - *Teach broader, more inclusive concepts before the narrower, more detailed concepts that elaborate upon them.*
   - *Use either a topical or a spiral approach to this conceptual elaboration.*
   - *Teach "supporting" content (principles, procedures, information, higher-order thinking skills, attitudes, etc.) together with the concepts to which they are most closely related.*
   - *Group concepts and their supporting content into "learning episodes" that aren't so large as to make review and synthesis difficult but aren't so small as to break up the flow of the learning process.*
   - *Give students some choice as to which concepts to elaborate upon first/next.*
2. *Theoretical elaboration sequence*
   - *Use this approach when the goals call for learning many related principles.*
   - *Teach broader, more inclusive principles before the narrower, more detailed ones that elaborate upon them.*
   - *Use either a topical or a spiral approach to this theoretical elaboration.*
   - *Teach "supporting" content (concepts, procedures, information, higher-order thinking skills, attitudes, etc.) together with the principles to which they are most closely related.*
   - *Group principles and their supporting content into "learning episodes."*
   - *Give students some choice as to which principles to elaborate upon first/next.*

3. *Simplifying conditions sequence*
  - *Use this approach when the goals call for learning a task of at least moderate complexity.*
  - *Teach a simpler version of a task (that is still fairly representative of all versions) before teaching progressively more complex versions.*
  - *Use either a topical or a spiral approach to this simplifying conditions sequence.*
  - *For procedural tasks focus on teaching steps; for heuristic tasks focus on teaching principles; and for combination tasks teach both steps and principles—in accordance with the way experts think about the task.*
  - *Teach "supporting" content together with the steps and/or principles to which they are most closely related.*
  - *Group steps/principles and their supporting content into "learning episodes."*
  - *Give students some choice as to which versions of the task to learn next.*

Major contributions. Detailed guidance for designing holistic sequences for several kinds of course content. Guidance for scope and sequence decisions for heuristic tasks, including heuristic task analysis methods.

—C.M.R.

The Elaboration Theory: Guidance for Scope and Sequence Decisions

The paradigm shift from teacher-centered and content-centered instruction to learner-centered instruction is creating new needs for ways to sequence instruction. In the industrial-age paradigm the need was to break the content or task down into little pieces and teach those pieces one at a time. But most of the new approaches to instruction, including simulations, apprenticeships, goal-based scenarios, problem-based learning, and other kinds of situated learning, require a more holistic approach to sequencing, one that can simplify the content or task, not by breaking it into pieces, but by identifying simpler real-world versions of the task or content domain. The elaboration theory was developed to provide such a holistic approach to sequencing that also makes the learning process more meaningful and motivational to learners. And it was developed to provide an approach that allows instructional designers (including teachers) to empower learners to make some scope and sequence decisions during the learning process.*

In this chapter I begin by discussing some basics about sequencing and when it is beneficial to use the elaboration theory. Then I discuss each of the different kinds of elaboration sequences, with particular emphasis on the simplifying conditions method.

What Do Sequencing Strategies Entail?

Decisions about sequencing are concerned with how to group and order the content. You cannot order the content without creating some kind of groupings to be ordered, and different kinds of sequences require different kinds of groupings. Therefore, decisions must be made about what content should be in each grouping. This is why educators often talk about "scope and sequence" together.** *Scope* is concerned with what to teach: the nature of the content.[1] It requires decisions about what the learner needs and/or wants to learn. Scope and sequence decisions involve several types of decisions regarding:

- the size of each group of content (learning episode):

- the components of each learning episode:

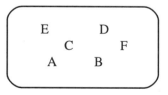

---

* Which common features of the new paradigm do you recognize here?

** Again we see the integration of curriculum theory and instructional theory.

[1] I use the term "content" to refer to everything that comes under "what to teach." It therefore includes whatever tasks you might teach as well as whatever knowledge, and the term "content analysis" includes "task analysis." It also includes generic skills and attitudes.

- the order of components within each episode:

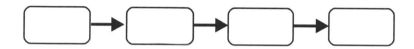

A | D
B | E
C | F

- and the order of episodes:

all of which influence the quality of the learning experience: its effectiveness, efficiency, and appeal.

Does Scope Make a Difference?

If you are in a training department for any of the three sectors (private, public, or nonprofit), the employees or customers need certain skills and knowledge to perform well. If you don't teach what they need, it doesn't matter how good the remaining aspects of the instruction are.

However, a K–12 or higher education context is very different, in that needs are much less clear and depend largely on values. Furthermore, students have interests that may be unrelated to the values that the community and the parents hold. And the benefits of the instruction may not become apparent until many years later. All these factors make it much more difficult to say whether scope makes a difference, or perhaps more accurately, what kinds of difference scope makes. Clearly, the differences made by scope will vary from one student to another and from one "stakeholder" to another in the educational system. (Stakeholders are all those who have a stake in the particular educational system, such as parents, employers, taxpayers, students, social service agencies, and so forth.) But ask any student or any stakeholder whether "what is taught" makes a difference to them, and you are almost certain to hear a resounding "Yes!"

General Concerns for Deciding on Scope

If scope does make a difference, how can you make sure that you select the right content?

Training Contexts.   For training contexts, the answer is fairly straightforward. You conduct a needs analysis. Much has been written elsewhere about how to conduct a needs analysis (see, e.g., Kaufman & English, 1979; Kaufman, Rojas, & Mayer, 1993; Rossett, 1987). But I would also like to suggest that the selection of goals for an organization to pursue be based as much on values as it is on needs. Issues relating to the quality of products and the ways in which customers will be treated are two cases in point that could have powerful influences over what to teach. More attention should be placed on values analysis in the instructional design process.

Education Contexts.   For K–12 and higher education contexts, it is more difficult to make sure that you select the right content, for all the reasons outlined earlier:

- needs are much less clear,
- needs depend largely on values,
- students have interests of their own, and
- benefits may not become apparent until many years later.

Furthermore, just as the business world has been evolving from standardization to customization, perhaps the content-selection process for the K–12 and higher education contexts should not require that students learn all the same things. Osin and Lesgold (1997) talk about "defining a required common curriculum and supporting additional student choices" (p. 642). Technology is evolving to the point where we can create flexible, computer-based learning tools that students can use—while they are learning—to create or modify their own instruction.* Therefore, much of the content selection that is now done by a teacher (or curriculum committee) for a whole "batch" of learners well ahead of the actual instruction could soon be done during the instruction as the multimedia systems and the teacher continuously collect information from individual learners and/or small teams of learners and use that information to present an array of sound alternatives to the learner(s),[2] about both what to learn next and how to learn it. This will require designing scope and sequence options in ways that are fundamentally different from the ways scope and sequence decisions have been made in the past.

Does Sequencing Make a Difference?

This is a very common type of question to ask, but it is the wrong type! The issue, as with most instructional strategies, is not whether it makes a difference, but when it makes a difference. The impact of sequencing depends upon two major factors: the strength of relationships among the topics and the size of the course of instruction.

---

*See e.g., chapter 17 by Merrill.
[2]These systems and the teacher can also provide guidance to the learner after she or he chooses from an unlimited set of alternatives.

Sequencing is only important when there is a strong *relationship among the topics* of the course. If a course is composed of several unrelated topics, such as word processing, computer graphics, and electronic spreadsheets, the order for teaching the topics is not likely to make much difference. On the other hand, when there is a strong relationship, the sequence will influence how well both the relationship and the content are learned. For example, there is an important relationship between the analysis and design phases in the instructional systems development (ISD) process. Some sequences take a fragmented approach that makes it difficult to learn the relationship and understand the content, whereas other sequences facilitate such learning by dealing with both phases simultaneously or spiraling frequently from one to the other.

Second, if there is a strong relationship among the topics, then, as the *size of the course* increases, so does the importance of sequencing. When the content requires more than a couple of hours to learn, sequencing is likely to begin to make a significant difference in the learners' ability to master it, because most learners will have a difficult time organizing so much content logically and meaningfully if it is poorly sequenced. However, when the content to be learned is minimal (e.g., less than a couple of hours), the human mind can compensate for weaknesses in the sequence.*

Types of Sequencing Strategies

Relationships Are the Key.   The importance of relationships is twofold. First, as was just mentioned, if no relationships exist, then sequencing doesn't matter. But, second, each method of sequencing is based upon a *single type of relationship*. For instance, a historical sequence is based upon the chronological relationship—a sequence is devised that follows the actual sequence of events. A procedural sequence, the most common pattern of sequencing in training, is based upon the relationship of "order of performance" of the steps in the procedure. A hierarchical sequence is based upon the relationship of learning prerequisites among the various skills and subskills that comprise a task. And the "simplifying conditions" sequence (described later) is based upon the relationship of the degree of complexity of different versions of a complex task.**

Furthermore, when a number of topics needs to be taught, two basic patterns of sequencing can be used that are fundamentally different: topical and spiral (see Fig. 18.1).

Topical Sequencing.   In topical sequencing, a topic (or task) is taught to whatever depth of understanding (or competence) is required, before moving to the next one. There are both advantages and disadvantages of topical sequencing.

---

* Did you recognize these two paragraphs as identifying two preconditions for all theories or methods of sequencing, not just the elaboration theory?
** Is this design theory or descriptive theory?

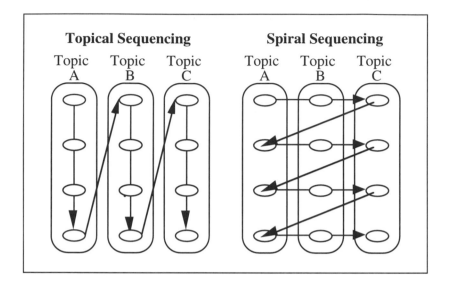

FIG. 18.1.   Topical and spiral sequencing. (From Reigeluth & Kim, 1993)

Learners can concentrate on one topic (or task) for in-depth learning without frequently skipping to new ones. And hands-on materials and other resources are all
used in one block of time, rather than being used at different points scattered over
several months or a year. However, once the class (or team or individual) moves on
to a new topic (or task), the first one is often forgotten. And the learners don't gain a
perception of what the whole subject domain is like until they reach the end of the
course (or curriculum). The weaknesses of topical sequencing can be compensated
for, to some extent, by incorporating instructional tactics for overview, review, and
synthesis.*

Spiral Sequencing.   In spiral sequencing (Bruner, 1960), the learners master
a topic (or task) gradually in several passes. The learner learns the basics of one
topic (or task), then another, and another, and so on, before she or he returns to learn
more about each topic, and this pattern continues until the necessary depth and
breadth are reached for all of them. The main advantage of spiral sequencing is its
built-in synthesis and review. The interrelationships among topics (or tasks) may be
learned more easily using the spiral approach because it allows similar aspects of

---

* Two issues were touched on here. To what extent do you think *all* methods of instruction have both
strengths and weaknesses? And to what extent can a method that has a certain weakness be comple-
mented with a method that compensates to some extent for that weakness?

the various topics (or tasks) to be learned close in time to each other. Furthermore, cycling back to learn more about an earlier topic (or task) provides a periodic review of the earlier one. On the other hand, the main disadvantage of spiral sequencing is disruption. To frequently switch topics disrupts the learners' thought development, as well as the efficient management of material resources.

Which one Is best?   Again, this is a very common type of question, but the wrong type! The issue is not which pattern of sequencing is best, but when each is best. Furthermore, in reality, neither topical nor spiral sequencing exists in a pure form. In an extreme case, spiral sequencing could entail presenting only one sentence on each topic (or task) before moving on to the next. The real issue lies in how deep or broad a slice a teacher or learner makes into one topic before going on to another. Rather than thinking of spiral and topical sequencing as two separate categories, it is useful to think of them as the two endpoints on a continuum. The instructional designer's (or the learner's) decision, then, is where on the continuum to place any given training program or curriculum (or when to select any given point on the continuum).*

When to Use the Elaboration Theory and Why

In both training and education contexts, much instruction focuses on complex cognitive tasks (with a focus on skills) and/or cognitive structures (with a focus on understanding).

Regarding complex tasks, the simplifying conditions method (SCM) sequencing strategy enables learners to understand the tasks holistically and to acquire the skills of an expert for a real-world task from the very first lesson (or module, or segment, etc.; I prefer Bruner's term, "learning episode," because it has a more holistic, less fragmented connotation). These skills enhance the motivation of learners and, therefore, enhance the quality (effectiveness and efficiency) of the instruction. The holistic understanding of a task results in the formation of a stable cognitive schema to which more complex capabilities and understandings can be assimilated. This is especially valuable for learning a complex cognitive task. Also, since the learners start with a real version of the task from the beginning, this method is ideally suited to situated learning, problem-based learning, computer-based simulations, and on-the-job training. Further, it can be used with highly directive instruction, highly constructivist instruction, or anything in between.

Regarding cognitive structures (understanding), the elaboration sequences help to build the cognitive scaffolding that makes subsequent, more complex understandings much easier to attain, through either directive or constructivist approaches to instruction. Therefore, this sequencing strategy also results in the formation of stable cognitive schemata to which more complex understandings are more easily added.

---

* Did you notice that *two* ways of transcending "either-or" thinking were offered here?

The limitations of the SCM and elaboration sequences are:

- The content must be fairly complex and large to make the approach worthwhile. With smaller amounts of content, these approaches won't make much difference in the quality of the instruction.
- The SCM sequences must be used with other sequencing strategies that provide guidance for within-episode sequencing. For example, procedural tasks require a combination of procedural and hierarchical approaches for within-episode sequencing. However, as an instructional theory that synthesizes existing knowledge about sequencing, the elaboration theory includes guidelines for using those other approaches with the SCM approach.

The net effect is that the SCM and elaboration sequences are powerful methods for complex content, but they are a bit more complex and hence more difficult to learn to design, though perhaps actually easier to design than alternatives once they are learned.

Furthermore, the SCM task-analysis procedures and the elaboration sequence content-analysis procedures are both very efficient. Because these procedures allow task/content analysis and sequence design to be done simultaneously, it is possible to do *rapid prototyping* so that the first learning episode can be designed and developed before any task or content analysis is done for the remaining episodes of the course or curriculum. A rapid prototype can provide a good sample for inspection and approval by clients, higher management, and other stakeholders, as well as for formative evaluation and revision of the prototype, which can strongly improve the design of the remaining episodes.

WHAT IS AN ELABORATION SEQUENCE?

The elaboration theory of instruction was developed to provide a holistic alternative to the parts-to-whole sequencing and superficial coverage of content that have been so typical of both education and training over the past five to ten decades.* It has also attempted to synthesize several recent ideas about sequencing instruction into a single coherent framework. It currently only deals with the cognitive and psychomotor domains, and not the affective domain.[3] It is founded on the notion that different sequencing strategies are based on different kinds of relationships within the content, and that different relationships are important for different kinds

---

* In this sense, it represents a different paradigm of instructional sequencing.

[3]However, there are strong indications that it can be, and indeed is, already intuitively being, applied in the affective domain. For example, Mark Greenberg and associates (see, e.g., Greenberg & Kusché, 1993) have developed the PATHS curriculum (Promoting Alternative THinking Strategies), an emotional literacy program designed to help children avoid the road to violence and crime. According to Goleman (1995), "the PATHS curriculum has fifty lessons on different emotions, teaching the most basic, such as happiness and anger, to the youngest children, and later touching on more complicated feelings such as jealously, pride, and guilt." (p. 278).

of expertise. So the kind of sequence that will most facilitate learning will vary depending on the kind of expertise you want to develop.

First, elaboration theory makes a distinction between task expertise and subject-domain expertise. *Task expertise* relates to the learner becoming an expert in a specific task, such as managing a project, selling a product, or writing an annual plan. *Domain expertise* relates to the learner becoming an expert in a body of subject matter not tied to any specific task, such as economics, electronics, or physics (but often relevant to many tasks). This is not quite the same as the distinction between procedural and declarative knowledge (J. R. Anderson, 1983).

Task Expertise

Tasks range from simple to complex. The elaboration theory is only intended for more complex tasks. It is based on the observation that complex cognitive and psychomotor tasks are done differently under different conditions, that each set of conditions defines a different version of the task, and that some of those versions are much more complex than others. Consequently, the elaboration theory offers the SCM to design a holistic, simple-to-complex sequence by starting with the simplest real-world version of the task and gradually progressing to evermore complex versions as each is mastered. For example, solving mathematical problems is easier when you are solving for one unknown than when there are two unknowns. The number of unknowns is a condition variable having two conditions: one unknown and two unknowns. And skills and understandings of differing complexity are required for each condition. So problems or projects that learners tackle should be ones that are within what Vygotsky (1978) called "the zone of proximal development"—close enough to the learner's present competence for the learner to be able to deal with successfully—and they should gradually increase in complexity.

But not all complex tasks are of the same nature. Some are primarily procedural (i.e., tasks for which experts use a set of steps, mental and/or physical, to decide what to do when, such as a high school course on mathematics or a corporate training program on installing a piece of equipment for a customer), and some are primarily heuristic (i.e., tasks for which experts use causal models—interrelated sets of principles and/or guidelines—to decide what to do when, such as a high school course on thinking skills or a corporate training program on management skills). Most tasks, however, are a combination of the two, somewhere on a continuum that ranges from purely procedural to purely heuristic tasks. The guidance offered by the SCM is a bit different for the procedural than for the heuristic elements of a task, because what must be learned (the content) is different, and the relationships within that content are different. The SCM is discussed in more detail later.

Before we proceed to a discussion of domain expertise, it may be helpful to clarify what I mean by a causal model, for it is important in upcoming discussions. A causal model is an interrelated set of cause–effect relationships, in which there are

---

* Did you recognize this as a situationality?

chains of causes and effects and there are usually multiple causes of the effects and multiple effects of the causes (see Fig. 18.2). These causal relationships are usually probabilistic rather than deterministic, meaning that the causal event will increase the probability of the effect occurring rather than necessitating (determining) that it will occur.

Fig. 18.2 shows part of a complex causal model related to the water cycle. Each box shows a change, either an increase (shown by a rising arrow) or a decrease (shown by a declining arrow) in some activity or condition. The arrows between boxes show the direction of causality. So, looking at the top of the diagram, you would read that "an increase in surface temperature causes (or, more accurately, increases the probability of) an increase in evaporation."

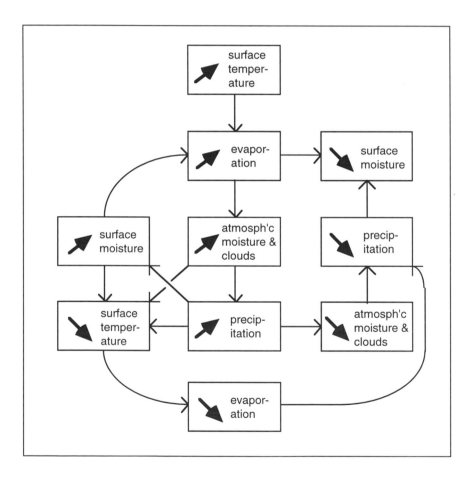

FIG. 18.2.   A partial example of a causal model related to the water cycle.

Domain Expertise

Domain expertise ranges from simple to complex, but also from general to detailed. And it is the general-to-detailed nature of domain expertise that allows the design of a holistic sequence that goes from simple to complex. The elaboration theory's sequencing guidance for domain expertise was derived primarily from Bruner's (1960) spiral curriculum and Ausubel's (1968) advance organizers and progressive differentiation, but it differs in several important ways from each and also provides greater guidance as to how to design such a sequence. An elaboration sequence starts with the broadest, most inclusive, most general ideas (which are also the simplest and generally among the first to have been discovered), such as the law of supply and demand in economics and Ohm's law in electricity. It gradually progresses to more complex, precise ideas, such as those that relate to maximizing profits on the supply side (marginal revenues and marginal costs) and to consumer preferences on the demand side of the law of supply and demand. This makes an elaboration sequence ideal for discovery learning and other approaches to the construction of knowledge.

But the elaboration theory recognizes two major kinds of domain expertise: conceptual (understanding what) and theoretical (understanding why). In their simplest form, these are concepts and principles, respectively, and in their more complex forms, they are conceptual knowledge structures (or concept maps) for "understanding what," and both causal models and "theoretical knowledge structures" (described later; see Fig. 18.4) for "understanding why." Although these two kinds of domain expertise are closely interrelated and are both involved to varying degrees in gaining expertise within every domain, the guidance for building a holistic, general-to-detailed sequence is different for each kind of domain expertise. Consequently, the elaboration theory offers guidance for sequencing the development of both kinds of domain expertise,* and both types of elaboration sequences can be used simultaneously if there is considerable emphasis on both types of domain expertise (knowledge structures) in a course. This is referred to as *multiple-strand sequencing* (Beissner & Reigeluth, 1994).

The conceptual elaboration sequence is described next, followed by the theoretical elaboration sequence and finally the SCM sequence.

The Conceptual Elaboration Sequence**

The conceptual elaboration sequence (Reigeluth & Darwazeh, 1982) is based on several observations. The first is that concepts are groupings or classes of objects, events, or ideas. For example, "tree" is a concept that includes all individual plants

---

* Here, a situationality has required breaking a general method down into more detailed kinds, each of which is used for a different parameter of that situational variable.

** As more detail is provided about this method, try to decide if it is parts, kinds, or criteria, as discussed in chapter 1, p. 10. Also, try to differentiate descriptive theory from design theory.

that meet certain criteria, most notably a woody stem. The second is that concepts can be broken down into narrower, less inclusive concepts that are either parts or kinds of them. For example, parts of trees include trunk, roots, branches, and leaves. Kinds of trees include deciduous and evergreen. And each of those parts and kinds can be further broken down into parts and kinds. The third observation is that people tend to store a new concept under a broader, more inclusive concept in their cognitive structures. The broader concept provides what Ausubel (1968) referred to as "cognitive scaffolding," and the process of learning that proceeds from broader, more inclusive and general concepts to narrower, more detailed concepts he called "progressive differentiation" because it entails a process of making progressively finer distinctions.

The kind of relationship upon which the conceptual elaboration sequence is based is one of inclusivity among concepts, with respect to either parts or kinds. Fig. 18.3 shows kinds of music. The inclusivity relationships are generally referred to as superordinate, coordinate, and subordinate relationships. In Fig. 18.3 classical music is subordinate to music, is coordinate to medieval music, and is superordinate to instrumental classical music. As you go further down in the conceptual structure to kinds of kinds of kinds (or parts of parts of parts), the concepts become progressively narrower and more detailed. Ausubel (1968) postulated that concepts are organized in our heads in this manner, so more stable cognitive structures are formed if you learn a broader, more inclusive concept before its subordinate concepts. Schema theory (R.C. Anderson, 1984; Rummelhart & Ortony, 1977) supports this notion, but with additional complexity. Please note that the lower concepts in a conceptual structure are not necessarily more complex or more difficult to learn. For example, children usually learn what a dog is long before they learn what a mammal is.

The conceptual elaboration sequence is one that starts by teaching (or discovering) the broadest, most inclusive, and general concepts that the learner has not yet learned, and proceeds to ever more narrow, less inclusive, and more detailed concepts, until the necessary level of detail has been reached. This kind of sequence might be used by a high school student interested in learning about the kinds and parts of animals and plants or by an employee interested in learning about the kinds and parts of equipment that the company sells. But how do you identify all these concepts and their inclusivity relationships? This is the purpose of a conceptual analysis. The result of such an analysis is a conceptual knowledge structure (see Fig. 18.3), which is often referred to as a taxonomy. The term "hierarchy" is sometimes used also, but this term miscommunicates because of the very different, more broadly accepted use of "hierarchy" to refer to a learning hierarchy (Gagné, 1968).

The conceptual elaboration sequence may be designed in either a topical or spiral manner. For a topical sequence, one could go all the way down one leg of the conceptual structure and gradually broaden out from there. For a spiral sequence, one could go completely across the top row, then across the next lower row, and so forth.

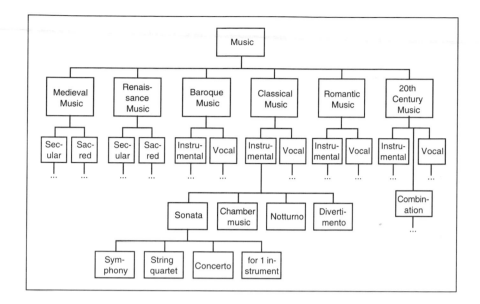

FIG. 18.3.   An example of a conceptual structure.

One point worth emphasizing is that the conceptual elaboration sequence doesn't violate the notion of learning prerequisites (hierarchical sequencing) because concepts higher in a conceptual knowledge structure contain some of the prerequisites for concepts below them but no prerequisites for any concepts above them (Wilson & Merrill, 1980).

For more about the conceptual elaboration sequence, see Reigeluth (in press).

The Theoretical Elaboration Sequence

The theoretical elaboration sequence is the second of the two sequencing strategies currently offered by the elaboration theory for building domain expertise. It is intended for courses that focus on interrelated sets of principles, which are usually elaborations of each other, such as a high school biology course that focuses on principles of genetics, life cycles, and bodily functions, or a corporate training program on how and why a piece of equipment works (not how to use it).

This sequencing strategy is based on several observations. The first is that principles are either causal relationships or natural-process relationships among changes in concepts. For example, the law of supply and demand indicates how changes in the supply of, and demand for, something influence its price, and vice versa (how changes in its price influence its supply and demand). The second is that principles, like concepts, exist on a continuum from broader, more general, and more inclusive ones to narrower, more specific, and less inclusive ones. For example, according to Michael Kelly[4], a fairly general principle is:

- Temperature change in an environment causes behavioral changes in certain organisms within that environment.

And two subordinate principles are:

- High temperatures in a desert environment cause certain organisms to be nocturnal.
- High temperatures in a desert environment cause certain organisms to undergo a period of estivation.

And this last principle could be further elaborated by identifying specific physiological changes that occur in a particular species when it estivates. Fig. 18.4 shows another example. So, unlike concepts, the broader principles are generally simpler and easier to learn than the narrower ones. This quality led principles to be the focus of Bruner's (1960) spiral curriculum. The third observation is that, as with concepts, people tend to store a new principle under a broader, more inclusive one in their cognitive structures. Again, Ausubel (1968) discovered that the broader principle provides "cognitive scaffolding" for the narrower, more complex principles, and therefore recommended the general-to-detailed sequencing strategy he called "progressive differentiation." But there is a fourth observation for principles that does not hold for concepts. Principles can be combined into causal models that reflect the complex, systemic, and often seemingly chaotic nature of most phenomena in the world (see Fig. 18.2).

The theoretical elaboration sequence starts by teaching the broadest, most inclusive, most general principles that the learner has not yet learned (which are also the simplest principles and generally the first to have been discovered); and it gradually progresses to ever more narrow, less inclusive, more detailed, more precise principles (which are also more complex and were generally discovered later). Examples were given earlier for economics (the law of supply and demand) and electricity (Ohm's law). This sequence continues until the desired level of complexity has been reached. The fact that this order reflects the order in which the principles were usually discovered, and could be most easily discovered by learners, makes this sequence ideal for problem-based learning and other discovery approaches.

But how does a teacher or designer identify all these principles and their inclusivity/complexity relationships? This is the purpose of a *theoretical analysis*. The result of such an analysis is a theoretical structure (see Fig. 18.4), which is different from a causal model (Fig. 18.2) in that it shows principles that elaborate on other principles (which provide more complexity and/or guidance on the same phe-

---

[4]In an assignment for a graduate course at Syracuse University.

When light rays pass from one medium into another (of different optical density):

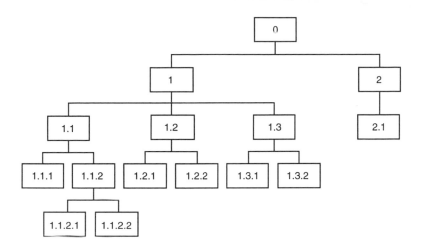

0   they behave unexpectedly.
1   they bend at the surface,
2   a straight object in both media looks bent at the surface.
1.1   the rays bend because they slow down in a denser medium or speed up in a less dense medium (C),
1.2   rays bend and change their distance from each other but remain parallel to teach other (A),
1.3   a portion of each ray is reflected off the surface, while the rest is refracted into the new medium (A),
2.1   the apparent position and size of an object usually change (A).
1.1.1   if they pass into a denser medium, the light rays bend toward the normal (B, D),
1.1.2   the greater the difference in optical density between two media, the more the light rays bend (D),
1.2.1   when rays bend toward the normal, they become farther apart (B, D),
1.2.2   the sharper the angle between a light ray and the surface, the more the ray bends (D),
1.3.1   the sharper the angle between a light ray and the surface, the more of each ray that is reflected and the less that is refracted (D),
1.3.2   if the angle is equal to, or sharper than, the critical angle, all of the light ray is reflected (B, E).
1.1.2.1 the index of refraction $(n) = c/c_r = (\sin i)/(\sin r)$ (D, E),
1.1.2.2 the relationship between the critical angle and the index of refraction is: $\sin i_c = 1/n$ (D, E).

Codes:
(A) What else happens?   (B) When?   (B) Why?   (C) Which way?   (D) How much?

FIG. 18.4.   An example of a theoretical structure.

nomena), whereas a causal model shows principles that combine with other principles (add new phenomena), usually at a similar level of complexity.

You can see in Fig. 18.4 that the kind of relationship upon which the theoretical elaboration sequence is based is one of the complexity with which a given causal phenomenon is characterized.* The more complex treatments (principles) are generally referred to as subordinate to the less complex ones. Therefore, the theoretical relationships are superordinate, coordinate, and subordinate, somewhat similar to conceptual relationships. For example, in Fig. 18.4, principles 1 and 2 elaborate on principle 0 because they each provide more detail about what happens when light rays pass from one optical medium into another of different optical density.

It should be noted that more detail can be provided by elaborating on either the causal factors or the resultant factors (effects) or both. And elaboration can occur by answering several different kinds of questions, such as:

- What else happens? or What else can cause this?
- When does this cause have this effect?
- Which way (direction) do things change?
- Why do they change?
- How much do they change? (See Fig. 18.4.)

The theoretical elaboration sequence may also be done in either a topical or a spiral manner. For a topical sequence, one could go all the way down one leg of the theoretical structure and gradually broaden out from there. For a spiral sequence, one could go completely across the top row, then across the next row down, and so forth.

For more about the theoretical elaboration sequence, see Reigeluth (1987; in press).

The Simplifying Conditions Method

For building task expertise, the SCM is a relatively new approach (though practitioners have long used it intuitively) that offers guidance for analyzing, selecting, and sequencing the "what to learn" (content). Briefly, SCM provides practical guidelines to make a very different kind of simple-to-complex sequence from the hierarchical sequence—one that is holistic rather than fragmented. Given that any complex task has some conditions under which it is much easier to perform than under others, an SCM sequence begins with the *simplest version* of the task that is still fairly representative of the task as a whole; then it teaches *progressively more complex versions* of the task until the desired level of complexity is reached, making sure that the learner is made explicitly aware of the relationship of each version to the other versions. Each version of the task is a class or group of complete,

---

* Have you noticed that the processes described here for breaking concepts and principles down into more detailed ones represent a more general case of the process described in chapter 1 (p. 10) of breaking methods down into more detailed parts, kinds, and/or criteria?

real-world performances of the task. This process contrasts sharply with the hierarchical approach to sequencing, which teaches all the prerequisites first and does not teach a complete, real-world task until the end of the sequence. Fig. 18.5 shows the differences between the hierarchical approach and the SCM approach.

For *procedural tasks,* the focus is on the steps (mental and/or physical) that experts use to decide what to do when. The SCM's selection (scope) and sequencing

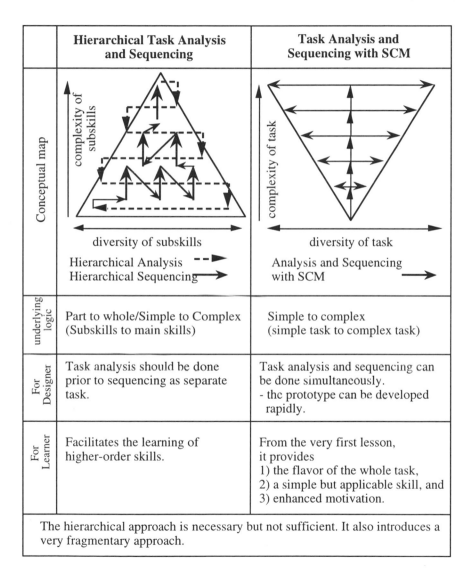

	Hierarchical Task Analysis and Sequencing	Task Analysis and Sequencing with SCM
Conceptual map	*(diagram: complexity of subskills vs. diversity of subskills)* Hierarchical Analysis --▶ Hierarchical Sequencing ⟶	*(diagram: complexity of task vs. diversity of task)* Analysis and Sequencing with SCM ⟶
underlying logic	Part to whole/Simple to Complex (Subskills to main skills)	Simple to complex (simple task to complex task)
For Designer	Task analysis should be done prior to sequencing as separate task.	Task analysis and sequencing can be done simultaneously. - the prototype can be developed rapidly.
For Learner	Facilitates the learning of higher-order skills.	From the very first lesson, it provides 1) the flavor of the whole task, 2) a simple but applicable skill, and 3) enhanced motivation.
The hierarchical approach is necessary but not sufficient. It also introduces a very fragmentary approach.		

FIG. 18.5.   Hierarchical approach and the SCM approach. (From Reigeluth & Kim, 1993)

methodology was derived primarily from the work of Scandura (1973) and Merrill (1976, 1980) on "path analysis" of a procedure. Every decision step in a complex procedure signals at least two different paths through the flowchart of the procedure (one of which is almost always simpler than the other), and it also represents at least two different conditions of performance.

In contrast, for *heuristic tasks* (Reigeluth, 1992; Reigeluth & Kim, 1993), the focus is on principles, guidelines, and/or causal models that experts use to decide what to do when (rather than using a set of steps).* Such heuristic tasks are characterized by great variations in the nature of an expert's performance, depending on the conditions of performance—so much so that experts do not think in terms of steps when they perform the task. This sequencing methodology was derived by Reigeluth primarily from the procedural SCM sequence.

Both types of SCM sequences can be used simultaneously if the task is a combination of both types of knowledge (procedural and heuristic). And SCM and domain-elaboration sequences can be used simultaneously as well. These are referred to as *multiple-strand sequences* (Beissner & Reigeluth, 1994).

The SCM (for both procedural and heuristic tasks) is composed of two parts: epitomizing and elaborating. Epitomizing is the process of identifying the simplest version of the task that is still fairly representative of the whole task. Elaborating is the process of identifying progressively more complex versions of the task.

The principles of *epitomizing* are based upon the notions of holistic learning and schema building. Therefore, epitomizing utilizes:

1. a whole version of the task rather than a simpler component skill;
2. a simple version of the task;
3. a real-world version of the task (usually); and
4. a fairly representative (typical or common) version of the task.

The epitome version of the task is performed by experts only under certain restricted (but usually real-world) conditions, referred to as the *simplifying conditions.*

The principles of *elaborating* are similarly based on the notions of holistic learning and assimilation-to-schema. Therefore, each subsequent elaboration should be:

1. another whole version of the task;
2. a slightly more complex version of the task;
3. equally authentic (or more so); and
4. equally or slightly less representative (typical or common) of the whole task.

The simplifying conditions are removed one by one to define each of the more complex versions of the task.

---

* This is a kind of learning that was not addressed much by the industrial-age paradigm of instructional theory but is receiving much attention in the new paradigm.

Since this is a relatively unknown approach to sequencing, some guidance for designing it is provided in the remainder of this chapter.

How to Design an SCM Sequence*

An SCM sequence is designed by integrating task analysis with design.** The analysis/design process centers around the questions, "What is the simplest version of the task that an expert has ever performed?" and "What is the next simplest version?" and so forth. As each version is identified, its place in the sequence is simultaneously determined.

In addition to this rule of thumb, you may find the following guidance helpful.*** Since designing an SCM sequence is more of a heuristic than a procedural process, the guidelines that follow include heuristics (bulleted) as well as steps (numbered), although, due to space limitations, I have not identified the full set of heuristics that an expert would use. Only the most important heuristics are included below. The procedural elements tend to predominate at the upper levels of analysis (the major phases of the task), but there comes a point at which it is no longer productive to break a given step into substeps, for that is not the way an expert thinks. Rather, you must identify the heuristics upon which an expert's performance of the step is based. I hope that the following portrayal will help to illustrate this nature of combination tasks.

Phase I. Prepare for Analysis and Design

1. Preparation. Lay the groundwork for your analysis and design.

1.1. Establish rapport with a SME (subject-matter expert).****
1.2. Identify the characteristics of the task in general.
1.3. Identify the characteristics of the learners in general.
1.4. Identify the delivery constraints (or fuzzy vision) of the instruction in general.

Phase II. Identify the First Learning Episode

2. Simplest version. Help the SME to identify the simplest version of the task that is fairly representative of the task as a whole and to describe the conditions that distinguish that version from all other versions.

- It may be helpful to start by identifying some of the *major* versions of the task and the conditions that distinguish when one version is appropriate versus another.

---

* Try to distinguish elements of instructional theory from elements of the ISD process in the following.
** The idea of integration is a common feature in the new paradigm.
*** Did you recognize this as method and sub-methods?
**** What is the relationship between 1.1 and 1? Between 1.1 and 1.2?

- Thinking of different conditions helps to identify versions, and thinking of different versions helps to identify conditions. Therefore, it is wise to do both simultaneously (or alternately).
- Ask the SME to recall the simplest case she or he has ever seen. The simplest version will be a class of similar cases. Then check to see how representative it is of the task as a whole.
- There is no single right version to choose. It is usually a matter of trade-offs. The very simplest version of the task is usually not very representative of the task as a whole. The more representative the simple version can be, the better, because it provides a more useful schema to which learners can relate subsequent versions.
- You may want to use some other criteria in addition to simple and representative, such as common (how frequently performed the version of the task is) and safe (how much risk there is to the learner and/or the equipment).

3. Organizing content.[4] Analyze the organizing content for this version of the task. How you do this will vary depending on the nature of the task: procedural, heuristic, or a combination of the two. (This is done now rather than later because it is important for determining whether this version of the task will be too large or too small for a single episode.)

- If primarily *procedural*, perform a procedural task analysis to identify substeps at the entry level of description and draw a flowchart for this version of the task. (For more guidance, see Merrill, 1976; 1980; Reigeluth, in press.)
- If primarily *heuristic*, use the process described in the next section of this chapter to identify guidelines and decision rules in a performance model and to identify explanations in explanatory models.
- If *combination,* do both: identify substeps, guidelines, decision rules, and explanations and portray each graphically.

4. Supporting content. Analyze supporting content for this version of the task. (This is also important to do now so that you can determine whether this version of the task will be too large or too small for a single episode.)

4.1 Identify information, understandings, skills, metacognitive/higher order thinking skills, and affective qualities (e.g., attitudes) that are directly relevant to this version of the task and have not yet been acquired by the learners.

4.2 Analyze those understandings, skills, metacognitive/higher order thinking skills, and affective qualities down to entry level. The procedural and hierarchical task analysis approaches work well for skills and higher-order skills, and the hierarchical approach can be fairly easily extended to identifying pre-

---

[4]In the case of a procedural task, the organizing content is steps, whereas for a heuristic task, the organizing content is principles (heuristics).

requisite understandings. But I cannot offer much guidance for analyzing affective qualities.

At this point, you have identified all the content that needs to be taught in the episode for this version of the task. However, if you use an instructional approach that is highly constructivist and requires much self-directed and self-regulated learning, then you will not be explicitly teaching any supporting content. Nevertheless, it is helpful for the teacher (or guide) to be aware of all this supporting content, to provide appropriate scaffolding to the learner when needed, or to help the learner identify appropriate resources for learning important supporting content.

5. Size. Make sure the amount of learning required for this version of the task fits the size of the episodes for your course.

5.1. Decide how big your episodes should be.
* Analyze the delivery constraints of the specific instructional situation, if any (such as 45-minute time blocks for class sessions).
* Be sure to keep in mind both in-class and "homework" time.
* Too big is bad. In considering the optimal size of your groupings of content, consider how long your learners can be actively engaged without a break. This will depend to some extent on such factors as the age of the learners, the difficulty/abstractness of the content, the motivational value of the instruction, and additional factors.
* Too small is bad. Also consider how long the learners should be allowed to work in order to not interrupt their concentration and engagement.
* For less time-bound learning environments, size of episodes should be determined more by the considerations that Bruner (1960) talks about: ensuring that the "pay-off" for the learner is commensurate with the effort the learner invests. Also, there will be little need to make the episodes equal in size.
5.2. Adjust the size of the episode to the target size.
* If its length is greater than the target, reduce the size of this episode, preferably by adding another simplifying condition. It is possible to create simplifying conditions that don't exist in the real world to accomplish this if necessary, but there are obvious negatives in doing so. However, it is often possible to compensate for those negatives. Alternatively, some supporting content could be removed from this episode, but don't remove any prerequisites for the organizing content.
* If its length is much smaller than the target, increase the size of this episode, preferably by removing a simplifying condition (which requires adding skills).

6. Within-episode sequence. If you have decided to provide much guidance to the learner, you will want to sequence the content selected for this episode. But, if you intend to use a problem- or project-based learning approach with very little guidance, you may require the learner to figure out what learning resources he or she needs when. Either way, you may want to consider some of the following guidelines as you either make suggestions to the learner or decide on a within-episode sequence for the learner.*

- Teach prerequisites just prior to the content for which they are prerequisite.
- Teach understanding (principles, causal models, or process models) prior to a related procedure.
- Teach coordinate concepts together.
- Teach content in the order in which it is used (e.g., a procedural sequence).

At this point, if you are using a rapid-prototyping approach to ISD, you are ready to design and develop the instruction for this learning episode (the epitome). Otherwise, you can continue to Phase III to design the scope and sequence for each of your remaining episodes.

Phase III. Identify the Next Learning Episode

7. *Next version.* Help the SME to identify the next simplest version of the task that is fairly representative of the task as a whole.

   7.1. Identify and rank-order all the simplifying conditions that distinguish the simplest version of the task from all the more complex versions.
   - Each simplifying condition eliminates some skills and knowledge from what an expert needs, to be able to perform the task. Different conditions correspond to different sets of skills and knowledge that vary in complexity. This allows the simplifying conditions to be ranked according to how much additional complexity each requires for performance of the task.
   - The rank-ordering of the simplifying conditions corresponds to an ordering of the versions of the task from simple to complex.
   - The rank-ordering of the simplifying conditions should be done using the same criteria you used in step 2: how simple and representative the resulting version of the task is and any other criteria you choose, such as how common it is and how safe it is.
   - Don't expect to be able to identify all of the simplifying conditions right away. As you proceed with the analysis, you will find additional conditions to add, no matter how thorough you try to be from the beginning.
   - These simplifying conditions are referred to as the "primary simplifying conditions" (PSCs) because they are identified first. (Secondary simplifying conditions, or SSCs, are discussed next.)
   - It is usually helpful to identify the full variety of versions of the task appropriate for this course.

---

* Hopefully, you have noticed many places where diversity of methods is either provided or accommodated by the elaboration theory.

7.2. Identify the next simplest and most representative version of the task (the next elaboration).

- This will typically be the next rank-ordered simplifying condition.
- If removing a PSC requires more new content than can be taught in one episode, then identify *SSCs* that can be included to reduce the complexity of the new version of the task that results when the PSC is removed.
- If SSCs are added, rank-order them.
- Note that episodes defined by removing a PSC (called "primary elaborations") must be learned after the simplest episode (the "epitome"), for they all elaborate on it. However, those episodes could be learned in any order in relation to each other, even though it is usually better to teach the simpler elaborations first. On the other hand, the episodes defined by removing SSCs (called "secondary elaborations") cannot be learned until after the related primary elaboration is learned, for they all elaborate on it.
- If you want to design a learner-controlled sequence, you can design the primary elaborations so that they can be selected in any order. However, sometimes this can result in a fair amount of redundancy, if skills learned in one elaboration are also required in another. Of course, computer-based instruction can be designed to eliminate any such redundancy, by keeping track of what has already been learned.

7.3. If SSCs are added, rank-order them (see step 7.1).

8. Organizing content, supporting content, size, and within-episode sequence. These steps are the same as steps 3–6 in Phase II.

9. Remaining versions. Repeat Phase III (except for step 7.1) for each remaining simplifying condition (primary, secondary, tertiary, etc.) until instructional time runs out or you have reached the level of expertise desired.

Again, I would like to emphasize that this characterization of the SCM analysis/design process is considerably abbreviated, especially with respect to the heuristic elements, but hopefully it gives some understanding, both by the guidance it offers and the illustration it provides.

Elaboration on Step 3: Organizing Content

Step 3 above called for analyzing the organizing content for the selected version of the task. For procedural content, there is an effective method already available: procedural analysis (see, e.g., Gagné, Briggs, & Wager, 1992, pp. 147–150; Merrill, 1976; 1980; Reigeluth, in press). But for heuristic tasks, I am not aware of much guidance for identifying the heuristics that an expert uses in performing any given version of a task. The major difference lies in the nature of the content that is analyzed, sequenced, and learned. Rather than a set of steps (with decisions and branches and paths), you must identify the underlying principles or causal models that experts use to perform the task. In work I have done, the following ideas have gradually evolved.

Experts use both descriptive and design (prescriptive) theories to guide their decisions. I refer to a design theory as a performance model (or set of performance models), each of which is a set of interrelated guidelines for attaining a given goal. And I refer to one kind of descriptive theory as an explanatory model (or set of explanatory models), each of which is an interrelated set of explanations as to why the guidelines work. This is usually related to another kind of descriptive model, which shows how a complex "object" works, for example, the human psyche in the task of psychotherapy, or a power plant in the task of power-plant maintenance and repair.

"Object" descriptive models are usually the easiest to analyze, because an expert tends to be fairly well aware of the way the "object" of interest works. Therefore, this is a good place to start. Explanatory descriptive models are easier to identify after you identify the performance models that they are to explain. Performance models are perhaps the most difficult to analyze, because experts are usually not overtly aware of many of the heuristics that guide their performances of the task, and it is easy to overlook whole sets of guidelines and explanations.

To address this problem, it is useful to use a top-down approach to analyzing a version of a heuristic task for an episode. The top, most general, level is the **goals** of the task (or subtask, if it is a combination task). For example, for the task "Determine the media for a course," the goals might include:

- the media will help the learner to master the objective;
- the media will be cost effective;
- the media fall within the constraints for the course development and implementation.

After identifying all the important goals, you can then think in terms of **considerations** for attaining each goal. Considerations are the major categories of causal factors that influence performance of the task. For example, for the third goal (within constraints), the considerations might include:

- budget,
- skills of the personnel available to teach the course, and
- availability of equipment for the course.

If there are lots of causal factors within a category (a consideration), then it is helpful to identify **subcategories** of causal factors. This helps to keep from overlooking some types of causal factors. Eventually, you are ready to identify specific **causal factors** for each category (or subcategory). For example, for the third consideration (equipment availability), the factors might include:

- amount of equipment,
- scheduling of equipment,
- alternative uses of equipment,
- features (capabilities) of equipment.

This is the lowest level of analysis you need to reach in the top-down process. Once you have identified causal factors, you need to analyze each causal factor to identify all **guidelines** an expert uses to perform this version of the task that involve the causal factor. For example, guidelines for the above factors might include (in respective order):

- If an insufficient amount of the equipment is available for the projected number of students, do not select that delivery system.
- If the equipment is not available at all the necessary times, do not select that delivery system.
- If the equipment is available and would otherwise go unutilized, there is a stronger need for you to select that delivery system.
- If the capabilities of the equipment do not meet the instructional needs, do not select that delivery system.
  (Note that these examples are intended to be illustrative, not exhaustive, and there may be more than one guideline for a given causal factor.)

You should also identify any **decision rules** an expert uses to combine the guidelines into a performance model. Finally, you are ready to identify specific **explanations** as to why each of the guidelines works and to combine the explanations into explanatory models.

In summary, these are some substeps for performing step 3 for heuristic or combination tasks:

1. Identify a *descriptive model* for any and all objects involved in performing the task.
2. Identify the *goals* for this version of the task under its conditions.
3. Identify all important *considerations* for attaining each goal. If there are a lot of causal factors for a consideration, identify *subconsiderations* for it.
4. Identify all important *causal factors* for each consideration (or subconsideration).
5. Analyze each causal factor to identify all *guidelines* (prescriptive principles) that an expert uses to perform this version of the task. Also identify any *decision rules* an expert uses to combine the guidelines into a performance model.
6. Identify *explanations* as to why each of the guidelines works and combine the explanations into explanatory models.

Space limitations prohibit listing the heuristics for performing each of these substeps. But please keep in mind that you should identify these components of task expertise even if you plan to take a constructivist approach to the instruction, for it will provide an understanding of the kinds of scaffolding that may be helpful to provide.

CONCLUSION

The purpose of the elaboration theory is to provide guidance for making scope and sequence decisions that support much more holistic approaches to learning, which is especially important for the new paradigm of instructional theories. It recognizes that different guidelines are needed for different instructional situations. At this point, the differences are based on different kinds of expertise to be developed, but the elaboration theory is definitely a work in progress, and much remains to be learned about sound guidance for making scope and sequence decisions. I hope that this progress report will stimulate others to help contribute to this growing knowledge base.

REFERENCES

Anderson, J. R. (1983). *The architecture of cognition.* Cambridge, MA: Harvard University Press.
Anderson, R. C. (1984). Some reflections on the acquisition of knowledge. *Educational Researcher, 13*(9), 5–10.
Ausubel, D. P. (1968). *Educational psychology: A cognitive view.* New York: Holt Rinehart & Winston.
Beissner, K. L., & Reigeluth, C. M. (1994). A case study on course sequencing with multiple strands using the elaboration theory. *Performance Improvement Quarterly, 7*(2), 38–61.
Bruner, J. S. (1960). *The process of education.* New York: Random House.
Gagné, R. M. (1968). Learning hierarchies. *Educational Psychologist, 6,* 1–9.
Gagné, R. M., Briggs, L. J., & Wager, W. W. (1992). *Principles of instructional design* (4th ed.), New York: Harcourt Brace Jovanovich College Publishers.
Goleman, D. (1995). *Emotional intelligence: Why it can matter more than IQ.* New York: Bantam Books.
Greenberg, M. T., & Kusché, C. A. (1993). *Promoting social and emotional development in deaf children: The PATHS project.* Seattle, WA: University of Washington Press.
Kaufman, R. A., & English, F. W. (1979). *Needs assessment: Concept and application.* Englewood Cliffs, NJ: Educational Technology Publications.
Kaufman, R. A., Rojas, A. M., & Mayer, H. (1993). *Needs assessment: A user's guide.* Englewood Cliffs, NJ: Educational Technology Publications.
Merrill, P. F. (1976). Task analysis: An information processing approach. *NSPI Journal, 15*(2), 7–11.
Merrill, P. F. (1980). Analysis of a procedural task. *NSPI Journal, 19*(2), 11–15.
Osin, L., & Lesgold, A. (1997). A proposal for the reengineering of the educational system. *Review of Educational Research, 66*(4), 621–656.
Reigeluth, C. M. (1987). Lesson blueprints based on the elaboration theory of instruction. In C. M. Reigeluth (Ed.), *Instructional theories in action: Lessons illustrating selected theories and models* (pp. 245–288). Hillsdale, NJ: Lawrence Erlbaum Associates.
Reigeluth, C. M. (1992). Elaborating the elaboration theory. *Educational Technology Research & Development, 40*(3), 80–86.
Reigeluth, C. M. (in press). *Scope and Sequence Decisions for Quality Instruction.*
Reigeluth, C. M., & Darwazeh, A. N. (1982). The elaboration theory's procedure for designing instruction: A conceptual approach. *Journal of Instructional Development, 5*(3), 22–32.

Reigeluth, C. M., & Kim, Y. (April 1993). *Recent advances in task analysis and sequencing.* Paper presented at the NSPI national conference, Chicago, IL.

Rossett, A. (1987). *Training needs assessment.* Englewood Cliffs, NJ: Educational Technology Publications.

Rummelhart, D. E., & Ortony, A. (1977). The representation of knowledge in memory. In R. C. Anderson, R. J. Spiro, & W. W. Montague (Eds.), *Schooling and the acquisition of knowledge.* Hillsdale, NJ: Lawrence Erlbaum Associates.

Scandura, J. M. (1973, August). Structural learning and the design of educational materials. *Educational Technology, 13,* 7–13.

Vygotsky, L. S. (1978). *Mind in society: The development of higher psychological processes.* (Edited by M. Cole, V. John-Steiner, S. Scribner, & E. Souberman). Cambridge, MA: Harvard University Press.

Wilson, B. G., & Merrill, M. D. (1980). General-to-detailed sequencing of concepts in a taxonomy is in general agreement with learning hierarchy analysis. *NSPI Journal, 19*(10), 11–14.

Unit 3 Fostering Psychomotor Development

FOREWORD

Although this unit has only one theory, it is one which integrates a wide variety of methods from a variety of theoretical perspectives. I encourage you to explore the extent to which the methods and principles (or guidelines) offered by this theory have counterparts in the cognitive domain. I also encourage you to think about whether this theory might represent an example of the kind of highly integrative theory that could benefit the other two domains (cognitive and affective).

—C.M.R.

19 The Development of Physical Skills: Instruction in the Psychomotor Domain

Alexander Romiszowski
Syracuse University

Alexander Romiszowski

Alexander Romiszowski, PhD, currently divides his time between the U.S., where he teaches Instructional Design and Development at Syracuse University, and Brazil, where he is a Director of TTS Consultants and AGITT Multimedia in Rio de Janeiro and a visiting researcher at the "School of the Future" Institute at the University of Sao Paulo. Among his many award-winning publications are: the "trilogy" *Designing Instructional Systems*, *Producing Instructional Systems*, and *Developing Auto-Instructional Materials*; the chapter on "Message Design for Psychomotor Task Instruction" in Fleming and Levie's *Instructional Message Design*; and, most recently, the anthology of *Instructional Development Paradigms*, co-edited with Charles Dills.

457

FOREWORD

Goals and preconditions. *The primary goal of this theory is to foster the development of psycho-motor (physical) skills. It is intended for all situations.*

Values. *Some of the values upon which this theory is based include:*

- *physical skills,*
- *automatizing physical skills,*
- *the integration of different approaches and apparently conflicting viewpoints.*

Methods. *Here are the major methods this theory offers:*

1. *Impart knowledge of what should be done.*
   - *For reproductive skills: use expository methods.*
   - *For productive skills: use experiential, discovery-learning techniques.*
2. *Develop the basic skill (step-by-step actions).*
   - *Demonstrate the skill.*
   - *Provide controlled practice.*
3. *Develop proficiency (flow, automatization, generalization)*

To impart knowledge:
   - *For tasks that require no new knowledge: Demonstrate without explanations.*
   - *For tasks that require limited new knowledge: Demonstrate and explain simultaneously.*
   - *For tasks that require much new knowledge but little new skill:*
     - *For mainly visual relationships: Use exploratory practice followed by expository review.*
     - *For a single, multi-stage movement: Demonstrate the sequential action pattern before providing practice.*
   - *Promote the mental rehearsal of the task.*
   - *Accompany demonstrations with verbal cueing of the steps.*
   - *Provide all demonstrations from the viewpoint of the performer.*

To provide practice:
   - *Teach integrated, coordinated tasks by the whole-task method.*
     - *But teach prerequisite subskills first.*
   - *Teach tasks made of relatively independent actions by the progressive-parts method.*
   - *Provide long, continuous practice sessions for productive tasks.*
   - *Provide short, spaced practice for reproductive tasks.*
     - *Use mental rehearsal between spaced practice sessions.*

- *Use forced pacing for high-speed tasks.*
- *Use a progression of specific performance goals during practice.*

To provide feedback on practice:
- *Provide after-the-fact knowledge of results rather than feedback that controls performance.*
- *Correct aspects of performance rather than just giving right/wrong information.*
- *For productive tasks, provide debriefing or reflection-in-action.*

To promote transfer:
- *The more productive a task is, the more variability the practice should have.*
- *Help the learner develop a motor schema having all the important attributes for performance of the task.*
- *Promote over-learning of the task.*
- *Don't progress to more difficult tasks too soon.*

To use task fidelity appropriately:
- *Use physical fidelity for reproductive tasks.*
- *Use functional fidelity for productive tasks.*
- *Use perceived fidelity rather than technical fidelity.*
- *Progress from lower to higher fidelity.*
- *Sacrifice fidelity when doing so will improve learning.*

To develop the "inner self":
- *Use relaxation exercises.*
- *Imagine being a known expert.*
- *Engage in appropriate self-talk.*

Major contributions. *Deals with all kinds of physical skills for all kinds of situations. Demonstrates how apparently conflicting viewpoints can be integrated into a coherent scheme that may meet practitiioner needs better than a more ideological fixation on one viewpoint (which has important implications for the cognitive domain).*

—C.M.R.

The Development of Physical Skills: Instruction in the Psychomotor Domain

INTRODUCTION

The Importance and Value of Physical Skills

Physical, or psychomotor, skills are in evidence whenever people perform practical activities in a competent manner, whether in the world of sports, the world of work, or the world of leisure. Despite such current socioeconomic tendencies as automation in the workplace, increased leisure time and the boom in home entertainment, the importance of physical skills to the individual and to society in general appears to be maintained and indeed perhaps increased.

In some respects, it would seem that today's world is the world of sports. Sports stars have taken on the societal roles that once were the prerogative of Hollywood film stars. More coverage than ever is given to sports in the mass media. In schools, sports education plays more prominent a role than ever in the past.

In the world of work, despite the elimination of many areas of skilled physical activity by robotics, it is often found that well-trained people can outperform the robots in both productivity and quality of work. Some companies that completely automated their production lines have now reverted to using human workers. Examples reported in the press include automobile assembly, electronics assembly, and microchip inspection.

In the everyday world, with increased leisure time, a greater number of people are involved in the arts and manipulative work of a semiartistic nature that requires the use of specific psychomotor skills. Also, the general rise in the standard of living of a society leads to rising costs of specialist labor, which in turn leads to growth in "do it yourself" home improvement and automobile maintenance, thus creating a need on the part of many people for the skills that before were the prerogative of a few.

The need to master new physical skills, which in the past tended to involve smaller numbers of learners and were typically learned once during their lifetime, has become a part of lifelong learning for a greater proportion of the population. Furthermore, whereas in the past the development of physical capabilities tended to occur in the earlier formative years, typically through a process of free participation in sports and other forms of activity or through apprenticeship to a "master" performer who was not necessarily a skilled instructor, today's fast-changing needs have tended to increase the importance of effectiveness and efficiency in the learning process and, therefore, the value of instruction.

The theme developed in this chapter is that the value of instruction in the psychomotor area lies in the value of the skills and competencies achieved by the learners, as perceived by the learners themselves, their employers, and society in general. This value is generated by the application of research-based principles of instruction drawn from several areas of learning theory. I hope that one spin-off value of this chapter will be to demonstrate the interrelatedness of psychomotor skills instruction with best practices in the cognitive, affective, and other domains of learning.*

Research and Theory on Instruction in the Psychomotor Domain

It is interesting to note that much of the research work reported here was accomplished in earlier years when, it seems, the psychomotor-learning domain was more popular with educational researchers. More recently, the mainstream literature on instruction has tended to neglect the psychomotor domain. Despite this apparent recent neglect, however, several fruitful lines of research and instructional models for the development of motor skills do exist in the literature.

Some of these models have kept close to the preindustrial apprenticeship model of skills development, which involved the forging of intimate relationships between a master performer and a novice or apprentice. This relationship was not based on formal instruction so much as on the delegation of tasks, the supervision of these by the master, and the supply of rich feedback, often including reflection on why things worked out or did not work out. These models have much in common with ideas recently popularized in the cognitive area, such as "reflection-in-action" and the "cognitive apprenticeship." It may not be surprising, therefore, that a review of successful practice in the teaching of psychomotor skills, as researched in the past, continues to be currently valid and indeed may be closer in philosophy to current (postindustrial) thinking about the process of learning and instruction than might at first be expected.

On the other hand, the area of physical activity is the area that is readily accepted as being validly measurable through objective measures of performance such as speed, productivity, error rate, etc. One can therefore place effective psychomotor training models within paradigms such as the one the performance technology movement has spawned. All in all, therefore, the analysis of current best practices of physical skills development is particularly interesting in revealing multiple paradigms that can be used as the philosophical and theoretical backdrop for practice. The motor skills domain, better than perhaps any of the others, can therefore illustrate the thesis that the process of instruction can be most adequately planned by some combination of several theoretical viewpoints.**

---

* This is certainly a consistent theme for the new paradigm of instructional theories.
** Hopefully, you recognized this notion of multiple perspectives and eclectic, systemic thinking as characteristic of the new paradigm.

LEARNING AND TEACHING OF PSYCHOMOTOR
SKILLS: BASIC CONSTRUCTS

The Skills Schema

Perhaps one of the weaknesses of much early work on skill acquisition has been the concentration on simple movements or on sequences of simple repetitive steps.* However, these are typically performed in real life as components of more complex activity. The importance of this view only began to be fully appreciated in the latter half of this century. A distinction was made by Poulton (1957), in the context of sports training, between "closed" and "open" tasks, the former requiring a response to a stable environment (e.g., bowling), and the latter requiring continuous adjustment to an unpredictable, changing environment, as during a football game.** Pioneering work in the 1960s at the Perkins factory in the United Kingdom identified the importance in the industrial context of "planning" or "strategy" skills (Wellens, 1974). These have also been referred to as "productive" skills in that they require the performer to produce a situation-specific response. We begin to see the trend toward the integration of instruction across the domains (see next paragraph) and also the blending, in practice, of ideas on instruction drawn from the apparently opposed camps of behavioral and cognitive psychology.

We may conceptualize a continuum of "reproductive-to-productive" skills as a basic model for the analysis of skills. The position of a given task on this continuum is of great importance to decisions about appropriate instructional methods. Fig. 19.1 presents a schema that combines a four-domain classification of skills with the reproductive–productive continuum. Whereas the domains may influence certain aspects of instructional decision making (e.g., media selection), the position of a task on the reproductive–productive continuum influences instructional decisions in much more fundamental ways, for example, in deciding between expository and experiential (or discovery-learning) instructional methods, or in the extent to which "deep processing" discussions are an essential part of the teaching method (Romiszowski, 1981).***

Another point illustrated by Fig. 19.1 is the potential for redefinition of the universe of learning objectives into more than the three traditionally accepted domains, adding a fourth domain related to the interpersonal skills area. This gives a model with four content-related domains, referring essentially to the skills of controlling your thinking, controlling your body, controlling your emotions, and con-

---

* Can the same not also be said of the early work in the cognitive domain?
** To what extent is this similar to the distinction between structured and ill-structured domains in the cognitive arena? And is it related to the key markers of a mechanistic view of the world in the industrial age and an "organic," systemic view of the world in the information age.
*** Did you recognize this as a situationality?

trolling other people's reactions.* The point of importance, however, is that the position of a given skill on the productive-to-reproductive dimension may be of greater importance in terms of instructional issues than its position in one or another of the four domains.**

The Skills Cycle

Many authors have observed that skilled activity involves a cycle of stages, commencing with the reception of information from the environment and leading to some action on the environment. Wheatcroft (1973), for example, describes the physical skill cycle as commencing with the formation of an idea or purpose in the mind of the performer. This leads to:

DOMAIN OR CATEGORY OF SKILLED ACTIVITY	THE SKILLS CONTINUUM	
	REPRODUCTIVE SKILLS	PRODUCTIVE SKILLS
	Knowledge content: applying standard procedures (algorithms)	Knowledge content: applying principles and strategies (heuristics)
COGNITIVE SKILLS • Decision making • Problem solving • Logical thinking, etc.	Applying a known procedure to a known category of "problem" (e.g., dividing numbers, writing a grammatically correct sentence).	Solving "new" problems or inventing a new procedure (e.g., proving a theorem, writing creatively).
PSYCHOMOTOR SKILLS • Physical action • Perceptual acuity, etc.	Repetitive or automated skills (e.g., typewriting, changing gear, running fast).	"Strategy" or "planning" skills (e.g., painting, defensive driving, playing football).
REACTIVE SKILLS • Dealing with oneself: (attitudes and feelings, habits and self-control)	Conditioned habits and attitudes: attend, respond (Krathwohl et al, 1964); approach and avoidance behaviors (Mager, 1968)	Personal control skills: developing a mental set or value system (Krathwohl, et al, 1964); self-actualization (Rogers, 1969).
INTERACTIVE SKILLS • Dealing with others: (social habits and skills)	Conditioned social responses (e.g., good manners, pleasant tone of voice, socialized behaviors).	Interpersonal control skills (e.g., leadership, supervision, persuasion, salesmanship).

FIG. 19.1.   The skills schema.

---

* Is the fourth domain a new one, wherein the third domain is in effect the affective domain, or do the third and fourth domains together constitute what has typically been called the affective domain?

** Identifying the most powerful situationalities is perhaps one of the most important things an instructional theory can do.

- the reception of relevant information,
- its correct perception and interpretation,
- a decision on the appropriate action to take,
- and, finally, the action itself.*

This is then followed by reception of further new information on the results of the action, perception, decision, further action, and so on. By incorporating in this model the aforementioned need to have previously gained knowledge of the procedure which is to be executed, the skill cycle can be represented as shown in Fig. 19.2 (Romiszowski, 1981).

This model enables one to distinguish between the automated, reproductive (reflexive, closed, etc.) skills and the more productive (strategy, planning, open, etc.) skills. Indeed, three basic categories of skilled behavior are postulated:

- Totally reflexive and automated skills (like typing), in which the sensory information that is perceived directly triggers a physical action without any significant involvement of the brain. The performance "loop" for such skills may be described as "S–1–4–R" in Fig. 19.2.
- Skills that depend on the recall of a possibly complex, but essentially algorithmic, procedure and the execution of a series of linked actions in sequence.

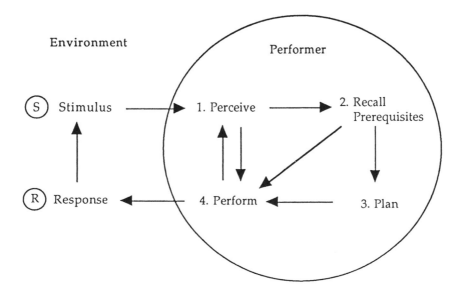

FIG 19.2.   A four-stage performance cycle.

_____

* Is this design theory or descriptive theory?

Many industrial and sports skills fall into this category. The performance loop for these skills can be described as "S–1–2–4–R."

- Skills that depend on the analysis of the incoming sensory information in order to formulate plans of action appropriate to the situation and, possibly, to evaluate alternative plans before deciding on the appropriate action. The performance loop for these skills is "S–1–2–3–4–R." Actually, this is a simplification, for a lot of internal looping may take place as well. For example, as performance is about to commence, internal control processes may sense that the external situation has changed and the planned response is no longer adequate, so the internal loop (1–2–3–4) is repeated. Also, as the planning (information processing) is performed, new insights, rules, or relationships may be remembered for future use (2–3–2–3–2, etc.).

The skills cycle draws our attention to the importance of considering such factors as perception, memory, intellectual skills, and cognitive strategies when we engage in the teaching of psychomotor skills. The similarity to the planning issues characteristic of the cognitive domain is quite striking. Also, when viewed in conjunction with the previously presented skills schema, we can see how the basic model may be applied across the whole universe of skilled activities.* Here are a few examples drawn from all four domains.

Perception. The performer may have a low level of "perceptual acuity," as for example:

- Cognitive skill: inability to "see" a word problem in math as such;
- Psychomotor skill: insufficient ability to distinguish color, tone, size, speed;
- Reactive skill: inability to notice the relevant events occurring around one;
- Interactive skill: inability to notice the reactions (including nonverbal responses) of other people to one's own actions.

Prerequisites. Inability to recall prerequisites may be caused by a lack of these prerequisites; that is, the performer simply does not know what to do in a particular situation. The relevant procedure has not been learned, or has been forgotten. Alternatively, the performer may fail to recall the relevant knowledge, although it is in store, due to a failure to interpret the perceived stimulus information in the correct way. The new information is compared with the stored experience (knowledge structures or schemata) and is misclassified. Thus the wrong procedure is recalled and applied:

- Cognitive skill: A given Portuguese noun is misclassified as to gender; this leads to the recall of the wrong form of the adjective to be coupled to it.

---

* This is related to the controversy over whether instructional theory should be domain-dependent or domain-independent (or some combination of the two).

- Psychomotor skill: A given road sign is misinterpreted by the motorist, leading to the recall of an incorrect strategy; the motorist accelerates instead of braking.
- Reactive skill: A student's examination errors are misinterpreted by the teacher as due to laziness, leading to the development of an unduly negative attitude towards the student in question.
- Interactive skill: A salesman misinterprets a potential customer's reactions and as a result applies an inappropriate selling strategy.

Planning.   The causes of failure in the planning of an action may be due to an inability to generate a set of possible alternative courses of action, or to make the best choice. The first implies an inability to use the relevant principles in order to "invent" alternative procedures (assuming, of course, that the relevant principles are previously known). The second implies an inability to evaluate the alternatives by "thinking through" the implications of each one. For example, a manager faced with an industrial relations problem may (or may not) consider all the alternative courses of action (sacking, warning, suspension, ignoring the problem) and may (or may not) evaluate correctly the hazards of each one (strikes, loss of productivity). A football player may (or may not) consider the range of possible plays open to him (run, avoid, pass, kick) and may (or may not) select the one that is most likely to succeed at that specific moment of the game.*

THE GENERAL PROCESS OF PSYCHOMOTOR SKILL LEARNING AND INSTRUCTION

Much has been written on the classification of motor tasks and skills in an attempt to create some form of taxonomy or schema that would assist workers in the psychomotor domain in a way similar to the two well-known taxonomies in the cognitive and affective domains (Bloom, Englehart, Hill, Furst, & Krathwohl, 1956; Krathwohl, Bloom, & Masia, 1964). An attempt to classify the models was made by Gilchrist and Gruber (1984), who identified no less than 12 different models in the literature. None of these models, however, seem to serve the same function as the Bloom and Krathwohl taxonomies of indicating a sequence or hierarchy of stages through which mastery progresses. Such a hierarchical model of stages to mastery is useful for the planning of instructional sequences and the development of appropriate evaluation instruments and criteria for each stage in the sequence.

A hierarchical model of skill development, based on very detailed experimental observation of industrial skills acquisition and the stages through which the mastery of industrial skills progresses was described by Seymour (1954, 1966). Similar

---

* Is this design theory yet?

descriptions have appeared more recently in the literature, apparently derived independently in other domains of skilled activity. Examples are Schmidt's (1975) schema-theory model of motor skill learning, the account given by Adler (1981) based on observations in sports activities and another by Gentner (1984) based on observations of the development of expertise in typing. The model presented below of five stages in the development of psychomotor skills is derived from the above research, particularly that of Seymour.* It has been successfully used as the basis for much practical skills training, including work by the present author (Romiszowski, 1974, 1981).

Stage 1: Acquiring knowledge of what should be done, to what purpose, in what sequence, and by what means. Further knowledge is acquired as the learning process progresses. What is required up-front is the minimum knowledge necessary to start performing the task in a meaningful manner.

Stage 2: Executing the actions in a step-by-step manner, for each of the steps of the operation. The characteristics of this stage are: there is a conscious application of the knowledge (i.e., the "what and how" aspects of the operation are controlled by the conscious thinking-out of each step); the perceptual information necessary to initiate and control action (the "when-to-do and how-well-done" aspects) is almost exclusively visual (sometimes auditory). The observable result of these two characteristics is that execution of the task is erratic and jumpy. Time taken on a given step may vary considerably between attempts.

Stage 3: Transfer of control from the eyes to other senses or to kinesthetic control through muscular coordination. The release of the sense of vision (at least partially) from the direct control of each movement allows for more efficient "advance planning" of subsequent movements in the sequence. The subsequent actions flow on directly without any apparent break between one movement and the next.

Stage 4: Automatization of the skill. This stage is characterized by a reduction of the need for conscious attention and "thinking through" of the actions. Performance becomes a set of reflex actions, one triggering the next, without direct conscious effort of the performer. The observable progress in this stage is that the performer may execute the task and at the same time be thinking or talking about other matters, even to some extent attending to other events in the environment, without this having any appreciable effect on the speed or quality of execution of the task.

---

* In what ways is this similar to Landa's phases of skill acquisition (see p. 342)? Should the two be similar?

Stage 5: Generalization of the skill to a continually greater range of appli-cation situations. This last stage applies to the productive/strategy/planning end of our skills continuum. In fact, most sports, most crafts, and most design skills are, at least in some respects, "productive." However well the basic physical skills involved are automated, one can still differentiate among football players on the basis of their gamesmanship, among motorists on the basis of their "road sense," and among lathe operators on the basis of how they strike the balance between speed and quality of work.*

The skills-mastery model presented above suggests three basic steps or stages in the overall instructional process (see Fig. 19.3).

Step 1: Imparting the knowledge content. This refers to the minimum knowledge required to understand why, when, and how to perform the task. It re-lates to the first stage of skill development as outlined in the previous section. Generally speaking, this would take place by means of expository methods. However, in the case of productive skills, it may be desirable to teach the underlying basic concepts and principles by means of experiential, or discovery-learning techniques. This is in line with general principles for instruction in the cognitive domain.

	REPRODUCTIVE SKILLS	PRODUCTIVE SKILLS
Step 1 **Imparting the essential** **knowledge content**	Expository or experiential methods may be used (dependent on the category of knowledge).	Experiential methods preferred (concept and/or principle learning is always involved).
Step 2 **Imparting the basic** **psychomotor skills**	Expository methods (demonstration and prompted practice), by either the "whole task" or "progressive parts" methods. Note: Imparting the knowledge and skills content may in some cases be combined in one step.	Expository methods (demonstration and prompted practice), generally by the "whole task" method. Note: This step may sometimes be omitted when the learner starts with well-developed pre-requisite psychomotor skills.
Step 3 **Developing proficiency** **(speed, stamina and** **accuracy) and generality** **(transferability to a range** **of situations or cases)**	Supervised practice of whole task or special simulation exercises. Continuing corrective feedback (knowledge of results and/or knowledge of performance).	Experiential methods (guided problem solving) across a varying range of cases or examples. Continuing reflective feedback (debriefing; reflection-in-action).

FIG. 19.3.   Instructional strategies for skills development.

* Is this skills-mastery model a descriptive model or a design model?

Step 2: Imparting the basic skill. This refers to the initial demonstration and controlled practice of the task being taught. It relates to the second stage of skill development as outlined in the previous section. The rationale here is that if there is a "best" method of executing the task, it should be demonstrated, or modeled, for the trainee. Unlike the conceptual learning in the previous stage, where exposure to "right and wrong" may be beneficial in sharpening the trainee's power of discrimination, there is no benefit for the trainee in practicing an incorrect movement. In some cases, where the amount of basic knowledge to be imparted is small, it is possible to combine the first two steps into one.

Step 3: Developing proficiency. This refers to the provision of appropriate conditions for further practice to mastery. It relates to the remaining three stages of skill development outlined in the previous section: transfer of control, automatization, and generalization. The first two of these are relevant in the case of skills that lie toward the closed, or reproductive, end of our skills continuum. The third relates to skills at the productive end. Typically, however, a complex skilled activity is composed of both reproductive and productive skill elements.* Car-driving involves the smooth changing of gears, acceleration, automatic glancing in the rear-view mirror, and also the roadcraft skills of judging safe distances between vehicles, selection of the appropriate gear for each situation, prediction of possible acts by other road users, and the adoption of appropriate defensive-driving strategies.**

INSTRUCTIONAL TACTICS FOR SPECIFIC SITUATIONS

In this section of the chapter, we shall examine the more specific research-based principles of instruction that underlie the basic model suggested above. We shall group these principles into four categories:

- information (explanation, demonstration, and guidance),
- practice (frequency, spacing, etc.),
- feedback (frequency, form, quality, etc.),
- transfer and generalization.

Imparting the Essential Information to the Trainee*

If the task is simple, with limited background knowledge, then demonstrate and explain simultaneously as an illustrated narrative. However, if the task requires little if any new knowledge to be learned, apart from the movement pattern of the ac-

---

* This is an important point that applies equally to the cognitive domain.
** Do these three steps represent a descriptive model or a design model?

tion, it may be effectively taught without explanations, simply by demonstrating a "model performance."

Experiments on the role of visual demonstration (and feedback) on the mastery of a movement task (Carroll & Bandura, 1982, 1987, 1990) support the importance of a clear and sufficiently repeated visual enactment of the task as the principal factor leading to effective learning. However, in the case of knowledge-based skills, it is important to support the demonstration by appropriate verbal explanation.

Complex tasks, involving a large amount of new knowledge but little new skill, are learned better through exploratory activity with outline notes or a physical model to follow. In addition, retention of a complex task involving procedural knowledge is better if the task is learned through exploratory practice followed by expository review, rather than through expository demonstration followed by practice.

Baggett (1983) compared the relative effectiveness of a number of alternative procedures for learning a model helicopter assembly task using different combinations of exposition and exploratory practice, with an assembled helicopter as a model guide, and with or without procedural instruction supplied by a narrated film. The results showed that immediate success was proportional to the total amount of exploratory practice received and was not dependent on having viewed the film. After an interval of one week, however, the most successful students were those who had the greatest amount of exploratory practice first and then viewed the film last.

A possible explanation could be drawn from the general literature on expository versus discovery learning. If there are some "general principles of model assembly" that can help across several phases of the assembly task, then learning is better when they are "discovered." The long-term effect of the film may be due to the promotion of deep processing and organization of the knowledge gained through the practical experience, even though the film script was not specifically designed to promote "reflection-in-action." Those who saw the film before practice had no relevant experience to reflect on; hence no deep processing was possible.**

Let the student observe a sequential action pattern before attempting to execute it.

Research on tracking skills, springing from wartime gunnery and radar needs, paints a picture that contrasts with the findings just discussed. A series of experiments carried out by Poulton (1957) showed that observation of a pursuit-tracking activity before practicing it significantly improved the accuracy of performance. Similar results have been obtained by other researchers (Carroll & Bandura, 1982).

Are these findings in opposition to those reported by Baggett? On the contrary, they can be seen to support each other at a higher level of generality. The discov-

---

* In this section, try to identify the methods and the situationalities.
** The importance of experience first is emphasized by a number of other theories (see especially chap. 16 by Kovalik & McGeehan).

ery-learning-based explanation of Baggett's findings, proposed above, is based on the hypothesis that learning methods which involve deeper mental processing of sensory information are more effective. The difference between the two experimental situations lies in the type of learning task that is being studied. In one case, the critical learning is of visual patterns and relationships among components. In the other, it is the sequence and timing of a single, multistage movement. In the first case, practical exploration presents the visual relationships among parts in a manner that is more conducive to mental representation of the critical information than is a film sequence. In the second case, a film (video) presents the sequence of the task in a manner that is more conducive to its mental representation.*

Promote and encourage the mental rehearsal of a task, to enhance its initial learning and long-term retention.

The use of mental rehearsal as a skills-training technique has a long history, for example, in thinking and talking through football strategies during a pregame briefing discussion. Often, these "think-through" sessions are taken further, each strategy being given a code name by which it can be evoked during the game. Sometimes the steps or components of the strategy are likewise named, so the players may recall the sequence, pace, or nature of each step by means of an appropriate code word.

Supply verbal coding, or cueing, of the steps in an action pattern accompanying a model demonstration, to help the learner to form a mental representation of the action.

Bandura and Jeffery (1973) found that verbal labels were particularly effective as symbolic codes in terms of long-term retention of a sequential movement skill. The findings suggest that some form of verbal cueing as an aid to the internalization of motor skills should in general be provided. These cues should be meaningful to the learners but as simple and nontechnical as possible. Carroll and Bandura (1990) showed that verbal coding or cueing was not in itself sufficient to overcome the defective instructional design of insufficient demonstration and practice opportunities. One might expect, therefore, that purely verbal instruction would in general be inadequate for the teaching of all but the simplest of physical tasks.

Demonstrate a task from the viewpoint of the performer.

Experimental support for this principle can be found in many studies (Greenwald & Albert, 1968; Roshal, 1961). Often, instructors may demonstrate a sequence of movements while facing a group of students. The students must then "invert" the demonstration in their minds. It is better to demonstrate exactly what the student will see when performing.

---

* So situationality resolved the apparent contradiction of findings.

Providing Opportunities for Practice

Teach integrated and coordinated activities by the "whole task" method.

Several studies suggest that learning is more effective when the task is practiced as a whole, allowing the separate movements to be coordinated in all the practice sessions (Knapp, 1963; McGuigan & MacCaslin, 1955; Naylor & Briggs, 1963). This finding seems to hold good in laboratory experiments, in real-life industrial skills, and in sports.

Tasks composed of a sequence of relatively independent actions are better learned by the "progressive parts" method.

In the "sequential parts" method, a four-step task (e.g., A–B–C–D) would be practiced in four stages, each concentrating on one of the parts (i.e., A alone, then B alone, and so on) until all parts had been practiced separately. In the progressive parts method, the stages of practice grow cumulatively, for example, A alone, then B, then A and B, then C alone, then A and B and C, then D, and finally the whole task A–B–C–D. Some research has shown both of these approaches to be equally effective and better than the whole task method for learning simple sequential tasks. However, the bulk of the research supports the superiority of the progressive parts approach for sequential tasks (Naylor & Briggs, 1963; Seymour, 1954; Welford, 1968).

Prerequisite subskills that are initially below "minimum threshold levels" should, however, be developed prior to the practice of the whole task.

Several examples of such pretraining exercises and their effectiveness in the industrial skills arena are given by Seymour (1954, 1966). Note that the pretraining of specific movement or perceptual subskills before their integration into a more complex pattern of activity is not the same as the practice of the activity itself in separate parts.

Provide continuous practice for highly coordinated and "productive" tasks, but spaced practice for repetitive and high-speed "reproductive" tasks.

Some studies suggest that for more complex tasks in which much decision making is involved or where there is a high level of coordination or rhythmic activity, long and continuous practice sessions are more effective than spaced practice (Welford, 1968). Singer (1982) showed that although spaced practice may show an advantage immediately after a series of trials, this advantage is largely lost over time. Other research suggests that spaced training sessions with short rest stops between every few trials is more effective in the case of repetitive high-speed skills of a reproductive nature (Lee & Genovese, 1988).

Learning is enhanced through mental rehearsal during rest intervals.

Theoretical justification has been provided by many writers (Luria, 1961; Meichenbaum & Goodman, 1971). Shasby (1984) reviews the research on this technique, finding it especially effective with young children who have problems with motor control. Whatever the theoretical explanations, the benefits can be reaped by encouraging learners to think through the procedures of novel tasks in between practice sessions and, in particular, in the intervals between the trials in a spaced-practice routine.

The forced pacing of high-speed tasks promotes more rapid progress to mastery.

When forced pacing is applied to the practice of high-speed industrial tasks (Agar, 1962) or to typing skills (Sormunen, 1986), learning rates are very significantly enhanced, and ultimate performance levels achieved may be much higher than under self-paced practice conditions. This principle is often overlooked due to too much emphasis on the principles of self-paced learning.* In tasks where speed is a criterion, the principle of allowing a student to progress "at his/her own pace" needs careful interpretation.

Setting a specific goal can lead to more rapid mastery of a skilled activity.

Barnett and Stanicek (1979) found that students who set personal goals in terms of scores in archery shared significant improvement as compared to students who did not set themselves such goals. Setting a specific "hard" goal for students on motor tasks leads to greater learning and performance improvement than just asking students to "do their best" (Locke & Bryan, 1966).

Feedback in Psychomotor Skills Instruction

In general, "learning feedback" (results information) promotes learning, and "action feedback" (control information) does not.

Annett (1959) found that subjects pressing down on a spring balance would not learn to exert a given pressure accurately despite many trials when they had the benefit of the scale supplying them with information. When the scale was covered while they made their attempt and then uncovered, they did learn. Thus, continuous knowledge, supplied visually, of the pressure being applied (action feedback) guaranteed error-free practice but did not result in the learning of the "feel" of applying the correct pressure. After-the-fact knowledge (of results) did promote progressively more accurate attempts and led to effective learning of the "feel" of executing the task (hence the term "learning feedback").

In general, feedback is more effective in promoting learning when it transmits more complete information.

Knowledge of the results (KOR) of a practice trial and knowledge of performance (KOP) (how the results were achieved) represent two ways in which the in-

---

* This helps to point out that most methods are not universally beneficial; there is almost always some situationality. It is wise to be skeptical of any instructional theorist who says that her or his approach should always be used.

structor may seek to correct the performance of a task. The supply of KOP is more effective (Wallace & Hagler, 1979). KOP only supplies information about the correctness of a response and possibly the direction and extent of an error. The KOP, in addition, may comment on or correct certain aspects of executing the process of the task.

When teaching productive skills, supply knowledge of performance through a process of "debriefing" or reflection-in-action.

In the case of skills involving a high level of strategy planning and decision making, the appropriate feedback not only may, but should, take the form of KOP. In these skills, it is not sufficient to compare results with expectations, but it is necessary to engage in an analysis of the causes of an observed discrepancy, reflect on the plans that were implemented, and evaluate the reasons for their shortcomings, all this leading to the synthesis of new plans or strategies for the next practice trial. Such reflective debriefing, either instructor-led or spontaneous, is now recognized as an essential element of the development of productive skills in any domain. In the psychomotor domain, this is exemplified in the sports context by the before- and after-game strategy discussions in the locker room. It is also apparent in the stress laid on the reflection-in-action approach to skill development in professions such as surgery (Schon, 1983, 1987).*

Teaching for Transfer

In general, variability of practice exercises enhances transfer and generalization of a motor skill, but this depends on whether the skill is reproductive (closed) or productive (open).

According to Gabbard (1984), a major prediction of schema theory is that "increasing the variability of practice on a given task will result in increased transfer to a novel task of the same movement class." However, experience in some sports and in many high-speed, repetitive industrial skills has not supported the variability-of-practice principle. One way to explain this is by means of our "skills continuum." The further an activity is toward the productive end of this continuum, the more important it is to practice across the range of variability in order to ensure effective transfer. The further the activity lies toward the reproductive end, the less permissible is variability in execution, and so the less valuable is variability of practice (indeed, it may be harmful).

In the case of teaching for transfer, the variability of the practice exercises should be so designed as to define, or refine, "motor concepts" and "motor schemata" in the learner's mind.

---

* You may recognize reflection as a common feature of the new paradigm of instructional theories, for the psychomotor as well as cognitive domains.

According to Schmidt's (1975) theory, a motor schema is a structure of interrelated "motor concepts" analogous to the structure of a cognitive schema. A concept in the cognitive domain is defined by a series of attributes that define its boundary more or less precisely. Just so, a motor concept, such as throwing a ball accurately, is defined and bounded by certain attributes, such as: distance to throw, force to apply, angle of release of the ball, and arm speed at the moment of release. These attributes are not, of course, defined verbally or mathematically, but are nevertheless known and interrelated within the player, so that any required distance of throw, as stimulus, produces an appropriate combination of the other attributes as response. The implication for instruction is that practice should be designed to vary in terms of all the critical attributes of the motor concept.

Transfer and retention of motor skills are improved by "overlearning."

Both practical observation and experimental evidence suggest that "the amount of transfer of learning is proportional to the amount of initial practice" (Gagné, 1954). Singer (1982) makes the further point that there is evidence that "overlearning" or "overpractice" is beneficial in terms of long-term retention, although there is a law of diminishing returns in force which may establish limits beyond which formally organized overpractice would not be cost effective.

Avoid too fast a progression to more difficult tasks. Information overload generally results in a deterioration of task execution.

Several approaches have been found to be helpful in avoiding or staving off the onset of information overload (Welford, 1976):

1. devising ways of "chunking" the incoming information so that more can be handled;
2. devising ways of helping the performer be selective in the information attended to;
3. devising ways of pacing the task so that information overload is avoided;
4. establishing realistic "threshold levels" for the performer and working within them.

These suggestions are most difficult to implement in competitive sports, where little control can be exercised over the information that will be received by the performer. In the case of industrial skills, however, much can be done by a process of systems engineering where man and machine are considered together.

INTEGRATING THE PERFORMER AND THE TASK

In this section, we discuss two additional and important aspects of the teaching and learning of physical skills, which are to some extent unique to the psychomotor domain, and which go beyond the bounds of the basic skills-development model presented earlier on. The two topics, placed together here under the concept of "integrating the performer and the activity being performed," may be seen as a special contribution of the field of research sometimes referred to as "man–machine studies." This field focuses on better adapting the work environment to the characteristics of the people who work there (for example, through ergonomic design of workspaces and tools) and on better adapting the people to the environment (for example, through various forms of psychological preparation). In the specific context of instruction, we focus on simulated work (and play) environments and on the "inner self" of the worker (or player).

The Question of Fidelity in Training Devices and Simulators

The common practice of putting emphasis on high fidelity to the real task in all respects is not a very cost-effective approach to training and may not even be the most effective approach irrespective of costs. *

Gagné (1954) argued that training effectiveness as a guiding principle should replace the "identical elements" principle first suggested by Thorndike (1903) in the design of training devices and simulators. The idea has taken a long time to catch on, but there is evidence that at last this has become the preferred orientation. One outcome of this work was the identification of the multiple factors that influence the optimal levels of fidelity that should be built into training devices. Below we examine these factors as well as the multiple aspects of the concept of fidelity.

It is important to distinguish between physical fidelity and functional fidelity. ** *Training effectiveness requires different levels of physical and functional fidelity.*

It would seem that physical fidelity (the "look and feel") is more important in the case of reproductive skills which involve little or no cognitive effort in their execution, while functional fidelity (realistic cause-effect relationships) is more important in the case of productive skills that depend on deeper cognitive processing of task information (Allen, Hays, & Buffardi, 1986).

It is also important to distinguish "technical fidelity" as defined by an expert, from "perceived fidelity" as experienced by a trainee. For effective training, it is the perceived fidelity that counts.

Technical fidelity is the extent to which the training device replicates the working of the real system. Perceived fidelity is the extent to which the device appears to do so to the trainee (Smode, 1972). The pursuit of perceptual fidelity focuses the trainer's attention on the trainee and allows for the implementation of less expensive and possibly more effective solutions by seeking to provide the sensory information required by the trainee in order to learn in the simplest and easiest-to-interpret technical manner.

---

* The issue of authentic, real-world task versus less realistic ones (including fantasy situations) was important for the cognitive domain, also (see, e.g., chap. 14 by Pogrow).

** This seems like a powerful way to resolve the conflicting views on fidelity.

Exact simulation of a task is often in conflict with effective training, since it precludes the implementation of effective instructional-design principles. Part-task training devices often overcome this problem, allowing sound design to be incorporated into simulated practice exercises.

As early as 1945, research demonstrated that the sacrificing of exact simulation can be necessary in order to enhance performance improvement (Lindahl, 1945). This approach was also strongly advocated by Gagné (1954), who favored component practice over total simulation and expressed doubts whether any skills were ever effectively learned "all at once" exclusively through practice on the job or on fully realistic simulators.

Progress to "full" (higher fidelity) simulation appears to be governed by several interacting factors: the context of the training, the task content, the learners, and the stage of learning.

Hays and Singer (1989) review the literature on such progressive sequences of exercises from the viewpoint of fidelity. Their review suggests that at least four factors are particularly important to take into consideration when planning progressions of exercises for the training of complex psychomotor tasks: the training context, the type of task, the trainees, and the sequence of progression to mastery. They stress, however, that the interaction of these factors is not yet fully understood and that much of the design process of simulators and part-task trainers is still based on trial-and-error.

Development of the Inner Self and Psychological Conditioning

Finally, we shall review some of the methods that are being applied with increasing frequency, particularly in the training of athletes and sports teams, to prepare the players psychologically for maximum performance. The aim is to develop greater levels of control over the inner self, that is, the feelings and beliefs that influence peak performance. Whereas the area of growth in application of these methods is in sports, we are beginning to see them applied also in the industrial skills arena, for example, in the growing practice of engaging in relaxation exercises and mental imagery prior to work.

Relaxation exercises, prior to engaging in skilled activities, tend to enhance performance levels.

The relaxation routines most often described in the literature (e.g., McAuley & Rotella, 1982; Rose, 1985) involve initial breathing exercises, sometimes with a musical background or with a planned effort to concentrate on the process of breathing itself. The breathing exercises are followed by some body exercises, especially of the shoulder and neck. After these initial exercises are complete, the main relaxation routines commence. Usually, there is an element of meditation involved in this stage. The immediate effects of such meditative relaxation some-times include a drop in body temperature and a slowing of the rate of heartbeat (Rose, 1985). The extent to which such changes in physiological processes affect later physical action is not clear, though Niddefer and Deckner (1970) documented some case studies that showed a positive effect on performance.

Thinking oneself into the role of a known expert performer and identifying as completely as possible with that role model tend to improve performance.

This has been suggested by Lozanov (1978) and others who have contributed to the methodologies variously termed "suggestology," "suggestopaedia," or "accel-erated learning." These methodologies propose that imagining you will be success-ful in what you are about to attempt is good, but imagining yourself to *be* someone who habitually is successful in that activity is even better. Lozanov's research dem-onstrates the efficiency of this approach across all the domains of learning. In the psychomotor skills arena, this methodology is used by encouraging the trainees to select and study a role model and then, just prior to competition, to actually become this role model in their imagination.

Engaging in appropriate "self-talk" with oneself (a form of "inner game") can have significant positive effects on performance.

Gallwey (1974), a professional tennis player and coach, has studied the problem of how human beings interfere with their own ability to achieve and learn. He postu-lates that every game is composed of two parts: the outer game, which is played against an external opponent to overcome external obstacles and to reach an exter-nal goal, and the inner game that takes place in the mind of the player and is played against such obstacles as lapses of concentration, nervousness, self-doubts, and self-condemnation.* Players are instructed to attend to aspects other than the tech-nical execution of the appropriate actions. In tennis, the player may be told to watch the ball (of course) but to consciously attend to the color of the ball or the beauty of its motion, letting the body and the sensory system automatically take care of the execution of the appropriate tennis stroke.

CONCLUSION: INTEGRATING INSTRUCTIONAL THEORY AND PRACTICE

The principles suggested by Gallwey would, in many respects, appear to run coun-ter to some of the other principles presented in this chapter. On the other hand, the inner game methodology has now been applied to a wide variety of sports, appar-ently with immense practical success. Perhaps the apparent conflict is not real if we remember some of the observations from the very first section of this chapter on the stages through which the mastery of a psychomotor skill progresses. Perhaps the

---

* To what extent is this similar to, or a kind of, metacognitive training?

automatization and increased fluidity of high-speed industrial skills, noted by Seymour (1954, 1966), and the observed ability of highly skilled typists to engage in conversations with neighboring typists without any noticeable deterioration in either speed or accuracy of their typing (Sormunen, 1986) are analogous to the tennis player in the state of "relaxed concentration" described by Gallwey.

Perhaps, furthermore, the integration of principles and research results from such different areas as psychology, physiology, psychiatry, ergonomics, work study, and engineering, which is a characteristic of the practice of psychomotor skills development, may serve as an example of the viability of integrating apparently conflicting viewpoints on the processes of learning and instruction, and of the possibility of treating the question of instruction and its planning as one integrated discipline, rather than as a series of disciplines divided by boundaries variously defined in terms of subject-matter domain, instructional objectives domain, or preferred philosophy of learning.* Maybe, in some respects, the area of physical skills instruction may serve as a model and as a form of intellectual "glue" for the field of instructional design as a whole.

REFERENCES

Adler, J. D. (1981). Stages of skill acquisition: A guide for teachers. *Motor Skills: Theory into Practice, 5*(2), 75–80.
Agar, A. (1962). Instruction of industrial workers by tape recorder. *Affarsekonomi, 10.*
Allen, J. A., Hays, R. T., & Buffardi, L. C. (1986). Maintenance training simulator fidelity and individual differences in transfer of training. *Human Factors, 28*(5), 497–509.
Annett, J. (1959). Learning a pressure under conditions of immediate and delayed knowledge of results. *Quarterly Journal of Experimental Psychology, 11,* 3–15.
Baggett, P. (1983). *Learning a procedure from multimedia instructions: The effects of film and practice.* Boulder, CO: Colorado University, Institute of Cognitive Science. (ERIC No. ED239598.)
Bandura, A., & Jeffery, R. W. (1973). Role of symbolic coding and rehearsal processes in observational learning. *Journal of Personality and Social Psychology, 26,* 122–130.
Barnett, M. L., & Stanicek, J. A. (1979). Effects of goal setting on achievement in archery. *Research Quarterly, 50,* 328–332.
Bloom, B. S. (1968). Learning for mastery. *Evaluation Comment, 1*(2), Los Angeles, CA: UCLA
Bloom, B. S., Englehart, M. D., Hill, W. H., Furst, E. J., & Krathwohl, D. R. (1956). *Taxonomy of educational objectives, Handbook 1: The cognitive domain.* New York: David McKay.
Carroll, W. R., & Bandura, A. (1982). The role of visual monitoring in observational learning of action patterns: Making the unobservable observable. *Journal of Motor Behavior, 14*(2), 153–167.
Carroll, W. R., & Bandura, A. (1987). Translating cognition into action: The role of visual guidance in observational learning. *Journal of Motor Behavior, 19*(3), 385–398.
Carroll, W. R., & Bandura, A. (1990). Representational guidance of action production in observational learning: A causal analysis. *Journal of Motor Behavior, 22*(1), 85–97.
Gabbard, C. P. (1984). *Motor skill learning in children.* ERIC No. ED293645.
Gagné, R. M. (1954). Training devices and simulators: Some research issues. *American Psychologist, 9*(7), 95–107.
Gallwey, W. T. (1974). *The inner game of tennis.* New York: Random House.
Gentner, D. R. (1984). *Expertise in typewriting.* CHIP Report, 121. La Jolla, CA: University of California, San Diego, Center for Human Information Processing. (ERIC No. ED248320.)

---

* This integrative viewpoint is an important aspect of the new paradigm of instructional theories and reflects systemic thinking.

Gilchrist, J. R., & Gruber, J. J. (1984). Psychomotor domains. *Motor Skills: Theory into Practice, 7*(1/2), 57–70.

Greenwald, A. G., & Albert, S. M. (1968). Observational learning: A technique for elucidating S-R mediation processes. *Journal of Experimental Psychology, 76*, 267–272.

Hays, R. T., & Singer, M. J. (1989). *Simulation fidelity in training system design.* New York: Springer-Verlag.

Knapp, B. N. (1963). *Skill in sport: The attainment of proficiency.* London: Routledge and Kegan Paul.

Krathwohl, D. R., Bloom, B. S., & Masia, B. B. (1964). *Taxonomy of educational objectives, Handbook 2: The affective domain.* New York: Longman.

Lee, T. D., & Genovese, E. D. (1988). Distribution of practice in motor skill acquisition: Learning and performance effects reconsidered. *Research Quarterly for Exercise and Sport, 58*(4).

Lindahl, L. G. (1945). Movement and analysis as an industrial training method. *Journal of Applied Psychology, 29*, 420–436.

Locke, E. A., & Bryan, J. F. (1966). Cognitive aspects of psychomotor performance: The effects of performance goals on levels of performance. *Journal of Applied Psychology, 50*, 286–291.

Lozanov, G. (1978). *Suggestology and outlines of suggestopaedia.* New York: Gordon & Breach.

Luria, A. R. (1961). *The role of speech in the regulation of normal and abnormal behavior.* New York: Liveright.

Mager, R. E. (1968). *Developing attitude toward learning.* Belmont, CA: Fearon.

McAuley, E., & Rotella, R. (1982). A cognitive-behavioral approach to enhancing gymnastic performance. *Motor Skills: Theory Into Practice, 6*(2), 67–75.

McGuigan, F. J., & MacCaslin, E. F. (1955). Whole and part methods in learning a perceptual motor skill. *American Journal of Psychology, 68*, 658–661.

Meichenbaum, D., & Goodman, J. (1971). Training impulsive children to talk to themselves: A means of developing self control. *Journal of Abnormal Psychology, 77*, 115–126.

Naylor, J. C., & Briggs, G. E. (1963). Effects of task complexity and task organization on the relative efficiency of part and whole training methods. *Journal of Experimental Psychology, 65*, 217–224.

Niddefer, R. M., & Deckner, C. M. (1970). A case-study of improved athletic performance following the use of relaxation procedures. *Perceptual and Motor Skills, 30*, 821–822.

Poulton, E. C. (1957). On prediction in skilled movement. *Psychological Bulletin, 54*, 467–478.

Rogers, C. R. (1969). *Freedom to learn.* New York: Merrill.

Romiszowski, A. J. (1974). *Selection and use of instructional media: A systems approach.* London: Kogan Page.

Romiszowski, A. J. (1981). *Designing instructional systems.* London: Kogan Page.

Romiszowski, A. J. (1993). Psychomotor principles. In M. Fleming and W. H. Levie (Eds.), *Instructional message design. Englewood Cliffs, NJ: Educational Technology Publications.*

Rose, C. (1985). *Accelerated learning.* Great Missenden, UK: Accelerated Learning Systems.

Roshal, S. M. (1961). Film mediated learning with varying representation of the task: Viewing angle portrayal of demonstration, motion and student participation. In A. A. Lumsdaine (Ed.), *Student response in programmed instruction.* Washington, DC: National Academy of Sciences, National Research Council.

Schmidt, R. A. (1975). A schema theory of discrete motor skill learning. *Psychological Review, 82*, 225–260.

Schon, D. A. (1983). *The reflective practitioner.* New York: Basic Books.

Schon, D. A. (1987). *Educating the reflective practitioner.* San Francisco: Jossey-Bass.

Seymour, W. D. (1954). *Industrial training for manual operations.* London: Pitman.

Seymour, W. D. (1966). *Industrial skills.* London: Pitman.

Shasby, G. (1984). Improving movement skills through language. *Motor Skills: Theory into Practice, 7*(1/2), 91–96.

Singer, R. N. (1982). *The learning of motor skills.* New York: Macmillan.

Smode, A. F. (1972). *Training device design: Human factors requirements in the technical approach.* Orlando, FL: Naval Training Equipment Center.

Sormunen, C. (1986). A comparison of two methods for teaching keyboarding on the microcomputer to elementary grade students. *Delta Pi Epsilon Journal, 28*(2), 67–77.

Thorndike, E. L. (1903). *Educational psychology.* New York: Lemcke and Buschner.

Wallace, S. A., & Hagler, R. W. (1979). Knowledge of performance and the learning of a closed motor skill. *Research Quarterly, 50*, 265–271.

Welford, A. T. (1968). *Fundamentals of skill*. London: Methuen.
Welford, A. T. (1976). *Skilled performance: Perceptual and motor skills*. Glenview, IL: Scott Foresman.
Wellens, J. (1974). *Training in physical skills*. London: Business Books.
Wheatcroft, E. (1973). *Simulators for skill*. London: McGraw-Hill.

Unit 4 Fostering Affective Development

FOREWORD

This unit opens with a chapter that helps the reader analyze and understand the theories in the unit. Chapter 20 presents a conceptual model showing six major dimensions of affective development (e.g., emotional, social, moral), along with major components having instructional value for each of those dimensions (e.g., knowledge, skills, attitudes). These should help the reader to understand the differences among the instructional-design theories regarding what to teach. Chapter 20 also provides an application model that shows eight of the more important dimensions on which instructional-design theories can differ from each other in the affective domain, such as the duration of the affective program and how integrated the topics are.

The first of the five theory chapters (21) is the one that overlaps most with the cognitive domain and in essence provides a bridge between the two domains. Then come chapters that focus on emotional development (22), attitude development (23), character development (24), and spiritual development (25). But these five theories only begin to deal with the breadth of the kinds of affective development for which guidance is sorely needed. And for the kinds of affective development that are represented here, these five chapters only begin to scratch the surface of the work that has been initiated by theorists all over the world.

Compared to the cognitive domain you might find it easier to explore the extent to which these chapters complement and support each other, as opposed to competing or conflicting with each other.

It is my hope that the inclusion of these five chapters will increase awareness of the importance of developing more guidance (instructional theory) for people interested in fostering affective dimensions of human learning and development. I also hope these chapters will show that it is possible to offer useful guidance in spite of the tremendous complexity of the affective domain.

As you read through the chapters in this unit, you might find it helpful to periodically review the list of questions on pp. 1–2.

—*C.M.R.*

483

20

Affective Education and the Affective Domain: Implications for Instructional-Design Theories and Models

Barbara L. Martin
Independent Consultant, Orlando, FL

Charles M. Reigeluth
Indiana University

AFFECTIVE EDUCATION: WHAT DOES IT MEAN?

In 1976, Bills stated that the definition of affect was so unclear and so unfocused, and measurement of it so difficult, that educators would not be able to adequately deal with it in their classrooms unless or until we came to a better understanding of what it was. In 1986, Martin and Briggs came to much the same conclusion. They listed 21 different terms associated with affect, including self-concept, mental health, group dynamics, personality development, morality, attitudes, values, ego development, feelings, and motivation. In 1990, Beane concurred:

> Little progress has been made toward developing a broad and coherent theory or framework that defines the place of affect in the curriculum.... To begin with, there is still disagreement about how to define affect, resulting in a wide variety of opinions about how it should be placed in the curriculum.... Nevertheless, the present disarray in the field demands such an attempt because almost everything we do in schools has to do with affect. (p. 2)

While we will not resolve these issues in this chapter or this book, we will provide a variety of perspectives about affective development and its place in learning and instruction, and we will describe some considerations that instructional devel-

485

opers and teachers can use as they decide whether or how to include affect in their instruction.

The term "affect" is widely known. Affective education deals broadly with students' experiences in school (Ackerson, 1991/1992) and is generally used to describe programs dealing with personal and social development. The following is a composite sampling of some ways of defining affect in education.

Affective education refers to education for personal-social development, feelings, emotions, morals, ethics; it is often isolated in the curriculum (Ackerson, 1991/1992; Beane, 1990).

Education for affect affirms that education is about becoming human, and therefore education must be about affect; it cannot be otherwise and cannot be separated from other aspects of the curriculum (Beane, 1990).

Affective development as a process refers to individual growth or internal changes to serve the "best" interests of individuals and society, while *affective development as an end-product* addresses the result(s) of that process: a well-adjusted or "affectively developed" person (*Education for Affective Development: A Guidebook on Programmes and Practices*, 1992).

Affective development education refers to a deliberate process of intervention in the development of students; it may include affect as part of particular subject areas (e.g., English or government), may be integrated into the curriculum, or may include separate courses of study for the development of affect as process or end-product.

Affective domain refers to components of affective development focusing on internal changes or processes, or to categories of behavior within affective education as a process or end-product.

WHY CONSIDER AFFECT?

Affect has been considered either overtly or covertly as a part of schooling for decades. It has emerged in many different forms, some more defensible and/or more effective than others, including humanistic education, moral development, student-centered learning, self-actualization, and values education, to name only a few. Affect has also emerged as a response to many different social needs, including racism, drug and alcohol abuse, and teen pregnancy. And it has emerged as a part of varying philosophical and curricular orientations, such as the child vs. the curriculum. Needs and times change, and affect becomes increasingly popular or unpopular.

Lickona states, in chapter 24 of this volume, that the philosophy of logical positivism in the middle of the 20th century eroded support for teaching character education. The same was true of other affective programs, as curriculum emphasis was placed on academic subjects, specifically science and math. In the 1960s, values education reappeared, as did Rogers' (1969) student-centered learning and Kohlberg's (1969) approach to moral development. Although these programs were not at all similar to each other, each refocused attention on what we are calling affective education.

When considering the inclusion of affect in schooling, Beane (1990) suggested that:

> the underlying theory appears to be this: When large-scale social problems appear, we may react with legal and legislative action, but in the long haul the best solution is to educate the present generation of young people to "cope" with their own problems and/or to help create a more ethical and moral society. (p. 3)

However, it is important to recognize that academic programs in public schools are only one of the many forums for teaching or learning affective behaviors. For children and adolescents, affective behaviors are addressed directly or indirectly in private and religious schools, summer camps, churches, and community and recreational activities, to name only a few. For adults, affective behaviors can be addressed or taught explicitly in places as diverse as parenting classes, corporate training programs, and volunteer organizations. While our focus in this unit of the book is on public schools, it is incumbent on all of us to remember that affective behaviors can be taught and developed in almost any setting, and at any age level, and that instructional-design theories should provide guidance for the full range of contexts, not just public schools.

When we do focus on teaching affective behaviors in public school settings, there are important issues that have to be considered due to any number of philosophical and social concerns. For example, whether affective objectives are overt or implicit, stated or unstated, planned or unplanned raises issues of what to teach and who is responsible for making those decisions. Likewise, what kinds of methods teachers use and whether those methods are direct or indirect can influence how receptive parents, students, and the community are to teaching in the affective domain. Other important issues that have to do with teaching in the affective domain include:

- affective development often takes a long time,
- indoctrination or brainwashing can be an ethical concern,
- sometimes the absence of behaviors is more important than the presence of behaviors (e.g., to abstain from unsafe or premarital sex),
- classical conditioning, operant conditioning, and persuavise communications may be powerful methods to instill or maintain affective behaviors,
- there may be some confusion about affect as a means for cognitive ends versus as ends in their own right.

All of these are important issues for instructional theories to address.

In spite of these issues, over the past several decades, renewed interest in affective education has grown to unprecedented levels in American public education (Beane, 1990). Why has this happened? The obvious answers lie in the explosion of substance abuse, teen pregnancy, gang violence, runaways, crime, the divorce rate, dropouts, eating disorders, all kinds of abuse, and other similar social problems. Within schools, interpersonal conflicts have increased dramatically, and lack of discipline (including the categories of fighting, violence, and gang activity) is one of the biggest problems confronting public schools (Johnson & Johnson, 1996).

A less obvious answer, however, is that modern theories of psychology and philosophy recognize more than ever the interrelationships among thoughts and feelings. Purposeful action is based on attention to both affect and cognition. Our emotions are tied to something, they have some referent, and they require reasoned (re)action and resolution (Beane, 1990; Goleman, 1995; Noddings, 1994). In fact, Tennyson and Nielson (1997), reporting the work of Brown, Collins, and Duguid (1989), Harre (1984), and Vygosky (1978), state that recently certain cognitive psychologist have "discovered" that the affective domain may actually dominate the cognitive. They suggest that this is seen in many constructivist ideas, such as situated cognition. Other educators who also espouse constructivist and postmodern positions are increasingly concerned with more holistic approaches to education. These are sometimes characterized as including a worldview that is less reductionistic, bureaucratic, and hierarchical and more student-centered, humanistic, and democratic (Hlynka, 1997; Lebow, 1997; Miller, 1994)—all markers of the new paradigm discussed in chapter 1.

Recent research on the architecture of the brain and how it works reveals that the brain is of two "minds:" the emotional and the rational (Goleman, 1995). Goleman, reporting the research of neuroscientists, states that while these two components of the brain often work in harmony, they are somewhat independent, each operating separately. Based on knowledge of evolution, we now know that the emotional center of the brain was the first to develop and is often the first to "engage" or kick in as we make decisions or face dilemmas. This often happens while the thinking brain is still coming to a decision. What this means for education and educational programs is that students must learn, and therefore be taught, to harness their emotions. This includes learning the difference between feelings and actions and the effects of this difference on behavior. Goleman (1995) calls this "emotional intelligence." He states that emotional intelligence can help students and society deal with the plethora of social problems previously mentioned (e.g., violence, depression, stress) by teaching students to manage their feelings, become more self-aware, improve their social and cognitive skills, and become more empathic.

Gray and LaViolette proposed another brain theory, called emotional/cognitive structures (ECS), that states that emotional nuances are the organizing structures for thought and knowledge (Ferguson, 1982). Sommers (Ferguson, 1982) conducted research that provides some validity to ECS. Regarding learning, Gray and LaViolette suggested that ignoring feelings may actually retard efficiency in learning and that understanding emotions may be the key to fostering more advanced cognitive organization. Similarly, Greenspan (1997) provides powerful evidence that "emotions, not cognitive stimulation, serve as the mind's primary architect" (p. 1). Greenspan's conclusions are based on many thousands of hours of observation and research on both normal and exceptional (e.g., autistic) children. According to Greenspan (1997):

These observations make clear that certain kinds of emotional nurturing propel them to intellectual and emotional health, and that affective experience helps them master a variety of cognitive tasks. According to experiments conducted by Stephen Porges of the University of Maryland and myself, parts of the brain and nervous system that deal with emotional regulation play a crucial role in cognition (Porges, Doussard-Roosevelt, Portales, & Greenspan, in press). (Pp. 9–10)

Emotions therefore not only become the complex mediators of experience but also serve an internal organizing and differentiating role. (p. 113)

Hence, rather than emotional development being separate from but equal in importance to cognitive development, it is an essential foundation for and component of cognitive development. This places it squarely within the traditional mission of public schools.

Another powerful reason for the inclusion of affect in the curriculum revolves around the values for a democratic society. Norton (1994) states:

In the United States, the decade of the 1980s brought vividly to the public awareness the precarious condition of the moral character of our people. The decade witnessed an unparalleled succession of exposures of moral corruption in government, business, finance, the professions, and evangelical religion. This has produced a public outcry for "more integrity" in our nation's leadership and its people, and has led some observers to speak of our "crisis of moral character." (p. 3)

Norton goes on to say that ethics and moral integrity are the cornerstones of education for a moral life. Integration of moral principles and shared values, such as human dignity, freedom, justice, caring, equality, peace, and honesty, into all aspects of American education, from elementary to higher education, is a must. Mere understanding of these important principles and values is not sufficient. Learning implies that individuals will behave in personally and socially responsible ways.

Why consider affect? We are more aware now than ever before of the holistic nature of learning, behavior, and human growth and development, as well as how our thoughts and feelings are interrelated and influence everyday decision making. Additionally, as a society, we place a high value on moral integrity and attention to the needs of others. It is important to us to have citizens who are productive and mentally healthy and honest, who are able to take care of themselves and their families, and who promote the welfare of others. Without attention to affect, schools are shortchanging students and, ultimately, society.

WHAT ARE THE DIMENSIONS OF AFFECTIVE LEARNING?

The answer to this question is important for several reasons. First, knowing what kinds of learning comprise the affective domain helps us to understand what the affective domain is and what it is not. Second, it provides a menu that helps educators to decide what is important to teach. And third, different kinds of affective learning may require different kinds of methods of instruction for fostering their development, and this is the major focus of instructional theory.

The most widely known and most often used taxonomy of the affective domain was developed by Krathwohl, Bloom, and Masia in 1964. Called the "affective taxonomy," it was based on the principle of *internalization*, the process by which an attitude or value becomes increasingly a part of the individual. Internalization is a fundamental concept in understanding the taxonomy because, from a theoretical perspective, the more a value or an attitude is internalized, the more likely that value or attitude is to influence behavior. The taxonomy consists of five major categories (each with subcategories) that reflect the concept of internalization. From least to most internalized, they are: Receiving, Responding, Valuing, Organization, and Characterization by a value or value complex (see Martin & Briggs, 1986, for a complete description of the categories and subcategories). The taxonomy was developed, in part, to help teachers write affective objectives for each of the five major categories as well as the subcategories, and to help them design affective measures. These objectives could be written to reflect the different levels of internalization, and they could be distinguished from cognitive objectives because they emphasized a feeling tone, an emotion, or a degree of acceptance or rejection of some phenomenon.

The five major categories of the taxonomy were intended to be hierarchical (building on each other); however evidence for the hierarchical validity of the taxonomy is sparce and unconvincing (Martin & Briggs, 1986). For curriculum and instructional development, whether or not the taxonomy is hierarchical is very important because, if affective objectives could be shown to build upon each other, then a "spiraling" sequence of affective behaviors could be built into any instructional program or curriculum.

The affective taxonomy has been criticized as being too general, too abstract, overly dependent on cognition, and limited in scope (Martin & Briggs, 1986). In addition, as a taxonomy, no instructional methods were included for fostering the development of the different affective outcomes. Regarding its limited scope, Krathwohl and associates (1964) indicated that they attempted to organize the taxonomy by many different organization schemes, including using affective constructs such as values, attitudes, emotions, and self-development, but they found that those constructs were too poorly defined to use. These definitional problems are still largely unresolved (Beane, 1990; Bills, 1976; Martin & Briggs, 1986).

A number of other affective taxonomies were developed (Brandhorst, 1978; Foshay, 1978; Gephart & Ingle, 1976; Hoepfner, 1972 ; Nunnally, 1978) and were reviewed by Martin and Briggs (1986). They range in scope from physiological and psychosocial responses to emphasizing self-development as a goal. These taxonomies also include a wide variety of affective constructs, including sentiments, interests, beliefs, emotions, social temperament, and visceral responses. Foshay (1978) described six domains of learning: intellectual, emotional, social, physical, aesthetic, and spiritual. He included two affective constructs, aesthetics and spirituality, that were not included in other taxonomies.

In part based on these taxonomies, Martin and Briggs (1986) developed their own affective taxonomy with self-development as the most inclusive of the affective constructs, and social competence, values, morals and ethics, continuing motivation, interest, attitudes, and emotions and feelings as subcomponents (Martin & Briggs, 1986, p. 448). While their taxonomy was intended to depict outcomes of learning in the affective domain, it was a means to an end. That is, they sought to show how the affective and cognitive domains were interrelated, but could not do so unless the affective domain was better described. Recognizing the definitional problems with affective constructs, they wrote:

> Perhaps an *alternate* way to think about the affective categories ... is to identify *goal or outcome categories* that cut across the [constructs]. Potential affective goals or outcomes for education and training might include:
>
> 1. Goals related to *positive attitudes toward subject area or disciplines* including aesthetics.
> 2. Goals related to the development of a *rational basis for attitudes and values*. These would include analytical thought about and decision making in the realm of morals and ethics.
> 3. Goals related to *affective processes*; those indicative or positive directional movement as perceived by the individual.
> 4. Goals related to *developing and sustaining interest and motivation* in vocational or avocational pursuits, as well as other areas that are important or are of interest to the learner. (p. 450)

Another conceptual model was developed by The Lethbridge Catholic Schools in Alberta, Canada, in 1989 (Lambert & Himsl, 1993). They undertook a project to identify affective qualities valued as significant outcomes of education. Based on reviews of literature and a survey of educators in Alberta, they devised a conceptual model that included what they refer to as indicators, but what we would call affective constructs (e.g., self-development) or dimensions (e.g., spiritual development) of the affective domain: self-worth, relating to others, world awareness, learning, and spiritual life. They present a conceptual model of interlocking circles that shows the interrelationships among these areas.

> The model represents the formation and growth of behaviors that display positive attitudes toward the SELF as they take place through the interrelated experiences of dealing with OTHERS, through a growing awareness of the WORLD, and through the process of LEARNING. The SPIRITUAL LIFE dimension unifies the other four, by identifying a purposiveness in life, its events and activities; it provides the hope that leads the learner on. (Lambert & Himsl, 1993, p. 17)

Last, in a cross-cultural study of 17 countries, *Education for Affective Development* (1992), the authors presented a conceptual model, or "map," of the content domains of affective development education. This model identifies five domains: the intellectual, aesthetic, physical, spiritual, and social. The social domain is further subdivided into two branches: (a) emphasis: the moral, legal, political, and conventional (e.g., manners, etiquette, social protocol) and (b) perspective: the individual, family, school, community, society, nation, and world. The first branch prompts the question: if social, with what emphasis (e.g., moral, political)? The second branch prompts the question: if social, from what perspective (e.g., individual, society)? The authors stated that, while all the domains are not equally valued across the 17 countries studied, nearly all the countries regarded education and intellectual performance as values, stressing one or the other or both. For example, some countries explicitly stated the desire that children should learn to love learning, that is, education itself is a value that should be promoted. Likewise, nearly all the countries valued intellectual performance. "Ideally then, children should associate intellectual aspects of education with positive affect also" (p. 28). The association of positive affect with education and cognitive learning in this cross-cultural study serves as a reminder of the interrelatedness of the domains.

These last two conceptual models of the affective domain place considerably more emphasis on the spiritual domain than do the taxonomies (with the exception of Foshay, 1978), and they are more explicit about a world rather than an individual view. This may be because of their international focus. Also, these models include a focus on either learning as a value or intellectual behaviors as a value, or both, within affective education. To some extent all the conceptual models address the individual and self-development, moral education, attention to social learning, and the development of positive values and attitudes (although these have different referents). Social learning sometimes has an emphasis on the cognitive aspects (e.g., learning skills for relating to others), and sometimes the emphasis is more specifically on understanding one's feelings and emotions and how they influence interpersonal relationships.

ANOTHER CONCEPTUAL MODEL
OF THE AFFECTIVE DOMAIN

It is apparent from the above review of taxonomies and conceptual models that the affective domain does not lend itself to neat, clear-cut classifications. It can be viewed many ways from many different perspectives and for many different purposes. Part of the reason for this is that everything is so interconnected, and the same elements are often connected in several different ways. Consequently, there is much merit to being aware of a wide variety of different conceptualizations of the affective domain, to give you a realistic understanding of its complexity and "fuzziness." Toward this end, we offer an additional conceptual model (see Fig. 20.1) that focuses on affective development as both a process that addresses individual growth and internal change and as an end-product that addresses the "affectively well-adjusted" person.

We feel that one of the most important considerations for understanding affective development is what we call the different *dimensions of development,* but each of these dimensions is so complex that we also feel it is important to identify some of the major *components* of each that are most relevant to instruction. Our model has six dimensions and three major components. The six dimensions are defined in Fig. 20.2 and each one represents a different aspect of affective development. The components are the elements that, when taken together, comprise affective development in each dimension. While there are many components, we have identified three that we believe are especially important, for they represent the interrelatedness of the domains, and we have left a fourth column in the model to remind the reader that there are many more components. The three major components are

DIMENSIONS	COMPONENTS OF INSTRUCTIONAL VALUE			
	Knowledge	*Skills*	*Attitudes*	*Others?*
Emotional Development	Knowing that others experience the same emotions you do, such as joy and anger	Recognizing emotions Controlling one's emotions	I want to be happy. I don't like to be angry.	?
Moral Development	Understanding moral & ethical rules of the culture, such as caring, justice, equality	Moral reasoning skills Problem-solving skills in the realm of morals	I want to be honest. I am in favor of having ethical standards.	?
Social Development	Understanding group dynamics and democratic ideals, such as the role of a facilitator	Social skills, including interpersonal communication skills	I want to interact positively with others. I am opposed to resolving disagreements by fighting.	?
Spiritual Development	Knowledge of religious precepts about the spiritual world, such as the nature of the soul	Skills for getting in touch with your inner self Ability to love others selflessly	I want a spiritual life. I am in favor of prayer to build a relationship with God.	?
Aesthetic Development	Understanding the subjective nature of aesthetics, such as the relationship between one's values and one's judgments	Skills for assessing aesthetic qualities Skills for generating aesthetic creations	I want to surround myself with things of beauty. I appreciate an elegant theory.	?
Motivational Development	Understanding internal and external rewards for sustained activity, such as joy and sense of accomplishment	Skills for developing one's interests, both immediate and life-long	I want a career that I enjoy. I am opposed to hobbies related to guns.	?

FIG. 20.1.   A conceptual model for affective development.

knowledge, skills, and attitudes (of which, we assert, attitudes is often the most important):

- *Knowledge:* understandings and information related to a dimension, for example, knowledge of terms, ideas, concepts, rules, and strategies as they apply to oneself and others;
- *Skills:* abilities that are based on aptitudes, relevant knowledge, and practice for competent performance, for example, self-control skills; and
- *Attitudes:* positive, neutral, or negative responses to or evaluations about a referent, usually represented as position (pro or con) and intensity (strong to weak), for example, liking, opposition, willingness, appreciation; attitudes may or may not result in action.

Other is an open-ended category that reflects additional components that comprise affective development, such as readiness, IQ, experience, teacher beliefs about affective education, and culture, to name just a few.

Dimensions of Development

Our selection criteria for including a dimension were twofold: (a) the dimension had to have a strong attitude or feeling component that had the potential to influence behavior, and (b) the behaviors that might be exhibited could be widely applied. The most obvious dimensions are emotional, moral (or ethical), social, and motivational development (see Fig. 20.2 for definitions). Some researchers have suggested that social development is a separate domain (e.g., Romiszowski, 1981), rather than a dimension of affective development. Heinich, Molenda, and Russell

Term	*Definition*
Emotional Development	Understanding your own and others' feelings and affective evaluations, learning to manage those feelings, and wanting to do so.
Moral Development	Building codes of behavior and rationales for following them, including developing prosocial attitudes, often in relation to caring, justice, equality, etc.
Social Development	Building skills and attitudes for initiating and establishing interactions and maintaining relationships with others, including peers, family, coworkers, and those different from ourselves.
Spiritual Development	Cultivating an awareness and appreciation of one's soul and its connection with others' souls, with God, and with all His Creation.
Aesthetic Development	Acquiring an appreciation for beauty and style, including the ability to recognize and create it; commonly linked to art and music, but also includes the aesthetics of ideas.
Motivational Development	Cultivating interests and the desire to cultivate interests, based on the joy or utility they provide, including both vocational and avocational pursuits

FIG. 20.2.   Definitions of the dimensions of affective development.

(1989) refer to it as the interpersonal domain. We include it here as a dimension of affective development because of the strong attitude component involved in so many human relationships.

But what about spiritual and aesthetic development? Are they significantly different from the other dimensions of affective development, and do they belong in the affective domain? Several researchers believe they are and do (Foshay, 1978; Education for Affective Development, 1992), and we largely agree because they meet our criteria. But it is important to point out that we view spiritual development as something distinct from religion. Spiritual development is concerned with increasing one's awareness that the spiritual realm is a plane of existence different from the physical realm, that all people have souls (spirit entities), and that all souls are interrelated, or one, with each other and with God. Spiritual development is tied in with one's ability to love all people and/or to develop conscious awareness of one's soul. Can someone develop spiritually without believing in God or without believing that human beings have souls? According to our definition, they are developing aspects of spirituality but are incomplete. However, exploration of that idea is beyond the scope of this chapter and left to individual readers to consider.

We have, therefore, included six dimensions of affective development in our model, because they meet our criteria and because we believe they are qualitatively different from each other in that they have different referents and focus on different contexts in which feelings and attitudes are expressed. But the six are highly correlated and interdependent, which will become apparent when you read the next four chapters of this book. They are also pervasive in the literature we reviewed, and we believe they capture the "essence or intent" of most descriptions and taxonomies of the affective domain.

Since it might be argued that emotions, as states of feeling, are a component of all the dimensions, we need to clarify why we have included emotional development as a separate dimension. In the emotional development dimension of our model, the focus is on emotions per se. In the other dimensions, the focus is on a feeling state in a particular context, so the same emotion may be applied in a different way for different purposes within each of the other dimensions. For example, understanding empathy as an emotion, experiencing it physiologically, learning its triggers, and valuing it are all parts of emotional development. However, having positive attitudes about empathy toward those who have been persecuted or discriminated against is part of moral development, because the focus is on right and wrong behavior. Similarly, favoring empathy as a way of maintaining positive relationships with others is part of social development, as is the skill of empathizing with others. In the last two examples, an individual may or may not be able to identify or label the feeling as "empathy," and that may or may not be important. What is important is whether the individual experiences positive, negative, or neutral feelings in that context; that is, do they have negative feelings about discrimination or do they feel neutral, or even positive?

But what about the many other concepts in the affective domain literature? Several that were frequently mentioned in the taxonomies and conceptual models we reviewed earlier are empathy, self-worth, and interests. Do they represent dimensions of affective development? In a certain sense, they and many other concepts are indeed in the affective domain and represent areas of possible (even desirable) human development. But are they qualitatively different from the other dimensions? Empathy seems to us to be a component that is an important part of several (perhaps all) of the other dimensions. Self-worth seems to us to be a major component of emotional development, and perhaps a component, or prerequisite, for social development and even for spiritual development. Interests, on the other hand, seem to us to be largely a separate area of affective development and therefore deserving of being considered as another dimension, which we have called motivational development (although it is important to keep in mind the somewhat narrower-than-usual definition of motivation that this represents).

By engaging in a similar analysis of other affective concepts, we have for now limited our list of dimensions to those shown in Figs. 20.1 and 20.2. But it should be kept in mind that other concepts could be viewed as additional dimensions, and each of the dimensions we have listed may have subdimensions as well as components—and certainly other components, for that matter.

Components of the Dimensions

Regarding the components of the dimensions of affective development, several researchers have identified knowledge, skills, and attitudes/values as particularly important (Martin & Briggs, 1986; Zimbardo & Leippe, 1991). For example, emotional development requires the development of certain attitudes and values, certain skills, and certain knowledge (understandings). This is also the case for moral development, and indeed for *all* the dimensions we have listed (see Fig. 20.1 for a brief sample), though the relative importance of each component varies from one dimension to another and within each dimension.

But certainly there are other components of each of the dimensions, beyond knowledge, skills, and attitudes, that often influence ways we can foster affective development, which is the purpose of instructional-design theory. We provided some examples: readiness, IQ, experience, teacher beliefs about affective education, and culture. Our intent in including this category is to make clear that, due to the complexity of the affective domain, our model is not complete, and that other components may be found to be as important to fostering affective development as the three on which we have focused our attention.

Of the three major components in our model, we believe attitudes are the crux of all the affective dimensions of development. An attitude can be defined as a state of readiness or as a learned predisposition to behave in a consistent way. It is made up of cognitive, affective, and behavioral elements (Kamradt & Kamradt, chap. 23 in this volume; Katz & Stotland, 1959; Zimbardo, Ebbeson, & Maslash, 1977). The *affective* element of an attitude is its core and refers to the emotional response to an attitude object, that is, how one feels about it. The *cognitive* element refers to an individual's belief or knowledge about the attitude object. The *behavioral* element refers to the tendency to act on the attitude. (Please note that the cognitive element of an attitude is different from the knowledge component of a dimension of affective development, and the behavioral element of an attitude is different from the skill component of a dimension of affective development. For example, the skill of controlling one's emotions is not the same as the behavioral tendency to act on a favorable attitude toward controlling one's emotions.)

Depending on how the three elements of an attitude are aligned, an attitude can be strong or weak, conscious or unconscious, isolated or highly integrated with other attitudes. The cognitive and affective elements of an attitude are most directly linked to its formation, whereas the behavioral element is most likely to influence an action orientation and is closely linked to the cognitive element. Even though the affective or evaluative/emotional response to the attitude object is thought to be central, attitudes cannot exist without some cognitive element: an object must be at least recognized to be evaluated. (see chap. 23 of this volume or Martin & Briggs, 1986, for a complete discussion of attitude development.) Therefore, each of the attitude components in our model contains cognitive, affective, and behavioral elements (subcomponents), which we have not represented in Fig. 20.1.

We would, again, like to emphasize that the conceptual model shown in Fig. 20.1 is a work in progress and limited to one perspective, and therefore is in great need of being supplemented by other conceptualizations of this complex and fuzzy domain. For example, we also find it helpful to think of affective development as including the internal person and the person as a social being. Although both internal growth and social development have been captured in our dimensions, these two aspects of development are not explicitly portrayed. Furthermore, we find it useful to define "self-development" as a growth process wherein all of the dimensions and their components within the affective domain merge to form a unique individual. We hope that you will find this conceptual model a useful addition to your current conceptualizations for helping you to understand and analyze the remaining chapters in this volume.

AN APPLICATION MODEL FOR AFFECTIVE DEVELOPMENT CURRICULA

Conceptual models help us to understand affective development, but this book is concerned with identifying ways of fostering affective development, which in most applications means designing educational programs and courses (curricula). Although conceptual models certainly help, a different kind of knowledge is needed: design theory (see chap. 1). The remaining chapters in this unit present a small sampling of the exciting work that is being done in this area today. Here, we offer an ap-

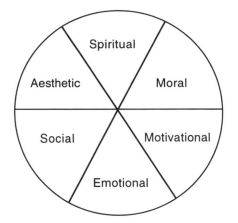

Dimensions of an Affective Development Curriculum

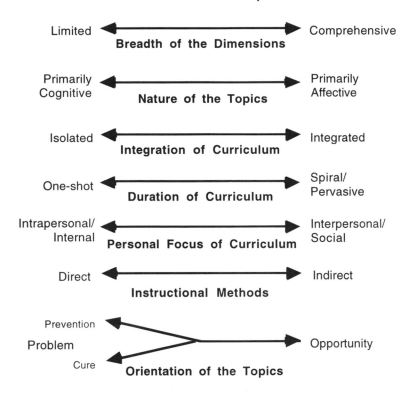

FIG. 20.3.   An application model for affective development curricula.

plication model to help you think about some of the design issues that are likely to be important in those design theories (see Fig. 20.3).

Our application model has seven primary design issues for the curriculum: *topics, orientation, breadth, integration, duration, personal focus, and instructional methods for the curriculum.* Each of these is described next, but we hope you will identify additional design issues, for this is certainly not an exhaustive list.

- *Dimensions of the affective curriculum* refers to which particular kinds of affective development (e.g., spiritual, moral, motivational) the program or course will address. You may use our conceptual model to frame the options, you may choose to use a different conceptual model, or you may choose to modify our model or another model; but some indication of the dimensions of affective development for the curriculum is important to an application model.
- *Breadth of the dimensions* refers to whether the curriculum is *comprehensive*, that is, encompassing multiple dimensions (e.g., moral, social, emotional, etc.), or whether it is *limited*, addressing only one or two dimensions.
- *Nature of the topics* refers to whether the topics are generally thought to be primarily *affective* or *cognitive*. Because the cognitive and affective domains are highly interrelated, almost any topic can be addressed from either domain. However, some topics are more typically thought of as affective and some as cognitive. For example, topics like conflict resolution, character education, and education for moral integrity are typically regarded as highly affective, whereas topics like managing planned change, World War II, geography, and geometry are more likely to be considered cognitive. Other topics that combine both domains (for example, in social studies, literature, and the humanities) might fall more nearly in the middle of the continuum, depending on its emphasis.
- *Integration of the curriculum* refers to how or whether affective topics/programs are integrated into the subject areas of the curriculum. An *isolated* curriculum has no attachment to regular school subjects and hence is taught as separate programs or courses, or it may be attached to one subject, for example, social studies. Furthermore, within the affective curriculum, the dimensions and their topics can be addressed separately (e.g., moral development only) or in any combination (e.g., moral and emotional; social and emotional; cognitive, emotional, and social; etc.) and become attached to a particular subject area or be distinct from it. An integrated curriculum is one that is fully combined with the other curricula in a school; the affective program is woven throughout the other curricula.
- *Duration of the curriculum* refers to how often a topic or dimension is taught. In a *one-shot* curriculum, it is taught once and may be used to serve a particular, limited need. In a *spiral* or *pervasive* curriculum, it is on-going throughout the school year and is elaborative (see Reigeluth, chap. 18).

- *Personal focus of the curriculum* refers to whether the course is intended to foster the development of internal (intrapersonal) topics/dimensions or social (interpersonal) ones. *Intrapersonal* topics are ones in which students develop individual cognitive and affective structures and meanings, whereas *interpersonal* topics are ones in which students develop relationships with others and therefore must engage with other people. Clearly, this distinction has important instructional implications. Although this issue can be seen as more of a dichotomy than a continuum, the continuum reflects the proportion of topics that are intra- versus interpersonal.

- *Instructional methods* can be either direct or indirect. *Direct* methods refer to specific activities and strategies that are planned for use during an instructional intervention (e.g., role playing, skill-building exercises, etc.). *Indirect* methods refer to interventions with planned outcomes but that are not necessarily classroom interventions. These might include modeling, changes in the school climate or environment, social supports, and so forth.

- *Orientation of the topics* refers to whether the purpose of addressing the topics is to address a *problem* (e.g., child abuse or teen pregnancy) or an *opportunity* (e.g., developing a hobby or making new friends), and if a problem, whether it is intended to prevent or to cure the problem. Although this design issue can be seen more as a dichotomy than a continuum, the continuum reflects the proportion of topics that are problem oriented versus opportunity oriented.

Courses and programs for affective development can be described and analyzed in reference to all eight design issues. Therefore, instructional theories in the affective domain should address these issues. Next, we identify several sample affective programs not represented in the following chapters, and we briefly describe them on the design issues listed above.

WHAT KINDS OF COURSES AND PROGRAMS EXIST IN AFFECTIVE EDUCATION?

In this section, we include a few examples of affective program that fit some of the parameters we have outlined in our models above. We have classified all the programs as primarily affective ("nature of the topic"), however, this is a judgment call on our part. While it appears that attitudes or values are being developed, the extent to which each program actually focuses on affective behaviors rather than cognitive skills is unclear.

Regarding the category "personal focus of the curriculum," we originally separated the programs into two broad groups: those with an intrapersonal focus and those with an interpersonal focus. Programs with an *intrapersonal/internal focus* are typically those that address self-concept, attitude change, and moral or character development. *Interpersonal/social programs* typically involve teaching problem-solving and critical thinking skills and often, but not always, include conflict resolution, effective communication skills, and managing emotions. However, you can hardly address one without the other, so intra-/inter-personal *focus* is a matter of degree. In the programs below we have used the intrapersonal label for those programs where individual or internal growth seems to take precedence, and we use interpersonal for programs with an immediate focus on developing social skills.

The *Celebration of Learning* **program** is based on the goals and objectives of the Lethbridge Catholic School District and those of Alberta Education (Lambert & Himsl, 1993). It focuses on both *intrapersonal behaviors* (e.g., self-worth, self-esteem, well-rounded person, problem-solving, creativity, happy and positive attitude, academic excellence, values) and *interpersonal skills* (communication with others and interpersonal relationships). The program is actually a means for teachers to monitor, observe, record, and report students' positive and negative affective indicators. There are lists of indicators that show signs of affective growth or decay in each target area. For example, positive self-worth indicators (growth) include "shows confidence," "assumes responsibility," and "develops talents." Decay self-worth indicators include "demeans self and gives up," "shirks responsibility," "wastes time and talents." Teachers observe students and affirm positive behaviors, and/or they make plans with students and parents to rectify decay behaviors. It is not mandatory that teachers use the program; it is offered to them. The program is *comprehensive* (breadth of focus) and *integrated* (integration of curriculum); plans may include *direct* or *indirect* "instructional methods," and it is *spiral* (duration) in nature. It addresses both *problems* and *opportunities* (orientation).

Nel Noddings' Moral Education (Norton, 1994) uses the teacher as a positive moral resource in the business of education, which is defined as "peoplemaking." Noddings claims that the primary aim of parents and educators is to enhance and preserve caring. She holds that moral education is both education that is moral and education in morality. Norton (1994) applies the term "affective apprenticeship" or "apprenticeship in caring" to her view of schooling. She outlines a method for apprenticeship in caring that is similar to the steps of cognitive apprenticeship: *modeling* to show the process by which morality may be achieved, *dialogue* in order to externalize the moral thinking of the teacher and students, and *practice*, which includes apprenticeship in the community. She argues that the same teacher should stay with students over a longer period of time and is opposed to grading as an intrusion on the caring relationship. Her program is highly *integrated*, uses some direct but primarily *indirect* instructional methods, including a restructuring of schools to support caring, and is *spiral or pervasive* (duration) in its delivery. The breadth of focus is *limited*, with primary attention being given to moral development.

Affective Self-Esteem: Lesson Plans for Affective Education (Krefft, 1993) is based on the notion that unacceptable social behaviors require the "alteration of the biochemistry of emotion" (p. iv). The goal of the program is to help students understand the nature of emotions and constructively manage them. The program includes a set of lesson plans that strongly encourages an interdisciplinary approach that can be either *integrated* into the curriculum or *segregated* in health science, biology, science, social studies, or language arts. The first four lesson plans contain the fundamentals, and it is advised that they be taught first. After that, separate units can be taught on guilt, fear, grief, and anger in any order, but may require adaptations if done out of order. The "breadth of focus" is *somewhat limited*, with emphasis on emotional development, although social and cognitive development are certainly included. The program is intended to *spiral* (duration) through the curriculum, and the "instructional methods" are mostly *direct*. It is aimed at prevention and cure (orientation).

Faith, Family, and Friends: Catholic Elementary School Guidance Program (Campbell, 1993). This program includes 18 topics ranging from understanding self and others to Christian education. Hence, it is very much involved with *intrapersonal* growth and development. However, a large part of the curriculum includes *interpersonal skills*, including stress management, moral decision making, substance abuse, communication, and conflict resolution. Specific competencies are provided under the categories of attitudes, skills, and concepts. It is *comprehensive* (breadth of focus), it is an *integrated* curriculum, it uses primarily *direct* methods of instruction, and the duration is *spiral*. Depending on the specific competencies under consideration, the program could be seen as providing a problem orientation (prevention and/or cure) or an opportunity for growth.

Conflict Resolution in Middle School: A Curriculum and Teaching Guide (Kreidler, 1994), enables teachers to help "middle school students become effective at handling conflict nonviolently and to use what they know about interpersonal conflict resolution to understand conflict in the larger world" (p. 1). Twenty conflict resolution skill lessons are provided, plus a thematic unit on diversity and conflict that describes how conflict is rooted in diversity. The curriculum is based on a model called the "peaceable classroom," a caring community that emphasizes cooperation, communication, affective education, appreciation of diversity, and conflict resolution. The focus of the program is on *social skills*; the breadth of focus is *somewhat limited*, dealing primarily with social development (interpersonal conflict), but it includes some cognitive, moral (a caring community), and emotional development as well. The curriculum is intended to be *integrated*, and the duration is *spiral* or *pervasive*, as the concepts are intended to be infused and reinforced in every aspect of a standard middle school curriculum. Its emphasis is on *direct* instructional methods, primarily cooperatively structured activities and class discussions. It is oriented toward *prevention* and *cure*.

Decision Skills Curriculum (Wills, reported in Botvin & Wills, 1985) is an intervention approach to preventing substance abuse based on combating the psychosocial stress factors that may predispose students to abuse substances such as alcohol and drugs. While there are hundreds of drug and substance programs available to educators, we report this one because it is based on the assumption that deterring substance abuse can be accomplished by changing coping skills and reducing stress. In this program attitudes and values are addressed directly, as are negative emotions that may lead to substance abuse. The program consists of eight modules taught over a two-week period and is taught by trained health educators with assistance from classroom teachers. The first module is a values-clarification exercise about the use of leisure time. Other modules included are: decision making, social influence, assertiveness, stress management, and the health consequences of smoking. The program is *one-shot* (duration), *isolated* (integration), and uses primarily *direct* instructional methods.

Additional Programs

There are literally hundreds, perhaps thousands, of programs that address the affective domain or components of affective education (see Goleman, 1995, and Strein, 1988, for some of them). There is no way we can describe even a small portion of them. However, we include next some descriptions of a few additional programs (or in one case a prescription for a program) to give you some idea of the range of programs that are available.

Multicultural Thematic Instruction (Fitzgerald, 1995) is a framework for designing affective instruction to meet the needs of middle-level students, many of whom are defined as "at risk." The role of identity development and self-concept are emphasized. A chart is provided linking middle school objectives, the framework for unit teaching, and learner needs.

Developing and Understanding Self and Others (DUSO) (Dinkmeyer, 1970); (Human Development Training Institute, reported in Strein, 1988) is one of 23 programs that Strein includes in a critical review of affective programs (the results will be presented in the next section). The program focuses on the development of self-concept and has an instrument, DUSO Affectivity Device, to measure self-concept.

The Character Development prescription of Etzioni (1993; 1994; also reported in Goleman, 1995). Etzioni is a social theorist who believes that character is the foundation of democratic societies and that emotional intelligence is the foundation for character development. "Schools, notes Etzioni, have a central role in cultivating character by inculcating self-discipline and empathy, which in turn enable true commitment to civic and moral values" (Goleman, 1995, pp. 285–286). Children need to learn about values and to practice them.

The PATHS Project (Greenberg & Kusché, 1993; also reported in Goleman, 1995) was designed to help boys who were prone to violence and crime identify and deal with their emotions. The curriculum has 50 lessons on different emotions (from basic emotions like anger to more complicated ones such as jealousy), and the lessons include how to recognize and monitor the emotions of self and others. The lessons are presented to all children in a class, not just those students who are prone to violence. PATHS stands for Parents and Teachers Helping Students.

Resolving Conflict Creatively (Lantieri, Patti, & Edelman, 1996; also reported in Goleman, 1995) is a prevention-based emotional literacy program that focuses on a specific problem: violence. Although originally intended to focus on how to settle schoolyard arguments that can escalate, Lantieri sees the program as having a much wider mission that includes conflict resolution through means other than passivity or aggression. Much of the program involves teaching students emotional basics.

Yale-New Haven Social Competence Promotion Program (Caplan et al., 1992; also reported in Goleman, 1995) is a social competence curriculum designed for students in the inner-city schools of New Haven, CT. There is a series of courses that cover problems such as emotional development, sex education, drug education, violence, and conflict resolution.

A *Mentorship Model for Students At-Risk* (Sapone, 1989) describes a teacher-education program that encourages university/school partnerships in the identification of at-risk students and the development of strategies and interventions to influence the self-esteem of those students. A mentoring model is suggested that can help students achieve personal worth and competence, and dignity in school and in life.

Values-Based Teaching Skills (Hall, Kalven, Rosen, & Taylor, 1995). This is a book that is designed to help teachers clarify their own values. In learning about their own values, they learn how to promote value development in their students. Specific objectives and exercises are included.

How Effective are these Programs? The Research Evidence

The research evidence concerning the success of affective education programs is mixed, although there are some data to suggest that problem-solving or social skill programs are generally more successful than programs that focus on intrapersonal or internal behaviors. In fact, Goleman (1995) reports very positive results (selected results are provided) for the following programs: *The PATHS Project* (Greenberg & Kusché, 1993) showed improved social and cognitive skills and improved classroom behavior; *Seattle Social Development Project* (Hawkins) showed more positive attachments to family and school and less drug-use initiation, less delinquency, and better scores; *Yale-New Haven Social Competence Promotion Program* (Caplan et al., 1992), showed improved problem-solving skills, better impulse control, and better coping skills; *Resolving Conflict Creatively* (Lantieri, Patti, & Edelman, 1996), showed less violence in class, a more caring atmosphere, and more empathy; *The Improving Social-Awareness-Social Problem Solving Project* (Elias) showed higher self-esteem, more prosocial behavior, and better self-control, social awareness, and social decision-making in and out of the classroom.

Other researchers, however, are more cautious in their endorsement of affective education programs. Strein (1988) compared 23 studies that evaluated the effectiveness of classroom-based, elementary school, affective education programs dating from 1970. He evaluated each study on methodological rigor, program type, grade level, program length, and the leader's profession. He states:

The lack of positive significant findings in the more carefully designed studies provides little support for the effectiveness of affective education programs in promoting changes on either behavioral or affective measures, especially for programs with an internal focus [e.g., self-concept]. Studies of social-cognitive problem solving programs produced promising results, but require further evidence of effectiveness. (p. 288)

Of the problem-solving programs, he states that these programs were weak in two outcomes: generalizing to real-life situations and maintenance of the behaviors over time. Longer programs did show increased treatment effects, but there were only three programs in this category.

In an extensive review of conflict resolution and peer mediation programs (ones with an interpersonal/social focus) in elementary and secondary schools, Johnson and Johnson (1996) reported that there has been an explosion of these types of programs since 1994 with no real evidence to support their use. While their findings have to be tempered due to the numerous problems with the individual research studies they report, their findings suggest that the programs do seem to be effective in teaching students integrative negotiation and mediation procedures. "After training, students tend to use these conflict strategies, and constructive outcomes tend to result" (p. 498).

It is difficult to make generalizations about the effectiveness of affective education programs based on these limited studies. However, the isolated data do seem to indicate that interpersonal programs are more likely to have long-term positive results than do programs that focus on intrapersonal (internal) changes, and that longer programs are more successful than shorter ones. This may provide some very limited support for the need to integrate affective programs into or across the curriculum and to have spiral rather than one-shot programs. Most importantly, the research and evaluation results show that there is promise, but that we still have a long way to go to develop powerful instructional-design theories and programs in the affective domain.

DECISION-MAKING FOR THE INSTRUCTIONAL DESIGNER AND TEACHER

The models we have developed, the sample programs provided, and the research results can help the teacher or instructional designer to design effective instructional plans that include affective goals. This can be accomplished within any unit or instructional sequence regardless of such issues as: (a) whether the subject matter is primarily cognitive or affective, (b) whether the topic is isolated or can be integrated into the curriculum, and (c) whether the instruction is one-shot or spiraling through the curriculum. Of course, whole affective courses and programs can be developed, too; it just takes a little more time and effort. As a summary, consider the following:

- The affective domain may be equally, if not more, important than the cognitive domain in promoting student learning, and the domain has overlapping dimensions of development that promote growth. These include emotional, moral, aesthetic, social, spiritual, and motivational development.
- Cognitive skills are an important part of the domain and must be addressed. For example, reason and intellectual knowledge come into play as students learn about themselves, make moral and value-laden decisions, learn how anger and emotion occur (e.g., triggers), identify cognitive referents of attitudes, and develop the skills for effective communication or conflict resolution. In addition, the simple love of learning or the enjoyment of subject matter has been stated as a worthy affective educational goal.
- The application model provided in Fig. 20.3 can be used as a guideline for issues to consider when thinking about program goals and methods, and the conceptual model in Fig. 20.1 can be used to help determine which dimensions should be addressed to accomplish those goals.
- Affective programs that are integrated into the curriculum, and are pervasive rather than one-shot, are reported to have longer lasting effects.
- There is some evidence to suggest that affective programs that focus on social-cognitive problem solving (e.g., interpersonal skills) tend to be more effective than programs that focus on intrapersonal (internal) growth, provided that the programs are long enough to be effective.
- The teacher and the instructional designer may need to acquire additional knowledge about and skills related to education in the affective domain. Both may need an expanded knowledge base about the affective domain, for example, what it is, more information about specific dimensions, what instructional strategies and methods are successful, how or whether to evaluate students in affective behaviors, and which evaluation techniques could be

TABLE 20.1
Instructional Methods

Direct Instructional Methods	Indirect Instructional Methods
Skill building	Moral apprenticeship
Discussion groups	Modeling
Keeping a journal	Mentoring
Role plays/simulations	Parental involvement
Activity sheets	Unstructured "learning environments"
Multimedia applications	Relaxation techniques, including mood music
Bulletin boards	Visualization
Providing examples and nonexamples	Altering the school climate/environment
Gaining new knowledge (reading, media)	
Lectures/telling	
Overt practice, e.g., community service	
Direct rewards	

used. In addition, teachers and designers may need new cognitive skills that will enable them to integrate affective programs into existing units, courses, or programs, or new skills in how to design complete new programs. Finally, teachers and designers may need to develop new attitudes about teaching in the affective domain and their own affective development.

- Both direct and indirect instructional methods have been used successfully. Table 20.1 lists several methods in each category.

WHY CONSIDER AFFECT?

At the beginning of this chapter we asked the question, "why consider affect?" To answer that question, we provided definitions of the affective domain, perspectives about affective education, and the definitions of several dimensions of the affective domain. We provided rationales for including the affective domain in instruction. We presented taxonomies and models, existing instructional programs, instructional methods and strategies, and research evidence. In pondering the question "why consider affect?," we became even more convinced that the affective domain is vitally important in all aspects of learning and that affective programs can have at least some positive influence on the lives of students of all ages as they grow and develop. We believe there are compelling reasons for including affective development in all types of learning environments. These include instructional sequences or programs for young students and older students, in corporate training, medical education, graduate education, and community education programs, to name a few. However, real impact on the lives of students will have maximum effect only when there is a concerted effort by educators and other stakeholders to infuse affective learning into all types of courses, programs, and curricula. Therefore, two questions remain: "Do you believe instruction in the affective domain can have a positive effect on students? If yes, what will you do about it?"

REFERENCES

Ackerson, C. (1991/1992). Affective objectives: A discussion of some controversies. *Instructional Development, 3*(1), 7–11.

Beane, J. A. (1990). *Affect in the curriculum: Toward democracy, dignity, diversity.* New York: Teachers College, Columbia University.

Bills, R. E. (1976). Affect and its measurement. In W. Gephart, R. Ingle, & F. Marshall (Eds.), *Proceedings of the National Symposium for Professors of Educational Research (NSPER).* Memphis, TN. (ERIC Document Reproduction Service No. ED 157 911.)

Botvin, G. J., & Wills, T. A. (1985). Personal and social skills training: Cognitive-behavioral approaches to substance abuse prevention. In C. S. Bell & R. Battjes (Eds.), Prevention research: Deterring drug abuse among children and adolescents. *NIDA Research Monograph, 63,* 8–49. (A RAUS Review Report.)

Brandhorst, A. R. (1978*). Reconceptualizing the affective domain.* W. Gephart (Ed.). (ERIC Document Reproduction Service No. ED 153 891.)

Brown, J. S., Collins, A., & Duguid, P. (1989). Situated cognition and the culture of learning. *Educational Researcher, 18*(1), 32–42.

Campbell, B. (1993). *Faith, family, and friends: Catholic elementary school guidance program* (Vols. 1–6). (ERIC Document Reproduction Service No. ED373277.)

Caplan, M., Weissberg, R. P., Grober, J. S., Sivo, P. J., Grady, K., & Jacoby, C. (1992). Social competence promotion with inner-city and suburban young adolescents: Effects of social adjustment and alcohol use. *Journal of Consulting and Clinical Psychology, 60*(1), 56–63.

Dinkmeyer, D. (1970). *Developing understanding of self and others* (Educational Program). Circle Pines, MN: American Guidance Service.

Education for affective development: A guidebook on programmes and practices. (1992). (ERIC Document Reproduction Service No. ED 371 904.)

Etzioni, A. (1993). *The spirit of community*. New York: Crown.

Etzioni, A., et al. (1994). *Character building for a democratic, civil society*. Washington, DC: The Communitarian Network.

Ferguson, M. (Ed.). (1982). New theory: Feelings code, organize thinking [Special issue, Part I]. *Brain/Mind Bulletin, 7*(6).

Fitzgerald. D. F. (1995). *Multicultural thematic instruction: One strategy for meeting middle learner's affective needs*. (ERIC Document Reproduction Service No. ED390859.)

Foshay, W. R. (1978). An alternative for task analysis in the affective domain. *Journal of Instructional Development, 1*(2), 22–24.

Gephart, W. J., & Ingle, R. B. (1976). Evaluation and the affective domain. In W. Gephart, R. Ingle, & F. Marshall (Eds.), *Proceedings of the National Symposium for Professors of Educational Research (NSPER)*. Phoenix, Arizona . (ERIC Document Reproduction Service No. 157 911.)

Goleman, D. (1995). *Emotional Intelligence*. New York: Bantam.

Greenberg, M. T., & Kusché, C. A. (1993). *Promoting social and emotional development in deaf children: The PATHS project*. Seattle, WA: University of Washington Press.

Greenspan, S. I. (1997). The growth of the mind. Reading, MA: Addison-Wesley Publishing Co.

Hall, B., Kalven, J., Rosen, L., & Taylor, B. (1995). *Values-based teaching skills: Introduction and implementation*. Rockport, MA: Twin Lights Publishers.

Harre, R. (1984). *Personal being: A theory for individual psychology*. Cambridge, MA: Harvard University Press.

Heinich, R., Molenda, M., & Russell, J. D. (1989). *Instructional media and the new technologies of instruction*. New York: Macmillan.

Hlynka, D. (1997, February). A post-modern perspective linking cognition and affect. In B. L. Martin & W. Wager (Co-Chairs), *Alternative perspectives linking cognition and affect: Implications for education*. Presidential Session presented at the annual conference of the Association for Educational Communications and Technology, Albuquerque, NM.

Hoepfner, R. (1972). *CSE-RBS test evaluation: Tests of higher order cognitive, affective, and interpersonal skills*. Los Angeles: Center for the Study of Evaluation.

Johnson, D. W., & Johnson, R. T. (1996). Conflict resolution and peer mediation programs in elementary and secondary schools: A review of the research. *Review of Educational Research, 66*(4), 459–506.

Katz, D., & Stotland, E. (1959). A preliminary statement to a theory of attitude structure and change. In S. Koch (Ed.), *Psychology: A study of science* (Vol. 3, pp. 423–475). New York: McGraw-Hill.

Kohlberg. L. (1969). Stage and sequence: The cognitive-developmental approach to socialization. In D. Golin (Ed.), *Handbook of socialization theory and research*. Chicago: Rand McNally.

Krathwohl, D. R., Bloom, B. S., & Masia, B. B. (1964). *Taxonomy of educational objectives: The classification of educational goals. Handbook II: Affective domain*. New York: Longman.

Krefft, K. (1993). *Affective self-esteeem: Lesson plans for affective education*. Muncie, IN: Accelerated Development.

Kreidler, W. J. (1994). *Conflict resolution in the middle school: A curriculum and teaching guide*. Field test version. (ERIC Document Reproduction Service No. ED377968.)

Lambert, E., & Himsl, R. (1993). *Signs of learning in the affective domain*. (ERIC Document Reproduction Service No. ED 360–081.)

Lantieri, L., Patti, J., Edelman, M. (1996). *Waging peace in our schools*. Boston, MA: Beacon Press.

Lebow, D. (1997, February). Bees do it better. In B. L. Martin & W. Wager (Co-Chairs), *Alternative perspectives linking cognition and affect: Implications for Education*. Presidential Session presented at the annual conference of the Association for Educational Communications and Technology, Albuquerque, NM.

Martin, B. L., & Briggs, L. J. (1986*). The affective and cognitive domains: Integration for instruction and research*. Englewood Cliffs, NJ: Educational Technology Publications.

Miller, R. (1994). Introduction. In D. M. Bethel (Ed.), *Compulsory schooling and human learning: The moral failure of public education in America and Japan* (pp. xi–xvi). San Francisco: Caddo Gap.

Noddings, N. (1994). Caring and moral capacities. In D. M. Bethel (Ed.), *Compulsory schooling and human learning: The moral failure of public education in America and Japan* (pp. 55–68). San Francisco: Caddo Gap.

Norton, M. K. (1994). Educating for head, heart, and hand: Recent research toward moral education. In D. M. Bethel (Ed.), *Compulsory schooling and human learning: The moral failure of public education in America and Japan* (pp. 31–43). San Francisco: Caddo Gap.

Nunnally, J. C. (1978). *Psychometric theory* (2nd ed.). New York; McGraw-Hill.

Porges, S. W., Doussard-Roosevelt, J. A., Portales, A. L., & Greenspan, S. L. (in press). Infant regulation of the vagal "brake" predicts child behavior problems: A psychobiological model of social behavior, Developmental Psychobiology.

Rogers, C. R. (1969). *Freedom to learn.* Columbus, OH: Charles E. Merrill.

Romiszowski, A. J. (1981). *Designing instructional systems.* London: Kogan Page.

Sapone, C. V. (1989). *A mentorship model for students at-risk.* (ERIC Document Reproduction Service Nno. ED314395.)

Strein, W. (1988). Classroom-based elementary school affective education programs: A critical review. *Psychology in the Schools, 25,* 288–296.

Tennyson, R., & Nielson, M. (1997, February). Complexity theory: Inclusion of the affective domain in psychological foundations for instructional design theory. In B. L. Martin & W. Wager (Co-Chairs), *Alternative perspectives linking cognition and affect: Implications for Education.* Presidential Session presented at the annual conference of the Association for Educational Communications and Technology, Albuquerque, NM.

Vygotsky, L. S. (1978). *Mind in society: The development of higher psychological processes.* (Edited by M. Cole, V. John-Steiner, S. Scribner, & E. Souberman). Cambridge, MA: Harvard University Press.

Zimbardo, P. G., Ebbeson, E. B., & Maslash, C. (1977). *Influencing attitudes and changing behavior* (2nd ed.). Menlo Park, CA: Addison-Wesley.

Zimbardo, P. G., & Leippe, M. R. (1991). *The psychology of attitude change and social influence.* Philadelphia: Temple University Press.

21

Recapturing Education's Full Mission: Educating for Social, Ethical, and Intellectual Development

Catherine Lewis
Marilyn Watson
Eric Schaps
Developmental Studies Center, Oakland, CA

Catherine C. Lewis

Catherine C. Lewis, a developmental psychologist, directs formative research at the Developmental Studies Center. She has authored more than two dozen articles on schooling, social development, and educational innovation. Her book *Educating Hearts and Minds* was named an outstanding academic book of 1995 by the American Library Association's *Choice*. She currently directs an NSF-funded study of the shift to student-centered science in Japanese elementary schools, and a study of the relationship between teachers' sense of community and educational change in six U.S. school districts.

Marilyn Watson

Eric Schaps

Marilyn Watson is program director at the Developmental Studies Center, Oakland, California. She received her MA and PhD degrees from the University of California at Berkeley, in education. Her primary role at DSC has been that of program director of the Child Development Project, DSC's school change project focused on fostering children's social, ethical and intellectual development. She is currently responsible for integrating the DSC's programs into teacher preparation. Previously, she was a preschool teacher and director of the Children's School at Mills College in Oakland, California.

Eric Schaps is founder and president of the Developmental Studies Center in Oakland, California. He is the author of three books and over 50 book chapters and articles on character development, school improvement, substance abuse prevention, and program evaluation. He serves on several boards and advisory panels, including those of the Bay Area School Reform Collaborative and the Bay Area Coalition of Essential Schools. He currently co-chairs the National Commission on Character Education of the Association of Teacher Educators. He earned his PhD in psychology from Northwestern University.

FOREWORD

Goals and preconditions. *The primary goal of this theory is to foster social and ethical, as well as intellectual, development—to build caring relationships, ownership, reflection, internal motivation, understanding of prosocial values, and academic development. The theory is intended for K-6 schools.*

Values. *Some of the values upon which this theory is based include:*

* *social and ethical development, as well as intellectual development,*
* *a school as a caring community of learners in which all children feel valued and emotionally attached to their school,*
* *a curriculum that fosters bonds among fellow students and interest in learning (intrinsic motivation).*

Methods. *Here are the major methods this theory offers:*
1. *Literature-based reading.*
   * *The books should be rich in social and ethical themes.*
   * *Use read-alouds (by the teacher) and partner reads (two students reading aloud).*
   * *Hold interesting and lively discussions about each book.*
   * *To teach reading, provide practice, modeling, opportunities to actively construct understanding, and comments from teachers and peers.*
   * *Use planning and reflection for application of core values.*
2. *Developmental discipline.*
   * *Draw on the desire to belong to a valued group rather than on self-interest, as the basis for discipline.*
   * *Begin the school year with children getting to know one another, and continue to build human relationships throughout the year.*
   * *Don't give punishments or rewards.*
   * *Have students help build and maintain class norms (values), not rules.*
   * *Address disciplinary problems with a problem-solving approach, including diagnosing the cause of the problem, repairing the damage they have done, and developing ways to prevent future occurrences. Model this approach, and help students to use it.*
3. *Cooperative learning.*
   * *Use group work in such a way as to build children's understanding and practice of social skills and ethical values.*
   * *Use group work in such a way as to build human relationships.*
   * *Foster internal motivation by addressing important subject matter, along with social and ethical themes.*
4. *Schoolwide activities.*

- *Use schoolwide activities to extend values of respect, fairness, and kindness beyond students' immediate group of classmates.*
- *Make sure schoolwide activities meet children's needs for friendship, contribution, and belonging, rather than pitting children against one another.*
- *Make students' families feel more welcome at school.*
- *Emphasize inherent interest and challenge rather than awards.*

Major contributions. Addressing the cognitive and affective in a thoroughly integrated manner—especially social and ethical development. Emphasizing self-discipline over external discipline.

—C.M.R.

Recapturing Education's Full Mission: Educating for Social, Ethical, and Intellectual Development

INTRODUCTION

What are education's goals? Over the past decade, we have asked educators and parents in communities across the United States what qualities they want their elementary-schoolers to have 30 years from now. Their answers point up the importance of social and ethical, as well as intellectual, development: "honest," "responsible," "kind," "motivated," "intelligent." Our informal experience is supported by national polls. When Americans were asked by the Gallup Organization to rate the relative importance of 25 possible goals for schools—everything from preparing students to assume high-paying jobs to promoting physical fitness—the public gave the second-highest ranking to the following goal: "To develop standards of what is right and wrong" (Elam, 1989). Only the essential academic mission, "To develop the ability to speak and write correctly," ranked higher. Another national poll revealed that Americans strongly approve of the teaching of core values in the public schools, including honesty (97% of respondents), democracy (93%), acceptance of people of different races and ethnic backgrounds (93%), caring for friends and family members (91%), and so forth (Elam, Rose, & Gallup, 1993).

But ask the question "What do you want your children to learn in school *this year?*" and, often, a very different picture emerges. Suddenly, adults are concerned that students learn to sit still, pass spelling tests, and take notes. Many adults who participate in this exercise discover a gap between their long-term goals of nurturing able, caring, principled adults and their current activities. In this chapter, we make the case that social, ethical, and intellectual development are all essential goals of schooling, and we lay out the instructional practices that support all three goals.*

What Are the Essential Outcomes of Schooling?

What skills, attitudes, and dispositions must children develop if they are to sustain a democratic society? Fig. 21.1 lists seven qualities of intellectual, social, and ethical development that we believe to be essential: that students become competent, knowledgeable, thoughtful, caring, principled, self-disciplined, and motivated from within. Remarkably diverse groups have come up with lists that overlap largely with the list in Fig. 21.1 (see, for example, Character Education Partnership, 1996; Etzioni, 1996). But aren't social and ethical development the job of families and religious institutions, not schools? We have argued elsewhere that schools cannot do a surgical strike on children's intellects (Lewis, Schaps, & Watson, 1995). Everything about schooling—what is taught, how it is taught, discipline, how students and teachers relate to one another—teaches children how we treat other human beings and what we truly value. We have no choice about whether to teach these lessons, but only whether we teach them deliberately and carefully (or leave them to be learned haphazardly, as part of an unintentional curriculum).**

What kind of instruction enables children to develop the qualities of intellect, attitude, and character shown in Fig. 21.1? Theory, basic research, and our own study of the Child Development Project (CDP) over the past 15 years suggest that a particular kind of classroom and school—one which we call a "caring community of learners"—is most likely to foster these qualities (Battistich, Solomon, Watson, & Schaps, 1997).*** In a caring community of learners:

- All children feel like valued community members and, in turn, they value the community and want to maintain their attachment to it.
- The community helps children understand and practice the values it wants them to develop, such as kindness, fairness, self-discipline, and personal commitment to learning.
- The curriculum is both important and engaging; it builds important knowledge, skills, and dispositions in ways that students find engaging.

---

* It is worth noting that in corporate training contexts there is a similar interest in social and ethical development as well as intellectual development of employees.

** This inextricable relationship between the affective and cognitive domains is a common theme in the new paradigm of instructional theories.

*** As you read on, try to figure out how the idea of a "caring community of learners" compares with Bielaczyc and Collins' notion of "learning communities" (chap. 12).

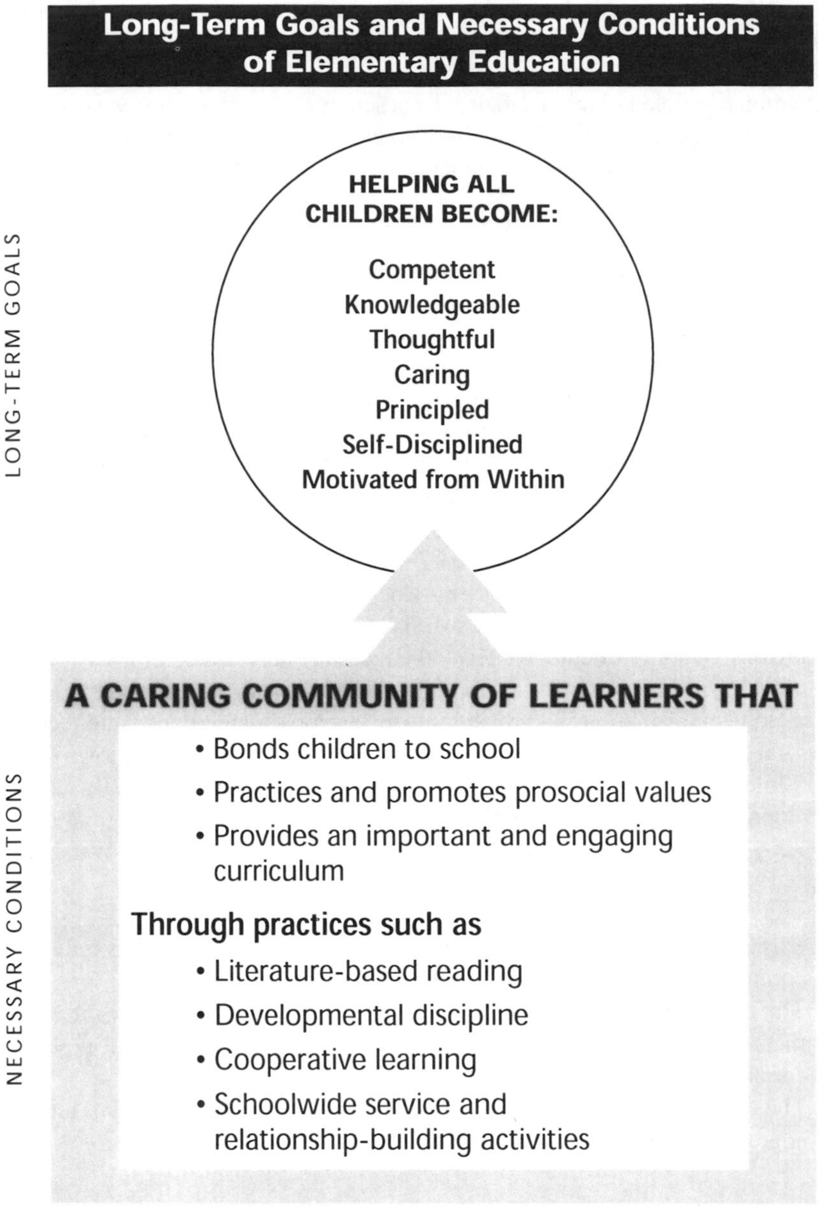
Long-Term Goals and Necessary Conditions of Elementary Education
LONG-TERM GOALS
HELPING ALL CHILDREN BECOME:
Competent
Knowledgeable
Thoughtful
Caring
Principled
Self-Disciplined
Motivated from Within
NECESSARY CONDITIONS
A CARING COMMUNITY OF LEARNERS THAT
• Bonds children to school
• Practices and promotes prosocial values
• Provides an important and engaging curriculum
Through practices such as
• Literature-based reading
• Developmental discipline
• Cooperative learning
• Schoolwide service and relationship-building activities

FIG. 21.1. Long-term goals and necessary conditions of elementary education.

Three bodies of theory and research underpin the "caring community of learners."

Intrinsic Motivation.   In the long run, children will be most likely to develop a personal commitment to actions they feel they have willingly chosen; they will be less likely to develop a commitment to actions they see as having been motivated by rewards, punishments, or other external constraints (Deci & Ryan, 1985; Lepper, 1983; Lepper, Keavney, & Drake, 1996). Hence, the caring community of learners emphasizes intrinsic motivation (such as the joy of learning, the satisfaction of helping others, the sense of personal accomplishment from challenging oneself) rather than extrinsics (such as stickers, points, and other rewards or punishments).*

Attachment and Internalization.   When school meets children's basic human needs for belonging, autonomy, and competence, children are likely to become attached to school, and to care about its values (Connell & Wellborn, 1991; Deci & Ryan, 1985; Battistich et al., 1997). Attachment to school provides an important source of motivation for children to learn and to develop ethically and socially because children are disposed to take on the values of groups they care about, be those schools or gangs. This kind of motivation has been called "internalized" motivation:** the willingness to act in ways consistent with one's values, long-term goals, or the welfare of a valued group, even when it is not immediately rewarding or satisfying to do so (Lepper, Sethi, Dialdin, & Drake, 1997; Rigby, Deci, Patrick, & Ryan, 1992). Such internalized motivation may present an important and relatively stable source of academic motivation, in contrast to "extrinsic" motivators (e.g., rewards and punishments) or "intrinsic" motivators (e.g., the inherent interest of tasks), which may fluctuate dramatically as, for example, the reward or activity that motivated children yesterday is old hat today. The caring community of learners seeks to foster the attachment of every child to the classroom and school community as a way to foster internalization of values, such as fairness, responsibility, and so forth, and the motivation to pursue them.

Theories of learning.   Modeling, practice, construction, and instruction all help children learn (Brandt, 1988/1989; Palincsar & Brown, 1984; Rosenshine & Meister, 1992). In the caring community of learners, learning takes advantage of all these approaches.*** Children are most likely to understand why things sink and float if, for example, they have opportunities to try experiments, talk about what they saw and thought, have their ideas challenged by others, and apply what they have learned to new situations and problems (Eylon & Linn, 1988). The same holds true for social and ethical learning. For example, children are most likely to become fair,

---

* Did you recognize this as a common feature in the new paradigm?
** Although this is different from the concept of intrinsic motivation, it is increasingly recognized as an important aspect of the new paradigm of instruction.
*** Did you recognize this as the diversity or multiplicity of methods theme that pervades the new paradigm?

responsible, and kind if they have daily opportunities to practice these qualities, to see others practice them, to actively consider and discuss what these qualities mean (for example, as they discuss literature, world events, or classroom conflicts); and to be challenged and stimulated by adults' thinking about these issues.

Goals Guiding Instructional Approaches in a Caring Community of Learners

There is no single right way to build a caring community of learners.* The three bodies of theory described above, combined with content goals (for example, what we want children to learn in language arts, mathematics, science, etc.) are consistent with many different instructional approaches. Yet there are many wrong instructional practices,** if our goal is to build a caring community of learners, and ultimately to foster children's intellectual, social, and ethical development. Many of the instructional practices used to build a caring community of learners, if used with a slightly different twist, can actually undermine community. This chapter takes up four instructional approaches that can be integral to building a caring community of learners: cooperative learning, developmental discipline, literature-based reading, and schoolwide activities. Before taking them up, we explore briefly the goals that must guide these activities if they are to promote children's ethical, social, and intellectual development:***

- to build close, caring human relationships among members of the classroom community and with the larger world outside;
- to build ownership: children's sense that they have a "say" in classroom life and learning;
- to build reflection: the habit of thinking deeply both about academic work and about one's behavior;
- to build internal motivation: a personal commitment to act on one's beliefs, even without external incentives;
- to build understanding of prosocial values such as kindness, fairness, and responsibility, and the capacity and habit of acting upon those values;
- to build academic development through construction, instruction, and practice.

Specific Instructional Approaches

Although we wrote earlier that there is no single right way to create a caring community of learners, we are struck by how tightly schools are constrained if they want to promote intellectual, ethical, and social development simultaneously.

---

* This is another manifestation of the diversity of methods theme.

** This is an important flip side of the "diversity of methods" coin that is frequently overlooked.

*** How many of these represent common themes in the new paradigm?

Schools serious about all facets of children's development often find they must reject practices that are widespread in American schools (reward systems, ability-grouping, teacher-made rules and consequences, a skill-and-drill curriculum) and to substitute methods that build children's attachment to school at the same time that they build academic learning.*

In the sections that follow, we highlight four instructional approaches that, taken together, go a long way toward building a caring community of learners. They form the core of the CDP, an approach to school change that we have studied intensively over the past 15 years, whose positive effects on children's social and ethical development have been well documented (Battistich et al., 1997; Battistich, Solomon, Watson, Solomon, & Schaps, 1989; Lewis, Schaps, & Watson, 1996); CDP's effects on academic development have been documented for performance assessments but not for standardized achievement tests (Solomon, Watson, Battistich, Schaps, & Delucchi, 1992).** Remarkably, the four approaches also form a good description of Japanese education, a system strongly focused on social and ethical, as well as intellectual, development[1] (Lewis, 1995).***

LITERATURE-BASED READING

Introduction: A Classroom Example of Literature-Based Reading

At Hazelwood School in Louisville, Kentucky, pairs of students are scattered around a second/third-grade classroom. Heads bent together, students brainstorm with their partners about why Widower Muldie, of the book *Wagon Wheels*, left his three sons behind when he set off across the wilderness in search of a homesite. Although this story**** of an African-American pioneer family is set in the rural America of more than 100 years ago, these inner-city students have little trouble diving into the assignment: to write a dialogue between Johnnie and Willie Muldie, ages 11 and 8, who are left in charge of their 3-year-old brother.

Teacher Laura Ecken sets the stage: "Let's imagine that we're Johnny and Willie. It's the first night all alone without Daddy. We've put little brother to bed and we're just sitting up talking to each other." Before students launch into their partner work, Mrs. Ecken asks the class to discuss "ways we can help our partners." Demonstrating remarkable forethought about the kinds of problems they may encounter, students

---

[1]The material we cover under literature-based reading tends to occur in a separate subject, moral education, in Japan; in addition, Japanese reading texts are also carefully chosen for their ethical and social themes.

* This helps clarify some of the major differences between the new paradigm and the industrial-age paradigm.

** This reflects the need for different measures to accompany a paradigm that pursues different goals.

*** As you study the four approaches that follow, try to decide which features are instructional theory and which are curriculum theory, as distinguished in chapter 1 (p. 14).

**** How does this use of stories differ from that in chapters 8 (Schank, Berman & Macpherson), 13 (Corno & Randi), and 14 (Pogrow)?

discuss a number of strategies for making the partner work go smoothly: "disagree without being mean," "if your partner says something that don't fit, then work it into another part," and "let your partner say all they want to say."

Several features of the students' work together over the next hour are striking. Students are intensely interested in figuring out what the Muldie boys might have said to each other; no grade or behavioral reward is offered for this task, nor is any needed. Students are friendly, helpful, and tactful as they work in partnerships, but also determined to write the best dialogue they know how. In one partnership, John says "We could talk about how much we miss Daddy." Cynthia counters: "But Daddy's only been gone for a day." After a few exchanges on this point, John and Cynthia agree to talk about "how much we're *going to* miss Daddy." In another partnership, Barry makes use of a strategy suggested by a classmate in the discussion preceding the task: "How about if we use your idea 'Will you help me hunt for food?' later, because right now we're talking about how the boys feel." Students seem remarkably comfortable questioning and expressing disagreement in their partnerships; the easy camaraderie extends to the many partnerships that cross racial and gender lines.

These students are reading *Wagon Wheels* as part of the literature-based reading program "Reading, Thinking, and Caring." As its title implies, the program is designed to foster children's development as thoughtful, able readers at the same time as it fosters their development as caring, principled individuals. It includes both read-alouds (books read aloud to the class by the teacher) and partner reads (books read by the students in pairs).

Educators who have watched the *Wagon Wheels* lesson on videotape are struck by how respectfully the students treat one another, how committed they are to telling the truth in their dialogues, and how deeply engaged they are in understanding the book. This doesn't just happen. Six major features of the literature program are designed to build caring community.

How Literature-based Reading Builds a Community of Learners

1. The selected books are rich in social and ethical themes.   The books raise issues common to children (such as friendship) and provide opportunities for children to empathize and deeply identify with children who are different from them in some way, for example; culture, race, religion, abilities, or economic circumstances. The books raise social and ethical issues such as honesty, courage, and compassion, and provide a nonthreatening format in which children can talk about these issues while discussing a work of literature. They can talk, for example, about why children tease a poor girl who wears the same dress to school every day (*The 100 Dresses*), how the courage to stand up against injustice emerges in a group of children during World War II (*Twenty and Ten*), or the importance of fairness and honesty in human relationships (*J.T.*). One teacher distinguishes an approach like "Reading,

Thinking, and Caring," in which children have a chance to explore ethical themes as they naturally arise in good literature, from a more heavy-handed approach:

> All the stories have—I hate to say, a "moral," because that sounds too much like *Leave It to Beaver*—but all the lessons and books all the way through have positive things for kids to pick up on. They're there even without the kids realizing it. They're not there like lessons and morals.

A second-grade teacher describes how the social and ethical situations encountered in books help build the caring community of the classroom:

> Today I said we were going to change partners for literature.... We had a discussion before the new partnerships about how we treat people when we get new partners. Someone mentioned how hurtful it would be to say that they didn't want to work with someone or to act like they didn't want to work with someone. Then another little boy said, "How would you know you wouldn't want to work with someone before you even get to know them?" Then another student in the class related it to the book we read at the beginning of the year, *Miss Maggie,* and said, "Nat thought he didn't like Miss Maggie because she was spitting tobacco and had a snake, but then he found out he did, and we could have experiences like that."

2. Read-alouds and partner reads provide an alternative to ability-grouping.   No matter how we attempt to disguise it, dividing a class into several ability-based groups for reading is likely to give children powerful messages about who is "smarter" and, by implication, "better." Partner-reading (in which children typically are paired with a partner to read for the duration of one book, either taking turns reading out loud or reading silently, depending on their reading level) avoids such stigmatization; with just two children per group, it also provides maximum out-loud reading time for each child while still allowing children to receive feedback and help from a peer. "Read-alouds," books that the teacher reads to the whole class, create an equal platform from which all class members (even the slowest readers) can contribute their ideas to the discussion, thereby connecting them to the classroom community.*

3. Read-alouds motivate children to develop their reading skills.
Learning to read is hard work. When children hear books read aloud, they learn that the pleasures of reading are worth the hard work it entails. Interesting and lively discussions about books further stimulate children's interest in reading. A sixth-grade teacher was surprised to find that several of the toughest students in her class, poor readers, eagerly sought out the book she was reading aloud, in order to read it on their own:

---

* In what ways are read-alouds similar to the idea of scaffolding discussed by Jonassen (chap. 10) and others?

Now I'm reading *The Outsiders* with my kids. Although it's a seventh-grade book, we use it. It's about gangs. It's about the Greasers and the Socials. It's about the feelings of a child who has murdered someone. We have a murder committed by a child about once a month [in this city]. It's about real stuff, and yet they get to see something positive. We're reading this as a read-aloud, and even the toughest kids are picking it up during free reading because they like it so much and want to pursue it.

4. Students learn through practice, modeling, opportunities to actively construct understanding, and comments from teachers and peers.

Reading is a complex skill, developed through many kinds of experiences: practice connecting symbol and sound, opportunities to hear phrasing and intonation modeled by a skillful reader, active attempts to make sense of what is read, and opportunities to compare one's own "sense" to that of other readers. The combination of read-alouds and partner-reads (and, at the youngest grades, phonics) enables children to gain these diverse kinds of experiences. Programs that rely largely on one method (e.g., phonics only, independent reading only) risk missing some contributors to children's development as readers.

5. Values govern children's work together.
Before students launched into their partner work, Ms. Ecken asked, "How can we help our partners?" Children came up with suggestions that reflect the classroom's core values of respect and responsibility (see "developmental discipline," below, for a discussion of how these become class values). After the partner work, students reflected as a whole class on how they worked together in partnerships. They asked: "What were the strengths of our work together; what were the rough spots?" These explicit discussions send a powerful message that it matters how students treat each other. Students talk about the values that will guide their work together; they figure out the concrete meaning of values like "respect" and "responsibility"; they try to put these into practice in the partnerships; and they reflect and get feedback from peers on how well they succeeded. These experiences are likely to build understanding of abstract values, as well as the skills and commitment to put these values into practice.

6. Literature provides a shared experience for the class.
A Japanese elementary school teacher described the most important goal of teaching as "to create happy memories" (Lewis, 1995, p. 36). Reading aloud to the class is one way to "create happy memories"—to create the kind of shared, positive experiences that bond children to one another and to school.

DEVELOPMENTAL DISCIPLINE

Introduction: A Classroom Example of Developmental Discipline

When teacher Ruby Tellsworth returned to her classroom after a break, she was surprised to find that her second-graders had convened a class meeting and were intently discussing a problem that had come up during recess. They listened carefully to one another's ideas and solved the problem, while she observed from the sidelines (Kohn, 1990a).

"Discipline," in most educational writing, refers to student obedience and to the strategies (such as rewards, point systems, and "consequences") that adults use to elicit obedience. By "discipline," we mean something quite different: the qualities of heart and mind that will enable children to sustain a humane, caring society, and the strategies that develop those qualities of heart and mind. The second-graders who spontaneously cut short recess to solve a class problem already show many of these qualities: a sense of responsibility for problems that threaten the common good; willingness to take initiative in solving these problems; and some skills (such as convening a community meeting) needed to work collaboratively toward solutions. How did the students develop these qualities?

Much of the answer to this question can be found in the qualities of the "caring community of learners" described early in this chapter: in the valued human relationships that make children want to behave responsibly; in the opportunities to understand and practice core values that occur throughout the curriculum and daily school life; in the emphasis on reflection and choosing to do right.

We call our approach "developmental discipline" because it focuses on children's development of the qualities of heart and mind needed to live in a democracy. In our view, the proper goal of a school discipline program is not simply to control children, but to kindle in them a personal commitment to ethical behavior.* As Fig. 21.2 illustrates, the heart of developmental discipline is children's social and ethical development. The additional goals of safety and efficiency in the classroom are pursued in ways consonant with these long-term goals, rather than in ways that undermine them. The systems of rewards and punishments that comprise discipline in many American schools can be dramatically effective in the short run. But in the long run, such carrot-and-stick approaches are counterproductive, because they undermine children's bonds to school and lessen children's willingness to act responsibly because it is the right thing to do. Several kinds of practices are central to developmental discipline.

Practices Central to Developmental Discipline

1. Practices that build human connections among members of the class (and school) community.

When children begin the school year by getting to know one another as people, there is, in the words of one teacher, "no opportunity for the picked-on child to emerge." As children have partner chats (brief chats in which, for example, each partner has one minute to talk about their favorite hobby while the partner listens),

---

* These two conceptions of discipline represent an industrial-age view and an information-age view, consistent with the key markers listed in chapter 1, p. 17.

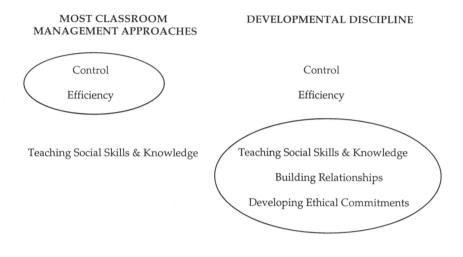

MOST CLASSROOM   DEVELOPMENTAL DISCIPLINE
MANAGEMENT APPROACHES

Control   Control

Efficiency   Efficiency

Teaching Social Skills & Knowledge   Teaching Social Skills & Knowledge

                                                Building Relationships

                                                Developing Ethical Commitments

FIG. 21.2.   Comparison of discipline goals.

children discover common interests as well as learn what matters to others. There are literally hundreds of brief activities that build human relationships in the classroom (Dalton & Watson, 1997), and many of these do double duty as activities that build academic skills. For example, butcher-paper "graffiti boards" where children have been invited to share their favorite books in various categories (adventure, nonfiction, fantasy, mystery, etc.) may build connections among students at the same time that they interest children in new books or new kinds of reading. Class charts, polls, interviews, and displays can all be ways of helping children get to know their classmates at the same time that they build core academic skills.

When teachers embrace the goal of building human relationships in the classroom, often they reject disciplinary practices commonly used in American schools: putting names of misbehaving children on the board, giving awards for good behavior, and point systems. Discipline that uses public sanctions, whether names on the board or "positive" incentives such as prizes, often has unwitting ill effects on relationships among children. We know a 5-year-old who tearfully insisted on revoking a classmate's birthday party invitation because the friend's name had been put on the blackboard for talking out of turn: "I can't invite a *bad person* to my birthday party." One teacher reflects on the change in her classroom after she stopped putting names on the board for misbehavior:

> Back in the days before the Child Development Project, when a child wouldn't come to the rug, I would put their name up on the board and fuss at them. What I didn't realize at the time was that I was causing that child to be an outcast.... We don't have those kinds of outcasts now.... If the people all over this city got to the point that the kids in my class are at, there would be no gangs. It's the outcasts who find belonging in gangs. No child is left out in this school. There is no child who doesn't belong.

Even "rewards" can end up humiliating children and undermining the friendships among them, as top earners come to be envied, and low earners to be seen as bad. (We know a teacher who stopped giving out daily "Good job!" slips because children who did not receive slips were derogated by their peers and even punished by some parents.) Even such seemingly benign stand-bys as "Look how nicely Darlene is sitting. Everyone should be sitting like Darlene" are invidious comparisons that, over time, erode the relationships among students. Contrast it with "Everyone check yourself out. See if you're sitting like we agreed we would sit."*

In addition to creating envy, systems of individual rewards and consequences may undermine discipline in another way: they create self-focus. Children become focused on the question "How am I doing?" not the equally important "How is our class doing?" When children are persistently focused on their own performance, as they must be in classrooms where certificates, prizes, and points are the currency of self-worth, it diverts their attention from the needs and feelings of others, the very grist of ethical development.

The goal of building human relationships means that students (and teacher) have many opportunities to get to know one another as people. It also means that practices found in other schools, for example, "Special Person of the Week," are often modified to better promote human relationships; for example, all class members become special person in turn, rather than as a reward for good behavior or grades. Many of the techniques that teachers traditionally use to maintain control, such as warnings and time-out, can be modified to avoid humiliating children. A kindergarten teacher we know practices time-out with a "twist" that emphasizes the teacher's continuing regard for the student: a beautifully ornate roll-top desk that children are invited to use as a "private office" until they feel able to return to the more distracting setting of the four-child table groups. To help a student who has persistent difficulties with self-control, some teachers work with the student to develop a private signal: some cue of body or voice that reminds the student to control a disruptive behavior such as talking or getting up, without public mention.

---

* The focus on making comparisons versus meeting a standard epitomizes a key difference between the two paradigms.

2. Students help build and maintain class norms.

Students and teacher start out the year, not with a teacher-made list of rules and consequences, but by asking "What kind of class do we want to be?" and discussing the rules that will allow them to live up to those aspirations (Developmental Studies Center, 1996). Often, this is not a simple process. Students may come up with detailed prescriptions—"no hitting, no cussing, no copying, no calling someone's mother a name"—and need help relating these specific don'ts to larger norms such as respect and responsibility. When students are invested in these shared norms, the role of the teacher changes.* The teacher is neither a boss, demanding obedience, nor a manipulator who bribes and coerces students into compliance, but a moral guide and model who helps students ask, "How does our current behavior live up to our aspirations for the class?" A principal describes the shift from rules to values:

> For years, I have approached discipline [by asking]: What did you do? Is that against the rules? What can you do about it? But this isn't enough any more—in fact, it really misses the point in a big way. It leaves out values entirely. I want the template for making decisions to be values NOT rules.

Motivation from within means that discipline is not something adults do to children; it is something willingly taken on by all class members. This mutual investment takes time, especially at the beginning of the school year. Coming to consensus about the norms that will govern the class, discussing problems that arise, and allowing children the latitude to find their own solutions all take longer than issuing orders and dispensing punishments. This can be agonizing for teachers who must daily juggle discipline with vital concerns about curriculum coverage. As one teacher in the midst of changing her disciplinary philosophy explained it to us,

> It was awful at first. I had given up putting names on the board or telling the kids that they would have to stay in at recess. So then I'd be standing up there and all the kids would be talking and I'm thinking, "What do I do now?" I'd like to stress that developmental discipline takes longer in the very beginning—by longer I'm talking about a minute here, a minute there—but those minutes sometimes seemed like hours.

Once shared norms have been established, problems provide an opportunity for all students to think about their behavior, "not just the 5 or 10 names I might have arbitrarily chosen to put on the board in the past when most of the class was talking," as one teacher described the change. Who among us, however well behaved, wouldn't benefit from thinking about how our recent behavior fits our ideals of kindness, respect, and responsibility?

In a class meeting that is one hallmark of developmental discipline, fourth-graders raised the concern that they had little time to play softball at lunch because they were wasting so much time choosing teams. They decided to split the

---

* Fundamental changes in the roles of teachers and students are central to the new paradigm of instruction.

class into teams rather than choose teams daily, and to switch the team at bat at the recess halfway point. Their teacher remarked, "They came up with that idea themselves. These experiences have shown them that they can do it for themselves. These solutions would not have worked if I had suggested them and imposed them." When children help forge a solution to a problem, they are likely to try to make it succeed, and in the long run their personal investment can save a great deal of time. In schools where CDP has been established for several years, teachers often note that students come to them from lower grades with stronger problem-solving skills and a greater sense of responsibility; so the payoff from investing in developmental discipline should not be measured over just one school year.

3. A problem-solving approach.

Many approaches assume that classroom discipline is something you must establish before learning can occur. We assume that discipline is learning—and that disciplinary problems, like other learning problems, demand a careful effort to understand the cause of the problem and to help students build the understanding, skills, and commitment needed to remedy the problem. Just as a student's poor write up of a science experiment may reflect many different root causes, from poor grasp of the scientific concept to poor writing skills to lack of motivation, misbehavior demands a careful differential diagnosis. Students may not know what behavior is expected, or they may know but lack self-control skills, or they may be so wrapped up in their own needs that they don't grasp the needs and feelings of those around them. Each root cause demands a different solution.* A teacher describes her shift to developmental discipline:

> My approach to discipline has really changed. Now if students do something that's a problem, I'll say to them, "I think we need to talk. Can I have a little bit of your time, maybe at recess, to talk?" I'll tell them that I think they're not themselves that day, and ask them whether something's wrong. You find out an awful lot that way. Maybe their bird died last night. They really appreciate the time devoted to their needs.

"I'm worried about you. Can we talk after school?" conveys a very different message from "That's once too many. Stay after school." When teachers can take the time to ask the child why a problem is occurring, this often yields unexpected rewards. "The biggest difference in my discipline is that now I think: Why is this child acting up? What might be going on that would make them act this way?" comments one teacher. Just listening to children can help them, by meeting their needs for attention, self, expression and human connection. A child's problems do not excuse bad behavior; but understanding why children misbehave can help adults maintain their threads to the most trying children.

In other words, a "problem-solving" approach means that teachers work to diagnose why misbehavior is occurring, and help children develop the skills, under-

---

* This is the essence of customization, and it is the essence of situationality.

standing, and human bonds* that will help them avoid similar problems in the future. A further part of problem solving is finding ways for students who have transgressed to reestablish themselves as caring, responsible people by, for example, repairing the damage they have done, or offering a genuine apology for a hurtful remark. "What can I do to make up for what I did wrong?" is a question many children naturally ask themselves—or will come to, in a supportive climate, where they hear people around them doing so. Comforting, apologizing, repairing, and restitution can all be powerful means of reestablishing one's sense of oneself as a "good child" after a transgression, particularly if they are heartfelt, rather than coerced.

Two Boys, One Chair: Developmental Discipline in Action

Many aspects of developmental discipline are proactive: Teachers work to help students know one another as human beings, think deeply about the values that guide life in the "class we want to be," and respectfully solve conflicts that arise. But, inevitably, problems occur, and luckily so, because like mistakes in other areas of learning, they provide valuable opportunities for students to build understanding and skills. What does developmental discipline look like in action? At Ruus School in Hayward, California, a video camera captured a struggle between two boys:

> Two kindergarten boys, Paul and Rayshon, sit wedged on the same chair, sneaking hostile sidelong glances at one another. A group activity, making a class caterpillar out of paper plate segments, is underway.
>
> "I'm sitting here," Rayshon whispers.
>
> "I am," answers Paul.
>
> "I am," says Rayshon.
>
> "I am," says Paul.
>
> Sizing up the conflict, Linda Rayford, their teacher, comes by and bestows a single paper plate on the pair. (Every other child is given his or her own.) "Here's one paper plate. You guys figure it out," she counsels, and continues on her rounds.

What is going on here? Typically, teachers intervene when they see conflict brewing. In this case, however, Ms. Rayford doesn't try to solve the problem. Indeed, she takes a step that makes the problem even more pressing: she gives the two boys a single plate to share. She treats the conflict as an opportunity for the two boys—and, as we'll see, their classmates as well—to learn how to get along with each other. We return to Paul and Rayshon, who struggle over a single chair, and now a single paper plate.

> When it becomes clear that the boys are not going to be able to move the dispute off dead center on their own, Linda Rayford returns and asks, "Do you have any ideas about how to solve the problem?"

---

* Of these three kinds of learning/development, skills were the only one that was addressed in any significant way by the industrial-age paradigm of instructional theory.

"I could ask Paul to please go to another chair," Rayshon volunteers.

"That's true," the teacher agrees. "Why don't you try that?"

"Paul, could you please go to another chair?" Rayshon asks, a look of hope lighting up his face. Paul, on the other hand, is scowling. He knows when he has been outfoxed. Lower lip thrust out, he stands up to leave, not saying a word.

"Wait a minute," Ms. Rayford gently stops him. "Paul, is this solution okay with you?"

Surprised, Paul blinks and shakes his head. No, it isn't.

"Rayshon," she translates, as she helps Paul back onto the chair, "He says he doesn't like that idea. What other solutions could you try?"

The boys are stumped. They stare blankly into space, uneasily ignoring one another. At this point, one of the other children sitting at their table looks up from his artwork and makes a suggestion. "I know. They could share," says Mark.

Interestingly, the two antagonists literally have a hard time hearing this idea. "Rayshon could leave," says Paul, when asked to repeat what was said. "Paul should go to another chair," Rayshon thinks he heard. The teacher has Mark reiterate his suggestion twice before the two boys grasp it and can accurately repeat what he is saying.

The two boys agree to follow Mark's suggestion of sharing the single paper plate. "I'll do one side, you do the other," Paul suggests, and Rayshon agrees. Because sitting squeezed together in a single chair is uncomfortable, Paul scoots a second chair up next to Rayshon. The boys decide to draw a line down the middle of the plate, and then each cheerfully sets to work on his half, trading crayons and remarks about what the other is drawing. When they finish (Paul checks with Rayshon to make sure he is done) the two take the plate up to the teacher to be mounted on the wall. She mounts it, quietly congratulating them on the way they worked out their conflict. Unselfconsciously Paul and Rayshon walk off together to look at butterfly cocoons and books in the classroom's science center.

After the last paper plate segment in the class caterpillar is mounted on the wall, Linda Rayford calls the class together for a wrap-up discussion of the project. In the course of the discussion, Paul volunteers to the group that he and Rayshon shared a plate.

"How did that come about?" the teacher asks.

"Because I like to share?" Paul answers in a quizzical voice. Apparently, he has forgotten the sequence of events that led to the collaborative effort.

"Rayshon, do you remember?"

"We had help with Mark," Rayshon recalls accurately. "He said we could get another chair and share the plate."

"And how did that work out?"

"Good," says Rayshon. "Fine," agrees Paul. At this, other children join in on the sharing theme, recalling who borrowed supplies from whom or swapped design ideas with whom during the activity. "I'm glad you decided to listen to Mark's suggestion," the teacher summarizes the discussion, addressing Paul and Rayshon again. "It was a good idea."

Principles of Developmental Discipline Illustrated
by "Two Boys, One Chair"

Paul and Rayshon's conflict over the chair initially kept them from their work. Under the disciplinary systems in place in many classrooms, their squabble might have landed both boys' names on the board—stigmatizing them in the eyes of classmates. In place of self-interest, developmental discipline draws on very different sources of motivation: the desire to belong to a valued group,* and the powerful impulses toward helpfulness, kindness, and responsibility that have been called "the brighter side of human nature" (Kohn, 1990b).

When Ms. Rayford stopped Paul from accepting a solution that he found unfair, she underlined a core value of their classroom: fairness. The first child to utter the magic word "please" did not automatically get his way. She also modeled the skills Paul and Rayshon needed to put this value into practice: asking questions, listening, noticing each other's body language.

Although one would never have guessed it from looking at their initial squabble over the chair, Paul and Rayshon were open to treating each other with consideration; they simply did not know how to do this in a situation of conflict. Ms. Rayford helped them learn these skills not just during the conflict but also during the subsequent class meeting, when she asked them to tell the class about their problem and how they solved it. That Paul had difficulty even recalling how he and Rayshon came to share the plate underlines how much children need opportunities to reflect on their behavior, and to revisit the lessons that (we hope) they have learned.

Linda Rayford didn't tell Paul and Rayshon how to settle their argument. Nor did she assume they had the skills to solve it. Rather, she highlighted the problem that lay before them, by giving them a single paper plate, and she modeled some of the skills that might help them solve the problem, such as assessing each other's reactions to a proposed solution and asking classmates for help. In other words, she handled the problem very much the way she might have handled a problem in writing or math: by highlighting the importance of the problem and asking questions that would help students think about the problem in a new way. But such skills are likely to take root firmly only if children value relationships with those around them and want to maintain those relationships.

In a more conventional setting, Paul and Rayshon's teacher might have asked both boys to sit elsewhere, or she might have conducted a brief investigation and awarded the chair to one of the boys. One or both boys would probably have ended up feeling like a loser, hardly a felicitous outcome if we care about human relations in the classroom. Further, a teacher-imposed solution would have deprived Paul and Rayshon of their feeling of "ownership."

---

* Self-interest versus belonging to a valued group—these are key markers of the industrial age and the information age, respectively; although to some extent belonging to a valued group is self-interest, reflecting the theme of the new paradigm often incorporating but reconfiguring rather than replacing the old.

Paul and Rayshon solved their squabble and went on to be friends. The ripples of their experience are likely to be many. Their bonds to teacher and classmates—who listened carefully and affirmed the importance of each child's needs—are likely to be deeper. Their skills for getting along with classmates and solving problems are likely to be greater. Their investment in a classroom community that met their needs, and their motivation to uphold its values, is likely to be stronger. In contrast, a teacher-imposed solution would likely have set off very different ripples: resentment, the humiliation of "losing" or being singled out as disruptive, a feeling that one's perspective has not been heard or valued, a belief that problems must be solved by an adult wielding power.*

Over time, most children in classrooms like Paul and Rayshon's will come to care deeply about shared values, will gain the skills to act on them, and will develop the human connections that make them want to do the right thing. They will be the citizens who care about the common good, and who actively work to keep democracy alive. The most remarkable feature of Paul and Rayshon's story is its ending: a month after their fight over the chair, the class caterpillar came down from the wall, and each boy asked to take home the half of the plate that the other had decorated.

COOPERATIVE LEARNING

Cooperative Learning and Classroom Community

Let's return to the students who have read Wagon Wheels and are writing dialogues about what the Muldie boys might have said to each other on their first night without Pa. Their work together illustrates the ways cooperative learning can build classroom community. We say "can" because cooperative learning doesn't necessarily build classroom community. Our approach to cooperative learning shares with other approaches the goal of building children's academic learning; it has three additional goals that are not necessarily shared by other approaches.

Goals of Cooperative Learning

1. To build children's understanding and practice of social skills and ethical values.   Children in Laura Ecken's class discussed the values that would guide group work, tried to put these into practice, and reflected on how well they had succeeded. Group work (groups of two, in the case of Wagon Wheels) provides a laboratory in which children can understand and practice humane values and re-

---

* This shows vividly how values are taught now in schools as part of the "hidden curriculum," but they are often values that, although perhaps needed in the industrial age (e.g., compliance), are often harmful in the information age (where, for example, initiative and responsibility are increasingly more important than compliance). It also shows that an instructional theory that only addresses the cognitive domain is sorely deficient—that we not only should not, but also cannot, separate the affective and cognitive domains.

ceive feedback on their efforts to put these values into practice. Some research suggests that cooperative learning benefits children socially, intellectually, and motivationally only if group members are helpful, friendly, collaborative, and show concern for each other. When small group members treat each other in a disrespectful, unfriendly manner, then increased work in small groups is actually associated with *decreases* in liking for school, intrinsic motivation, academic achievement, and experience of the classroom as a caring community (Battistich, Solomon, & Delucchi, 1993).

2. To build human relationships.

In cooperative learning, children are joined in a collaborative endeavor, rather than pitted against one another in competition. Ideally, working together on shared goals builds relationships among the children who work together, as they get to know one another and help one another. Because human relationships among all class members are a goal in a caring community of learners, our version of cooperative learning does not encourage competition between groups. Too often, competition undermines human relationships between competing groups and stigmatizes the children who are least able, for whatever reason, to contribute to their group's competitive standing.

3. To foster internal motivation.

Though set in frontier America, *Wagon Wheels* has compelling themes for today's inner-city students: Why might a father have to leave his children in order to provide for them? What does it feel like, as a child, to be given adult responsibility? What are the ways that children can help and protect their younger siblings? Ms. Ecken further sparked students' interest by asking them to imagine how they would feel if they were the Muldie boys and to write a dialogue between the boys. One can imagine how different the situation would have been if the chosen work of literature were trite, or if the task were to recall unimportant story details.* In other words, internal motivation is most easily fostered by important subject matter, presented in ways that help children grasp its importance.**

Two more points about internal motivation should be mentioned. First, we are struck by the fact that most children find social and ethical themes deeply compelling: Even children who show little enthusiasm for standard academic activities often enter eagerly into discussions of what a friend is, why children tease, or what is right and wrong. Thus, highlighting social and ethical themes may well make a curriculum more intrinsically motivating for students. Second, although social and ethical issues are central to much children's literature, we are struck by the fact that most available curriculum materials for literature-based instruction fail to capitalize on this strength, either by choosing works that are trivial in theme or by focusing

---

* By using methods that simultaneously pursue social, ethical, and intellectual goals, efficiency is enhanced so that the "additional" goals require very little in the way of extra time and effort. This kind of integration and synergy are characteristic of systemic thinking and the information-age paradigm.

** What other theories emphasize this?

on recall of factual information or formal literary analysis, ignoring the social and ethical questions that are at the heart of many works of literature.

SCHOOLWIDE ACTIVITIES

Schoolwide activities can support—or unwittingly undermine—teachers' efforts to build supportive human relationships, commitment to humane values, and the other instructional goals laid out at the beginning of this chapter.* The redesign of a school science fair illustrates how teachers can reshape traditions to better serve their instructional goals.

Traditionally, the science fair at a California elementary school had been a time for upper-grade students to make projects and compete for schoolwide awards. In contrast, this year's "family science festival" transformed the school, for an evening, into a hands-on science museum. Students and a record number of family members explored the mysteries of bubbles, magnets, and kitchen chemistry—activities planned and hosted by each class. As teachers worked to redesign the science fair, three aspirations guided them. First, they had been looking for ways to deepen and strengthen children's bonds to the school. With gang violence escalating sharply among the city's teenagers, these elementary school teachers wanted to create a school that would be more appealing than gangs by meeting children's needs for friendship, contribution, and belonging in a constructive way. Rather than pitting children against one another, the new science fair would join children in a shared, meaningful pursuit: planning an interesting, informative science festival. Every child could gain, academically and socially, from contributing to this effort, and there would be no "losers."

Second, teachers had been seeking ways to make students' families feel more welcome at school, including the 50% of parents who spoke a first language other than English. They recognized that families play a critical role in children's development, and were eager to provide an inviting and inclusive experience for as many family members as possible. The competitive science fair had provided mixed messages about family involvement: How much family help constituted "cheating?" By creating winners and losers, it had painfully reminded some parents of their own failures in school. In contrast, the new format unambivalently welcomed families. As others have noted, "Nobody flunks museum," (museum founder Frank Oppenheimer, quoted in Gardner, 1991).

Finally, teachers had become uncomfortable about using awards to motivate science learning. They had noticed that students were more interested in the awards than in the scientific content of the projects. Spurred on by research on the negative impact of rewards, the faculty chose to emphasize the inherent interest and challenge of designing hands-on science exhibits.

---

* This is systemic thinking in action.

As teachers redesigned the science fair, they carefully considered students' bonds to one another and to the school, their science learning and motivation, and their relationships with family members. In other words, they considered students' ethical, social, and intellectual development, and they sought to promote these by redesigning a school tradition, the science fair, so that it better served their goals of building human relationships, student ownership, intrinsic motivation, and so forth.

Students in American schools are typically tracked by age, and often by academic achievement, native language, and in other ways as well. Schoolwide activities can be an important way of helping children learn to extend values of respect, fairness, and kindness beyond their immediate group of classmates. For example, students might interview "the people who help us at school" and post pictures and interviews of administrators, custodial staff, secretaries, aides, and other adults. This activity makes members of the school community more human to one another, enables children see how they are helped by others, and builds schoolwide norms of helping.

We have a favorite group of slides that shows fifth-grade and kindergarten "buddies' classes" going on a field trip together, touring a museum. A snapshot from the bus ride home shows a kindergartner fast asleep, snuggled up against the shoulder of his fifth-grade buddy. Who can doubt that such experiences promote children's attachment to school? For children who have the benefit of a good buddies program or other schoolwide activities that help children to know one another as people, contribute in meaningful ways to the welfare of others, and learn the excitement of creating something bigger than one can create alone, school is likely to become a motivating, valued place. But like cooperative learning, schoolwide activities foster the caring community of learners only if they are designed with that goal in mind.

CONCLUSION

We have set out social, ethical, and intellectual development as essential goals of schooling, argued that building a caring community of learners enables schools to foster all three facets of development simultaneously, and described four instructional approaches that build the caring community of learners. Despite substantial evidence that the caring community of learners supports children's social, ethical, and intellectual development, the effort to spread such an approach faces daunting obstacles (Lewis et al. 1995; Lewis, Watson, & Schaps, 1997). The principles we have outlined—a focus on human relationships as well as intellectual development, on internal motivation, and on the importance of children's emotional attachment to school—run counter to an increasingly narrow focus on academic outcomes in American education (Schaps, 1997). The temptation is great to boost academic achievement scores in the short run by competition, prizes, and drill-and-skill curriculum that, in the long-run, undermine children's bonds to school and their relationships with one another.

The mission of social, ethical, and intellectual development complicates teachers' lives because it means that it is no longer enough to ask only whether a new curriculum increases students' subject-matter knowledge; we must also ask whether it fosters their bonds to fellow students and their interest in learning. It complicates researchers' lives because those who have traditionally worked in isolation from one another, for example, specialists in subject matter, pedagogy, school climate, and motivation, must all see the big picture.* But it offers the hope that we can escape the historical pendulum swing between academic and social development (Lewis et al., 1995) and more closely align our practices today with our aspirations for tomorrow.

ACKNOWLEDGMENTS

The work described in this paper has been funded by grants from: The William and Flora Hewlett Foundation; The San Francisco Foundation; The Robert Wood Johnson Foundation; The Danforth Foundation; Stuart Foundations; The Pew Charitable Trusts; The John D. and Catherine T. MacArthur Foundation; The Annenberg Foundation; Spunk Funk, Inc.; DeWitt Wallace-Reader's Digest Fund, Inc.; Louise and Claude Rosenberg, Jr.; and the Center for Substance Abuse Prevention, U.S. Department of Health and Human Services. We have drawn on William Boly's writing about the Child Development Project as a resource for this chapter.

REFERENCES

Battistich, V., Solomon, D., & Delucchi, K. (1993). Interaction processes and student outcomes in cooperative learning groups. *Elementary School Journal, 94,* 19–32.
Battistich, V., Solomon, D., Watson, M., & Schaps, E. (1997). Caring school communities. *Educational Psychologist, 32,* 137–151.
Battistich, V., Solomon, D., Watson, M., Solomon, J., & Schaps, E. (1989). Effects of a program to enhance prosocial behavior on children's social problem-solving skills and strategies. *Journal of Applied Developmental Psychology, 10,* 147–169.
Brandt, R. (1988/1989, December). On learning research: A conversation with Lauren Resnick. *Educational Leadership, 47,* 12–16.
Character Education Partnership. (1996). *Character education in the U.S. schools: The new consensus.* Alexandria, VA: Author.
Connell, J. P., & Wellborn, J. G. (1991). Competence, autonomy, and relatedness: A motivational analysis of self-system processes. In M. R. Gunnar & L. A. Sroufe (Eds.), *The Minnesota Symposia on Child Development, 23* (pp. 43–77). Hillsdale, NJ: Lawrence Erlbaum Associates.
Dalton, J., & Watson, M. (1997). *Among friends.* Oakland, CA: Developmental Studies Center.
Deci, E. L., & Ryan, R. R. (1985). *Intrinsic motivation and self-determination in human behavior.* New York: Plenum.
Developmental Studies Center. (1996). *Ways we want our class to be.* Oakland, CA.
Elam, S. M. (1989, June). The second Gallup/Phi Delta Kappa poll of teachers' attitudes toward the public schools. *Phi Delta Kappan, 70,* 785–798.
Elam, S. M., Rose, L. C., & Gallup, A. M. (1993, October). The 25th annual Phi Delta Kappa/Gallup poll of the public's attitudes toward the public schools. *Phi Delta Kappan, 75,* 137–152.
Etzioni, A. (1996, May). Virtue should be seen, not just heard. *Education Week,* p. 40.

---

* This is a strong advocacy for systemic thinking, an essential aspect of the new paradigm.

Eylon, B., & Linn, M. C. (1988) Learning and instruction: An examination of four research perspectives in science education. *Review of Educational Research, 48*, 251–301.

Gardner, H. (1991). *The unschooled mind*. New York: Basic Books.

Kohn, A. (1990a, January). The ABC's of Caring, *Teacher Magazine*, 52–58.

Kohn, A. (1990b). *The brighter side of human nature*. New York: Basic Books.

Lepper, M. R. (1983). Social control processes and the internalization of social values: An attributional perspective. In E. T. Higgins, D. N. Ruble, & W. W. Hartup (Eds.), *Developmental social cognition: A sociocultural perspective* (pp. 294–330). New York: Cambridge University Press.

Lepper, M. R., Keavney, M., & Drake, M. (1996). Intrinsic motivation and extrinsic rewards: A commentary on Cameron and Pierce's meta-analysis. *Review of Educational Research, 66*, 5–32.

Lepper, M. R., Sethi, S., Dialdin, D., & Drake, M. (1997). Intrinsic and extrinsic motivation: A developmental perspective. In S. S. Luthar, J. A. Burack, D. Cicchetti, & J. R. Weisz (Eds.), *Developmental psychopathology: Perspectives on adjustment, risk, and disorder* (pp. 23–50). New York: Cambridge University Press.

Lewis, C. (1995). *Educating hearts and minds: Reflections on Japanese preschool and elementary education*. New York: Cambridge University Press.

Lewis, C., Schaps, E., & Watson, M. S. (1995). Beyond the pendulum: Creating challenging *and* caring schools. *Kappan, 76*, 547–554.

Lewis, C., Schaps, E., & Watson, M. S. (1996). The caring classroom's academic edge. *Educational Leadership, 53*, 16–21.

Lewis, C., Watson, M. S., & Schaps, E. (1997, March). *Conditions for school change: Perspectives from the Child Development Project*. Paper presented at the meeting of the American Educational Research Association, Chicago, IL.

Palincsar, A. M., & Brown, A. L. (1984). Reciprocal teaching of comprehension-fostering and comprehension-monitoring activities. *Cognition and Instruction, 2*, 117–175.

Rigby, C. S., Deci, E. L., Patrick, B. C., & Ryan, R. M. (1992). Beyond the intrinsic-extrinsic dichotomy: Self-determination in motivation and learning. *Motivation and Emotion, 16*(3), 165–185.

Rosenshine, B., & Meister, C. (1992, April). The use of scaffolds for teaching higher-level cognitive strategies. *Educational Leadership, 49*, 26–33.

Schaps, E. (1997, January). Pushing back for the center. *Education Week*, p. 20.

Solomon, D., Watson, M., Battistich, V., Schaps, E., & Delucchi, K. (1992). Creating a caring community: Educational practices that promote children's prosocial development. In F. K. Oser, A. Dick, & J. L. Patry (Eds.), *Effective and responsible teaching: The new synthesis* (pp. 383–395). San Francisco: Jossey-Bass.

22 Self-Science: Emotional Intelligence for Children

Karen Stone-McCown
The Nueva School and 6 Seconds

Ann Hathaway McCormick
The Learning Company and Learning Design Company

Karen Stone-McCown

Ann Hathaway McCormick

Karen Stone-McCown began her career as a nurse. She studied at Stanford University before establishing the Nueva School in 1967. She earned her MA in education from the University of Massachusetts under a Ford Foundation grant, reflecting her interest in affective education, a topic on which she consults and leads workshops. Karen introduced Self-Science to Nueva as part of the curriculum and co-authored a book entitled *Self-Science, the Subject is Me*. Karen founded *6 Seconds*, a non-profit organization that offers training and materials on emotional intelligence. Karen also co-founded the Learning Design Company, an educational software and web company.

Ann McCormick taught elementary school in poverty-area schools, earning her doctorate in education at the University of California at Berkeley. She conducted research in effective teaching and founded the Learning Company, an educational software company where she lead design of 16 national prize-winning products. She co-founded the Learning Design Company where she creates multimedia learning products. Ann has consulted on schools of the future, appeared on television, and worked with educational leaders in 18 nations. She consulted to the Special Office of the President of the United States and Members of Parliament in England.

FOREWORD

Goals and preconditions. The primary goal of this theory is to foster children's emotional development. At a more detailed level, goals include: (1) legitimizing self-knowledge as valuable subject matter, (2) developing a trusting attitude toward members of one's class, (3) becoming more aware of the multiple and layered feelings one has, (4) developing communication skills for affective states, (5) disclosing one's thoughts and feelings, (6) enhancing self-esteem, (7) accepting responsibility for one's attitudes and actions, (8) becoming aware of one's major concerns/worries/anxieties, (9) recognizing one's present behavioral patterns and learning styles, and (10) experimenting with alternative behavioral patterns, such as choosing optimism and hope. This theory was developed for a school with grades 1–8 and requires support from the administration, teachers, and parents for a Self-Science course to succeed.

Values. Some of the values upon which this theory is based include:
- self awareness, impulse control, persistence, zeal, self-motivation, empathy, and social deftness as survival skills for working and loving,
- addressing each child's individual needs,
- a safe, trusting environment for fostering emotional development.

Methods. The major methods of this theory are:
The "Trumpet Process," which includes the following steps for students to take:
1. Share experiences, to provide a common reference point for discussion.
2. Inventory your responses: what did you think, feel, and do?
3. Recognize your patterns of unique behavior.
4. Own your patterns and understand how each serves you.
5. Consider the consequences of each pattern (benefits and costs).
6. Allow alternative patterns—explore the options.
7. Evaluate the alternatives.
8. Choose the best one for each situation.

Teaching methods:
- Use an appropriate class structure, such as two teachers working as a team, class size of 12-15, class sessions of 40-50 minutes, content is determined by each child's circumstances, begin each class by gaining a sense of the mood of the group, avoid the tendency of the teacher to take over the discussion.
- Create a safe environment by having a focusing activity that builds trust and collaboration; also build trust by expressing feelings openly, labeling actions clearly, giving feedback and reassurance, participating in games, and being sensitive to each child's needs.

- *Set ground rules, especially for how communication takes place: respect the confidentiality of other students, no "killer" statements, communicate during conflicts, use I-messages, don't require a new student to participate.*
- *Use questioning techniques, focusing on what, not why, and focusing on similarities and differences in students' responses, with an underlying premise of respect for the thoughts and feelings of others.*
- *Use such teaching techniques as dialogue, role-playing, social experiments, simulations from real life, games with rules, guided fantasy, expression through art, and keeping a journal.*

Variable teaching methods:
- *For Grades 1–2, help students become aware of the variety, intensity, and shifting of their feelings.*
- *For Grades 3–4, help students become aware of the tension caused by concern for social acceptance.*
- *For Grades 5–6, help students to set healthy boundaries within their families and social groups.*
- *For Grades 7–8, help students to build healthy images of their emerging adult self, their friendships, and their choices in the world.*

Major contribution. *Proven techniques for fostering children's emotional development in grades 1–8.*

—C.M.R.

Self-Science: Emotional Intelligence for Children

What is the effective value of a knowledge of externals if we lack an equally deep personal insight? Can there be wisdom even about the objective world around us in the absence of wisdom about the world within? Can there be any mature understanding of others without self-knowledge … ? Education without self-knowledge can never mean wisdom and maturity: but self-knowledge in depth is a process, like education itself, and is never finished. (Kubie, 1968, p. 225)

INTRODUCTION

Each day's newspaper brings us sad and violent news involving children and their families. Many breakdowns in society are so commonplace that they don't make the news: young people are afraid of being mugged in the restroom at school; metal detectors are placed at the school doors; drive-by shootings on the freeway are news only when a celebrity is involved; 60% of new marriages end in divorce; emotional abuse is on the rise; toddlers in crowded childcare centers are not fed regularly and babies are not picked up all day; children experience depression, eating disorders, and aggressiveness.*

Daniel Goleman, a Harvard Psychologist and journalist, addresses issues of emotional ineptitude, desperation, and recklessness in our families and our communities in his book, *Emotional Intelligence*. Pointing out some of the problems of society, Goleman (1995) says:

> Each day's news comes to us rife with such reports of the disintegration of civility and safety, an onslaught of mean-spirited impulse running amok. But the news simply reflects back to us on a larger scale a creeping sense of emotions out of control in our own lives and in those of the people around us. No one is insulated from this erratic tide of outburst and regret: it reaches into all of our lives in one way or another. (p. x)

Goleman states that perhaps the saddest facts in his book are based on research:

> A massive survey of parents and teachers shows a worldwide trend for the present generation of children to be more troubled than the last: more lonely and depressed, more angry and unruly, more nervous and prone to worry, more impulsive and aggressive. If there is a remedy, I feel it must lie in how we prepare our young for life ... bringing together mind and heart in the classroom. (p. xiii)

But despite the bad news, the last 10 years has seen a burst of scientific studies of emotion, discussed in detail by Goleman (1995). He describes how we can manage our emotional life with intelligence. He says, "Our passions, when well exercised, have wisdom. They guide our thinking, our passions, our survival. But they can easily go awry, and do so all too often." (p. xiv)

What Is Emotional Intelligence?

Goleman (1995) discusses recent brain and behavioral research and qualities that mark people who excel in real life—those whose intimate relationships flourish and who are stars in the workplace. "Emotional Intelligence," he says, includes "self-awareness and impulse control, persistence, zeal and self-motivation, empathy and social deftness," basic capacities needed if individuals are to thrive and if society is to prosper.

Importance of an Emotional Intelligence Curriculum

Because an emotionally intelligent populace is so important to society, and because the traditional family unit and the churches are not guiding people as they have in

---

* These problems were much smaller or even nonexistent in the industrial age. These societal changes represent much of the stimulus for a new paradigm of education that directly addresses the affective domain, especially emotional development.

the past, developing a curriculum to teach emotional intelligence in school seems of utmost importance. The demands of a global economy pose unprecedented demands on our children just when family structures are breaking down. In the past, individuals could be socialized to function in a small, local sphere where people had expectations and a sense of community that guided action. Today, society is changing vastly, and many of our children are left without basic guidance for living well day to day.

In educational discussions we use such terms as "self-esteem," "helping children reach their potential," and "educating for life." Out in traditional classrooms, however, we see Bob sitting in the back row every day, totally uninvolved in what is going on; Tom laughing at everything, including history, grades, and girls; Susan always being the first to put her hand up; Maria copying from others every chance she gets. Teachers seem weary. There is, day after day, processing of information about the external world with seemingly little regard for the person who has to do the processing in order for learning to take place.

If Martians were to look in on this situation, they might observe that what is being taught and what is being learned are sometimes as far apart as Earth and Mars, and that acquisition of survival skills such as those we need for working and loving are often left to chance. They might well ask, "Where do young people learn the techniques of survival? Where do they learn how to relate to themselves and others? To communicate? To solve problems? To take responsibility for their own learning?"

Fortunately, children can learn to relate more successfully to themselves and others and, according to Goleman (1995), the emotional lessons children learn actually sculpt their brain's circuitry.

Absence of Such a Curriculum

A self-science curriculum is important because few opportunities are available for children to learn emotional intelligence skills in school, though more and more businesses are offering seminars and coaching for adults.

Goleman (1995, p. 305–309) lists key programs that teach emotional intelligence with the experience they have obtained. Although these programs have shown improvement in problem-solving skills, involvement with peers, impulse control, improved behavior, more sharing, and other important social skills, the teaching of emotional competencies is not a mainstream subject in most schools. Shortly after completing his book *Emotional Intelligence,* Goleman gave a talk for the Nueva School community, which he described in chapter 16 of his book, and said that Nueva had contributed to inspiring the book. We will describe how we teach emotional intelligence at Nueva and the theory behind it.

THE NUEVA SCHOOL

For 25 years we have been meeting at the Nueva School, just south of San Francisco. Once or twice a week, with small groups of children in grades 1–8, teachers and students have been exploring what a school (or some community group) can do to fulfill its promise to educate young human beings.

At Nueva we have been trying to create a school climate* and a course to be taught alongside the traditional three R's. We call the course, "Self-Science: The Subject Is Me."

We make these basic assumptions:

- Learning requires thinking, feeling, and action and begins with experiencing.**
- The more conscious one is of what one is experiencing, the greater the potential for self-knowledge.
- The more self-knowledge one gains, the more likely it is that one can respond positively to one's self and others.

When we put these assumptions to work at Nueva (not without our full share of meanderings and mistakes), a curriculum emerged. Nueva's school psychologist, Hal Dillehunt, and Karen Stone-McCown (with input from Nueva's Director, James Olivero) wrote a handbook, *Self-Science: The Subject is Me* (Stone-McCown & Dillehunt, 1978) that tells how to teach the program, with lesson plans, suggestions concerning classroom management strategies, record keeping, evaluation, and sample journal excerpts to communicate some of the flavor and excitement of a self-science group in action.

SELF-SCIENCE

The Purpose and Importance of Self-Science

Self-Science is an experience-based program designed for children from the first through the eighth grades. It's purpose is to equip children with affective and cognitive skills*** that broaden their understanding and functioning in all learning and social situations.

One need not look too closely at current societal problems to find indications of less than total success in the areas of self-knowledge and interpersonal relationships.

In describing self-science at Nueva, Goleman (1995) states,

The classes themselves may at first glance seem uneventful, much less a solution to the dramatic problems they address. But that is largely because, like good child rearing at home, the lessons imparted are small but telling, delivered regularly and over a

---

* School climate or culture is increasingly being recognized as an important dimension of the new paradigm of instructional theory. At Nueva, they recognized that a course alone would not be enough. Which other theories in this volume address climate or culture? And how do their suggestions differ from Nueva's and each other's?

** Do you remember which other theories called for beginning the learning process with experiencing? Is the nature of this experience different from the others?

*** Note that affective development requires cognitive development, as well as vice versa.

sustained period of years.* That is how emotional learning becomes ingrained; as experiences are repeated over and over, the brain reflects them as strengthened pathways, neural habits to apply in times of duress, frustration, hurt. And while the everyday substance of Emotional Literacy classes may look mundane, the outcome, decent human beings, is more critical to our future than ever. (p. 263)

Families have long been the primary teachers of children, especially when it comes to social and emotional skills. Schools have traditionally supported the family by teaching academic skills. Self-science offers an opportunity to support and expand the learning to include the teaching of emotional competence. The most effective kind of education for children occurs when families and schools are partners in learning.** We have never met a parent or a teacher (or even a child) who did not think that human beings would benefit from more self-awareness, self-control, motivation, empathy, and social skills.

Theoretical Roots

Self-science has theoretical roots in both the cognitive and affective domains. When we began teaching self-science 25 years ago, we were concerned about learning all we could about how children change their ways of thinking and how they develop socially and emotionally. We sought out advisors, including Ralph Tyler, Head of the Behavioral Sciences Research Laboratory, and Ernest R. Hilgard, Head of the Psychology Department at Stanford University, to guide us in understanding this theory and research.

We reviewed writings of many authors, such as Carl Jung about unconscious processes, archetypes, and the self. We reviewed the research of Jean Piaget about developmental stages and learning processes. We met with Abraham Maslow about his schema of hierarchical needs and self-actualization, and with Anna Freud about her psychoanalytic work, primarily with children. We talked with Eric Erikson about the drive for identity and the tasks of children at various stages such as trust vs. mistrust and identity vs. role confusion. We studied Jerome Bruner's work and particularly appreciated the spiral curriculum he describes.

We were seeking ways to design a school for tomorrow's children, and all our advisors, including Nobel Laureate in Physics, Luis Alvarez, renowned violinist Yehudi Menuhin, and 10 other major contributors to society, told us that the school needed to address children's emotional and social needs as well as their intellectual needs.

---

* Contrast this with the typical one-shot, add-on approach we often see for addressing drug abuse, teen pregnancy, and so forth. This contrast represents additional key markers distinguishing the industrial and information ages. We have already noted how professional development for teachers is undergoing a similar shift from the one-shot, add-on approach to an integrated, long-term program. What other examples can you identify in these instructional theories?

** Partnerships (collaboration) represent another key marker of the new paradigm (see chap. 1, p. 17). Parents and community were typically excluded from schools in the industrial-age paradigm of education, and this is just beginning to change.

Over the years, self-science teachers stayed abreast of contemporary theory and research through reading and taking classes and workshops, and many taught courses for teachers at local universities. Theories and research most interesting to self-science teachers at Nueva were those of the constructivists, who portray learning as a process of creating one's own experiences, through both personal explorations and social interactions, which matches the Nueva philosophy. Teachers were also fascinated by new research on the brain's functioning and by the writings of Howard Gardner, who values interpersonal and intrapersonal intelligence, the major focus of self-science. We feel self-science teachers need to be knowledgeable about theories based in biology, social learning, and psychoanalytic literature, as well as informed about learning models, approaches, techniques, classroom management, and assessment.

Learning Goals

The self-science program consists of a sequence of lessons grouped under 10 major goals, listed in Fig. 22.1. The goals should be followed in sequence when they are first introduced because they build upon one another over time. Each of these goals is part of a lifelong learning process.* The term "approaching" used in reference to goals is meant to convey to self-science teachers the idea that process learning is very much like seed planting. There may or may not be evidence that learning is taking place immediately.

An example of self-science in action illustrates how some of these goals come together. A 6-year-old boy who began to recognize a pattern of his said, "I need my parents to help me all the time." The teacher and the group helped him develop a greater understanding of his pattern in the following discussion. "You're 6, still a child, and sometimes you need your parents to help you. Are there things you can do to help yourself? What are they? What do your friends do? Let's ask them. Would you be willing to try something new that you can do yourself? Let's talk about it next time and see how it worked." The self-science teachers and class helped the child become aware of an issue in his life, express how he felt, develop communication skills, try a new behavior, and take greater responsibility for himself, all in a manageable way for a 6-year-old.

While there is a skill-based sequence to the self-science curriculum and teachers have activities planned to meet the goals they have in mind, they are responsive to the social and emotional needs of children and adjust the program according to "what's up" at the beginning of each class.** Teachers can address issues of immediate importance to the children and still reach the goals of self-science over time.

---

* Note how intertwined instructional theory and curriculum theory are.

** Which other theories emphasized such flexibility and adaptation to learners' individual needs? Of course, this reflects the key marker, customization, discussed in chapter 1. Also, notice that the flexibility is tempered with some structure: "there is a skill-based sequence … ," transcending the "either-or" mindset.

Philosophy Underlying the Goals

There isn't anything radical about the self-science concept. In practice, it merely extends traditional classroom values. The extended values are in no way meant to supplant the traditional ones. They are meant to supplement what already works. An overriding value that guides all of self-science is the concept that development of emotional intelligence is as important as the development of academic intelligence. Every human being is capable of learning the skills needed for emotional literacy; the sooner we begin, the more successful we will be as human beings.

We believe that everyone is doing the best they can, given their level of awareness and their life experience. That may sound as if we believe people can't do any better than they are doing. Quite the contrary. If we want to help someone learn about changing their patterns and responses in life, we do so by increasing their level of awareness or expanding their life experience. If every parent and every teacher practiced this belief, think how different the life of a child would be. Children would live in a climate of trust and deep respect, where we believe learning takes place most productively. Teachers and parents can support learning by figuring out how to effectively increase children's life experience in a given situation and by deepening our level of awareness, rather than by criticizing and blaming. This tenet is at the core of self-science.

Fig. 22.2 conveys how the self-science program fits within the broader context of traditional instruction.

DECIDING WHAT TO TEACH

There is a cognitive structure to self-science, the "trumpet process," which helps us decide what to teach. As the scientific method is a tool for making discoveries about the physical world, the trumpet process is a tool for making discoveries about and acting on issues having to do with emotion and "inner space." Goals for the self-science curriculum have been outlined in Fig. 22.1. The first five goals help students work toward a group cohesiveness as well as toward learning certain skills. The next five goals are built around the trumpet process. The trumpet in fact provides the cognitive guidelines for making sense of the affective experiences in the lessons. It offers the focal point for questions the teacher or group may ask, questions that help each child understand and internalize their experiences, as well as become aware of the processes of the group as a whole. Fig. 22.3 lists the individual concerns and steps for learning.

The Trumpet Process

Step 1. Share Experiences. The child participates in various exercises or games that provide the class with a common reference point for discussion. Having common affective experience facilitates sharing of concerns.

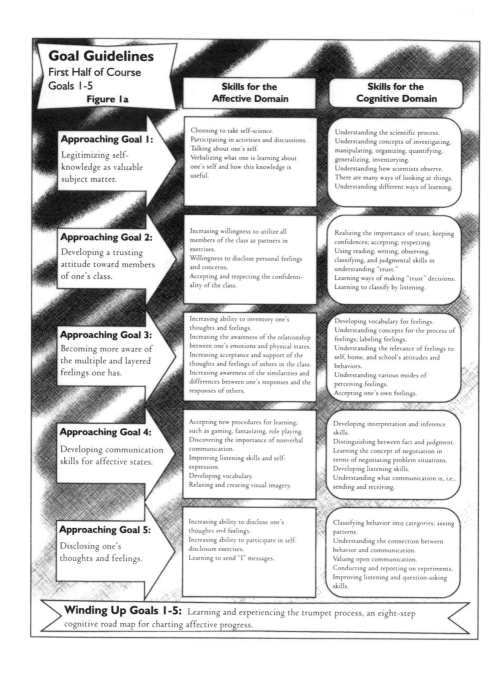

Goal Guidelines
First Half of Course
Goals 1-5
Figure 1a

	Skills for the Affective Domain	Skills for the Cognitive Domain
Approaching Goal 1: Legitimizing self-knowledge as valuable subject matter.	Choosing to take self-science. Participating in activities and discussions. Talking about one's self. Verbalizing what one is learning about one's self and how this knowledge is useful.	Understanding the scientific process. Understanding concepts of investigating, manipulating, organizing, quantifying, generalizing, inventorying. Understanding how scientists observe. There are many ways of looking at things. Understanding different ways of learning.
Approaching Goal 2: Developing a trusting attitude toward members of one's class.	Increasing willingness to utilize all members of the class as partners in exercises. Willingness to disclose personal feelings and concerns. Accepting and respecting the confidentiality of the class.	Realizing the importance of trust; keeping confidences; accepting; respecting. Using reading, writing, observing, classifying, and judgmental skills in understanding "trust." Learning ways of making "trust" decisions. Learning to classify by listening.
Approaching Goal 3: Becoming more aware of the multiple and layered feelings one has.	Increasing ability to inventory one's thoughts and feelings. Increasing the awareness of the relationship between one's emotions and physical states. Increasing acceptance and support of the thoughts and feelings of others in the class. Increasing awareness of the similarities and differences between one's responses and the responses of others.	Developing vocabulary for feelings. Understanding concepts for the process of feelings; labeling feelings. Understanding the relevance of feelings to self, home, and school's attitudes and behaviors. Understanding various modes of perceiving feelings. Accepting one's own feelings.
Approaching Goal 4: Developing communication skills for affective states.	Accepting new procedures for learning; such as gaming, fantasizing, role playing. Discovering the importance of nonverbal communication. Improving listening skills and self-expression. Developing vocabulary. Relaxing and creating visual imagery.	Developing interpretation and inference skills. Distinguishing between fact and judgment. Learning the concept of negotiation in terms of negotiating problem situations. Developing listening skills. Understanding what communication is, i.e., sending and receiving.
Approaching Goal 5: Disclosing one's thoughts and feelings.	Increasing ability to disclose one's thoughts and feelings. Increasing ability to participate in self-disclosure exercises. Learning to send "I" messages.	Classifying behavior into categories; seeing patterns. Understanding the connection between behavior and communication. Valuing open communication. Conducting and reporting on experiments. Improving listening and question-asking skills.

Winding Up Goals 1-5: Learning and experiencing the trumpet process, an eight-step cognitive road map for charting affective progress.

FIG. 22.1. Ten major goals.

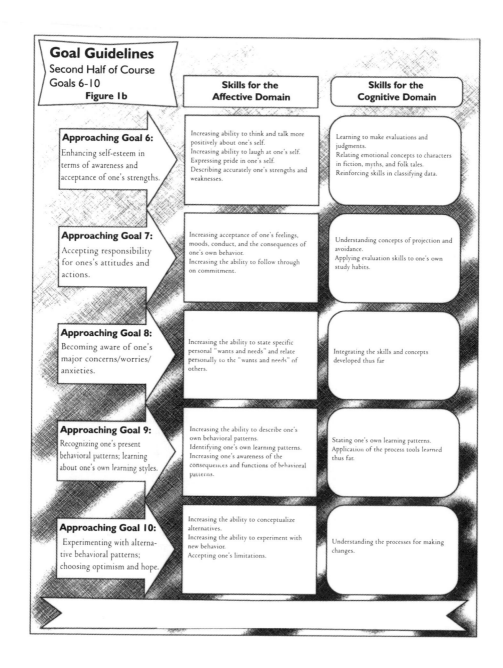

Goal Guidelines
Second Half of Course
Goals 6-10
Figure 1b

	Skills for the Affective Domain	**Skills for the Cognitive Domain**
Approaching Goal 6: Enhancing self-esteem in terms of awareness and acceptance of one's strengths.	Increasing ability to think and talk more positively about one's self. Increasing ability to laugh at one's self. Expressing pride in one's self. Describing accurately one's strengths and weaknesses.	Learning to make evaluations and judgments. Relating emotional concepts to characters in fiction, myths, and folk tales. Reinforcing skills in classifying data.
Approaching Goal 7: Accepting responsibility for ones's attitudes and actions.	Increasing acceptance of one's feelings, moods, conduct, and the consequences of one's own behavior. Increasing the ability to follow through on commitment.	Understanding concepts of projection and avoidance. Applying evaluation skills to one's own study habits.
Approaching Goal 8: Becoming aware of one's major concerns/worries/ anxieties.	Increasing the ability to state specific personal "wants and needs" and relate personally to the "wants and needs" of others.	Integrating the skills and concepts developed thus far
Approaching Goal 9: Recognizing one's present behavioral patterns; learning about one's own learning styles.	Increasing the ability to describe one's own behavioral patterns. Identifying one's own learning patterns. Increasing one's awareness of the consequences and functions of behavioral patterns.	Stating one's own learning patterns. Application of the process tools learned thus far.
Approaching Goal 10: Experimenting with alternative behavioral patterns; choosing optimism and hope.	Increasing the ability to conceptualize alternatives. Increasing the ability to experiment with new behavior. Accepting one's limitations.	Understanding the processes for making changes.

```
┌─────────────────────────────────────────────┐
│   Self-Science Extends Classroom Practice    │
│                  Figure 2                     │
└─────────────────────────────────────────────┘
```

Traditional Classroom Values

1. Learning about the world is the legitimate subject matter for the school.

2. Remembering, planning, and interpreting are important.

3. Learning words and concepts for, and learning how to negotiate, the world of ideas and things is important.

4. Critical judgment and evaluation (and earned respect for performance) are central in the learning process.

5. Talking, thinking, and reading about experiences and ideas are central in the learning process.

6. Well-thought-out expression about subject matter is valued in the learning process.

Self-Science Extended Values

+ Learning about one's self (thoughts, feeling, behaviors) is legitimate in school.

+ Experiencing the present moment, the here-and-now of students and teacher, is important.

+ Learning words and concepts for, and learning how to negotiate, one's emotions is important.

+ Nonjudgmental acceptance and respect is central to the process of individual personal growth.

+ Experiencing one's self and one's surroundings is central to personally important learning.

+ Appropriate, nonmanipulative disclosure of thoughts and feelings is valued and facilitates personal growth in self and others.

FIG. 22.2.   Self-science extends classroom practice.*

Step 2. Inventory Responses.   The child examines and explores what happened during that experience, asking, "How did I respond? What was unique? What was common?" This stage may be the most complex part of the trumpet process and requires the ability to ask questions in three main areas: "What did you think? How did you feel? What did you do?"

Step 3. Recognize Patterns.   As the inventory process becomes more elaborate, patterns of unique student behavior emerge and are evident in thought, feeling, and action. All people exhibit behavior patterns, but most people need help in identifying and understanding their patterns. Learning about one's patterns is difficult. Most children need to be made aware of a given pattern on at least three separate occasions before they recognize its existence. In this step, the child asks, "What is typical of me?" The teacher asks, "What are you doing right now? What did you just do? Do you usually do that?" The teacher can focus on patterns in the class. For example, in a primary-level class, boys tend to sit on one side of the circle and girls on the other. The teacher might ask, "Has anyone noticed where we choose to sit in

---

*This figure shows how the new paradigm expands and incorporates many aspects of the industrial-age paradigm.

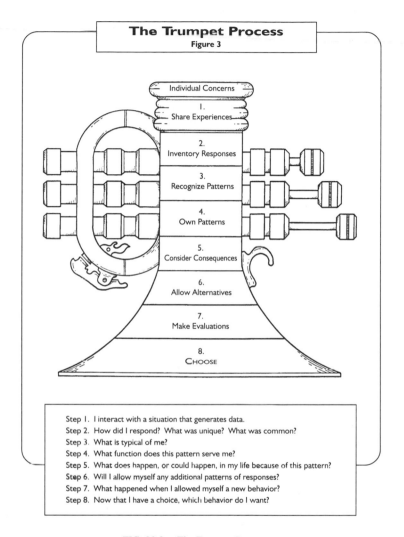

FIG. 22.3.   The Trumpet Process.

our class?" At least some of the students will identify the pattern. The teacher can then discuss the nature of patterns, the fact that we all have them, and that some patterns serve us well and some do not.

Step 4. Own Patterns.   Children examine the functioning of their patterns, understand how a particular pattern serves them, and accept that it is theirs (own it). A socially positive pattern, such as volunteering to clean the white board, is easy for the child to grasp, because the child is quickly aware of rewards. Many children, however, find it difficult to discover the benefits that may accrue from a socially negative pattern, such as bullying other children. The teacher may need to help them understand that even socially negative patterns serve the possessors in some way.*

Step 5. Consider Consequences.   The teacher encourages the child to ask, "What happens or could happen in my life because of this pattern?" The child examines the price one pays for a particular pattern. The teacher helps the child to understand what benefits come at what costs and to analyze how the rewards and consequences balance out. As all patterns have positive aspects, they also have negative aspects. Most people have at least one socially positive behavior pattern and generally think only of the "good" things derived from this pattern. Nevertheless, something is given up for this pattern, a price is paid. Even cleaning the white board has some costs for the child.

Step 6. Allow Alternatives.   The group supports the child in helping to search for alternative modes of responding. The teacher often asks children, "What else might you do?" They think of as many ideas as possible without evaluating them right then. Using their imaginations in this way helps children realize there is more than one approach to any situation.

Step 7. Make Evaluations.   "What happens when I allow myself a new behavior?" Once alternatives have been generated, the child begins evaluating them by discarding the most obviously inappropriate ideas. When only one or two alternatives remain, the child commits to trying one. After trying the chosen alternative, each child reports the results to the group, using the trumpet process to evaluate the new behavior.

Step 8. Choose.   The child asks, "Now that I have a choice, which behavior do I want to use?" Conscious choice is the most important element in this final step. Children must be aware of making decisions and must take responsibility for them.** The issue is not whether people choose one alternative over another or that they supplant one pattern with another. The purpose is to expand the range of choices children have so they can learn to choose an appropriate pattern according to specific circumstances. Repeating old patterns may be appropriate in some circumstances but not in others.

---

* This is similar to the Kamradt & Kamradt idea (chap. 23) that all of one's attitudes meet some need that person has. Other aspects to follow here have resemblance to the Kamradt & Kamradt theory of attitude development. See if you can spot them.

** Hopefully, you recognized this as self-regulated learning, a key common characteristic of the new paradigm of instructional theory.

DECIDING HOW TO TEACH

The values of self-science call for using process-oriented, experiential methods such as games and visualization vs. content-oriented methods such as teacher presentations, textbook reading, and answering questions. Self-science values the synergy and learning that come from the interactions of a whole group rather than individuals working or learning alone or in response to the teacher.* Self-science recognizes that mistakes are an opportunity for learning, not an opportunity for judging, criticizing, or blaming.**

In self-science, teaching is asking rather than telling; teachers encourage curiosity, exploration, redefinition, questioning, and multiple solutions rather than right answers. In self-science there may be a common theme, topic, or experience that is shared, but the specific content that the class explores arises from the group rather than being predefined.

Establishing an appropriate culture is as important as offering the course for certain periods each week. The methods we offer are intended to accomplish both a way of creating a "self-science-friendly" culture within a school and a way of teaching classes in self-science.

In this section, we will describe the structure of the self-science class, some useful ground rules, and some teaching techniques for classes, including communication techniques in general and specific activities, with samples of teaching at four levels from first to eighth grades.

Use an Appropriate Class Structure

Ideally, two teachers, sometimes aides or volunteers, work as a team in self-science classes. Team-teaching is helpful for noticing what is happening in the group, for balancing each other, and for debriefing afterwards, discussing what worked and what did not work and anticipating future objectives. Teaming is vital when a teacher is a novice in self-science.

The size of the group is an important factor in determining whether or not each student learns experientially. Small groups ensure the opportunity for each individual to be actively involved. The optimum class size is 12-15 students.*** Group

---

* Notice the avoidance of "individuals working or learning alone," yet the focus on flexibility and adaptation to learners' individual needs that I commented on in an earlier editor's note. This is a fine example of transcending "either-or" thinking.
** What other theories have advocated this view? It is a strong reflection of the difference between a paradigm focused on learning rather than sorting (see chap. 1, pp. 19–21).
*** This recommendation of two teachers for 12-15 students reflects a significantly different student-teacher ratio than most schools have today, and it is a ratio that could not be afforded, based on our current conceptions of roles in education. This points out the need for rethinking those roles. Perhaps the second person could be a much less expensive apprentice teacher. Or perhaps other "classes" in the school could utilize methods that work with a considerably higher student–teacher ratio. These considerations reflect the need for systemic thinking: identifying changes in other parts of the system that will make this part more workable.

awareness and self-awareness reinforce each other; by sharing ideas and generating choices, the group becomes a unit of support for learning and a place for creative solutions. Class sessions last about 40-50 minutes.

In self-science, the content is wide open and is determined by each child's real-life circumstances, issues, concerns, and interests. Self-science class is always stimulating and exciting because no two sessions are ever the same; the content comes from the participants and is alive.

One way to begin a class is to ask each child, "On a scale from one to ten (where ten is wonderful), how are you feeling today?" or "What color are you, what animal, which car are you today?" By doing this, the teacher gains a sense of the mood of the group and can respond to their tone.

If students are very excited, perhaps because they just had a big test, they need a more active experience so they can let off steam. Too much dialog wouldn't work well when they are "wired." If a trauma has occurred in a child's life, such as a death in the family, a suitable activity would be a quieter, more sensitive one.

The teachers have several activities (described later) "up their sleeves" at any given time so they can respond to the group. Inevitably, a classmate will ask someone with a high score (either end) why the person is feeling that way, and the discussion is off and running. The student might say, "I'm a 10 because today's my birthday," and the teacher might go on to ask the group what birthdays symbolize for them or what kinds of things make them feel really good about themselves.

While teachers "go with what's up" with the children, they set limits on how much the children decide about what the class will do, particularly when an emotionally charged situation is concerning the children, such as a weather disaster. The teacher chooses a comforting exercise, like tape recording each child's story, asking, "Where were you when it happened and what/who were you concerned about?"

One of the hardest parts of teaching self-science can be avoiding the tendencies to take control, wield authority, and moralize, which some teachers have been conditioned to do in classrooms. The teachers maintain order and set limits, but think of themselves more as facilitators who lead and demonstrate how to negotiate and keep the process going, rather than acting as a manager who is concerned with controlling and directing students.* A teacher never lets go of the class, but moves toward greater initiative from the group and less direction from the teacher as time goes on.

In self-science, nonjudgmental acceptance and respect are central to the process of personal growth. Indeed, they are central to simply hearing and seeing accurately and, thus, to learning. So each lesson usually contains a focusing activity which builds trust and a sense of the group working together.** When there are urgent issues, teachers assure children, "We will get back to that." Having two teachers in the self-science class allows one teacher to note things the group will address later.

---

* How does this new role for teachers compare with the new roles offered by other theories in this volume? Does there have to be a new role for teachers to have a new paradigm of instruction?

** Trust is a key element of building cooperative relationships between teachers and students, in place of the adversarial relationships that were typical of industrial-age schools (see chap. 1, pp. 17–19).

Teachers can model trust by expressing their feelings openly, labeling actions clearly but not labeling children, and giving feedback and reassurance so there are no hidden surprises. Teachers build trust by participating in games as a member of the group and demonstrating flexibility by choosing from both sexes for partners in an activity. The more you can let children in on what you are doing or attempting to do, the safer the group will feel.

Be What You Teach

A self-science teacher's role exceeds simply creating a safe environment. Preparing to teach self-science requires more self-reflection than preparing to teach most subjects. Children learn from the style of the teacher. Who you are and what you personally demonstrate is a great part of what you are teaching.

The teacher needs to be willing to act as a participant, not solely as a facilitator, to show respect for the students and enthusiasm for the values of self-science. Besides modeling "emotional intelligence," the teacher must be able to help the children examine their patterns, see the consequences, seek alternatives and make choices.

The teacher must be sensitive to each child's needs so that the child finds resolution with every matter he or she introduces or witnesses. An issue may be addressed in the self-science class, but the teacher must be able to ascertain when additional exploration in another setting, such as with family and/or professional resources, is needed. All teachers make these kinds of decisions in their classrooms.

Committed, interested, and willing teachers who are qualified to lead a self-science class are essential to a successful program. Just as someone who lacks reading skills cannot teach reading, someone with little emotional intelligence is unlikely to be able to lead a successful self-science class.*

Set Ground Rules

It helps to set some ground rules in a self-science class. These mainly have to do with how communication takes place. They apply to the child's whole experience in school, not just to self-science classes.

Trust and Privacy. Children learn how trust works in self-science. They can talk about what happened in self-science class with their families and about what they shared in class, but they may not quote other children. They know that if a matter of their health or safety is of concern, teachers will act in their behalf. Since the discussions that come up in self-science are private, and building the atmosphere of trust so important, visitors are rarely allowed in the sessions. It's helpful to have a

---

* This raises the need for very different kinds of teacher training and teacher selection criteria. A critical aspect of a new paradigm is that it requires significant changes in virtually all other parts of the educational (or training) system. It requires systemic change.

sign on the door that says, "Do not disturb" and see that it's respected by staff, students, and parents.

Killer Statements.   Not only during self-science but throughout school, students agree that no "killer statements" are allowed. Killer statements are verbal as well as nonverbal communications that hurt, criticize, demean, or reject oneself or others. Such statements kill another person's spirit or soul. "You're stupid" is an example of a killer statement. Children learn to recognize killer statements and call one another on using them so that all are protected from negative feelings.

Direct Contact.   Self-science teachers encourage students to speak directly with the person with whom they had a conflict, issue, or any kind of incomplete communication. The child might wish the teacher's support in doing this; however, the teacher encourages the child to initiate discussion with the other individual so as to have resolution rather than an ongoing difficulty.

I-Messages.   Children are taught to use "I-messages," for instance, "I feel _____ when you (do a specific behavior)." "I feel angry when you lie to me." "I feel sad when you leave me out." Next children state what they want, "I want you to tell me the truth." "I want you to include me." Older students can also identify and express consequences. "I felt disappointed when you didn't call me on the telephone last night as you promised. I want you to keep your agreements with me. If you don't, I will find it hard to trust you."

New Students.   If a new student joins the class, he or she is not required to participate. A child absorbs a great deal simply by observing. The teacher might afterwards take the student aside and ask if anything had occurred in the class that the child needed help with understanding or wished to learn more about.

Use Questioning Techniques

The opportunity to learn pivots on the cognitive inquiry process. By "learn" we mean, "make a conscious appraisal of the ideas generated during the activity." Asking questions puts the focus on learning rather than teaching. One self-science technique for effective questions is asking "what" not "why" questions. We have found that "why" questions lead to non-productive, defensive, and circular responses, whereas, "what" questions encourage precise observation in a nonjudgmental way, permitting open discussion.

What do you see?
What do you hear?
What are you thinking?
What do you feel?

What just happened?

What did you just do?

What were you feeling about that?

What do you mean by... ?

What if... ?

What would be the consequences of that (thought, feeling, action)?

What other possibilities are there?

Would you really do that or are you just talking?

Do you do this often?

Would you do the same thing over again?

These are the kinds of questions to use over and over. Not only will you help students sharpen their cognitive skills, but you will model appropriate and healthy modes of coping and analytical behavior.

Our second general questioning technique is to constantly use the expectations of the lessons to focus on similarities and differences in response. "Does anyone else in our group feel the same (differently)?" This kind of question creates awareness of self and others; builds reassurance by sharing similar thoughts and feelings, and enhances self-esteem by permitting recognition of differences. There is an underlying premise of respect for the thoughts and feelings of others.

Use Teaching Techniques

When a community has agreed on the goals of their self-science program, teachers will constantly invent new ways of teaching to meet the needs of their students. Some examples of teaching techniques that have proven effective in self-science classes include dialogue (in this case, high-quality discussion), role playing, social experiments, simulations from real life, games with rules and an outcome, guided fantasy, expression through art, and keeping a journal, all of which can be used at any age level. Later, we will give some examples of how to vary teaching for children at four levels (which correspond to Nueva's class groupings for most subjects).

Dialogue.   Since self-science classes have communication as a goal, children need to engage in constructive discussions in the group. Self-science dialogue often revolves around events that arise in the lives of the children, for example, a birthday, a new sibling, a holiday, a test, the death of a pet, a fight with a friend or news story that concerns them. Discussions in self-science are not adult-driven; the teacher acts as a facilitator, working to unfold the children's views. Children know that their time to speak is limited, although sometimes they may forget and need to be reminded. Having a signal to tell them it's time to wind up what they are saying is helpful. Children learn to really listen to the person who is speaking and consider how to respond to that person in a helpful way or to ask a question that will add depth to the discussion, rather than just thinking about what they will say when it's their turn. Listening is often one of the most neglected communication skills.

Role-Playing. Role playing provides an opportunity to be someone or something else. This technique is useful for exploring emotionally laden topics, for seeing other points of view, for examining alternatives, and for discovering consequences. When the goal is to generate self-awareness, students can play themselves and then have the opportunity of seeing other students playing them. The teacher might say, "Sarah, role play how you express frustration." Then to another student, "Now, you play Sarah." Sarah may see herself as assertive while others experience her as aggressive. The teacher then asks, "Do others see you as you see yourself?" When the intent is to aid the student in seeing another point of view, the teacher might cast the student in a role directly in conflict with his or her own position. Because role playing provides grist for follow-up discussions, it is advisable to keep the period of role playing brief.

Social Experiments. An experiment in self-science is an activity that includes observation of a phenomenon, data gathering, reporting results, and making conclusions. For example, children are divided into small groups and each group is given a deck of cards. The instructions are: "Build a three-story house of cards. Pay attention to your inner dialog and your interactions within the group." The teachers note the children's frustration levels rising as they attempt to add the third story and it falls down, over and over. The teachers stop the experiment after some negative interactions but before things get out of hand. Then the teachers help the students record and analyze data on the blackboard, "What did you notice about yourself? What did you notice about other people?" Then they would discuss conclusions about their patterns in relation to frustration. "Is this your normal pattern? What are the consequences? What are alternative ways of responding to frustration?"

Simulations. A simulation involves the recreation of an event in a simplified way so that children have a common experience to discuss. When children come to school, the teacher might say, "Today children with brown eyes are going to be treated as special. They will be first in line and first to select the sports equipment. The children with blue eyes will be called on last, will be given snack only if there is enough, and will clean up the room during recess." Then, throughout the day, the teacher and children enact the simulation. Naturally, this brings about strong feelings very quickly and the children are eager to discuss their thoughts and feelings, which brings up issues related to fairness, prejudice, and discrimination. Teachers ask, "When do you experience this in your life? What if you had to live this way every day? Where else does this happen? What can we do about prejudice and discrimination?" Simulation activities like this one require preparation, follow-up, and the cooperation of the other teachers involved with the children.

Games. Self-science games are activities that have rules and an outcome, but not necessarily a winner or a loser. Games can be designed to address any of the ten goals of self-science. The "M&M" game, for example, is popular with all ages. Students work in pairs. They are given a cup with M&Ms and the following directions: "The purpose of this game is for everyone to win. You take turns arm wrestling with your partner, and each time someone wins, they get an M&M. When all the M&Ms are gone, the game is over."

The following questions elicit individual and group understanding about listening to directions, attitudes toward winning and losing, individual patterns, competition, attitudes toward others, and consequences. "What did you think the rules of the game were? How did you play? How did your partner play? How were you feeling during the game? How do you think your partner was feeling during the game? Is this what you usually do when you play a game? What was the consequence of your pattern?" Typical patterns range from one child winning all the M&Ms, to partners where no one wins an M&M, to pairs who quickly understand that allowing each other to win results in sharing the M&Ms. Teachers can help children see how this applies to other areas of their lives as well as to the ways of the world.

Guided Fantasy. Fantasy is a process of creating mental images (imagination). Fantasy is used in self-science to help students gain a clearer recognition and overview of their strengths, personality resources, capacities, and potentialities. The first step is to spend a few minutes making a general list of personality strengths. The class breaks into groups of five or six. Focusing on one group member at a time, each group member is to bombard the member with the strengths they see. One member of the group acts as a recorder, listing the strengths and giving them to the person when the group has finished. This is a time to share only positives. After the list of strengths has been completed, the teacher asks, "How would you see Sam functioning five years from now if he used all his strengths and potentialities?" The group then shares all their fantasies and dreams about Sam. The teacher also asks, "What is your fantasy for yourself?"

Expression Through Art. Art is another form of communication. Children fold paper, draw, make clay sculptures or sand paintings in self-science to become more aware of their feelings, to express how reality looks from their perspective, and to create a vision of future possibilities. For example, children can draw pictures of feelings they have inside and those they have outside. They talk about their excitement (outside) about dressing up for Halloween, and their fear (inside) that they might get scared and cry in the haunted house. They draw these feelings, which helps them express themselves, and remember that they can feel more than one way at a time. The teacher asks questions to help children learn how they can align inside and outside feelings.

Keeping a Student Journal.   Students sharpen their powers of observation and awareness by keeping private journals, and entries are shared only if the student wishes. The journals also serve to provide a sense of progress for the students as they note increased vocabulary skills, improved problem-solving skills, recognition of their patterns, and an understanding of the consequences of those patterns to themselves and others.

Vary Teaching for Different Age Levels

The focus of self-science classes varies with the developmental level of the children. The following are sample activities to illustrate how the program can be varied to meet the needs of different age groups.*

First and Second Grades.   First- and second-graders are becoming aware of the variety, intensity, and shifting of their feelings. The following activities help to make this awareness concrete and to assist children, for example, in answering the question, "How are you?" with a more specific answer than "I'm fine." Brainstorm "feeling" words and post them on a list that can be extended as awareness increases and vocabulary improves. Draw a "feeling continuum" on the board to include angry, upset, sad/calm, indifferent, bored, happy, excited. Ask each child to put their initials under the word that describes how they feel right now and to add any word that better describes their feelings. Help children appreciate that two or more feelings can exist simultaneously; let them create a painting or a pair of paintings or drawings that express both the dread and the excitement of the first day of school.

Third and Fourth Grades.   Just as first- and second-graders are learning to put names on their "inside" and "outside" feelings, thus getting a concrete sense of the inherent tension there, third- and fourth-graders are in the process of developing greater awareness of the group and of the tension caused by concern for social acceptance: "inclusion" or "exclusion." The "consensus game" can be used often to make group decisions and to build a sense of contribution to community. Perhaps the group must decide on a speaker, a class mascot, or a new color to paint the classroom. In the case of choosing a color, the teacher (or a child) goes around the circle and each person names their color of choice (individuals may choose the same color) with no additional comments by anyone. Go around continuously until one color is agreed upon. If an impasse is reached between two colors, only the leader may ask for a show of hands to indicate if one color is absolutely unacceptable to anyone. If so, the color is no longer available. Repeat with a show of hands for the second color. The teacher should note as much non-verbal communication as possible. When consensus is reached, ask for feedback on the process. Ask questions

---

* Obviously, this is getting into situationalities. Try to identify whether any of the following methods are parts or kinds or criteria of methods described earlier.

such as, "Was this process difficult or easy? When would consensus be useful? When would it not be useful in making a decision?"

Fifth and Sixth Grades. Fifth- and sixth-graders are still tied to their families but they are reaching out for their peers, and they are learning to set healthy boundaries within their families and social groups. Thus, the "privacy blocks" game offers an appropriate activity. In this game, students will take a look at the criteria they use to determine their own patterns of sharing. Put a diagram of the privacy blocks on the board. It is a series of concentric squares dealing with what you share and to whom. In the center square is "self," then "intimates" (close friends and family), "friends" (school, community), "acquaintances," "everyone." Ask the students to put a key word in the appropriate box for several different instances. "Who would you tell if you cheated on a test?" (Key word: *cheat.*) "If your parent were diagnosed with cancer?" (Key word: *cancer.*) "If your best friend shoplifted?" (Key word: *shoplift.*) Follow this exercise with journal writing or group discussion.

Seventh and Eighth Grades. Seventh- and eighth-graders are focused on becoming adults, on their emerging self, on their friendships and gender roles, and on the choices they are confronted with in the world. The "animal fantasy" game is an exercise that is tuned to the self-conscious adolescent. Teachers instruct students to find a comfortable spot or posture and close their eyes. "Imagine a huge forest, and in the middle of the woods is a large open field. The animal that is you and the animal that is a person you dislike are in the center of the field. What are you thinking/feeling/doing?" Pause and give the students time to create the image. "Let the scene fade. Now have the large open field appear again. This time the animal that is you is with the animal that is the person you love the most. What are thinking/feeling/doing?" Pause again. "When you are ready, return to this room and slowly open your eyes."

Immediately after the exercise, ask the students to describe in detail what happened during the fantasy. Students should be encouraged to share reactions with the group and to consider questions such as the following, "How did you feel during each of the encounters? Is this the way you usually react to these people? What did you learn about yourself from your reactions? How were your thoughts and feelings similar to and different from other members of the group?"

PRECONDITIONS FOR SUCCESS*

Before teachers and administrators consider initiating a self-science program, they should explore and clarify their own responses to these major questions:

- Are the goals of self-science consistent with my personal values?

---

* These are what were called "preconditions" in chapter 1 and in the chapter forewords.

- Are the goals of self-science philosophically consistent with the values of the school where I teach?
- Do teachers have the following leadership qualifications for self-science?

Love of children: They are interested in children's emotional and social development; they can be child centered rather than subject centered.

Self-knowledge: The more they know about themselves, the greater is their ability to help children learn about themselves.

Openness: They are willing to share their feelings and thoughts, and willing to say, "I don't know."

Warmth: They have a friendly, caring manner, are relaxed in most situations, and can help others feel relaxed.

Acceptance: They accept themselves and others, acknowledge the feelings of self and others as valid, accept the good and bad in all of us, possess a willingness to stand up for the child, and have the ability to listen.

Support: They are nondefensive, trustworthy, supportive; a child needs to feel support in order to gain the security to venture into the unknown, a truism for people generally.

Flexibility: They are able to alter a course of action to flow with the mood of the class, and to respond constructively to the unexpected.

Sensitivity: They are perceptive to individual members of the class and how their behavior is affecting the group; sensitivity also implies being perceptive to self, one's own feelings, and how they may be affecting the class; sensitivity allows one to be a key observer of the moment, the "here and now."

Respect: They can let kids figure things out for themselves, they can listen to children.

Teachers and administrators need two kinds of support to gain acceptance for a self-science curriculum within the school. First, they need agreement from the administration, as well as other teachers and parents, that the teaching of emotional intelligence is important and valued. Second, they need to identify at least one other person on the staff who is willing to support their efforts.

It is necessary to get agreement about whether self-science is an elective class or a required class and whether teachers will work with a coleader. Finally, it is necessary to determine how children will be assessed. There is a range of possibilities from a pass–fail system based on attendance and completed assignments, to anecdotal reports by students and teachers about behavior changes, to a parents' survey response form, to children checking their own journals and assessing their own progress, to using standardized measures of self-esteem.

CONCLUSION

In the "Emotional Intelligence" chapter about the Nueva School Self-Science program, Goleman (1995) states,

> as a society we have not bothered to make sure every child is taught the essentials of handling anger or resolving conflicts positively—nor have we bothered to teach empathy, impulse control or any of the other fundamentals of emotional competence. By leaving the emotional lessons children learn to chance, we risk largely wasting the window of opportunity presented by the slow maturation of the brain to help children cultivate a healthy emotional repertoire.

It is difficult to imagine a situation in which a self-science curriculum would not benefit children. If children gain emotional competence at an early age, they are more likely to have fulfilling lives and to be better members of their families and communities and better citizens of the world. We have found self-science to be an exciting journey for both teachers and students. Goleman (1995) writes:

> Despite high interest in emotional literacy among some educators, these courses are as yet rare; most teachers, principals, and parents simply do not know they exist. The best models are largely outside the education mainstream, in a handful of private schools and a few hundred public schools. Of course no program, including this one, is an answer to every problem. But given the crises we find ourselves and our children facing, and given the quantum of hope held out by courses in emotional literacy, we must ask ourselves: Shouldn't we be teaching these most essential skills for life to every child—now more than ever? And if not now, when? (pp. 286–287)

REFERENCES

Goleman, D. (1995). *Emotional intelligence*. New York: Bantam Books.
Kubie, L. (1968). In R. Porter (Ed.), *The role of learning in psychotherapy*. Boston: Little, Brown.
Stone-McCown, K., & Jenson, A. L. (1998). *Self-science: Teaching emotional intelligence*. San Mateo, CA: Six Seconds.

23 Structured Design for Attitudinal Instruction

Thomas F. Kamradt
Elizabeth J. Kamradt
Indiana University

Tom Kamradt

Beth Kamradt

Tom Kamradt holds a degree in Philosophy from the University of Illinois and has been involved in the design of instructional systems since 1971. His work has included a diverse range of audiences and subject matter, including the mentally and physically handicapped, pilots, and air traffic controllers. In 1984 he founded TechniQuill, Inc., an entrepreneurial consulting company which delivers training and productivity solutions to major corporations in the U.S. and Europe.

Beth Kamradt holds a degree in Microbiology from Penn State University and a degree in Instructional Systems Technology from Indiana University. She has lectured at Indiana University and has been an encore presenter at the International Society for Performance and Instruction on the topic of attitudinal instruction. She is presently a managing director in the newly established Unisys Corporation University.

563

FOREWORD

Goals and preconditions. The primary goal of this theory is to help a learner change an attitude. It is intended for situations in which the learner is willing to reconsider an existing attitude.

Values. Some of the values upon which this theory is based include:
* attitude development or change,
* learners having a choice as to whether or not to work on changing an attitude,
* events to help the learner maintain a new attitude and transfer it to real-life situations.

Methods. Here are the major methods this theory offers:

General Strategy

Simultaneously move all three components of the attitude (affective, cognitive, and behavioral) the same amount in the same direction, using rapid shifts in instructional tactics, from one component to another.

Offer a safe environment in which to try on the new attitude.

Specific Tactics

1. Activate the attitude: Present a situation which calls for its use (behavior).
   * Can be direct or indirect activation.
   * The action should be slightly inconsistent with the learner's existing attitude and in the direction of the target attitude (adjust if necessary). This creates dissonance.
2. Diagnose the dissonant component(s) by asking:
   * How did that situation make you feel? (affective)
   * What were you thinking? (cognitive)
   * Why did you do what you did? (behavioral)
3. Address whichever component is most dissonant.
   * If affective, use operant conditioning techniques.
   * If cognitive, use persuasion.
   * If behavioral, use demonstrations and practice for the action.
4. Consolidate the attitude at one point on the continuum before proceeding.
   * Include explicit transfer events and an organizational development plan.

Major contributions. Is a highly ethical, humane approach. Recognizes the interdependence of the three components of an attitude. Is personalized to address the most dissonant component first. Recognizes that every attitude is a tool which its owner uses to resolve a need.

—C.M.R.

Structured Design
for Attitudinal Instruction

INTRODUCTION

In our travels across the corporate landscape, we have found the word "attitude" emblazoned on the following items: pencils, pens, pen holders, memo pads, newsletters, posters, balloons, T-shirts, hats, calendars, flags, banners, plaques, trophies, and a racing car. Most of these sightings have been quite recent and their frequency is increasing. Often the word appears in a short phrase, such as, "My *attitude* is the difference!" Just as often it appears by itself, implying that the message and its significance are obvious.

This phenomenon reflects an important trend in the conduct of both business and education: the widespread recognition that attitude is a critically important success factor. But the use of "Attitude!" as a pop icon also reveals a serious problem. Though we may have an intuitive sense of what we mean when we sing the praises of attitude as a performance goal, our efforts often prove to be misguided and fruitless when we try to actually *do* something to affect attitude.

The discipline of instructional systems design is striving to address this challenge, but thus far it has not supplied us with the kind of objective, repeatable methods we employ when performance objectives lie in the traditional domains of cognitive, psychomotor, or affective skills. This chapter describes the lesson design portion of a comprehensive, structured model for the creation of attitudinal instruction. The complete model includes a functional definition of attitude, techniques for the objective measurement of attitudes, a method for attitudinal needs analysis, a means to apply analysis findings directly to the lesson design process, and a detailed posttraining evaluation capability.

Our goal in the development of this model has been twofold:

- To retain the rigor that accounts for the strength and success of contemporary instructional-design techniques, namely, repeatable methods leading to predictable results;
- To disseminate the skills required for effective attitudinal instruction to a wide audience of educators and designers who have not found success, or perhaps have not attempted to succeed, in this area.

Instructional designers who have been taught that the role of instruction is to close the performance gap between *what is* and *what should be* will probably find the transition to our methodology an exciting one and not nearly the gigantic leap one might expect. Applying our model will not require you to abandon methods whose value has already been proven. In addition to being structured, the model is holistic in two significant ways:

- It is consistent with the recommendations of the major authors who have defined the standards of contemporary instructional systems design.
- It offers an integrated approach involving all dimensions of the learner that are relevant to learning and performance.

We begin by considering some fundamental perspectives.

How Attitudes Function

An attitude can be viewed as a fundamental entity containing elements of all three learning domains: cognitive, psychomotor, and affective (Fig. 23.1).* Just as an atom is a fundamental unit of matter, one that cannot be subdivided by any practical means, we propose that an attitude is the fundamental unit of learning. An atom does have components, however: electrons, protons, neutrons, and, if your physics training is up to date, quarks. Similarly, bits of cognitive, psychomotor, and affective learning are the components of attitudes. They do not normally exist apart from an attitude, nor is there any practical means to separate them. Attitudes are what the learner learns and, therefore, what the effective teacher must teach.

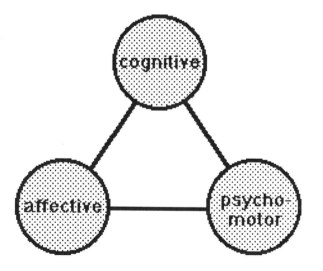

FIG. 23.1.   Components and structure of a discrete attitude.

* This should be a familiar key marker of the new paradigm by now.

This idea may fly in the face of habit for instructional designers accustomed to assigning each distinct piece of subject matter to a particular domain of learning. This popular practice has been helpful, not because the learner contains compartmentalized domains, but because our present teaching methods are domain specific. Within the learner, the subject matter, whatever it is, is stored within attitudes. We will elaborate on this further, but for now let's simply differentiate between cognitive, psychomotor, and affective *domains* within subject matter and cognitive, psychomotor, and affective *components* of attitudes.

Within an attitude, the three components interact through an explicit structure and process (Fig. 23.2). The effect is that an attitude functions as a tool that its owner can use to achieve a benefit. Viewing attitudes as tools created to implement a unique personal strategy is central to this model. The benefit, generally speaking, is the resolution of a need.* The existence of need states has been well documented by many authors. We will rely on Maslow's (1943) hierarchy in this chapter, but any comparable system is equally compatible with this model.

A latent attitude becomes activated by an unresolved need state. Needs are not themselves part of an attitude, and we do not perceive our needs directly. Rather, a need stimulates a feeling in the affective component of all pertinent attitudes (Fig. 23.2a). For example, a nutritional need stimulates a feeling of hunger in the affective component of all attitudes that might be useful in obtaining food. The feeling is typically a combined physical and emotional perception. The nutritional need and the hunger are not one and the same. Rather, nutrition is the need and hunger is a signal. We should also avoid confusing the signal with the concept or idea of hunger. The signal resides completely within the nonverbal affective component of the attitude. It is perceived identically whether we are talking about a mature adult or a preverbal infant. Of course, the complexity of our needs and the resulting variety of signals expand as we mature. At the upper end of Maslow's hierarchy, an unmet need for social or intellectual growth might result in a feeling of dissatisfaction (with a job, locality, relationship, etc.) or, perhaps, ambition. All of our readers can probably appreciate the distinction between gut-level feelings of dissatisfaction or ambition and the cognitive concepts connoted by these words.

Once the need state is signaled by the affective feeling, activation of the cognitive component follows quickly (Fig. 23.2b). The cognitive component serves two major purposes, the first of which is to give the feeling a name—to elevate it to the level of an idea. This makes it possible for us to enlist the full depth of our reason and experience in our effort to resolve the need. For example, in addition to considering immediate or obvious solutions to hunger, we also might choose to consider long-term solutions such as restocking the refrigerator, baking a loaf of bread, or planting a garden.

---

* How is this similar to the Stone-McCown and McCormick idea that all patterns serve their possessors in some way (chap. 22, p. 549)?

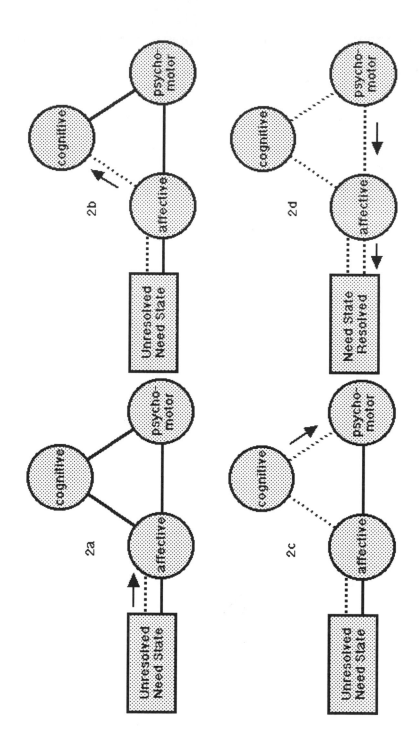

FIG. 23.2.   Process within an attitude.

The second purpose of the cognitive component is to choose a course of action from the available alternatives (Fig. 23.2c). Our perception of the level of risk, the likelihood of success, and numerous other factors responds to the circumstances at hand to make one course of action seem superior to other options.

Once a course of action is chosen, it is implemented (Fig. 23.2d). This is the psychomotor component of an attitude. Many authors have suggested that the doing of the chosen behavior is not actually part of an attitude, but rather a result of it. For reasons that will become clear when we discuss lesson design, we believe behavior is an integral part of an attitude. We view the attitude tool not as a passive implement, but as a very automatic tool with a built-in capacity for efficacy.

If the chosen behavior succeeds at satisfying the need, the attitude will return to latency. The owner of the attitude will judge it, probably subconsciously, to be a "good" attitude.* It has allowed him to succeed at resolving a critical personal need within the framework of what was possible. Because the value of the attitude has been proven, he will defend it if it is attacked. Its owner will perceive any threat to the attitude as a direct threat to the critical human need it was designed to resolve.

If the behavior fails to resolve the need state, its owner will hurriedly implement an alternative attitude. The first attitude, if deemed to be at fault, will not return to latency, but will remain accessible and malleable in a subconscious effort to improve it. Mental and emotional energy will be expended until the attitude is refined or a suitable replacement attitude is constructed.

Attitudes function at lightning speed and, with few exceptions, we use them subconsciously. Invoking judgment and experience we have previously stored in an attitude permits us to respond quickly and effectively to myriad situations within a complex, rapidly changing environment. This, we suggest, is the principal benefit of having attitudes. Without them, it would be necessary to carry on a detailed and time-consuming rational analysis of every situation we encounter before we could act. Given the complexity of our environment, we would be effectively paralyzed. The depth of our past experience, instead of simplifying things, would cause the problem to grow geometrically, since more experience means there would be that much more data to analyze. By applying our attitudes instantaneously and subconsciously, we free our conscious minds to deal with truly novel events for which no attitudinal learning has occurred.

Though we use our attitudes subconsciously, we can normally access them consciously if we so choose. If someone were to question you immediately after you acted on one of your attitudes, you could probably answer these questions with little effort:

- How did that situation make you feel?
- What were you thinking?
- Why did you do what you did?

---

* Note that it is behavioral theory that explains the rationale for this.

Answering these questions would be possible even though you probably would have no recollection of consciously evaluating the situation or choosing your response. In fact, your initial reply to the questioner might be, "Isn't it obvious?" These three questions are tied directly to the affective, cognitive, and psychomotor components, respectively, of the active attitude. The answers to them describe both the content of a particular attitude and the process for applying it, and they are keys to the effective teaching of attitudes.

A Functional Definition of Attitude

An attitude is a psychophysical structure that stores related bits of affective, cognitive, and psychomotor learning in a manner that allows instantaneous, subconscious access by its owner. This structure functions as a tool that allows its owner to respond quickly and effectively to environmental situations related to the satisfaction of fundamental personal needs.

Narrative Examples

Because attitudes contain both rational and nonrational components, no purely expository description of them can convey fully what we are trying to describe. As with a novel or a symphony, the nature of an attitude can only be apprehended fully in the experience of it. We believe attitudes are pervasive in human nature, accounting for the great majority of our behavioral choices. A beneficial exercise for anyone wishing to teach attitudes is to learn to recognize and interpret their own attitudes as they move through the events of their day. These examples provide a guide:

- On your lunch break, you take time before eating to return a book you borrowed from your Aunt Mary. She greets you in her doorway and invites you to stay for lunch. Upon hearing her invitation, you experience an immediate, visceral desire to leave. But your discomfort is in no way visible to Aunt Mary. Instead, she sees a sweet smile of regret come over your face as you look into her eyes and say, "Oh, I wish I could Aunt Mary, but I have to use my lunch break to prepare for an afternoon meeting with my boss. I'm really sorry, perhaps some other time."

  Your gut sensation to get away quickly *signals* (affective) you that staying threatens a core need. You *know* (cognitive) your aunt is lonely and often uses her generosity to garner companionship. You also *know* (cognitive) this violates your need for private time and responsible self-management. So you *choose* (cognitive) to *make an excuse* (psychomotor). But not just any excuse will do. You know that Aunt Mary is easily offended and very persistent. But she also has great respect for your job, so you choose the only excuse that will succeed without offending. You are fully prepared to implement your "demanding people versus my private time" attitude before her invitation has fully left her lips, and it works as expected. Afterward, you have no recollection of evaluating the situation or your possible responses.

- You're working a tight deadline on a critical project and will probably have to stay at your desk late into the night. You hear the voice of a new employee in a nearby cubicle complaining that she's been given an assignment she is not prepared for. You immediately go to her cube and volunteer your assistance, assuring her you'll work with her until she's off to a good start.

Your desire to go quickly to the newcomer's aid *signals* (affective) you that a core need is affected by hearing her complaints. You experience a gut level memory of the *frustration* (affective) you felt when you first started your job. You *know* (cognitive) her complaints are probably legitimate and disconcerting for her. You *believe* (cognitive) your responsibility to your fellows workers is more important than any project, so you *stop* (psychomotor) what you are doing and *go* (psychomotor) to help. Later, when you return to your own desk, you have no recollection of considering the consequences of your action on your own project.

Variable Proportion, Dissonance, and Consistency

The attitudinal nature of the preceding examples is readily apparent because the situations both involve a strong affective component. But if *all* our learning is stored in the form of attitudes, what are the attitudes involved in seemingly emotionless tasks like changing a tire?

We believe that all learning contains all three attitudinal components, but, within an attitude, the components typically do not exist in equal proportion (Fig. 23.3). We call this the principle of variable proportion. The task of changing a tire is primarily a psychomotor task with a small amount of supporting cognitive knowledge. The affective component seems minimal, and, as teachers, we are satisfied with the level of proficiency that can be developed using the psychomotor instructional methods of demonstration and practice. Conversely, a songwriter has a task that is affect-dominant. The cognitive and psychomotor skills needed to master musical notation are minimal in comparison to a songwriter's need to be able to feel the emotional impact of what he or she writes. A legal researcher has a job that is cognitive-dominant, with affective and psychomotor components secondary. All three components are present in the attitudes that store these dissimilar abilities, but in different proportions.

In addition to variable proportion driven by the nature of the subject matter, individual learners may have attitudinal component preferences incorporated into their learning styles. A person with a superior ability to develop the cognitive component of their attitudes might find greater success in a cognitive-dominant field such as engineering, whereas a person with a superior ability to develop the psychomotor component might do best in the construction industry. When a person who has a very strong component preference in their learning style finds a way to focus exclu-

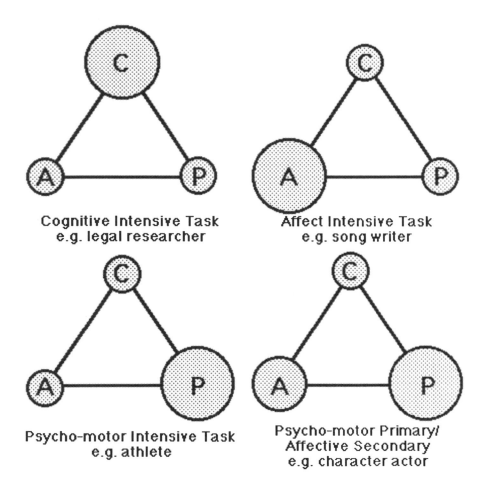

Cognitive Intensive Task
e.g. legal researcher

Affect Intensive Task
e.g. song writer

Psycho-motor Intensive Task
e.g. athlete

Psycho-motor Primary/
Affective Secondary
e.g. character actor

FIG. 23.3.   Principle of variable proportion.

sively on a subject that has a very strong matching domain dominance, they may achieve a reputation as a master performer ("prodigy") with little apparent effort. However, in our opinion, too much significance has been attached to this limited situation. Studying the learning methods of master performers is not the holy grail of performance development for those of us whose interests and attitudes reflect a more balanced makeup of affective, cognitive, and psychomotor components.

Consider this scenario: You are traveling alone in an unfamiliar area far from home. Your tire blows out on a deserted road just as darkness is falling. A nearby town has a reputation as a dangerous place. Though you desperately want to fix the tire and be on your way, you sit frightened in your car for several minutes before summoning the courage to begin. Then, while changing the tire, you make several key mistakes. You forget to set the parking brake. You lose one of the lug nuts. You forget to set the safety latch on the jack. The proficiency you demonstrated when you were taught to change a tire has somehow left you.

Such a performance failure is usually explained as some sort of interference. We suspect there is much more going on here, and we refer to it as *attitudinal dissonance*. Attitudinal dissonance is the inability of an attitude, by virtue of its design or its implementation, to resolve the need it was created to resolve. The task of changing a tire does have an affective component, whether it was addressed in the instructional process or not. For the person in this scenario, the signal to use the attitude which incorporates her tire-changing skill is tied to her basic human need to be safe, secure, and self-reliant. But on a dark, deserted road, following the learned procedure (i.e., attitude) could very easily lead to increased danger.

Typically our attitudes have a high degree of internal *consistency*, which is the opposite of dissonance (Fig. 23.4). Most of the time, in most situations, we find our attitudes are very reliable strategies for pursuing our personal needs. The affective signal, the cognitive concept, and the chosen behavior all share a tight and durable fit with each other. If an attitude is lacking in consistency or if its reliability becomes questionable, we invest a great deal of mental-emotional energy in refining it to a higher level of consistency. If a circumstance arises in which the interaction of the three components of an attitude fails to resolve the need it was expressly designed to resolve, we experience attitudinal dissonance. In the flat tire scenario, the need to be safe and secure seemed threatened by the activity of changing the tire, the exact opposite of the purpose for which the attitude was created. This particular person sat frozen in fear, doing nothing. Apparently, no alternative attitude was available. Another person might have made some other choice, such as using a cellular phone to summon help.

An attitude which is inherently dissonant, and whose consistency is damaged beyond repair is a dysfunctional attitude. For example, an infant who is routinely given food when it cries for affection can become, in adulthood, an overeater who experiences constant feelings of loneliness. The affective signal that calls for affection has been paired by conditioning to the cognitive belief that obtaining food is the solution, a strategy doomed to failure in adult life. Retraining dysfunctional attitudes is an important capability of this model, but it is outside the scope of our present discussion.

Human beings learn and retain what they learn because it is useful to them. A student cannot be taught effectively from the perspective that he or she is analogous to a filing cabinet or a memory bank, needing only to have the correct information entered and organized properly in order to achieve a desired performance level. Human learners make intrinsic, subliminal value judgments about the content of their learning. These judgments support and protect the full range of our Maslowian needs, with primary deference to the lowest level needs. They always include the ability to discriminate whether some piece of learning might be beneficial or harm-

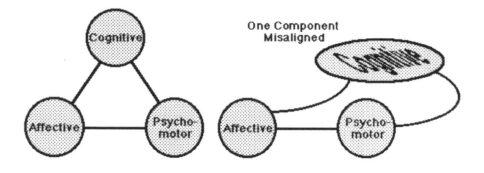

FIG. 23.4.   Internal consistency versus dissonance.

ful in a particular circumstance (affective components) and varied scenarios for how, and how not, to implement the learning for optimum effectiveness (cognitive and psychomotor components).

The bottom line of the principle of variable proportion is that all three attitudinal components are present, to some degree, in all learning and performance efforts. If the instructional process does not fully and correctly integrate all three components, learners will subconsciously fill in the blanks with information drawn ingenuously from their own experience and temperament. This distorts the instructional plan, leading to unpredictable performance outcomes. Contemporary, domain-focused instructional techniques do well at integrating cognitive and psychomotor components, but they consistently fail to properly integrate the affective component. In other words, they don't teach complete attitudes. Instead, after expertly teaching two of the three attitudinal components, we allow ourselves to blame low-performing learners for *their* attitude deficiencies.*

Attitudinal Needs Analysis**

Attitudinal needs analysis expands the scope of conventional needs analysis. The *what is* and *what should be* are expressed as specific attitudes (more commonly, sets of attitudes) explicitly defined in all three components. The process for conducting attitudinal needs analysis is beyond the scope of this chapter, but we must discuss the outputs it produces, since they drive the lesson-design process.

---

* This is typical of the industrial-age mindset, and it indicates why the affective domain is so important to integrate into the new paradigm of instructional theories.
** Is this a part of instructional theory or of the ISD process?

Related attitudes can be thought of as existing on a continuum of degree (Fig. 23.5a). The continuum is bounded on its ends by two attitudes representing opposite extremes. This is a second form of attitudinal consistency called *external consistency*. Previously, we discussed internal consistency, wherein the three components are well integrated within an attitude to produce a reliable effect. External consistency refers to the relationship of discrete attitudes positioned adjacent to each other along the continuum. Consider attitudes regarding racial diversity. At the "left" extreme of the continuum is an attitude constructed something like this:

- affective: feelings of fear, danger, serious threats to its owner's very survival;
- cognitive: people of other races are antagonists and competitors; desirable behavior options focus on subduing people of other races;
- psychomotor: segregation, violence, genocide, race war;

At the "right" extreme of the continuum is an attitude constructed something like this:

- affective: feelings of brotherhood, respect, sharing, appreciation, commonality, curiosity leading to social and intellectual growth;
- cognitive: people of other races are like me in every way that matters; behavior options include any and all bonding opportunities including intermarriage;
- psychomotor: seek proximity, seek interdependence, seek mutual respect, support intermarriage.

Sequenced along the continuum between these extremes are thousands of intermediate attitudes, reflecting the full range of possible attitudes on the subject of racial diversity. External consistency is, essentially, the absence of any rift or fracture along this continuum. If the various attitudes are correctly identified and expressed by the analysis process, each discrete attitude will clearly "fit" between two other attitudes that are highly similar to it (Fig. 23.5). Despite the similarities within each triad of attitudes, the question of which attitude belongs in the center, which belongs to the left, and which belongs to the right will be readily answered by examining the internal components of each attitude and their functional relationships. Furthermore, not only will the complete, discrete attitudes reflect this consistency, but the same regular gradient of similarity will be found by comparing component to like component. The techniques for analyzing the individual components are conventional. Conditioning and extinguishing scenarios explain the affective component, cognitive analysis explains the cognitive component, and behavioral analysis explains the psychomotor component.

Here is an example of an attitude (A) which might be found somewhere near the middle of the continuum described previously:

- affective: feelings of tolerance and respect;

(a)

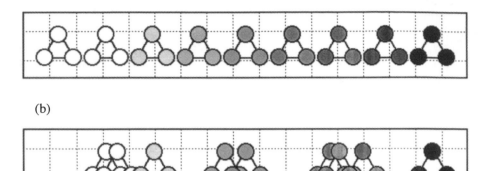

(b)

FIG. 23.5.   (a) Theoretical distribution of attitudes on a continuum; (b) Empirical
distribution measured by needs analysis.

- cognitive: people of other races are very much like me except in skin color
  and cultural values; desirable behavior options focus on acceptance and
  communication;
- psychomotor: acknowledge and respect the similarities and differences in
  other races whenever the opportunity arises.

Here is an example of an attitude (B) that might be found immediately adjacent
to attitude A, on its left:

- affective: feelings of tolerance and respect for many, but not all, members of
  another race;
- cognitive: people of other races are very much like me except in skin color
  and cultural values, which makes some of them unwelcome by virtue of
  being too different; desirable behavior options focus on cautious acceptance on an individual basis;
- psychomotor: getting to know a person of another race well before respecting
  them.

Here is an example of an attitude (C) that might be found immediately adjacent
to attitude A, on its right:

- affective: feelings of tolerance, respect, and commonality;
- cognitive: people of other races are very much like me except in insignificant
  ways; desirable behavior options focus on acceptance, sharing, and social
  bonding;

- psychomotor: acknowledge and respect the similarities and differences in other races whenever the opportunity arises; seek out avenues that develop understanding and a sense of community.

Notice how similar A, B, and C are when viewed as complete, discrete attitudes. Notice, too, how comparing component to like component among A, B, and C reveals an equally strong similarity. Nevertheless, it is clear that B is most like the left extreme of the continuum when compared to A and C, and C is most like the right extreme when compared to A and B. In our experience, we have come to believe that all attitudes can be analyzed in this manner. If unusually fine gradations of attitude are identified in the analysis process, constructing a continuum of the data becomes more difficult. But careful attention to this step gives us the benefit of being able to define equally fine gradations in performance goals and instructional points.

The output document of the needs analysis process is a simple two-dimensional matrix we call an *attitude map*. It describes a continuum like the one in Fig. 23.5b, but in verbal terms. The labels "affective component," "cognitive component," and "psychomotor component" are placed on the X-axis. On the Y-axis are the improvised names of all the attitudes encountered during data collection. Two attitudes are identified as the "positive" and "negative" extremes of the attitude being analyzed. They are described, component by component, in the top and bottom rows. The remaining attitudes are carefully sequenced between these extremes. In describing the components of each attitude, we ask our respondents to use "feeling" words in the affective box, "idea" and "concept" words in the cognitive box, and "action" words in the psychomotor box. We then constrain ourselves to transfer their data to our final maps using identical terminology.

Conceptually, a completed map gives us a comprehensive picture of an individual's or a group's attitudinal makeup as it relates to the subject matter of the planned intervention. Physically, the final maps may vary considerably in length, depending on the complexity of the planned intervention and the size and attitudinal diversity of the audience.

Obstacles to Learning

There are two critical obstacles that must be overcome if we are to achieve our goal of a predictive methodology based on structured techniques:

1. Most of us are quite sure that our attitudes are already as "good" as they can be, and we defend them fiercely against any suggestion that they can be improved.
2. Instructional systems design provides us with many techniques that teach to the affective, cognitive, and psychomotor components of attitudes, but it currently offers very little guidance for teaching attitudes as fundamental entities.

Attitudes are our personal strategy for living, for being who we are. We rely on our attitudes because they have repeatedly proven their worth at allowing us to pursue our needs and values with maximum success and minimum discomfort. Since infancy we have each been building a very special collection of attitudes, and we have done so with great care. "Sure, every attitude doesn't work every time, but I don't see any better options than the ones I've chosen. If I did, I'd be happy to change my attitude and, actually, I've done so many times. But in the here and now, I can say with absolute certainty I've adopted all the attitudes that look like they're good for me and rejected all those that do not. You think I need to change somehow? You think it would be good for me? If I thought there were a better way, I would have found it myself long ago. You don't understand who I am, or what I really want and need, so why should I trust you?"

Who of us doesn't react much like this when we sense an attitude of ours is being tampered with? Even people who admit their lives are unhappy and ineffectual are often the first to insist that there is no other "way to be me" that doesn't come at too high a cost. But the pressure is unrelenting. Not only do we judge our own attitudes by *what's good for me*; we also judge other people's attitudes by *what's good for me!* The result? While we innocently go about trying to develop good, healthy attitudes for ourselves, we must deal with a pressure cooker of people and institutions that want us to adopt attitudes that are good for *them!*

The world has three commonplace strategies, all of them flawed, for tampering with our attitudes. We suspect you will recognize them almost instantly. We have nicknamed them:

- the revival preacher,
- the debate champion,
- the dictator.

The company is doing poorly. Sales, profits, and quality are all down. The anointed one seizes on a strategy to turn things around. Employees are herded into the auditorium for a day-long, nonstop revival. Speeches are given about how grandpa founded this company and nursed it through the depression. We are asked to turn to our neighbor and share a hug and a tear to symbolize our interdependence. We chant a motto or sing a song to refocus ourselves on the dream of industry dominance. At the end of the day, everyone goes home with a chest full of pride, passion, and commitment.

But something is wrong. A week later nothing has changed. Many employees experience an embarrassed feeling of having been seduced. What's wrong is that the revival preacher tries to change attitudes by tugging on the affective component alone, hoping that belief and behavior will somehow follow along. Supported by the camaraderie of the revival tent, we tolerate this dissonance briefly. But our natural appetite for attitudinal consistency soon takes command. While trying to realign our cognitive and behavioral components to the new affect, we discover there is really no logical reason (cognitive) to change our ideas about the company or the way we do our jobs (psychomotor). Like a stretched rubber band, we release our tension by reasserting the original, consistent attitude.

The debate champion tries to change your attitude with a superior argument. "Doesn't it make sense that ... ?" "Just use your common sense and you'll realize my way is better!" He tugs on the cognitive component, hoping that affect and behavior will come along. And often, after a long stretch of relentless argument, you give up. "OK, you're right, I'll do it your way." But the next day everything is back the way it was. Your aversion to attitudinal dissonance and your appetite for consistency take command and your original attitude (i.e., performance) reasserts itself. You tried it his way and it just didn't feel right, so that's that.

The dictator has the right to control your behavior. "I'm your boss. I sign your paycheck, so you'll do it my way. End of discussion." Of course, he has that right because you gave it to him. Maslow wisely realized that physical and safety needs belong at the bottom of the hierarchy. Most of us only begin to develop attitudes for creative self-fulfillment when our food supply is secure. So we elect to tolerate a dictator manipulating some of our attitudes some of the time. But dictatorships sow the seeds of revolution. When our coerced behavior threatens our own attitudes, we intensify our commitment to our beliefs (cognitive) and the affective accouterments that are so intimately tied to who we are. We reluctantly accept the attitudinal dissonance and continuous stress it causes us, believing that some day an opportunity for consistency will present itself. The stress causes performance failures that can only be corrected by increased dictatorial threats, and a vicious cycle is begun. Eventually the dictator's attitudinal training system crumbles under its own weight.

We blamed these travesties on the world, but they are also promoted by instructional design that allows subject matter to dictate a domain-specific instructional strategy. People can and do change their attitudes. They do it frequently and they do it willingly. To tap into this willingness in a structured training environment, we must develop a strategy that scrupulously avoids the pitfalls of the revival preacher, the debate champion, and the dictator. Though each of them seized upon a different attitudinal component, they all fell prey to the same self-protective mechanism built into every attitude.

The rubber band, mentioned previously, is an apt analogy for this mechanism (Fig. 23.6). In an internally consistent attitude, the rubber band assumes its natural, relaxed shape and the components are aligned symmetrically in a triangle. In a dissonant attitude, one or more components is misaligned causing the rubber band to stretch and distort the symmetry, which is analogous to consistency. If we could somehow *simultaneously* move all three components of an attitude exactly the same amount in exactly the same direction, the learner could adopt a new, improved attitude without ever experiencing the attitudinal dissonance that stretches the rubber band and triggers resistance (Fig. 23.7). Regrettably, at present, we lack an instructional technology to accomplish this.

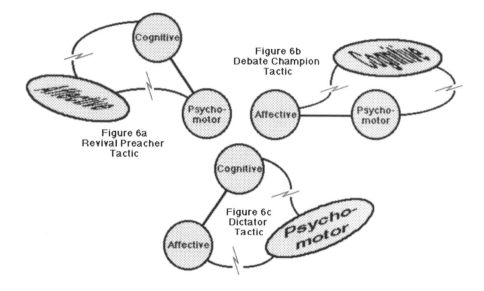

FIG. 23.6.   (a) Revival preacher tactic; (b) debate champion tactic; (c) dictator tactic.

A HOLISTIC INSTRUCTIONAL STRATEGY

In the absence of technology offering true simultaneity, we propose a practical and effective alternative. The alternative is based on using the domain-specific instructional methods we do possess in a way that emulates the teaching of a complete attitude. Specifically, we must alternately nudge each component of an existing attitude a small amount in the direction of the matching component in the target attitude. This certainly causes dissonance and motivates learners to protect their existing attitudes, but if we quickly and effectively shift our instructional focus from one component to the next, nudging each an identical amount in an identical direction until all three have been addressed, the dissonance can be promptly relaxed (Fig. 23.8).

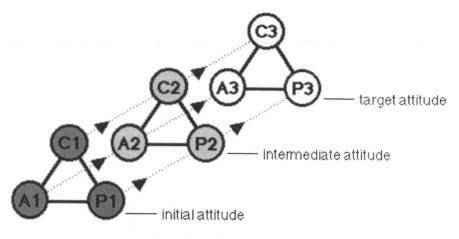

FIG. 23.7.   Developmental attitude shifts.

This strategy assumes that our natural aversion to attitudinal dissonance is not absolute. Most people will tolerate a limited degree of dissonance under certain very restrictive conditions:

1. They will not risk significantly damaging a proven attitude. If exposing a proven attitude to a change process threatens to leave its owner without an effective tool, he or she will not cooperate. Remember, any threat to a proven attitude is perceived as a direct threat to the critical human need it was designed to resolve.
2. They must believe there is a possibility of achieving an improved attitude. *Improved* means the new attitude not only must resolve the underlying need every bit as well as the attitude being surrendered, it must also offer a clear *additional* benefit which the old attitude did not possess.
3. The dissonance must be confined to the shortest possible period of time.

To meet these conditions, we base our lesson designs on three essential features:

1. We offer the learners the *opportunity* to change, *if they wish to*. We never insist or even suggest that they avail themselves of the opportunity. Everyone is free to leave or to sit through the intervention without participating, no questions asked. Attitudes are a unique personal strategy for success. No one, ethically, has the right to command the attitudes of another.* We also promise everyone that, if they do participate, they are free at any time to discard their newly learned attitudes and re-adopt their old ones without recrimination.

---

* This is certainly not an industrial-age viewpoint, which is based more in top-down control (see chap. 1).

582

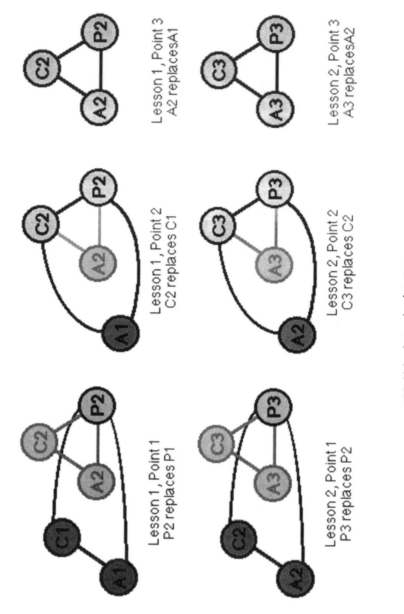

Lesson 1, Point 1
P2 replaces P1

Lesson 1, Point 2
C2 replaces C1

Lesson 1, Point 3
A2 replacesA1

Lesson 2, Point 1
P3 replaces P2

Lesson 2, Point 2
C3 replaces C2

Lesson 2, Point 3
A3 replacesA2

FIG. 23.8.   Instructional strategy.

Successful attitudinal instruction must always be a win-win, risk free proposition. The worst case outcome must be no more severe than a learner completing the intervention with the same functional set of attitudes that he or she began with.

2. We enable the learners to vividly encounter both their present attitude and a potential new attitude, which has been carefully chosen to be an attractive replacement. Most will typically object to the new attitude at least three times, defending the track record of the existing attitude component by component. Through a process called the "two-sided encounter," we offer them a safe environment in which to "try on" the new attitude and form an opinion about whether it effectively satisfies the same need as the old attitude and offers valuable additional benefits.

3. We utilize rapid shifts in instructional tactics as the learner's defenses shift from one attitudinal component to another, sometimes many times in the span of a minute.

Activation

In addition to meeting these three criteria,* the lesson design must also provide a way to activate the attitude in question, so that all of its components are accessible to the learner and the teacher. An attitude is activated by a situation that calls for its use. For example, if the attitude in question relates to interpersonal behavior (perhaps the learner is missing meetings or using sexist language), role-play exercises might be appropriate. If the attitude relates to some object (perhaps the learner is abusing equipment or wasting supplies), using the real objects in the classroom might prove activating.

If direct activation is not possible, an indirect method often works just as well. The indirect method is based on vividly imagining a situation that calls for the attitude. Consider this exercise. Your teacher might say to you, "Please explain the importance of turning in your work on time."

Most people would respond by pausing a few seconds to power up the cognitive component of their attitude, that is, their beliefs and experiences. Their response would probably be full of pauses and the most important reason might not come out first. They might attempt to describe some of their feelings, but they probably wouldn't feel them directly. Though they probably do have a positive, functional attitude about timeliness, they access it inefficiently at best when it is not activated. Now consider hearing this request from your teacher:

> Close your eyes. Imagine yourself standing at the door of your boss's office. You're holding a report you've written that's two weeks late. You pause before knocking and take a deep breath. Your arms feel heavy. Eventually you knock, walk in, and put the

---

* Here is a clear case of methods as criteria, as discussed in chapter 1 (p. 10).

report in her hand. She slowly looks up and your eyes meet. Why would you not want to do this?*

This time you are able to respond fully, immediately, and effortlessly, answering the key questions:

- How did that situation make you feel?
- What were you thinking?
- Why did you do what you did?

The second form of the request has vividly engaged all three components of your timeliness attitude, if only through the power of imagination.

Setting Objectives

The instructional goal is always to motivate the learner to freely adopt an attitude that is nearer to the "positive" end of the attitude continuum than his or her initial attitude, as measured by needs analysis. Choosing the right target attitude for each lesson and right-sizing the overall intervention involve a number of subtleties that we have learned more from experience than theory. People will accept significant attitudinal development with surprising speed and willingness if the three core design principles are strictly adhered to. Design a win–win, risk-free intervention that offers positive growth without ignoring critical human needs, and you may be astounded, as we have been, at the power of this approach.

Each time the learner adopts an improved attitude, the rubber band reverts to a state of complete relaxation. This allows yet another lesson, with a new and even "better" target attitude, to begin without residual resistance. Put another way, attempting to nudge any component of the initial attitude shown in Fig. 23.7 to the position of the like component in the target attitude would probably stretch the initial attitude's rubber band to the breaking point. The learner would defend the attitude by refusing the instruction. But to nudge each component only as far as the intermediate attitude might be entirely acceptable to the learner, who has one eye focused on the growth opportunity and the other focused on the risk to his or her core needs. Once the intermediate attitude is decisively adopted, repeating the same process from this new starting point could motivate the learner to adopt the target attitude with equal ease and without ever placing resistance-triggering tension on the rubber band.

We have found that an instructor who is experienced with this model can conduct an intervention with a group of as many as 20 learners and still routinely achieve a 90% adoption rate of the target attitude set. Of course, this assumes a nearly optimal design. Time must be allotted and instructional events must be designed to give adequate opportunity for slower adopters to be in sync with rapid adopters at each intermediate attitude juncture. Equally important, the instructor

---

* How is this similar to the idea of stories included in several other theories in this volume?

must be able to assess whether the group is moving forward more or less in unison at each intermediate juncture. To train more than 20 learners, we use the results of the attitude needs analysis to select subgroups for sessions of about 20 participants.

The size of the transition between the initial and intermediate attitudes, and between the intermediate and target attitudes, begins as an informed guess about how large a transition the learner will decisively adopt. There are, however, checkpoints built into the instructional process that indicate whether an intermediate attitude should be dynamically redefined as the instruction proceeds. Depending on the goals of the intervention and the makeup of the audience, fig. 23.7 might need to be redrawn to include any number of intermediate attitudes. An intervention with a large number of attitudinal transitions is often not only more successful but also faster than one with fewer transitions, which may seem counterintuitive.

Identifying the specific content of the intermediate and target attitudes is also a function of intervention goals and audience makeup. It is not always desirable to have an audience that globally shares a common set of attitudes. If the audience contains several subgroups, there likely will be members who can testify to the value and practicality of the attitudes being proposed to others. In such a situation, the intervention strategy is not to move the entire group to a particular point on the continuum, but to move each subgroup a similar amount in a positive direction.*

If the audience does reflect a homogeneous set of attitudes, there will be a great opportunity for honest and heartfelt expressions about the perception of risk, as well as the perceived benefits of change. Such expressions are valuable for providing a supportive, risk-free learning environment.** What is missing is an accessible model of the target attitude. We have found that learners who share common attitudes often share common heroes, either within the organization or outside of it. So we create a flip-chart model of the attitude set (explicitly defined in all three components) of an agreed-upon hero. When using our model to develop attitudes within sales organizations, we typically find that the audience shows an uncanny ability to describe, attitude by attitude, how the perennial winner of the sales trophy is different from themselves. Before being offered attitudinal instruction, they frequently end their descriptions with a reflective statement like, "But that's him, not me."

An Instructional Model

As long as the essential features described previously are adhered to, there is room for an immense amount of variety and creativity in choosing instructional events.*** Let's consider a few useful preliminary exercises before we move to the steps required by the model.

---

* This is a form of customization characteristic of the new paradigm of instructional theories.
** Which other instructional theories have advocated a similar learning environment?
*** Hopefully, you recognized this as diversity or multiplicity of methods.

We typically begin with an exercise, either verbal or written, designed to provide a real-time validation of the needs analysis. This exercise also acquaints the audience with using a critical approach based on the three key questions that identify the components and processes built into their attitudes. Usually, we simply describe situations relevant to the subject of the intervention and ask, "How do you like to handle this situation?" If the exercise is couched in positive terms, participants will be enthusiastic about relating the merits of their expertise (i.e., attitudes).

If their responses lack specific references to one or more attitudinal components, we ask them component-focused questions until they have described a complete attitude:

- How does using this approach make you feel? (affective)
- Why does this approach make sense to you? (cognitive)
- What do you actually do in this situation? (psychomotor)

If their description of the affective component does not clearly identify which underlying need it signals, we ask them directly, "What personal value, in the most basic terms, is enhanced when you handle this situation the way you described?"

Searching for growth opportunities is another valuable preliminary exercise. Appropriate opportunities for attitudinal intervention must not only provide a benefit to the sponsor of the intervention, they must also benefit the owner of the attitude, *in the owner's opinion*. This is an ethical constraint we place on ourselves to ensure that no one is threatened with the loss of a tool that is essential to their life strategy.

We begin the search by reinforcing the audience for their cooperation and asking a leading question. For example, "I've heard some excellent attitudes described: good, reliable ways of doing your job and living your life that serve you well. Each of the attitudes you've described is your own personal creation and you should be proud of your ability to create and live by beneficial attitudes. Do any of you believe the attitude you described is the best possible attitude for that situation—that it is absolutely beyond improvement?" Few people answer affirmatively to this question. (If someone does, other members of the audience will be happy to critique the attitude by explaining why they haven't adopted it for themselves.) Next, we ask them to focus on an attitude (pertinent to the intervention) they believe can be improved and describe its shortcomings. A large percentage of the shortcomings will fall into four categories:

- The attitude doesn't work often enough.
- The attitude works but has some negative consequences.
- The attitude doesn't generalize well to other situations.
- The attitude conflicts with another valued attitude.

These preliminary exercises enable the instructor to assess whether the baseline and target attitudes assumed by the intervention design accurately represent the attitudinal makeup of the audience.

At this point, we enter the critical phase of the instruction and begin applying the precepts of the model. *Step 1* is activation of the existing attitude. The most reliable activation technique is to ask the learner to perform some action (psychomotor) that is slightly inconsistent with their existing attitude and in the direction of being consistent with the target attitude. In other words, the requested action should be consistent with a carefully selected intermediate attitude. (The intervention design, of course, must ensure that the action is feasible.) This request stimulates mild dissonance and prepares the learner to mount a defense. In the activated state, all components of the existing attitude become accessible to both learner and teacher by way of the key component-specific questions.

Typically, the learner objects immediately before, during, or after performing the requested action. A phrase such as "Yes, but ... " often prefaces the objection and may be repeated several times. We have consistently found the moment of activation to be an impressive, visible drama. "Yes, but let me tell you why doing that worries (affective) me.... " "Yes, but let me tell you why my way makes more sense (cognitive).... " "Yes, but I don't think doing (psychomotor) that will work." It is the poignancy of activation which causes us to conclude that the behavioral component is an intrinsic part of an attitude.

- If the learner has no objection, the requested action is too consistent with the existing attitude. The instructor should be prepared to switch to an intermediate attitude that is closer to the target attitude.
- If the learner absolutely refuses to perform the action, the action is too inconsistent with the existing attitude. The instructor should be prepared to switch to an intermediate attitude that is closer to the existing attitude.*

Step 2 is the two-sided encounter. If the objection is component or need specific, respond to it with feedback that is carefully focused on the same component or need, using appropriate instructional techniques (see table 23.1). For example:

1. If the learner objects by saying, "Doing this doesn't make sense because ... ," use cognitive instruction to offer a plausible rationale by which the action does make sense. Be prepared to back up the proposed rationale with events predesigned into the instructional plan.
2. If the learner objects by saying, "Doing this is impossible (or dangerous, or impractical, or any action-based objection)," use psychomotor development to demonstrate and practice the action in a way that alleviates the objection.

---

* This requires flexibility or adaptability based on situationality.

3. If the learner objects by saying, "I don't want to do this because it makes me feel frightened (or embarrassed, or angry, or any affect-based objection)," use operant conditioning techniques to demonstrate that the aversive feeling can readily be avoided and that positive affective feelings can readily be achieved.*

Less commonly, a learner may object in a way that is directly need based: "If I do that, I'll be fired; then I'll lose my house, my car, (etc.)." As before, the design of the intervention must include the capacity to allay the objection, which can be particularly challenging if the need is at the survival level. Recently, we were attempting to develop empowerment and initiative attitudes in a group of store managers employed by a company that had embraced highly directive "Theory X" practices for decades. The behavior we suggested was to take the leather-bound "bibles" of company regulations off the managers' desks and place them in the trash. The objections were immediate and vehement. As part of our design, we had the president of the division conspicuously seated in the back of the classroom. Amidst the din of objections, the president (by design) picked up the trash bin and carried it to each participant, saying, "Trash the book. I want you to!" Twenty years of attitudes about how to succeed in that company succumbed that very day.

If the learner's objection does not point to a particular attitudinal component (e.g., "I'd rather not"), give general encouragement by citing the support of the group, the prevention of the expected aversive consequences, or the game-like nature of the lesson. If the learner repeats a general objection, solicit a component-specific objection. But do nothing to directly attack the learner's existing attitude. Instead, acknowledge their absolute right to retain the attitude if they so choose.

Be prepared to spend as much time addressing objections within each component as the learner wants you to. Also, be prepared to shift the instructional focus from component to component as frequently as the learner wants you to. If the learner begins to run out of objections without reaffirming the initial attitude, progress is being made. The learner is "trying on" a new attitude and discovering that the underlying need can be met by an alternative attitude that lacks the shortcomings of their initial attitude. Ask component-specific questions about the learner's perceptions to verify that a consistent, functional attitude is being formed. Ask for a repetition of the action. Oftentimes the learner, now convinced of the win–win possibility, will restate the intermediate attitude or propose a more attractive alternative: "So, you're saying, if I handle this situation this way, I'm actually (learner states rationale) and I should feel (learner states new positive affective sensations) and I don't ever need to feel (learner states prior negative affective sensations)?"

When the objections have subsided and the learner is willing to practice the action repeatedly, test the functionality of the new attitude. The attitude has been decisively adopted if the learner can:

---

* Did you recognize these as situationalities for selecting different methods?

TABLE 23.1

Attitude Component	Content Examples	Type of Learning	Example Learning Events
Psychomotor	Athletics, computer keyboard and mouse usage, manual tool manipulation, musical instrument operation, dancing	Motor Skill Learning* 1. Imitation 2. Manipulation 3. Precision 4. Articulation	• demonstration • step-by-step instruction • practice with guided feedback
Cognitive	Facts, concepts, principles, rules	Cognitive Learning+ 1. Knowledge 2. Comprehension 3. Application 4. Creation	• recall pre-requisite or related knowledge • present new information • present model examples • present close-in non-examples • provide novel situations for application and generalization of new knowledge (e.g. experiments, case studies)
Affective	Pain, hunger, anxiety, friendship, love, pride, embarrassment, fun, competitiveness	Conditioning ++ 1. Operant 2. Respondent	• present stimulus • elicit response • reinforcing or extinguishing contingency efforts (e.g. A reward or punishment scenario)

*Adapted from Benjamin S. Bloom, ed. *Taxonomy of Educational Objectives, handbook 1: Cognitive Domain.* New York: David McKay Company, 1956.

+ Adaptation based upon published works of E. Simpson (University of Illinois) and R. H. Dave (National Institute of Education, New Delhi, India).

++ See work by: Skinner, B. F. (1938). *The Behavior of Organisms.* New York: Appleton-Century-Crofts. (1969) *Contingencies of Reinforcement: A Theoretical Analysis.* Englewood Cliffs, NJ: Prentice-Hall.

1. perform the action without clumsiness or hesitation,
2. explain the rationale without confusion,
3. acknowledge feelings which attest to a satisfied need state.

Transfer Events and Organizational Development

To motivate a person to willingly set aside attitudes that have proven safe and reliable for years is a significant accomplishment, and often a necessary one in today's business and educational environments. With some practice in this methodology, you can expect to see your students leave the classroom exuding feelings of renewal, even if you only set out to teach them how to change a tire. The discovery of a path that offers personal and professional growth without placing fundamental human needs at risk is an exhilarating experience that we all would choose, if only we had a teacher who could show us the way.

But, as every good teacher knows, the world is the most formidable classroom of all. People who have experienced this methodology commit to their new attitudes with a resiliency that is far beyond anything that can be achieved by the revival preacher, the debate champion, or the dictator. But that commitment is neither eternal nor absolute. If a learned attitude does not deliver on its promise, our ceaseless quest for consistency will restart the formative process until a better attitude is found.

To minimize this risk, all of our interventions include explicit transfer events and an organizational development (OD) plan. The transfer event has four components: support, threats, exceptions, plans.

Support is the support of the teacher and the other participants in the intervention. These are the only people who were present when risks were being taken and discoveries were being made. Membership in this group is an ongoing asset that supports the implementation of newly learned attitudes, even after the intervention has physically dispersed.

Threats are factors known to be hostile to the newly learned attitudes. By identifying and acknowledging these threats while still in the classroom, appropriate defenses can be planned and ready.

Exceptions are situations which may appear to call for the newly learned attitudes, but which are inappropriate for the application of those attitudes. Learning when and when not to apply new attitudes requires practice, and identifying exceptions while still in the classroom can protect new attitudes from unnecessary risks.

Plans are efforts made by the participants in the intervention to weave support, threat, and exception factors into a conscious, plausible scenario for utilizing their new attitudes and enjoying the benefits of them without placing them at unnecessary risk.

The OD plan is an acknowledgment that, in most organizations, the intervention participants will return to an environment that rewards not their new attitudes, but their old ones. Indeed, the old attitudes may very well have been created as tactics needed to prosper in that organization. If the organization continues to reward the old attitudes, rather than renewing itself as it has asked its employees to do, those attitudes will soon be readopted.

Each specific organizational factor brings its influence to bear primarily on one specific attitudinal component. Performance reward systems and job design directly affect core personal needs. Management style, culture, and social dynamics directly affect affective attitude components. The vision of leadership, mission statements, and personnel policies directly affect cognitive components and task flows, and procedures and equipment directly affect psychomotor components. Internal and external consistency is essential in the design and implementation of all organizational factors if the organization desires the benefits of a healthy and productive attitude set in its members.

REFERENCES

Maslow, A. H. (1943). A theory of human motivation, *Psychological Review*, 370–396.

24 Character Education: The Cultivation of Virtue

Thomas Lickona
State University of New York at Cortland

Thomas Lickona

Thomas Lickona is a developmental psychologist and professor of education at the State University of New York at Cortland, where he currently directs the Center for the Fourth and Fifth Rs (Respect and Responsibility). He holds a PhD in psychology from the State University of New York at Albany and has done research on the growth of children's moral reasoning. He is a past president of the Association for Moral Education and now serves on the board of directors of the Character Education Partnership. Of his many books, *Educating for Character* has been praised as "the definitive work in the field" and was named winner of a 1992 Christopher Award for "affirming the highest values of the human spirit."

591

FOREWORD

Goals and preconditions. *The primary goals of this theory are to develop good people, good schools, and a good society, where "good" is construed as having virtues like honesty, justice, empathy, caring, perseverance, self-discipline, humility, and others. It was developed for K–12 schools.*

Values. *Some of the values upon which this theory is based include:*
- *the reality of objective moral truth—that virtues are objectively good human qualities,*
- *the acquisition of objectively worthwhile virtues as an important educational goal,*
- *context as influencing the choice of which virtues to teach,*
- *behavior as the ultimate measure of character,*
- *knowing the good (the cognitive side), desiring the good (the emotional side), and doing the good (the behavior side) as important to character development,*
- *being comprehensive and objective in teaching virtues,*
- *a whole-school effort to create a community of virtue for fostering character development,*
- *students' active participation and responsibility for constructing their own characters, but also adults' exercise of moral authority and leadership,*
- *transmitting a moral heritage of tested virtues, but also equipping students to think critically about how to apply the virtues in cases of value conflicts.*

Methods. *Here are the major methods this theory offers as a comprehensive approach to character development:*

Classroom strategies

1. *Teachers should respect and care about their students, set a good example, and provide directive moral guidance.*
2. *Create a caring classroom community by helping students to know each other as persons; respect, care about, and affirm each other; and feel a valued member of the group.*
3. *Help students develop moral reasoning, self-discipline, and respect for others.*
4. *Involve students, through regular class meetings, in shared decision-making.*
5. *Teach virtues through the curriculum by "mining" it for its moral potential.*
6. *Use cooperative learning to give students regular practice on important social and moral competencies while learning academic material and to contribute to the development of a cohesive and caring classroom community. Students should regularly reflect on how well they cooperated, and should develop guidelines.*

7. *Help students develop the "conscience of craft" (desire to do a good job), including self-discipline, persistence, dependability, diligence, and responsibility, by setting a good example, combining high expectations and high support, engaging all learners, and assigning regular and meaningful homework.*
8. *Teach students what the virtues are, how their habitual practice will lead to a more fulfilling life, and how each of us must take responsibility for developing our own character.*
9. *Teach students how to resolve conflicts.*

Schoolwide Strategies

1. *Develop students' caring beyond the classroom through exposure to altruistic role models and continuing opportunities for service (in face-to-face relationships) in their schools and communities.*
2. *Create a positive moral culture in the school by defining, modeling, teaching, and upholding the school's character expectations in all areas of school life. Participatory school democracy is a powerful tool for mobilizing the peer culture on the side of virtue.*
3. *Recruit parents and the community as partners in character education.*

Major contributions. The understanding that there are some objectively worthwhile virtues that should be a central part of the K–12 curriculum. The importance of a whole-school effort. The use of both directive and constructivist goals and methods.

—C.M.R.

Character Education:
The Cultivation of Virtue

A headmaster remembers that above the door to the main classroom building where he went to school, the following words were engraved:

> Be careful of your thoughts,
> for your thoughts become your words;
> Be careful of your words,
> for your words become your deeds;
> Be careful of your deeds,
> for your deeds become your habits;
> Be careful of your habits,
> for your habits become your character;
> Be careful of your character,
> for your character becomes your destiny.
>
> —Anon

One of the most important ethical developments of recent times has been a renewed concern for character. Scholarly discussion, media attention, and everyday conversation have all focused attention on the characters of our elected leaders, our fellow citizens, and our children. The psychiatrist Pittman (1992) writes:

> The stability of our lives depends upon our character. It is character, not passion, that keeps marriages together long enough to do their work of raising children into mature, responsible, productive citizens. In this imperfect world, it is character that enables people to survive, to endure, and to transcend their misfortunes. (p. 63)

The renewed attention to character is especially evident in the current resurgence of character education. Character education can be defined as the deliberate effort to cultivate virtue. Virtues are objectively good human qualities, good for the development and well-being of the individual and good for the whole human community. Because they are intrinsically good, virtues transcend time and culture; justice, honesty, and kindness always have been and always will be virtues.

In its underlying philosophy, character education asserts the reality of objective moral truth,* the notion that some things are truly right and others truly wrong.

---

* Objectivist and subjectivist viewpoints have battled for the public's minds and hearts, unable to transcend "either-or" thinking. Just as we are coming to recognize that there are well structured and ill-structured domains in the cognitive arena, so we are perhaps beginning to realize that there are objective moral truths as well as some subjective and relative dimensions in the ethical arena.

Objective truth, as philosophers Kreeft and Tacelli (1994) point out, is truth that is independent of the knower. That Lincoln was President during the Civil War is objectively true, even if someone doesn't know it. That adultery is wrong, racism is wrong, torture is wrong, date rape is wrong, cheating is wrong, and the unjust taking of innocent life is wrong are objective moral truths, even if many people do not realize it. Objective moral truths have a claim on our conscience and behavior.

The History of Character Education

The idea of objective, knowable moral truth is very old. The theologian Dulles (1950), in an essay describing his journey at Harvard University from atheistic materialism to Christian belief, says it was the writings of Plato and Aristotle that first convinced him that virtue is real and that only a virtuous life can be fulfilling. Dulles writes:

> Plato, whom I read extensively during the summer of my sophomore year, dispelled from my mind the illusion that morality was nothing but a tissue of artificial conventions. He proved conclusively that man is able to discern, in a sure intuition of objective reality, the excellence of virtues such as wisdom, justice, courage, and temperance. He then went on to demonstrate that these virtues are always and everywhere better than their opposites, that the good has a claim on our obedience, that evil is on no account to be done, and that those who do it are liable to punishments in a future life. Plato convinced me that man is not fully a man unless he subjects his passions to his will and his will to the dictates of right reason. My own experience confirmed this lesson. It took this kind of self-mastery, I noticed, to study on an evening which could have been more pleasantly spent in a barroom or a bull session. And such self-mastery was nobler and more satisfying than merely following the path of sensual self-indulgence. (p. 71)

Throughout most of American history, cultivating the virtues that make for a noble and fulfilling life has been a primary purpose of schooling. Horace Mann, considered the father of the common school, argued that the highest goal of education was character and that schools should teach virtue before knowledge (McClelland, 1992). Modeling good character was considered the first responsibility of teachers. Within the school curriculum, books like the *McGuffey Readers* gave pupils a daily diet of inspiring tales about honesty, hard work, thriftiness, kindness, patriotism, and courage.

Instruction in virtue through edifying stories, the teacher's good example, and discipline remained a major mission of public schools until the middle of the 20th century. At that point, powerful forces converged to reshape the Zeitgeist and erode support for teaching character. Prominent among these was the philosophy of logical positivism, which asserted that value statements such as "stealing is bad" and "kindness is good" could not be proven in the way that scientific claims could be proven; therefore, moral claims had no status as objective truth. As a result of positivism, morality was made to seem purely a matter of subjective and variable opinion, not a matter for public debate and certainly not for public transmission through the schools.

In the 1960s, the nation felt the effects of a worldwide surge of "personalism." Personalism celebrated the worth, autonomy, and subjectivity of the person. It emphasized individual rights and freedom over responsibility. Personalism rightly protested societal oppression and injustice (racism, sexism, and institutional corruption) and advanced human rights, but it had a destructive downside: It delegitimized moral authority in all realms (school, family, church, and government), further eroded belief in objective moral norms, led people to become preoccupied with self-fulfillment, weakened social commitments such as marriage and parenting, and fueled the socially destabilizing sexual revolution.

At the same time, the rapidly intensifying pluralism of American society raised the question, "*Whose* values should we teach?" Finally, the increasing secularization of the public arena, notably Supreme Court rulings against promoting religion in public schools, caused people to worry, "Won't moral education get you into religion and violate the First Amendment?" When much of society came to think of morality as being entirely subjective, not something a pluralistic society could ever agree on, and not something we could legitimately teach in our secular democracy, public schools retreated from their once central role as character educators.

In the late 1960s, values education reappeared but in a very different form: values clarification (Raths, Harmin, & Simon, 1966). Values clarification was positivism and personalism "gone to school." It rejected the notion of objective, universally valid values; it argued instead that people create values out of their personal experience. Hence the teacher's role should be nonjudgmental, teaching students a "process" for clarifying their own values. No distinction was made between nonmoral values ("Do you like to read the Sunday comics?") and moral values ("Where do you stand on capital punishment?"). Value judgments of all kinds were reduced to personal preference. Faced with students who defended moral choices from shoplifting to having sex to belonging to a Satanic cult as their self-chosen values, teachers using values clarification as their framework felt powerless to respond.

During the 1970s, values clarification got some competition from ethically sounder approaches—such as Kohlberg's "moral dilemma discussions" (see, for example, Reimer, Paolitto, & Hersh, 1979) and an approach called "rational decision making" that was developed by moral philosophers (see, for example, Hall & Davis, 1975). These cognitive approaches rejected value clarification's moral relativism and attempted to help students develop more systematic and principled moral reasoning. But the focus of these methods was still on process—thinking skills—rather than on moral content (learning what's right and then practicing it until it became habit). Teachers using these cognitive methods did not see it as their responsibility to model, teach, or otherwise encourage particular moral behaviors.

The Character of Character Education*

The current character education movement is driven by several factors: the breakdown of the family as a moral socializer of children; the growing negative influence of the mass media culture as a shaper of youth values; the public perception that the country is in a period of moral and spiritual decline; and troubling youth trends showing a rise in juvenile violence, dishonesty, drug abuse, self-centeredness, and sexual activity (Kilpatrick, 1992; Lickona, 1991).** Character education is also a reaction against the process-centered, nondirective, and overly cognitive values education methods of recent decades, methods that are now seen as part of the problem.

Character education is a return to the conscious attempt to help students acquire objectively worthwhile virtues. Students don't decide for themselves what is right and wrong; rather, the school stands for virtues like respect and responsibility and promotes them explicitly at every turn. Character education is not just talk; thinking and discussing are important, but the bottom line is behavior, taken to be the ultimate measure of character. Character education is not a separate course, though that can be part of it. Rather, it is a whole-school effort to create a community of virtue, where behaviors such as respect, responsibility, honesty, kindness, diligence, and self-control are modeled, taught, expected, celebrated, and continuously practiced in everyday interactions.***

A core theoretical principle guiding character education is Aristotle's: Virtues are not mere thoughts but habits we develop by performing virtuous actions. We become kind by doing kind deeds, self-controlled by exercising self-control.**** Acting on that principle, character educators seek to help children to perform kind, courteous, and self-disciplined acts repeatedly, until it becomes relatively easy for them to do so and relatively unnatural for them to do the opposite.

The Goals of Character Education

Character education has three goals: good people, good schools, and a good society.

The first goal asserts that we need good character to be fully human. We need strengths of mind, heart, and will and qualities like good judgment, honesty, empathy, caring, perseverance, and self-discipline to be capable of love and work, two of the hallmarks of human maturity.

The second goal asserts that we need schools that embody good character. Schools are better places—certainly more conducive to teaching and learning—when

---

* As you read on, try to identify what is instructional theory and what is curriculum theory, as discussed in chapter 1, p. 14.

** Here we see fundamental changes in society as a driving force for fundamental changes (a new paradigm) in education.

*** Again, the issue of culture or climate appears as an important method variable.

**** This is reminiscent of Pogrow's metaphor of the brain as a muscle (chap. 14).

they are civil, caring, and purposeful communities that model, teach, and uphold high standards of conduct in all phases of school life.

The third goal asserts that character education is essential to the task of building a moral society. Societal problems, such as violence, dishonesty, greed, family disintegration, the growing number of children living in poverty, the battering of women, and the moral contradiction of defending vulnerable and dependent human life after birth while permitting its destruction in the womb, have deep roots and require systemic solutions. But it is not possible to build a virtuous society if virtue does not exist in the minds, hearts, and souls of individual human beings. The school, like the family and the church, is one of the potential seedbeds of virtue.

The Content of Character

Schools embracing character education begin with the proposition that character education aims to foster virtue and that virtues are objectively good human qualities. That general proposition leads to a more specific question: What virtues should a school teach as the basis of good character?*

The ancient Greeks named four "cardinal virtues": prudence (which enables us to judge what we ought to do), justice (which enables us to give other persons their due), fortitude (which enables us to do what is right in the face of difficulties), and temperance (which enables us to control our desires and avoid abuse of even legitimate pleasures). In his book *Character Building: A Guide for Parents and Teachers*, British psychologist Isaacs (1976) offers a more elaborate scheme: 24 virtues, grouped according to developmental periods during which the different virtues should be given special emphasis: (a) Up to 7 years: obedience (respecting legitimate authority and rules), sincerity (truth telling with charity and prudence), and orderliness (being organized and using time well); (b) From 8 to 12 years: fortitude, perseverance, industriousness, patience, responsibility, justice, and generosity; (c) From 13 to 15 years: modesty (respect for one's own privacy and dignity and that of others), moderation (self-control), simplicity (genuineness), sociability (ability to communicate with and get along with others), friendship, respect, patriotism (service to one's country and affirmation of what is noble in all countries); and (d) From 16 to 18 years: prudence, flexibility, understanding, loyalty, audacity (taking risks for good), humility (self-knowledge), and optimism (confidence). A recent book, *The Heart of Virtue,* by DeMarco (1996), recommends 28 virtues, from care and chastity through temperance and wisdom.

Some character education schools stress the "hard virtues" of self-discipline, hard work, perseverance, and self-control; others emphasize the "soft virtues" of empathy, kindness, compassion, and tolerance. In choosing virtues to teach, schools should aspire to be comprehensive and objective. The governing criterion should be: What truly serves the best interests and development of the child?

---

* Clearly, this is an issue for curriculum theory.

Consider a virtue that is controversial: obedience. Some critics of character education have reacted negatively to schools' teaching obedience, treating it as akin to raising good Nazis. But unquestioning, Nazi-like obedience is a corruption of the virtue. Properly understood, obedience means, as one elementary school teaches it, "following rules when it does not go against justice." Obedience to rules and laws is our general duty, but justice may conflict with obedience, as when our boss tells us to lie, cheat, or steal. Correctly taught, then, obedience is not blind; it requires moral judgment and personal responsibility.*

The choice of which virtues to teach is also influenced by context. In democratic societies, for example, character education should logically include "democratic virtues" such as respect for individual rights, concern for the common good, reasoned dialogue, regard for due process, tolerance of dissent, and voluntary participation in public life—virtues that are important to the kind of character needed for democratic citizenship. In a similar way, a religious context profoundly affects how the virtuous life is conceived. The great saints, for example, saw humility as the essential foundation for all the other virtues. "On the degree of our humility," wrote the philosopher von Hildebrand (1948),

> depends the measure in which we shall achieve freedom to participate in God's life.... Every virtue and every good deed turns worthless if pride creeps into it—which happens whenever in some fashion we glory in our goodness.... Humility involves the full knowledge of our status as creatures, a clear consciousness of having received everything we have from God. (p. 150)

Religious schools can teach faith-based reasons for leading a moral life (achieving union with God in this life and the next) and lessons about the ultimate source of goodness (God's grace) that, in a public school, can only be studied as a worldview, not taught as truth. But even public schools do well to challenge students, drawing on their full intellectual and cultural resources, including their faith traditions, to develop a vision of the purpose of life that will guide them in the task of developing their personal character. Without such a vision, the quest for character lacks a philosophical rudder.

The Psychological Components of Character

In addition to defining the content of character, schools also need a psychology of character. What are the psychological components required for living the moral life? Character must be broadly conceived to encompass the cognitive, affective, and behavioral aspects of morality: moral knowing, moral feeling, and moral action.** Good character consists of knowing the good, desiring the good, and doing the good:

---

* Hopefully, you recognized this as transcending "either-or" thinking: we need to deal with both the objective and the subjective (or relative).

** Again we see the inseparability of the cognitive, affective, and psychomotor domains.

habits of the mind, habits of the heart, and habits of behavior. We want our children to be able to judge what is right, care deeply about what is right, and then do what is right, even in the face of pressure from without and temptation from within.

The cognitive side of character includes at least six components: moral alertness (does the situation at hand involve a moral issue requiring moral judgment?), understanding the virtues and what they require of us in specific situations, perspective taking, moral reasoning, thoughtful decision making, and moral self-knowledge: all the powers of rational moral thought required for moral maturity.

People can be very smart about matters of right and wrong, however, and still choose the wrong. The emotional side of character serves as the bridge between moral judgment and moral action. This emotional side includes at least five components: conscience (the felt obligation to do what one judges to be right), self-respect, empathy, loving the good, and humility (a willingness to both recognize and correct our moral failings).

There are times when we know what we should do, feel strongly that we should do it, and yet still fail to translate moral judgment and feeling into effective moral behavior. Moral action, the third part of character, involves three additional components: moral competence (including skills such as listening, communicating, cooperating, and solving conflicts); moral will (which mobilizes our judgment and energy and is at the core of self-control and courage); and moral habit (a reliable inner disposition to respond to situations in a morally good way).

A COMPREHENSIVE APPROACH TO CHARACTER DEVELOPMENT

In order to develop character in its cognitive, emotional, and behavior dimensions, schools need a comprehensive approach. A comprehensive approach challenges schools to: (a) identify the character development opportunities present in every phase of classroom and school life and (b) plan deliberate ways to use those opportunities to foster character development and to minimize school practices that are antithetical to good character.

At the State University of New York at Cortland, our Center for the 4th and 5th Rs (Respect and Responsibility) defines a comprehensive approach in terms of twelve mutually supportive strategies, nine that are classroom-based and three that are schoolwide. These methods are both direct (e.g., explaining the virtues, modeling them, leading students in the study of the virtues, and encouraging them to practice the virtues) and indirect (e.g., providing real moral experiences such as cooperative learning, conflict resolution, and service learning that help students understand and practice the virtues). This comprehensive approach regards adults' moral authority and leadership as an essential part of character education, but also values students' active participation and responsibility for constructing their own characters. There is an effort to transmit a moral heritage of tested virtues but also to equip students to think critically about how to apply the virtues to future moral challenges (e.g., combatting the destruction of the environment and solving the problem of abortion in a way that both respects preborn life and supports women).*

There is also a recognition that critical thinking is needed to deal with value conflicts: life vs. liberty, loyalty vs. justice, individual freedom vs. the common good, and economic development vs. the protection of the environment, to name just a few. Character education holds that in everyday ethical life, most of the moral choices we have to make are not complex dilemmas, but it also acknowledges that there are occasions when one needs prudent judgment and moral imagination to discern how to do justice to competing virtues. "What should I say to someone I don't really like," asked a third-grader in a classroom discussion, "when that person comes up to me on the playground and says, 'Do you like me?'" A classmate responded with a way to integrate truthfulness and kindness: "I'll tell you what I do; I say, 'There are some things I like about you and some things I don't, and I can say that about everybody I know.'" This exchange illustrates how children can often help each other learn how to apply the virtues to the moral complexities they encounter.

To summarize: Character education seeks to develop virtues: moral qualities that are good for the individual and good for society. Schools should develop the full range of virtues that constitute mature character and should develop the cognitive, emotional, and behavioral aspects of each virtue. To develop character in this comprehensive sense requires a comprehensive approach, one that makes use of all phases of the school's moral life as opportunities for character development. A comprehensive approach to character education includes direct approaches (e.g., the curriculum) and indirect approaches (e.g., a positive moral environment), adult authority and student responsibility, passing on a legacy of moral wisdom and developing critical thinking, and helping students practice doing the right thing in clear cases and helping them figure out integrative solutions to moral problems where virtues conflict.

In the rest of the chapter, I would like to explain and illustrate each of the 12 classroom and school strategies in this comprehensive model. (See *Educating for Character*, Lickona, 1991, for a fuller discussion.)

Classroom Strategies in the Comprehensive Approach

1. The Teacher as Caregiver, Moral Model, and Moral Mentor.

In classrooms, as in families, our moral impact on children depends greatly on the quality of our relationship with them. In their relationships with their students, teachers can exert positive moral influence in three ways: respecting and caring about their students, setting a good example, and providing directive moral guidance.

---

* Again, this paragraph contains several examples of transcending "either-or" thinking, with a consequent focus on diversity of methods.

For example, Molly Angelini, a former fifth-grade teacher, made courtesy an important virtue in her classroom. She treated all of her students with a high level of courtesy and modeled courteous behavior toward anyone who came into their classroom. If her students called a classmate a name, she required them to write a letter of apology to the offended person. She taught them to say, "Pardon me?" instead of "What?" or "Huh?" when they wished something repeated. When they went to lunch, she instructed them to greet the cafeteria workers by name and to thank them when they put the food on their trays. Most importantly, she taught her children that all these behaviors were not mechanical gestures but meaningful ways of respecting other people.

2. Creating a Caring Classroom Community.*

Children need caring attachments to adults, but they also need caring attachments to each other. When their own needs for belonging and affirmation are met, they are more likely to care about others.

At any grade level, teachers can take steps to create a caring classroom community by helping students to: (a) know each other as persons; (b) respect, care about, and affirm each other; and (c) feel a valued membership in the group.**

For example, Hal Urban, who teaches high school history and psychology, does three simple things at the start of each class that take only five minutes but go a long way toward developing a moral community in the classroom. First, he asks, "Who has good news?" After a few students share good news, he asks, "Would anyone like to affirm anyone else?" Students become comfortable doing that. Finally, he asks students to take a seat different from the one they had in the previous class and take a minute to get to know their new neighbor better. He finds that building a class community also contributes to an atmosphere of trust that increases students' participation in discussion. At the end of the semester, when asked on course evaluations what they will remember about the course 10 years from now, many students write that they will remember the way Mr. Urban began each class.

3. Moral discipline.

Discipline, if it is to serve character development, must help students develop moral reasoning, self-discipline, and respect for others. Rules should be established in a way that enables students to see the moral standards (e.g., courtesy and caring) behind the rules. The emphasis should not be on extrinsic rewards and punishment*** but on following the rules because it's the right thing to do: because it respects the rights and needs of others.

---

* Which other theories emphasize this? Does this conception differ in any ways from each of the others?

** Here the method is broken down into more detailed methods. Are they parts, kinds, or criteria, as defined in chapter 1, p. 10? Be sensitive to this issue for each of the remaining strategies.

*** This is a fairly common theme in the new paradigm of instructional theories.

For example, Kim McConnel, on the first day of school, puts her sixth-graders in groups of four. She asks each group to write down, on a large sheet of paper, classroom rules that "will help us: get our work done, feel safe, and be glad we're here."

When they are finished, the small groups tape their lists of suggested rules on the blackboard. Drawing from all the lists, the teacher helps the class come up with a list that will serve as "our class rules."

Regardless of whether students help to create the rules, a teacher using moral discipline ensures that students understand the moral basis of the classroom rules. Moreover, consequences for rule-breaking should teach a moral lesson (for example, why the offense was wrong) and foster virtues (such as honesty, a sense of fairness, and a willingness to take responsibility for one's actions). They should require students, whenever possible, to make appropriate restitution so they learn that when they do something wrong, they should take positive action to set things right.*

4. Creating a Democratic Classroom Environment.

This means involving students, on a regular basis, in shared decision-making that increases their responsibility for making the class a good place to be and to learn. The chief means of creating a democratic classroom is the class meeting.

For example, As a student teacher of tenth-grade English, Martha Bigelow began the semester by holding a class meeting in all of her classes to present, discuss, and have students sign a contract for classroom behavior. As she progressed through her first unit on the play *A Raisin in the Sun*, however, she found that one of the contract expectations, "Come prepared for class," was not being met by more than half of the students in two of her classes.

She immediately held another class meeting to discuss this problem. In her words: "I stated the numbers of people not finishing their homework and the importance of finishing the homework in order to have a good discussion of the play. I explained that it was very disappointing and frustrating for me to be spending several hours preparing for class while so many students were coming unprepared. I said it seemed to me that they didn't care about the class."

Students reacted strongly to this last statement, insisting that they *did* care; they came to class, didn't they? Teacher Bigelow replied that just showing up wasn't enough. Students then talked about all the reasons why they didn't get the homework done: they had baseball practice after school, they had a job at Burger King, they liked to watch TV when they got home, and so on, and by the time they did everything else, they were too tired to do homework. So Ms. Bigelow helped them work out time management strategies that included a planned time for homework in their daily schedules. In subsequent classes, she also spent more time explaining assignments and their importance. Most students did better after that, but not all. She held another class meeting, and this time students suggested that homework should be graded to provide an additional incentive to get it done. Doing this brought about

---

* Stone-McCown and McCormick emphasize many of these same points.

a further improvement. "The idea of class meetings," Martha Bigelow commented, "was the most important thing I learned this semester. It makes students feel that their opinions are valuable and that they can help solve a problem." Class meetings of this sort implement a principle often ignored: If we want students to develop responsibility, they must have responsibility.

5. Teaching Virtues Through the Curriculum.

Mining the academic curriculum for its moral potential requires teachers to look at their grade-level curriculum and ask, "What are the moral questions and character lessons already present in the subject I teach? How can I make those questions and lessons salient for my students?" A science teacher can design a lesson on the need for precise and truthful reporting of data and how scientific fraud undermines the scientific enterprise. A social studies teacher can examine questions of social justice, actual moral dilemmas faced by historical figures, and current opportunities for civic action to better one's community or country. A literature teacher can have students analyze the moral decisions and moral strengths and weaknesses of characters in novels, plays, and short stories. A mathematics teacher can ask students to research and plot morally significant societal trends (e.g., violent crime, teen pregnancy, homelessness, children living in poverty). All teachers can engage students in the study of men and women who have achieved moral or intellectual distinction in their fields.*

Teaching character through the curriculum also includes making thoughtful use of published character education curricula. The Heartwood Ethics Curriculum for Children (The Heartwood Institute, 1994) uses ancient and contemporary classics in children's literature from around the world to foster seven character qualities: justice, respect, honesty, courage, loyalty, hope, and love. Facing History and Ourselves (Facing History and Ourselves National Foundation, 1994), initially developed for eighth-graders and later adapted to high school and college levels, uses history, film, and guest speakers to study the Holocaust and to ask students to look within themselves to probe the universal human tendency toward prejudice and scapegoating. Choosing to Participate (Stoskopk and Strom, 1990), which grew out of the Facing History curriculum, has students study all the ways people have historically participated, through human service, politics, social activism, and other voluntary activity, in creating a society that seeks justice and dignity for all its members. Students are then encouraged to conceive and to carry out social action projects of their own. *The Art of Loving Well* (The Boston University Loving Well Project, 1993), described by its creators as an "anti-impulse curriculum" for junior high and high school English and health classes, uses an anthology of short stories, poems, essays, and folk tales to help students reflect on romance, love, commitment, and marriage. In a federally funded evaluation that used anonymous self-report questionnaires to survey several thousand students, 92% of those stu-

---

* To a certain degree, this represents the idea of integrated curriculum.

dents who experienced the Art of Loving Well curriculum were still sexually abstinent two years later, compared to 72% of the control group.

6. Cooperative Learning.

Cooperative learning gives students regular practice in developing important social and moral competencies, such as the habit of considering the perspectives of others, the ability to work as part of a team, and the capacity to appreciate others, at the same time that they are learning academic material. Cooperative learning also contributes to the development of a cohesive and caring classroom community by breaking down ethnic, racial, and other social barriers and by integrating every student into the small social structure of the cooperative group.

Cooperative learning, in order to be effective as an academic and character-building strategy, must be designed to include both interdependence and individual accountability.* Every member of the group must be needed, and everyone must independently demonstrate mastery of the material at the conclusion of working together. The format should vary (e.g., learning partners, team testing, jigsaw learning, small-group projects, whole-class projects, etc.). Time should be spent teaching students the skills and roles they need to cooperate effectively. Time must also be spent engaging students in reflecting on how well they cooperated on a given assignment and how they can make needed improvements the next time. The class can develop guidelines that will help prevent problems and provide criteria for reflecting on their efforts. For example, teacher Betty House and her fifth-graders developed the following guidelines: "GROUP MEMBERS CONTRIBUTE THEIR BEST WHEN ... (1) We are kind to each other, (2) There are no put downs, (3) We listen to and try to use everyone's ideas, (4) Everyone has a job to do, (5) No one goofs off, (6) People don't complain, (7) Someone compliments me."

7. The Conscience of Craft.

Our personal character often affects the lives of others through the quality of the work we do. When we do our work well, other people benefit; when we do it poorly, others suffer. One of the most important "voices" of conscience, therefore, is the conscience of craft, the voice that says: "Do a good job." It is a mark of people's character, Syracuse University professor Greene (1985) observes, when they take care to perform their jobs and other tasks well.

A student's schoolwork affords the opportunity to develop this conscience of craft and the work-related qualities of character: (a) self-discipline, including the ability to delay gratification to pursue future goals; (b) persistence in the face of discouragement; (c) dependability, including a public sense of work as affecting the lives of others; (d) diligence; and (e) responsibility (including making the most of one's education). Teachers help students develop these work-related character qualities when they set a good example of responsible work through their own

---

* This should sound familiar.

teaching (e.g., being well prepared and on time, returning student work promptly with appropriate feedback, and giving extra help where needed), combine high expectations and high support, provide a curriculum that engages all learners, and assign regular and meaningful homework.

8. Ethical Reflection.

This strategy focuses on developing the various qualities that constitute the cognitive side of character. Especially important is teaching students what the virtues are, how their habitual practice will lead to a more fulfilling life, and how each of us must take responsibility for developing our own character. For example, the psychologist Cronin (1995) has designed a junior high school curriculum centered on helping students increase their awareness of their own behavior. Students are encouraged to set small daily goals for improvement in their practice of a particular virtue such as respect, cooperation, or generosity (e.g., to give help before it's asked, or to defend someone against negative gossip). At the end of the day, they self-assess and, if they choose, record their progress in a personal journal. This daily goal-setting is considered important for self-awareness and good habit formation.

9. Teaching Conflict Resolution.

Teaching students how to resolve conflicts without force or intimidation is a vitally important part of character education for two reasons: (a) conflicts not settled fairly will prevent or erode a moral community in the classroom; and (b) without conflict resolution skills, students will be morally handicapped in their interpersonal relationships now and later in life and may end up contributing to violence in school and society.

There are a great many ways to teach conflict resolution skills in the classroom. Susan Skinner, a kindergarten teacher at Heathwood Hall Episcopal School in Columbia, South Carolina, uses two methods she finds effective. When two children have a conflict, she stops the action and uses it as a teachable moment. She invites two other children (not the ones involved in the dispute) to come to the front of the class to role-play a positive solution to the conflict. She then asks the whole class for their suggestions. Finally, the two children who were involved in the conflict are invited to act out a positive solution that draws on what they have just seen and heard. These skills have the best chance of becoming part of a child's character when they are learned early and practiced often. But effective training is still possible at the adolescent level, where the stakes are even higher because conflicts may explode into deadly violence.

Schoolwide Strategies in the Comprehensive Approach

1. Caring Beyond the Classroom.

Character education must extend students' caring beyond the classroom into larger and larger spheres. Students can be helped to develop their awareness of the needs of others, their desire to help, and the skills of helping through exposure to altruistic role models and through continuing opportunities for service in their schools and communities. Service opportunities with the potential to develop character are those that involve students in face-to-face helping relationships so that they experience the fulfillment of touching another's life.

An exemplary service learning program can be found at the Stuart Country Day School in Princeton, New Jersey. Sister Joan Magnetti, (cited in Lickona, 1991) headmistress, describes the service opportunities for their high school students:

> Our students read to the blind, work with kids in inner-city neighborhood houses, help in soup kitchens, rebuild houses, and spend two weeks in Appalachia. Many have also interviewed their congressional representatives regarding social issues. Since we believe this kind of education should ideally have an international dimension, we've also sent many students to Bogota. Our goal is to prepare our students for leadership by exposing them to the moral imperatives in the world today. (p. 320)

2. Creating a Positive Moral Culture in the School.

The moral culture of a school is defined by its operative values, ones that are reflected in actual school practices and behavior (e.g., do people respect each other? help each other? pay attention to moral problems in the school environment?). Operative values are true norms: what people expect of everybody else and are willing to help uphold. The school's moral culture is important because it affects moral behavior (a positive moral culture pulls behavior up, whereas a negative culture pulls it down) and because it affects character development (a positive moral culture makes it easier to develop good character).

Creating a positive moral culture in the school involves defining, modeling, teaching, and upholding the school's character expectations in all areas of school life. Part of this effort is mobilizing the peer culture on the side of virtue. One of the most effective ways to do that is participatory school democracy that involves students in sharing responsibility for the moral environment of the school.

For example, in Heath Elementary School, a K–8 school in Brookline, Massachusetts, principal Ethel Sadowsky (1991) instituted a weekly "community meeting" of all the fourth- and fifth-graders, who had just studied the American Constitution. Principal Sadowsky helped students see the parallel between the rules and regulations needed to govern a nation and the need for a fair and effective way of solving conflicts and other problems that arise in a school. She then invited students to place written suggestions for community meeting topics in a large manilla envelope on her office door. Suggestions submitted included saving seats in the lunchroom, cutting into lunch lines, unfair use of playground space, and lack of soap in the bathrooms.

When they held their first meeting, lack of soap in the bathrooms was chosen as the first problem to work on. The large group was divided into small groups, 10 students to a group, each with an adult leader (a teacher, administrator, or student teacher). The adults were to facilitate the problem-solving process: 10 minutes would be used to generate possible solutions, each of which would then be examined in the light of four "guideposts": (a) Is the solution fair to everyone? (b) Is it safe? (c) Is it necessary? (d) Is it workable? The principal gave each adult leader a description of the problem:

> Students complain that there is no soap in the bathrooms. The custodians resist stocking bathrooms with soap because it disappears immediately. They are also unwilling to install soap dispensers because they are quickly broken. How can we, the Heath Community Meeting, help to make sure that if we install soap dispensers, they will be used for washing and not be broken? What problems are likely to arise, and what can we do about them? What are *you* willing to do? (Sadowsky, 1991, p. 99)

In the small-group discussions, the children's imaginations took flight. Proposed solutions included employing a guard to watch the dispensers, installing television monitors, hiring fingerprinters, having the custodians check the dispensers every 5 minutes, putting alarms on the dispensers, and getting a watchdog to patrol the bathrooms. "Fortunately," principal Sadowsky (1991) writes, "a student in each group emerged to point out the pitfalls of such solutions. In the group I led, one student argued persuasively against the fingerprinting idea on both practical and libertarian grounds. She pointed out that it would be very expensive to do all that fingerprinting and that someone might be accused of breaking a dispenser whose fingerprints were on it but who had used it appropriately. The small size of the discussion groups, and using the guideposts to evaluate solutions, helped to elicit thoughtful criticism."

When the small groups came together at the next weeks community meeting, the following consensus was reached: (a) The soap dispensers would be installed; and (b) Heath community meeting members would go in pairs to every classroom, explain the problem about the lack of soap, and describe how the community meeting had met to work out a solution. They would request cooperation from all their schoolmates by saying, "The soap dispensers are for everybody's use, and if they get broken, no one will have them."

A month after the soap dispensers were installed and being used in the intended way, one of them was destroyed. An eighth-grade boy, angry because he had failed a science test, went into the bathroom and punched the dispenser off the wall. A first-grader happened to be in the bathroom at the same time and observed this act. He had listened very carefully to the community meeting partners' presentation in his classroom about how everyone had a responsibility to help make the dispenser solution work. He said to the eighth-grader who broke the dispenser, "You're dead meat." He then came to the office and reported the culprit. The eighth-grader, to his credit, admitted his wrongdoing and agreed to pay for a new dispenser.

The dispensers survived the year. Other problems addressed in a similar way through Heath's community meeting included being rushed at lunch, inequitable access to playground space and equipment, and a lack of a safe place to lock bikes that students rode to school.

Participatory school democracy makes it possible for students to play an active part in creating a positive moral culture in the school. It sends the message: "This is *our* school. If we've got a problem, we should fix it." Giving students real responsibility for real problems develops all three parts of character: moral knowing, because students are engaged in making moral judgments about what's right and fair and in coming up with effective solutions to real-life challenges; moral feeling, because students are helped to care about issues of rights and responsibilities in the school; and moral action, because students are being given opportunities for taking moral action.

3. Recruiting Parents and the Community as Partners in Character Education.*

Three ideas here are key: (a) Parents are a child's first and most important moral teachers, and the school must do everything it can to support parents in this role; (b) Parents must in turn support the school's efforts to develop good character; (c) The impact of the school–parent partnership is enhanced when the wider community (e.g., churches, businesses, youth organizations, local government, and the media) promotes the virtues that make up good character.

Schools can support parents in their role as character educators in several ways. They can tell parents how vital they are in their child's character development. They can help parents understand how character is formed (by what children see, hear, and are repeatedly led to do). They can share what research shows regarding the difference that parents make in children's moral development and what parenting approaches are effective. They should involve parents on the school's character education committee, survey all parents to seek their input, and clearly communicate the school's core values and character education plans to all parents. They can help parents participate directly in the character education of their children through school-based activities (e.g., family film nights) and home-based activities suggested by the school. Home-based activities can be parent initiated (e.g., dinner discussion topics or bedtime stories) or child-initiated (e.g., school assignments where children interview their parents concerning their attitudes about drugs, their views on friendship, what values they were taught growing up, etc.).

One of the areas where cooperation between home and school is crucial is sex education. Currently, sex is the area of young people's lives where they often display the poorest character and the lowest levels of respect, responsibility, and self-control. It is not an exaggeration to suggest that more young people are at risk from premature sexual activity than from any other single threat to their physical, emotional, and spiritual welfare. As a nation, we have one of the highest teen pregnancy rates in the developed world and the highest teen abortion rate (about

---

* You may recognize this as another common feature in the new paradigm.

400,000 a year). One-third of sexually active teen girls are infected with chlamydia (one of the leading causes of infertility) or human papilloma virus (the cause of nearly all cervical cancer).

As a culture, we are gradually emerging from the sexual revolution to recover the wisdom that chastity, or sexual self- control, is part of good character, a virtue that serves the individual and common good. However, many schools, even those committed to educating for character, lack a consistent educational philosophy governing their approach to sex education. In most areas of school life, they are likely to be appropriately directive, guiding students to morally correct conclusions (it's wrong to lie, cheat, steal, be racist, etc.) as character education recommends. But when it comes to sex education, they send a mixed moral message: "Don't have sex, but here's how to do it safely." Schools say they have to teach students how to use contraceptives because many students will have sex no matter how much the school stresses abstinence. But in an area such as drug education, schools would never say, "If you decide to do drugs, here's how to practice safer drug use: Buy your stuff from someone you trust; don't mix drugs and alcohol; and get your clean needles from the school nurse." As a general rule, if the school judges something to be wrong (harmful to self and others) it doesn't teach students how to do it.

Two groups, the Character Education Partnership (1997) and the Medical Institute for Sexual Health (1996), have each recently articulated principles of "character-based sex education" to try to help schools apply character education principles to the sexual domain. Through ethical reasoning, medical evidence, and real-life stories, character-based sex education helps young people come to the conclusion that abstinence is the only medically safe and morally responsible choice for an unmarried teenager.

EVALUATING CHARACTER EDUCATION

As the character education movement gains momentum, questions of evaluation loom larger. In thinking about evaluation, it is helpful to identify three kinds of results schools hope for when they undertake character education:

1. Improvements in student character that can be observed or documented within the school environment.   Schools often begin character education programs because they hope to make the school a better place by effecting a positive change in student attitudes and behavior. Evaluation in this area asks questions such as: Has student attendance gone up? Fights and suspensions gone down? Vandalism declined? Drug incidents diminished? Attitudes toward cheating, and self-reported frequency of cheating, improved? One can assess such before-and-after-the-program differences by keeping records of observable behavior and by anonymous questionnaires that measure student moral judgment (for example, "Is cheating on a test wrong?"), moral commitment ("Would you cheat if you were sure you wouldn't get caught?") and self-reported moral behavior, ("How many times have you cheated on a test in the past year?").

2. Character effects beyond the school environment. This is a measure of generalization. Here evaluation asks: to what extent do students, when they are outside the school, engage in prosocial behaviors such as helping others in need? Stand up for a moral belief? Refrain from antisocial behaviors such as shoplifting? Refrain from high-risk behaviors such as drinking and driving and sexual intercourse? These behaviors outside the school environment, like in-school behaviors, can be assessed through anonymous self-report surveys.

3. Life outcomes after graduation. This is a measure of the school's enduring effects on character. To what extent do graduates become faithful spouses and responsible parents? Law-abiding citizens? Productive and contributing members of their communities? This third area can be assessed only through longitudinal research typically beyond the capacity of schools themselves. Other agencies can and must undertake such evaluations.

What does the available research tell us about the effectiveness of character education? The best of the evaluation research has sought to measure all three facets of character: cognitive, attitudinal, and behavioral outcomes.

For example, Solomon, Watson, Battistich, Schaps, and Delacchi (1992) The Child Development Project in California has conducted a longitudinal experimental study of a character program that combines cooperative learning, teaching empathy through literature, positive role models, developmental discipline, involving students in helping relationships, and parent involvement. By the end of elementary school, students who experienced the program, compared to those who did not:

- showed more spontaneous acts of helping and encouraging their classmates (a measure of the behavioral side of character);
- were better at thinking of prosocial solutions to hypothetical social conflicts (a measure of the cognitive side of character);
- were more committed to democratic values such as the belief that all members of a group have a right to participate in decisions affecting the group (a measure of the emotional or attitudinal side of character).

Recent research also supports the effectiveness of school, family, and community partnerships, as opposed to only school-based efforts, in one of the most challenging areas: changing student attitudes toward and use of drugs and alcohol. Pentz (1989) reports a study of 20,000 sixth- and seventh-graders that compared a well-regarded school-based drug education curriculum with a program that combined the school curriculum with family involvement (students interviewed their parents and role-played refusal skills at home) and community involvement (extensive media support). The more comprehensive approach was significantly superior in slowing early adolescent use of marijuana, cigarettes, and alcohol.

The greatest danger facing character education, as educational researchers Aspy and Aspy (1996) observe, is that severe social problems will be met with only weak educational efforts. When weak efforts fail to ameliorate the problems significantly, people will say, "We tried character education, and it failed." The scale of our character education efforts must therefore be commensurate with the seriousness of the moral problems that confront us. This means that all formative institutions—including families, faith communities, youth organizations, government, and the media—must join with schools to build the character of our young and, ultimately, one hopes, the character of our culture.*

REFERENCES

Aspy, C., & Aspy, D. (1996). The case for a strong values education program in public schools. *Journal of Invitational Theory and Practice, 4,* 7–24.

Boston University Loving Well Project. (1993). *The art of loving well.* Boston: Author.

Character Education Partnership. (1997). *Character-based sex education in the public schools.* Alexandria, VA: Author.

Cronin, P. (1995). *A manual for character education.* Chicago: Metro Achievement Center.

DeMarco, D. (1996). *The heart of virtue.* San Francisco: Ignatius Press.

Dulles, A. R. (1950). Coming home. In J. A. O'Brien (Ed.), *Where I found Christ.* (pp. 63–81). Garden City, NY: Country Life Press.

Facing History and Ourselves National Foundation. (1994). *Facing history and ourselves: The Holocaust and human behavior.* Brookline, MA: Author.

Greene, T. (1985). The formation of conscience in an age of technology, *American Journal of Education, 94,* 1–38.

Hall, R., & Davis, J. (1975). *Moral education in theory and practice.* Buffalo, NY: Prometheus Books.

The Heartwood Institute. (1994). *Heartwood: An ethics curriculum for children.* Pittsburgh, PA: Author.

Isaacs, D. (1976). *Character building: A guide for parents and teachers.* Dublin, Ireland: Four Courts Press.

Kilpatrick, W. (1992). *Why Johnny can't tell right from wrong.* New York: Simon & Schuster.

Kreeft, P., & Tacelli, R. K. (1994). *Handbook of Christian apologetics.* Downers Grove, IL: InterVarsity Press.

Lickona, T. (1991). *Educating for character.* New York: Bantam Books.

McClelland, B. E. (1992). *Schools and the shaping of character: Moral education in America, 1607–present.* Bloomington, IN: ERIC Clearinghouse for Social Studies.

Medical Institute for Sexual Health. (1996). *National guidelines for sexuality and character education.* Austin, TX: Author.

Pentz, M. A. (1989). A multicommunity trial for primary prevention of adolescent drug abuse. *Journal of American Medical Association, 261,* 3259–3266.

Pittman, F. (1992). On character, *Networking* (newsletter), 63.

Raths, L., Harmin, M., & Simon, S. (1966). *Values and teaching.* Columbus, OH: Charles E. Merrill.

Reimer, J., Paolitto, D., & Hersh, R. H. (1979). *Promoting moral growth: From Piaget to Kohlberg.* New York: Longman.

Sadowsky, E. (1991). Democracy in the elementary school. In J. Benninga (Ed.), *Moral, character, and civic education in the elementary school.* (pp. 84–106). New York: Teachers College Press.

Solomon, D., Watson, M., Battistich, V., Schaps, E. & Delacchi, K. (1992). Creating a caring community. Educational practices that promote children's prosocial development. In F. K. Oser, A. Dick, & J. L. Patry (Eds.). *Effective and responsible teaching: The new synthesis.* (pp. 383–396). San Francisco: Jossey-Bass.

Stoskopk, A. L., & M. S. Strom. (1990) *Choosing to participate.* Brookline, MA: Facing History and Ourselves National Foundation.

Von Hildebrand, D. (1948). *Transformation in Christ.* Manchester, NH: Sophia Institute Press.

---

* This idea of collaboration with other institutions concerned with youth is an important aspect of systems thinking and reflects a key marker of the information age.

25 Adolescent Spiritual Development: Stages and Strategies

Joseph Moore
New England Consultants

Joseph Moore

Joseph Moore is the president of New England Consultants in Ministry, Inc., and directs a reintegration program for young offenders in Plymouth County in Massachusetts. He holds a masters degree in religious studies and another in counseling. For thirty years he worked within Roman Catholic parishes and schools as a youth minister, campus minister, and director of adolescent religious education and development. He is the author of fifteen books: included among these are two popular religious education programs for teenagers: *Choice*, published by Paulist Press, and *Connect*, published by Silver Burdett & Ginn.

FOREWORD

Goals and preconditions. The primary goal of this theory is to foster spiritual development. It is intended for use with adolescents.

Values. Some of the values upon which this theory is based include:
- the young person as gradually advancing in perfection in (somewhat artificial) stages,
- fostering spiritual development, especially in adolescents,
- student-centered, psycho-educational methods.

Methods. These are the major methods this theory offers for each of the three stages of spiritual development:

The Purgative Stage

The goal is to cleanse oneself from a false sense of self, particularly from low self-esteem.
1. Use inventories that "measure" self-esteem as a springboard for discussion about self-worth.
2. Hold retreats for adolescents that deal with self-image and nurture a sense of self-worth.
    - Have a talk by an older teen or young adult on their own defense mechanisms or "masks" and the destructive power of the flight from self.
    - Have small-group discussions on their own defenses.
    - Have students verbalize or write concrete affirmative statements about each other.
3. Have students be members of a peer ministry team to help them feel significant in the lives of others.

The Illuminative Stage

The goal is to help adolescents move from self-preoccupation to establishing and nourishing a relationship with God.
1. Impose a regimen of silence and short periods of meditation.
    - Use "fantasy trips" and breathing exercises as preludes to meditation.
    - Use guided meditation until the adolescent is able to meditate on his or her own.
2. Do "scripture sharing" in which a circle of trusting friends read a section of scripture and discuss how it applies in their own lives.
3. Hold a weekend retreat that uses such methods as guided meditation, journal keeping, solitude, scripture sharing, and shared prayer to foster a personal relationship with God.
4. Have an adult mentor or guide assist the adolescent in establishing a personal relationship with God.
    - The adult needs to initiate the mentoring relationship.

The Unitive Stage

The goal is to help adolescents come to feel at one with God and all His living creation.

1. *Provide cultural exposure in groups, entailing direct human interaction with (a) people of a lower income level and/or (b) people having significant differences within the same income level, and have group reflection on the experience.*
2. *Hold a weekend retreat on topics of social justice, using talks, audio-visual material, and small-group discussion.*
3. *Expose adolescents to the broad spectrum of social issues by offering them speakers and films on a variety of topics, being sure to communicate the complexity of issues, not just the point of view we would like them to reach.*

Major contributions. *Holds spiritual development as an important dimension for instructional theory to address. Conceives of stages of spiritual development, each of which requires different methods of instruction.*

Special Comment. This chapter deserves three special comments.

First, spiritual development is conceived here as the gradual advancement of the soul, and as such is distinct from religious education. It is something which all religions seem to address to some extent.* But it can also occur in the absence of any religion. Fostering spiritual development does not require advocacy of any particular religion. And it has nothing to do with religious doctrine or indoctrination.

Second, the inclusion of this chapter in this volume does not in any way imply that spiritual development should be included in public education. Human learning and development of all kinds are fostered in many kinds of settings other than public education, and all the theories in this book can be applied in many different settings. The choice of setting in which to apply a theory is independent of the theory itself. But the belief that religion should not be taught in public schools does not dictate that we should omit from instructional theory any and all guidance for fostering spiritual development, for it might be highly valued in other settings.

Third, most of the existing guidance for fostering spiritual development has come from organized religions. It is natural that experts in such guidance would view it from the perspective of their respective religions. The author of this chapter writes from a Christian perspective, but I hope that the reader will be able to look beyond any trappings of Christianity to see the more universal ideas he offers for fostering spiritual development.

—*C.M.R.*

---

*For an example of stages of spiritual development from a Buddhist perspective, see *Ox Herding at Morgan's Bay*, by Master Sheng-Yen.

Adolescent Spiritual Development: Stages and Strategies

Most religions recognize the concept of spiritual development.[1] For example, in the history of Christianity since the time of the Fathers, it has been common to distinguish three principal degrees in the spiritual life: the purgative, the illuminative, and the unitive. Spiritual writers since earliest Christian times have supported the idea that the soul gradually advances in perfection and that progress in a relationship with the Lord is gradual.* St. Paul declares that adults need stronger food than children, distinguishing between those who are already "spiritual" and those who, though Christian, are "still carnal" (1 Corinthians 3:1-2). Cassian has three degrees: servile fear, mercenary hope, and filial love (Conferences XI, 6-12), and St. Bonaventure speaks of the purgative, illuminative, and perfective in the exercise of meditation. In "Ascent of Mount Carmel," John of the Cross writes about the first night of the senses, which leads to the second night of the spirit, which leads to the third degree of perfect union.**

In today's society,*** it seems that adolescents are encountering greater difficulty than ever in developing spiritually and establishing a relationship with the Lord. So it is that I would like to speak about adolescent spiritual development. I will attempt to ascribe contemporary meaning to the traditional three stages (the purgative, illuminative, and unitive), in the light of modern psychology

---

[1]Since my experience is primarily Christianity, I will draw my examples from it, but the ideas are more universal.

* This idea of gradual advancement of the soul, herein referred to as spiritual development, is very different from the more familiar conception of religious education. An interesting question to ponder is whether separation of church and state requires a separation of spirituality and state. The frequent reference to God by our forefathers in the United States (from the Declaration of Independence to inscriptions on our currency), could indicate that they might not have interpreted it as requiring such separation.

** The concept of a person advancing in spiritual development is perhaps even more pronounced in Far Eastern religions, and an argument could be made that their knowledge of methods to foster spiritual development is more advanced than in Christianity or Islam (see e.g., *Autobiography of a Yogi*, by Paramahansa Yogananda; *Faith in Mind: A Guide to Ch'an Practice*, by Master Sheng-Yen).

*** In the industrial-age society, machines represented an extension of our physical capabilities. In the emerging information-age society, technology represents an extension of our mental capabilities. What might be next? There are some who have proposed that the next major stage of societal evolution will represent an enhancement of our spiritual capabilities, including our ability to see our oneness with God, with all people, and with all of creation. But whether or not that happens, spiritual development may be the most important of all the kinds of human learning and development, yet, it is probably the one to which we devote the least attention.

and research on spiritual development. I will further suggest specific strategies for helping young people to "progress" or move on in their spirituality.

While we recognize the relative artificiality of "stages," I find it helpful to focus on them for the purposes of strategizing youth ministry and planning religious education. Yes, it is true that we all fluctuate between stages of spiritual and emotional growth during our entire lives. We sometimes behave like spiritual or emotional infants and at other times like adults. Most often we are somewhere in the middle. It is certainly true that we cannot confine the spirit of God to neatly defined stages that sound good on paper. But because we do think logically and because there is surely some merit to the concept of advancing gradually in a relationship with God, I offer you the following suggestions for your work with adolescents, regardless of the religion to which you may subscribe.

I think it is helpful to think logically about adolescent spiritual and emotional growth for the purpose of structuring experiences and retreats and planning curricula. It is helpful as long as we proceed with the twinkle in our eye that indicates our awareness that the Spirit can transcend all our neatly defined human categories whenever he wishes. And so let us proceed with a contemporary view of the spiritual stages and concrete suggestions for furthering spiritual growth among youth.

1. THE PURGATIVE STAGE*

Let me begin with a contemporary perspective on the purgative stage, bringing to bear upon our traditional understanding some insights from psychology. To "purge" means literally "to cleanse" and, in a spiritual sense, to cleanse from sin. If we might speak of sin as the failure to be our true selves, the children of God, we can discuss purgation as a getting rid of, a washing away of, our untrue or false selves. In psychology we might use the term "mask" or "facade" to connote an unauthentic or deceitful persona. I would like to think of the "purgative" stage as cleansing oneself from a false sense of self, particularly from low self-esteem.** This perspective comprises the major component of doing spiritual direction with adolescents.

St. Bernard of Clairvaux, in his treatise on "The Love of God," asserts that the first stage in loving God is to develop a healthy self-love, and appreciation of our individual uniqueness in this world. Yet Strommen, in his cross-denominational study of 7,000 teenagers, *The Five Cries of Youth* (Strommen, 1974) points out that low self-esteem is one of the root problems of young people. This phenomenon manifests itself in a variety of ways: distress over school-related relationships, academic problems, and problems with family members and with the opposite sex. I would concur with Strommen that low self-esteem is the basis of so many adolescent

---

* Which of the following ideas are descriptive theory and which are design theory?

** It should not come as a surprise that emotional development and other aspects of psychological development are inextricably interrelated with spiritual development, given the importance of interrelationships that we have seen between the cognitive and affective domains in earlier chapters.

issues, including spiritual ones. There is research to indicate that if a person feels unloved and unworthy, they will also feel that God doesn't care much about them and certainly doesn't answer their prayer (Strommen, 1974).

There is also research to indicate that high schools in this country do not help matters. Researchers polled 28,000 seniors and surveyed them again two years later. In general, self-esteem had improved dramatically (National Center for Education Statistics, 1984). When you are in high school, it and its culture determine what a "successful" person is. Outside of school a young adult feels freer to define himself or herself. In another study of 46,000 young people in grades 6–12, less than half reported that they "feel good about themselves" (Search Institute, 1993). Reflect upon the huge demands that young people so often place on themselves as you read this letter from a suicide victim's parent (The Samaritans).

On a Son's Death

I'm not a writer, I'm a mother. My son, Adam Johnson, my youngest child, whom I loved and treasured, committed suicide two weeks ago. I grieve for his loss and wish he were here so I could tell him. I also feel that there was something more I could have done so that he could be here now and we could benefit from his living.

But he is not, and we are. We are left to transform our lives from his death.

The first step in the transformation is acceptance. We are not always strong and we are not always perfect.

Adam was no exception.

Adam was beautiful, witty, charismatic. His determination helped him to become a fine athlete. But he was also afraid, hungry for affection and recognition, and he was lonely.

His friends, and even those of us in his family, admired the first set of qualities and were, at times, ignorant of his sensitivity. Adam did his best to hide it. He was ashamed of being human, and we must feel partly responsible for this. For all of us have created an environment where strength is greatly admired and vulnerability is judged a limitation. We don't acknowledge it in ourselves and don't see it in others.

Achievements do not fully represent us. How terrible that those of us who are looked up to as examples and guides cannot step down, drop a role, and ask for help, fearing that this step is a fall. By admiring people for their own achievements and seeing only their power, we rarely know and understand them. We may achieve, but achievement fades or passes and we are all left with the tender, suffering core, which we may hide and run from, or choose to expose. And in exposure, we reach our fullest humanity.

—A mother in Minneapolis

James Fowler, in his research on the stages of faith (Durka & Smith, 1986), places most people between ages 12 and 18 in the "synthetical conventional" stage, as he calls it. At this stage the young person is concerned with the interpersonal, and God can be viewed as a friend as one emerges from childhood. This research underscores the centrality of self-esteem to establish relationships in the world. It also offers the spiritual guide a starting place. In Christianity, one can stress the friendship of Jesus and his personal interest in each person. Certain sections of the Gospel can be used effectively to establish this image of Lord as friend: Matthew 6:25-34; Matthew 7:7-11; Matthew 11:28-30; Matthew 12:46-50; Luke 10:38-42; Luke 15:11-32; John 11:1-44; John 14:1-31; John 15:1-17.

Although this stage, according to Fowler, can span the breadth of the teenage years, I believe that it corresponds to what we have called here "the purgative stage," or Stage 1. I believe that adolescents who progress on their spiritual journey can begin to experience Fowler's next stage, called "individuating-reflexive faith." This occurs when an individual internalizes authority and the criteria for determining truth and at the same time accepts affiliation with a group and its ideology. The young person in this stage pays strong attention to personal experience and the experience of peers.

John Westerhoff, in his book, *Will Our Children Have Faith* (1976), considers the adolescent to be in the stage of "affiliative faith" or "religion of the heart." In this stage, belonging to a community is very important in order to fulfill our need to be wanted and accepted. Places of worship, so adult dominated in terms of meaningful roles, face a real challenge in helping young people to have a truly meaningful place in church life. For example, in Christianity we tell young people that at Confirmation they become Christian adults, and yet so often we abandon them in parish or congregational life at that point and fail to assist them in making a significant contribution to the community. One function a spiritual guide of teenagers can fulfill is to work on developing post-Confirmation rules for youth in the parish: a place on the parish/congregation council and parish committees, liturgical functions as well as input in liturgy planning, a challenge to peer ministry as well as to those suffering with the church family.

I agree with Strommen (1974) that at this stage the primary role of the youth minister or spiritual guide is the "ministry of friendship." According to St. Bernard it is impossible to advance in the love of God if one first does not grow to love oneself in some fundamental way (Dwyer, 1980). Thus, it seems to me that in the "purgative" stage we should focus our energies on personal relationships with young people which affirm their worth and values, as well as choosing strategies that develop an affirming community* and foster a positive self-image. Nelson (1984) talks about spiritual guides at this stage as being "midwives," that is, adults who help young people to see their own value and calling.

Strategies for Stage 1

Self-Image Inventories

For group discussion in class or a religious education grouping or for one-to-one conversation, inventories that "measure" high and low self-esteem can be very helpful. It isn't that self-image can be accurately measured, but such devices serve

---

* Again, the idea of community emerges as a method. As you read on, try to see how this conception of community compares and contrasts with the many other conceptions in earlier chapters.

as a good springboard for discussion. For samples of self-image inventories see Moore (1991, 1993a, 1993b).

Self-Growth Retreats*

Some churches have retreat evenings, days, and weekends, which have as their primary concern the building up of the individual and thereby the church community. I believe it is impossible to stress more than one major issue on a retreat. Themes can be interwoven, but I feel retreats are most effective when a focus is carefully chosen and everything on the retreat points to this focus. When several themes are given equal attention, I believe it dilutes the experience and minimizes the impact. And for Stage 1, I am calling for a retreat experience that deals with self-image and does not need to apologize for not being a "sufficiently religious" theme. Standard church rituals can easily be an integral part of such a retreat, but their theme should also be to nurture a sense of self-worth. (In Stages 2 and 3 I will be suggesting different retreats with different goals.)

There is a variety of exercises that enhance self-worth. One place to begin to chip at false senses and low opinions of the self is to talk about defense mechanisms or "masks." Erikson (1968) talks about the fundamental task of adolescence as being to discover one's true self: identity formation. This task, often threatening to the young person, can elicit a number of defense mechanisms. Some suggested by Logan (1978) are: (a) escapes (parties, T.V., etc.); (b) taking on a role (e.g., athlete, scholar); (c) engaging in expressions that reinforce the present state of confusion (e.g., sex, drugs); and (d) adopting a negative identity opposed to adults and authority figures.

A good way to approach this matter on retreat is to have a talk by an older teen or young adult on their own "masks" and the destructive power of the flight from self. The speaker can stress the need to accept one's uniqueness and individuality and to grow in self-esteem. Small-group discussions can follow the talk in which the young people discuss their own defenses.

Also, on self-growth retreats, exercises in which students have to verbalize or write concrete affirmative statements about each other are very helpful. One creative technique is to send positive notes to other retreatants, to say or write one positive adjective about other group members. Positive verbal feedback, especially by the peer group, can offer tremendous healing for a teenager with low self-esteem. We are surely manifestations of the love of God when we build each other up in this fashion.

Peer Ministry

Being a member of a peer ministry team that assists younger teenagers with one-to-one counseling or religious activities (like retreats) can tremendously enhance a young person's sense of self. The feeling of being significant in the life of

---

* As you read through this section, try to identify where this method is being broken into more detailed parts, kinds, or criteria, and look for situationalities.

others is an immeasurable experience. In a short paper summarizing the findings of a project, "Training Youth to Reach Youth," Strommen (1978) reports that for youths trained in peer ministry their own self-esteem increased, their concern over personal faults decreased, and they showed a striking increase in their sense of self-regard.

Although I will discuss prayer more explicitly in Stage 2, let me conclude Stage 1 by remarking that shared prayer in a group can be very helpful for young people in areas previously mentioned:

1. It can teach them a way to grow in a more personal friendship with God.
2. It can help them to realize that their own concerns are also shared by others—that they are not so "strange" after all.
3. It can offer them, if it is an ongoing prayer group, a sense of security and support for building a healthier self-image rooted in faith: faith in oneself, faith in others, and faith in God.

2. THE ILLUMINATIVE STAGE

The second stage, the "illuminative," literally means "filled with light." When an object is illuminated we can see it clearly, as it truly is. In this case the object is ourselves. Once we have dropped our defenses, our low self-image, or our inflated ego, we can begin to perceive ourselves as we are in truth: as God sees us. Another way to speak about the second stage is to say that I perceive myself as lovable because I am loved with the everlasting love of God. In the illuminative stage a person can begin to take the focus off himself or herself and being to look to God. It is the reduction of self-preoccupation that frees a young person to begin to develop a mature relationship with the Lord. As discussed earlier, it is my contention that a teenager must first deal with the self before a significant relationship with God can develop.

In early adolescence a person tends to turn to God to relieve anxiety and to gain a sense of security. In later adolescence the teenager is capable of deeper sharing and deeper intimacy on both the human and "spiritual" planes. Having mustered enough of a positive identity, the young persons have enough inner resources to break out of the constant surrounding of themselves with a group and to "walk up the mountain" alone. While God is certainly present in the group, we also need to encounter Him individually for a personal relationship to flower. In the "synthetic conventional" stage of Fowler, God is thought of as a "friend." A study of young Catholics (Fee, Greeley, McCready, & Sullivan, 1980, Table 3.1, p. 55) indicates that today's youth have very "warm" and immanent images of God and Jesus.

Westerhoff (1976) feels that "provided that the needs of affiliative faith have been met during late adolescence, persons may expand into 'searching' faith" (p. 96). This is when religion of the "head" becomes religion of the heart. This is often accompanied by an exploration of our earlier understanding of our own tradition, and it is during this period of intellectual struggle and experimentation that the young person feels the need for commitment. It is my feeling that a religiously mature teenager, who is a junior or senior in high school, can move in and out of this stage that Westerhoff describes.

Goldman (1964) states that between ages 13 and 17 the experience of God is "felt" by young people (p. 240). And Elkind (1974) remarks that "the search for privacy and the belief in personal uniqueness leads to the establishment of an I-thou relationship with God as personal confidant to whom one no longer looks for gifts but rather for guidance and support" (p. 93). Elkind (1985) has also said that because of new mental abilities, teenagers need a break from institutional religion to be able to have a private conversation with God as a personal friend who won't "squeal." Elkind feels they need this break and that we should allow it. Nelson (1984) would characterize the spiritual director's role at this stage as an "adoption agency," inviting young people to make faith their own.

In a papal document on catechesis Pope John Paul II (1979) asks the following crucial question:

> How are we to reveal Jesus Christ, God made man, to this multitude of children and young people, reveal him not just in the fascination of a first fleeting encounter but through an acquaintance, growing deeper and clearer daily, with him, his message, the plan of God that he has revealed, the call he addresses to each person, and the kingdom that he wishes to establish in this world with the "little flock" of those who believe in him?

This statement is a challenge to all of us in youth ministry and adolescent religious education. How can we as adults help young people to establish and nourish a relationship with, and commitment to, God? Presuming that we have done some groundwork in the psychological realm (the purgative stage), I will suggest some examples of practical steps that we can take in this second stage of spiritual growth.

Strategies for Stage 2

Asceticism

The first strategy I would like to speak of is asceticism, or a sense of discipleship. "Disciple" and "discipline" come from the same root. What young people need first to progress or deepen spiritually is assistance in taking the spotlight off the self and focusing on the Lord. Piveteau (1938) wrote that young people are dulled to the spiritual because our civilization has banished silence. Teenagers are immersed in a world of constant noise. The most noticeable thing about media is the increased fragmentation bombarding the senses: more and more pieces of information packed into shorter and shorter time segments.*

Young people, I believe, need a discipline, a regimen imposed upon them from outside themselves—a regimen of silence and short periods of meditation. They

---

* This is certainly an information-age phenomenon that methods for spiritual development did not have to grapple with in earlier times.

need our help in creating space and a place for a personal conversation with the Lord. They are too self-centered, distracted, immersed in noise, and fragmented to do this on their own—at least at the outset. Eventually they will need to develop their own inner discipline, but not at first. We need to create prayer times when we meet them in groups, not just where prayer is verbally shared, but also where silence is observed so that, like Elijah, they might come to know that God speaks not in a crashing noise but in a gentle whisper—and that to hear that whisper an inner stillness is absolutely essential.

As preludes to meditation, "fantasy trips," where a leader takes people on an inner journey of their mind, can be of real help. I would emphasize here that these fantasy trips are preliminary to contemplation and serve the function of teaching inner stillness and the possibility of inner adventure. Also, breathing exercises and other exercises often used in stress reduction can be helpful preliminaries to meditation and contemplation.

Adolescence is not too soon to teach the difference between meditation (which involves cognition and focusing on a Gospel story or image of God) and contemplation, which involves the senses and a passivity of God's voice where the intellect is "stilled." A Quaker meeting is a great field trip for teenagers to observe a group of people in the practice of contemplation. As for teaching meditation, a leader who guides a young person (or a group of youths) through a fantasy trip or reflection upon a Gospel story is helpful in teaching the technique of meditation. "Guided meditation" may be necessary for some time before an adolescent is able to meditate on his or her own. A discussion about the images of God a young person holds can help meditation. Phillips' book, *Your God is Too Small* (1971), although quite dated, is still relevant today.

Bible Sharing

A second strategy for "advancing" into the illuminative stage is Bible sharing. Sharing the Scriptures, as opposed to Bible study, involves developing a circle of trusting friends who can read a section of Scripture and then verbalize how they see a practical application between God's word and their own lives, both personally and collectively. This sharing on a spiritual level can do much to help a person of any age grow in a deeper understanding of God. For teens, the use of Scripture is particularly helpful because it is so concrete, something for them to "sink their teeth" into. A study of 508 teenagers from the Princeton Religion Research Center (1984) concludes that only one in eight Christian teenagers reads the Bible daily. Thirty percent of those interviewed say that they have never even opened a Bible. And so we have much work to do in helping youth grow in a thirst and love of the word of God.

Retreat

A third strategy is to have a retreat that focuses specifically on a relationship with the Lord. This type of weekend would have time for guided meditation, journal keeping, solitude, Bible sharing, shared prayer, penance, and Eucharist. The talks and exercises revolve around a personal relationship with the Lord. For example, in the "Jesus Circle" exercise, retreatants locate themselves in relationship to Jesus, the center, and label all the inner circles as obstacles that separate us from him.

Journal keeping, where a young person records his or her own thoughts and feelings about God as well as the movements of the Spirit within them, can be a helpful form of reflection both on a retreat and on a daily basis. Like a regular time for prayer, the habit of journal keeping aids young people in the asceticism needed for deepening their friendship with the Lord. Journal keeping also helps us to recognize patterns (both good and bad) in our personal lives.

Spiritual Direction and Modeling

Last, I would like to discuss spiritual direction and modeling as additional strategies at this stage. It is helpful for teenagers to have an adult mentor or guide assist them into this journey of a personal relationship with God. Most teenagers will not seek out spiritual direction on their own, and so my suggestion is that the structure be provided to them. A spiritual direction program can be offered in a Catholic high school through the religion department or perhaps in conjunction with an elective course on prayer. In parishes this might be achieved by giving the sponsor a meaningful role in preparation for confirmation. Spiritual direction for adolescents will also involve some basic psychological counseling. But it is also a real opportunity to teach a young person how to pray Scripture, how to keep a journal, how to set aside time for daily prayer, and how to practice meditation and contemplation. A spiritual guide can help a young person move from the "gimme God" mentality of immature prayer to an understanding of prayer as communication in a relationship.

The modeling provided by a spiritual director is just as significant as anything he or she might say. Who God is for you, what He means in your real life, and how you speak about and act out of your own faith will have a very positive impact upon the adolescents with whom you are working. Brother Roger of Taize remarks

> Or how can we create a prayer open to all? Often a single individual who dares to remain alone in a church, for a long time if necessary, becomes by his or her perseverance a living call to seek God.... A single person is enough. (Schutz, 1979, p. 27)

To conclude this discussion of the illuminative stage, I wish to make it clear that, although we may be able to provide countless opportunities for adolescents to get to know God better, they may choose not to move into a deeper relationship with Him. We may offer them prayer courses, teach them how to meditate, and take them on a retreat, but we simply cannot manipulate them into a conversion or movement away from self-preoccupation. Groome (quoted in Hutchinson, 1984) writes:

> Coming to know God, for people of any age, is a process that has more to do with questions than with answers. We need to honor the "no's" of young people capable of making moral decisions. Consider the "no" of the rich young man. Jesus didn't argue with

him or insist that he was making a mistake. He honored the young man's decision even though it saddened him. (p. 22)

3. THE UNITIVE STAGE

The third stage, the unitive, connotes that we experience ourselves "united": at one with the living God, at one with all of his living creation. Rather than being restricted to flashes of feeling at peak moments in life, the word "stage" implies that this "at-one-ment" is a sustained perspective.

In some way the surrender of the control of one's existence seems to me to be necessary for a complete entry into this spiritual level. As Jesus said to Peter:

> I tell you most solemnly,
> when you were young
> you put on your own belt
> and walked where you liked;
> but when you grow old
> you will stretch out your hands
> and somebody else will put a belt around you
> and take you where you would rather not go. (John 21:18)

It is the paradox that in being vulnerable we become strong. It is the "wounded healer" concept of which Nouewen (1979) writes so poignantly when he says that our mutual confession "and sharing of weakness becomes a reminder to one and all of the coming strength" (p. 94).

For adolescents, life is experienced as an adventure of which they are in charge. They are planning careers, colleges, lifestyles, and other dimensions of their own futures as if they possessed total control over their existence. The exception to this would be a middle class teenager whose life has been dealt a heavy blow over which he or she has had no control: the death of a parent, the divorce of a parent, the experience of a serious illness. Another exception might be an urban teenager who grows up in an environment where violence and traumatic loss are commonplace. But even teens who undergo serious tragic events still have not accumulated sufficient life experience to teach them the lesson of spiritual surrender. So in some sense an adolescent is simply not able to enter the unitive stage. But I would like us, for our purposes of strategizing opportunities of youth spiritual development, to look at the unitive stage in a limited but fresh sense connected to a more global world view.

Fowler suggests that in later adolescence and early adulthood the "individual reflexive" stage of faith becomes characteristic. At this point the individual begins to assume responsibility for his or her own commitment, lifestyle, and beliefs. It is also characterized by a broader world view. As a corollary to Fowler's thesis, I would also suggest that in later adolescence, after the self-identity issues have been dealt with to some degree, a young person is capable of growth in empathy and in, the emotional arousal that leads one person to help another person. Being aware of their own gifts (as enumerated by St. Paul in 1 Corinthians 12), adolescents are capable of being deeply moved to exercise their giftedness for the benefit of another. But youth need spiritual direction and encouragement to feel their connectedness to all their brothers and sisters on the earth. They need personal experiences and encounters that will knock down their barriers of bias and a narcissistic nationalism. Particularly middle and upper middle class youth need to move out of their "suburban hothouses" to take the pain of the disenfranchised, the suffering, and the poor.

For those of us in youth ministry, this presents a great challenge to our creativity and energies. Strommen (1979) reports that one in five teenagers is prejudiced and leads an unreflective life. They see themselves as more conservative than their parents in terms of race relations. They are not moved when minorities are mistreated; money is a high value for them, viewing it as a means to acquire what they want for themselves. One can only speculate how much this selfishness has escalated since Strommen re-did his research in the mid 1980s! In their research on the differing goals for Christian education/youth ministry in various denominations, the staff of the Boys Town Center for the Study of Youth Development found that social justice is a low priority for Roman Catholic parents and educators (Hoge & Petrillo, 1982). And yet the document, "A Vision of Youth Ministry," published by the United States Catholic Conference (U.S.C.C.) Department of Education over 20 years ago (1976), states that "justice and service" is one of the seven essential components of youth ministry. This critique, delivered by Warren (1994) to the national convention of the TEC ("Teenagers Encounter Christ") retreat movement, speaks eloquently to this issue:

> I have been concerned about the vision or portrait of Jesus being presented in many different programs for middle-class youth. This Jesus tends to be a middle-class Jesus, representing the dominant concerns of the moderately well-off and privileged. The dominant concern of the middle class tends to be greater comfort, and thus the middle-class Jesus is presented as the one who comforts. Overlooked is the Jesus who not only comforts but who also confronts and challenges, Jesus the upsetter. The middle-class Jesus is not the "Man For Others"; the middle-class Jesus is the Man *for us*. If there is any challenge of accepting him as a sign of God's love for us. Obviously it is essential to understand Jesus as God-with-us and as God's special gift to us. Accepting Jesus as God's love embodied is an important first step on the road to discipleship. Yet, to go no further is to remain with a middle-class and, ultimately, false image of Jesus. The gospels remind us in many ways that Jesus offers us not so much the Jesus-Hug, as a call for ourselves to embrace the poor and the weak and those who do not fit. In the gospels, Jesus continually calls attention, not to himself, but to the social situations that needed to be changed and to the people who suffered in these social situations, the poor. (p. 94)

I am continuing the thesis that we can help young people move somewhat progressively into a deeper level of spirituality. The first order of business is to deal with the self, discussed in the purgative stage. The second challenge is to foster a personal relationship with God, discussed in the illuminative stage. The third and final challenge for those of us who structure and strategize youth ministry and adolescent religious education is to see the face of the Lord in the suffering of humanity, discussed in the unitive stage. It is this third stage that perhaps has been paid the least attention in the past and that summons all Christians to loving action for the world. Again, though the stages are somewhat artificial concepts, and we are all constantly dealing with self, God, and others throughout a Christian lifetime. It nonetheless seems helpful to me to structure the emphasis of our religious education ministry with youth. And so we will now move to a discussion of some of the possible structures that will help teenagers to think globally while acting locally.

Strategies for Stage 3

This stage is the most challenging in terms of developing strategies for the spiritual development of young people. This is partly due to the advanced nature of Stage 3 and partly because, up until recently, very little attention has been paid to developing a global consciousness among youth.

Cultural Exposure

Probably the most effective strategy is what I will call "cultural exposure." By this I mean a person is exposed to a culture other than his or her own by direct human interaction. In most cases this means introducing middle-class youth to people of a lower socioeconomic level. Serving lunch at a soup kitchen, tutoring in the inner city, or going to Haiti or Central America with college students to minister for a week are all examples of cultural exposure. Another form of cultural exposure is to connect people within the same income level who have significant differences, e.g., the mentally retarded, the elderly, or the physically challenged who are ministered to by teenagers as part of, for example, a Christian service course of a Confirmation project. This direct human contact has real impact on young people who are already extremely impressionable. The formation of a relationship through ministry will be embedded in the consciousness of the adolescent for years to come. My suggestions for this strategy are the following:

1. That direct human interaction be considered the essential component of any "education service" class or project. (Babysitting a neighbor's child free of charge is certainly generous of a teenager but should not be placed in the category of "cultural exposure.")
2. That "cultural exposure" be experienced in community, i.e., that it be an experience not in isolation but with other teenagers and adult leaders who can help the young person reflect on the experience. Reflection is so important.*

---

* You may have recognized this as a common feature in many instructional theories in the new paradigm: direct experience followed by reflection. It is what I refer to as the action-reaction-reflection cycle.

Teenagers are easily overwhelmed by the poverty or suffering of others and feel extremely helpless and anxious. Reflection in community can help them put the experience into some sort of psychologically meaningful perspective. A group project for a week in Appalachia with a few adult leaders is a good example of service in community with the opportunity for reflection.

Retreat

A second strategy, which could be meaningfully developed as it has been for Stages 1 and 2, is the retreat weekend format. Personal talks could be given by teenagers and adults on such topics as peace, discrimination, sexism, and poverty. Sharing groups could discuss the talks and create strategies to deal in concrete ways with some of the issues raised. There is an increasing supply of audiovisual material emerging from various publishers in the area of social justice. Prayer services and other rites could revolve around the themes of the retreat.

Speakers and Films

A third suggestion or strategy is to expose young people to the broad spectrum of social issues by offering them speakers and films on a variety of topics. Although less direct than cultural exposure, speakers, films, and other media offer the opportunity to provide teenagers with the proper data and information they need to make moral choices on issues of justice. Sometimes we downplay the cognitive in this area of social justice and fail to explain the complexity of various issues in order to manipulate the point of view we ourselves would like young people to reach. But this is certainly a disservice to them. All the research on moral education indicates that young people need to have all the facts and then to wrestle with the various alternatives if they are ever to arrive at moral maturity.* This is true in matters of "personal" morality, and it is true in the realm of moral judgments regarding social issues.

SUGGESTIONS FOR PUBLIC SCHOOLS
AND AGENCIES

Public schools and agencies certainly contribute to the spiritual development and growth of young people. Any group activities that foster self-esteem, the experience of community, and responsibility for the world, are implicitly spiritual. The absence of mentioning the connection between a community-building activity, for example, and faith doesn't mean that faith is not being nourished. Homework assignments, classroom activities, outreach projects, community service, peer helping, negotiation-skills training, and much much more can all foster the development of a teenager's spirituality. Parents, too, by their love and affirmation

---

* Lickona expressed a similar view in chapter 24.

of young people, by their modeling and teaching of moral values, and by demanding participation in and celebration of family life as well as the human family, are sharing in the spiritual development we have been discussing here.

REFERENCES

Durka, G., & Smith, J. (1986). *Emerging issues in religious education* (pp. 187–208). New York: Paulist Press.

Dwyer, V. (1980, April). *The spiritual dimension of the educator.* Order of Cistercians of the Strict Observance O.S.C.O. address at the National Catholic Education Association N.C.E.A. Convention, New Orleans, LA.

Elkind, D. (1974). *Children and adolescents.* New York: Oxford University Press.

Elkind, D. (1985, March). *Teenagers in Crisis,* lecture delivered at St. Joseph College, West Hartford, CT.

Erikson, E. (1968). *Identity, youth and crisis.* New York: Norton.

Fee, G. D., Greeley, A., McCready, & Sullivan. (1980).*Young catholics.* New York: Sadlier.

Goldman, R. (1964). *Religious thinking from childhood to adolescence.* London: Rutledge.

Hoge, D., & Petrillo, M. P. (1982). Desired outcomes of religious education and youth ministry in six denominations. In Wych & Richter (Eds.), *Religious education ministry with youth.* (chap. 5). Birmingham, AL: Religious Education Press.

Hutchinson, G. (1984, September). Shared Christian praxis. *Religion Teachers Journal.*

John Paul II. (1979). Conference. Washington, DC.

Logan, R. (1978). Identity diffusion and psycho-social defense mechanisms.*Adolescence,* 13, 503–507.

Moore, J. (1991). *Personal growth* [minicourse, session 3]. Morristown, NJ: Silver, Burdette, & Ginn.

Moore, J. (1993a). *Confirmation journal* [minicourse, session 14]. Mahwah, NJ: Paulist Press.

Moore, J. (1993b). Friend for the journey [youth ed.]. Cincinnati: St. Anthony Messenger Press.

National Center for Education Statistics. (1984, February). Self-esteem rises after high school. *Group,* p. 17.

Nelson, J. (1984, March 31). Religious devotion among youth. Presentation delivered at St. Joseph College, Hartford, CT.

Nouewen, H. J. M. (1979). *The wounded healer.* New York: Image Books.

Phillips, J. B. (1971). *Your God is too small.* New York: Macmillan.

Piveteau, D. (1938). Youth, atheism and catechesis. *Lumen Vitae,* 38, 427.

Princeton Religion Research Center. (1984, April). Study Title Here, *Goosecorn,* 4.

The Samaritans. *On a son's death.* (Speech available from the Samaritans, 500 Commonwealth Ave., Kenmore Square, Boston, MA 02215)

Schutz, R. (1979, May). "*Fête et Saisons.*"

Search Institute. (1993). *The troubled journey.* Minneapolis, MN: Author.

Strommen, M. (1974) . *The five cries of youth* (chap. 2). New York: Harper and Row.

Strommen, M. (1978, July 22). *A futuristic approach to youth ministry.* Presentation delivered at the New England Conference on Youth Ministry, Stonehill College.

Strommen, M. (1979). *Cry of the prejudiced.* (chap. 5). New York: Harper and Row.

U.S.C.C. Department of Education. (1976). *A vision of youth ministry.* Washington, DC.

Warren, M. (1984). New stage in weekend retreat for teenagers. *Origins,* 14(6), 94.

Westerhoff, J. (1976). *Will our children have faith?* (pp. 94–96). New York: Seabury Press.

Unit 5 Reflections and Future Research

Foreword

Chapter 1 emphasizes the differences between descriptive theory and design theory. The improvement of descriptive theories revolves around validity, whereas the improvement of design theories revolves around preferability—which methods are better than the alternatives, given your goals, conditions, and values. One of the consequences of this difference is that different kinds of research methodologies are required for improving each of these two kinds of theory. Most of the research methodologies developed to date were designed to advance descriptive theory. The first chapter in this unit (chap. 26), addresses this problem by describing a kind of action research or developmental research that seems to hold promise for advancing design theory. It is my hope that this chapter will raise awareness of the need for, and will stimulate the development of, additional methodologies for advancing design theory, by researchers and practitioners alike. Many theorists in this book seem to have used similar theory-development methodologies, and I am particularly excited by the Corno and Randi approach (chap. 13).

The remaining chapter in this unit (chap. 27), provides some reflections on the collection of theories in this volume. It should be helpful for gaining a broader perspective of the "forest" that contains these individual theories (the "trees").

—C.M.R.

26

Formative Research: A Methodology for Creating and Improving Design Theories

Charles M. Reigeluth
Theodore W. Frick
Indiana University

In chapter 1, Reigeluth described design theory as being different from descriptive theory in that it offers means to achieve goals. For an applied field like education, design theory is more useful and more easily applied than its descriptive counterpart, learning theory. But none of the 21 theories described in this book has yet been developed to a state of perfection; at the very least, they can all benefit from more detailed guidance for applying their methods to diverse situations. And more theories are sorely needed to provide guidance for additional kinds of learning and human development and for different kinds of situations, including the use of new information technologies as tools. This leads us to the important question, "What research methods are most helpful for creating and improving instructional-design theories?" In this chapter, we offer a detailed description of one research methodology that holds promise for generating the kind of knowledge that we believe is most useful to educators—a methodology that several theorists in this book have intuitively used to develop their theories.

We refer to this methodology as "formative research," a kind of developmental research or action research that is intended to improve design theory for designing instructional practices or processes. Reigeluth (1989) and Romiszowski (personal communications, April, 1988) have recommended this approach to expand the knowledge base in instructional-design theory. Newman (1990) has suggested something similar for research on the organizational impact of computers in schools. And Greeno, Collins, and Resnick (1996) have identified several groups of researchers who are conducting something similar that they call "design experiments," in which "researchers and practitioners, particularly teachers, collaborate in the design, implementation, and analysis of changes in practice." (p. 15) Formative research has also been used for generating knowledge in as broad an area as systemic change in education (Carr, 1993; Naugle, 1996).

We intend for this chapter to help guide educational researchers who are developing and refining instructional-design theories. Most researchers have not had the opportunity to learn formal research methodologies for developing design theories. Doctoral programs in universities tend to emphasize quantitative and qualitative research methodologies for creating descriptive knowledge of education. However, design theories are guidelines for practice, which tell us "how to do" education, not "what is."

We have found that traditional quantitative research methods (e.g., experiments, surveys, correlational analyses) are not particularly useful for improving instructional-design theory, especially in the early stages of development. Instead, we have drawn from formative evaluation and case-study research methodologies in the development of formative research methods. Researchers familiar with these qualitative methods should recognize them. However, they should keep in mind that the purpose is different here, and hence we must consider additional methodological concerns.

We first discuss three criteria for evaluating research that aims to create generalizable design knowledge: effectiveness, efficiency, and appeal. Then we provide a detailed description of the formative research methodology, including designed cases, in vivo naturalistic cases, and post facto naturalistic cases. Finally, we address methodological issues of construct validity, data collection and analysis procedures, and generalizability to a design theory.

CRITERIA FOR EVALUATING RESEARCH
ON GENERALIZABLE DESIGN KNOWLEDGE

In research on descriptive theory, the major methodological concern is validity: how well the description matches the reality of "what is." In contrast, for a design theory (or a guideline, model, etc.), the major concern is *preferability*: the extent to which a method is better than other known methods for attaining the desired outcome. But what is "better"? What constitutes preferability? As discussed in chapter 1, the criteria you use depend on your values, or more appropriately, they should depend on the values of all those who have a stake in the application of the design theory. Those values array themselves on at least three dimensions: effectiveness, efficiency, and appeal (cf. Frick & Reigeluth, 1992; Reigeluth, Volume 1, 1983). Each of these is discussed next.

Effectiveness.   Often the most important aspect of effectiveness is the extent or degree to which the application of the theory (or guideline or method) attained the goal in a given situation. This is usually measured on a numerical scale in either a norm-based or a criterion-based manner (cf. Mager, 1984). Another aspect is the dependability with which it attained the goal over repeated trials. Dependability is measured by looking at probabilities. Analysis of patterns in time (APT) is a useful methodology for examining multiple cases and estimating probabilities (Frick, 1983; 1990). A third aspect is the breadth of contexts (or situations) in which it attains the goal. Different methods are often preferable for different situations, and, indeed, it is the provision of different methods for different situations that raises the design knowledge above the level of a method or model to that of a design theory.

Efficiency.   This has to do with "bang for the buck," which includes two elements: a measure of the "bang" (effectiveness) and a measure of the "buck" (cost, either in money or time, or some other cost, or a combination of costs). For instructional-design theory, we must consider human time, effort, and energy required, as well as the cost of further resources needed, such as materials, equipment, or other requirements of the setting needed for instruction.

Appeal.   This is an issue of how enjoyable the resulting designs are for all people associated with them. For instructional-design theory, this includes teachers and students, support personnel, and perhaps even administrators and parents. Appeal is independent from effectiveness and efficiency.

These three criteria—effectiveness, efficiency, and appeal—may be valued differently in different situations, because stakeholders' wants and needs are likely to differ. Therefore, all three criteria should be manifest in the research design for generating design knowledge. We need to look at how a particular design theory holds up on all three dimensions when continuing to refine it, and perhaps even generate different variations within the theory for different value weightings on the three criteria. For example, certain methods may be preferable when efficiency matters little compared with effectiveness, whereas other methods may be preferable when efficiency (e.g., low cost or short instructional time) is more important than effectiveness.

Finally, it should be patent that the development and testing of design theories is not a one-trial endeavor. It is a matter of successive approximation. Such theories continue to be improved and refined over many iterations. The Montessori system of education is a good example (Montessori, 1964; 1965). An educational-design theory can be useful early in its life, once initially substantiated as having instrumental value, and then continue to be refined and modified over many generations of educators who apply it.

Given these criteria for evaluating a research methodology for creating design theory, which include the preeminence of preferability over validity, how can one conduct research that addresses these criteria? The remainder of this chapter is devoted to offering some guidance for using the formative research methodology, based on about a dozen studies that have used variations of this methodology.

FORMATIVE RESEARCH

Formative evaluation (sometimes called field testing or usability testing) is a methodology for improving instructional resources and curricula (Bloom, Hastings, & Madaus, 1971; Cronbach, 1963; Scriven, 1967; Thiagarajan, Semmel, & Semmel, 1974). It entails asking such questions as "What is working?", "What needs to be improved?", and "How can it be improved?" (Worthen & Sanders, 1987, p. 36). Using it as the basis for a developmental or "action" research methodology for improving instructional-design theories is a natural evolution from its use to improve particular instructional systems. It is also useful to develop and test design theory on other aspects of education, including curriculum development, counseling, administration, finance, and governance.

The underlying logic of formative research as discussed by Reigeluth (1989) is that, if you create an accurate application of an instructional-design theory (or model), then any weaknesses that are found in the application may reflect weaknesses in the theory, and any improvements identified for the application may reflect ways to improve the theory, at least for some subset of the situations for which the theory was intended. There are notable similarities to the logic of experimental design, in which one creates an instance of each parameter of an independent variable, one collects data on the instances, and one generalizes back to the independent-variable concepts. Replication with diverse students, content, and settings is necessary in both cases. However, for formative research the guiding questions are, "What methods worked well?" "What did not work well?" and "What improvements can be made to the theory?"

In the formative research methodology, an instance (or application) of a theory is created or identified. The design instance is based as exclusively as possible on the guidelines from that theory. For example, for an instructional-design theory, a course might be developed based solely on that theory, using as little intuition as possible. The application (the course in this case) is then formatively evaluated using one-to-one, small-group, and/or field-trial formative evaluation techniques (Dick & Carey, 1990; Thiagarajan, Semmel, & Semmel, 1974). The data are analyzed for ways to improve the course, and generalizations are hypothesized for improving the theory.

Formative research has been used to improve existing instructional-design theories and models, including the elaboration theory (English, 1992; Kim, 1994), a theory to facilitate understanding (Roma, 1990; Simmons, 1991), a theory to foster awareness of ethical issues (Clonts, 1993), a theory for designing instruction for teams (Armstrong, 1993), and a theory for the design of computer-based simulations (Shon, 1996). It has also been used to improve instructional systems development (ISD) models, such as Keller's (1987) process for the motivational design of instruction (Farmer, 1989). Furthermore, it has been used to improve educational systems design (ESD) models for school systems engaging in systemic change (Carr, 1993; Khan, 1994; Naugle, 1996). The methodology has proven valuable for identifying ways to improve these theories and models, and it could also be used to improve theories and models in virtually all fields of education.

METHODOLOGICAL PROCEDURES
IN FORMATIVE RESEARCH

Formative research follows a case study approach as outlined by Yin (1984). Specifically, the design is typically a holistic single case: one application of the theory. The study is exploratory in nature because there is "no clear, single set of outcomes" (Yin, 1984, p. 25). Yin believes that a single case study is appropriate when "a how or why question [has been] asked about a contemporary set of events" (p. 20), which includes how to improve a design theory. This type of methodology lends itself well to researcher-teacher collaboration.

Specifics of the research methodology vary depending on the kind of formative research study. Over the past 7 years, we have gradually refined several methodologies for formative research, through the conduct of a dozen studies (Armstrong, 1993: Carr, 1993; Clonts, 1993; English, 1992; Farmer, 1989; Khan, 1994; Kim, 1994; Naugle, 1996; Roma, 1990; Shon, 1996; Simmons, 1991; Wang, 1992).

Case studies can be classified as designed cases or naturalistic cases, depending on whether the situation under investigation is manipulated in any way by the researcher. Formative research is a *designed case* if the researcher instantiates the theory (or model) and then formatively evaluates the instantiation. Alternatively, it is a *naturalistic case* if the researcher (a) picks an instance (or case) that was not specifically designed according to the theory but serves the same goals and contexts as the theory, (b) analyzes the instance to see in what ways it is consistent with the theory, what guidelines it fails to implement, and what valuable elements it has that are not present in the theory, and (c) formatively evaluates that instance to identify how each consistent element might be improved, whether each absent element might represent an improvement in the instance, and whether removing the elements unique to the instance might be detrimental. Furthermore, for naturalistic cases, the methodology varies depending on whether the observation is done during or after the practical application. This makes three major types of formative research studies:

- *designed cases,* in which the theory is intentionally instantiated (usually by the researcher) for the research;
- *in vivo naturalistic cases,* in which the formative evaluation of the instantiation is done during its application, and;
- *post facto naturalistic cases,* in which the formative evaluation of the instantiation is done after its application.

Within each of these three types, the methodology also varies depending on whether the study is intended to develop a new design theory (one that does not yet exist) or to improve an existing theory. Table 26.1 shows these variations.

TABLE 26.1

Kinds of Formative Research Studies

	For an Existing Theory	*For a New Theory*
Designed Case	Designed case for an existing theory	Designed case for a new theory
In Vivo Naturalistic Case	In vivo naturalistic case for an existing theory	In vivo naturalistic case for a new theory
Post Facto Naturalistic Case	Post facto naturalistic case for an existing theory	Post facto naturalistic case for a new theory

For a designed case to improve an existing theory, the methodological concerns center within the following process:

1. Select a design theory.
2. Design an instance of the theory.
3. Collect and analyze formative data on the instance.
4. Revise the instance.
5. Repeat the data collection and revision cycle.
6. Offer tentative revisions for the theory.

For a designed case to develop a new theory, the process changes a bit:

1. (Not applicable.)
2. Create a case to help you generate the design theory.
3. (Same as for an existing theory.)
4. (Same as for an existing theory.)
5. (Same as for an existing theory.)
6. Fully develop your tentative theory.

For both in vivo and post facto naturalistic studies, the process is still different:

1. (Same as for a designed case, for either a new or existing theory.)
2. Select a case.
3. Collect and analyze formative data on the case.
4. (Not applicable.)
5. (Not applicable.)
6. (Same as for a designed case, for either a new or existing theory.)

Next is a description of each of these kinds of formative research, beginning with the most common one, a designed case to improve an existing theory.

Designed Case to Improve an Existing Theory

While there is often much variation from one such case study to another, the following is a fairly typical process for conducting this type of formative research study.

1. Select a design theory.

You begin by selecting an existing design theory (or model) that you want to improve.

> For example, Robert English, a teacher at a university in Indiana, selected the elaboration theory of instruction (Reigeluth & Stein, 1983) for his dissertation study (English, 1992).

2. Design an instance of the theory.

Then you select a situation that fits within the general class of situations to which that design theory (or model) applies, and you design a specific application of the design theory (called a "design instance"). This instance may be a product or a process, or most likely both. It is important that the design instance be as pure an instance of the design theory as possible, avoiding both of the two types of weaknesses (omission: not faithfully including an element of the theory; and commission: including an element that is not called for by the theory). This is an issue of construct validity, and its counterpart in experimental design is ensuring that each of the treatments is a faithful representation of its corresponding independent-variable concept.

The design of the instance can be done either by the researcher (as participant) or by an expert in the theory (with the researcher as observer), preferably with the help of a subject-matter expert (usually the teacher for the course used in the instance). In either event, it is wise to get one or more additional experts in the theory to review the instance and ensure that it is a faithful instance of the theory. If you find yourself or the expert in the theory having to make decisions about which the theory offers no guidance, make special note of all such occurrences, as areas of guidance that should be added to the design theory later. It is also wise to get one, or preferably several, additional subject-matter experts to review the instance for content accuracy.

> For example, Robert English picked a basic college course on electricity that he was regularly teaching. He took four chapters from the textbook for the course and resequenced them according to the elaboration theory. Then he had one of the authors of the theory (Reigeluth) review the sequence for validity of representing the elaboration theory's guidelines.

3. Collect and analyze formative data on the instance.

Next, you begin data collection by conducting a formative evaluation of the design instance (see, e.g., Dick & Carey, 1990). The intent is to identify and remove problems in the instance, particularly in the methods prescribed by the theory. In some situations, design and implementation of the instance occur simultaneously, in which case the data are collected during the design process (or alternatively, design occurs during the data collection process). In other situations, design and development of an instance are completed before implementation begins, in which case data collection comes as a separate phase of activity. In still other situations, you can do a combination: some small-scale testing of parts as you design the instance, then larger scale testing of the whole when it is completed.

> In the case of English's study of the elaboration theory, design and development were completed before the implementation began, because it is hard to test a macro-level sequence before its design is completed.

First, you should prepare the participants, so that they will be more open in providing you with the data you need. This can be done by explaining that you are testing a new method, that you want them to be highly critical of it, and that any problems encountered will be due to weaknesses in the method, not to deficiencies in themselves. Try to establish rapport with them, and in one-to-one formative evaluations, try to get them to think aloud during the process (in this case, the instructional process).

> For example, Robert English explained to the students that a new course design was being used and that they were being asked for their reactions to it. He told them that any mistakes they made or any misunderstandings encountered would be due to deficiencies in the course rather than to their learning ability. Before instruction actually began, he established rapport with the learners to increase their comfort level enough to interact and make frank comments, and he encouraged them to be as critical as possible. He also asked the students to think aloud and to make notes on the material while proceeding.

Three techniques are useful for collecting the formative data: observations, documents, and interviews. *Observations* allow you to verify the presence of elements of the design theory and to see surface reactions of the participants to the elements. *Documents* on both elements (methods of instruction, in this case) and outcomes can help you to make judgments about the value of elements of the theory. For example, test results can help you to gauge how much learning occurred and what types of learning occurred. Newspaper reports of effects on the community can provide new insights about the value of certain elements or triangulation for elements on which you already have some outcome data, assuming the effects reported in the newspaper reflect the criteria you have established for assessing preferability, as discussed earlier.

But usually the most useful data come from *interviews* with the participants. Both individual and group interviews, or interactions, allow you to probe the reactions and thinking of the participants (such as teachers and students). They help you to identify strengths and weaknesses in the design instance, but they also allow you to explore improvements for elements in the design instance, to explore the likely consequences of removing elements from, or adding new elements to, the instance, and to explore possible situationalities (ways that methods should vary for different situations, such as kinds of learning, learners, learning environments, and development constraints for research on instructional-design theories). Although such data, as conjecture from the participants, are always suspect, they can also be highly insightful and useful. At a minimum they will likely provide some hypotheses worthy of testing with subsequent participants and situations. Interviews can be done during or after the implementation of the instance, or both.

Interactions with the participants *during* the implementation of the design instance should be guided by a set of questions that progress from very open-ended ones to very targeted ones. These questions should be tailored to the design theory under investigation and should strive to collect data about how to improve the specific guidelines in the theory, including adding new guidelines that may better attain the goals targeted by the theory. Therefore, for instructional-design theory, the questions should focus on identifying particular aspects of the implementation of the design instance that helped or hindered learning and finding ways to improve weak elements. The questions should be used flexibly and responsively, as they are prompted by such cues as facial expressions (e.g., a quizzical look) and used at break points in the implementation of the instance. If participants experience difficulties with certain elements of the instance, it is usually wise to help them overcome those difficulties before they proceed, so that future data will not be tainted by earlier weaknesses in the instance.

A different set of open-ended questions should be used *after* the implementation of the design instance. They should ask the participants such things as what they did and did not like about the various elements of the instance, what helped them, what did not help them, whether they felt that the materials and activities were appropriate for their needs, what changes they would make if they could, and whether they felt they attained the objectives. The purpose of the debriefing questions is to give the participants an opportunity to reflect on and evaluate the implementation of the design instance as a whole, to point out any strengths and weaknesses not mentioned before, and to make any additional comments. They should be strongly encouraged to point out weaknesses. Reliability or consistency across participants should be assessed so the point of saturation can be determined.

One additional point is worth mentioning here. Participants sometimes forget details about the design instance, and they have to be reminded where a particular element came in the overall process. Once shown, they usually have a lot to say. We suggest, then, after the first open-ended questions, to have the participants trace back through the process to specifically recall their impressions. It can be particularly helpful to show the participant a videotape of the process.

Usually, the most useful data come from one-on-one interviews with participants during the implementation of the design instance, because you avoid the memory-loss problem of interviews after the fact and you can overcome problems that might jeopardize data collection in the remainder of the implementation.

But interviews during the implementation have less external validity because of their intrusiveness. As in formative evaluation, we recommend starting with the richer but less valid data-collection technique (one-on-one interviews during the implementation of the design instance) and moving to progressively less rich but more representative techniques (small-group and field trials with interviews afterwards) to confirm the richer findings. It is usually helpful to record the interviews. And, in the more authentic trials for which the interviews are conducted afterwards, it is often helpful to video-record the implementation of the design instance and have the participant comment about it while viewing the tape. Also, "member checking" (Guba & Lincoln, 1981) should be done with each participant as soon as possible after the information is recorded. One technique for member checking is to show each participant a typed summary of the information he or she contributed and discuss its accuracy.

> English used all three techniques, but concentrated on interviews with students. He used the one-to-one interviews to explore ways to help each student with difficult content, and he recorded all comments made. There were two phases in his study: an "interactive" data-collection phase, which entailed interacting with each student during the instructional process, and a "noninteractive" data collection phase, which entailed interacting with each student (different students from Phase 1) only in a debriefing session after the instruction. Phase 1 data were richer, and Phase 2 data were used to check the validity of the results from Phase 1.

The data collection should always focus on how to improve the design theory. We have found it beneficial to focus on what should not be changed (strengths), as well as what should be changed (weaknesses). Wherever weaknesses are found, it is, of course, important to get the learners' (or users') suggestions for ways to overcome those weaknesses, or at the very least their reactions to any ideas you have about how to overcome each weakness. Several iterations of data collection are strongly advised (equivalent to increasing the number of subjects in an experimental study), to assess dependability of results. In these iterations, it is wise to systematically vary the situation (types of people and conditions) as much as you can, within the limits of the class of situations for which the theory is intended. This enables you to identify situationalities (different methods for different contextual conditions) and enhances external validity (generalizability).

> English's data included strengths, weaknesses, and suggestions for improvement to the theory. Also, English interviewed a total of 10 students in Phase 1 before reaching saturation, and three students in Phase 2. The students in each phase were evenly distributed across the intelligence spectrum.

Data analysis should be conducted during the data-collection process, if possible, to identify consistency of data across students. Of major concern is identifying the principal strengths and weaknesses in the instruction and what improvements could be made to the theory. Data analysis involves three activities: data reduction, data display, and conclusion drawing (Miles & Huberman, 1984). Data reduction is "selecting, focusing, simplifying, abstracting, and transforming the 'raw' data ... " (Miles & Huberman, 1984, p. 21). The analytical procedure outlined by Miles and Huberman (1984) focuses on categorizing the data by the types of observations made during the implementation of the design instance or the types of answers to questions during debriefing. Summary information could be placed in a series of matrices (such as those developed by Roma, 1990) which specify relevant situational characteristics (e.g., the students, content, and context) and array categories of data (e.g., elements of the theory) across them. Each cell would then represent either a positive/negative or yes/no response, depending on the nature of the data. Specific recommendations for improvement could be keyed to each weakness identified in the matrix and described in detail apart from the matrix. Many of the matrix categories cannot be determined prior to the study, as the majority of questions are open-ended.

One potential problem with open-ended questions is that many of the cells you end up with in the matrices may not be filled, because some students might not offer any data on some categories. This would make it difficult to draw adequate conclusions for all categories across types of situations (e.g., students, content, and contexts). One way to eliminate this problem is to use a combination of both open-ended and directed questions during data collection. This mixture could contribute information about specific aspects of the design instance from all participants and would, therefore, increase the number of filled cells. But it would be impossible to predict all categories of information, so we do not recommend the use of *only* directed questions. Our suggestion is to start with open-ended questions, and then use directed questions for certain important issues you know of in advance of the study or that emerge very early during data collection.

4. Revise the instance.

Next, you make revisions in the instance of the design theory, based on the data you collected. These revisions do not have to wait until you finish all the data collection and analysis. If you make the revisions as soon as you feel fairly confident in their value, then you can use them in your remaining data collection, perhaps even showing both versions of the design instance to the same student for comparative evaluation. You should also take note of the nature of the revisions, for they represent hypotheses as to ways in which the design theory itself might be improved.

5. Repeat the data collection and revision cycle.

Several additional rounds of data collection, analysis, and revision are recommended, again systematically varying the situation (people and conditions) as much as you can from round to round, within the boundaries of the theory. This is a way of confirming the earlier findings, and it enhances external validity (generalizability), which is so essential for justifying changes in the design theory itself. During this process, you are likely to find that a method that works very well for some situations may not work as well as an alternative method for other situations.

Such "situationalities" are important discoveries in a research effort to improve a design theory and better meet the needs of practitioners.

6. Offer tentative revisions for the theory.

Finally, you should use your findings to hypothesize an improved design theory. Naturally, your suggestions will not become "knowledge" until they have been more thoroughly replicated and validated. Additional formative research studies will provide the needed replication, but experimental studies are a form of research well suited to validation (or refutation!).

Designed Case to Develop a New Theory

This kind of formative research differs from the previous one primarily in that you do not start with an existing design theory. This means that you must skip Step 1 above entirely. Second, you must greatly modify Step 2 so as to design the best case (counterpart to an instance of a design theory), without a design theory for guidance. The purpose of this is to be able to use a concrete case from which to build grounded design theory, based largely on experience and intuition. Several of the theories in this book seem to have been developed using the basics of this kind of approach (e.g., Corno & Randi, chap. 13; Nelson, chap. 11; Perkins & Unger, chap. 5; Pogrow, chap. 14; Schwartz, Lin, Brophy, & Bransford, chap. 9), though the use of this approach would naturally have been intuitive rather than explicit. Steps 3, 4, and 5 remain virtually unchanged, but step 6 must now be a process of inductively developing a new design theory, rather than modifying an existing theory. The new steps 2 and 6 are as follows.

2. Create a case to help you generate the design theory.

You begin by selecting a situation that fits within the general class of situations to which you want your new design theory (or model) to apply. Then you design the best case you can for that situation, using experience, intuition, and trial and error, often in combination with knowledge of related descriptive, scientific knowledge of education. This case may, of course, be a product and its implementation, or a process, or most likely both. The case must be created by the person who will be developing the design theory, because intimate familiarity with the case is essential for developing good grounded theory. As you develop the case, you should develop a tentative design theory in parallel. For each element you decide to include in your case, you should generate guidelines for selection and use of that element and incorporate them into your theory, so that your case will become an instance of the theory.

6. Fully develop your tentative theory.

Finally, you should use your findings to revise and elaborate your tentative design theory. It is unlikely you will have been able to test your theory for the full range of situations for which the theory is intended, so there will likely be holes and other inadequacies in the theory. You should try to identify and describe all such inadequacies when you offer your theory to the public. And you should offer a research agenda that identifies the types of developmental studies you think would help most to further develop the theory.

Naturalistic Formative Research Studies

A naturalistic formative research study differs from a designed study in that you (the researcher) do not create a design instance or case. It is a naturalistic (in the general sense of the term) form of research, in that you observe a case that someone else has created. The case could be one that you study throughout its occurrence, which we call an *in vivo* naturalistic study, or it could be one that you study after the fact, which is called a *post facto* study. The major difference between post facto and in vivo studies is that observation is not possible in post facto studies (except perhaps through video segments), and interviews are more difficult to arrange and less likely to yield accurate and complete data, due to the passage of time. In either event, if it is a purely naturalistic study, there is no opportunity to revise the case based on your data (step 4 above) nor to try out the revision (step 5). A naturalistic case can be used either to improve an existing design theory or to create a new one (that doesn't exist yet). Here are the details for conducting a naturalistic study.

1. *(Same as for a designed case, for either a new or existing theory.)*

2. *Select a case.*

Instead of creating an instance (for research on an existing theory) or case (for research to develop a new design theory), you select a case that is about to begin (for an in vivo study) or a case that has been completed (for a post facto study). For research on either an existing or a new theory, the case should be in a situation that fits within the general class of situations to which the theory applies. This case may be a product or a process, or most likely a combination of the two. For testing an existing theory, it is helpful for the case to be as close as possible to being an instance of the theory; i.e., it will contain many of the elements that are called for by the theory. And it is wise to get one or more experts in the theory to observe the case to identify what elements are faithful instances of elements of the theory.

3. *Collect and analyze formative data on the case.*

Next, you collect and analyze formative data on the case. For research on an existing theory, there are three major kinds of data you want to collect, based on the presence and absence of elements in the theory and in the case. One is for elements that are present in both the theory and the case. You should identify the strengths, weaknesses, and possible improvements for elements of the theory that were used in the case. Can those elements be improved in the case (and, by inference, in the theory)? Another is for elements that are present in the theory but absent in the case.

You should identify the consequences of the case not using specific elements of the theory. Should those elements have been used? The third is for elements that are absent in the theory but present in the case. You should identify the strengths, weaknesses, and possible improvements for elements in the case that are not in the theory, including situationalities as well as methods. Should those elements be added to the theory? For research to develop a new theory, only this third kind of data is relevant. You need to rely heavily on your intuition, experience, and knowledge of relevant descriptive theory to develop hypotheses as to what might generalize from this case and how far it might generalize, including situationalities.

These three kinds of data can be collected through the three techniques discussed earlier: observations, interviews, and documents. Observations help you to judge which elements of the theory are present in the case and which are missing, as well as to see surface reactions of the participants to those elements. However, for *post facto* studies, observation will likely only be possible if video tapes were made of the case. Interviews (both individual and group) allow you to probe the reactions and thinking of the participants and to explore improvements for the case. Although these are difficult for post facto studies, it is usually possible to find and interview some people who were involved in the case. Finally, documents on both methods and outcomes can help you to make judgments about the value of elements of the theory.

As with the designed cases described earlier, the data collection should always focus on how to improve the case, even though you cannot actually make any such improvements to it. This entails identifying strengths, so that you know what not to change, as well as identifying weaknesses, for which you should look for specific improvements. Several replications of data collection are strongly advised (equivalent to increasing the number of subjects in an experimental study), to assess reliability of results. Again, we recommend the technique of saturation. Also, by varying contextual factors in each round, you can look for situationalities and breadth of generalizability.

Steps 4 and 5 are not applicable, and Step 6 is the same as for a designed case study, for either a new or existing theory.

Examples of post facto formative research include Khan (1994) and Wang (1992). Furthermore, Collins and Stevens' (Volume I, 1983) cognitive theory of inquiry teaching is an example of a design theory developed through post facto naturalistic formative research. Collins and Stevens obtained transcripts of a variety of "interactive" teachers—ones who used "some form of the case, inquiry, discovery, or Socratic method" (p. 250). And they "abstract[ed] common elements of those teachers' teaching strategies, and ... show[ed] how these can be extended to different domains" (p. 250).

These cases outlined above do not represent all the possible kinds of formative research methodologies, and they belie the fact that these are not mutually exclusive nor "hard and fast" categories. In fact, many formative research studies have elements of more than one of these kinds. Also, there is room for wide variation within each category. But there are methodological issues they all have in common, as well as some that are unique to each.

METHODOLOGICAL ISSUES FOR FORMATIVE RESEARCH

Case studies have been criticized in the past for their lack of rigor. However, this concern can be addressed by attending to three classes of methodological issues: (a) construct validity, (b) sound data collection and analysis procedures, and (c) attention to generalizability to the theory.

Construct Validity

Construct validity is concerned with "establishing correct operational measures for the concepts being studied" (Yin, 1984, p. 37). The concepts of interest in formative research are the methods offered by the design theory, any *situations* that influence the use of those methods, and the indicators of strengths and weaknesses (criteria for outcomes). The operationalization of the methods and analysis of relevant situations should be done by an expert in the theory, and preferably reviewed by one or two other experts in the theory, to assure their construct validity. As was mentioned under step 2 above, there are two ways in which construct validity can be weakened: omission (not faithfully including an element of the theory) and comission (including an element that is not called for by the theory).

The indicators of strengths and weaknesses should include the effectiveness, efficiency, and appeal of the methods, as discussed earlier. The indicators of effectiveness should be developed by an expert in measurement for the particular goals of the design instance or case, and reviewed by another. The indicators of efficiency should be developed by someone who is expert in measuring time and expense for both designing and using the methods, and those indicators should be reviewed by another expert. The indicators of appeal should be developed by an expert in motivational measurement and reviewed by another.

Sound Data Collection and Analysis Procedures

The soundness of the data collection and analysis procedures is influenced by two major factors: the thoroughness or completeness of the data and the credibility or accuracy of the data. These two factors overlap to some degree, but it is helpful to think of them as two separate issues (cf., Rubin, 1994, on usability engineering).

Thoroughness of the data can be enhanced through a number of techniques, including advance preparation of participants, an emergent data-collection process, gradually decreasing obtrusivity, iteration until saturation, and identification of strengths as well as weaknesses.

First, participants often require *advance preparation* because they may have difficulty critiquing the design instance or case. For example, students tend to blame their learning problems on themselves rather than on their instruction. And even if they see problems with the instruction, students are often hesitant to criticize it in the presence of one who may have some ego investment in it. Therefore, it is important—before the implementation of the design instance or case begins—to prepare the participants to be critical. Furthermore, establishing rapport with the participants will tend to make them more open to sharing all their reactions.

Second, because you have little idea as to what weaknesses and areas of improvement you may find in the theory, it is important that your data-collection process be *emergent*, that your quest for data be flexible and responsive to your findings, starting with open-ended probes (e.g., questions, observations, documents) and gradually becoming more targeted in response to promising leads.

Third, it is helpful to start with fairly obtrusive probes (that interrupt the implementation of the design instantiation) in your early rounds of data collection (e.g., with your first students in one-to-one interactions) and gradually become *less obtrusive* to confirm the earlier findings under conditions that have greater external validity (with later students).

Fourth, it is generally wise to continue the rounds (or iterations) of obtrusive probes until you have reached the point of *saturation* (where new rounds of data collection merely confirm prior findings and yield no new findings); (cf. Merriam, 1988).

Finally, to be thorough, you should be sure to collect information about the *strengths* as well as the weaknesses of the design instance or case, and about what should not be changed as well as what should.

Credibility of the data can also be enhanced through a variety of techniques, including triangulation (Lincoln & Guba, 1985), chain of evidence, member checks (Guba & Lincoln, 1981), and clarification of the researcher's assumptions, biases, and theoretical orientation (Merriam, 1988).

First, *triangulation* entails using multiple sources of evidence (data) and cross-validating each source against the other sources. In a formative research study, the multiple sources of evidence are, first of all, multiple participants (e.g., students). Data should be collected in additional rounds (iterations) with different participants until considerable consistency of results (saturation) is obtained across participants. (This is a clear point of overlap with the thoroughness of the data.) And multiple sources of evidence should be collected for each participant (e.g., observations of a student during learning, interviews with the student, and the student's productions—tests, papers, project reports). We recommend that some objective measures be utilized for evaluating the design instance or case, to get some sense of the general acceptability of the outcomes (e.g., pre- and posttests for measuring the effectiveness of instruction, and similarly objective measures for efficiency and appeal).

Second, all data-collection procedures should be clearly and precisely documented to establish a *chain of evidence*, and, as Yin suggests, the study should be performed as if someone is looking over the shoulder of the investigator.

Third, *member checks* usually entail taking data and interpretations back to the participants. Through further dialogue with participants, errors or misconceptions by the researcher can be corrected, interpretations clarified, and emphases modified.

Finally, clarification of the *researcher's assumptions*, biases, and theoretical orientation should be done early in the research report, and every attempt should be made to make these views explicit.

Attention to Generalizability to the Theory

Finally, rigor in formative research is increased by enhancing ways that the results can be generalized to the theory. There are two major tools for doing this: recognizing situationality and replicating the study.

Situationality can be explored in at least two ways: (a) Whenever you find different results in different rounds (iterations), look for differences in the situation (e.g., for a study on instructional design, the nature of the learner, of what is being learned, of the learning environment, and of the development constraints). (b) Purposely vary elements of the situation in your rounds of data collection to see if the results differ. These findings can allow you to hypothesize situationalities for the theory you are testing. When situationalities are incorporated into the theory, the theory becomes useful for a broader range of situations. At a very minimum, your research report should describe as completely as possible the situations under which the theory was applied in your study, so that others may draw conclusions about situationalities.

Replication is necessary to confirm the findings of any formative research study. With sufficient replications, hypotheses about improvements to the design theory gain sufficient evidence to warrant changes in the theory. Naturally, the replications should systematically vary all situational elements that may cause different methods to be preferable.

CONCLUDING REMARKS

Educational practitioners often find it difficult to utilize the kind of theoretical knowledge that is typically created by educational researchers. It is our observation that most educational research has resulted in descriptive knowledge. If this were true in each of the physical sciences, we would have primarily research in, say, physics or biology, with little research in mechanical engineering or medical practice.

Most of this chapter was devoted to describing various formative research methodologies for improving design theories, with our particular experience primarily in the area of instructional-design theories. Specifically, we described two methodologies for designed case studies: one for improving existing theories and one for developing new theories. And we described two methodologies for naturalistic case studies: one for in vivo studies and one for post facto studies, both of which can be used either for improving existing theories or developing new theories. These methodologies are based on knowledge gained from a dozen formative research studies that have been conducted over the past eight years.

It is our contention that to improve educational practice we need more—and better quality—research on design theory. It is our hope that this chapter and volume will encourage more educational researchers to team with practitioners in conducting formative research, for this type of work shows great promise for advancing design theory that can better meet educators' needs and enhance our ability to reverse the status quo in which "The history of educational reform is one of consistent failure of major reforms to survive and become institutionalized" (Pogrow, 1996, p. 657).

It is not a simple matter to overcome the apparent biases towards descriptive knowledge of education to the exclusion of other types. Therefore, we also hope this chapter will encourage more foundations and agencies to fund this type of research and more professional journals to accept this kind of research for publication, for those organizations have great influence over the kinds of studies that researchers conduct.

REFERENCES

Armstrong, R. B. (1993). *The Team Instructional Prescriptions (TIP) Theory: A set of integrated models for prescribing instructional strategies for teams.* Unpublished dissertation, Indiana University Graduate School, Bloomington, IN.

Bloom, B., Hastings, T., & Madaus, G. (1971). *Handbook on formative and summative evaluation of student learning.* New York: McGraw-Hill.

Carr, A. A. (1993). *Selecting community participants for systemic educational restructuring: Who should serve?* Unpublished dissertation, Indiana University Graduate School, Bloomington, IN.

Clonts, J. (1993). *Formative evaluation of an instructional theory for increasing awareness of ethical issues.* Unpublished dissertation, Indiana University Graduate School, Bloomington, IN.

Collins, A. (1992). Toward a design science of education. In E. Scanlon & T. O'Shea (Eds.), *New directions in educational technology* (pp. 15–22). Berlin: Springer-Verlag.

Collins, A., & Stevens, A. L. (1983). A cognitive theory of inquiry teaching. In C. M. Reigeluth (Ed.), *Instructional-design theories and models: An overview of their current status* (pp. 247–278). Hillsdale, NJ: Lawrence Erlbaum Associates.

Cronbach, L. (1963). Evaluation for course improvement. *Teachers College Record, 64,* 672–683.

Dick, W., & Carey, L. (1990). *The systematic design of instruction.* Glenview, IL: Scott, Foresman.

English, R. (1992). *Formative research on the elaboration theory of instruction.* Unpublished dissertation, Indiana University Graduate School, Bloomington, IN. See also English, R. E., & Reigeluth, C. M. (1996). Formative research on sequencing instruction with the elaboration theory. *Educational Technology Research & Development, 44*(1), 23–42.

Farmer, T. (1989). *A refinement of the ARCS motivational design procedure using a formative evaluation methodology.* Unpublished dissertation, Indiana University Graduate School, Bloomington, IN.

Frick, T. W. (1983). *Non-metric temporal path analysis: An alternative to the linear models approach for verification of stochastic educational relations.* Unpublished doctoral dissertation, Indiana University Graduate School, Bloomington, IN.

Frick, T. W. (1990). Analysis of patterns in time: A method of recording and quantifying temporal relations in education. *American Educational Research Journal, 27,* 180–204.

Frick, T. W., & Reigeluth, C. M. (1992, February). *Verifying instructional theory by analysis of patterns in time.* Paper presented at the annual conference of the American Educational Research Association, San Francisco, CA.

Greeno, J. G., Collins, A., & Resnick, L. B. (1996). Cognition and learning. In D. C. Berliner & R. C. Calfee (Eds.), *Handbook of Educational Psychology* (pp. 15–46). New York: Macmillan.

Guba, E. G., & Lincoln, Y. S. (1981). *Effective evaluation.* San Francisco, CA: Jossey-Bass.

Keller, J. M. (1987, November). The systematic process of motivational design. *Performance & Instruction, 26*, 1–8.

Khan, B. (1994). *Post facto formative research on the educational systems design (ESD) process.* Unpublished dissertation, Indiana University Graduate School, Bloomington, IN.

Kim, Y. (1994). *Formative research on the Simplifying Conditions Method for task analysis and sequencing of instructional content.* Unpublished dissertation, Indiana University Graduate School, Bloomington, IN.

Lincoln, Y. S., & Guba, E. G. (1985). *Naturalistic inquiry.* Newbury Park, CA: Sage Publications.

Mager, R. (1984). *Measuring instructional results.* Belmont, CA: Lake Publishing.

Merriam, S. B. (1988). *Case study research in education: A qualitative approach.* San Francisco, CA: Jossey-Bass.

Miles, M. B., & Huberman, A. M. (1984). *Analyzing qualitative data: A source book for new methods.* Beverly Hills, CA: Sage Publications.

Montessori, M. (1964). *The Montessori method.* New York: Schocken Books.

Montessori, M. (1965). *Spontaneous activity in education.* New York: Schocken Books.

Naugle, L. (1996). *Formative research of the Reigeluth process model and an effort to initiate school restructuring.* Unpublished dissertation, Indiana University Graduate School, Bloomington, IN.

Newman, D. (1990). Opportunities for research on the organizational impact of school computers. *Educational Researcher, 19*(3), 8–13.

Pogrow, S. (1996). Reforming the wannabe reformers: Why education reforms almost always end up making things worse. *Phi Delta Kappan, 77*, 656–663.

Reigeluth, C. M. (1983). Instructional design: What is it and why is it? In C. M. Reigeluth (Ed.), *Instructional-design theories and models: An overview of their current status* (pp. 3–36). Hillsdale, NJ: Lawrence Erlbaum Associates.

Reigeluth, C. M. (1989). Educational technology at the crossroads: New mind sets and new directions. *Educational Technology Research & Development, 37*(1), 67–80.

Reigeluth, C. M., & Stein, F. S. (1983). The Elaboration Theory of Instruction. In C. M. Reigeluth (Ed.), *Instructional-design theories and models: An overview of their current status* (pp. 335–382). Hillsdale, NJ: Lawrence Erlbaum Associates.

Roma, C. (1990). *Formative evaluation research on an instructional theory for understanding.* Unpublished dissertation, Indiana University Graduate School, Bloomington, IN.

Rubin, J. (1994). *Handbook of usability testing: How to plan, design, and conduct effective tests.* New York: Wiley.

Scriven, M. (1967). The methodology of evaluation. *In AERA Monograph Series on Curriculum Evaluation, No. 1* (pp. 39–89). Chicago: Rand McNally.

Shon, M. (1996). *Formative research on an instructional theory for the design of computer-based simulations for teaching causal principles.* Unpublished dissertation, Indiana University Graduate School, Bloomington, IN.

Simmons, J. (1991). *Formative evaluation research on an instructional theory for teaching causal principles.* Unpublished dissertation, Indiana University Graduate School, Bloomington, IN.

Thiagarajan, S., Semmel, M. I., & Semmel, D. S. (1974). *Instructional development for training teachers of exceptional children: A sourcebook.* Minneapolis, MN: Leadership Training Institute/Special Education, University of Minnesota.

Wang, S. W. (1992). *The process for creating and maintaining a Montessori public educational system in an urban community.* Unpublished dissertation, Indiana University Graduate School, Bloomington, IN.

Worthen, B., & Sanders, J. (1987). *Educational evaluation: Alternative approaches and practical guidelines.* New York: Longman.

Yin, R. K. (1984). *Case study research design and methods.* Beverly Hills, CA: Sage Publications.

27 Current Progress, Historical Perspective, and Some Tasks for the Future of Instructional Theory

Glenn E. Snelbecker
Temple University, Philadelphia, PA

This volume offers a sampling of currently available instructional theories and describes the nature of the respective theories and features that may be important for anyone who wants to conduct research or use instructional theories in a practical situation. As in chapter 2 and elsewhere (e.g., Snelbecker, 1985), I use the term *instructional theories* instead of instructional-design theories and models. I prefer instructional theories because it is important to distinguish between the kinds of instruction that we are trying to design (reflecting instructional theories) and processes by which we design and develop instruction (especially reflecting design and development activities and views or theories). In Volume 1 (Snelbecker, 1983a), I suggested several groups of people who are somehow involved with instructional theory, and noted that they have divergent as well as common interests. I use the term *knowledge producer* to refer to theorists and researchers, and the term *knowledge user* to refer to instructional designers and instructors. I identify those groups again here as a reminder that we need to recognize ways in which people may differ in their expectations about and reactions to instructional theories.

There are three main sections in this chapter. In the first, I offer some observations about the respective unit groups and various instructional theories described in this volume. In the second section, I suggest that in order to understand the current work as well as to identify potential future paths in the construction and use of instructional theory we should consider earlier theories and research, not only work in recent decades but also work completed earlier in this century. This section

653

includes a comparison of Volume 2 theories with those presented in Volume 1. In the third section, I identify two sets of challenges and tasks that can facilitate improved construction and use of instructional theory, briefly identified here by these keywords: *taxonomy*, and *technology*.

INSTRUCTIONAL THEORIES: CURRENT PROGRESS

What can be said about this collection of instructional theories? I first make some general comments about the theories in this volume; then, I comment on the respective units in the course of addressing the individual theory chapters.

Some Observations About This Collection of Instructional Theories

This is an impressive array of contemporary instructional-design theories and models. Collectively, they illustrate both common features and diverse views prevalent concerning instructional theory and the potential practical application of our evolving knowledge about designing instruction. They also reflect trends of a more general nature (i.e., beyond instructional theory) discussed in both "education" and "training" contexts. These trends include the following:

- Contemporary emphases on cognitive processes.
- Growing recognition about the role of affect in education and training.
- Questions about how we can effectively conceptualize and address learners' individual characteristics.
- Comparatively little apparent concern about potential impact of relevant differences among instructors and about instructional delivery system characteristics.
- Awareness about the potential impact of sociocultural characteristics on the process and outcomes of instruction.
- General agreement about the desirability of improving the effectiveness of instruction but contrasting views about how this can be done.

There are two general suggestions to consider while reading these theory chapters, whether the reader is an instructor who wants to apply ideas from one or more theories, an instructional designer, a researcher, or an individual developing an instructional theory. First, while reading these chapters it is important to realize that the respective authors were limited by space in the extent to which they could describe their views about instructional theory. Thus, the current chapters can be thought of as "samplers" or executive summaries about work in progress, and their bibliographies can be used to obtain further details about the respective theories.

The second suggestion is an extension from my comments in chapter 2. In chapter 2, I proposed that, whether we elect to draw ideas mainly from one theoretical perspective or from several, we should be aware of various available instructional theories as well as of the features of any given theory. Thus, when reading a particular theory chapter it is suggested the reader consider at least two aspects: (a) how the particular theory fits in the overall array of instructional theories now available, and (b) what "added value" can be derived from the particular theory. The key features and the "added value" generated by each theory are highlighted in the foreword section at the beginning of each theory chapter in this volume. Thus, when commenting on the theories, I focus on ways that each theory contributes to the overall array of instructional theories by drawing attention to (a) some "ideas" and (b) some "issues" that are important not only for that particular theory but also for the ongoing development of instructional theories.

Observations About Units and Individual Theories

Although cognitive theories were represented in Volume 1, it is quite clear, especially here in Unit 2, that instructional theory today is considerably less influenced by behavioral theory than had been the case earlier. Instead, heavy emphasis on cognitive processes, in one manner or another, seems to be typical of the current trend in the development of instructional theories. However, it seems important here to suggest that we might be missing some valuable ideas if we totally dismiss some of the conceptual foundations and the practical ideas that have been, and are being, based on behavioral theories. Although chapter 19 (this volume) displays some concern with behavioral processes, it seems evident that readers who want to utilize behavioral theories will need to consult Volume 1 and other sources.

In chapter 4, Gardner partly reflects the author's ideas about multiple intelligences, but the author also offers a number of additional ideas in this chapter. In the context of a century of debates about "how many" kinds of intelligence exist (e.g., only or mainly a general factor vs. more specific factors), Gardner not only advocates recognition of multiple intelligences, but also contends that these "multiple intelligences" provide a basis for addressing curricular matters as well as instructional methods. This raises a number of issues for the instructional theory community to consider, such as: Should all instructional theories include designation of particular curriculum topics? Does Gardner identify the particular instructional outcomes and goals that more instructional theorists should address? Should we expect a given instructional theory to be relevant only for certain curricular goals? Or, might there be "multiple" goals for respective instructional theories, and "multiple" instructional theories for respective curricular goals?

Chapter 5, "Teaching and Learning for Understanding," by Perkins and Unger, makes a strong case for facilitating students' "understanding," and they report results of their efforts to identify practical implications of their theory. Perkins and Unger offer a number of practical ideas about how students' understanding can be facilitated, and suggest reasons why their methods should "work." However, they acknowledge that "understanding" may be less of a central concern with some forms of instruction and learning than with others. Their approach raises a number of issues, such as: Does the fact that an individual "understands something" mean that he or she *will* be able to use it? If the person does not demonstrate learning, does that mean he or she does not "understand" it? How does an instructor know when to facilitate understanding, and when to focus on other kinds of learning?

In chapter 6, Hannafin, Land, and Oliver indicate that "open-endedness" can refer to the learning goals—means through which learning goals are pursued or taught, or both learning goals and means. A number of related concepts, components, and methods are described and illustrated. These authors contend that student-centered learning and learner-centered design have been and are growing, and suggest that teachers need to know how to provide open learning environments. Among the questions posed by this approach are: How can teachers be "prepared" to address the challenges of open-ended possibilities? What kinds of in-service preparation plus classroom-based resources may be needed to support this kind of approach? Although the authors did not seem to identify this prospect, it seems likely that an open-ended approach is particularly likely to occur in conjunction with Internet and other technology resources. This conceivably will lead to situations where "teacher does not always know best," where students may know more about some aspects of technology than teachers do. How will their approach aid instructors in coping with these "unfamiliar" contexts?

Chapter 7 by Mayer identifies three contrasting views of learning and instruction: learning as response strengthening, as knowledge acquisition, and as knowledge construction; and he proposes that instructors should focus on the third type—knowledge construction. Mayer identifies foundations for his approach and suggests techniques to facilitate students' "selecting, organizing and integrating" strategies for knowledge construction. He also identifies transfer of learning and learning-how-to-learn as important goals. Left unstated is the extent, if any, to which other forms of learning and instruction are needed and appropriate.

Chapter 8 by Schank, Berman, and Macpherson proposes that schools are in need of radical change. These authors, as well as the authors of other Unit 2 chapters, are especially critical of "fact-based" instruction and learning. Schank, Berman, and Macpherson offer their "goal-based-scenarios" and simulations as an "ideal" means to help students learn various subjects at any age and in any context. They present case-based reasoning (CBR) as their theory about how people learn and as the foundation for the techniques they advocate. However, they also acknowledge that CBR is not necessarily the only way that people learn. Here and elsewhere in this volume, readers are presented with unanswered questions about when, where, why, and how an instructor can "know" what kind of learning is appropriate for his students.

In chapter 9, Schwartz, Lin, Brophy, and Bransford offer ideas they have derived from classroom, corporate, and training settings in work conducted by the Cognition and Technology Group at Vanderbilt (CTGV). They advocate finding a middle ground so that some instructional decisions are made by instructional designers and other decisions are made by teachers and learners. They use a computer program (STAR Legacy) as the context in which to design and implement their ideas because it enables them to study flexibly adaptive instructional designs, and because it enables them to help students (at novice and advanced levels) to think about how people learn and about how instruction might be designed. In this chapter (as well as in other Volume 2 chapters) is something of a contradiction. On the one hand, there is a suggestion that we need to design instruction, but on the other hand there is the admonition that we need to be flexible. A resulting issue concerns decisions as to when we need to go with the plans and when we need to be flexibly adaptive. This same issue is relevant to consideration of theories more generally: When are we expected to "follow" the theory (whichever theory one might select) and when are we expected to adapt or even depart from that theory?

Chapter 10, by Jonassen, continues the theme, addressed also by authors of other Unit 2 chapters, that we need to encourage and support students constructing and structuring their developing ideas and understandings. He proposes a constructivist learning environment (CLE) as a generic context in which students, in groups as well as alone, can be aided in interpreting and solving various kinds of problems. He contends that CLEs can provide a context for question-/issue-based, case-based, project-based, or problem-based forms of learning. Using scaffolding and other techniques, learners at various levels of proficiency can be aided in formulating their own ideas and understandings. Here are some questions that come to mind as we anticipate further theory development about how CLEs "should" be organized: At that future, advanced level of our understanding about how to design "good" CLEs and about what kinds of learning outcomes are likely to occur with respective CLEs, will we reach a point where it looks like we are providing too much structure to the learners? Stated another way, will CLEs then be criticized for being "too objective" and for fostering predictable learning outcomes?

Nelson's chapter 11 combines cooperative learning with problem-based learning environments. Although Jonassen and other authors address "social" aspects of cognitive operations, this chapter especially emphasizes social interactions as a central aspect of instruction. Using her Collaborative Problem Solving theory, Nelson offers "comprehensive guidelines" that are applicable throughout the learning process and other suggestions in the form of "process activities" that are more situation or phase specific. One contribution of this chapter is a set of guidelines about facilitating group engagement in problem solving. But Nelson's approach prompts questions concerning the extent to which what is "good" for group interaction may or may not be "good" for at least some *individual* students, and questions about the extent to which instruction might become so "group oriented" that personalization of instruction might be diminished.

Chapter 12, by Bielaczyc and Collins, continues this focus on social interactions as an important aspect of instruction. An underlying theme is a goal to advance group or collective knowledge in a way that enhances individual knowledge. On the one hand, I find the ideas offered in this chapter to be interesting; on the other hand, given my experiences in working with various kinds of groups, I am a bit reluctant to make predictions about how the views expressed here will consistently work out as planned with different groups. Taking a more positive attitude about prospects for using these ideas, questions come to mind about the extent to which these ideas about "face-to-face groups" might also be useful with group interactions on the Internet. Group interactions, both as mediated through the Internet and while using various technology resources, constitute matters that increasingly more instructional designers are likely to face as the Internet and other technology resources are more commonly used as an integral part of instruction.

In chapter 13, by Corno and Randi, the focus is on individual learners, especially on the manner in which each learner is self-regulated. The first paragraph of this chapter immediately grabbed my attention; here the authors question whether our attempts to "design" instruction might be in conflict with attempts to have students regulate their own learning. This is the kind of dilemma to which I referred when I talked about future prospects for chapter 10 ideas. If (as I proposed in this volume) we view instructional theories as providing us with general guidelines rather than rigid ideas that we must systematically follow, it would seem that we can both "design" instruction and facilitate self-regulated learning by students. This poses an interesting issue for the instructional-design community: How can we help "novice" instructional designers to learn about and to use instructional theories without causing them to feel that one must almost rigidly follow and apply any given theory? In a sense, it would be "tough" to live without theories (because we would not have the guidance afforded by theories), but it's also easy to have theories "overcontrol" us as we try to use them. Perhaps solutions will emerge as we help novices to see that applications of theories involve iterations, going back and forth between theories and practical applications, rather than moving only in one direction from the theory to the practical context.

Pogrow's chapter 14 focuses on development of thinking skills but addresses students who have special needs. Pogrow advocates using the Higher Order Thinking Skills program and SuperMath, a 2-year pre-algebra program, as the main basis for instruction of this student group, rather than the remedial work and other approaches often used with these student groups. Pogrow expresses caution about depending too much on theories, and he particularly notes that there may be many different ways to apply" a theory in a particular practical situation. But then with those cautions stated, he suggests that one can design a "highly creative yet directive learning environment" for this group of students. He also cautions that violating "key situational parameters" can lead to failure of otherwise well-designed learning environments. This leads to an issue of general concern in the design of instruction: if, as I have suggested previously, we need not strictly adhere to a theory, how can we know when we may be missing some critical element, an element without which that theory will not be successfully applied?

In chapter 15, Landa proposes the Landamatics Instructional Design Theory and Methodology for Teaching General Methods of Thinking. In contrast with some of the social interactions and the social constructivist positions taken in some Unit 2 chapters, Landa focuses particularly on cognitive processes at the individual level. A common example of this approach consists of identifying the cognitive operations that can be discerned in "experts" on a given topic, contrasting ways in which "novices" typically differ from experts in their cognitive processes, and then organizing the experts' cognitive processes so that they can be taught to novices. The success of this approach is dependent on how well the instructor is able to discern these respective cognitive operations. This approach differs from some other cognitive theories that tend to emphasize the situation-specific or contextualized nature of cognitive operations; this author focuses on cognitive operations that are more general in nature, although they are applied to particular contexts. This raises questions about the generalizability of instructional principles and guidelines across contexts and student groups. It raises questions about the manner in which we decide which learning processes need to be considered explicitly with regard to particular situations and which may be applicable across contexts.

In chapter 16, Kovalik and McGeehan make a strong case for using neuropsychology research and theory as a major basis for formulating instructional theories. The Integrated Thematic Instruction (ITI) approach is proposed as a model for curriculum as well as instruction, in a way that is somewhat consistent with Gardner's focus on curricular goals in chapter 4. These authors identify "brain research about learning" as a major foundation for their ITI instructional model. Six brain basics range from acknowledgment of the role of emotions and personality in learning, to the influence of experience on intelligence and the role of multiple intelligences, and to meaningful patterns and organized mental programs as a feature of brain behavior activities. Some issues for the instructional-design community that are triggered by the focus of chapter 16 on the brain are as follows: To what extent does this approach (as well as other contemporary theories based on neuropsychology information) fully take into account the hierarchical, interdependent nature, and complexity of the nervous system? Especially for theories that focus mainly on "construction" of information or other higher cognitive processes, to what extent are other potentially important aspects of brain behavior functioning being overlooked?

Chapter 17 describes recently developed features of Merrill's Component Display Theory (CDT). Some of these features evolved during attempts to explore automation of instructional-design processes through computer-based implementation of CDT. This chapter describes methods for representing knowledge as knowledge objects and elements (slots) of knowledge objects, which serve as components of subject matter content (or, knowledge). Instructional Transaction Theory offers ideas about ways in which instructional methods can be used to attain selected curricular goals while maintaining some degree of adaptability and flexibility. This theory involves rather explicit identification of transactions, learner guidance, and other details involved in aiding students to attain various learning outcomes. Merrill's approach, with such careful attention to instructional details, illustrates a problem that seems inevitable for any theory that is "mature," namely: identifying instructional processes in such detail makes it subject to being criticized as involving "too much structure" for learners. In a sense, the more we know and are able to articulate about any instructional theories, the more the respective theories will be viewed as being too highly structured and even "mechanistic."

In chapter 18, Reigeluth represents another example of a more mature theory that can be subject to the same kinds of criticism about its details just mentioned regarding Merrill's theory. In this chapter, Reigeluth advances the view that it is not "whether" sequencing makes a difference but rather "when it makes a difference and when it doesn't." Reigeluth offers general views and some guidelines so that designers and instructors can more likely have sequencing make a positive difference in learners' activities and outcomes. One issue prompted by this chapter involves questions as to how designers and instructors can "handle" the diverse sequencing strategies and guidelines that may be identified for any instructional events. Reigeluth's theory and guidelines can help instructors and designers, but the more knowledge we accumulate in this area, the more options and decisions we need to consider. Another issue involves questions about the extent to which the learner (rather than a designer or an instructor) should be aware of and actually make sequencing decisions. In brief, to what extent should the individual learner or groups of learners be able to make these sequencing decisions?

Unit 3, "Fostering Psychomotor Development," and chapter 19, generate some interesting issues. In chapter 19, Romiszowski briefly notes illustrative instances in which psychomotor skills are involved in sports, leisure, and work contexts. He proposes that psychomotor skill instruction should take into account the long-established learning theories that previously have been used as a foundation for instruction and should also examine and modify them in light of contemporary contributions from cognitive psychology. Furthermore, he emphasizes the interrelations among psychomotor, cognitive, affective, interpersonal, and other learning domains. The views expressed about the interrelations among these various learning domains prompts the question: Should not instructional designers consider the interrelations among learning domains with regard to virtually all forms of instruction and instructional design?

Unit 4, "Fostering Affective Development," consists of five theory chapters. Chapter 21, by Lewis, Watson, and Schaps, makes the case for regarding affective education as a necessary component of kindergarten through Grade 12 education. As have some other chapter authors, they raise questions about the "essential outcomes" of schooling. A major theme, from their perspective, is to create an environment that will foster a "caring community of learners." Moreover, they contend that this kind of community will foster social, ethical, and intellectual development. The authors identify some issues that need to be considered, namely that this approach is not really compatible with some trends today toward *narrowing* the scope of academic outcomes. This approach presents additional problems and challenges for teachers and for researchers because of the considerably more complex processes and outcomes that are involved.

Stone-McCown and McCormick's chapter (chap. 22), displays some of the features addressed in Gardner's multiple intelligences approach, but their main conceptual foundation is related to Goleman's concept of "emotional intelligence." This chapter summarizes 25 years of experiences with "Self-Science: The Subject is Me," which involved weekly meetings that focused on helping small groups of children to develop affective and cognitive skills that could broaden their understanding and functioning in learning and social situations. Among the issues generated as a result of reading this chapter are the following: Is this program sufficiently different from other "self-esteem" ventures that it might be more successful in achieving its goals? To what extent might the same goals be attained by integrating some of these techniques with academic learning under conditions in which participants have some reasonable prospects of being successful academically and of feeling better about themselves and their interpersonal relationships?

On many occasions, I have heard teachers and trainers complain that their students or clients "have an attitude," as though an "attitude" is almost automatically something "bad." In chapter 23, Kamradt and Kamradt present "having an attitude" as an important goal of instruction. This approach does raise questions that instructional designers need to consider: When and how should we acknowledge that "attitudes" are sufficiently important to justify having them identified as goals for instruction? Should we devise separate or integrative instructional techniques (i.e., the latter involving affective and cognitive goals)? To what extent, if at all, should attitudes be considered important to evaluate learners' achievement?

Lickona's chapter 24 quite clearly announces that character education is (again) an important educational outcome. I added "again" because character education (also sometimes identified as moral/ethical/citizenship education) had been considered to be an important aspect of education prior to the 20th century but has been "up and down" in "popularity" among educators and in society in general throughout much of the 20th century. A number of distinctive features can be found in chapter 24, such as the assertion that there "is truth that is independent of the knower," and that character education should be viewed both as a goal and as a means to facilitate various aspects of intellectual development and academic achievement. It seems likely that some of the views advocated in this chapter will "clash" with some contemporary authors who take social constructivism to such an extreme that few or no "objective truths" are accepted, and that any attempts to "cultivate character" may be deemed suspect as possibly inappropriate manipulation of students' views.

But chapter 25 is the one that most clearly moves farthest from the narrowing views that education should only focus on academic or intellectual pursuits. In this chapter, Moore proposes that the teaching of spirituality (more commonly to be found only in religion-based schools) should be approached more developmentally. Moore attempts to identify goals and instructional methods that are sufficiently "universal" that they cut across established religion boundaries. In a footnote at the beginning of his chapter, Moore acknowledges that the examples and ideas he offers are, of course, influenced by his own views about spirituality and religion. Moore cites other adolescent development literature to bolster the case he makes for spiritual education. One may agree with much of what he says, but it seems likely that this very broad view of educational goals and priorities may stimulate instructors and other educators to re-examine their personal views on this topic, the emphases and priorities resulting from this expanded curriculum, and time management issues to incorporate this kind of program.

HISTORICAL PERSPECTIVE

This section reviews some of the history of instructional theories as a context for considering the Volume 2 theories, our current status of instructional theories, and preparation needed for the future construction and use of instructional theories. I have selected five benchmarks with which to compare the Volume 2 theories: The beginning of the 20th century, mid-century, the early 1970s, the early 1980s (when Volume 1 was being prepared), and the late 1990s (when this volume is being prepared). At each benchmark, I consider the focus and scope of theory, and the extent of interest in applying psychological theory to instructional practices. Particularly for the earlier benchmarks, I focus on psychological theory, especially psychological learning theory, due to the considerable influence of psychological learning theory on the origin and construction of instructional theory.

Beginning of the 20th Century

There was a little ditty concerning changes in the focus of psychology that I learned when I was a graduate student. Although I cannot recall the author or source while writing this chapter, I can recall that it characterized psychology as having lost its soul at the turn of the century and as having lost its mind by the 1930s with the advent of behavioral psychology's influence. Two main bases for this ditty can be identified. First, 19th-century discussions of moral issues and character development more or less disappeared or at least were "de-emphasized" as psychology was emerging as a science. Second, the early 20th-century discussions of what we now call "cognitive" topics faded into the background as comprehensive learning theories, especially those with behavioral psychology as a theoretical foundation, began to dominate much of theory construction in psychology. However, it should be noted that there were some behavioral psychologists, such as Edward Chance Tolman, who were expressing interest in cognitive processes at least as early as the 1930s.

From the latter part of the 19th century and the early part of the 20th century, psychology was gradually separating from philosophy and emerging as a science and discipline that focused particularly on sensation and perception. At that point, learning processes had not been a common focus of study, and instructional theory apparently was not even contemplated as an area of interest. In response to various requests, William James offered "talks with teachers" (in person and in print) in an attempt to describe some ways in which psychology could provide helpful ideas to educators. Others (cf. Snelbecker, 1985) attempted to identify ways in which psychology might be of assistance in planning instruction. For example, Thorndike acknowledged psychology's role as a "pure science" but also proposed that there should be research directed toward the practical application of psychological principles in education. Dewey (1900) earlier had cited psychology and education relationships as an example of how psychology might help address various social problems. Maria Montessori was one of a number of people who developed educational theories or approaches that some people today view as examples of early attempts to have instruction at least partly based on psychological information (cf. Snelbecker, 1985).

Perhaps more formalized relations between psychology and instruction were partly limited because of ongoing debates about the nature of psychology as a comparatively newly identified science. Although there was an initial expectation that there would be only one science of psychology, there soon were several schools of psychology whose proponents contended that their school should be this unifying force within psychology. Moreover, there was general anticipation that this emerging theory of psychology would provide a framework with which to understand a wide range of problems in psychology. Thus, there was little primary or direct involvement by most psychologists of that period in practical applications to instructional practices, or to most other practical matters at that time.

Mid-20th Century

By the middle of the 20th century it was apparent that psychological theories were becoming narrower in scope, leading to the emergence of "miniature models" (e.g., theories that addressed only certain kinds of learning rather than being depicted as the foundation for all kinds of learning processes). Before mid-century, "applied" psychologists mainly were identified with measurement rather than with planning instruction or other interventions. Partly as the result of the need to train large numbers of military personnel during and following World War II, a number of experimental psychologists who had been conducting basic research found themselves involved in identifying more effective means for planning instruction. By the late 1950s, there were instances in which a learning theory was used as the foundation for planning instruction—in some cases this involved behavioral learning theory and in other cases newly emerging cognitive theory.

These efforts to provide improved training later led to the emergence of some early instructional theories—including, for example, the work of B. F. Skinner, and Robert Gagné (cf. Snelbecker, 1985). Although these early instructional theorists attempted to demonstrate how their approaches could be used in education as well as in training, for reasons that are not really clear the ideas they developed were more extensively accepted in business, government and military training contexts as well as in some areas of professional education (e.g., health professions) than they were in K–12 education contexts.

Somewhat separate from these "training" activities, another foundation for early instructional theories can be found in K–12 education contexts. Some authors point to work by Ralph Tyler as early as the 1930s as an important foundation for the emergence of instructional theories. But it was only in the late 1950s and early 1960s that there were organized attempts to support the development of instructional theories. A number of Association for Supervision and Curriculum Development (ASCD) activities and publications illustrate contributions to the emergence of formalized instructional theories. For example, some ASCD meetings in the early 1960s focused on instructional theory, and an ASCD commission on instructional theory was formed in 1964 and remained active through 1967. One of the ASCD publications proposed criteria for instructional theories (Gordon, 1968).

Whereas the approaches of Skinner and, to a lesser extent, of Gagné were extensively influenced by behavioral learning theory, Jerome Bruner, in a series of publications (e.g., Bruner, 1960, 1966a, 1966b), espoused the use of emerging cognitive theories as the preferred basis for formulating instructional theory. Reviews of documents from that period support the impression that it was the nature of the particular groups involved in exploring applications of psychological theory, rather than the inherent nature of the respective psychology theories being considered, that led to this early "tilt" of behavioral learning theory for training contexts and of cognitive theory for education contexts. There are so many similarities between instructional principles in training and education contexts that any given psychological theory might constructively be used in both education and training contexts (cf. Snelbecker, 1988).

Early 1970s

In the late 1960s and early 1970s, while working on a book originally planned to address "learning theories and their potential applicability in education," I found sufficient evidence of organized attempts to construct instructional theories that I added "instructional theory" to the book title and focus (Snelbecker, 1985). For the most part, the early, formally identified instructional theories that could be identified at that time were primarily constructed essentially as "by-products" of work initiated for other purposes. Most were derived from psychological theories of learning in one way or another. A few, such as Carl Rogers' "freedom to learn" theory, represented a reaction against the then-dominant influence of psychological learning theories and were mainly derived from counseling and psychotherapy theories or variants of personality theories. I was able to identify five representative instructional theories and their main conceptual foundations as follows:

1. Behavior modification and instructional technology which was mainly based on operant theory and classical conditioning theory.
2. Cognitive construct instructional theories were considerably influenced by Jerome Bruner's advocacy for the development of instructional theories and by his growing interest in cognitive processes.
3. Principles of learning instructional theories were an attempt, illustrated by Richard Bugelski's work, to derive implications for instruction from various learning theories and research.

4. Task analysis instructional theories were based on Robert M. Gagné's approach in which instructional-design principles would be based on different learning theories depending on the type of learning involved.
5. Humanistic psychology and instructional theories had an instructional design for all kinds of situations that would be based on a view that emphasizes the "whole person" with ideas derived from counseling and psychotherapy theories or from variants of personality theory.

During this same time period (late 1960s and early 1970s) several authors were identifying emergent *teaching models* (also called *teaching theories* or *teaching styles*). Examples of this work include the original edition of Joyce and Weil's (1996) *Models of Teaching* and an earlier version of Mosston and Ashworth's (1990) *The Spectrum of Teaching Styles: From Command to Discovery*, both of which were published in the early 1970s. Both instructional theories and teaching models minimally have common features because they were, and are, constructed to improve instruction. The sets of instructional theories and teaching models even have some common theories (e.g., some cognitively oriented theories in both groups, some behavioral psychology-oriented theories in both groups). But there are comparatively few cross citations between the respective bodies of literature for these two groups, and their research tends to be published in separate journals. This "gap" between instructional theories and teaching models existed in the early 1970s and seems to have continued over the years up to the present time.

Early 1980s

The first volume of this series was written and published in the early 1980s. Authors of the Volume 1 instructional theories displayed major interest in characteristics of and influences on instruction. This was a significant departure from earlier periods when instructional theory more or less resulted as a by-product of research and theory on some other topic (e.g., psychological studies of learning or counseling theories). In his section "About This Book," the volume editor announced:

> This book is dedicated to increasing our knowledge about how to improve instruction. It is founded on the premise that the process of learning can be made easier and more enjoyable. During the past 25 years, a young discipline has developed to so improve instruction.... The major purpose of this book is to encourage the building of a *common knowledge base* that integrates the independent and piecemeal "knowledge bases" that presently characterize this discipline. (Reigeluth, 1983, p. xi)

There were other important signs of the commitment to and support for this newly established discipline for knowledge users as well as for knowledge producers. It seemed clear that instructional theories were addressing practical matters along with conceptual issues, rather than strictly adhering to some "pure science" formulation of ideas and construction of theories that may or may not have some practical value. For example, some Volume 1 instructional theories partly reflected the influence of behavioral psychology learning theories, and the growing influence of cognitive psychology was evident not only in cognition-oriented theories but to some extent in all of the theories of that period. But those theories also displayed a balance between trying to understand instruction and trying to find ways to use such knowledge effectively in practical situations.

Late 1990s

There has been a period of approximately 15 years between preparation and publication of the two volumes of *Instructional Design Theories and Models: An Overview of Their Current Status*. It seems useful to compare similarities and differences in the theories contained in these two volumes. An important similarity is that Volume 2 theories continue the trend, already evident in Volume 1, for the authors to have a major commitment to developing instructional theories as a primary interest, rather than as a by-product of their theory construction about learning, personality development or some other topic. This is important, both conceptually and practically, because it increases the likelihood that the authors will focus on important aspects of instruction in formulating their ideas, rather than on trying to force instructional processes and outcomes to fit a theory from some other area.

There are several ways in which Volume 2 theory chapters differ from those in Volume 1. First, the Volume 2 theories are even less dependent on psychology learning theories than were the Volume 1 theories, even though some "distance" between instructional theories and learning theories already was apparent and growing at the time that Volume 1 was prepared. The Volume 2 theories quite obviously draw from more diverse practical and theoretical resources than was apparent with the Volume 1 theories.

Earlier in this chapter, I referred to the ditty that portrayed psychology as having lost its soul and its mind early in this century. The Volume 2 theories provide a basis for conjecturing that we now have regained not only our mind but also our feelings and perhaps our soul. This presents us with a trade-off: With a broader scope of theories to address internal mental operations and to include affective and spiritual facets, we attain a "richer" interpretation of instructional theory's domain. However, we also obligate ourselves for some complexities that will, almost inevitably, (a) require even more complex theories than was the case with Volume 1 theories, and (b) trigger age-old debates about whether instruction should include feelings and values or whether instruction should focus only on narrowly designated "academic" topics.

The second difference I note involves the extent to which a given theory is supposed to address instruction in general rather than being limited to particular contexts or types of instruction. Volume 1 authors were reasonably careful in designating a restricted scope for their theories. The Volume 2 theory authors have been even more modest than Volume 1 authors in identifying those facets of instruction for which their conceptualizations are most likely to be relevant. The editor's "foreword" sections for each theory chapter should also assist readers in identifying places and ways in which each theory most likely is applicable.

A third difference is that there are almost three times as many theories offered in Volume 2 as there were in Volume 1. On the one hand, a larger "pool" of instructional theories gives the reader more choices; on the other hand, that means that the reader has the major responsibility in selecting theories to be used in a given situation. This fact prompted me to think of the many times that graduate students have complained about the number of theories they had to study and understand. I suspect that such complaints may grow, rather than diminish, as readers contemplate the growing array of instructional theories. By providing "foreword" sections before each theory chapter, Reigeluth (designated as "C.M.R." at the end of each foreword) has aided readers in identifying the particular emphases and features of the respective theories. But the fact that some additional help may be needed has prompted me to offer some suggestions later in this chapter about ways that instructional theory developers and users might be aided in "sorting through" the respective theories to make informed decisions.

FUTURE CHALLENGES AND TASKS

Some general, overlapping questions come to mind when reflecting on our current understanding about instruction. What is needed to stimulate research and to facilitate improved construction of instructional theories? What can be done to foster appropriate practical applications of this growing body of knowledge about instruction? What challenges exist and what tasks need to be addressed to help both knowledge producers and knowledge users benefit from, and contribute to, this growing body of knowledge about instruction? I identified two sets of challenges and tasks for the "instructional theory community" that, hopefully, will benefit knowledge producers and knowledge users. For brevity I summarily noted them as *taxonomy*, and *technology* (or, more specifically, *instructional technology*).

Taxonomy

Over the past several decades that I have been observing the development and use of psychotherapy theories, I have noted that in the course of about 25 years there was an increase from 36 psychotherapy theories (Harper, 1959) to more than 400 (Goldfried, Radin, & Rachlin, 1997; Karasu, 1986). In chapter 2 of this volume I briefly described some steps that have been taken by producers and users of psychotherapy theories to understand and cope with this proliferation of theories, including the formation of a Society for the Exploration of Psychotherapy Integration.

A brief examination of Volume 2 indicates 24 instructional theories. However, if one were to consider a few collections of theories that are not clearly identified here, the number of instructional theories that can be said to exist in the late 1990s would certainly exceed twice that. For example, there is work in Europe and in other countries around the world that would add many more theories. If one were to include the various collections of "teaching theories and models," even more theories that are relevant for instruction could readily be identified. Even if the number of instructional theories does not grow at the geometric rate found with psychotherapy theories, it seems likely that in the not too distant future we will possibly have hundreds of instructional theories to ponder.

The first set of challenges and tasks that I pose can be stated this way:

> *Challenge:* How can we (knowledge producers and knowledge users) be aware of, understand and utilize this growing body of information about instruction?

> *Tasks:* Explore prospects for developing a "taxonomy" that can serve as a system for classifying currently available theories and recognizing needs for further theory development. I suggest that our task will most likely be to develop some generally accepted taxonomy or other means for classifying instructional theories.

Development of such a taxonomy could be quite useful, but it will take a great deal of work, and it most likely will have to be constructed by people representing the various constituencies interested in instructional theories. There already exist a number of attempts to classify instructional theories or teaching models. In one of my earliest attempts at classification, I identified instructional theories in terms of the learning theories or other theories on which their instructional theories were based (Snelbecker, 1985). In Volume 1, the respective chapters by Gropper (1983) and Landa (1983) represent two approaches to identifying what particular theories do and do not address. It is not yet clear to me whether those two approaches would be useful with Volume 2 theories.

There are other attempts to classify theories that are not as explicitly linked to the words *instructional theories*. For example, Joyce and Weil (1996) identified four families of models as a way to classify teaching models. They group various approaches, respectively, into social, information-processing, personal, and behavioral systems families. Mosston and Ashworth (1990) present a Spectrum of Teaching Styles based mainly on "the decisions that are made by the teacher and those that are made by the learner" (p. 3). Scriven's (1994) paper on duties of the teacher represents another set of ideas that might be used in developing a taxonomy of instructional theories. Scriven's DOTT (duties of the teacher) list is based on analyses of what teachers actually do. This includes one section on instructional competence, but of course the DOTT list goes considerably beyond explicitly instructional duties. One might want to consider classifying instructional theories at least partly in terms of the kinds of learning outcomes on which they focus. If so, it might be useful to watch for an updated version of Bloom's widely cited *Taxonomy of Educational Objectives*; a series of e-mail comments on AERA and European listservs indicate that a group has been working on a revised taxonomy for the past few years.

Technology, Especially Instructional Technology

Another challenge-task set stems from the reciprocal relation between instructional theory and instructional technology—a relation that offers both opportunities and obligations for the instructional theory community. As was the case with the first challenge-task set, this second topic has important implications for knowledge producers as well as knowledge users.

It is almost impossible not to be aware of the considerable extent to which the word *technology* often has been used when discussing instruction, education, or training issues. However, not everyone defines the term the same way. That problems with the definition of technology, especially instructional technology, are not really new is reflected in the report, a quarter century ago, of an official U.S. Commission on Instructional Technology (cf. McMurrin, 1970; Tickton, 1970/1971). That Commission cautioned that it would be wrong to think of technology only as machines and "gadgetry," and that considering the various forms of media, hardware, and software in isolation would not be adequate. They proposed that a broader approach "holds the key to the contribution technology can make to the advancement of education" (McMurrin, 1970, p. 19). They proposed this definition of instructional technology:

> It is a systematic way of designing, carrying out, and evaluating the total process of learning and teaching in terms of specific objectives, based on research in human learning and communication, and employing a combination of human and non-human resources to bring about more effective instruction. (McMurrin, 1970, pp. 5, 19)

With this broader definition, *instructional theory* is an important, integral part of *instructional technology*. But even if one elects to use a narrower definition for *technology*, there is a close reciprocal relation between instructional technology and instructional theory. Good learning experiences involving technology can best be based on a sound instructional theory for several reasons. For one, an instructional theory can help us to think about instruction in an organized way; instructional theory can help "inform" us about what is likely to happen, and why it might happen, with different kinds of teaching–learning activities, and can help indicate appropriate ways to evaluate the implementation and impact of instructional technology resources. Conversely, these practical applications of instructional theory provide important opportunities for knowledge producers to "test" instructional theories, to identify needed modifications in our conceptualizations about instruction, and can generally foster development of better instructional theories. Chapter 26 by Reigeluth and Frick, provides some general guidelines and some specific examples of ways in which instructors can both (a) assess the utility of an instructional theory for their practical situation and (b) generate ideas about how that theory might be improved. For more extensive discussions about theory-technology and theory-practice issues than is possible here, readers may want to review comments by

Seels (1997) and Salisbury (1988), along with additional papers in the journal issues where those two papers were published.

A close relation between instructional technology and instructional theory may be detected in a series of discussions over the past few decades concerning the extent, if any, to which some form of technology (television, computers, multimedia systems, the Internet, etc.) can facilitate learning. Many discussions since the middle1980s have been stimulated by and/or have made reference to a 1983 *Review of Educational Research* paper by Richard Clark, "Reconsidering Research on Learning from Media." In that paper and in a series of subsequent papers (e.g., Clark, 1992, 1994), Clark took and maintained the position that technology *as a delivery system* really should not be expected to have any meaningful impact on instruction. In brief, as I understand his position, Clark contended that it is what we do with the delivery system—the instructional methods used, the ways that the instruction is designed—that will influence learning. Van Horn (1998) suggested that the "instructional design used to structure tomorrow's schools will be unlike today's designs" (p. 556). Van Horn did not specify, in this article, whether he agrees or disagrees with Clark's position. However, his emphasis on using the *interactivity* afforded by technology capabilities lent support to the view that whether technology will influence learning will quite likely depend on the kinds of teaching-learning activities that we design with the technology.

Here is the second challenge and task set:

> *Challenge*: How can we use instructional theory to design instructional technology applications constructively, and how can we use instructional technology applications to foster further development of instructional theory?
>
> *Tasks*: Identify ways to help ensure that "curriculum and instruction drive technology" instead of having "technology drive curriculum and instruction." Indicate how instructional theories can aid instructors in deciding when, where, and how to use technology resources; also indicate limitations of instructional theories in doing this. Candidly identify changes, improvements, or modifications needed in instructional theories, and indicate what other theories and models may be required along with instructional theories. Indicate ways to decide which instructional theory should be selected. Find means whereby technology applications may provide a basis for testing and modifying instructional theory. Just as instructional practices may need to be modified in light of ideas from theories, consider what changes are needed in the instructional theories in light of their uses with technology-supported instruction.

This instructional technology–instructional theory relation is especially evident in interesting ways as schools and universities develop plans to acquire and use new technology resources. Although the usual comments about being cautious in generalizing from anecdotal information apply here, I share some of my observations because they may indicate emerging patterns in the direction of greater emphasis on instructional theories.

During the 1980s, two National Science Foundation-funded projects were conducted to prepare K–12 computer teachers and teacher technologists (cf. Aiken & Snelbecker, 1991; Snelbecker, Bhote, Wilson, & Aiken, 1995). For the past several years I have been a participant in technology planning activities at university and K–12 school levels. I have noticed that the words *instructional technologist* and *instructional design* have been occurring with much greater frequency in the late 1990s than was the case throughout the 1980s. In earlier years when personal computers were first becoming available in education and training contexts, instructors and other educators seemed to be fascinated about having computers available. More recently, these same professionals appear to be asking why and how computers and other technology resources might facilitate instruction, rather than merely being satisfied with having computers available.

Quite importantly, in both training and education contexts, I keep hearing such statements as: "Curriculum and instruction should drive technology; technology should not drive curriculum and instruction." What has fascinated me is that it is often not an instructional theory enthusiast who makes comments like these; instead, on many occasions I've been hearing "technology types" offering such comments. For example, in both kinds of contexts people whose expertise is with computers, the Internet, and other technology resources have stated that they already know about hardware and software, but that we now need to have a better understanding about the ways, if any, that technology-supported learning really helps students.

Thus, in university and school technology planning sessions, I have observed a growing number of people contending that buying hardware and software is not enough. Increasingly more people are contending that technology purchasing decisions should be based on how those resources can be expected to have an impact on teaching and learning. Statements and activities involving two higher education associations illustrate how "teaching" and "learning" are becoming more closely associated with "technology." For the past several years, the American Association for Higher Education (AAHE) has been sponsoring a listserv and otherwise encouraging and supporting technology planning at colleges and universities throughout the United States. The AAHE listserv moderator (Gilbert, 1998), who also actively participates in these technology planning activities around the country, stated that the AAHE uses a three-part approach to technology planning after AAHE observed during the previous 15 years that none of the three had worked alone. AAHE encourages a combination of top-down (presidential or provostial leadership), bottom–up (individual faculty working with little institutional support), and "infection" model (publicize the work of the pioneers and wait for others to be infected by their enthusiasm) approaches. Most importantly, the university or college entity that facilitates this three-part approach is known formally as the Teaching, Learning, and Technology Roundtable—not a "technology planning roundtable." Somewhat similarly, an announcement about an institute on transforming teacher education (which I recently received from the American Association of Colleges for Teacher Education while preparing this chapter) displays primary emphasis on "teaching and learning" rather than on "technology."

It seems likely that we can anticipate various questions and issues that relate to the construction and use of instructional theories from a growing number of school as well as university "teaching, learning, and technology" groups. Instructional theories can be helpful not only in designing instruction, but also in identifying appropriate means for evaluating positive and negative impact of technology resources. Instructional theory can also be useful in designating how various aspects of technology-supported instruction can be expected to enhance "usual" ways of providing instruction and in identifying at least some ways in which current and emergent technologies might transform both the process and the outcome of instruction. For example, we need to consider, respectively, what a "stand-up" instructor, a computer, a multimedia system, the Internet, and other means of providing instruction have to offer. This position is similar to the view I expressed in chapter 2, where I suggested that we need to identify the "added value" that the various theories offer us.

Elsewhere (Snelbecker, 1993), I made two other suggestions. I contended that we should select theories on the basis of the needs and characteristics of the practical context, and that we should use design and development strategies that can accommodate different kinds of theories, even "competitive" theories such as constructivist and behavioral learning views, in the same practical context. We have opportunities and obligations to find ways to design the instruction so that we can capitalize on the particular features of these different "delivery systems." Those opportunities and obligations can also help us to re-examine and enhance our emerging instructional theories. Just as instructional theory might be useful in transforming (or, "re-engineering") instruction, those same applications might help guide us in transforming our views and even the manner in which we conceptualize instruction. Thus, instructional technology applications constitute an opportunity and an obligation for the instructional theory community.

SUMMARY

This volume contains a wide array of instructional theories. The number of theories we see here plus those that almost certainly will be forthcoming in future years represent a "mixed blessing." It is great to have so much information available, but this growing body of information can seem overwhelming at times. It seems inevitable that knowledge producers as well as knowledge users will need assistance in getting an overview of our body of knowledge about instruction to put a given theory into a broader perspective and to recognize the contributions of the respective theories. It seems likely that technology-related learning ventures will represent growing opportunities for applying instructional theories. But those opportunities also will involve obligations to test out and to improve the instructional theories that we have now and that we will develop in the future.

REFERENCES

Aiken, R. M., & Snelbecker, G. E. (1991). Hindsight: Reflections on retraining secondary school teachers to teach computer science. *Journal of Research on Computing in Education, 23*(3), 444–451.

Bruner, J. (1960). *The process of education.* New York. Random House.

Bruner, J. (1966a). Learning about learning: A conference report. *Cooperative Research Monograph, 15.*

Bruner, J. (1966b). *Toward a theory of instruction.* Cambridge, MA: Belknap.

Clark, R. E. (1983). Reconsidering research on learning from media. *Review of Educational Research, 53,* 445–459.

Clark, R. E. (1992). Media use in education. In M.C. Alkin (Ed.), *Encyclopedia of Educational Research* (pp. 805–814). New York: Macmillan.

Clark, R. E. (1994). Media will never influence learning. *Educational Technology Research and Development, 42,* 21–29.

Dewey, J. (1900). Psychology and social practice. *Psychological Review, 7,* 105–124.

Gilbert, S. W. (1998, March 9). Listserv moderator's comment on an e-mail message distributed by AAHE's listserv, aahesgit@list.cren.net.

Goldfried, M. R., Radin, L. B., & Rachlin, H. (1997). Theoretical Jargon and the Dynamics of Behaviorism. *The Clinical Psychologist, 50*(4), 5–12.

Gordon, I. J. (1968). *Criteria for theories of instruction.* Washington, DC: Association for Supervision and Curriculum Development.

Gropper, G. L. (1983). A metatheory of instruction: A framework for analyzing and evaluating instructional theories and models. In C.M. Reigeluth (Ed.), *Instructional-design theories and models: An overview of their current status* (Vol. 1, pp. 37–53). Hillsdale, NJ: Lawrence Erlbaum Associates.

Harper, R. A. (1959). *Psychoanalysis and psychotherapy: 36 systems.* Englewood Cliffs, NJ: Prentice-Hall.

Joyce, B., & Weil, M. (1996). *Models of teaching* (5th ed.). Needham Heights, MA: Simon & Schuster.

Karasu, T. B. (1986). The specificity versus nonspecificity dilemma: Toward identifying therapeutic change agents. *The American Journal of Psychiatry, 143*(6), 687–695.

Landa, L. N. (1983). Descriptive and prescriptive theories of learning and instruction: An analysis of their relationships and interactions. In C. M. Reigeluth (Ed.), *Instructional-design theories and models: an overview of their current status* (Vol. 1, pp. 55). Hillsdale, NJ: Lawrence Erlbaum Associates.

McMurrin, S. M. (1970). *To improve learning: A report to the president and the congress of the united states by the commission on instructional technology.* Washington, DC: U.S. Government Printing Office.

Mosston, M., & Ashworth, S. (1990). *The spectrum of teaching styles: From command to discovery.* New York: Longman.

Salisbury, D. F. (1988). Introduction to special issue. *Journal of Instructional Development, 10*(4), 2.

Scriven, M. (1994). Duties of the teacher. *Journal of Personnel Evaluation in Education, 8*(2), 151–184.

Seels, B. (1997). Introduction to special section: Theory development in educational/instructional technology. *Educational Technology, 37,* 3–5.

Snelbecker, G. E. (1983). Is instructional theory alive and well? In C. M. Reigeluth (Ed.), *Instructional-design theories and models: An overview of their current status* (Vol. 1, pp. 437–472). Hillsdale, NJ: Lawrence Erlbaum Associates.

Snelbecker, G. E. (1985). Contrasting and complementary approaches to instructional design. In C. M. Reigeluth (Ed.), *Instructional-design theories in action: Lessons illustrating selected theories and models,* (pp. 321–337). Hillsdale, NJ: Lawrence Erlbaum Associates.

Snelbecker, G. E. (1988). Instructional design skills for classroom teachers. *Instructional Development, 10*(4), 33–40.

Snelbecker, G. E. (1993). Practical ways for using theories and innovations to improve training. In G. M. Piskurich (Ed.), *The ASTD handbook of instructional technology* (pp. 19.3–19.26). New York: McGraw-Hill.

Snelbecker, G. E., Bhote, N. P., Wilson, J. D., & Aiken, R. M. (1995). Elementary versus secondary school teachers retraining to teach computer science. *Journal of Research on Computing in Education, 27*(3), 336–347.

Tickton, S. G. (Ed.). (1970/1971). *To improve learning: An evaluation of instructional technology* (2 volumes). New York: R. R. Bowker.

Van Horn, R. (1998). Power tools: Tomorrow's high-performance courseware: A rough sketch. *Phi Delta Kappan, 79*(7), 556–558.

Postscript

Given that this volume represents but a small sampling of the amount of work being done on the new paradigm of instructional theory, I have already initiated work on a Volume III; and I would like to encourage the reader to inform me of any work that you think might be important to include. You can contact me at reigelut@indiana.edu. You can also comment about, and view others' comments about, these and other instructional-design theories at my theory Web site: www. indiana.edu/~idtheory.

I concluded work on this volume with a sense of excitement about the amount of creative and sorely needed work being done to offer guidance for the design of approaches to learning and human development that are learning focused rather than sorting focused, as discussed in chapter 1. But I am also left with a sense of the tremendous amount of work that remains to be done to provide teachers, trainers, software designers, textbook authors, and all others concerned with fostering human learning and development with appropriate levels of guidance for helping people learn.

It is my hope that this volume will contribute in some small way to encouraging more people to work in this area, more journals to publish work of this kind, more funders to support work in this area, and more policymakers and practitioners to implement work of this kind. I would especially like to encourage the development of electronic performance support systems that can help practitioners select and apply the most appropriate design theories for their particular goals, conditions, and values.

—C.M.R.

Author Index

Subject Index

A